T0223964

Lecture Notes in Computer Science 1493

Edited by G. Goos, J. Hartmanis and J. van Leeuwen

Springer
Berlin
Heidelberg
New York
Barcelona
Budapest
Hong Kong
London
Milan
Paris
Singapore
Tokyo

Jonathan P. Bowen   Andreas Fett
Michael G. Hinchey (Eds.)

ZUM '98: The Z Formal Specification Notation

11th International Conference of Z Users
Berlin, Germany, September 24-26, 1998
Prooceedings

Springer

Volume Editors

Jonathan P. Bowen
The University of Reading, Department of Computer Science
Whiteknights, P.O. Box 225, Reading, Berkshire RG6 6AY, UK
E-mail: j.p.bowen@reading.ac.uk

Andreas Fett
Daimler-Benz AG, Research and Technology
Software Technology Laboratory
Alt-Moabit 96a, D-10559 Berlin, Germany
E-mail: andreas.fett@dbag.bln.daimlerbenz.com

Michael G. Hinchey
University of Nebraska at Omaha, Department of Computer Science
College of Information Science and Technology
6001 Dodge Street, Omaha, NE 68182-0500, USA
and
University of Limerick
Department of Computer Science and Information Systems
National Technological Park, Castleroy, Limerick, Ireland
E-mail: michael.hinchey@ul.ie

Cataloging-in-Publication data applied for

Die Deutsche Bibliothek - CIP-Einheitsaufnahme

The Z formal specification notation : proceedings / ZUM '98, 11th
International Conference of Z Users, Berlin, Germany, September
24 - 26, 1998. Jonathan P. Bowen ... (ed.). - Berlin ; Heidelberg ;
New York ; Barcelona ; Budapest ; Hong Kong ; London ; Milan ;
Paris ; Singapore ; Tokyo : Springer, 1998
 (Lecture notes in computer science ; Vol. 1493)
 ISBN 3-540-65070-9

CR Subject Classification (1991): D.2, I.1.3, F.3.1, D.1, G.2, F.4.1

ISSN 0302-9743
ISBN 3-540-65070-9 Springer-Verlag Berlin Heidelberg New York

© Springer-Verlag Berlin Heidelberg 1998
Printed in Germany

Typesetting: Camera-ready by author
SPIN 10638889   06/3142 – 5 4 3 2 1 0   Printed on acid-free paper

Preface

In a number of recent presentations – most notably at FME'96[1] – one of the foremost scientists in the field of formal methods, C.A.R. Hoare, has highlighted the fact that formal methods are not the only technique for producing reliable software. This seems to have caused some controversy, not least amongst formal methods practitioners.

How can one of the founding fathers of formal methods seemingly denounce the field of research after over a quarter of a century of support? This is a question that has been posed recently by some formal methods skeptics.

However, Prof. Hoare has not abandoned formal methods. He is reiterating, albeit more radically, his 1987 view[2] that more than one tool and notation will be required in the practical, industrial development of large-scale complex computer systems; and not all of these tools and notations will be, or even need be, formal in nature.

Formal methods are not a solution, but rather one of a selection of techniques that have proven to be useful in the development of reliable complex systems, and to result in hardware and software systems that can be produced on-time and within a budget, while satisfying the stated requirements.

After almost three decades, the time has come to view formal methods in the context of overall industrial-scale system development, and their relationship to other techniques and methods. We should no longer consider the issue of whether we are "pro-formal" or "anti-formal", but rather the degree of formality (if any) that we need to support in system development. This is a goal of ZUM'98, the 11th International Conference of Z Users, held for the first time within continental Europe in the city of Berlin, Germany.

How formal should the system development process in industry be in practice? The answer to this is likely to depend on the organization concerned, and even within an organization with consideration of the project in question, the personnel involved, standards that must be satisfied, and many other issues. Clearly valid answers range from "completely informal" to "full formal development". It might be thought as software development moves towards being a fully fledged engineering discipline that increasingly the answer would tend more towards the latter; unfortunately that is not necessarily the case.

How much formality should we be introducing to our students? At this stage in the evolution of formal development methods, it might be hoped that the answer to this would be rather uniform. Surprisingly, the range of answers is diverse, ranging from "none" to "a large amount of formality". This diversity is of great concern. Surely we should be united and agreed on the level of formality to which our students need to be introduced so that they are prepared for future research and industrial practice? Again, this is not the case, although we argue here that it should be: for formal methods to

---

[1] C.A.R. Hoare, How did software get so reliable without proof?, Springer-Verlag, *Lecture Notes in Computer Science*, **1051**:1–17, March 1996.

[2] C.A.R. Hoare, An overview of some formal methods for program design, *IEEE Computer*, **20**(9):85–91, September 1987.

become routine in appropriate development environments and scenarios, we require a skilled workforce that can bring concepts and ideas from academic investigation into realistic (industrial) development processes.

While not everyone involved in the software development process needs to be a formal methods expert, a certain minimum appreciation of formality and underlying mathematics is required by all involved in system development. An Educational Issues Session, organized by Neville Dean, and run as part of this conference, addresses these and other issues.

Our invited speakers for ZUM'98 are drawn from Germany, the UK, and the USA, both from industry and academia. Klaus Grimm of Daimler-Benz AG opens the conference with a discussion on the industrial requirements for the efficient development of reliable embedded systems. He is responsible for all research work carried out at Daimler-Benz AG in the area of software engineering. Ib Sørensen of B-Core (UK) Limited is a leading promulgator of formal methods technology and was the original instigator of the first ever Z User Meeting in December 1986 at Oxford University. Nancy Leveson of the University of Washington, USA is well-known for her work in the area of safety-critical systems, including the application of formal methods where appropriate. Ernst-Rüdiger Olderog at the University of Oldenburg, Germany has research interests concerning the development and application of formal methods to the design of correct systems. His contributions include work on semantic models and their combination, formal specification with associated verification techniques, and transformational design.

Tool demonstrations are being organized by Wolfgang Grieskamp (Technical University of Berlin) throughout the main meeting. In addition, there are associated activities both before and after the main meeting. Tutorials are being organized beforehand, by David Till, City University, UK. In the afternoon after the end of the main conference, the 4th in a series of associated Educational Issues Sessions is to be held, organized by Neville Dean of Anglia Polytechnic University, Cambridge, UK as in previous years.

The location of ZUM'98 has been influenced by the active use of Z in industry and academia in Berlin. The conference is organized by the Z User Group, but is generously aided and supported by a number of organizations, many based in Germany. The cooperation of Daimler-Benz AG, GMD (the German National Research Center for Information Technology) and the Technical University of Berlin has been extremely helpful in the local organization of the event. The event is being held within the Technical University of Berlin. Wolfgang Grieskamp has been especially helpful in the coordination of the local organization, and deserves a special vote of thanks.

Daimler-Benz AG (Germany) has provided substantial financial support. Praxis Critical Systems (UK) continues to provide a valuable and appreciated service in the running of the Z mailing list. FACS, the Formal Aspects of Computer Science specialist group of the British Computer Society (BCS), supports the Z User Group by providing publicity for meetings to its members.

This is the first time that we have been able to accept all contributions to the proceedings in electronic form suitable for processing using the LaTeX 2_ε document preparation system. As a result we have been able to publish the proceedings in a more uniform style than has previously been possible and an electronic version will be made available. On-line information concerning the conference is available under the following URL (Uniform Resource Locator):

```
http://www.fmse.cs.reading.ac.uk/zum98/
```

This will be kept up to date after the conference with any relevant information, and provides links to further on-line resources concerning the Z notation such as other Z User Meetings and formal methods in general.

Reading, Berlin and Omaha   Jonathan Bowen, Andreas Fett

July 1998   (Programme Co-Chairs)

                                   Mike Hinchey

                                (Conference Chair)

Programme Committee

The following people were members of the ZUM'98 programme committee:

Ali Abdallah, The University of Reading, UK
Jonathan Bowen, The University of Reading, UK
Paolo Ciancarini, University of Bologna, Italy
Neville Dean, Anglia Polytechnic University, UK
John Derrick, The University of Kent at Canterbury, UK
Mark d'Inverno, University of Westminster, UK
Andy Evans, University of Bradford, UK
Andreas Fett, Daimler-Benz AG, Berlin, Germany
David Garlan, Carnegie-Mellon University, USA
Wolfgang Grieskamp, TU Berlin, Germany *
Henri Habrias, University of Nantes, France
Jonathan Hammond, Praxis Critical Systems, UK
Ian Hayes, University of Queensland, Australia
Stephan Herrmann, GMD, Germany *
Mike Hinchey, University of Nebraska at Omaha, USA and Limerick, Ireland
Hans-Martin Hörcher, Vossloh System-Technik GmbH, Germany
Jonathan Jacky, University of Washington, USA
Stephan Jähnichen GMD and TU Berlin, Germany *
Randolph Johnson, National Security Agency, USA
Kevin Lano, Imperial College, London, UK
Shaoying Liu, Hiroshima City University, Japan
Jean-Francois Monin, France Telecom CNET DTL/MSV, France
Peter Pepper, TU Berlin, Germany *
Norah Power, University of Limerick, Ireland
Alf Smith, DERA Malvern, UK
David Till, City University, London, UK
Sam Valentine, University of York, UK
Matthias Weber, Daimler-Benz AG, Berlin, Germany *
Jim Woodcock, Oxford University, UK
John Wordsworth, IBM Hursley UK Laboratories, UK

* Those marked with an asterisk also helped with the local organization under the leadership of the local coordinator, Wolfgang Grieskamp.

External Referees

We are grateful to the following people who aided the programme committee in the reviewing of papers, providing additional specialist expertise:

Michel Allemand, University of Nantes, France
Eerke Boiten, The University of Kent at Canterbury, UK
Robert Büssow, TU Berlin, Germany
Stelvio Cimato, University of Bologna, Italy
Roger Duke, The University of Queensland, Brisbane, Australia
Kay Fuhrmann, Daimler-Benz AG, Berlin, Germany
Robert Geisler, TU Berlin, Germany
Mike Gordon, University of Cambridge, UK
Jim Grundy, Australian National University, Canberra, Australia
Jan-Juan Hiemer, Daimler-Benz AG, Berlin, Germany
David Jackson, Praxis Critical Systems, UK
Torsten Klein, Daimler-Benz AG, Berlin, Germany
Frank Lattemann, Daimler-Benz AG, Berlin, Germany
Eckard Lehmann, Daimler-Benz AG, Berlin, Germany
Cecilia Mascolo, University of Bologna, Italy
Bill Stoddart, University of Teesside, UK
Carsten Sühl, GMD FIRST, Germany
Alain Vailly, University of Nantes, France
Kirsten Winter, GMD FIRST, Germany

Sponsors

The 11th International Conference of Z Users greatly benefited from the cooperation and sponsorship of the following organizations:

Daimler-Benz AG
GMD FIRST
Technical University of Berlin
Praxis Critical Systems

Tutorial Programme

The following tutorials were scheduled on the day prior to the main conference (23rd September 1998):

Developing Safety-Critical Embedded Systems: The ESPRESS Approach
Wolfgang Grieskamp, Maritta Heisel, Thomas Santen, and Matthias Weber,
The ESPRESS Project, Germany

Effective Use of Z/EVES
Mark Saaltink, ORA, Canada

Educational Issues Session

The following informal talks were presented at a half-day session held immediately after the conference (26th September 1998):

What and How to Teach

Z on the Web
Jonathan Bowen, The University of Reading, UK

Mental models of Z
Neville Dean, University of East Anglia, UK

What makes a good specification case study? (Panel Discussion)
Norah Power, University of Limerick, Ireland

Assessment Issues

Collaborative work to answer a test on formal specification in B
Henri Habrias, University of Nantes, France

Managing Z coursework on-line
Zarina Shukur, Edmund Burke, and Eric Foxley, University of Nottingham, UK

Poster

Table of Contents

Semantic Theory

Theory and Standards

Reasoning and Consistency Issues

Refinement

Object Orientation

Appendices

Industrial Requirements for the Efficient Development of Reliable Embedded Systems

(Extended Abstract)

Klaus Grimm

Daimler-Benz AG, Research and Technology, Software Technology Laboratory
Alt-Moabit 96A, D-10559 Berlin, Germany
Tel: +49 30 39982 226   Fax: +49 30 39982 107
Email: Klaus.Grimm@dbag.bln.daimlerbenz.com

1   Introduction: Crucial Conditions and Requirements

Software-based systems are gaining in importance in almost all business units of the Daimler-Benz Group. In numerous units differentiation between the competitors is achieved mainly by innovative functions implemented in software. Furthermore, a lot of important business processes are based on software solutions. Hence, the quality of the systems as well as the efficiency of the development and business processes are decisive for competition.

Important conditions are:

- the increasing use of software in safety-related areas,
- the increasing complexity of the systems,
- the high cost for system development and maintenance,
- the demands to be met by the systems themselves as well as the development pro-cess, given by various standards and legal requirements.

The most important requirement resulting from this is system dependability, i.e. relia-bility and safety. Nevertheless, this dependability has to be achieved in an efficient way by means of appropriate process models, methods and tools.

2   State of the Art

At present, several different notations, methods and tools are being used for each of the development tasks such as specification, design and testing. Most of the specification measures are based on graphically represented notations like Structured Analysis and Statecharts. These notations are a widely accepted compromise between preciseness and automation capabilities on the one hand, and usability and intuitive understanding on the other.

Practical experience shows that the use of mathematically sound formal methods is likely to improve the quality of specifications significantly. It ensures that the problem to be solved as well as the solution planned are investigated and described much more precisely, and computer support for further constructive and analytical development steps is facilitated to a greater extent. However, most of the formal approaches require a sound mathematical background training or at least a deep mathematical understanding, and the effort to introduce these concepts into new or current projects is generally very high.

At Daimler-Benz, there is currently no regular use of formal methods like VDM or Z, but some promising practical trials are being carried out in various fields of application. A number of research projects were set up to investigate the strengths and weaknesses of formal methods in general and Z in particular, and to evaluate different specification and verification approaches based on formal methods. The results have been or will be reported at the corresponding conferences. The main topics of research and application and the current experience are briefly listed in Section 4 below.

3 Specific Requirements

Based on the experience gained with the research work and the practical trials of formal methods Daimler-Benz Research has put forward a list of requirements which have to be fulfilled by (new) processes, methods and tools to ensure an efficient development of dependable software-based systems. The most important requirements are:

- A sound process model has to be defined based on relevant standards and guidelines. It has to regulate all development steps, milestones, reviews and responsibilities.
- A methodological support for the whole development process is required, providing a high degree of formalization and automation. Errors have to be avoided or at least uncovered at the earliest possible stage, in particular by integration of a powerful verification and validation concept as well as animation and visualization utilities even at specification level. Furthermore, an efficient change management has to be provided based on appropriate tracing mechanisms. Last but not least, the development has to be supported by a powerful configuration management.
- The notations and methods have to be easily learnable for well-trained users. To avoid totally new investments and to enable the user to continue to work in an accepted methodological environment, new formal notations have to be integrated – or at least combined – with established well-accepted graphical methods and notations.
- All methods and notations have to be supported by appropriate tools forming an open development environment with a comfortable user interface and without major breaks or gaps. This environment should be based on commonly used established tools.
- If required, the documents produced during system development have to be easily understandable by partners, customers and licencing authorities.
- Comprehensive, user-friendly guidelines for the application of the methods and tools have to be provided as well as appropriate documents for tutorials.
- The methodological framework as well as the tool environment have to prove adequate and powerful when applied to representative industrial case studies.
- The methods and tools have to be capable of being easily integrated into the existing development processes. For this reason, they also have to comply with all

national and international development standards relevant to the specific application. At best, methods and tools are widely accepted and commonly used to form an ideal basis for national and international cooperations.
- The benefits of the use of new approaches have to be described and calculated on the basis of the practical trials.

4 Current Research Work

The research work carried out at Daimler-Benz in the field of software engineering for embedded systems is strongly oriented towards these requirements. The focus is not to invent new methods or tools but to gain advantages over competitors by sound company-internal processes as well as methods and tools which are combined in an efficient way to form an integrated development environment. Furthermore, one of the most decisive factors is the extensive know-how of the engineers and managers of their processes and the current best methods, tools and technologies. The most important job of the research departments is to support the business units to gain and consolidate a top position in these fields of software technology. Only in areas where a new method or tool is required to ensure a better position, is a new solution developed within the company.

As a consequence, important elements of the improvement of the current practice are:

- the investigation of new technological trends,
- the evaluation of innovative technologies, methods and tools,
- the detailed analysis of the current development processes including appropriate process improvement activities,
- the identification of major technological and methodological deficiencies,
- the closing of these gaps by means of innovative research-based concepts,
- the introduction of those concepts, methods and tools into the current development processes and practices which are best suited for the specific application,
- comprehensive coaching in the use of these methods and tools.

A specific research field is directed at the use of formal methods in the development of safety-related software-based systems. Following the above-mentioned requirements no absolutely new notations are defined, but the established methods providing a descriptive graphical representation are enhanced by and combined with appropriate formal notations. These formal notations are introduced only at those places where the existing approaches do not provide sufficient abstraction, preciseness or automation capabilities.

For instance, Statecharts are widely accepted especially in the field of vehicle electronics but have shortcomings mainly with respect to the level of abstraction of the specification of operations. Therefore, Z is used to specify these operations as well as the state space including the initial state, the communication channels, and the invariants with respect to system behaviour. Data flow diagrams are used to describe the system environment. The system behaviour is specified by means of Statecharts, with both notations supported by the STATEMATE tool. Semantics are being defined for the combination of the two notations, and powerful analysis mechanisms are being developed to provide several consistency and completeness checks [2]. This development approach has been applied successfully to an intelligent cruise control system [1].

Another research project is focused on the integration of SA/RT and Z. The functional decomposition of the system is described by means of data flow diagrams, the functional behaviour by state transition diagrams. Z is used to specify the interfaces, the state space including initial state and data, and the system functions. This development approach has been successfully applied to two real-world projects: one in the field of space systems in terms of a component of the Columbus Software, the other one in the area of defence systems.

In addition, research work is being carried out to improve the specification of embedded real-time systems by means of an interval temporal logic [4]. Furthermore, another focus is the verification and validation of embedded systems based on formal methods. Model checking techniques are investigated to ensure an effective verification of formal specifications [3], and innovative algorithms are developed to automate test case design and test evaluation as extensively as possible [5].

5   Conclusions

All in all, the experience gained with the practical application of these research results is promising. The notations proved to be applicable to representative real-world problems, and improvements in terms of preciseness and degree of automation of the system development could be shown. Nevertheless, the transfer of the approaches crucially depends on the acceptance by the users. This requires comprehensive education and coaching. Furthermore, experiments have to be carried out to prove the real benefit of the use of formal methods in terms of development time and cost over the whole system's life cycle. The result should be a guideline for the specific use of formal methods regarding the system characteristics as well as the safety and reliability requirements of the system and its components.

References

1. M. Conrad and D. Wetter. An Adaptive Cruise Control System – A Case Study for the Industrial Use of Formal Methods. Workshop on Formal Design of Safety Critical Embedded Systems, Munich, Germany, 16–18 April 1997.
2. W. Grieskamp, M. Heisel, and H. Dörr. Specifying Embedded Systems with Statecharts and Z: An Agenda for Cyclic Software Components. In E. Astesiano, editor, Proceedings of Formal Aspects of Software Engineering (FASE '98), 30 March – 1 April 1998. To appear.
3. J. Hiemer and K. Fuhrmann. Formal Verification of Statemate-Statecharts. In Proceedings of the Int. Conf. on Tool Support for System Specification, Development, and Verification. Malente, Germany, 2–4 June 1998. To appear.
4. F. Lattemann and E. Lehmann. A Methodological Approach to the Requirement Specification of Embedded Systems. In M.G. Hinchey and S. Liu, editors, Proceedings of 1st IEEE Int. Conf. on Formal Engineering Methods, pages 183–191, IEEE Computer Society, 1997.
5. H. Singh, M. Conrad, and S. Sadeghipour. Test Case Design Based on Z and the Classification-Tree Method. In M.G. Hinchey and S. Liu, editors, Proceedings of 1st IEEE Int. Conf. on Formal Engineering Methods, pages 81–90, IEEE Computer Society, 1997.

How to Combine Z with a Process Algebra*

Clemens Fischer

University of Oldenburg, FB Informatik
P.O. Box 2503, 26111 Oldenburg, Germany

Email: Fischer@Informatik.Uni-Oldenburg.de

Abstract. The specification language Z has been designed to describe data and functional aspects of systems, but it does not define a semantics for specifications in a distributed setting. Process algebras, on the other hand, concentrate on the behaviour of communicating agents. For this reason the combination of Z with a process algebra recently got a lot of attention. In this paper we summarise and categorise the different approaches and identify pitfalls and shortcomings in existing combinations. Thereby we give an overview over the many possible answers to the question: 'What is the behavioural semantics of a Z specification?'

1 Introduction

Z is a very successful language – at least compared with a lot of other formal techniques. It is used in realistic case studies and has a very active user group. The language is strong at describing functional or data aspects of systems. But it was not designed for the description of concurrent, communicating or distributed systems. Although Z is often used for this purpose, this is not supported by the language itself. Strictly speaking, a Z schema has no behavioural semantics. According to the draft standard [30], a Z specification introduces a universe of names and associated values. But the way input and output parameters are processed is not defined nor is the triggering condition (i. e. the guard) of an operation clear. Consequently authors differ in the behavioural interpretation of Z schemas. Often these aspects are even kept implicit, which is clearly against the spirit of a *formal* method. E. g. the question whether the triggering condition of an operation is the precondition or not is a source of endless confusion. Standard data refinement rules [36] imply that an operation can always be invoked; thus the precondition is not the guard. But as this interpretation is often not useful for concurrent systems, various different approaches are used (see [37] for a summary).

To define the behavioural semantics of Z formally, it is attractive to combine it with a formalism specialised in concurrency; like process algebras, which are, on the other hand, weak at specifying complex data aspects. Thus the combination can be used to design wide spectrum specification languages, taking the best of two worlds. This has been done for CCS [27] and Z in [19, 38], and for CSP [21] and Z in [14, 32], and for Object-Z [10] and CSP in [15, 35]. However, in the same way as the informal behavioural interpretations of Z differ, we now see a variety of different formal definitions.

---

* This research is supported by the German Ministry for Education and Research (BMBF) as part of the project UniForM under grant No. FKZ 01 IS 521 B2.

In this paper we investigate in general which design decisions must be taken when combining Z with a process algebra and we categorise the existing work according to the decisions taken there. Although there is not *one* single superior combination, we are able to identify criteria for a good combination of Z and a process algebra, and we spot omissions and pitfalls in existing definitions.

We start our investigation with a demonstration of the different approaches based on a common case study. The remaining sections introduce the major problems that occur when Z is combined with a process algebra; i.e. style of semantics, granularity of Z operations, guards, the meaning of input and output parameters and types of channels and parameters.

In this paper we do not consider timed process algebras. Work on this topic is only taken into account when it has implications for the untimed case. However, the problems discussed here are also relevant for the combination of Z with timed process algebras.

2   Case Study

To explain the different approaches, we introduce a simplified specification of a UNIX connectionless socket. Sockets transmit sequences of bytes with some maximal length.

$$\mid max : \mathbb{N}_1$$

$$Byte == 0 \ldots 255$$
$$MSG == \{m : \text{seq} \, Byte \mid \#m \leq max\}$$

The order of messages is not preserved in connectionless sockets. Thus we store just the bag (i.e. multiset) of pending messages.

```
┌─ StateSoc ─────────────        ┌─ InitSoc ─────────────
│ s : bag MSG                     │ StateSoc
└───────────────────────         ├──────────────────────
                                  │ s = [[ ]]
                                  └──────────────────────
```

The UNIX system call *sendto* is used to send an array of bytes via a socket. The return value is the number of bytes that could be stored in the socket. For simplicity we omit file descriptors here. We divide the specification into two parts: First we only consider the normal case, then possible errors are specified. The schema *sendto* is then specified by disjunction.

—*sendto_normal*—

$\Delta StateSoc$

$d? : MSG$ [the message]

$l? : \mathbb{Z}$ [length of the message]

$q! : \mathbb{Z}$

$\lceil$Length of the message that is stored inside the socket. $q! = -1$ if an error oc-$\rceil$
$\lfloor$curred. Thus $l? = q!$ is the normal behaviour.$\rfloor$

$l? \leq \#d?$

$0 \leq q! \leq l?$

$\lceil$The value of $q!$ is chosen nondeterministically. It depends on the amount of$\rceil$
$|$memory the operating system can use and how much memory is used by other$|$
$\lfloor$processes.$\rfloor$

$q! > 0 \Rightarrow s' = s \uplus [\![1..q! \lhd d?]\!]$ [Only the first $q!$ bytes of $d?$ are stored.]

$q! = 0 \Rightarrow s' = s$

—*sendto_error*—

$\Delta StateSoc$

$d? : MSG$

$l?, q! : \mathbb{Z}$

$l? \leq \#d? \wedge q! = -1$ [If an internal error occurs, the value -1 is returned.]

$s' = s \vee \exists n : 1..l? \bullet s' = s \uplus [\![1..n \lhd d?]\!]$

[If an error occurs a message may or may not be stored.]

$sendto \mathrel{\hat=} sendto\_normal \vee sendto\_error$

The system call *recvfrom* is used to read messages from a socket. For lack of space we
ignore errors here.

—*recvfrom*—

$\Delta StateSoc$

$n? : \mathbb{Z}$

$\lceil$The maximal number of bytes that can be received. $n?$ should be the number of$\rceil$
$\lfloor$bytes that are allocated in the memory to store the message.$\rfloor$

$l! : \mathbb{Z}$ [The length of the message.]

$d! : MSG$

$\exists x : s \bullet (s' = s \uplus [\![x]\!] \wedge$ [x is taken out of the bag of stored messages.]

$\qquad d! \text{ prefix } x \wedge$

$\qquad l! = \#d! = min\{n?, \#x\})$

[If $n? < \#x$ holds only a prefix of x is sent back.]

This completes the Z specification. However, important aspects of the behaviour of a
socket are not captured yet. E. g.

1. What happens if *recvfrom* is used when s is empty? UNIX sockets can be used in
    two modes: *recvfrom* can either be blocking until a message arrives or it returns the
    value -1 if no message is pending.

2. What happens if we call *sendto* with parameters such that $\#d? < l?$ holds? In this case the system might read more bytes than actually allocated in the memory.

This kind of question is clarified if the combination with a process algebra is taken into account. In the following we show how the socket specification might look like in different combinations.

Smith [35] gives a CSP semantics for Object-Z [10] classes. The class socket could be as follows.

```
┌─Socket─────────────────────────────────────────────────────
│ ┌──────────────────────────────  ┌─INIT──────────────────
│ │ StateSoc                        │ InitSoc
│ └──────────────────────────────  └───────────────────────
│
│ ┌─sendto───────────────────────  ┌─recvfrom──────────────
│ │ ...                             │ ...
│ └──────────────────────────────  └───────────────────────
│
│ The definition of sendto and recvfrom are the same as above; but ΔStateSoc is
│ replaced by Δ(s). This delta list specifies the variables that can be changed by an
│ operation.
└───────────────────────────────────────────────────────────
```

The sequence $\langle(sendto,f),(recvfrom,g)\rangle$ with the functions $f = \{l \mapsto 3, d \mapsto \langle 2,4,6,8\rangle,$ $q \mapsto 3\}$ and $g = \{n \mapsto 10, d \mapsto \langle 2,4,6\rangle, l \mapsto 3\}$ is a possible trace of the CSP semantics of the class *Socket*. Following Smith, the operations *sendto* or *recvfrom* cannot occur if $\#d? < l?$ or $s = \varnothing$ hold.[1]

The combination in [15] – called CSP-OZ – is based on the same idea, but extends the class with the declaration of the interface and an optional CSP process.

```
┌─Socket─────────────────────────────────────────────────────
│ channel sendto : [d? : MSG; l? : ℤ; q! : ℤ]
│ channel recvfrom : [n? : ℤ; l! : ℤ; d! : MSG]
│ ...                          [State, initialisation and operations as above.]
│ com_sendto ≙ sendto
│ com_recvfrom ≙ recvfrom
│   ┌The keyword com indicates that the operation recvfrom is blocking if no message┐
│   └is pending.                                                                    ┘
└───────────────────────────────────────────────────────────
```

The CSP semantics of *Socket* is almost the same as in the work of Smith. However, differences in the interpretation of the parameters lead to divergence in the case $\#d? > l?$. By using other keywords, CSP-OZ allows the specification of non-blocking operations and explicit guards.

Mahony and Dong [26] propose a combination of Object-Z and timed CSP, called TCOZ. Instead of identifying operations and channels, as it is done in the two approaches above, they map parameters to channels individually. The operation *sendto* would be specified as

---

[1] He also does not support the separation of *sendto_normal* and *sendto_error*. Both operations would be visible for a user of the class socket.

---
sendto

$\Delta(s)$

$d?: MSG$ **on** $sendto_1$

$l?: \mathbb{Z}$ **on** $sendto_2$

$q!: \mathbb{Z}$ **on** $sendto\_out$

$sendto\_normal \lor sendto\_error$

This schema could engage in the trace

$$\langle(sendto_2,3),(sendto_1,\langle2,4,6,8\rangle),(sendto\_out,3)\rangle \quad \text{or}$$
$$\langle(sendto_1,\langle2,4,6,8\rangle),(sendto_2,3),(sendto\_out,3)\rangle$$

for example. Mahony and Dong use extra syntax to separate the guard from the effect of an operation. Thus both, blocking and non-blocking mode can be specified. The case $\#d? < l?$ is modelled by divergence.

Roscoe, Woodcock and Wulf [32] suggest a translation of Z into CSP. Therefore they have to divide every operation schema into two schemas: one for the input and one for the output parameters. On this basis they translate Z to CSP. The idea is to code the state of the Z specification into the parameter of a CSP process. We use Z notation to manipulate parameters although this feature is not worked out in [32].

$$Socket = S([\![\,]\!])$$
$$S(s) = \quad (sendto\_in?l?d \to \bigsqcap q: -1..l \bullet sendto\_out!q \to$$
$$\textbf{if } q > 0 \textbf{ then } S(s \uplus [\![1..q \lhd d!]\!]) \textbf{ else } S(s) \sqcap S(s \uplus [\![1..q \lhd d!]\!]))$$
$$\square \ (recvfrom\_in?n \to$$
$$\bigsqcap x: s \bullet recvfrom\_out!(1..min\{n,\#x\} \lhd x)!(min\{n,\#x\})$$
$$\to S(s \uplus [\![1..min\{n,\#x\} \lhd x]\!]))$$

The notation '$sendto\_in?l?d$' stands for receiving two values over the channel $sendto\_in$; the symbol '$\bigsqcap q: -1..l$' denotes the nondeterministic choice of q out of the set $-1..l$; by '$recvfrom!x!y$' the values x and y are sent over the channel $recvfrom$. The symbol '$\square$' stands for the external choice. The name $sendto\_in$ is our invention; no standard mapping from Z operations to CSP event names is suggested in [32].

Note that the above CSP process is the result of a (non-automatic) translation procedure which defines a semantics of the above Z specification. It is not suggested in [32] to use CSP as specification language which replaces Z.

Taguchi and Araki [38] would start with our initial Z specification and make references to the schema names within CCS process definitions.

$$Socket = InitSoc.S$$
$$S = \quad sendto\_in(d?,l?).sendto.\overline{sendto\_out}(q!).S$$
$$+ recvfrom\_in(n?).recvfrom.\overline{recvfrom\_out}(l!,d!).S$$

The process (or agent) S can perform the input action $sendto\_in$, which binds the received values to the identifiers $d?$ and $l?$. Again any name could be used instead of *sendto_in*. Note that we could also write $sendto_2(d?).sendto_2(n?)$ if input parameters are not passed in one step (non-atomic value passing). The dot '.' is used in CCS for the same purpose as the arrow '→' in CSP: action prefixing. The action *sendto* refers to the above Z schema. It results in a state where b and $q!$ are changed according to the Z specification. The over-lined *sendto_out* is an output event. The choice operator '+' offers the choice between the actions *sendto* and *recvfrom*. In this simple example the meaning is the same as the CSP operator '□'. Taguchi and Araki only use the blocking view. The system would deadlock after receiving $\#d? < l?$.[2]

The language CCZ by Galloway [16] is similar to this approach, although specifications are structured in the spirit of Object-Z. A CCZ specification of a socket can be found in Fig. 1. The semantics of the agent definition is similar to the Taguchi and Araki approach.[3]

$$Socket \overset{def}{=}$$

State *StateSoc* **where**

$$\_StateSoc_____$$
$$s : \mathbb{P}\,MSG$$

Initialisation *InitSoc* **where** ...   [*InitSoc* from above]

Operations

...   [*sendto_normal, sendto_error*, ... from above]

Agents

$$\text{main} \overset{def}{=} \quad sendto\_in(d? : MSG; \, l? : \mathbb{Z}); \, \mathbf{Z}(sendto); \, \overline{sendto\_out}(q!); \, \text{main}$$
$$+ \, recvfrom\_in(n? : \mathbb{Z}); \, \mathbf{Z}(recvfrom); \, \overline{recvfrom\_out}(l!, d!); \, \text{main}$$

Fig. 1. CCZ specification of a socket

We can now start to look at the different approaches in more detail.

3   Syntactical versus semantical Combination

Combination of formal languages means to design something new with an emphasis on reusing existing formalisms. The more existing syntax, semantics, methods and tools can be reused, the better is the combination. For the existing integrations of Z and process algebras we can differentiate two basic styles which we propose to call *syntactical* and *semantical combination*.

A syntactical combination starts with defining syntax by combining the syntax of Z and a process algebra and then defines the semantics of the new language by lifting

---

[2] It is possible to handle the case $\#d? < l?$ separately and to model also divergent behaviour. But this has to be done explicitly by the specifier.

[3] We omitted extra declarations of output variables which is necessary in CCZ.

existing definitions. This was done for the combinations of Z and CCS by Taguchi and Araki [38] and Galloway [16]. They mix Z and CCS syntax, define an appropriate labelled transition system that reflects the state of Z variables and CCS processes and give transition rules for all operators (e. g. parallel composition). Mahony and Dong [26] work in a similar fashion with Object-Z and Timed CSP.

A semantical combination, on the other hand, takes some part of a Z specification and identifies this with a process. Thus Z can be seen as an alternative way of describing a process. The best basis for this style of combination happens to be some object-oriented extension of Z, like Object-Z, because classes are the natural candidate to be identified with a process. E. g. Smith [35] and Fischer [15] define CSP semantics for Object-Z classes. Roscoe, Woodcock and Wulf [32] and Fischer [14] have worked on semantical integrations of pure Z and CSP.

The syntactical combinations provide a deeper integration of Z and the process algebra. It is possible to access variables of the Z part within process algebra expressions which is impossible for a semantical integration. The reason for this is the absence of global variables in the underlying process algebra. Consequently the state of the Z specification can only be changed by Z operations in a semantical integration.[4]

However, the price to pay for the liberal variable handling of a syntactical integration is the extra complexity of redefining semantics for process algebra operators. Although these redefinitions are simple liftings of existing rules, they are an obstacle for tool reuse.

In a semantical combination, Z and the process algebra are more separated. Thus for transformations and analysis that affect one part alone, existing tools can be reused without any change. For a deeper tool integration, only the semantic embedding has to be represented. E. g. for the language CSP-Z [14] first model checking results based on FDR [12] are already available [29]. The translation from Z to CSP in [32] is also used to analyse a Z specification with FDR.

For a syntactical combination tool reuse seems to be more difficult although we have to wait for more work on tool integration before we come to clear statements on this topic. But the trade off between an expressible language from a syntactical integration and simple tool reuse of a semantical integration is a major challenge for future research in this area.

4   Refinement Rules

Both, Z and process algebras, come with a notation of refinement, which allows to prove that an implementation is correct with respect to some specification. The embedding of Z into some process algebra relates the refinement rules of both worlds. I. e. let $[\![S]\!]_P$ be the semantics of the Z specification S in the process algebra P and let $\sqsubseteq_Z$ and $\sqsubseteq_P$ be the refinement relations on Z and P respectively. We then expect that for any Z specifications C and A the refinement relation is respected by $[\![.]\!]_P$:

$$A \sqsubseteq_Z C \quad \Longrightarrow \quad [\![A]\!]_P \sqsubseteq_P [\![C]\!]_P$$

---

[4] It is possible to mimic global variables by process algebras. The trick is to define each variable as a process. But the semantic complexity is enormous.

The exact formalisation of these rules gives important insights in the details of a combination. This was worked out for combinations of Object-Z and CSP in [13,33].

Weak Refinement Process algebras usually have a concept of local events. E. g. the CSP process $P \setminus L$ (P hide L) behaves like the process P but all events from the set L ('local events') happen spontaneously and are concealed from the environment. Z itself does not have the concept of a local operation, but it is nevertheless used informally in some case studies (e. g. a telecommunications protocol in [39]). Z refinement rules that take local operations into account are called weak data refinement rules [8]. The combination of Z with a process algebra allows a correctness proof for weak data refinement rules. Let $\sqsubseteq_W^O$ denote weak data refinement with the set of local operations O and let $Events(O)$ be the set of corresponding process algebra events. Then

$$(A \sqsubseteq_W^O C) \Rightarrow (\llbracket A \setminus Events(O) \rrbracket_P \sqsubseteq_P \llbracket C \setminus Events(O) \rrbracket_P)$$

should hold for all specifications C and A. Such rules are proven for CSP-OZ in [13]. The weak refinement rules in [8] fail this test because the introduction of infinite occurrence of local operations is not considered there.

5   Granularity of Z Operations

An event of a process algebra is the basic atomic step a system can perform. From the Z point of view, a system evolves by executing operations. Thus a key issue for this paper is the relation between events and operations.

From Sec. 2 we can identify three possibilities which we propose to call as follows.

- The *single event approach* makes a one to one correspondence between operations and events. Thus every occurrence of the operation *sendto* is modelled by a single event *sendto.f* with some function f assigning values to the parameters. It is used in [35, 14, 15] and already in the trace semantics of Object-Z [10, 34].
- The *double event approach* takes a more implementation oriented point of view. It introduces an event for reading the input values and one for sending the output parameters. The double event approach is advocated in [32].
- Finally, the *multi event approach* is even more detailed. Any (type correct) channel can be used to process a parameter. There is no fixed connection between Z operations and process algebra events. This approach is used in [38, 16, 26]. As it is possible to process more than one parameter with a single event, the multi event approach can easily simulate the double event approach.

The choice between the three approaches depends on the kind of system that should be modelled and the abstraction level that is used. The single event approach is useful for a high abstraction level. E. g. from the point of view of a user of a socket the system call *sendto* is atomic and therefore the single event approach is the suitable abstraction level. Furthermore, method calls of object-oriented languages are examples where the single event approach can be useful.

The double event approach is nearer to an implementation as we can actually observe two events. E. g. from the point of view of the operating system, the two event approach is appropriate as it is possible to model overlapping calls of *sendto* from different users.

The multi event approach is useful for systems where value passing is not atomic or overlapping methods calls do matter. E. g. a polling based controller that reads some input values in an arbitrary order, calculates a state transition and sends out the output parameters is modelled closely with a multi event approach.

However, the double- and multi event approaches have a pitfall: Every operation involving transmission of parameters is split into two or more events: first input parameters are received and then output is sent. If for a possible communication partner the splitting of the corresponding operation has to be done in reverse order since input and output are switched then partners in a parallel composi-

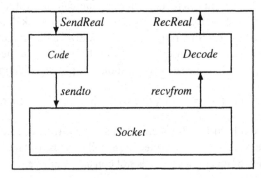

Fig. 2. Transmission of real numbers using sockets

tion fail to synchronise. We explain the problem with the following example. We want to use sockets to transmit real numbers. The overall structure we are aiming at can be found in Fig. 2. The component *Code* receives some real number (represented by integer values for the exponent and the mantissa), codes it somehow into a sequence of bytes and uses a socket connection to send it to *Decode* where the original number is restored. The structure corresponds to the CSP process (*Code* $\|$ *Socket* $\|$ *Decode*) $\setminus$ {*sendto, recvfrom*} where $\|$ denotes parallel composition of processes.

In Fig. 3 we have specified *Code* using CSP-OZ, which uses a single event approach. Also in the multi event approach of [16, 38] we have no problem:

$\_code\_$
$exp?, man? : \mathbb{Z}$
$d!, l! : \mathbb{Z}$

$l! = \#d! \land d! = f(exp?, man?)$
  [The injective function f to code real numbers as bytes is not specified here.]

The schema *code* translates a real number into a sequence of bytes. This schema can be used within CCS:

$$Code \stackrel{def}{=} SendReal(exp?, man?).code.\overline{sendto\_in}(d!, l!).sendto\_out(q?).Code$$

Note that we do not need an extra store like *next* because we have direct access to the variables within the CCS process. Thus this is an example for the bigger flexibility of a syntactical over a semantical combination.

```
Code
  channel SendReal : [exp?, man? : ℤ]
  channel sendto : [d! : MSG; l! : ℤ; q? : ℤ]
  main  = SendReal → sendto → main
                [The CSP process main restricts possible occurrence of operations.]
```

next : MSG

effect_SendReal
$\Delta(next)$
$exp?, man? : \mathbb{Z}$

$next' = f(exp?, man?)$

effect_sendto
$\Delta()$
$d! : \text{seq } Byte$
$l!, q? : \mathbb{Z}$

$l! = \#d! \land d! = next$

We omit the specification of the injective function f that translates integers to sequences of bytes. The keyword **effect** indicates that *SendReal* and *sendto* are non-blocking.

Fig. 3. Specification of *Code* in CSP-OZ

However, every approach that sticks to the 'first input then output order' like [32], cannot specify the operation *sendto* from *Code* directly. It is not possible simply to interchange the input and output parameters as it is done above. The schema

sendto
$\Delta State$
$d! : MSG$
$l!, q? : \mathbb{Z}$

$\ldots$

generates the events $\langle sendto\_out.?q, sendto\_in.!(d, l) \rangle$ because the order of reading input and writing output parameters is fixed in the semantics. But this does not match the traces from the specification of the socket above and runs into deadlock. The only solution is to use two schemas to handle input and output parameters separately.

To avoid these complications it might be useful to provide two kinds of schemas to cover both orders of parameter passing.

6   Guards and undefined Behaviour

Formalisms like B [1], VDM [24], Statecharts [20], action systems [5] or the guarded command language [9] have a syntactic construct to distinguish the guard (or triggering condition) of an operation from its effect. The guard is a boolean expression defining when an operation can be executed.

Z, however, does not have this separation, as it was originally designed for the description of sequential systems where operations can always be executed. If for a given state and input parameters no final state and no output parameters are defined the result of the operation is not predictable. E. g. the outcome of the operation *Div*

$$
\begin{array}{l}
\underline{\_Div}\underline{} \\
\quad z, z' : \mathbb{N} \\
\quad in?, out! : \mathbb{N} \\
\hline
\quad out! = in?\,\mathrm{div}\,z \wedge z' = z
\end{array}
$$

used with $z = 0$ is not specified and thus – in the standard, established interpretation – any behaviour is allowed. We call this the *non-blocking view*. The precondition

$$\mathrm{pre}\,S = S \setminus (x'_1, \ldots, x'_m, y_1!, \ldots, y_n!)$$

(where x_i are the state variables and y_j the output parameters of S) characterises the states and input parameters some result of the operation is defined for. Therefore standard data refinement rules [36] allow not only the reduction of nondeterminism but also a weaker precondition. E. g. the operation Div_2

$$
\begin{array}{l}
\underline{\_Div_2}\underline{} \\
\quad z, z' : \mathbb{N} \\
\quad in?, out! : \mathbb{N} \\
\hline
\quad z = 0 \Rightarrow out! = 0 \\
\quad z \neq 0 \Rightarrow out! = in?\,\mathrm{div}\,z \\
\quad z' = z
\end{array}
$$

is a refinement of *Div*.

However, to describe communicating and distributed systems it is necessary to express that an operation is disabled and cannot occur. E. g. if a socket is used in blocking mode the execution of the system call *recvfrom* is delayed if no message is pending. Therefore a lot of authors simply use the precondition as the guard of an operation [10, 8, 16, 35, 38]. We call this the *blocking view*. Consequently the data refinement rules differ in this aspect; the precondition of refined operations must be equivalent to the abstract one.

But this approach is too simple as we can see at the socket example. A part of the precondition of the operation *sendto* from Sec. 2 is the condition $l? \leq \#d?$, i. e. $l?$ should not be bigger than the length of the message. However, memory requests beyond the allowed bounds are common errors in C based programs. The socket cannot prevent a user from sending wrong parameters. Thus here the established non-blocking view exactly reflects standard UNIX implementations: In case of $l? > \#d?$ something unpredictable will happen.

Furthermore, it is a standard recommendation of software engineering methods to specify normal behaviour and exceptional behaviour separately. E. g. the operation *Div* from above specifies only the standard behaviour whereas Div_2 catches the exception of a division by 0. As Div_2 is a refinement of Div in the non-blocking view all proofs and validations that have been done for the system where Div is used are also true when we turn to Div_2. In the blocking interpretation this is no longer true. There is no refinement relation between Div and Div_2 and consequently the separation of normal behaviour and exceptional behaviour is not well supported by using only this view.

Thus neither blocking nor non-blocking view alone are enough to use Z in a distributed context and we have to capture two aspects in combination of Z and a process algebra:

- The guard of an operation.
- Undefined behaviour if an operation is enabled but no transition is defined for this case. Undefined behaviour is called divergence in a process algebra.

Mahony and Dong [26] argue along the same line. They interpret schemas as non-blocking and introduce extra syntax to specify what they call the 'state guard'.

For the same purpose, two keywords are introduced in CSP-OZ [15]: enable and effect. The schema enable_op specifies the guard of the operation *op*. It must contain unprimed state variables only, whereas the schema effect_op may contain primed and unprimed state variables. It specifies the transition that can take place if the operation *op* is executed. This solution is flexible enough to model all other existing interpretations via suitable abbreviations. E. g. the schema com_op abbreviates the standard blocking view: effect_op = pre com_op and enable_op = com_op. Other views, like the firing condition approach suggested by Strulo [37] can be integrated in the same way.

The semantic complexity of this solution is small; at some point in the integration the guard has to be computed anyway.

The data refinement rules for CSP-OZ are worked out in detail in [13] establishing the proof indicated in Sec. 4: A concrete Object-Z class C refines an abstract class A if for all operations *op* (under some suitable abstraction relation) the following holds:

1. Every transition possible for effect_op_C is either allowed by effect_op_A or pre effect_op_A does not hold (reduction of nondeterminism).
2. pre effect_op_A implies pre effect_op_C (reduction of divergence).
3. effect_op_C and effect_op_A are equivalent.

In the case of the non-blocking view we have enable_op = *true*; thus these rules coincide with the standard Z data refinement rules.

All other existing combinations have either shortcomings concerning this point or they are not precise about the guard. The combination in [35] sticks to the blocking view, and so do [16, 38]. However, due to the flexibility of a syntactical combination, Taguchi, Araki and Galloway can model the divergent case in their combinations. But a designer has to explicitly specify it for *every* occurrence of an operation.

7   Input and Output Parameters

As we have frequently done above, the decorations ? and ! are used to separate input and output parameters of an operation. Unfortunately we are again in the situation that the

Z standard does not define a semantics for these decorations. But the intuition behind Z parameters is as follows:

- An input parameter is solely controlled by the environment. If an operation is enabled all possible input values must be accepted. Thus an operation should not block on input values for which no transition is defined. E. g. using *sendto* with $l? > \#d?$ should lead to undefined behaviour (non-blocking input parameters).
- An evaluation of an output parameter, on the other hand, should only be done by the operation. The communication partner must accept any possible value. E. g. any possible value for $q!$ must be accepted from a process using *sendto*. This has to be reflected by a nondeterministic choice over different values for output parameters in the underlying process algebra.

This should be reflected by the refinement rules we expect. An implementation can restrict the choice between different output parameters and could be more defined on input values.

$$
\begin{array}{l}
\hline
\text{\_\_}sendto\_error_2 \text{_____} \\
\quad \Delta StateSoc \\
\quad d? : MSG \\
\quad l?, q! : \mathbb{Z} \\
\hline
\quad l? > \#q? \wedge q! = -1 \wedge s' = s \\
\hline
\end{array}
$$

The schema $sendto_l \triangleq sendto\_normal \vee sendto\_error \vee sendto\_error_2$ should implement *sendto* from Sec. 2 because $sendto_l$ is defined for more input parameters.

The double and multi event approaches model this behaviour naturally. Input values are received before the actual transition is executed which itself can choose any output parameter independently from the environment. However, the expected refinement rules do only hold if undefined input parameters lead to divergence.

For the single event approach it is tricky to get the desired rules. A possible solution is worked out in [15]. The proof of the expected refinement rules can be found in [13]. Note that it does not make sense to use input variables within enable schemas, as this would place an unwanted restriction on the input parameters and falsify the expected refinement rule.[5]

The trace semantics of Object-Z [34] and the combination with CSP in [35] does not reflect the distinction between input and output parameters semantically.

Simple Parameters Non-blocking input parameters in Z stem from the non-blocking view of Z operation schemas. However, several authors found it useful to restrict possible input values for specifications in a distributed setting. E. g. CCZ allows to restrict possible input values arbitrarily. A closer look at the socket example discovers a similar necessity. UNIX offers a blocking mode for the operation *sendto*. If a message is too long to be stored internally *sendto* blocks until enough memory is available. Thus in this mode the operating system and the user both have influence on the value of $l?$. For this

---

[5] For this reason, input parameters are also hidden by the precondition in CSP-OZ [15].

reason, a new kind of parameters were introduced in CSP-OZ: *simple parameters*. They can be influenced by the environment *and* the system. Syntactically they are represented by the declaration of undecorated values in an operation schema. A specification of the guard for *sendto* could be as follows.

```
┌─enable_sendto ──────────────────────────────────────────────
│  l : ℤ                                    [l is now a simple parameter]
│ ─────────────────────────────────────────────────────────────
│  l ≤ free_mem
│      [free_mem is some variable storing the amount of memory the socket can use.]
└──────────────────────────────────────────────────────────────
```

Simple parameters can also be used to address different sockets in parallel, an aspect we have ignored so far. A UNIX socket is handled like a file. Thus every system call of *sendto* and *recvfrom* must hand over a valid file descriptor. We would extend the Object-Z specification of a socket with a simple parameter describing the file descriptor.

Simple parameters can result in deadlocks, input parameters might lead to divergence. Therefore a syntactically difference between these aspects is sensible. However, CCZ can easily model the desired effect without introducing a third kind of parameter – given that CCZ is extended with non-blocking schemas to capture divergence.

8   Types and Parameters

Z provides flexible and standardised constructs to express types. Process algebras, on the other hand, do not have standard notations for types. It is therefore natural to use Z to define types of channels or parameters of processes in a combined language.

This is done systematically for CCZ [16] where Z is established as a value calculus of value passing CCS (see also [19]). Other approaches do not handle this point formally.

However, there is a technical problem with the use of Z types for process algebra channels. As we are interested to prove that an operation is defined completely and cannot diverge, we have to deal with the following case. The type *Byte* that is used for the declaration of messages in the socket example is a subrange of the integers. Therefore $d? : \text{seq} \, Byte$ has the same type as $\text{seq} \, ℤ$ and thus the predicate $d? = \langle 257 \rangle$ is type correct. The schema $[d? : \text{seq} \, Byte]$ is equivalent to $[d? : \text{seq} \, ℤ \mid \forall x : \text{ran} \, d? \bullet x \in 0..255]$.

The point is, what happens if we try to transmit the sequence $\langle 257 \rangle$ via a socket. As we argued above, no input parameter should be refused. Thus the socket would diverge. However, this does not model the UNIX implementation correctly. In CCZ every parameter must be declared explicitly thus avoiding the problem. CSP-OZ uses extra syntax to declare channels. This declaration is used to define the set of events in the underlying process algebra. E. g. the message $\langle 257 \rangle$ cannot be used as an event.

Other approaches are not explicit about this point. But simply deriving channel types from Z operation schemas does not help here.

9 Related Work

Combining Z with a process algebra is a special case of the combination of state based and event based formalisms [4, 23, 25, 28, 40]. This work has already influenced the formulation of Z data refinement rules. Thus work on the combination of Z with a process algebra can be seen as an instantiation of these basic results. However, capturing all aspects of Z operations with input, output and perhaps even simple parameters goes beyond existing approaches on the combination of state and event based formalisms.

Derrick, Bowman, Boiten and Steen [7, ?] work on the connections between Z and LOTOS [6] specifications. They use Z and LOTOS to specify different aspects of a system and define consistency rules between both views. This is based on a translation of LOTOS to Z which obviously does not define a behaviour semantics of Z specifications. Investigating their consistency rules on the basis of an integration of Z into some process algebra is an interesting topic for further research.

The language ZCCS was proposed by Galloway and Stoddart [18, 19]. They introduce Z as the value calculus of value passing CCS; i. e. data manipulation, types and parameters of CCS agents are described in Z. It is a quite deep integration of Z and CCS and reuses standard semantics of both languages. However, as the authors admit, they just use Z as a formalism to define functions and types, but they do not reflect the standard Z style of defining invariants and operations on some state space. E. g. the operation *sendto* from above cannot be modelled straight forward in ZCCS. This was the motivation to develop the successor of ZCCS, the language CCZ, which we have discussed intensively above.

Heisel and Sühl [22] suggest a syntactical combination of Z and timed CSP with a multi event approach. However, in contrast to the syntactic combinations of CCS and Z discussed above, they do not define operators like parallel composition for the combined language. This work has a very strong focus on real time properties and does not bring new aspects for the untimed case.

Sometimes it is suggested to define a behavioural semantics for Z without considering other languages (e. g. [11]). Our work is based on the assumption that the dynamic behaviour of a Z specification can be understood best on the basis of a mature theory of distributed systems. E. g. to use local operations, a theory for hiding operations has to be reinvented in pure Z. For the same reason we have not discussed translations of a process algebra into Z, like [3].

10 Conclusion and further Research

This paper gives an overview on different existing approaches and general principles on combining Z with a process algebra. All aspects are explained by the example of UNIX sockets. As this communication mechanism is widely used in Internet applications, we see it as a benchmark for the modelling capabilities of a specification language. For all existing approaches we could identify at least some omission or shortcoming. A summary of the classification can be found in Tab. 1. As general guidelines that should hold for all combinations we worked out the following:

	[38]	[16]	[26]	[35]	[15]	[32]
Name		CCZ	TCOZ		CSP-OZ	
Process Algebra	CCS	CCS	Timed CSP	CSP	CSP	CSP
Z Dialect	Z	Z	Object-Z	Object-Z	Object-Z	Z
kind of combination Sec. 3	syntax	syntax	syntax.	semant.	semant.	semant.
Granularity of Operations Sec. 5	multi	multi	multi	single	single	double
Mapping Operations to Channels	CCS syntax	CCS syntax	extra syntax	identity	extra syntax	
Guard Sec. 6	precon.	precon.	extra syntax	precon.	extra syntax	
Parameters Sec. 7	in/out	in/out	in/out	simple	in/out/ simple	in/out
Refinement Rules				[33]	[13]	
Z types for channels formalised Sec. 8	no	yes	no	no	no	no

Table 1. Classification of different approaches on combining Z with process algebras

- As extra structure on pure Z specifications is needed anyway, some structured or even object-oriented extension of Z provides a better starting point than using just Z.
- It should be possible to specify the guard of an operation separately from the effect. Otherwise the expressibility of the language is limited and the separation of the specification of the normal behaviour from the error case is not supported smoothly.
- The characteristics of input and output parameters should be captured in the semantics. Simple parameters can be introduced to enhance the expressibility of the language.
- The general pattern of Z data refinement (extended with the one extra condition concerning guards) should be proved for a concrete combination. Although this has not been done for all existing combinations yet, we expect that this rule is universal. This is notable, because concrete combinations may vary in basics like the event concept.
  Weak data refinement is a powerful extension of data refinement. Such a rule should hold in any combination.

While these principles are generally applicable, we found the following trade offs.

- A semantic integration, where only the embedding of Z is defined but the process algebra is not touched, is simpler and therefore supports simple tool reuse. A syntactical integration on the other hand provides a deeper integration and allows a more flexible use of the language.

- The single event approach is more abstract whereas the multi event approach models realistic systems more closely. The double event approach can easily be modelled by a multi event approach. Therefore it can be considered as a special case of the multi event approach.

  The problem with the single event approach is the complicated semantics to capture the behaviour of input and output parameters correctly. When using the multi event approach one has to take care that input and output events may occur in any order.

Both aspects are interesting topics for further research. As tool support has a major influence on the success of a formal method, language combination should eventually result in tool combination. But tool integration is usually more time consuming than pencil and paper work. A slight change in the language to be combined – maybe formalised easily on paper – is a potential source for tool complications. For this reason every theoretical work on the combination of Z and a process algebra must carefully justify any extension or change in the existing languages. A lot of research is still needed to simplify tool combination while preserving expressibility of the language.

Concerning the trade off between a single and a multi event approach, the ideal methodology would start with the abstract view of a single event approach and translate this to a multi event approach on some later step. Specifications using the single event approach are easier to analyse as far less states and interleavings of traces have to be considered. However, on a lower abstraction level only the multi event approach is realistic. The notion of *action refinement* [2, 17, 31] provides a suitable background for this investigation.

Acknowledgements. I would like to thank G. Smith, B. Mahony, J. Dong and J. Derrick for fruitful discussions on topics related to this paper. H. Fleischhack, S. Kleuker, M. Schenke and H. Wehrheim read preliminary versions of this paper and made valuable comments.

References

1. J.-R. Abrial. *The B-Book: Assigning Programs to Meanings*. Cambridge University Press, 1996.
2. L. Aceto and M. Hennessy. Adding action refinement to a finite process algebra. *Information and Computation*, 115(2):179–247, December 1994.
3. M. Benjamin. A message passing system: an example of combining CSP and Z. In J.E. Nicholls, editor, *Z User Workshop, Oxford 1989*, Workshops in Computing, pages 221–228. Springer-Verlag, 1990.
4. M.J. Butler and C.C. Morgan. Action systems, unbounded nondeterminism, and infinite traces. *Formal Aspects of Computing*, 7:37–53, 1995.
5. R.J.R. Back and K. Sere. Stepwise refinement of action systems. *Structured Programming*, 12:17–30, 1991.
6. T. Bolognesi, J. van de Lagemaat, and C. Vissers, editors. *LOTOSphere: Software Development with LOTOS*. Kluwer Academic Publishers, 1995.
7. J. Derrick, H. Bowman, E.A. Boiten, and M.W.A. Steen. Comparing LOTOS and Z refinement relations. In R. Gotzhein and J. Bredereke, editors, *Proceedings FORTE'96*, pages 501–516, 1996.
8. J. Derrick, E.A. Boiten, H. Bowman, and M.W.A. Steen. Weak refinement in Z. In J.P. Bowen and M.G. Hinchey, editors, *ZUM'97: The Z Formal Specification Notation*, volume 1212 of *Lecture Notes in Computer Science*, pages 369–388. Springer-Verlag, 1997.

9. E. W. Dijkstra. *A Discipline of Programming*. Prentice-Hall, 1976.

10. R. Duke, G. Rose, and G. Smith. Object-Z: A specification language advocated for the description of standards. *Computer Standards and Interfaces*, 17:511–533, 1995.

11. A.S. Evans. An improved recipe for specifying reactive systems in Z. In J.P. Bowen and M.G. Hinchey, editors, *ZUM'97: The Z Formal Specification Notation*, volume 1212 of *Lecture Notes in Computer Science*, pages 275–294. Springer-Verlag, 1997.

12. Formal Systems (Europe) Ltd. *Failures-Divergence Refinement: FDR2 User Manual*, Oct 1997.

13. C. Fischer and S. Hallerstede. Data-Refinement in CSP-OZ. Technical Report TRCF-97-3, University of Oldenburg, June 1997.

14. C. Fischer. Combining CSP and Z. Technical Report TRCF-97-1, University of Oldenburg, January 1997.

15. C. Fischer. CSP-OZ: A combination of Object-Z and CSP. In H. Bowmann and J. Derrick, editors, *Formal Methods for Open Object-Based Distributed Systems (FMOODS '97)*, volume 2, pages 423–438. Chapman & Hall, 1997.

16. A.J. Galloway. *Integrated Formal Methods with Richer Methodological Profiles for the Development of Multi-Perspective Systems*. PhD thesis, University of Teesside, School of Computing and Mathematics, August 1996.

17. U. Goltz, R. Gorrieri, and A. Rensink. Comparing syntactic and semantic action refinement. *Information and Computation*, 125(2):118–143, 15 March 1996.

18. A.J. Galloway and H. Habrias. Integrating NIAM, JSD, CCS and Z. Rapport de Recherche IRIN – 130, Université de Nantes, Institut de Recherche en Informatique de Nantes, France, 1996.

19. A.J. Galloway and W. Stoddart. An operational semantics for ZCCS. In M.G. Hinchey and Shaoying Liu, editors, *International Conference of Formal Engineering Methods (ICFEM)*. IEEE Computer Society Press, 1997.

20. D. Harel. Statecharts: A visual formalism for complex systems. *Science of Computer Programming*, 8(3):231–274, 1987.

21. C.A.R. Hoare. *Communicating Sequential Processes*. Prentice-Hall International, 1985.

22. M. Heisel and C. Sühl. Formal specification of safety-critical software with Z and real-time CSP. In E. Schoitsch, editor, *Proc. 15th International Conference on Computer Safety, Reliability and Security*, pages 31–45, 1997.

23. He Jifeng. Process refinement. In J. McDermid, editor, *The Theory and Practice of Refinement*. Butterworths, 1989.

24. C.B. Jones. *Systematic Software Development using VDM*. Prentice Hall, 1990.

25. M.B. Josephs. A state-based approach to communicating processes. *Distributed Computing*, 3:9–18, 1988.

26. B.P. Mahony and J.S. Dong. Blending Object-Z and Timed CSP: An introduction to TCOZ. In *The 20th International Conference on Software Engineering (ICSE'98)*, pages 95–104. IEEE Computer Society Press, April 1998.

27. R. Milner. *Communication and Concurrency*. Prentice Hall International Series in Computer Science, 1989.

28. C.C. Morgan. *Programming from Specifications*. Prentice Hall International Series in Computer Science, 1990.

29. A. Mota and A. Sampaio. Model-checking CSP-Z. In *Proc. European Joint Conference on Theory and Practice of Software*, volume 1382 of *Lecture Notes in Computer Science*, pages 205–220. Springer-Verlag, 1998.

30. J. Nicholls. Z notation. Draft Version 1.2, ISO, September 1995.

31. A. Rensink and R. Gorrieri. Action refinement as an implementation relation. In M. Bidoit and M. Dauchet, editors, *TAPSOFT '97: Theory and Practice of Software Development*, volume 1214 of *Lecture Notes in Computer Science*, pages 772–786. Springer-Verlag, 1997.

32. A.W. Roscoe, J.C.P. Woodcock, and L. Wulf. Non-interference through determinism. In D. Gollmann, editor, *ESORICS 94*, volume 875 of *Lecture Notes in Computer Science*, pages 33–54. Springer-Verlag, 1994.

33. G. Smith and J. Derrick. Refinement and verification of concurrent systems specified in Object-Z and CSP. In M.G. Hinchey and Shaoying Liu, editors, *International Conference of Formal Engineering Methods (ICFEM)*, pages 293–302. IEEE Computer Society Press, 1997.

34. G. Smith. A fully abstract semantics of classes for Object-Z. *Formal Aspects of Computing*, 7:30–65, 1995.

35. G. Smith. A semantic integration of Object-Z and CSP for the specification of concurrent systems. In J. Fitzgerald, C.B. Jones, and P. Lucas, editors, *FME'97: Industrial Applications and Strengthened Foundations of Formal Methods*, volume 1313 of *Lecture Notes in Computer Science*, pages 62–81. Springer-Verlag, 1997.

36. J.M. Spivey. *The Z Notation: A Reference Manual*. Prentice Hall International Series in Computer Science, 2nd edition, 1992.

37. B. Strulo. How firing conditions help inheritance. In J.P. Bowen and M.G. Hinchey, editors, *ZUM '95: The Z Formal Specification Notation*, volume 967 of *Lecture Notes in Computer Science*, pages 264–275. Springer-Verlag, 1995.

38. K. Taguchi and K. Araki. The state-based CCS semantics for concurrent Z specification. In M.G. Hinchey and Shaoying Liu, editors, *International Conference of Formal Engineering Methods (ICFEM)*, pages 283–292. IEEE Computer Society Press, 1997.

39. J.C.P. Woodcock and J. Davies. *Using Z: Specification, Refinement, and Proof*. Prentice-Hall International Sereies in Computer Science, 1996.

40. J.C.P. Woodcock and C.C. Morgan. Refinement of state-based concurrent systems. In D. Bjørnjer, C.A.R. Hoare and H. Langmaack, editors, *VDM '90: VDM and Z – Formal Methods in Software Development*, volume 428 of *Lecture Notes in Computer Science*, pages 340–351. Springer-Verlag, 1990.

The Specification and Refinement of an Environmental Model

Bill Stoddart

School of Computing and Mathematics, University of Teesside, UK

Email: W.J.Stoddart@tees.ac.uk

Abstract. When specifying a reactive system, we need to consider both the system itself, and the environment it operates in. A suitable formalism for such a task is the Event Calculus, a theory of synchronised state machines which lends itself to diagrammatic representation and which can be conveniently formulated in Z. In this paper we describe an approach to behavioural refinement in the Event Calculus. We consider a gas burner, starting with an outline description of its physical behaviour, then refining this by adding additional details and constraints. Each refinement step is achieved by adding a new (and simple) state machine to our existing model.

1 Introduction

We use a gas burner case study to discuss some aspects of the specification of a reactive system. Such a system can be modelled in terms of the interaction between a control system and its environment. In our case the "environment" will be represented by the physical behaviour of the gas burner. The motivation for creating a model which includes both the control system and its environment is that it provides us with a mathematical model of overall system behaviour which we can interrogate to determine whether safety and availability properties will be satisfied.

In this paper we concentrate on modelling the physical behaviour of the burner. We begin with an outline model of burner behaviour in terms of a state machine diagram. We then add timing details and additional constraints by a series of refinement steps. Each step is achieved by adding another state machine to our model.

The first series of refinement steps produce a more detailed model of the burner's physical behaviour. However its physical behaviour alone does not ensure safe operation, so we continue the refinement process by adding further constraints that express required safety properties.

In previous papers on the Event Calculus we have used communicating state machines to model systems with concurrent components (e.g. a distributed seat booking system). In refining an environmental model we use the same mathematical formulation but our motivation is completely different. We are using the properties of synchronized state machines to achieve behavioural refinement: i.e. to add details of further events and impose further behavioural constraints on events that have already been introduced.

2   The Event Calculus

The Event Calculus is a theory of communicating state machines. It makes extensive use of diagrams and provides a translation from diagrams to the model based notations Z and B. Its *raison d'être* is to provide an expressive and easily understandable notation for adding behavioural aspects to model based specifications. Such aspects include how a system reacts to its environment, how it may be decomposed into concurrent components, where inputs come from and outputs go to, and in what order its operations should be performed.

We posit the basic types [*MACHINE,STATE,EVENT*]. The behaviour of a machine *m* is characterised by:

- its set of possible initial states,
- its next state relation ψm, which has type *STATE* × *EVENT* $\leftrightarrow$ *STATE*,
- its repertoire, *repertoire m*, which is a set of events that includes all the events used to form its next state relation, but may include other events also.

An Event Calculus system consists of a set of machines which may communicate by means of shared synchronized events. For an event to occur, each machine that has that event in its repertoire must be ready to take part in the event. When an event does occur, every machine that has that event in its repertoire changes according to one of the possibilities offered by its next state relation. The others are not affected.

We can factor the state of a machine into a behavioural state, which may be figuratively represented by the position of a counter on a state machine diagram, and an internal data state, represented (in Z terminology) by a binding written on the counter. Transitions may be associated with a schema or schema text whose pre-condition acts as a firing condition for the transition, and whose update describes the change to the internal data state when the associated transition takes place. We may also parametrize events, e.g. with input/output values which can also be "seen" in the schema associated with the transition. In a model of Z to which real numbers have been added, the Event Calculus can be extended to model systems that evolve in continuous time. Full details of the Event Calculus are given in [22, 21, 23, 24]. Some details helpful (we hope) to an understanding of the material in this paper will be given as we go along.

A closely related technique for specifying reactive systems is the action systems formalism [1, 4, 5]. The approach of [5] resembles the Event Calculus in modelling communications through shared events. [1] emphasizes the importance of building a mathematical model of both the system and its environment, as does [15], which includes a gas burner case study.

3   The Gas Burner, Outline Behaviour

To start the burner we first ignite a pilot light by means of an electric coil. Only when the pilot is alight will a physical interlock on the burner allow the main valve to open and main ignition to occur. An outline model of the burners behaviour is given as an Event Calculus state machine in Figure 1.

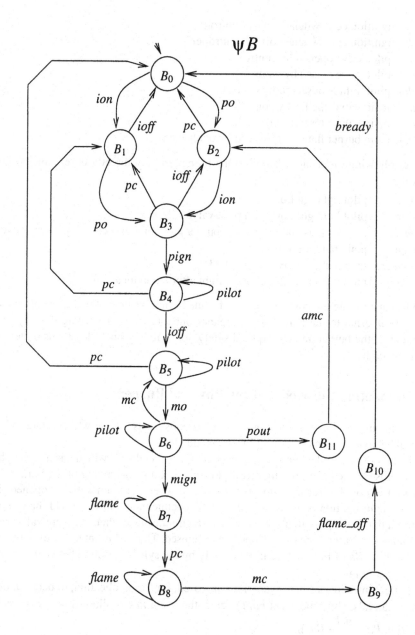

Fig. 1. Gas Burner

In this state machine the following events model communications with the controller:

> *ion*   ignition coil switched on by controller
> *ioff*   ignition coil switched off by controller
> *po*   pilot valve opened by controller
> *pc*   pilot valve closed by controller
> *pilot* pilot light is observed by controller
> *mo*   main valve opened by controller
> *mc*   main valve closed by controller
> *flame* main burner flame is observed by controller.

The following events are internal to the burner and not directly observable by the controller.

> *pign*   pilot light ignition
> *pout*   pilot light goes out with pilot valve still open
> *amc*   autonomous main close: the burner autonomously closes its main valve
> *mign*   main burner ignition
> *flame_off* the main flame is extinguished
> *bready* burner becomes ready to re-light after a previous burn.

When specifying the control software for the burner we cannot make use of events which are internal to the burner. In this paper our interest is specifying the physical behaviour of the burner and its required safety constraints. This task puts us under no such constraint.

4   Completing the Model of the Physical Burner

Our outline model does not contain any timing constraints. Those which relate to the physical behaviour of the burner will now be added.

The main valve of the burner is connected to a bi-metal strip which ensures that the valve is closed unless the pilot light is lit. From the outline behaviour of the burner we see that it is possible for the pilot light to go out when the main valve is opened. In this case main ignition is not achieved. Our first refinement will be to add the timing constraint that if the pilot light goes out in such circumstances then the main valve will autonomously close before two seconds have elapsed. The constraint is imposed by the state machine *Ba* of Figure 2, or more exactly by the synchronisation between *Ba* and machine *B* of Figure 1.

Figure 2 introduces a new event *tick*, supposed, for this application, to occur at one second intervals. Until the event *pout* occurs, the event *tick* is allowed to occur freely (transition $Ba_0 \xrightarrow{tick} Ba_0$).

The event *pout* is a shared event which can only occur when machines *B* and *Ba* are in states B_6 and Ba_0 respectively. If it does occur the machines make the state transitions B_6 to B_{11} and Ba_0 to Ba_1.

After the event *pout*, machine *Ba* allows at most one tick to occur before the event *amc*. This illustrates our basic technique for expressing timing constraints: if we require

$$\psi Ba$$

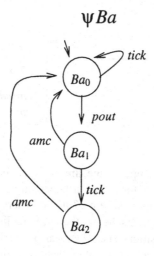

Fig. 2. Timing Constraint: if the pilot light goes our while the main valve is open, the main valve will autonomously close within two seconds.

an event to occur within a certain time we limit the number of ticks that can occur before that event. *amc* is also a shared event, which machine B is ready to take part in when in state B_{11}. Thus *amc* is forced to occur before two clock ticks.

We add further constraints that refer to the shut down of the burner. After the main burner is extinguished, the burner becomes ready for re-use within 60 clock ticks. This constraint has the same form as the previous one, but the requirement to deal with sixty seconds rather than two seconds makes it too laborious to express in terms of a primitive state machine. Instead we use a machine which has both behavioural state and internal data state. We introduce Z schemas to describe its possible data states and its initial data state.

$$
\begin{array}{|l}
\hline
\_Timer_____ \\
lapsed, limit : \mathbb{N} \\
\hline
lapsed \le limit \\
\hline
\end{array}
\qquad
\begin{array}{|l}
\hline
\_TInit_____ \\
Timer \\
\hline
lapsed = 0 \\
\hline
\end{array}
$$

We need operations to start the timer and to register a clock tick:

<table>
<tr><td>

Start _____

$\Delta Timer$

$lapsed' = 0$
$limit' = limit$

</td><td>

Tick _____

$\Delta Timer$

$lapsed' = lapsed + 1$
$limit' = limit$

</td></tr>
</table>

The state machine that imposes the timing constraint is shown in Figure 3. The states of this machine are factored into a behavioural component (Bb_0 or Bb_1) and a data component (a binding of schema *Timer*). Where the machine has a transition labelled with an event and a Z schema, the "pre-condition" of the schema acts as a firing condition for the transition. The schema also describes any change to the internal data state of the machine that occurs when the transition takes place. Transitions that are just labelled with an event cause no change of internal state: they can be thought of as having $\Xi Timer$ as their default schema.[1]

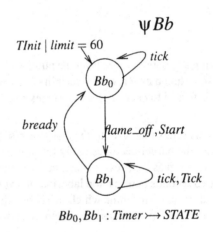

$$Bb_0, Bb_1 : Timer \rightarrowtail STATE$$

Fig. 3. Timing Constraint: the burner becomes ready for re-use within 60 clock ticks of being extinguished.

----

[1] The initial data state, given by the schema text *TInit* | *limit* = 60, is the binding:
$\langle | lapsed \leadsto 0, limit \leadsto 60 | \rangle$. The behavioural states Bb_0 and Bb_1 are functions from possible data states of Bb to *STATE*. E.g. the initial state of machine Bb is: $Bb_0 \langle | lapsed \leadsto 0, limit \leadsto 60 | \rangle$
Each transition in a machine with internal state represents a set of primitive transitions. For example the transition $Bb_0 \xrightarrow{\text{flame\_off}, Start} Bb_1$ represents the set of transitions:
$\{ Start \bullet (Bb_0(\theta Timer), flame\_off) \mapsto Bb_1(\theta Timer') \}$

The next constraint to be imposed is: if the main valve is closed whilst the burner is ignited, then the flame will be extinguished immediately. This restraint is context sensitive in the sense that we are not interested in restraining what happens after any closure of the main valve: our interest is limited to what happens on closing the main valve when the burner is ignited. We impose this constraint with the machine of Figure 4. Initially (in state Bc_0) we allow time to pass and the main valve to close with no constraint. However, when main ignition occurs the machine enters a state which requires *flame_off* to occur immediately the main valve closes.

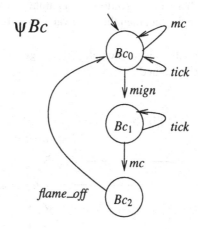

Fig. 4. Timing Constraint: the flame is extinguished immediately the main valve is closed.

This completes our environmental model: we have now described the behaviour of the physical burner.

5   Safe Operation

Although the physical behaviour of the burner incorporated some safety mechanisms, these are not enough to ensure safe operation. For this we also require certain safety conditions:

- the main valve must close between five and six seconds of opening if main ignition is not obtained
- when the main valve is closed following a failed attempt at ignition, ten seconds must elapse before it is opened again.
- the pilot valve should only be opened when the ignition coil is on.

In the final implementation, the imposition of these restraints will be the responsibility of the burner control software. What we are aiming to do here is to give a formal expression to these constraints so that we have something against which to formally judge the specification of the control system.

For the temporal constraints we define a guard for the timeout condition.

```
_ Timeout _____
  ΞTimer
 _____
  lapsed = limit
```

We can now express our temporal safety constraints using the machines of Figure 5 and 6. In Figure 5 the timer functions as a watchdog, which is triggered by the opening of the main valve. If neither a main ignition or an autonomous close is obtained by the time the timeout condition is true, then the main valve must be closed by the controller (event *mc*).

In Figure 6 the timer acts as a simple delay. It is triggered when *mo* is followed by *mc* without ignition being obtained.

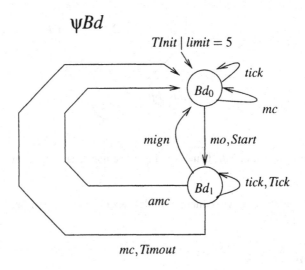

$$Bd_0, Bd_1 : Timer \rightarrowtail STATE$$

Fig. 5. Safety Constraint: the main valve must close between five and six seconds of opening if main ignition is not obtained.

Finally we add the constraint that the pilot valve should only be opened when the ignition coil is on. The critical word here is *opened*. We do not prevent the valve being open when the coil is off, but we prevent the action of opening it.

We first define some types to describe the state of valves and switches.

$$VALVE ::= open \mid closed$$
$$SWITCH ::= on \mid off$$

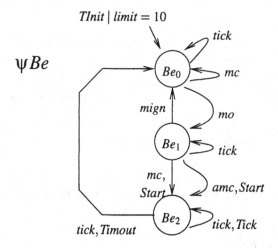

Fig. 6. Safety Constraint: when the main valve is closed following a failed attempt at ignition, ten seconds must elapse before it is opened again.

We give a state schema which records the state of the pilot valve and ignition coil.

```
┌─ Ignition ─────────────────
│ pilot : VALVE
│ coil : SWITCH
└────────────────────────────
```

```
┌─ IInit ────────────────────
│ Ignition
├────────────────────────────
│ pilot = closed
│ coil = off
└────────────────────────────
```

We need operation schemas to register the changing states of the pilot valve and ignition coil. The operation to open the pilot valve includes the pre-condition that the coil should be on.

```
┌─ IOn ──────────────────────
│ ΔIgnition
├────────────────────────────
│ coil' = on
│ pilot' = pilot
└────────────────────────────
```

```
┌─ IOff ─────────────────────
│ ΔIgnition
├────────────────────────────
│ coil' = off
│ pilot' = pilot
└────────────────────────────
```

$$
\begin{array}{|l}
\hline
\_PO _____ \\
\;\Delta Ignition \\
\hline
\;coil = on \\
\;pilot' = open \\
\;coil' = coil \\
\hline
\end{array}
\qquad
\begin{array}{|l}
\hline
\_PC _____ \\
\;\Delta Ignition \\
\hline
\;pilot' = closed \\
\;coil' = coil \\
\hline
\end{array}
$$

We can now impose our constraint with the machine of Figure 7.

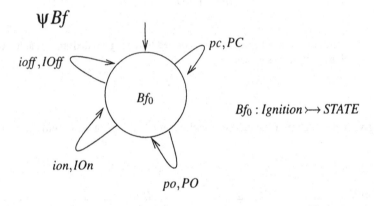

$Bf_0 : Ignition \rightarrowtail STATE$

Fig. 7. Constraint: during the ignition phase the pilot valve should not be opened unless the ignition coil is on.

The machine *Bf* has a single parametrized state Bf_0. To see in detail how the constraint is imposed via the pre-condition of schema *PO*, consider the transition $Bf_0 \xrightarrow{po,PO} Bf_0$. This represents the following set of primitive transitions:

$$\{PO \bullet (Bf_0(\theta Ignition), po) \mapsto Bf_0(\theta Ignition')\}$$

which contains the following members:

$\{$
$(Bf_0(|pilot \leadsto closed, coil \leadsto on|), po) \mapsto Bf_0(|pilot \leadsto open, coil \leadsto on|),$
$(Bf_0(|pilot \leadsto open, coil \leadsto on|), po) \mapsto Bf_0(|pilot \leadsto open, coil \leadsto on|)$
$\}$

Any transition which does not satisfy the pre-condition of the schema *PO* is simply filtered out by the set comprehension. The result is that the meaning of a pre-condition in an Event Calculus transition is that of a guard.

6   Comparison of the Event Calculus and Process Algebras

Process algebras such as CCS [11, 17] and CSP [14] provide concepts and notations for a deep study of concurrency and communication. Why use the Event Calculus when instead we could use a ready made process algebra and adopt Z as its value calculus?

This section is to say why the Event Calculus is useful, how it differs from a process algebra, and how it resembles one.

In process algebra terms the state machine B_a of Figure 2 could be described using the following set of mutually recursive equations:

$$Ba_0 = (tick \rightarrow Ba_0 \mid pout \rightarrow Ba_1)$$
$$Ba_1 = (tick \rightarrow Ba_2 \mid amc \rightarrow Ba_0)$$
$$Ba_2 = (amc \rightarrow Ba_0)$$

The symbols $\rightarrow$ and $\mid$ are read as "then" and "choice". The first of the equations says that process Ba_0 can engage in event *tick* and remain the process Ba_0, or can engage in the event *pout* and become the process Ba_1. There is an obvious correspondence between the process Ba_0 and the state Ba_0 in Figure 2, but in the process algebra formulation the notions of machine, state and system have been subsumed into the single idea of process. The state machine representation of machine B_u being in state Ba_0 is resumed, in the process algebra form, by the process Ba_0 whose definition provides an account of its future behaviour. This allows us to express the dynamic creation and absorption of processes. For example a process P that engages in event c then becomes process Q running in parallel with process R would be defined as:

$$P = (c \rightarrow (Q \parallel R))$$

In developing the Event Calculus [20] our main aim was to provide a support for the dialogues that occur between system designers and other engineers, bearing in mind the need for cross disciplinary communication and the fact that even specialised engineers must cover a wide range of competencies and have only a limited time to spend on each one. State machines are easily understood and accepted by many engineers. They are amenable to graphical representations which can serve as a focus for discussions. It is easier to focus an engineer's attention on a state machine diagram than on a set of process algebra equations.

The expressive power of state machines corresponds closely to what is required in many problem domains. There is little chance of a gas burner evolving into two concurrent gas burners, nor of the software that controls it needing to evolve into two concurrent controllers. Even where a problem is amenable to solution through the dynamic creation of processes we may prefer to take a more static approach to avoid the problem of formally ensuring the availability of dynamically allocated resources.

Thus state machines provide a good conceptual tool for approaching a large number of problems, and they are easy to represent in Z. It is also easy to factor a machine's state into a behavioural state, which may be notionally represented by the position of a counter on a state machine diagram, and an internal data state, represented by a binding written on the counter. To codify a complete process algebra theory in Z would be far more complex. To codify the whole of Z in a process algebra would be unthinkable.

To construct an integrated formalism which incorporates the formal proof rules of both systems is possible but also appears to be complex [12, 13] and inevitably involves much duplication in the encoding of basic concepts required in both formalisms. The Event Calculus is a compromise which provides reasonable expressive power together with a graphical representation that can be easily translated into Z.

In its use of synchronised events to model communication the Event Calculus borrows very heavily from process algebra, and due to its use of n way synchronisation has more resemblance to CSP that CCS (which limits itself to two way synchronisations). A particular use of n way synchronisation illustrated in our case study is the use of *tick*. All machines that are able to engage in the *tick* event must do so in a single synchronised action.

7   A Comparison of the Event Calculus with other Treatments of Concurrency in Z

In comparing the Event Calculus with other treatments of concurrency, we should first note that the case study treated in this paper, in which synchronised state machines are added to an environmental model to express timing constraints, is a little atypical. A more usual Event Calculus model is one in which the functionality of a system is described in terms of communicating concurrent sub-systems, each of which encapsulates its own data within a secure interface. For example in [23] we specify the functionality and real time properties of a scalable distributed seat booking system in terms of booking agents, booking clerks and a reservations data base, and in [19] we specify an invoicing system in terms of an invoice clerk, an inventory clerk and an orders clerk.

In contrast to the distributed approach of the Event Calculus most of the work on modelling concurrency in Z has used a global model of state. e.g. [6, 8–10, 7, 16].

For example Andy Evans in [8–10] develops an approach in which a specification has both static and dynamic parts. The static part is syntactically identical to a classical Z specification, with the difference that schema pre-conditions are interpreted as guards rather than as true pre-conditions. This means that rather than exhibiting divergent (unknown) behaviour if invoked outside its pre-condition, an operation simply does not fire unless its pre-condition is true. The static specification is used to define a a set of possible system traces, expressed in terms of bindings from the state space. The dynamic part of the specification consists of restraints which prune the set of traces defined by the static specification. For example one such constraint might be to impose fairness. This provides us with an improved ability for reasoning about the dynamic behaviour of the system. For example if operation *Op* establishes Q and *Op* is continuously enabled, the fai

In [6] the operations in a specification are characterised as either internal (able to fire when their pre condition is true) or external (forming part of the user interface). Invocation of an interface operation which takes an input may result in a series of internal operations becoming enabled and firing, one or more of which may deliver some results. This model requires a careful formulation of refinement, which the authors refer to as weak refinement to distinguish it from classical Z refinement.

We have argued in [13] that the classical Z style of specification neglects the importance of the *behavioural* dimension of a specification, and we prefer an approach which
is considerably further removed from the classical style of Z specification than the work
cited above.

More specifically, we feel it is essential to have a formalism which can directly
describe:

- the order in which events and operations occur
- where inputs come from and outputs go to
- how a system interacts with its environment and how component sub-systems interact
- the data state, invariant and operations of data encapsulated within a concurrent
  component.

Needless to say, no approach has all the advantages, and it could be said that using
the Event Calculus can lead to a premature and inappropriate division of a system into
concurrent components, and that it is likely to produce models with properties which are
not directly specified but which emerge from the interaction of components. These are
possible weaknesses that must be born in mind by any who decide to use it or any similar
formalism. Experience shows however that many systems are inherently concurrent
(different machines in an automated factory or TV studio, different departments in a
bank...) so that concurrency emerges even at the level of requirements investigation. We
discuss the issue of stating and verifying emergent properties of concurrent systems in
[25].

One of the referees enquired whether we had considered using Coloured Petri Nets
to visualise our systems, as is done in [8]. In fact the main difference of approach has
less to do with the formal tools used than with the approach to systems modelling. In
[8] the dining philosophers problem is modelled by a Coloured Petri net in which each
philosopher and fork appears as a constant and in which state changes are modelled
by changing the sets *eating* and *thinking* (of philosophers) and the set *free_forks* (of
forks). This fits naturally with modelling a system by means of a global state space.
Our inclination would rather have been to model each philosopher and the table as
separate state machines, each encapsulating an internal data state which records the set
of forks currently in their possession. Philosophers would communicate with the table
by means of an exchange of forks.

8   Some Properties of Behavioural Refinement

Behavioural refinement can be understood in terms of an observer, equipped with a
specification A and observing a system implemented from a specification B. We say
that A is behaviourally refined by B if there is no possibility of our observer noting
anything which conflicts with specification A.

Furthermore, we assume that our observer only perceives events in the repertoire
of A. This means that in behavioural refinement we can introduce behaviour based on
new events, as well as place restrictions on the existing behaviour of the system being
refined. We use the notation $A \sqsubseteq_B B$ for A is behaviourally refined by B. If *traces* s

denotes the possible event traces of a system s (in the spirit of CSP a possible definition of behavioural refinement[2] is:

$$SYS == \mathbb{P} \, MACHINE$$

$$\_ \sqsubseteq_B \_ : SYS \leftrightarrow SYS$$

> $\forall sys1, sys2 : \mathbb{P} \, MACHINE \bullet sys1 \sqsubseteq_B sys2 \Leftrightarrow$
> $repertoire\, sys1 \subseteq repertoire\, sys2 \,\wedge$
> $\forall t : traces\, sys2 \bullet t \upharpoonright repertoire\, sys1 \in traces\, sys1$

In the Event Calculus a system is a set of state machines, and the parallel composition of systems is simply a matter of forming the set union of the two systems. What is important about a system is its behaviour. We distinguish two equivalence classes. If there is no way to tell two systems S, T apart by observing their behaviour, we say they are observationally equivalent: written as $S \simeq T$. A stronger requirement than observational equivalence is that we should be able to replace one with the other when either is used as a component in a larger system. We call this property equivalence, $S \approx T$. An example will be given to show the difference between these concepts.

The relations $\simeq$ and $\approx$ form equivalence classes of systems. By an abuse of language we will sometimes refer to an equivalence class of systems as if it were a single system. For example we will talk about the system $STOP_{EVENT}$, which has an empty next state relation and a repertoire equal to $EVENT$.

$STOP_{EVENT}$ plays an important role in this theory of refinement, as does $NULL$, the system with an empty next state relation and an empty repertoire. These systems form the infimum and supremum of a refinement lattice. For any system S we have.

$$NIL \sqsubseteq_B S \sqsubseteq_B STOP_{EVENT}$$

We can state the following obvious laws:

$$S \simeq T \Leftrightarrow S \sqsubseteq_B T \wedge T \sqsubseteq_B S$$
$$S \cup NIL \approx S$$
$$S \cup STOP_{EVENT} \approx STOP_{EVENT}$$
$$S \approx T \Rightarrow S \simeq T$$
$$S \sqsubseteq_B S$$
$$S \sqsubseteq_B S \cup T$$
$$S \sqsubseteq_B T \wedge T \sqsubseteq_B U \Rightarrow S \sqsubseteq_B U$$
$$S \sqsubseteq_B T \Rightarrow (S \cup U) \sqsubseteq_B (T \cup U)$$

The last two laws tell us that we can perform both stepwise and a piecewise refinement.

Since every parallel composition constitutes a refinement, and since we have been able to achieve all the refinements of our case study through parallel composition, we

---

[2] The definition given is really only adequate for deterministic systems. We are currently researching a more complete definition that incorporates non-determinism and probabilistic choice.

might wonder whether *any* refinement required could be achieved by such means. The machines of fig. 8 show us that it cannot. The behaviours of A and B are indistinguishable in terms of observable actions, and thus $\{A\} \simeq \{B\}$. However machine B is non-deterministic. We have $\{B\} \approxeq \{A\} \cup \{B\}$ but there is no system X such that $\{A\} \approxeq \{B\} \cup X$. To see this consider that if such a system did exist it would need to have some transition on a, say $X_i \xrightarrow{a} X_j$ which would necessarily give rise to the following transitions in $\{B\} \cup X$:

$$\{B_0\} \cup X_i \xrightarrow{a} \{B_0\} \cup X_j$$
$$\{B_0\} \cup X_i \xrightarrow{a} \{B_1\} \cup X_j$$

If the second of these transitions occurs, system $\{B\} \cup X$ will enter a state where event b is disabled. Machine A has no such state so we cannot have $\{B\} \cup X \approxeq \{A\}$.

Also, although A and B are observationally equivalent, they are not equivalent as they cannot be used interchangeably as components of a larger system. To see this note that $\{B, C\}$ can reach a deadlocked state $\{B_1, C_1\}$, whereas $\{A, C\}$ can never deadlock.

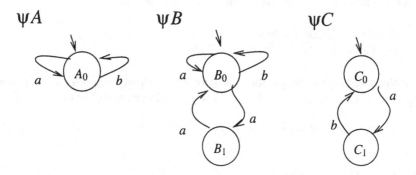

Fig. 8. Refinement and non-determinism

If we limit ourselves to deterministic systems, observational equivalence becomes identical to equivalence. Furthermore, we can always obtain any required refinement by parallel composition. This follows from the result (see [14]) that a deterministic system can be uniquely characterised by its possible traces and its repertoire.

Thus for deterministic systems we have the additional law:

$$S \sqsubseteq_B T \Rightarrow \exists U : SYS \bullet S \cup U \approxeq T$$

In a model which contains composite transitions involving operations described by Z schemas or schema texts, behavioural refinement can be performed by doing operational refinement on these operations. What is known in Z as the "syntactic precondition" of an operation can play two roles,[3] that of a true pre-condition, and that of

---

[3] As it can in classical Z specifications, where the syntactic pre-condition of a stand alone operation schema is interpreted as a true pre-condition, but the syntactic pre-conditions of schemas in a schema disjunction are guards.

a guard. Operational refinement permits us to loosen pre-conditions and tighten guards. Since we do not distinguish these concepts syntactically in Z we must be a little careful in applying these refinement rules to the Event Calculus.

A little explanation will help. A true pre-condition is part of the instructions for using an operation rather than part of the instruction itself. It is the responsibility of the user of an operation to do so in a context where its pre-condition is guaranteed to be true. If we consider a transition:

$$S_i \xrightarrow{\ e,OP\ } S_j$$

then if we choose to interpret pre Op as a true pre-condition we incur the proof obligation that pre Op can be inferred by the fact of being in behavioural state S_i. Obviously if this is established pre OP has no effect of filtering out transitions and plays no role as a guard. We may loosen pre Op without affecting our specification in any way.

We conclude this section with a remark on the use of behavioural refinement in the specification of the burner's control software. Let us give names to the models of physical and safe behaviour we developed in our case study:

$Burner == \{B, Ba, Bb, Bc\}$
$SafeBurner == \{B, Ba, Bb, Bc, Bd, Be, Bf\}$

When we develop the specification of a control system, *Controller*, it must constrain the burner to operate in a safe manner. The proof obligation that ensures this is:

$SafeBurner \sqsubseteq_B Burner \cup Controller$

9   Over Refinement

It is perfectly possible to over refine, e.g. to the point of deadlock. Given $A \sqsubseteq_B B$ our refinement technique guarantees that restrictions on the behaviour of A (e.g. the main valve will not open before the pilot valve is lit) will be maintained in B, but it does not guarantee that B will have any behaviour at all.

The situation is similar to operational refinement in B or the Refinement Calculus [2, 18, 3] where an operation may be refined to the point of non-feasibility. The supremum of the operational refinement lattice is *magic*, a non-implementable operation which will establish any condition we may care to name. This corresponds with the deadlocked system $STOP_{EVENT}$ in behavioural refinement.

The danger of over refinement of operations is mitigated to some extent by the impossibility of implementing a non-feasible specification. This ensures that a mistake in the specification of an operation which renders it non-feasible will never be translated into code. Exactly the same situation exists in our theory with respect to *temporal feasibility*. The deadlocked system $STOP_{EVENT}$ is non-implementable, since to implement it would stop the passage of time as modelled by the event *tick*. It corresponds to *magic* in the refinement theory of sequential programs.

10   Conclusions

We have given the outline specification for the behaviour of a gas burner as an Event Calculus state machine. We have added timing and imposed a series of constraints through a process of "behavioural refinement". In this way we developed a complete model of burner behaviour and the further restrictions required for its safe operation.

Each constraint was imposed by the addition of a simple state machine to our model. No refinement proof obligations were incurred since the parallel composition of machines is automatically a behavioural refinement in this system. This encourages us to proceed in small refinement steps, with each refinement consisting of the addition of a state machine to impose a particular constraint. The ability to refine in small steps allows us to concentrate on one thing at a time and lessens the chance that we will make errors when developing our specification. Of course we incur an obligation to show that over refinement (temporal infeasibility) has not occurred.

A model of the burner control software was not developed, but we articulated the proof obligation such a system would have to satisfy to comply with our model of safe operation.

References

1. J.-R. Abrial. Extending B without Changing it (for Developing Distributed Systems). In H. Habrias, editor, *Proc. 1st B Conference*, 1996. ISBN: 2-906082-25-2.
2. J.-R. Abrial. *The B Book*. Cambridge University Press, 1996.
3. R. J. R. Back. Correctness preserving program refinements. *Tract 131, Mathematish Centrum*, 1980.
4. M. Butler and M. Waldén. Distributed System Development in B. In H. Habrias, editor, *Proc. 1st B Conference*, 1996. ISBN: 2-906082-25-2.
5. M. Butler. An approach to the design of distributed systems with B AMN. In J. P. Bowen, M. G. Hinchey, and D. Till, editors, *ZUM '97: The Z Formal Specification Notation*, volume 1212, Lecture Notes in Computer Science, pages 223–241, Springer-Verlag, 1997.
6. J. Derrick, E. Boiten, H. Bowman, and S. Steen. Weak Refinement in Z. In J. P. Bowen, M. G. Hinchey, and D. Till, editors, *ZUM '97: The Z Formal Specification Notation*, volume 1212, Lecture Notes in Computer Science, pages 369–388, Springer-Verlag, 1997.
7. M. Engel. Specifying Real Time Systems with Z and the Duration Calculus. In J. P. Bowen and J. A. Hall, editors, *Z User Workshop, Cambridge 1994*, pages 282–294, Springer-Verlag, 1994.
8. A. S. Evans. Visualising Concurrent Z Specifications. In J. P. Bowen and J. A. Hall, editors, *Z User Workshop, Cambridge 1994*, Workshops in Computing, pages 269–281, Springer-Verlag, 1994.
9. A. S. Evans. Specifying and Verifying Concurrent Systems Using Z. In M. Naftalin, T. Denvir, and M. Bertran, editors, *FME '94: Industrial Benefit of Formal Methods*, volume 873, Lecture Notes in Computer Science, page 366-380, Springer-Verlag, 1994.
10. A. S. Evans. An Improved Recipe for Specifying Reactive Systems in Z. In J. P. Bowen, M. G. Hinchey, and D. Till, editors, *ZUM '97: The Z Formal Specification Notation*, volume 1212, Lecture Notes in Computer Science, pages 275–294, Springer-Verlag, 1997.
11. P. C. Fencott. *Formal Methods for Concurrency*. Chapman & Hall, 1995.

12. A. J. Galloway and W. J. Stoddart. An Operational Semantics for ZCCS. In M. G. Hinchey and Shaoying Liu, editors, *Proc. International Conference of Formal Engineering Methods (ICFEM)*, IEEE Computer Society Press, 1997.

13. A. J. Galloway and W. J. Stoddart. Comparative Formal Methods. In *Proc. INFORSID*, 1997.

14. C. A. R. Hoare. *Communicating Sequential Processes*. Prentice Hall International Series in Computer Science, 1985.

15. K. Lano. Specifying Reactive Systems in B AMN. In J. P. Bowen, M. G. Hinchey, and D. Till, editors, *ZUM '97: The Z Formal Specification Notation*, volume 1212, Lecture Notes in Computer Science, pages 242–274, Springer-Verlag, 1997.

16. B. Mahoney and I. Hayes. A Case Study in Timed Refinement: A Mine Pump. *IEEE Transactions on Software Engineering*, 18(9):817–826, September 1992.

17. R. Milner. *Communication and Concurrency*. Prentice Hall International Series in Computer Science, 1989.

18. C. C. Morgan. *Programming from Specifications*. Prentice Hall International Series in Computer Science, 1990.

19. W. J. Stoddart. An Event Calculus Treatment of the Invoicing of Orders. In H. Habrias H and A. J. Galloway, editors, *International Workshop on Comparing System Specification Techniques*. IRIN, Université de Nantes, France, 1998. ISBN: 2-906082-29-5.

20. W. J. Stoddart and P. Knaggs. The Event Calculus, (formal specification of real time systems by means of Z and diagrams). In H. Habrias, editor, *5th International Conference on putting into practice methods and tools for information system design*. University of Nantes, France, 1992.

21. W. J. Stoddart. The Event Calculus, extensions for modelling hybrid systems. Technical Report tees-scm-2-96, University of Teesside, UK, 1996.

22. W. J. Stoddart. The Event Calculus, vsn 2. Technical Report tees-scm-1-96, University of Teesside, UK, 1996.

23. W. J. Stoddart. An Introduction to the Event Calculus. In J. P. Bowen, M. G. Hinchey, and D. Till, editors, *ZUM '97: The Z Formal Specification Notation*, volume 1212, Lecture Notes in Computer Science, Springer-Verlag, 1997.

24. W. J. Stoddart, S. E. Dunne, and P. C. Fencott. Modelling Hybrid Systems in Z. In H. Habrias, editor, *Z Twenty Years on: What is its Future?*, pages 11–25, IRIN, Université de Nantes, France, 1995.

25. W. J. Stoddart, S. E. Dunne, A. J. Galloway, and R. Shore. Abstract State Machines: Designing Distributed Systems with State Machines and B. In D. Bert, editor, *B'98: Recent Developments in the Use of the B Method*, volume 1393, Lecture Notes in Computer Science, Springer-Verlag, 1998.

Formal Derivation of Finite State Machines
for Class Testing

Leesa Murray, David Carrington, Ian MacColl, Jason McDonald, and Paul Strooper

Software Verification Research Centre
Department of Computer Science and Electrical Engineering
The University of Queensland, St Lucia, Australia 4072

Email: {leesam,davec,ianm,jasonm,pstroop}@csee.uq.edu.au

Abstract. Previous work on generating state machines for the purpose of class testing has not been formally based. There has also been work on deriving state machines from formal specifications for testing non-object-oriented software. We build on this work by presenting a method for deriving a state machine for testing purposes from a formal specification of the class under test. We also show how the resulting state machine can be used as the basis for a test suite developed and executed using an existing framework for class testing.

To derive the state machine, we identify the states and possible interactions of the operations of the class under test. The Test Template Framework is used to formally derive the states from the Object-Z specification of the class under test. The transitions of the finite state machine are calculated from the derived states and the class's operations. The formally derived finite state machine is transformed to a ClassBench testgraph, which is used as input to the ClassBench framework to test a C++ implementation of the class. The method is illustrated using a simple bounded queue example.

1 Introduction

The purpose of specification-based testing is to derive testing information from a specification of the software under test, rather than from the implementation. Although it is possible in theory to formally refine such a specification into an implementation, this rarely happens in practice. However, when the implementation is developed informally from a formal specification, the specification can assist with testing, by allowing us to derive test inputs and the expected outputs for the implementation.

Although a considerable amount of work has been done in the area of class testing [2], most of this work is not formally based. In this paper, we present a method for specification-based class testing, in which we use an Object-Z specification [8, 7] of the class under test to generate a state machine that allows us to test the class implementation. Explicitly, we focus on the use of the formally derived finite state machine for practical work, that is, actually using the finite state machine to generate and execute test cases, and evaluate test results. In previous work it is not clear that finite state machines derived from specifications have actually been used to test implementations.

In [22], we introduce object-orientation to the Test Template Framework [25, 26] – a framework originally designed for non-object-oriented specification-based testing.

We achieve this by deriving testing information (test inputs and expected outputs) from Object-Z specifications and by inheriting testing information from parent classes. However, that work involves testing at the operation level. Our goal here is to focus on testing the class as a whole. We achieve this by deriving a class's finite state machine from its specification, which allows us to formulate sequences of the class's operations to conduct testing. The Test Template Framework does not execute tests; it is used to generate testing information. By using it to formally derive finite state machines for classes, we are providing a basis for test execution in a framework such as ClassBench [12, 13].

ClassBench is a testing framework that models the class under test as a finite state machine. This model is referred to as a *testgraph* and represents a subset of the states of the class and the transitions between them. Currently a testgraph is developed informally in the ClassBench framework. ClassBench executes tests by traversing the testgraph and comparing the state of the class under test to the expected state supplied by an oracle class, to evaluate test results. We present the initial results of work on transforming the class's formally derived finite state machine to a ClassBench testgraph, which we use to test the class implementation. The Test Template Framework [22] and ClassBench [17] both provide support for genericity and inheritance, and therefore do support object-oriented testing. However, the derivation of finite state machines for classes, which is the focus of this paper, deals with class testing.

In Section 2 we specify class *Bounded_Queue*[*G*], which is used throughout to illustrate our method. The Test Template Framework is introduced in Section 3. Section 4 details the process of deriving the states and transitions of a class's finite state machine from its Object-Z specification. This section concludes with the derived finite state machine of our example class. Section 5 addresses the reachability of states in finite state machines derived from specifications. The process of transforming a finite state machine to a testgraph for use in the ClassBench framework is presented in Section 6. Related work is compared to our work in Section 7. In Section 8 we conclude with a discussion of our achievements and plans for future work.

Throughout this paper, when referring to specification items we use italics – *Extend*, and implementation items are presented in typewriter font – Extend.

2 Example - Specification of *Bounded_Queue*[*G*]

Our example class, *Bounded_Queue*[*G*], is a generic class representing a first-in-first-out abstract data type. *Bounded_Queue*[*G*] is contrived to demonstrate the problem of unreachable states in finite state machines discussed in Section 5. The Object-Z specification of *Bounded_Queue*[*G*] is shown in Figure 1.

An Object-Z class is represented as a named box with optional generic parameters (here class *Bounded_Queue* with generic parameter *G*). A class contains an unnamed state schema, an initialisation schema (*INIT*) and zero or more operations (five in this case). Inputs to operations are decorated with ? and outputs are decorated with !. Pre-state variables are unprimed and post-state variables are primed (′). Operations that are permitted to change the state of the class have a delta list (denoted by Δ) in their declarations. The list identifies those variables that are 'open', that is, that do not have

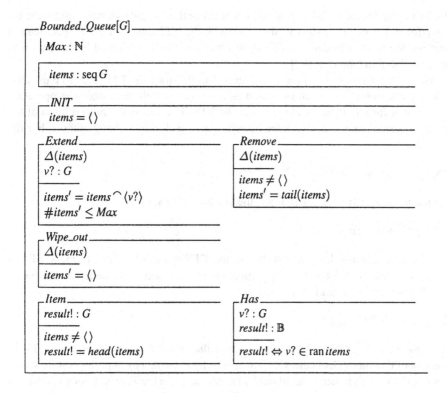

Fig. 1. The Object-Z Specification of *Bounded_Queue*[G].

their unprimed and primed forms equated. An Object-Z operation is disabled outside its precondition, in contrast to Z where precondition violation gives an undefined result.

We represent a queue as a sequence of elements, *items*. The *INIT* schema specifies that a *Bounded_Queue*[G] is initially empty. The *Extend* operation appends an element to the queue provided the size of the queue is less than *Max*, a constant whose value is set by the environment. The specification of *Extend* is contrived to illustrate steps in our method for deriving finite state machines. Such a restriction on the addition of elements to a queue would usually form part of the class invariant. *Remove* removes the first element of a non-empty queue, leaving the rest of the queue as the result. *Wipe_out* deletes all elements from the queue. *Item* returns the first element of a non-empty queue. *Has* checks if a given element, $v?$, is an element of the queue, returning *true* if it is and *false* otherwise. *Item* and *Has* do not change the state of the queue.

3 Test Template Framework

Our approach to specification-based testing is based on the Test Template Framework (TTF) [15, 25, 26]. The TTF is a formal, abstract model of non-object-oriented testing, used to derive a hierarchy of test information from a model-based formal specification.

The hierarchy includes test inputs and expected outputs (oracles), but is not used directly for test execution. Most of the work with the TTF has used the Z specification notation. We have extended the TTF to accommodate object-oriented features such as those available in Object-Z [22].

We use the *Extend* operation from Figure 1 to illustrate the TTF. The TTF uses the valid input space (VIS) of an operation as the source of all tests since the operation is undefined for any inputs that are not in the VIS. The VIS is the precondition of the operation's schema and is computed by hiding the final state and any outputs. For the example,

$$VIS_{Extend} \; \hat{=} \; [items : \text{seq}\, G; \; v? : G \mid \#items < Max]$$

The input space (IS) of an operation is the signature of its VIS.

$$IS_{Extend} \; \hat{=} \; [items : \text{seq}\, G; \; v? : G]$$

The basic unit for defining test data in the TTF is a test template (TT). A TT is a constrained subset of the VIS and is expressed as a Z schema. We define a type for all TTs derived for the operation *Extend*:

$$TT_{Extend} \; == \; \mathbb{P}\, VIS_{Extend}$$

Test templates are organised into a hierarchy called the test template hierarchy (TTH). The root of this hierarchy is the VIS. The hierarchy is created by applying testing strategies to existing TTs to derive additional TTs. A strategy in the TTF identifies a particular technique for deriving test cases. The TTF encourages the use of multiple strategies to build the TTH, both traditional techniques such as input partitioning and boundary analysis, and specialised techniques that exploit the specification notation [26]. The TTH for *Extend* is formally declared as:

$$\mid TTH_{Extend} : TT_{Extend} \times STRATEGY \nrightarrow \mathbb{P}\, TT_{Extend}$$

where *STRATEGY* is the set of all possible testing strategies.

For our example, we choose to apply a type-based strategy to partition the VIS into cases where the queue is empty and where it is nonempty. The resulting templates are:

$$TB_1 \; \hat{=} \; [VIS_{Extend} \mid items = \langle \rangle]$$
$$TB_2 \; \hat{=} \; [VIS_{Extend} \mid items \neq \langle \rangle]$$
$$TTH_{Extend}(VIS_{Extend}, Type\_based) = \{TB_1, TB_2\}$$

Naming of the TTs reflects the testing strategy used.

The second strategy applied is boundary analysis for the cases where the cardinality of *items* is either the maximum permitted (*Max* − 1) or less than the maximum. Only template TB_2 can be partitioned so we obtain two further templates:

$$BA_{2.1} \; \hat{=} \; [TB_2 \mid \#items = Max - 1]$$
$$BA_{2.2} \; \hat{=} \; [TB_2 \mid \#items < Max - 1]$$
$$TTH_{Extend}(TB_2, Boundary\_analysis) = \{BA_{2.1}, BA_{2.2}\}$$

At this stage our test template hierarchy is:

```
VIS  Extend  ─────┬──── TB 1
                  └──── TB 2 ──────┬──── BA 2.1
                                   └──── BA 2.2
```

TTs are derived until the tester is satisfied that the subdivisions of the VIS are adequate to achieve satisfactory testing. From each leaf TT, we derive an instance template that uniquely defines a single test case. If we instantiate the queue to store integer values with $Max = 5$, possible instance templates for *Extend* are:

$IT_1 \mathrel{\hat=} [TB_1 \mid items = \langle\rangle \land v? = 0]$
$IT_2 \mathrel{\hat=} [BA_{2.1} \mid items = \langle 1,2,3,4\rangle \land v? = 0]$
$IT_3 \mathrel{\hat=} [BA_{2.2} \mid items = \langle 1,2\rangle \land v? = 0]$

The formal specification can also be used as an oracle to determine the success or failure of each test. We derive oracle templates to precisely describe suitable output for a given input. An oracle template is calculated by

$$(operation \land T) \restriction OS_{operation}$$

where T is replaced by a test or instance template and $OS_{operation}$ is the output space of *operation*. For example, the output space of *Extend* and the oracle for IT_1 are:

$$OS_{Extend} \mathrel{\hat=} [items' : seq\, G]$$

$$oracle_{IT_1} \mathrel{\hat=} (Extend \land IT_1) \restriction OS_{Extend} \equiv [items' : seq\, G \mid items' = \langle 0\rangle]$$

The derivation of the test template hierarchies for the other operations of *Bounded_Queue[G]* appears in [21]. No testing strategies were used for *Remove* and *Item*, as we chose not to partition their valid input spaces. The cause effect strategy [26] was used in the derivation of the test template hierarchy for *Has* and partition analysis [26] was used for *Wipe_out*.

4   Derivation of Finite State Machines

This section details the derivation of a finite state machine from an Object-Z specification. We address the derivation in two parts: derivation of the states of the class's finite state machine; then the transitions. The process is illustrated using *Bounded_Queue[G]* and the section concludes with the complete finite state machine of *Bounded_Queue[G]*.

4.1   Derivation of States

We use the Test Template Framework to derive test templates and oracles for the class's operations. From the class's *INIT* schema, and each operation's test templates and oracles, we derive the states of the class's finite state machine. When deriving test templates from an operation's specification, we partition the operation's input space. The states that result from test templates only guarantee that some operation of the class can be executed in each state. However, there is no guarantee that the state reached after the operation terminates will be a member of the set of states derived from test templates. Therefore it is also necessary to use the oracles of the operations to derive the states of the finite state machine. We only consider oracles for operations that change the state of the class, as operations that do not change the state cannot contribute any new states. Considering test and oracle templates gives more equivalence classes, that is, a finer grained partition of the class's state space. The collection of states gained from the *INIT* schema, test templates and oracles provides the states for the class's finite state machine, and these are referred to as *state templates*.

We derive the states from the leaf test templates of each operation's test template hierarchy by using schema hiding to restrict the signatures of the templates to be only the state variables. Hiding involves removing the input variables from the template's declaration and existentially quantifying them in the template's predicate.

To derive states from oracles, we rename the primed state variables to their un-primed equivalents. Any output variables in the oracle templates are hidden and the templates simplified, so only state variables appear in the templates' declarations.

Once the set of state templates is derived, we consider whether the templates are disjoint. If they are not, it is necessary to resolve any overlap of states so that we have a maximal partition[1] of the class's state space. To achieve this, we apply Dick and Faivre's [5] transformation of a disjunction into disjoint components. This method uses equivalences of the form:

$$A \lor B \equiv A \land B \lor \neg A \land B \lor A \land \neg B$$

to obtain non-overlapping partitions.

If the *INIT* schema is partitioned in the process of formulating disjoint templates, the subscript *INIT* is added to the names of the resulting templates. This allows us to track those templates that are initial states of the class's finite state machine. This process for deriving the states of a finite state machine from an Object-Z specification is illustrated using our example class *Bounded_Queue[G]*.

Deriving the States of *Bounded_Queue[G]*.
The state template derived from *Bounded_Queue[G]*'s *INIT* schema is

$$ST_{Init} \cong [items : \mathrm{seq}\, G \mid items = \langle\rangle]$$

The derivation of test templates for *Bounded_Queue[G]*'s *Extend* operation is shown in Section 3. The test template derivations for the other operations are similar and appear

---

[1] By maximal partition, we mean there is no overlap of states and together the states completely cover the class's state space.

in [21]. The resulting leaf test templates of *Bounded_Queue[G]*'s operations are:

$TT_{Extend_1} \mathrel{\widehat{=}} [items : \text{seq} \, G; \, v? : G \mid items = \langle \rangle]$

$TT_{Extend_2} \mathrel{\widehat{=}} [items : \text{seq} \, G; \, v? : G \mid items \neq \langle \rangle \land \#items = Max - 1]$

$TT_{Extend_3} \mathrel{\widehat{=}} [items : \text{seq} \, G; \, v? : G \mid items \neq \langle \rangle \land \#items < Max - 1]$

$TT_{Remove_1} \mathrel{\widehat{=}} [items : \text{seq} \, G \mid items \neq \langle \rangle]$

$TT_{Wipe\_out_1} \mathrel{\widehat{=}} [items : \text{seq} \, G \mid items = \langle \rangle]$

$TT_{Wipe\_out_2} \mathrel{\widehat{=}} [items : \text{seq} \, G \mid items \neq \langle \rangle]$

$TT_{Item_1} \mathrel{\widehat{=}} [items : \text{seq} \, G \mid items \neq \langle \rangle]$

$TT_{Has_1} \mathrel{\widehat{=}} [items : \text{seq} \, G; \, v? : G \mid v? \in \text{ran} \, items]$

$TT_{Has_2} \mathrel{\widehat{=}} [items : \text{seq} \, G; \, v? : G \mid items = \langle \rangle]$

$TT_{Has_3} \mathrel{\widehat{=}} [items : \text{seq} \, G; \, v? : G \mid v? \notin \text{ran} \, items \land items \neq \langle \rangle]$

To formulate state templates, we take each test template and hide the input variables, which results in schemas that have only the (unprimed) state variables in their declarations. We assume that G, the generic parameter of *Bounded_Queue[G]*, contains sufficient elements to allow simplification of our state templates in the finite state machine. Upon refinement of G to a concrete type, the states are reviewed [26]. For the same reason, we assume that $Max > 4$ [2].

$ST_1 \mathrel{\widehat{=}} TT_{Extend_1} \setminus (v?) \equiv [items : \text{seq} \, G \mid items = \langle \rangle]$

$ST_2 \mathrel{\widehat{=}} TT_{Extend_2} \setminus (v?) \equiv [items : \text{seq} \, G \mid \#items = Max - 1]$

$ST_3 \mathrel{\widehat{=}} TT_{Extend_3} \setminus (v?) \equiv [items : \text{seq} \, G \mid items \neq \langle \rangle \land \#items < Max - 1]$

$ST_4 \mathrel{\widehat{=}} TT_{Remove_1} \equiv [items : \text{seq} \, G \mid items \neq \langle \rangle]$

$ST_5 \mathrel{\widehat{=}} TT_{Wipe\_out_1} \equiv [items : \text{seq} \, G \mid items = \langle \rangle]$

$ST_6 \mathrel{\widehat{=}} TT_{Wipe\_out_2} \equiv [items : \text{seq} \, G \mid items \neq \langle \rangle]$

$ST_7 \mathrel{\widehat{=}} TT_{Item_1} \equiv [items : \text{seq} \, G \mid items \neq \langle \rangle]$

$ST_8 \mathrel{\widehat{=}} TT_{Has_1} \setminus (v?) \equiv [items : \text{seq} \, G \mid items \neq \langle \rangle]$

$ST_9 \mathrel{\widehat{=}} TT_{Has_2} \setminus (v?) \equiv [items : \text{seq} \, G \mid items = \langle \rangle]$

$ST_{10} \mathrel{\widehat{=}} TT_{Has_3} \setminus (v?) \equiv [items : \text{seq} \, G \mid items \neq \langle \rangle]$

We calculate oracles for the operations that change the state of the class. This ensures that all post states of operations are included in our finite state machine. The calculation of *Extend*'s output space is shown in Section 3. Calculation of the output spaces of the other operations is similar and is shown in [21]. After the calculation of the oracles, state templates are formed by renaming the primed state variables to their

---

[2] At this point it is only necessary to assume $Max > 2$, but in subsequent sections we need to assume $Max > 4$.

unprimed equivalents. Recall that we only calculate oracles for operations that change the state: *Extend*, *Remove* and *Wipe_out* in this case.

$Oracle_{ST_1} \stackrel{\wedge}{=} (Extend \wedge ST_1) \restriction OS_{Extend} \equiv [items' : seq\,G \mid \#items' = 1]$

$ST_{11} \stackrel{\wedge}{=} [items : seq\,G \mid \#items = 1]$

$Oracle_{ST_2} \stackrel{\wedge}{=} (Extend \wedge ST_2) \restriction OS_{Extend} \equiv [items' : seq\,G \mid \#items' = Max]$

$ST_{12} \stackrel{\wedge}{=} [items : seq\,G \mid \#items = Max]$

$Oracle_{ST_3} \stackrel{\wedge}{=} (Extend \wedge ST_3) \restriction OS_{Extend}$
$\equiv [items' : seq\,G \mid \#items' > 1 \wedge \#items' < Max]$

$ST_{13} \stackrel{\wedge}{=} [items : seq\,G \mid \#items > 1 \wedge \#items < Max]$

$Oracle_{ST_4} \stackrel{\wedge}{=} (Remove \wedge ST_4) \restriction OS_{Remove} \equiv [items' : seq\,G]$

$ST_{14} \stackrel{\wedge}{=} [items : seq\,G]$

$Oracle_{ST_5} \stackrel{\wedge}{=} (Wipe\_out \wedge ST_5) \restriction OS_{Wipe\_out} \equiv [items' : seq\,G \mid items' = \langle\rangle]$

$ST_{15} \stackrel{\wedge}{=} [items : seq\,G \mid items = \langle\rangle]$

$Oracle_{ST_6} \stackrel{\wedge}{=} (Wipe\_out \wedge ST_6) \restriction OS_{Wipe\_out} \equiv [items' : seq\,G \mid items' = \langle\rangle]$

$ST_{16} \stackrel{\wedge}{=} [items : seq\,G \mid items = \langle\rangle]$

One reason for the contrived specification of *Extend* is to illustrate the important role that oracles have in the formation of states. If we did not use oracles, classes might not be fully tested as operations might not be executed in all possible states. Without oracles, we would not have the state template ST_{12}, which specifies a full queue. Without ST_{12}, there is no guarantee that we will test a full queue. As a result, we may not generate tests from the finite state machine to examine the class's behaviour when the queue is full. Other templates such as ST_5 include ST_{12} as a special case, but there is no guarantee that this special case will be chosen, so we need ST_{12} to ensure the *Extend* operation is fully exercised.

The set of state templates for *Bounded_Queue*[G] so far is

$\{\ ST_{Init} \stackrel{\wedge}{=} [items : seq\,G \mid items = \langle\rangle],$
$\quad ST_2 \stackrel{\wedge}{=} [items : seq\,G \mid \#items = Max - 1],$
$\quad ST_3 \stackrel{\wedge}{=} [items : seq\,G \mid items \neq \langle\rangle \wedge \#items < Max - 1],$
$\quad ST_4 \stackrel{\wedge}{=} [items : seq\,G \mid items \neq \langle\rangle],$
$\quad ST_{11} \stackrel{\wedge}{=} [items : seq\,G \mid \#items = 1],$
$\quad ST_{12} \stackrel{\wedge}{=} [items : seq\,G \mid \#items = Max],$
$\quad ST_{13} \stackrel{\wedge}{=} [items : seq\,G \mid \#items > 1 \wedge \#items < Max],$
$\quad ST_{14} \stackrel{\wedge}{=} [items : seq\,G]\}$

We now transform this set into a set of disjoint state templates. ST_{Init} and ST_4 partition ST_{14} ($ST_{14} \equiv ST_{Init} \vee ST_4$) so ST_{14} is discarded. ST_{Init} is disjoint from all other state templates. Templates ST_2 and ST_3 are disjoint, but ST_2 and ST_4 are not, so we apply Dick and Faivre's [5] transformation.

$$ST_2 \vee ST_4$$
$$\equiv ST_2 \wedge ST_4 \vee \neg ST_2 \wedge ST_4 \vee ST_2 \wedge \neg ST_4$$
$$\equiv [items : seq\,G \mid \#items = Max - 1] \wedge [items : seq\,G \mid items \neq \langle\rangle] \vee$$
$$\qquad [items : seq\,G \mid \#items \neq Max - 1] \wedge [items : seq\,G \mid items \neq \langle\rangle] \vee$$
$$\qquad [items : seq\,G \mid \#items = Max - 1] \wedge [items : seq\,G \mid items = \langle\rangle]$$
$$\equiv [items : seq\,G \mid \#items = Max - 1] \vee$$
$$\qquad [items : seq\,G \mid items \neq \langle\rangle \wedge \#items \neq Max - 1] \vee$$
$$\qquad [items : seq\,G \mid false]$$
$$\equiv ST_2 \vee [items : seq\,G \mid items \neq \langle\rangle \wedge \#items \neq Max - 1]$$

Therefore we have a new state template,

$$ST_{17} \;\widehat{=}\; [items : seq\,G \mid items \neq \langle\rangle \wedge \#items \neq Max - 1]$$

and ST_4 is excluded from our set of templates as it is partitioned by ST_2 and ST_{17} ($ST_4 \equiv ST_2 \vee ST_{17}$).

Details of the remainder of the transformation are shown in [21]. Our resulting set of state templates for *Bounded_Queue*[G] is

$$\{\; ST_{Init} \;\widehat{=}\; [items : seq\,G \mid items = \langle\rangle],$$
$$\quad ST_2 \;\widehat{=}\; [items : seq\,G \mid \#items = Max - 1],$$
$$\quad ST_{11} \;\widehat{=}\; [items : seq\,G \mid \#items = 1],$$
$$\quad ST_{12} \;\widehat{=}\; [items : seq\,G \mid \#items = Max],$$
$$\quad ST_{18} \;\widehat{=}\; [items : seq\,G \mid \#items > 1 \wedge \#items < Max - 1],$$
$$\quad ST_{19} \;\widehat{=}\; [items : seq\,G \mid \#items > Max]\}$$

4.2 Derivation of Transitions

In the previous section, we partitioned a class's state into state templates to be used as the nodes of the class's finite state machine. We derive the transitions of the finite state machine by considering each pair of states and checking whether the pair is related by an operation. In this section, we present a formal model of this process and give examples. The model is extended in Section 5 to include reachability.

We take the set of all states of the class under test as given, we define operations as relations on states, and we identify a class as a set of operations.

$[State]$

$Op == State \leftrightarrow State$

$$| \quad class : \mathbb{P}\,Op$$

A valid transition in a finite state machine occurs when a pair of states (s_1, s'_2), is related by an operation. For each valid transition identified, an arc labelled with the operation's name, beginning in state s_1 and terminating in state s'_2, is added to the class's finite state machine.

Each operation requires n^2 (where n is the number of states) valid transition calculations. This work is mechanical, but detailed and tool support would be of great assistance. However, automation of this process is beyond the scope of this paper.

Deriving the Transitions of *Bounded_Queue[G]*.

We choose two possible *Bounded_Queue[G]* transitions to illustrate the derivation of valid and invalid transitions of a class. To show that (ST_{Init}, ST'_{Init}) are not related by *Extend* and therefore do not form a valid transition in *Bounded_Queue[G]*'s finite state machine, we prove

$\exists IS_{Extend}; \ OS_{Extend} \bullet ST_{Init} \wedge Extend \wedge ST'_{Init}$

$\equiv \exists items, items' : seq G; \ v? : G \ |$

$\quad\quad items = \langle \rangle \wedge items' = items ^\frown \langle v? \rangle \wedge \#items' \leq Max \wedge items' = \langle \rangle$

$\equiv$ false

with IS_{Extend} and OS_{Extend} as the input and output spaces of *Extend* ([*items* : seq G; v? : G] and [*items'* : seq G]) respectively.

On the other hand, to show that (ST_{Init}, ST'_{11}) are related by *Extend* and therefore form a valid transition, we prove

$\exists IS_{Extend}; \ OS_{Extend} \bullet ST_{Init} \wedge Extend \wedge ST'_{11}$

$\equiv \exists items, items' : seq G; \ v? : G \ |$

$\quad\quad items = \langle \rangle \wedge items' = items ^\frown \langle v? \rangle \wedge \#items' \leq Max \wedge \#items' = 1$

$\equiv$ true

The complete derivation of the *Bounded_Queue[G]* transitions appears in [21].

ST_{Init} is the only initial state of *Bounded_Queue[G]* as it was not partitioned during the derivation. We represent initial states by an incoming arc that does not originate in a state and has no label. The resulting finite state machine of class *Bounded_Queue[G]* is shown in Figure 2. Note that the finite state machine maintains assumptions made during the generation of templates, namely, that *Max* is at least 5 and that the generic type *G* contains sufficient elements.

5 Reachability

As *Bounded_Queue[G]* illustrates, it is possible to derive a finite state machine from a class's specification that contains unreachable states. By unreachable, we mean states that cannot be reached from the initial state via a sequence of transitions. ST_{19} is an example in Figure 2. The goal of generating a finite state machine for a class is so we can construct sequences of tests to exercise the class. We are not only interested in testing each operation in isolation but also testing interactions between operations. While a class's specification may generate unreachable states, and it may be possible to execute operations in these states and perform legal transitions, if the interaction of the class's operations does not allow us to reach these states they cannot be tested.

To formally identify reachable states, we first specify all possible paths that are present in the class's finite state machine.

$Path == \{ ss : seq State \ | \ \forall i : 2 .. \#ss \bullet \exists op : class \bullet (ss(i-1), ss(i)) \in op \}$

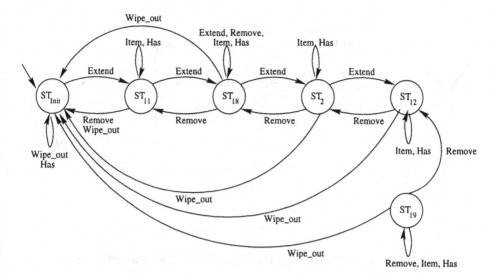

Fig. 2. Class *Bounded_Queue[G]*'s Finite State Machine.

We are interested in those paths that begin in an initial state of the finite state machine. We call these realisable paths.

$$initial : \mathbb{P}\,State$$

$$Realisable == \{p : Path \mid head(p) \in initial\}$$

where *initial* is the set of initial states of the finite state machine and *head(p)* returns the first state of the path *p*, thus giving us a set of paths where each path begins at an initial state.

From *Realisable*, we can identify those states of the class's finite state machine that are reachable, since all states in a realisable path are reachable states.

$$Reachable == \mathrm{ran}(\bigcup Realisable)$$

Reachable therefore consists of the states that occur in at least one realisable path. Any states of the finite state machine that are not elements of *Reachable* are eliminated along with any arcs that originate or terminate in them. The resulting finite state machine for *Bounded_Queue[G]* is shown in Figure 3.

6   Testing Classes

A formally derived finite state machine for a class allows us to identify the allowed interactions of its operations and possible sequences of tests. This section shows how such a finite state machine can be used as the basis of a test suite for a state-based testing framework such as ClassBench [12, 13].

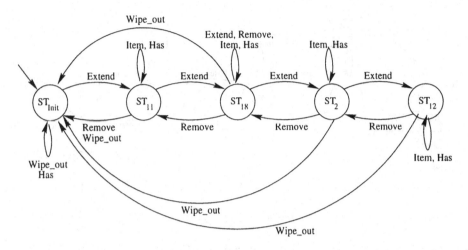

Fig. 3. Class *Bounded_Queue[G]*'s Finite State Machine with Reachable States.

For each ClassBench test suite, the tester must provide three components: a *test-graph*, an Oracle class, and a Driver class. The testgraph is a finite state machine that models a subset of the possible states and transitions of the Class Under Test (or *CUT*). The testgraph nodes correspond to states of the CUT and the arcs to the transitions; there is one distinguished node, the start node, that represents the initial state of the CUT.

The Oracle class is derived from the Object-Z specification of the CUT [18]. The oracle inherits the CUT's implementation and augments its operations to check the CUT's state is always consistent with the specification. The oracle also checks the values of any outputs, reporting an error if they do not comply with the specification.

The Driver class is called by the framework as the testgraph is traversed. The Driver must provide two functions. The Driver::arc() function performs the state transitions associated with each testgraph arc. The Driver::node() function checks that the CUT behaviour is correct for the state corresponding to the current testgraph node. At run-time, the framework automatically traverses the testgraph, calling Driver-::arc() each time an arc is traversed, and calling Driver::node() each time a node is reached. The ClassBench traversal algorithm guarantees arc and node coverage of the testgraph.

Before we can test the class with ClassBench, we must implement the class and transform the formally derived finite state machine into a ClassBench testgraph. Since ClassBench tests C++ implementations, we have chosen C++ as the implementation language. In the implementation, we must also decide on values for the class constants and generic parameters. Even though the class can be implemented as a generic class in C++ using templates, we cannot test it unless we instantiate the generic parameters. For this example, we have given *Max* a value of 5, and chosen the type int (integer) to replace the generic parameter *G*.

We must also transform the state machine to a ClassBench testgraph. In the formally derived finite state machine, a state typically represents a set of states that is considered to be an equivalence class. In a ClassBench testgraph, a node represents one state. Therefore, we must transform the finite state machine states to testgraph nodes. To achieve this, we choose one state for each set of states in the finite state machine.

Bounded_Queue[G]'s finite state machine has a single initial state, which becomes the start node of the testgraph[3]. The result of transforming the states of *Bounded_Queue* *[G]*'s finite state machine (shown in Figure 3), to testgraph nodes is shown in Figure 4. The initial node is distinguished by an incoming arc that has no source node. Above each node in the testgraph we identify the queue that it represents, and below each node we identify the finite state machine state from which it is derived.

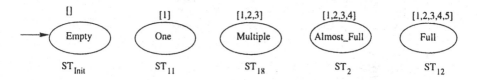

Fig. 4. Class *Bounded_Queue[G]*'s Testgraph Nodes (for *Max* = 5).

In a testgraph, all nodes should be reachable. An arc, or transition, in a finite state machine represents the execution of one operation call. An arc in a testgraph represents a sequence of calls. For example, Extend2 in Figure 5 is implemented by calling the Extend operation of *Bounded_Queue[G]* twice; the first call adds 2, and the second adds 3. We must also cover the finite state machine's transitions that change the state of the class. Transitions that do not change the state, such as the *Has* and *Item* transitions in Figure 3, are tested by including them in Driver::node().

At present, ClassBench does not allow an arc to have the same source and desti-nation nodes. ClassBench also does not permit two arcs to have the same source and destination nodes, as *Remove* and *Wipe_out* do between states ST_{11} and ST_{Init} in Fig-ure 3. To overcome these problems, we duplicate nodes in our testgraph as we have done to node Empty in Figure 5. The complete testgraph for *Bounded_Queue[G]* that achieves coverage of the transitions of its finite state machine in Figure 3 is shown in Figure 5. Of particular interest is arc Extend2, because it represents two transitions in *Bounded_Queue[G]*'s finite state machine. Extend2 begins in node One (derived from state ST_{11}) and terminates in node Multiple (derived from state ST_{18}). In the finite state machine, there is an *Extend* transition from ST_{11} to ST_{18}, and one from ST_{18} to itself. Arc Extend2 in the testgraph absorbs both of these transitions, as it has two calls to the Extend operation. The first call translates to the ST_{11} to ST_{18} *Extend* transition in the finite state machine. The second call translates to the *Extend* transition from ST_{18} to itself.

---

[3] A finite state machine may have more than one initial state, but a testgraph has only one start node, and this node must correspond to the unique initial state of the class implementation. Note that this may mean that some of the other initial states of the finite state machine become unreachable, which can be addressed by adding arcs to the testgraph.

The derived testgraph was used to test *Bounded_Queue[G]*'s implementation us-ing ClassBench. During the testing, the ClassBench traversal algorithm generated 41 calls to `Driver::node()` and 36 calls to `Driver::arc()`. This testing achieved 100% statement coverage of *Bounded_Queue[G]*'s implementation, showing that the choice of one concrete state in the testgraph for each equivalence class (state) in the finite state machine, adequately exercised the class's implementation.

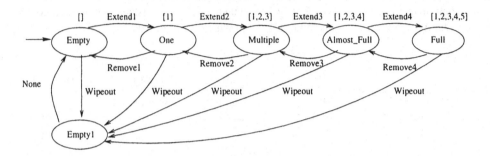

Fig. 5. Class *Bounded_Queue[G]*'s Testgraph.

7 Related Work

In this section, we discuss related work on the formal derivation of finite state machines from specifications for testing purposes, the generation of finite state machines from Object-Z specifications, and the use of finite state machines for testing classes.

Our work builds on that of Dick et al. [1, 5] who provide a method for generating test cases and for constructing a finite state machine from a model-based specification. Using partition analysis, they reduce the specification to disjunctive normal form. The transitions of the finite state machine are a set of expressions, termed sub-operations, that are derived from the partition analysis. The states of the finite state machine are the disjoined before and after states of the sub-operations. The sub-operations correspond to our consideration of pairs of states in *Op* in Section 4.2. We extend their work by using an object-oriented notation, Object-Z, and by using the resulting finite state machine as input for a test execution framework.

Hierons [11] describes the generation of a finite state machine from a Z specifica-tion. The input domain is partitioned using the category-partition method of Ostrand and Balcer [24]. The Test Template Framework, in contrast, permits use of a variety of testing strategies, including category-partition. Hierons calculates states for the finite state machine by rewriting the specification as disjoined input and output predicates (ef-fectively preconditions and postconditions). The transitions are determined by pairwise consideration of states as operation pre- and postconditions. The effect is similar to the machine constructed by Dick et al. Hierons also notes previous work on test control and test sequencing from finite state machines but does not pursue these aspects. We are using ClassBench for test control and sequencing.

Dong, Zucconi and Duke [6] informally generate a finite state machine from an Object-Z specification. Their motivation is to highlight the system behaviour in a non-trivial specification, that is, supporting comprehension rather than testing. States are formed from a permutation of the cross product of the possible values of the critical state variables of the class. Transitions are Object-Z operations with instantiated pre-conditions.

Bosman and Schmidt [3] use finite state machines to test classes. Their method uses state machines that result from Statecharts [10] used in object-oriented analysis and design techniques. A *design fsm* for a class is generated from the state diagrams and defines the expected outcomes of test cases. A *representation fsm* is an abstraction of the class's implementation and is used to drive the testing of the class. It also provides a mapping between the design and implementation of the class. Their approach is similar to ours but starts from a behavioural rather than a model-based specification. Object-Z is richer for constraining underlying state, whereas Statecharts are stronger for constraining behaviour. Their tool support appears less developed than ClassBench.

Hong et al. [14] apply conventional data flow testing techniques to class testing. A finite state machine is used to specify class behaviour and is transformed into a flow-graph of data member definitions and uses. The finite state machine is developed as a component of the overall system model in contrast to our approach of deriving the state machine from a formal specification. Application of data flow testing techniques to specification-based testing is a novel aspect of this work. Our approach permits use of a range of test derivation strategies rather than being restricted to a single class of techniques, and uses a model-based notation rather than a behavioural notation.

McGregor and Dyer [19, 20] describe a technique for constructing the finite state machine of a subclass from the finite state machine of its parent class. They use Objectcharts [4], an object-oriented variant of Statecharts, and restrict the inheritance relationship of classes to subtyping. The focus of this work is test case generation from behavioural notations, with a particular emphasis on reuse through inheritance. Transition coverage is considered as a criterion for test adequacy but use of the state machine for test execution is not discussed.

Turner and Robson's [28] state-based testing technique uses finite state machines for test case generation. Finite state machines are constructed to model the internal representation of a class, in contrast to Bosman and Schmidt, and McGregor and Dyer, who use a state machine constructed for object-oriented analysis and design. This work highlights the importance of considering state in object-oriented testing. In our approach, the Test Template Framework provides access to both the state of the class and the local parameters of an operation. Testing strategies can be applied to either.

Gao et al. [9] also construct a state model specifically for testing. The model is similar to Objectcharts and it is unclear how it is derived from a class design specification.

8   Conclusions

We have described a method for the formal derivation of a finite state machine for a class from its Object-Z specification. Test inputs and outputs derived from the class's operations using the Test Template Framework comprise the states of the finite state machine. Transitions are calculated to determine operation execution and termination. The finite state machine provides us with a mechanism for testing the class as it details the possible interactions of the class's operations. By using the finite state machine in a testing framework such as ClassBench, the tests are executed as ClassBench traverses the finite state machine. The derived finite state machine must undergo a transformation to be suitable for use with ClassBench. Initial details of this transformation process are provided and a formalisation of this transformation is work in progress [16, 23].

Others have formally derived finite state machines from model-based specifications, but not from object-oriented specifications. Finite state machines generated from object-oriented analysis and design diagrams are used to aid in the testing of classes, but the generation of the finite state machine is not formal. By formally deriving the finite state machine from the class specification, we have a representation of the expected behaviour of the class. Executing this expected behaviour by way of a transformed finite state machine in ClassBench enables us to test an implementation effectively. The example used to illustrate the formal derivation of a finite state machine is deterministic. However, Object-Z allows the specification of non-deterministic operations, the Test Template Framework and finite state machines handle non-determinism, as does ClassBench [23].

Work currently under investigation is the development of a tool to support and partially automate the Test Template Framework. Plans for future work include an open tool set that allows us to link the Test Template Framework and ClassBench, so that we have integrated tool support for testing object-oriented software based on formal specifications.

Acknowledgements

The authors wish to thank the anonymous reviewers for their constructive comments and suggestions. This work is supported by Australian Research Council grant A4-96-00282. Ian MacColl is supported by an Australian Postgraduate Award and a Telstra Research Laboratories Postgraduate Fellowship. Jason McDonald is supported by an Australian Postgraduate Award.

References

1. J. Bicarregui, J. Dick, B. Matthews and E. Woods. Making the most of formal specification through animation, testing and proof. *Science of Computer Programming*, 29:53–78, 1997.
2. R. Binder. Testing object-oriented software: a survey. *Software Testing, Verification and Reliability*, 6:125–252, 1996.
3. O. Bosman and H. Schmidt. Object test coverage using finite state machines. In C. Miggins, R. Duke and B. Meyer, editors, *Technology of Object-Oriented Languages and Systems (TOOLS 18)*, pages 171–178, Prentice Hall, 1995.
4. D. Coleman, F. Hayes and S. Bear. Introducing Objectcharts or how to use Statecharts in object-oriented design. *IEEE Transactions on Software Engineering*, 18(1):8–18, 1992.
5. J. Dick and A. Faivre. Automating the generation and sequencing of test cases from model-based specification. In J.C.P. Woodcock and P.G. Larsen, editors, *FME '93: Industrial Strength Formal Methods, 5th International Symposium of Formal Methods Europe*, Volume 670 of *Lecture Notes in Computer Science*, pages 268–284, Springer-Verlag, 1993.

6. J. Dong, L. Zucconi and R. Duke. Specifying Parallel and Distributed Systems in Object-Z: The Lift Case Study. *International Workshop on Software Engineering for Parallel and Distributed Systems*, pages 140–149, IEEE Computer Society Press, 1997.

7. R. Duke, G. Rose and G. Smith. Object-Z: A specification language advocated for the description of standards. *Computer Standards and Interfaces*, 17:511–533, 1995.

8. R. Duke and G. Rose. *Formal Object-Oriented Specification and Design Using Object-Z*, Academic Press, Formal Methods Series, to appear 1998.

9. J.Z. Gao, D. Kung, P. Hsia, Y. Toyoshima and C. Chen. Object State Testing for Object-Oriented Programs. *Computer Software & Applications Conference (COMPSAC 95)*, pages 232–238, 1995.

10. D. Harel. Statecharts: A visual formalism for complex systems. *Science of Computer Programming*, 8(3):231–274, June 1987.

11. R. Hierons. Testing from a Z Specification. *Software Testing, Verification and Reliability*, 7:19–33, 1997.

12. D.M. Hoffman and P.A. Strooper. The testgraph methodology: Automated testing of collection classes. *Journal of Object-Oriented Programming*, 8(7):35–41, November-December 1995.

13. D.M. Hoffman and P.A. Strooper. ClassBench: A methodology and framework for automated class testing. *Software Practice and Experience*, 27(5):573–597, May 1997.

14. Hyoung Seok Hong, Yong Rae Kwon and Sung Deok Cha. Testing of object-oriented programs based on finite state machines. In *Proc. Asia-Pacific Software Engineering Conference (APSEC '95)*, pages 234–241, 1995.

15. I. MacColl, D. Carrington and P. Stocks. An experiment in specification-based testing. In *Proc. 19th Australasian Computer Science Conference (ACSC '96)*, pages 159–168, 1996.

16. I. MacColl, L. Murray, P. Strooper and D. Carrington. *Specification-based object-oriented testing: A case study*. Technical Report 98-08, Software Verification Research Centre, The University of Queensland, Australia, 1998. Submitted to ICFEM'98.

17. J. McDonald and P.A. Strooper. Testing inheritance hierarchies in the ClassBench framework. In *Proc. Technology of Object-Oriented Languages and Systems (TOOLS USA '96)*, 1996. In press.

18. J. McDonald. *Translating Object-Z specifications to passive test oracles*. Technical Report 98-04, Software Verification Research Centre, The University of Queensland, Australia, 1998. Submitted to ICFEM'98.

19. J. McGregor and D. Dyer. A Note on Inheritance and State Machines. *SIGSOFT Software Engineering Notes*, 18(4):61–69, October 1993.

20. J. McGregor. Constructing Functional Test Cases Using Incrementally Derived State Machines. *11th International Conference and Exposition on Testing Computer Software*, pages 377–386, 1994.

21. L. Murray, D. Carrington, I. MacColl, J. McDonald and P. Strooper. *Formal Derivation of Finite State Machines for Class Testing*. Technical Report 98-03, Software Verification Research Centre, The University of Queensland, Australia, 1998.

22. L. Murray, D. Carrington, I. MacColl and P. Strooper. Extending Test Templates with Inheritance. In P. Bailes, editor. *Proc. 1997 Australian Software Engineering Conference (ASWEC '97)*, pages 80–87, IEEE Computer Society Press, 1997. Available in extended form as Technical Report 97-18, Software Verification Research Centre, The University of Queensland, Australia, 1997. URL:
http://svrc.it.uq.edu.au/Bibliography/svrc-tr.html?97-18

23. L. Murray, J. McDonald and P. Strooper. *Specification-based class testing with ClassBench*. Technical Report 98-12, Software Verification Research Centre, The University of Queensland, Australia, 1998. Submitted to APSEC'98.

24. T. Ostrand and M. Balcer. The category-partition method for specifying and generating functional tests. *Communications of the ACM*, 31(6):676–686, June 1988.
25. P. Stocks and D. Carrington. A framework for specification-based testing. *IEEE Transactions on Software Engineering*, 22(11):777–793, November 1996.
26. P. Stocks. *Applying formal methods to software testing*. PhD Thesis. Department of Computer Science and Electrical Engineering, The University of Queensland, Australia, 1993.
27. C. Turner and D. Robson. *State-Based Testing and Inheritance*. Technical Report TR-1/93, Computer Science Division, University of Durham, UK, 1993.
28. C. Turner and D. Robson. A state-based approach to the testing of class-based programs. *Software – Concepts and Tools*, 16:106–112, 1995.

Using B to Specify, Verify and Design Hardware Circuits (Extended Abstract)

Ib Holm Sørensen

B-Core(UK) Limited
Kings Piece, Harwell OX11 0PA, UK

Email: B@b-core.com
URL: http://www.b-core.com/

1 Introduction

This talk reports on the results of a 1 year collaborative research programme between B-Core(UK) Ltd and AWE (Aldermaston Weapon Establishment, Hunting-Brae) to develop an approach and a set of tools for the formal mathematical design and implementation of hardware circuits. The abstract specification and all designs are done within the framework of the B formal development method [2–5] and its supporting tools [1], while the hardware implementations are produced by utilizing the capabilities of VHDL [6, 7] and its supporting synthesis tools [8].

2 VHDL

VHDL (the VHSIC – Very High Speed Integrated Circuit – Hardware Description Language) supports the precise description of the structure and the behaviour of hardware circuit.

VHDL has several purposes; firstly it is a description and a conceptual modelling tool; secondly it allows the descriptions to form the basis for simulations, which can exhibit the described behaviour before the actual hardware is produced; thirdly the descriptions can be verified against mathematically stated requirements using program verification techniques; and finally descriptions can form the basis for a highly automated production of hardware circuits.

The reasons for using a language like VHDL for developing hardware circuits are the same as the reasons for using a High Level Language for developing sequential programs. However, while the target for HLL is a single sequential process, the target for VHDL is a collection of connected concurrently operating processes, and additional issues which are not present in the world of design of sequential programs need to be addressed in any work on methods and tools for supporting the use of VHDL in producing hardware circuits. These issues include notions such as *events* and *concurrency*.

3 The Adopted Approach

The design of single sequential process systems, where there is no interference in the thread of execution in the target implementation, has been successfully addressed by many model oriented specification techniques (e.g VDM, Z and B) and the use of Pre and Post conditions to describe the building blocks (sub-routines or collections of sub-routines) of such system, has proved its suitability, is relatively mature, and is widely used as a technique for mathematically specifying behaviours of such systems.

Within a development process for sequential systems we use the model oriented specification techniques and its associated mathematically based notations for the conceptual modelling and verification stages of the software development process. Limited simulation and testing can also be carried out within this framework. Programming languages are only used as a stepping stone for generating executable code - i.e. the programming language is the link between a purely mathematical world and the real world of electronics.

Within our project we sought to adopt the same approach for the development of hardware. We needed a purely mathematical framework and notation for the conceptual modelling and verification stages of the hardware design process – leaving VHDL and its supporting tools the role of *mapping* mathematical models to hardware circuits.

The specification of concurrent systems and the development of a mathematical framework for supporting the formal specification and formal analysis of such systems have been amply researched within the academic community, and many formalisms are available.

We could have turned our attention to these formalisms (e.g Concurrent Sequential Processes) and used these as a basis for our work; however, we took the decision to base it on AMN (Abstract Machine Notation) and the B Method which originally have been designed (like VDM and Z) to address the specification and development of systems of sequential programs.

This decision was based on

1. The availability of a practical tool (The B-Toolkit) which already supported many of the aspects which the development of sequential programs and the development of concurrent systems share.

2. The economy of having one methodology, one notation and one set of integrated tools for designing systems, (whether they are hardware or software) within an industrial development team.

3. The potential to delay decisions about whether a particular design or sub-component design should be implemented in software or hardware; furthermore components implemented in hardware in one version of the system can be implemented in software in the next.

4. The apparent similarities of the AMN pseudo-programming style and VHDL, which should ease the take-up of our new development process.

5. The fact that the notion of *concurrency* is supported in AMN through its notions of multiple (or simultaneous) assignment $v1, v2 := e1, e2$ and through the availability of the '$\|$' operator within its mathematical framework. In other mathematical framework the same notions are supported simply through use of predicate conjunction $v1' = e1$ & $v2' = e2$ or Schema Conjunction (in Z).

4 Formal Development in B

The traditional approach to program verification, which can be applied to VHDL, is to use the *semantics* of the programming language to *assign meaning to particular programs* and then prove that these programs meet their formal mathematically stated requirements with reference to the *assigned meaning*. In the development of the B, Jean Raymond Abrial did take a different approach, namely, that of *assigning programs to meaning*. In B all specifications and low level designs are done entirely within a relatively simple mathematical framework and supported by a single notation (AMN). This means, that in the proofs about even the lowest level design we need not consider the full semantics of any particular programming language. This approach is particularly important when utilizing a complex programming language like VHDL. AMN has been designed to look like a pseudo-programming notation around some very simple and intuitive *laws of programming* with formal analysis and verification in mind. This approach – we believe – makes the formal verification of even complex system, manageable and much more attractive. The basis for B is an extension of Dijkstra's weakest precondition calculus [9, 10].

The objective of B refinement and its divide-and-conquer based design process is to arrive, from an abstract specification, at a detailed formally verified design in which *off-the-shelf* formal 'mathematical models' are combined using the operators from the underlying mathematical calculus. Implementation in the executable target language are then *assigned* to the design using translation tools. The *off-the-shelf* 'mathematical models' and their assigned implementations pre-exist in extensible libraries within the B-Toolkit.

The formal verification of designs against their abstract specification is based on the refinement techniques developed for Z [11] and implemented within the B-Toolkit.

5 The Achievements

A result of our project is that an approach has been developed by which digital circuits can be described in standard AMN simply by adopting a particular style of specification.

The approach is currently developed to a stage where abstract design of hardware circuit – which is essentially a collection of concurrently operating sequential processes – can be described in AMN.

In order to exhibit the behaviour of the specified system the abstract AMN design can be Animated, using the standard Animator available in the B-Toolkit.

The abstract description of the system can be refined to lower level designs which utilize some very simple built-in library components. Most designs can be formally verified to meet their specification using the B-Toolkit Proof Obligation Generators and the B-Toolkit Provers which implement the existing refinement rules for AMN.

Finally, the design can be automatically translated into VHDL by a new translator integrated into a special version of the B-Toolkit. By allowing translation of AMN descriptions which employ the notions of parallelism (through '||'), concurrently operating processes can be produced.

The traceability components within the B-Toolkit have, for the VHDL version, been extended so VHDL code fragments produced by the translator can be 'traced' back into their abstract AMN specifications.

6 The Changes to AMN and the B-Toolkit

The results have been achieved with only a few changes to AMN and a few additions to the original B-Toolkit.

No fundamental changed have been made to AMN or the B-Method. A few changes have been made to the syntax of AMN to make descriptions more manageable, e.g. literal bit-strings can be used to describe a total function over an initial segment of the natural numbers.

More specifically "110" is $\{\ 0 \mapsto '0', 1 \mapsto '1', 2 \mapsto '1'\ \}$

where '0' and '1' are the only members of a new type *std_logic*.

The set *std_logic* is introduced by a library component available with the B-Toolkit. A small enhancement has also been made to the static analysis performed by the B-Toolkits type checker. In this analysis, ranges of numbers (e.g., 0..7) are being used to detect range errors. E.g.:

in a context where vec : 0..7 $\to$ BITS, bit : BITS, msb = 15

the assignment vec := "110" is invalid, so is bit := vec(msb)

7 Introducing Concurrency

The ';' operator within AMN is used to impose sequentiality within the processes, while the '||' operator is used to model the concurrent operation of separate processes. Sharing of state variables is limited to the scheme of one writer (process) and many readers which is already a concept supported by the AMN structuring mechanism SEES. Interference is controlled by synchronizing the processes behaviour in such a way that the variables are read only at the beginning of processes' execution and written into only at the end of their execution.

The concurrency within the VHDL resulting from an automatic translation is achieved by allowing the use of '||' in the designs that forms the basis for the translation.

8 The Elements of the Design Approach

The individual operating components in our conceptual AMN model of a system encapsulates internal *signals*. The traditional approach of abstract specification and subsequent refinement can be used, on one hand to manage complexity and on the other to ensure that we can refine our abstract specification confidently and achieve a simple formulation of our systems which can be automatically and confidently translated into the target implementation language (VHDL). These components operate internally as sequential processes with no interference, and all the existing rules of data and algorithm refinement, which are well known from Z and B, can be used. We call these components PROCESS Machines.

A PROCESS Machine can be refined, its operation being finally implemented using a sequential algorithm and functions available from a set of pre-defined PACKAGE Machines (packages of useful functions). The PROCESS Machines' internal state data is, in its lowest level of design, provided through the importation of pre-defined SIGNAL Machines (a signal with useful operations).

In a design the operations from PROCESS Machines can be arranged in a SIMPLE MODULE machine with the parallel but conditional 'invocation' of the processes' operations (i.e. using '||' and 'IF .. THEN .. END').

SIMPLE MODULE machines, which correspond to sub-components in a hardware circuit with their own input and output 'wires', can be arranged into COMPOUND MODULE machines which determine the 'wiring' connections between these sub-components.

In hardware systems the notion of 'events' plays a central role. For example, a state transition can be conditional on the occurrence of an event (e.g. 'a rising edge' is the event where a 2-valued logic signal changes from 'low' to 'high'). This notion of events is supported by the use of EVENT Machines – which allow for event value changes to be used in conditional statements.

Parameterized PACKAGE-, SIGNAL- and EVENT-Machines are all made available in a B-Toolkit library, and constitutes the bottom level building block for a design of a hardware system within the B-Toolkit.

The PROCESS-, SIMPLE_MODULE- and COMPOUND_MODULE-Machines are produced by the designer by 'filling' in pre-defined templates.

The machines and their refinements are arranged in a hierarchy using the standard INCLUSION and IMPORTATION mechanisms in AMN, and sharing is achieved through the use of the SEES mechanism.

This hierarchy of machines is automatically translated into VHDL, by using translation rules for the combinators (e.g. ';', '||') of AMN and instantiating the particular PACKAGE-, SIGNAL- and EVENT-Machines used in the lowest level of design.

9   Future Work

So far we have only conducted some relatively small development using this approach, and the proof of correctness has only been selectively applied to the refinement of PROCESS Machines.

In the next stage of the work we will undertake a much more ambitious exercise in developing a processor, in order to test how well the approach scales up to the design of systems of significant complexity.

As mentioned above, the refinement of the PROCESS-Machine follows the standard B approach for developing sequential algorithms, and the standard methods and tools for verifying correctness of refinements do apply. However, the approach we have adopted for specifying SIMPLE- and COMPOUND MODULE-Machines falls outside the capabilities of the B Method.

Future work will seek to identify how best to extend the notions of refinement within the B framework, in order to deal will refinement of MODULES whose actual input-output 'functions' are achieved through the a repeated concurrent invocation of operations from several PROCESS Modules.

An example of this approach will be available at the conference and my talk will include a demonstration of the developed technology.

10   Commercial Concerns and Acknowledgement

The AMN language, originally devised by Jean-Raymond Abrial, and its supporting B tools are the property of B-Core(UK) Limited. The B-Toolkit product is available from B-Core.

The work presented in this paper is carried out by David Neilson of B-Core and the author on behalf of Aldermaston Weapon Establishment (AWE), Hunting Brae. The developed technology is integrated with the B-Toolkit but is not part of B-Core's commercial B-Toolkit release.

Significant input to the design of the approach for using B to develop hardware has come from AWE, and I would especially like to thank Dave Thomas, Wilson Ifill, Alun Lewis and Neil Watkins for their help and guidance.

References

1. B-Core(UK) Limited. *B-Toolkit User Manual Version 3.4* (available from B-Core (UK) Ltd. on request), 1996.
2. J-R. Abrial. *The B Book – Assigning Programs to Meanings.* Cambridge University Press, 1997.
   This book contains the mathematical basis for the B-Method.
3. J-R. Abrial, M.K.O. Lee, D.S. Neilson, P.N. Scharbach and I.H. Sørensen. *The B-method (software development).* In W.J. Prehn, S. Toetenel, editors, *VDM 91: Formal Software Development Methods,* Springer-Verlag, Lecture Notes in Computer Science, Volume 552, pages 398–405, 1991.
4. K. Lano. *The B Language and Method.* Springer-Verlag, 1996.
5. J.B. Wordswoth. *Software Engineering with B.* Addison-Wesley, 1996.
   This is the definitive guide to software engineering with B.
6. P.J. Ashenden. *The Designer's Guide to VHDL,* 1996.
7. IEEE. *Standard VHDL Reference Manual,* IEEE Standard 1076-1993, 1993.
8. TransEDA Limited. *TransGATE VHDL for Synthesis,* 1992.
9. E.W. Dijkstra. Guarded commands, nondeterminacy and formal derivation of programs. *Communications of the ACM,* 18(8), 1975.
10. C.C. Morgan *Programming from Specifications,* 2nd edition. Prentice Hall International Series in Computer Science, 1994.
11. J. He, C.A.R. Hoare, J.W. Sanders. *Data Refinement Refined.* In B. Robinet and R. Wilhelm, editors, *Proc. ESOP 86,* Lecture Notes in Computer Science, volume 213, pages 187–196, Springer-Verlag, 1986.

Z on the Web Using Java

Jonathan P. Bowen and David Chippington

The University of Reading, Department of Computer Science
Whiteknights, PO Box 225, Reading, Berks RG6 6AY, UK

Email: J.P.Bowen@reading.ac.uk
URL: http://www.cs.reading.ac.uk/people/jpb/

Abstract. Displaying the formal Z notation within a World Wide Web browser using standard HTML (HyperText Markup Language) pages is problematic because of the non-standard fonts used in Z, making it difficult to view Z documents on-line for some. This paper presents a solution to this problem. The formal text is formatted using a specially developed Java applet where the Z specification to be displayed is specified as a parameter to the applet, following the Z Interchange Format in the draft Z standard. A separate Java application program may be used to create and edit the Z specification. Other possible solutions and future directions are also discussed.

1 Introduction

The World Wide Web (WWW) [2] has been phenomenally successful over the past few years, expanding exponentially in use and allowing easy access to a wide range of digital resources around the world via the global Internet 'network of networks'. The Web allows ready access to resources for educational, business, marketing, publicity and other purposes.

The underlying formatting language is HTML (HyperText Markup Language), a relatively simple Document Type Definition (DTD) of the Standard Generalized Markup Language (SGML, ISO 8879). HTML has been under continuous development since its introduction. Early versions included little support for characters not in the ISO Latin 1 character set, which extends the standard 7-bit ASCII code for characters, but is still encoded using only 8 bits, limiting the number of characters available severely. The most recent recommendation for HTML is Version 4.0 [23]. Section 24.3 of this draft standard covers *character entity references for symbols, mathematical symbols, and Greek letters*. This uses Unicode 2.0 names and encodings which may be up to 16 bits, thus vastly increasing the number of possible symbols available.

The Z notation [3, 22] is a stylized form of mathematics that is amenable to a standardized syntax and computer processing. Indeed, Annex E of the draft Z standard specifies a proposed ASCII Z Interchange Format for the exchange of Z specifications between tools [29]. This is based on SGML and an experimental tool to handle this format has been built [15]. A major problem for the display of Z within HTML is the use of many mathematical symbols, most in general use in standard mathematics, but some specific to Z itself. It has been suggested as part of the Z standardization effort [6] that all Z symbols could be included in the Unicode encoding for greater portability of Z specifications [30].

Despite possible developments in the future, the fact remains that none of the currently widely used WWW browsers can display Z symbols, schemas, etc., satisfactorily without some form of auxiliary help. Thus the majority of users of the Web cannot view on-line Z documents easily and conveniently at the moment. However, there is a desire by researchers and others to publish formal specifications using Z and other mathematically based notations on the World Wide Web in a convenient form for as wide a readership as possible [19].

Z documents can be placed on-line in POSTSCRIPT [1] format (or increasingly the more recent PDF format), but most Web browsers are not configured to display such documents directly. They must be set up to run an appropriate viewer program when a POSTSCRIPT file is detected (typically through the filename extension ".ps"). While POSTSCRIPT viewers are fairly common on Unix-based systems (e.g., *GhostView*), they are typically less readily available on most Windows-based systems (e.g., *GSView*). The problem is even more acute if a DVI format file is placed on-line, as output directly by the LATEX document preparation system [17] which is used to generate many Z documents at the moment, especially in academia.

Additionally, POSTSCRIPT files can be large and are thus often compressed using the Unix *compress* utility (extension ".z") or the GNU *gzip* program (extension ".gz") to reduce loading time and to save file space. Again, it is possible for Web browsers to be configured to automatically uncompress such files, but the naive user will not necessarily be able to do this easily, particular on a Windows-based system.

Even if a Web browser is configured correctly, there can be loading speed problems in practice if a Z document in POSTSCRIPT format is accessed, especially across national boundaries where Internet connections can be overloaded. In any case, there is a significant overhead in running a POSTSCRIPT or DVI viewer compared to viewing on HTML directly, even if network delays are minimal.

2   Potential Solutions

A number of options are available to the implementor attempting to solve the problem of accessing and displaying an on-line Z document directly within a Web browser window, each with various advantages and disadvantages.

The simplest approach is to use in-line graphical image files containing the desired Z specification, interspersed with informal explanatory text in standard HTML. Probably the easiest way to achieve this is using the LATEX2HTML tool [10, 11]. This allows Z specifications written using the LATEX document preparation system [17] to be converted to HTML directly where possible and into in-line GIF images (the most standard graphics format in Web pages) where it is not. LATEX 'styles' such as those available with the commercial *f*UZZ [21] and the free ZTC [28] Z type-checking tools allow the relevant fonts to be loaded. Unfortunately this is often problematic since Z uses non-standard fonts and the result of using LATEX2HTML on Z specifications can easily produce flawed results (e.g., missing fonts, or fonts of incorrect size).

An alternative would be to have a set of GIF images for the individual mathematical symbols and schema boxes and to include these in-line as needed. It would be desirable to have a tool to convert from some source format (e.g., Z Interchange Format or LaTeXsource) to the matching HTML, which would not be very readable. This approach would also allow the relatively easy and possibly automated inclusion of hyperlinks for cross-referencing of names (e.g., of schemas, etc.), enabling convenient traversal of the specification by the reader.

A problem with using GIF images included in Web pages is that they are in general of low quality when printed on paper since they are typically designed for low resolution screen display. An advantage is that the approach works with any graphical WWW browser, whatever its vintage, since in-line GIF images have been supported by all graphical browsers since the early free *mosaic* browser from NSCA.

A more sophisticated approach is to use the Z Browser [18] which is now available in the form of a Web browser 'plug-in'. This allows the plug-in program to control a specified portion of the Web page directly. In the case of the Z Browser plug-in, a portion of Z specification is displayed. A plug-in for DVI output from LaTeX documents is available for Unix [20], and thus could potentially be used to display Z specifications written using LaTeX. A disadvantage of this approach is that plug-ins are machine specific. In the case of the Z Browser plug-in, it is only available on PCs running under Windows 95 and Windows NT. Additionally, plug-ins only work on more recent browsers, such as later versions of *Netscape* and Microsoft's *Internet Explorer*. However these are now widely available.

A platform independent approach could be achieved by using a CGI (Common Gateway Interface) program to generate portions of Z specification dynamically as in-line images, using parameters to pass a description of the Z to be displayed. Using this approach would be worth investigation and could work well for smaller specifications. For example, the MINSE project has demonstrated that the approach is convenient with small mathematical expressions [16]. However large specifications would require considerable transmission of information from the client's browser to a Web server, possibly located far away on the Internet. This could slow loading time dramatically if the network is heavily loaded and/or the available bandwidth is limited. The approach also depended on the availability of a central server on the network to run the CGI program. If that server or its network connection malfunctions, all documents making use of the server become inaccessible. In addition, the use of graphical images means noticeably low quality when the document is printed.

Many recent graphical Web browsers now support the inclusion of Java programming language [12] 'applets' (mini application programs) within Web pages. Like plug-ins, these control a specified portion of the display Web page in which they are embedded. Unlike plug-ins, applets written in Java and compiled into intermediate Java byte code are platform independent. WebEQ takes this approach for mathematics in general [14], but is very slow and can be unreliable on early Java-enabled browsers. IDVI is a Java applet that displays DVI output from LaTeX documents within Web pages [9], and thus could potentially be used to display Z documents within Web pages.

A major problem with Java applets at the moment is the speed of loading and execution, although this is improving as new Java enabled Web browsers become available (e.g., using "Just In Time" compilation). There are also various versions of Java available (and more to come); only earlier versions (e.g., Version 1.0) are well supported by widely used Web browsers. Later versions, even Version 1.1, are not so well supported yet. If course this is likely to change, but only relatively slowly for many due to the inertia of installation of new browsers once users have a working Web browser.

The rest of this paper describes a specialized applet for displaying Z specifications and an associated Java application tool which can be used to interactively generate the required HTML source code and embedded applets with suitable parameters. This paper only gives an overview of the facilities available. For readers requiring more detail, much fuller information is available elsewhere [7].

3 Z Display Applet

The major front-end software that interfaces the display of Z specification material to the end user running a client Web browser is implemented as a Java applet named ZDisplay. The call to this software is embedded directly in the HTML source of the Web page in which the Z is to be displayed using the standard <APPLET ...> ...</APPLET> markup (see later for further details).

Initialization of the Z display includes loading of Z fonts as images. Updating of the display buffer is done in a separate area before it is painted to the display to avoid flickering effects. Full details are available in a report [7].

Figures 1 and 2 (on pages 70 and 71) show two example screen dumps using the *Netscape* and Internet Explorer Web browsers respectively. Both show part of Spivey's well known Birthday Book example from the Z Reference Manual [22], illustrating compatibility with the two main graphical Web browsers employed by the majority of users.

Figure 3 (page 72) shows the HTML source for the Birthday Book applet. This reads its input from a file named "bb.txt", the contents of which are shown in Figure 4 on page 73. This uses a syntax based on the ASCII Z Interchange Format in Annex E of the draft Z standard [29], particularly for the symbol names.

4 Z Creator Application

The ZCreator application allows the generator and editing of the source descriptions for Z specification blocks that are to be subsequently embedded within an HTML document. Like the ZDisplay applet, it is written in the Java programming language which means it is highly portable. Unlike ZDisplay, ZCreator is a stand-alone application rather than an applet so that it can read and write files without any security issues. Applets are not allowed to read or write local files since this could cause security problems if invoked remotely.

Figures 5 and 6 on page 74 show screen shots of the ZCreator application under Unix and Windows respectively, illustrating the portability of the application. There are minor differences in the graphical presentation, but the functionality is essentially the same in each case.

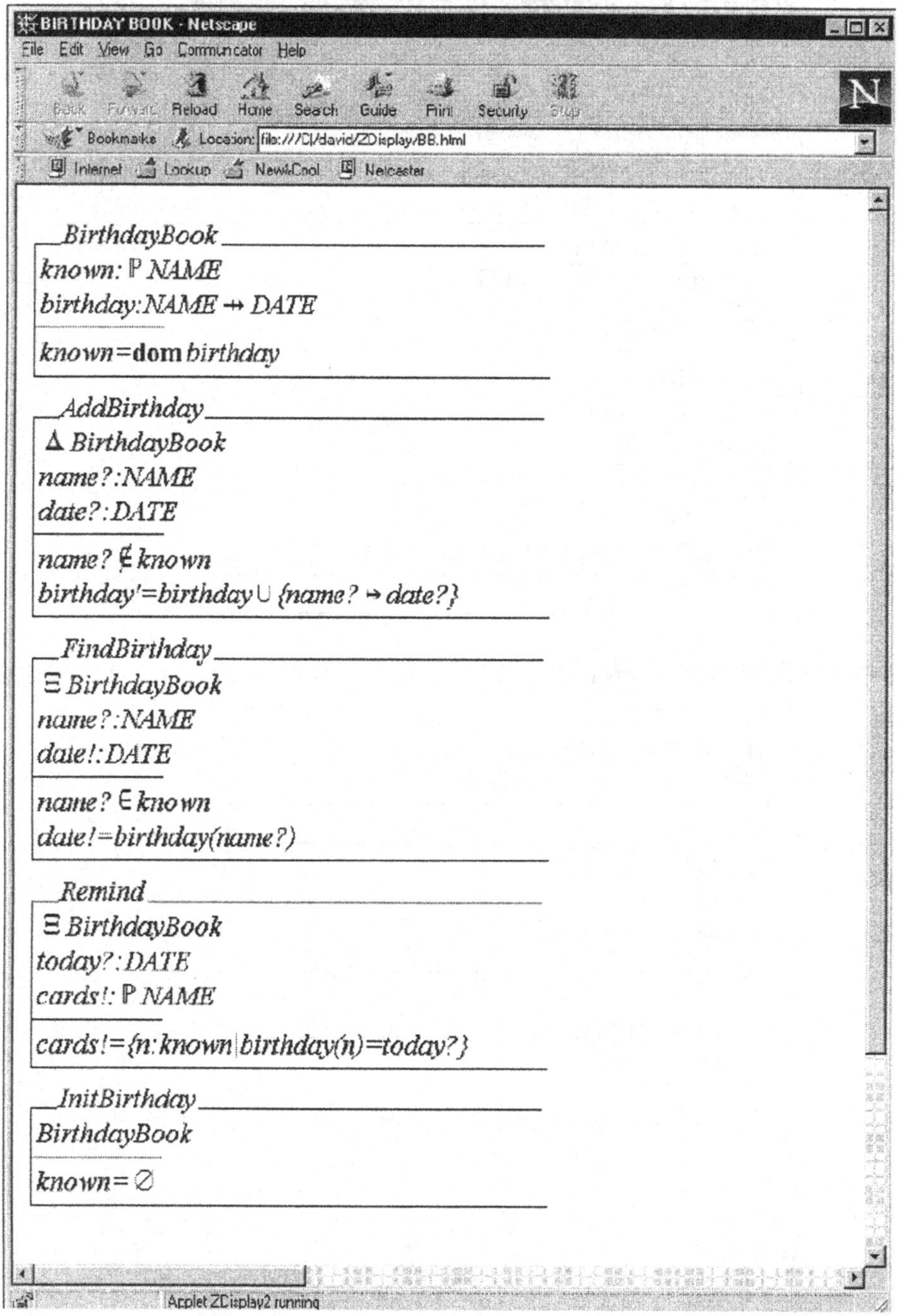

BIRTHDAY BOOK - Netscape

File Edit View Go Communicator Help

Back Forward Reload Home Search Guide Print Security Stop

Bookmarks Location: file:///C|/david/ZDisplay/BB.html

Internet Lookup New&Cool Netcaster

$$
\begin{array}{l}
\_\_BirthdayBook_____ \\
known: \mathbb{P}\ NAME \\
birthday: NAME \nrightarrow DATE \\
\hline
known = \mathbf{dom}\ birthday
\end{array}
$$

$$
\begin{array}{l}
\_\_AddBirthday_____ \\
\Delta\ BirthdayBook \\
name?:NAME \\
date?:DATE \\
\hline
name? \notin known \\
birthday' = birthday \cup \{name? \mapsto date?\}
\end{array}
$$

$$
\begin{array}{l}
\_\_FindBirthday_____ \\
\Xi\ BirthdayBook \\
name?:NAME \\
date!:DATE \\
\hline
name? \in known \\
date! = birthday(name?)
\end{array}
$$

$$
\begin{array}{l}
\_\_Remind_____ \\
\Xi\ BirthdayBook \\
today?:DATE \\
cards!: \mathbb{P}\ NAME \\
\hline
cards! = \{n:known \mid birthday(n) = today?\}
\end{array}
$$

$$
\begin{array}{l}
\_\_InitBirthday_____ \\
BirthdayBook \\
\hline
known = \varnothing
\end{array}
$$

Applet ZDisplay2 running

Fig. 1. ZDisplay Birthday Book example applet screen dump (*Netscape* browser).

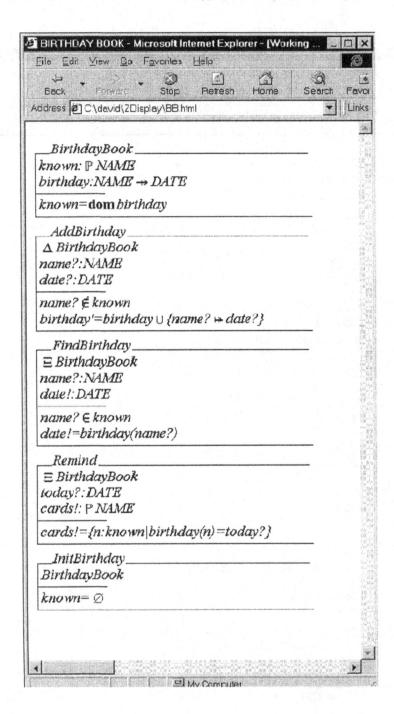

Fig. 2. ZDisplay Birthday Book example applet screen dump (*Internet Explorer* browser).

```
<HTML>
<HEAD>
<TITLE>BIRTHDAY BOOK</TITLE>
</HEAD>
<BODY>
<APPLET CODE="ZDisplay.class" WIDTH=2000 HEIGHT=694>
<PARAM NAME="input" VALUE="file">
<PARAM NAME="filename" VALUE="bb.txt">
<PARAM NAME="back" VALUE="white">
<PARAM NAME="fontsize" VALUE="16">
</APPLET>
</BODY>
</HTML>
```

Fig. 3. HTML source for Birthday Book example applet.

To the left of the ZCreator display window, buttons allow specification blocks to be selected for editing. In the centre at the top, the source to the Z specification block currently selected may be edited. Below this is a formatted display of the Z specification being edited. In this case it is part of the Birthday Book example again from [22]. To the right are buttons allowing Z symbols not available on a standard keyboard to be input directly, without the need to remember the ASCII name used for the symbol.

5   Z Creator/Display Language

The Z specification blocks and symbols are specified using a markup language following the Z Standard ASCII syntax for interchange of Z specifications [29, 30]. This is passed to the ZDisplay applet as a parameter either within a named on-line file or included directly in-line. Figure 8 on page 76 shows an example of HTML code calling the ZDisplay applet, including the ASCII names for the various Z symbols that are available. The applet has a number of named parameters:

- NAME="input" can take a value of "file" for input from a file (as named by the optional "filename" parameter) and "param" for input in-line from the "spec" parameter (see below).
- NAME="back" allows the background colour to be set.
- NAME="fontsize" allows the size of the text to be determined.
- NAME="spec" enables the Z specification to be included in-line instead of within a file as illustrated in Figure 3.

Figure 7 (page 75) shows the equivalent output using the Netscape Web browser when formatting HTML input calling the ZDisplay applet as listed in Figure 8.

The following markup is also available to start, delineate and end major sections in a Z specification:

```
\&StartSchema BirthdayBook
\known : &pset NAME
\birthday : NAME &pfun DATE
\&Line
\known = &TextSymS dom &TextSymE birthday
\&EndSec

\&StartSchema AddBirthday
\&Delta BirthdayBook
\name? : NAME
\date? : DATE
\&Line
\name? &notin known
\birthday' = birthday &cup {name? &map date?}
\&EndSec

\&StartSchema FindBirthday
\&Xi BirthdayBook
\name? : NAME
\date! : DATE
\&Line
\name? &isin known
\date! = birthday(name?)
\&EndSec

\&StartSchema Remind
\&Xi BirthdayBook
\today? : DATE
\cards! : &pset NAME
\&Line
\cards! = { n:known | birthday(n) = today? }
\&EndSec

\&StartSchema InitBirthday
\BirthdayBook
\&Line
\known = &empty
\&EndSec
```

Fig. 4. Input file for Birthday Book example applet.

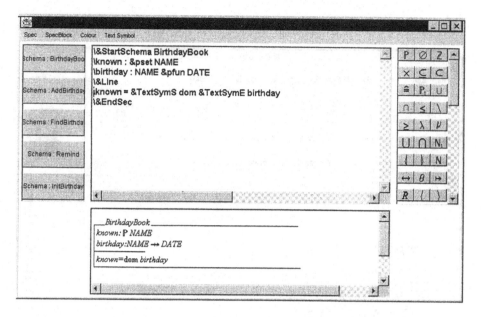

Fig. 5. ZCreator application for creating and editing Z specifications (under Unix).

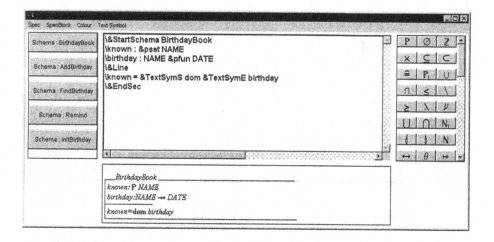

Fig. 6. ZCreator application for creating and editing Z specifications (under Windows).

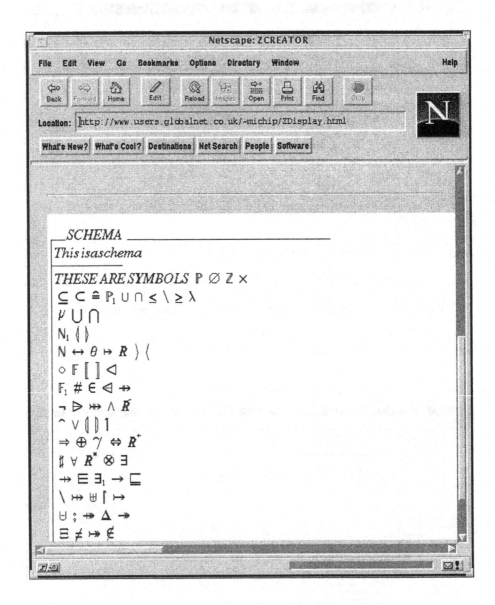

Fig. 7. ZDisplay specification language symbols output under Netscape.

```
<APPLET CODE="ZDisplay.class" WIDTH=2000 HEIGHT=450>
<PARAM NAME="input" VALUE="param">
<PARAM NAME="back" VALUE="white">
<PARAM NAME="fontsize" VALUE="16">
<PARAM NAME="spec" VALUE="
\&StartSchema SCHEMA
\This is a schema
\&Line
\These are symbols:
\&pset &empty &int &cart
\&sube &sub &horiz &pset1 &cup &cap &le &sdiff &ge &lambda
\&mu &Bigcup &Bigcap
\&nat1 &openbind &closbind
\&nat &rel &bind &map &iter &lang &rang
\&compfn &fset &lbag &rbag &dres
\&fset1 &num &isin &dsub &fpfun
\&isnot &rres &rsub &fpinj &and &relinv
\&concat &or &limg &rimg &extract
\&rArr &oplus &distconc &iff &trans
\&multi &forall &reflex &bagsc &exist
\&pfun &bagmem &exist1 &rarr &sbrel
\&sh &pinj &bagun &proj &rarrtl
\&bagd &scomp &psur &Delta &Rarr
\&Xi &ne &bij &isnotin
\&EndSec">
</APPLET>
```

Fig. 8. ZDisplay specification language symbols.

- &StartSchema – start a standard vertical Z schema. The following text word is taken as the name of the schema (e.g., *BirthdayBook*). If no name is required, the keyword &NoTitle may be used instead.
- &StartGeneric – start a generic construction definition. The following word is taken as the generic parameters (e.g., $[X, Y]$). If no parameters are required, the keyword &NoTitle may be used as for &StartSchema.
- &StartAxiomatic – start an axiomatic description definition. There are no parameters.
- &StartSpecText – start standard Z text section. Again, there are no parameters as following text.
- &StartText – allows the inclusion of informal text between formal Z specification text.
- &Line – include a dividing line between the declaration and predicate part of a vertical schema box, generic construction or axiomatic description.
- &EndSec – end any of the sections started by &Start... above.

It is possible to select the colour of text until the end of the section (or a subsequent colour change) if desired. E.g.: &red, &blue, &black and &white.

A text-based Z symbol may be placed in specification sections using the delimiters &TextSymS ... &TextSymE. For example, "dom *birthday*" may be coded as:

```
&TextSymS dom &TextSymE birthday
```

This disambiguates such symbols from standard text by displaying the text in a different font (bold Roman instead of italic).

To start a new line, the "\" character should be used. It is convenient to include this at the start of lines in the source file or parameter string.

6   Future Improvements

The ZDisplay applet and ZCreator program have been developed as a proof of concept. Approximately three months effort were expended in their implementation and documentation [7]. There are still major barriers in their practical use, but none are insurmountable. The following problems (together with suggested solutions) remain:

− Java is still rather slow when run as an applet within a Web browser. The first time Java is invoked can result in a delay while it is loaded. "Just In Time" (JIT) compilation to native code and other optimizations, together with the increasing performance of computer hardware, may help to solve this problem in future Web browsers.

− Many people may wish to print a Z document viewed within a Web browser, the output of Java applets is typically not shown when a Web page is sent to a printer. Future Web browser may address this problem, which is general and not specific to Z. ZDisplay could be used to generate a GIF image for subsequent static use.

− Currently the ZDisplay applet does not support hyperlinks within Z schemas. This is a useful feature which could be included with extra Java coding. Manual hyperlinks could be added in a similar manner to the existing HTML coding for internal anchor hyperlinks (<A HREF=#*anchor*>*text*</A>). Automatic links could be added to link names with their original definitions to aid the reading of large specifications. As an alternative, hyperlinks for GIF images of Z text could be supported using HTML image maps.

− The structural markup syntax used here is simpler than the Z Interchange Format in Annex E of the draft Z standard [29]. For example, <SCHEMADEF STYLE=vert> ...</SCHEMADEF> is the standard syntax for a vertical schema. Updating the Java applet to follow the Z standard syntax more closely is possible with some Java programming effort. It would also be possible to parse other widely used formats directly (e.g., LaTeX document preparation system Z specification source [17]), perhaps by selection of a parameter option to the applet or by having more than one applet available.

− Currently Z symbols are implemented as GIF images which must be read and loaded individually. There are many Z symbols, so this is a slow process. A particular applet could just load the symbols it required to speed up this process. In addition, GIF images do not print very well because the resolution is aimed at screen display rather than paper quality. In the future it is likely that more (or even all) Z symbols will be supported by HTML using Unicode. A proposal exists as part of the Z standards initiative to help ensure just this [30].

- ZCreator is a stand-alone tool that does not interface directly with any other Z tool. There is a large amount of legacy Z specification written using the LaTeX document preparation system [17] (and other word processing tools). It would be helpful to be able to convert from (and to) other formats (e.g., LaTeX source). Such conversions could be done within ZCreator using additional Java code, or as a separate program written in Java or any other suitable programming language.

The work presented here has some general utility beyond Z in the display of any notation with non-standard symbols and formatting. It could be adapted to other formal notations if desired, but not without considerable effort in its current form.

Similar work on "displets" described in [8] covers some of the issues mentioned above (e.g., inclusion of hyperlinks, adherence to the Z Interchange Format syntax and conversion from LaTeX format). It may be worth coordinating future developments.

7   Conclusion

Software to generate and display Z specification on the World Wide Web using the Java programming language [12] has been presented. A graphical ZCreator application, written in Java, generates Z specification code based on the Z Interchange Format from the draft Z standard [6]. A ZDisplay applet for displaying Z within HTML pages is available, entirely configured via parameter values supplied to it within the associated Web page. The code may be generated by ZCreator, hand-written, or produced from elsewhere. These utilities are functional as they stand, but could be developed further for realistic use, as discussed in the previous section.

The Web is changing extremely rapidly and facilities available are dramatically different even within a year. Recent work on an Extensible Markup Language (XML) [13, 25], a subset of SGML designed for easy implementation, may well subsume HTML in the medium to long term. This allows user-definable markup, as opposed to the fixed HTML markup periodically updated by the World Wide Web Consortium (W3C) A Mathematical Markup Language (MathML) [26, 27], a native XML application, is available as a W3C proposed recommendation. Amaya [24], W3C's browser/editor, supports MathML.

It remains to be seen how well MathML will support a language like Z. For example, schema boxes and special symbols may be problematic depending on the flexibility of the facilities made available in MathML. Other work has considered how Z could fit into XML, as well as using Java for display of Z [8]. A goal of XML is to be very generic, so it is likely that convenient display of Z using this approach will be possible at some point in the future; exactly when that will be is difficult to predict but the time-scale is likely to be years rather than months. In the meantime, interim measures may be appropriate.

Further information on the work presented in this paper and links to many of the other approaches to presenting Z and mathematics in general on the World Wide Web [4] may be found under the following URL (Uniform Resource Locator), maintained by one of the authors:

`http://www.fmse.cs.reading.ac.uk/z/java/`

References

1. Adobe Systems Incorporated. *PostScript Language Reference Manual.* Addison-Wesley Publishing Company, 2nd edition, 1990.
2. T. Berners-Lee. World Wide Web past present and future. *IEEE Computer,* 29(10):69–77, October 1996.
3. J. P. Bowen. *Formal Specification and Documentation using Z: A Case Study Approach.* International Thomson Computer Press, 1996.
4. J. P. Bowen. Proposed extensions in HTML for Z. Part of the Virtual Library, Z section, 1998. URL:
   `http://www.comlab.ox.ac.uk/archive/z/html-z.html`.
5. J. P. Bowen and M. G. Hinchey, editors. *ZUM'95: The Z Formal Specification Notation, 9th International Conference of Z Users, Limerick, Ireland, September 7–9, 1995, Proceedings,* volume 967 of *Lecture Notes in Computer Science.* Springer-Verlag, 1995.
6. S. M. Brien and J. E. Nicholls. Z base standard. Technical Monograph PRG-107, Oxford University Computing Laboratory, Wolfson Building, Parks Road, Oxford, UK, November 1992. Accepted for standardization under ISO/IEC JTC1/SC22.
7. D. Chippington. Presentation of Z specifications on the World Wide Web. Final Project Report 3/CS/6N – Computer Science Project, The University of Reading, Department of Computer Science, UK, 5 May 1998. URL:
   `http://www.fmse.cs.reading.ac.uk/z/java/report/`.
8. P. Ciancarini, C. Mascolo, and F. Vitali. Visualizing Z notation in HTML documents. In J. P. Bowen, A. Fett, and M. G. Hinchey, editors, *ZUM'98: The Z Formal Specification Notation,* volume 1493 of *Lecturer Notes in Computer Science,* pages 81–95. Springer-Verlag, 1998. In this volume. URL:
   `http://www.cs.unibo.it/~fabio/displet.html`.
9. G. A. Dickie. About IDVI, 18 October 1996. URL:
   `http://www.geom.umn.edu/java/idvi/`.
10. N. Drakos. From text to hypertext: A post-hoc rationalisation of LATEX2HTML. In *Proc. 1st World Wide Web Conference,* Geneva, Switzerland, May 1994. CERN. URL:
    `http://cbl.leeds.ac.uk/nikos/doc/www94/www94.html`.
11. N. Drakos. The LATEX2HTML translator, 23 February 1998. URL:
    `http://www-dsed.llnl.gov/files/programs/unix/latex2html/`.
12. D. Flanagan. *Java in a Nutshell: A Desktop Quick Reference.* O'Reilly & Associates, 2nd edition, 1997.
13. P. Flynn et al. Frequently Asked Questions about the Extensible Markup Language: The XML FAQ, 1998. URL:
    `http://www.ucc.ie/xml/`.
14. Geometry Technologies, Inc. WebEQ: Putting math on the Web, 1998. URL:
    `http://www.webeq.com/`.
15. D. M. Germán and D. D. Cowan. Experiments with the Z Interchange Format and SGML. In Bowen and Hinchey [5], pages 224–233.

16. Ka-Ping Yee. Mathematical expressions on the WWW, 1996. URL:
    http://www.lfw.org/math/.
17. L. Lamport. *LᴬTEX User's Guide & Reference Manual: A document preparation system.*
    Addison-Wesley Publishing Company, 2nd edition, 1993.
18. L. Mikušiak, M. Adamy, and T. Seidmann. Publishing formal specifications in Z notation
    on the WWW. In M. Bidoit and M. Dauchet, editors, *TAPSOFT'97: Theory and Practice
    of Software Development*, volume 1214 of *Lecturer Notes in Computer Science*, pages 871–
    874. Springer-Verlag, 1997.
19. L. Mikušiak, V. Vojtek, J. Hasaralejko, and J. Hanzelová. Z browser – tool for visualization
    of Z specifications. In Bowen and Hinchey [5], pages 510–523.
20. K. Peeters. nDVI: A DVI viewer plugin for Netscape (Unix), 8 October 1997. URL:
    http://norma.nikhef.nl/~t16/ndvi_doc.html.
21. J. M. Spivey. *The ƒUZZ Manual.* Computing Science Consultancy, 34 Westlands Grove,
    Stockton Lane, York YO3 0EF, UK, 2nd edition, July 1992.
22. J. M. Spivey. *The Z Notation: A Reference Manual.* Prentice Hall International Series in
    Computer Science, 2nd edition, 1992.
23. World Wide Web Consortium (W3C). *HTML 4.0 Specification*, 18 December 1997. REC-
    html40-971218, W3C Recommendation. URL:
    http://www.w3.org/TR/REC-html40/.
24. World Wide Web Consortium (W3C). Amaya – W3C's browser/editor, 10 July 1998. URL:
    http://www.w3.org/Amaya/.
25. World Wide Web Consortium (W3C). Extensible Markup Language (XML), 1998. URL:
    http://www.w3.org/XML/.
26. World Wide Web Consortium (W3C). HTML math overview, 1998. URL:
    http://www.w3.org/Math/.
27. World Wide Web Consortium (W3C). Mathematical Markup Language (MathML), 24
    February 1998. PR-math-19980224, W3C Proposed Recommendation. URL:
    http://www.w3.org/TR/PR-math/.
28. Xiaoping Jia. *ZTC: A Type Checker for Z – User's Guide.* Institute for Software Engineering,
    Department of Computer Science and Information Systems, DePaul University, Chicago, IL
    60604, USA, 1994.
29. Z Standard. Annex E – Interchange Format, 9 August 1995. Draft 1.2. URL:
    ftp://ftp.comlab.ox.ac.uk/pub/Zforum/ZSTAN/versions/part2.ps.
30. Z Standard. Annex A – Lexis, December 1997. Draft 1.3. URL:
    ftp://ftp.comlab.ox.ac.uk/pub/Zforum/ZSTAN/drafts/lexis.ps.

Visualizing Z Notation in HTML Documents

Paolo Ciancarini, Cecilia Mascolo, and Fabio Vitali

Department of Computer Science, University of Bologna
Mura Anteo Zamboni, 7, I-40127 Bologna, Italy

Tel: +39 51 354506   Fax: +39 51 354510
Email: {ciancarini,mascolo,vitali}@cs.unibo.it

Abstract. The use of the WWW as a communication medium for software engineers is limited by the lack of tools for writing, sharing, and verifying formal notations. For instance, the Z specification language has a a rich set of mathematical characters, and requires graphic-rich boxes and schemas for its specifications. It is difficult to integrate Z specifications and text on WWW pages written with the current versions of HTML, and traditional tools are not suited for the task.

We present a Java-based tool for rendering Z specifications within HTML documents that can be shown on every WWW browser with Java capabilities. Being a complete rendering engine, text parts and Z specifications can be freely intermixed, and all the standard features of HTML (such as links, etc.) are available outside and inside Z specifications. Furthermore, the extensibility of our engine allows additional notations to be supported and integrated with current ones.

1   Introduction

The use of the WWW as an environment for software design introduces new problems and challenges to the specification community: the use of the WWW to support software process work-flows, sharing specification documents, allowing read and write access, and providing hypertextual links among documents is a hot topic [8, 14].

The typographical rendering of WWW documents is usually defined using the HTML markup language [1, 13]. HTML provides textual support for elements such as input fields, buttons, choice lists, etc. along with structural and formatting commands for text within the data format of network documents.

This has allowed both complex interfaces and proper and traditional text content to be described in ASCII-based source documents. On the other hand, HTML only allows a few elements, that is, those that are explicitly defined in the standard. Whenever authors' needs exceed the capabilities of the elements already defined in HTML, a different approach needs to be used: either the existing tags are abused for a different purpose than that for which they were created, or an image is used, or a Java applet is created providing the desired functionality.

Specification languages like Z [16] are often based on specialized notations (mathematics and logic symbols): it would be useful to be able to give a visual interpretation of these symbols and to allow them to be displayed on WWW pages.

The purpose of this paper is to report on a Java rendering engine for HTML data that we have implemented. The engine allows typographical and graphical support for standard HTML documents, and can easily be extended to include support for additional notations. We have added a complete graphical and typographical support for formal specification documents written in Z. The rendering engine we are describing is a completely autonomous piece of code that can work on unmodified Java-enabled browsers such as Netscape Communicator or Microsoft Internet Explorer.

Using our engine, it becomes possible to integrate full-blown Z specifications and plain text chunks using HTML and HTML-extensions that can be browsed and displayed in any WWW browser that is Java-enabled.

The paper is structured as follows: in Section 2 we summarize the state of the art of the rendering of Z documents as hypertexts. In Section 3 we describe the idea of extending HTML with Java using the *displets* concept. Section 5 explains how our Z browser works from the point of view of the user, whereas Section 4 describes the implementation details of the tool. In Section 6 we draw some conclusions and sketch our future work.

2   Creating Z specifications

2.1   Writing, printing and visualizing Z specifications

Several tools exist to this date to help software designers write, test, and share their Z specifications. A complete guide to all the existing tools for Z can be found at http://www.comlab.ox.ac.uk/archive/z.html.

We can divide these tools in four main categories: fonts, browsers, editors, and type checkers.

True Type fonts for Z are available to use with common word processors on many platforms including Windows and Macintosh, but fonts of course only give access to the special mathematical characters of the Z language, forcing users to use non-specific features of available tools to create the graphic boxes of schemata and other Z elements.

Customizable formatters such as LaTeX [10] are the most common tools to write Z specifications. General style files for LaTeX such as oz.sty, fuzz.sty and ztc.sty, have been published to precisely render Z specifications.

Logica has created a syntax-driven WYSIWYG editor for Z on MS Windows platforms. Such an editor also integrates a type checker and forces the production of well-formed Z specifications by providing facilities for building, editing, checking, and viewing Z specification documents. Being WYSIWYG, the editor can display the Z constructs and symbols as they would appear on a printed page.

Z Browser, an application for displaying Z specifications that runs on MS Windows, is presented in [12]. The tool is aimed at Z novices, and is integrated with a complete help system for Z grammar and notation.

Zola, by IST, is an integrated editing tool for Z that runs on Sun OS and Solaris. Zola is a WYSIWYG editor that automates the construction, syntax checking and visual layout of Z documents.

Several analysis tools also exist for Z specifications. For instance, CADiZ [7] is an integrated suite of tools for creating Z documents. It understands source files in LaTeX and Word for Windows, and can visualize implicit Z expressions (i.e. schema calculi) by showing their expansions.

Finally, the ZTC [18] type checker accepts LaTeX-formatted Z specifications as well as text-based ones. ZTC also suggests using a special syntax based on concatenation of ASCII characters for mathematical symbols.

2.2   Hypertext and Z specifications

There are several good reasons to provide hypertext functionalities to Z specifications. A complex specification is intrinsically composed of many connected chunks (schemas, etc.) that refer to each other in a peculiar, often unpredictable way. Furthermore, the idea of literate programming requires that schemas and texts interleave freely, so that the reader is provided with a narrative explanation of the most complex schemas, and a formalized and exact specification of vaguer descriptions. These remarks naturally call for a hypertext solution.

Moreover, collaboration and sharing are even better reasons for providing hypertext support to Z specifications: formal specifications are but one step in the complex process of system design, verification, and implementation [5]. Modern development processes are enacted by teams of people that cooperate, interact, and discuss. Being able to create, access, and verify formal specifications within the usual tools of our everyday work, publish them, connect them to the other deliverables of the design and implementation processes would allow a tighter integration between formal design and actual implementation [3].

Till recently, Z specifications could only be visualized on the WWW by creating images in one of the supported inline formats, such as GIF. This leads to a very cumbersome and unnatural creation process, since the Z specifications have to be created in a different environment than the text, and furthermore non-specialized graphic editors have to be used in order to produce graphically acceptable schemas. It is also a very unnatural and clumsy way of accessing the information: an image of a schema is a completely opaque object, where the subparts, the texts, and the formulas are completely inaccessible; it is a bitmap that cannot be further processed because the content and meaning have been lost: the content of a schema cannot be searched, the specifications cannot be indexed, analyzed or verified.

A first attempt to show Z specifications on the WWW was described in [11], designing a plug-in for Netscape and Internet Explorer that accepts Z specifications written using one of the existing LaTeX styles.

Although this approach is very original it has two main limitations: first, visualizing Z documents requires the availability of the plug-in, which is architecture-dependent (it only exists for MS Windows). Secondly, the LaTeX format is alien to the available SGML-based formats suggested for the WWW: in fact, writing Z schemas in LaTeX requires a different syntax and approach than writing the surrounding free-flow text in HTML, and the specifications live independently of the host document. The first problem has been addressed: the Z browser is becoming a Java applet, which is architecture-independent and can be run on most computers of the current generation.

We know that also J. Bowen and others at the University of Reading are working on a Java applet to visualize Z schemas (http://www.fmse.cs.reading.ac.uk/z/java/). Our approach, detailed in Section 5, is related but with noteworthy differences.

2.3   The advantages of markup languages

HTML has been extremely successful in allowing unsophisticated network users to become authors of fairly complex documents, even in the absence of widespread editing tools. Nonetheless, there has been in the past two or three years a widespread awareness ([15]) that HTML has reached its potential, and that a change of paradigm was necessary.

The major drawback of HTML is that it allows only a pre-specified set of elements. Authors can only use these elements, and have to limit their authoring needs to what is available within the existing language, or to force these elements beyond their intended meaning.

HTML is an application of the Standard Generalized Markup Language [15], that is, a class of documents conforming to the SGML Document Type Definition (DTD) that describes 'HTML documents'. SGML, being a meta-language describing classes of documents rather than one specific class, is free of the above mentioned limitations of HTML: by appropriately creating a custom class of documents, and defining the legal elements therein, authors can provide support for any kind of rhetorical need, however complex and arcane. Metalanguages 'allow groups of people or organizations to create their own customized markup languages for exchanging information in their domain (music, chemistry, electronics, hill-walking, finance, surfing, linguistics, knitting, history, engineering, rabbit-keeping, mathematics, etc.)' – see http://www.ucc.ie/xml/.

Unfortunately, SGML is considerably more complex to learn and use than HTML, and it has been said that this would prevent its generalized adoption. Therefore the SGML working group of the Word Wide Web Consortium was asked to develop a new mark-up meta-language, namely the eXtended Markup Language (XML) [9], to take the place of SGML on the Web. XML documents would have to be straightforwardly usable over the Internet, compatible with SGML, and easy to create.

Interestingly, in the Z community an SGML-based language for Z specifications already exists: the Z Interchange Format (ZIF for short) [2] defines a portable representation of Z, that can be used by all tools supporting SGML. The ZIF is basically a Document Type Definition (DTD), namely an SGML specification defining the syntax of documents that contain Z specifications. In [6] a study of the usage of the ZIF was presented, according to which ZIF can be fruitfully used to create editors for Z documents using standard SGML tools, and that Z specifications encoded using ZIF could easily be included in other SGML documents.

XML documents are valid SGML documents. Most existing SGML DTDs can be used with no modifications in an XML environment. Notably, the Z Interchange Format is one of such DTDs.

It is therefore possible to use the definitions specified in the ZIF within XML tools, in order to create web-friendly visualizations of Z specifications. Alternatively, XML tools allow the HTML tag set to be described and extended as needed. By joining the HTML DTD with the ZIF DTD, and producing a capable browser, it is possible to write HTML documents that contain Z specifications as markup items, instead of images, thereby keeping all the useful properties that markup has over bitmaps.

In this paper we report about one such tool, that allow the display of standard HTML documents enriched with Z specifications, using a markup extension of HTML directly derived from ZIF.

3 Displets and HTML extensions

Displets were proposed in [17] as a way to extend HTML documents using Java. The HTML language was extended on a per-document basis by defining new tags as needed, and providing Java classes to take care of their graphical display. While not providing all the functionality and flexibility of a full meta-markup language such as XML (Sect. 2), HTML extended with displets could allow all kinds of specialized notations and graphical effects while at the same time leveraging over the existing and well-known set of elements defined by HTML.

Our first experiment with rendering arbitrary, non-text-based markup extensions [17] was to modify an existing browser to allow the parsing and the visualization of new HTML-like elements. To do so, we took an early version of the HotJava browser, whose source code was freely available, and modified it so that it could accept on-the-fly extensions of the HTML DTD and load the appropriate classes (called *displets*) whenever the newly defined tags were to be displayed. That experiment was extremely limited, in that we used an old version of the Java language, and worked only on a specific version of a specific browser. Furthermore, we heavily relied on the existing rendering architecture of the browser and just provided a minimal effort implementation (basically a displet was just a sequence of drawing instructions for the visualization of the elements).

In [4], on the other hand, we reported about the DispletManager applet, a general, extensible rendering and architecture we have been working on, which can be used for both extensions to HTML and straight XML documents. This architecture is embodied in a Java applet that can be run within any Java-enabled browser such as Netscape Communicator or MS Internet Explorer.

Fundamental design requirements for the rendering engine were:

- it must be possible to create special code for rendering arbitrarily odd data types, in particular non-textual data (*displets*).
- all displets must easily integrate with each other: a chart element may have a mathematical formula as one of the labels, and some staff notation as another, where some notes may act as hypertext links.
- the rendering engine must work both for extended HTML and for straight XML, and the displet classes must be identical.

Figure 1 shows the general structure of the DispletManager applet. The document chunk to be displayed, be it HTML or XML, is loaded by the displet manager and parsed by the appropriate parser. The resulting tree is then recursively (depth-first) analyzed: the appropriate displet classes are activated to create the rendering (i.e., the display object) of their element on the basis of the rendering of their sub-elements. No class is allowed direct access to the screen: on the contrary, each displet creates a (set of) off-screen bitmap(s) that its ancestor can pass, ignore, modify or add to.

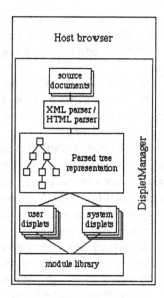

Fig. 1. The general structure of the `DispletManager` applet

3.1   Extending HTML

Extending HTML is important whenever one needs to provide graphical support for some previously unsupported notation, within a document that can be easily mapped onto plain HTML. The Z notation is one such case, but many others can be devised. The displet manager allows any kind of extension to HTML. In order to extend the HTML tag set, it is necessary to specify the new tags and a bit of syntax constraints, and associate them the corresponding Java classes that will take care of the creation of the visual object.

The following is an example of a simple HTML document with a simple extension for displaying text in reverse video:

```
<applet code="DispletManager.class" align="baseline"
 width="500" height="200">
<param name="def" value="
  <tag name='reverse' hasEndTag nonNesting
  src='example/reverse.class'>
  </tag>
">
<param name="HTMLcode" value="
  <body>
  <p>This is an example of a text rendered in
  <reverse>reverse</reverse></p>
  </body>
">
</applet>
```

The `DispletManager` is an applet that has two arguments: the first contains the definition of the new tags (in this case, the tag `<reverse>`), while the second one contains the HTML document that has to be displayed, and that includes the extension previously defined.

The standard HTML elements are all pre-defined, and have their own displet classes that are automatically loaded. The 'def' parameter of the applet allows the definition of the new elements, providing some simple syntactical support and the URL of the displet code in charge of providing its rendering.

Upon loading the applet, the displet manager will start the HTML parser and patch it with the elements defined in the 'def' parameter. It will then parse the 'HTMLcode' parameter, verifying that the new elements are being used according to the given grammar. The 'def' parameter acts as a simplified DTD for the new tags: it allows to specify the names, attributes, inclusion rules and minimization features allowed for the new elements, as well as the URL of the Java code containing the rendering applet.

The resulting tree then is examined and the proper displet for each node is activated. Each displet is required to produce a (list of) bitmaps of its content. Each displet may sets parameters and wait for the displet of its sub-elements to return their bitmaps, before producing its own. For instance, the displet for the <P> tag in HTML (that defines a paragraph) sets some values (such as margins, line spacing, font and size) that may affect its sub-elements, waits for all of them to return their bitmaps (one for each word, because <P> combines whole words into lines) and then creates its own list of bitmaps (one for each line).

Figure 2 shows how the above mentioned document looks on the screen:

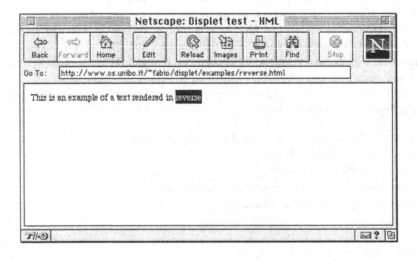

Fig. 2. Rendering a simple displet

We are using a modification and update of a beta version of an old Sun HTML parser. Currently, the HTML displet package contains displets for all HTML 3.2 tags, except tables. Anchors and form elements are included and work correctly. This allows authors to use standard HTML elements within the special elements they define: for instance, it is possible to have styled text, form elements or hypertext links within a Z schema.

4 The rendering engine

The rendering engine used by the DispletManager applet consists of a set of Java classes that provide the rendering for the appropriate document elements. These classes are all subclasses of the DocElement class, which provides the framework of the rendering procedure.

We are using Java 1.0 because it is supported by most browsers currently in use. We are developing a version for Java 1.1

All classes provide a createBitmap() method, whose purpose is to create and return the bitmap of the flow object of the considered markup element on the basis of the bitmaps of its sub-elements. The createBitmap() method is usually not seen by the implementer of new classes, and provides the following functionalities:

- an active drawing environment is managed. The drawing environment is a set of parameters that are used by the rendering methods of the classes in order to decide how to create the bitmaps. For instance, a paragraph-like class may set some parameters that will be used by itself, such as margins, line spacing, alignment, etc., and some that will be used by its sub-elements, such as font name, font size, font color, etc. The createBitmap() method allows a displet to set its own attributes with the setParams() method, and restores the previous situation when the displet is finished. Since createBitmap() methods are recursively activated, this creates a stack that provides the proper parameters at any level of recursion.

- the rendering of sub-elements is managed. The presence/absence of the element in the XSL rule, or some internal decisions for the HTML displet, may cause or prevent the rendering of the sub-elements of the current element.

- the rendering of the element is managed. After the bitmaps of the sub-elements of the element have been created (if appropriate), the createBitmap() method calls the render() method, which in turn creates the final bitmap (or set of bitmaps) that will be returned. Different classes will implement render() differently: for instance, the render() method of a block element will collect the bitmaps of its sub-elements in a vertical stack (one above the other), and provide a single bitmap of the whole element, while the render() method of a paragraph will collect its sub-elements side-by-side in lines of the given width, and provide a bitmap for every line it has created; this allow the element containing the paragraph to decide how much of the paragraph to display at a time (for instance, in case of scrolling).

- active elements are specified and created. Active elements are those that will need to react to user and system events after they have been displayed. For instance, form elements and anchors have an associated behavior that is activated when the user selects them.

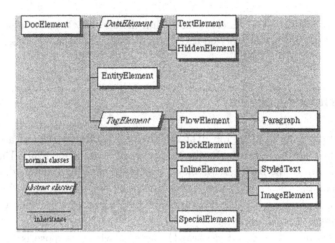

Fig. 3. The inheritance structure of the module library

Figure 3 shows the inheritance structure of the classes of the module library. Doc-Elements can either be data, entities or tag elements. *DataElement* classes are used for the content of markup elements, i.e., #PCDATA in SGML and XML DTDs. They can either be text or hidden elements. EntityElements are provided for the management of XML and HTML entities such as & or the definition of new ones. *TagElements* are used for the creation of the structure flow objects of the document: they are either flow objects, block objects, inline elements or special elements.

- A block element is a single object that stands alone in the vertical layout of the document. Paragraphs or tables are block elements. A flow element is a block element that is built piecemeal: while plain block elements are built from start to end before the createBitmap() returns, flow elements build each of their sub-element and return, and are called as many times as there are sub-elements. This allows long and complex elements to be rendered only for the possibly small section that is actually displayed. For instance, HTML and BODY are considered flow elements, so that the display of an HTML document can start as soon as the first object is completed, and be interrupted when the available display space is filled.

- Inline elements are elements that can be put side by side with their siblings. Inline elements are used within block elements and may be text-based, images or something else. The StyledText class allows the specification of text runs of arbitrary styles. Inline elements specify the places where they can be broken by creating as many bitmaps as break points. This allows the containing paragraph or block element to determine where the line should be broken.

- Special elements are completely tailorable. While in the previous classes displet programmers can only overload the setParams() and render() methods, here all methods are overloadable, and can be customized.

As an example, this is the complete source code of the reverse displet:

```
package example;
import displet.*;

public class reverse extends StyledText {
        public void setParams(StyledTextParams p) {
                Color c = p.fgColor;
                p.fgColor = p.bgColor ;
                p.bgColor = c ;
        }
}
```

The reverse displet is a subclass of the StyledText, which is a subclass of the InlineElement class. These are classes for text-based objects that behave as in-line elements (eg. bold, italic, etc.). As it can be seen, the programmer of such a displet only has had to specify a parameter and have the render() method of its superclass handle all the details. The displets for showing Z specifications are shown in the following section.

5   The Z browser

The main extension to HTML we have considered using displets is the implementation of the complete ZIF DTD. Authors writing Z specifications can create documents containing their Z specifications in a markup language similar to HTML and completely intermixable with plain text and other HTML features such as links, tables, etc.

The ZIF format defines several elements (tags) for the building blocks of the language, such as schemas, definitions, etc., and several entities (literal macros) for the special characters inherited from mathematics and logics. Each element is implemented by a displet that creates a bitmap where the content of the element is appropriately composed and the graphical elements such as boxes, lines, etc. are then added. Entities on the other hand are elements of a graphical alphabet that is contained in a single GIF image and is loaded with the displets.

The following is an example of a Z schema using the Z Interchange Format:

```
<schemadef>
    BirthdayBook
    <decpart>
        <declaration> known: &pset; NAME</declaration>
        <declaration> birthday: NAME &pfun; DATE </declaration>
    </decpart>
    <axpart>
        <predicate>known = &dom; birthday</predicate>
    </axpart>
</schemadef>
```

A schema is defined by a tag called schemadef, which contains three elements: the name of the schema, a declaration part and an axiom part. The declaration part contains one or more declarations, and the axiom part contains zero or more predicates.

Appropriate ordering and nesting of elements is enforced by the DTD, and is checked when parsing the document. The notations '&pset;', '&pfun;' and '&dom;' are three entities (respectively, the partial set symbol, the partial function symbol and the domain symbol) that will be substituted by the corresponding element in the graphical alphabet containing all the relevant Z symbols. The displet manager can appropriately show document bits as the previous one in a WWW browser.

Since many Z specifiers use LaTeX to produce their Z documents, we have developed an off-line translator called 'Zed2HTML' that transforms Z specifications written in LaTeX using style oz.tex into a corresponding HTML document with the appropriate extension.

Of course, the well known LaTeX2HTML translator is of little help, as it ignores all LaTeX commands that cannot be immediately transferred into standard HTML.

For instance, given the following Z specification (the basic Birthday Book example from [16]):

$$[NAME, DATE]$$

$$
\begin{array}{|l}
\hline
\_\,BirthdayBook\,\underline{} \\
\quad known : \mathbb{P}\,NAME \\
\quad birthday : NAME \nrightarrow DATE \\
\hline
\quad known = \mathrm{dom}\,birthday \\
\hline
\end{array}
$$

corresponding to the following LaTeX source document:

```
\documentclass[italian,12pt,twoside,openright]{report}
\usepackage{amsfonts}
\usepackage{oz}

\begin{document}

\begin{zed}
[NAME, DATE]
\end{zed}

\begin{schema}{BirthdayBook}
known: \power NAME\\
birthday: NAME \pfun DATE
\where
known = \dom birthday
\end{schema}
\end{document}
```

The Zed2HTML application transforms the previous LaTeX example in the corresponding extended HTML document:

```
<applet code="DispletManager.class" align="baseline"
```

```
width="300" height="700"><param name="def" value="

<tag name='givendef' hasEndTag
          nonNesting
          src='zpack/givendef.class'>
</tag>

<tag name='schemadef' hasEndTag
          nonNesting
          src ='zpack/schemadef.class'>
    <attr name='id' value=cdata >
    <attr name='group' value=nmtoken >
    <attr name='style' value='vert, horiz' >
    <attr name='purpose' value='state, operation, datatype' >
</tag>

<tag name='decpart' hasEndTag
          nonNesting
          in ='schemadef'
          src ='zpack/decpart.class'>
</tag>

<tag name='axpart' hasEndTag
          nonNesting
          in ='schemadef'
          src ='zpack/axpart.class'>
</tag>

<tag name='declaration' hasEndTag
          nonNesting
          in ='decpart'
          src ='zpack/declaration.class'>
</tag>

<tag name='predicate' hasEndTag
          nonNesting
          in ='axpart'
          src ='zpack/predicate.class'>
    <attr name='label' value=cdata >
</tag>

<entity name='pset' data='#185' font='zpack/zfont.14.gif'>
<entity name='pfun' data='#193' font='zpack/zfont.14.gif'>
<entity name='dom' data='dom' font='TimesRoman%14%Plain'>

"><param name="cod" value="

<body>
<givendef>
    <a name='name'>NAME</a>,
```

```
        <a name='date'>DATE</a>
</givendef>
<p>
<schemadef>
    BirthdayBook
    <decpart>
        <declaration> known: &pset; <a href='#name'>NAME</a> </declaration>
        <declaration> birthday:
            <a href='#name'>NAME</a> &pfun;
            <a href='#date'>DATE</a>
        </declaration>
    </decpart>
    <axpart>
        <predicate>known = &dom; birthday</predicate>
    </axpart>
</schemadef>
</body>
"></applet>
```

The output of Zed2HTML is the HTML specification of the *DispletManager* applet. As in the previous example, two parameters are specified: the definition of the new tags and entities according to the ZIF DTD, and the source document of the actual schema. When run on a WWW browser, the previous documents is shown as in Figure 4.

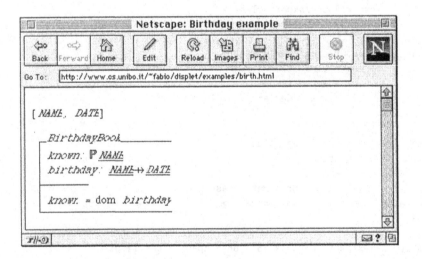

Fig. 4. Visualization on the WWW of a Z schema

A number of issues concerning the HTML document have to be noted:

– In the tag definition part, the new tags are specified with some syntax constraints (for instance, the element <declaration> requires the end tag, cannot nest with other declarations, and is only defined within the element <axpart>), and the name of the displet class that should take care of its rendering.

- Entities are defined either as textual substitution in specific fonts (such as the &dom; entity, which corresponds to the string 'dom' written using the font TimesRoman 14), or as elements of a graphical alphabet corresponding to a single GIF image. The displet manager will then download the image, and select and cut the appropriate bitmap from it depending on the position in the alphabet as specified by the entity code in the definition. Thus, in the example, the image of the 'partial function' character is the 185th element of the image 'zfont.14.gif'.

- Z elements and plain HTML elements freely intermix: it is possible to put standard HTML tags within Z schemas, for instance an author may require that some declarations of a schema are written in bold. The Zed2HTML translator automatically connects types used in declarations to their definitions using plain HTML links. The author may freely add or modify the available links and HTML features.

6   Conclusions

We have presented a tool for visualizing Z specifications on the WWW: it fits every browser supporting Java under any platform. The tool is based on HTML extended with 'displets'.

The advantage of having a Z browser that fits all platforms is essentially that sharing of Z documents is encouraged by the diffusion of WWW on the Internet.

A possible application can be a groupware tool for editing and versioning formal documents; such a tool could be integrated with other software tools in order to improve the specification phase of the software process.

The reuse of parts of documents obviously benefits from having these hypertextual Z documents. The tools will also improve the search of pieces of specifications in complex documents: every element in the Z specification can be labeled or linked to other pieces of documents or to a URL on the Internet.

Extended HTML also allows more links for an element (hot word). A possible application of this could be on Z generic schemas: a generic schema specification can provide different links for the parameters of the schema; the links can show the possible schemas or variables that can be substituted for the parameters.

HTML can be further extended in order to include new symbols and integrate Z specification with other notations: new Java classes have to be written for the new symbols.

A displet site is being created at:

    http://www.cs.unibo.it/~fabio/displet.html

The site contains the code for the rendering engines, examples for both HTML and XML, and a list of all the displets we have created so far.

Acknowledgements: We would like to acknowledge the help and contribution of Alfredo Rizzi, Stefano Pancaldi, and the help and suggestions of Michael Bieber and Chao-Min Chiu.

References

1. J. Bannan. *Intranet Document Management*. Addison-Wesley, 1997.

2. S. Brien and J. Nicholls. Z Base Standard, November 1992. Programming Research Group.

3. P. Ciancarini, A. Fantini, and D. Rossi. A multi-agent process centered environment integrated with the WWW. In *Proc. 6th IEEE Workshops on Enablings Technologies: Infrastructure for Collaborative Enterprises (WETICE)*, pages 113–120, Boston, June 1997. IEEE Computer Society Press.

4. P. Ciancarini, A. Rizzi, and F. Vitali. An extensible rendering engine for XML and HTML. *Computer Networks and ISDN Systems*, 30(1-7):225–238, 1998.

5. M. Fraser, K. Kumar, and V. Vaishnavi. Strategies for Incorporating Formal Specifications in Software Development. *Communications of the ACM*, 37(10):74–86, October 1994.

6. D. German and D. Cowan. Experiments with the Z Interchange Format and SGML. In J. Bowen and M. Hinchey, editors, *ZUM'97: The Z Formal Specification Notation*, volume 967 of *Lecture Notes in Computer Science*, pages 224–233, Limerick, Ireland, September 1995. Springer-Verlag, Berlin.

7. D. Jordan. CADiZ – Computer Aided Design in Z. In S. Prehn and W. Toetenel, editors, *VDM 91: Formal Software Development Methods*, volume 551 of *Lecture Notes in Computer Science*, pages 685–690. Springer-Verlag, Berlin, October 1991.

8. G. Kaiser, S. Dossick, W. Jiang, and J. Yang. An Architecture for WWW-based Hypercode Environments. In *Proc. 19th Int. Conf. on Software Engineering (ICSE 17)*, pages 3–13, Boston, MA, May 1997.

9. R. Khare and A. Rifkin. XML: A Door to Automated Web Applications. *IEEE Internet Computing*, 1(4):78–87, July/August 1997.

10. L. Lamport. Verification and Specifications of Concurrent Programs. In J. deBakker, W. deRoever, and G. Rozenberg, editors, *A Decade of Concurrency*, volume 803 of *Lecture Notes in Computer Science*, pages 347–374. Springer-Verlag, Berlin, 1993.

11. L. Mikusiak, M. Adamy, and T. Seidmann. Publishing Formal Specifications in Z notation on the WWW. In M. Bidoit and M. Dauchet, editors, *TAPSOFT'97: Theory and Practice of Software Development*, volume 1214 of *Lecture Notes in Computer Science*, pages 871–874, Lille, France, 1997. Springer-Verlag, Berlin.

12. L. Mikusiak and al. Z Browser: A Tool for Visualization of Z Specifications. In J. Bowen and M. Hinchey, editors, *ZUM'97: The Z Formal Specification Notation*, volume 967 of *Lecture Notes in Computer Science*, pages 510–525, Limerick, Ireland, September 1995. Springer-Verlag, Berlin.

13. S. Ressler. *The Art of Electronic Publishing*. Prentice Hall, 1997.

14. W. Scacchi and J. Noll. Process-Driven Intranets – Life Cycle Support for Process reengineering. *IEEE Internet Computing*, 1(5):42–51, September/October 1997.

15. C. Sperberg-McQueen and R. Goldstein. HTML to the Max: A Manifesto for Adding SGML Intelligence to the World-Wide Web. In *Proc. 2nd International WWW Conference: Mosaic and the Web*, 1994. (Electronic proceedings.)

16. J.M. Spivey. *The Z Notation. A Reference Manual*. Prentice Hall International Series in Computer Science, 2nd edition, 1992.

17. F. Vitali, C. Chiu, and M. Bieber. Extending HTML in a principled way with *displets*. *Computer Networks and ISDN Systems*, 29(8-13):1115–1128, 1997.

18. Xiaoping Jia. *ZTC: A Type Checker for Z – User's Guide*. Institute for Software Engineering, Department of Computer Science and Information Systems, DePaul University, Chicago, IL 60604, USA, 1994.

On the Semantic Relation of Z and HOL

Thomas Santen[*]

GMD FIRST
Rudower Chaussee 5, D-12489 Berlin, Germany
Email: santen@first.gmd.de

Abstract. We investigate the relation between the semantic models of Z, as proposed by the Z draft standard, and of the polymorphic version of higher-order logic that is the basis for proof systems such as HOL and Isabelle/HOL. Disregarding the names in schema types, the type models of the two systems can be identified up to isomorphism. That isomorphism determines to a large extent how terms of Z can be represented in higher-order logic. This justifies the soundness of proof support for Z based on higher-order logic, such as the encoding $\mathcal{HOL\text{-}Z}$ of Z in Isabelle/HOL.

The comparison of the two semantic models also motivates a discussion of open issues in the development of a complete semantics of Z, in particular concerning the type system, generic constructs, and approaches to base the semantics of Z on a small kernel language.

1 Introduction

Many users of Z like to think of the language as a first-order predicate logic augmented with "set theory". In this intuitive view of Z, it often remains vague what the exact nature of "set theory" is.

Publications about Z, in particular the Z reference manual [13] and the Committee Draft of the Z standard [8], make it clear that the set theory of Z is a typed one, and type-checkers like *f*UZZ [12] help users validate their specifications.

A number of proof tools have evolved that aim at a more powerful tool support for Z. A recent overview of existing provers for Z [7] distinguishes two categories of tools: encodings within a more general logical framework, and special implementations. While that report does not reveal to what extent the special implementations use the type system of Z, the majority of the logical frameworks used to support Z are typed, and three of them [2, 5, 6] are based on polymorphic higher-order logic, as it is implemented in the HOL system [3] and in the HOL variant of the generic theorem prover Isabelle [9]. See [6] for a survey on different approaches to encoding Z in HOL.

The present work establishes a formal relationship between the semantics of Z and that variant of higher-order logic. Although it has emerged from work on one of the above-mentioned proof systems, namely $\mathcal{HOL\text{-}Z}$ [6], this research also contributes to the ongoing discussion on the semantics of Z: it shows that, under a marginal revision of the "traditional" semantic view of Z, the models of the two type systems are isomorphic modulo names in schema types.

[*] This research is funded by the German ministry BMBF, project ESPRESS (grant 01 IS 509 C6).

To facilitate a comparison of the two formalisms, we recapitulate the semantic model of Z in Section 2 and of HOL in Section 3. Section 4 establishes a relation between the type models of the two languages. Section 5 sketches how the relation between the type models extends to relations between terms. A discussion of possible consequences for the Z semantics concludes the paper.

2 The Semantics of Z

The following presentation of the semantic model of Z is based on the Committee Draft of the ISO standard for Z [8], in particular Section 5. We slightly rephrase the definitions given there to facilitate a comparison with the semantic model of HOL in Section 4.1.

The semantic model is described in terms of Zermelo-Fraenkel (ZF) set theory, which is untyped and more expressive than Z and HOL.[1] Like the Z standard [8], we use symbols familiar from Z to denote ZF expressions, but care should be taken not to confuse expressions of Z and of ZF.

Names. For both languages, we assume the same two disjoint sets of identifiers exist: TyNames is a countably infinite set of *type names*, and Names is a countably infinite set of *constant names*. We further assume that both sets are totally ordered such that we can obtain a unique, increasingly ordered sequence for every set of identifiers. The orders on identifiers serve us to distinguish representations of schema types and bindings of Z, in Section 4. Distinguishing identifiers of types and constants is not strictly necessary but it eliminates a source of confusion in semantic descriptions. For Z, the set of type names TyNames is just a means to describe the semantics, because there is no way to denote types in the language of Z (see also Section 2.4).

2.1 Types

The types of a specification are built from a set $\Gamma \subseteq$ TyNames of type names, the *given set names* [8] or *basic types* [13]. The set Z of integers is declared in every specification. Therefore, each set of basic type names contains a distinguished element Z^t, which is the type of the elements of Z. We use the notation S^t to denote the type of the elements of a set S. We use similarly marked symbols for set operations to denote the corresponding operations on types.

Definition 1 (Z-Types). *Let Γ be a set of given set names. The set* ZTypes^Γ *of Z-types over Γ is defined inductively as follows:*

1. given set names are Z-types

$$\Gamma \subseteq \mathsf{ZTypes}^\Gamma$$

2. for each $\sigma \in \mathsf{ZTypes}^\Gamma$, the type of sets over σ, its power set type, *is a Z-type*

$$\mathbb{P}^t \sigma \in \mathsf{ZTypes}^\Gamma$$

---

[1] In ZF, the expression $\{1, \{2\}\}$ denotes a set, but it is not typable, and thus illegal, in both, Z and HOL.

3. *for all* $n > 1$, $\sigma_1, \ldots, \sigma_n \in \mathsf{ZTypes}^\Gamma$, *the n-ary product of these types is a Z-type*

$$\sigma_1 \times_n^t \ldots \times_n^t \sigma_n \in \mathsf{ZTypes}^\Gamma$$

4. *all* finite *partial functions mapping variable names to types are Z-types*

$$\mathsf{Names} \nrightarrow \mathsf{ZTypes}^\Gamma \subseteq \mathsf{ZTypes}^\Gamma$$

All types defined this way are distinct.

Case 3 of the definition introduces different types for tuples of different lengths, e.g. triples (x, y, z) and nested pairs $(x, (y, z))$ have different types.

Case 4 defines the types of schemas. The *signature* of a schema is a finite set of pairs associating the variable names with their type, i.e. the set of schema signatures over Names is the set of finite functions mapping names to types.

$$\mathsf{Signature}^\Gamma = \mathsf{Names} \nrightarrow \mathsf{ZTypes}^\Gamma$$

2.2 Values and Typed-Values

Every type of ZTypes^Γ is mapped to a set of values, its *carrier*. The carriers are defined inductively on the structure of ZTypes^Γ. The basis of this definition is a set $\mathcal{W}_0$ of carriers of the given set names. We require that the set of integers is a member of $\mathcal{W}_0$, and that the type Z^t is interpreted in $\mathcal{W}_0$ in a standard way. The union of all carriers of ZTypes^Γ forms the set $\mathcal{W}$ of *values*. A type and a value will be assigned to each expression in a Z-specification.

Definition 2 (Interpretation of Given Set Names). *Let Γ be a set of given set names, and let $\mathcal{W}_0$ be a set of carriers for the given sets. An* interpretation *of Γ into $\mathcal{W}_0$ is a total surjective function*

$$\mathsf{Carrier}_0 : \Gamma \twoheadrightarrow \mathcal{W}_0$$

mapping Z^t to the integers:

$$\mathsf{Carrier}_0\, \mathsf{Z}^t = \{\ldots, -2, -1, 0, 1, 2, \ldots\}$$

The interpretation of Z^t is fixed, but there are no further assumptions on the interpretation of given set names. In particular, the Z standard explicitly notes that the empty set is a valid interpretation [8, page 18], and $\mathsf{Carrier}_0$ is not necessarily injective.

Definition 3 (Interpretation of Z-Types). *Let $\mathsf{Carrier}_0$ be an interpretation of Γ. The interpretation of types* based on $\mathsf{Carrier}_0$ *is a total function mapping the types in ZTypes^Γ to sets, their* carriers. *Its graph is defined inductively on ZTypes^Γ:*

$$\Gamma \lhd \mathsf{Carrier} = \mathsf{Carrier}_0 \tag{1}$$

$$\mathsf{Carrier}\,(\mathsf{P}^t\,\sigma) = \mathsf{P}\,(\mathsf{Carrier}\,\sigma) \tag{2}$$

$$\mathsf{Carrier}\,(\sigma_1 \times_n^t \ldots \times_n^t \sigma_n) = (\mathsf{Carrier}\,\sigma_1) \times \ldots \times (\mathsf{Carrier}\,\sigma_n) \tag{3}$$

$$\mathsf{Carrier}\,\{x_1 \mapsto \sigma_1, \ldots, x_n \mapsto \sigma_n\} = \{\upsilon_1 : (\mathsf{Carrier}\,\sigma_1); \; \upsilon_n : (\mathsf{Carrier}\,\sigma_n) \\ \bullet \{x_1 \mapsto \upsilon_1, \ldots, x_n \mapsto \upsilon_n\}\} \tag{4}$$

The set (Carrier σ) *is called the* carrier *of* σ. *The set* $\mathcal{W}$ *of* Z-values *based on* Carrier$_0$ *is the union of all carriers.*

$$\mathcal{W} = \bigcup(\text{ran Carrier})$$

An interpretation of types conforms to the interpretation of given set names. It maps power set types and product types to the power sets and products of the carriers of their component types, respectively. The interpretation of a schema signature is a set of *bindings*, which map the variable names in the domain of the signature to elements of the carriers of the corresponding types in the signature's range. The set of bindings, therefore, is the set of finite functions from names to values.

$$\text{Binding}^\Gamma = \text{Names} \nrightarrow \mathcal{W}$$

Note the similarity of (3) and (4). We can rewrite the choice of values in (4) using (3):

$$\bigwedge_{i=1}^{n} \upsilon_i \in (\text{Carrier}\,\sigma_i) \Leftrightarrow (\upsilon_1,\dots,\upsilon_n) \in (\text{Carrier}\,\sigma_1) \times \dots \times (\text{Carrier}\,\sigma_n)$$
$$\Leftrightarrow (\upsilon_1,\dots,\upsilon_n) \in \text{Carrier}\,(\sigma_1 \times_n^t \dots \times_n^t \sigma_n)$$

Pairs of types and values form *typed-values*,[2] which serve us to give meanings to expressions and predicates. More specifically, the set TyVal is the set of type-value pairs whose members are related by Carrier.

$$\text{TyVal} = \{\sigma : \text{ZTypes}^\Gamma;\ \upsilon : \mathcal{W} \mid \upsilon \in (\text{Carrier}\,\sigma)\}$$

2.3 Genericity

With generic constants and generic schemas, Z provides a way of parameterizing parts of specifications. To capture their semantics, the Z standard introduces generic types and generic typed-values, which are total functions mapping power set types to types and typed-values of power set types to typed-values, respectively.

More formally, the *generic type* of a generic construct with n parameters is a function mapping an n-tuple of power set types to a type

$$\text{GenTypes}_n^\Gamma = \underbrace{\text{PowTypes}^\Gamma \times \dots \times \text{PowTypes}^\Gamma}_{n} \longrightarrow \text{ZTypes}^\Gamma \tag{5}$$

where $\text{PowTypes}^\Gamma = \{\sigma : \text{ZTypes}^\Gamma \bullet \mathbb{P}^t \sigma\}$ is the set of types in Case 2 of Definition 1. The set of all generic types is the union of the generic types with any finite number of parameters.

$$\text{GenTypes}^\Gamma = \bigcup_{n \in \mathbb{N}} \text{GenTypes}_n^\Gamma$$

---

[2] The Z standard [8] calls typed-values "elements". This leads to an imprecise language, such as "the set of all elements". We therefore prefer to call pairs of types and values "typed-values".

The set Gen_TyVal of *generic typed-values* with n parameters, similarly, is a function mapping n-tuples of typed-values of power set type to typed-values. A generic typed-value must be type-consistent, i.e. it must map typed-values of the same types to the same type. The set of all generic typed-values is the union of these sets.

$$type\_consistent_n \; \varphi = \{\sigma_1, \dots, \sigma_n : \mathsf{PowTypes}^\Gamma; \; \sigma' : \mathsf{ZTypes}^\Gamma; \; \upsilon_1, \dots, \upsilon_n, \upsilon' : \mathcal{W}$$
$$| \; ((\sigma_1, \upsilon_1), \dots, (\sigma_n, \upsilon_n)) \mapsto (\sigma', \upsilon') \in \varphi$$
$$\bullet \; (\sigma_1, \dots, \sigma_n) \mapsto \sigma'\}$$
$$\in \mathsf{GenTypes}^\Gamma_n$$

$$\mathsf{Gen\_TyVal}_n = \{\varphi : \mathsf{Pow\_TyVal}_n \longrightarrow \mathsf{TyVal} \; | \; type\_consistent_n \; \varphi\}$$

$$\mathsf{Gen\_TyVal} = \bigcup_{n \in \mathbb{N}} \mathsf{Gen\_TyVal}_n$$

where $\mathsf{Pow\_TyVal}_n = \{\sigma : \mathsf{PowTypes}^\Gamma_n; \; \upsilon : \mathcal{W} \; | \; (\sigma, \upsilon) \in \mathsf{TyVal}\}$ is the set of typed-values of power set type.

The family of predicates *type_consistent_n* φ requires type-consistency of generic typed-values: the set of "component-wise projections" $(\sigma_1, \dots, \sigma_n) \mapsto \sigma'$ of the members of φ to their types must be a generic type. Thus, applying a generic typed-value to different typed-values of the same types results in typed-values of the same type.

2.4 Environments

The Z standard defines the semantics of Z in a denotational style using environments that describe the context in which language constructs are interpreted. An *environment* is a partial finite function mapping names to elements or generic elements.

$$\mathsf{Env} = \mathsf{Names} \nrightarrow (\mathsf{TyVal} \cup \mathsf{Gen\_TyVal})$$

From each environment $\eta \in \mathsf{Env}$, we can construct a *type environment* in a canonical way by projecting the component typed-values of η to their (generic) types.

$$\mathsf{Tenv} = \mathsf{Names} \nrightarrow (\mathsf{ZTypes}^\Gamma \cup \mathsf{GenTypes}^\Gamma)$$

A *situation* is an environment that does not contain generic typed-values.

$$\mathsf{Situation} = \mathsf{Names} \nrightarrow \mathsf{TyVal}$$

The environment corresponding to a paragraph that introduces a given set illustrates that types do not have denotations in Z. The given set declaration

$$[G]$$

semantically denotes an environment that maps the name $G \in \mathsf{Names}$ to a typed-value:

$$\{G \mapsto (\mathbf{P}^t \, G^t, \mathsf{Carrier}_0 \, G^t)\}$$

Thus, G denotes a value of power set type $\mathbf{P}^t \, G^t$, namely the set $\mathsf{Carrier}_0 \, G^t$.

Table 1. Semantic functions of Z

	Type	Value	Meaning
Expression	$[\![\_]\!]^T$: Tenv $\nrightarrow$ ZTypes$^{\ulcorner}$	$[\![\_]\!]^V$: Env $\nrightarrow$ $\mathcal{W}$	$[\![\_]\!]^M$: Env $\nrightarrow$ TyVal
Predicate	$\{\![\_]\!\}^T$: $\mathbb{P}$ Tenv	$\{\![\_]\!\}^V$: $\mathbb{P}$ Env	$\{\![\_]\!\}^M$: $\mathbb{P}$ Env
Schema	$(\![\_]\!)^T$: Tenv $\nrightarrow$ Signature$^{\ulcorner}$		$(\![\_]\!)^M$: Env $\leftrightarrow$ Situation
Paragraph	$\langle\![\_]\!\rangle^T$: Tenv $\nrightarrow$ Tenv		$\langle\![\_]\!\rangle^M$: Env $\leftrightarrow$ Env

2.5 Semantic Functions

Table 1 summarizes the semantic functions defined in the Z standard [8]. The meaning of an expression in an environment, which gives meanings to the free variables of the expression, is an element of TyVal, i.e. a well-typed value. Two semantic functions determine the meaning of an expression. The first, $[\![\_]\!]^T$, determines the type of an expression, the second, $[\![\_]\!]^V$, determines its value. The semantic functions are *partial*. Their domains are the expressions that are well-typed or value-defined, respectively. The *meaning* $[\![\mathcal{E}]\!]^M$ of an expression $\mathcal{E}$ is the pair of the type and the value of the expression – if that pair is a member of TyVal. Thus, we have three semantic functions for expressions. The first row of Table 1 shows their signatures.

Because the definitions of the type and the value of an expression are independent, there exist value-defined expressions that are not well-typed. Still, requiring the meaning of an expression to be in TyVal guarantees that only well-typed expressions are in the domain of $[\![\_]\!]^M$:

> An expression is well-defined in those environments in which it is well-typed and value-defined. [8, page 37]

Combining type and value considerations also serves us to determine the meaning of predicates (c.f. Table 1). A predicate is *well-typed* if all the expressions it contains are well-typed. Interpreting it as a predicate of ZF defines its truth value. Thus, the value of a predicate $\mathcal{E}$ may be "true" in an environment η, i.e. $\eta \in \{\![\mathcal{E}]\!\}^V$, even if it is not well-typed in that environment, i.e. $te(\eta) \notin \{\![\mathcal{E}]\!\}^T$. An example is the predicate $\neg\,(x \in x)$, which is ZF-true but not well-typed. Like for expressions, the meaning function $\{\![\_]\!\}^M$ ensures that only well-typed predicates are considered *true* in Z:

> The environments in which a predicate is true are exactly those environments in which the predicate is well-typed and is ZF-true. [8, page 61]

A predicate is equivalent to *false* in the environments in which it is well-typed and ZF-false.

The type of a schema in a type environment is its signature, its meaning is the pair of its signature and the set of bindings that fulfill its property.

A Z-specification consists of a sequence of *paragraphs*, such as constant declarations and schema definitions. The type of a paragraph P maps type environments to type environments, its meaning is a binary relation $\langle\!\langle P \rangle\!\rangle^{\mathcal{M}}$ on environments: a pair of environments (η_1, η_2) is in $\langle\!\langle P \rangle\!\rangle^{\mathcal{M}}$ if η_2 extends η_1 by the names introduced in P and associates these names to meanings consistent with the predicates in P.

Finally, composing the semantics of a specification's paragraphs and applying the resulting relation to the empty environment gives us the meaning of a specification: it is the set of all environments whose domains are the names introduced in the specification and whose values are well-typed and consistent with the predicates of the specification: if $Spec = P_1 \ldots P_n$, then the semantics of $Spec$ is $\{\eta : \mathsf{Env} \mid (\varnothing, \eta) \in (\langle\!\langle P_1 \rangle\!\rangle^{\mathcal{M}} \, \mathring{\varsigma} \ldots \mathring{\varsigma}$
$\langle\!\langle P_n \rangle\!\rangle^{\mathcal{M}})\}$.

3   Higher Order Logic

Although HOL and Z are both strongly typed languages, the type system is a much more prominent feature in HOL than in Z.

We base our presentation on [3, Part III]. After introducing the standard semantic universe of HOL, we will consider types and their semantics. A presentation of the semantics of terms follows, and finally, we introduce theories, which group types and terms to logical entities. Like the presentation in Section 2, the semantics of HOL can be formalized in Zermelo-Fraenkel set theory.

3.1   Semantic Universe

The semantics of HOL is based on a set theoretic model, the *standard model* of HOL. We describe this model in terms of a fixed set $\mathcal{U}$ of non-empty sets, the *universe*. It is closed under subsets and products, it contains an infinite element, and each of its member-sets contains a distinguished element.

Definition 4 (HOL-Universe). *A universe $\mathcal{U}$ of HOL is a set with the following properties:*

Inhab *Each element of $\mathcal{U}$ is a non-empty set.*
Sub *If $X \in \mathcal{U}$ and $\varnothing \neq Y \subseteq X$ then $Y \in \mathcal{U}$.*
Prod *If $X, Y \in \mathcal{U}$, then $X \times Y \in \mathcal{U}$.*
Pow *If $X \in \mathcal{U}$, then $\mathsf{P}\, X \in \mathcal{U}$.*
Infty *$\mathcal{U}$ contains a distinguished infinite set $\mathbb{I}$.*
Choice *There is a distinguished element $ch \in \prod_{X \in \mathcal{U}} X$. The set $\prod_{X \in \mathcal{U}} X$ consists of (dependently-typed) functions mapping each element X of $\mathcal{U}$ to an element of X. Thus, for all $X \in \mathcal{U}$, $ch\, X \in X$.*

The existence of a universe is provable in Zermelo-Fraenkel set theory with the Axiom of Choice, which reassures us that the semantics of HOL is based on solid ground.

The assumptions on $\mathcal{U}$ imply that the sets of *total* functions over elements of the universe are also in the universe, and that we can distinguish a one-element and a two-element set:

Fun *If $X, Y \in \mathcal{U}$, then $X \longrightarrow Y \in \mathcal{U}$.*
Unit *$\mathcal{U}$ contains a distinguished one-element set 1.*
Bool *$\mathcal{U}$ contains a distinguished two-element set 2.*

3.2 Types

Genericity in the form of polymorphism is a central concept of HOL. In addition to atomic types, we also have type constructors that map types to types. To model type constructors, we assume a countably infinite set TyVars of *type variables* whose elements are distinct from type names and constant names.

The basis of HOL's type system are type structures. They contain atomic types and type constructors that are used to build more complex types.

Definition 5 (Type Structure, Type Constant). *A type structure Ω is a set of type constants. A* type constant *is a pair (v, n), where $v \in$ TyNames is a type name and $n \in \mathbb{N}$ is the* arity *of the type constant. No two distinct type constants have the same name: if $(v, n_1) = (v, n_2)$, then $n_1 = n_2$.*

Type constants of arity 0 are *atomic types*, and type constants of positive arity are *type constructors*. The types over a type structure Ω are type variables, atomic types, instances of type constructors, and function types.

Definition 6 (Types). *The set* Types$_\Omega$ *of types over a type structure Ω is defined inductively:*

1. *TyVars $\subseteq$ Types$_\Omega$.*
2. *If $(v, 0) \in \Omega$, then $v \in$ Types$_\Omega$.*
3. *If $(v, n) \in \Omega$, $n > 0$, and for all $1 \leq i \leq n$: $\sigma_i \in$ Types$_\Omega$, then $(\sigma_1, \ldots, \sigma_n)v \in$ Types$_\Omega$.*
4. *If $\sigma_1, \sigma_2 \in$ Types$_\Omega$, then $\sigma_1 \to \sigma_2 \in$ Types$_\Omega$.*

Mapping types to elements of the universe $\mathcal{U}$ defines the semantics of types.

Definition 7 (Model of a Type Structure). *A model M of a type structure Ω maps each type constant $(v, n) \in \Omega$ to an n-ary function on $\mathcal{U}$.*

$$M(v) : \mathcal{U}^n \to \mathcal{U}$$

A model of a type structure is the basis to determine the meaning of types over the type structure. The concept of a type-in-context deals with the type variables of a type. A *type context* αs is a finite – possibly empty – list of distinct type variables. A *type-in-context* is a pair, written $\alpha s.\sigma$ of a type context αs and a type σ, where all type variables of σ appear in αs. The *canonical* context of a type σ contains exactly the type variables of σ, sorted with respect to the order on TyVars (c.f. Section 2).

Using type contexts, we define the meaning of a type by induction on the type structure.

Definition 8 (Meaning of a Type). *Let M be a model of a type structure Ω. For each type $\sigma \in$ Types$_\Omega$ and each type context αs of length n, we define a function*

$$[\![\alpha s.\sigma]\!]_M : \mathcal{U}^n \to \mathcal{U}$$

by induction on the structure of σ:

1. $[\![\alpha s.\alpha_i]\!]_M$, where α_i is the ith element of αs, is the ith projection function mapping $(X_1, \ldots, X_n) \in \mathcal{U}^n$ to X_i.
2. $[\![\alpha s.\sigma_1 \to \sigma_2]\!]_M$ maps $Xs \in \mathcal{U}^n$ to the set of all total functions from $[\![\alpha s.\sigma_1]\!]_M(Xs)$ to $[\![\alpha s.\sigma_2]\!]_M(Xs)$.
3. $[\![\alpha s.(\sigma_1, \ldots, \sigma_n)v]\!]_M$ maps $Xs \in \mathcal{U}^n$ to the set $M(v)(S_1, \ldots, S_n)$, where $S_i = [\![\alpha s.\sigma_i]\!]_M(Xs)$.

The meaning $[\![\sigma]\!]_M$ *of type* σ *with canonical context* αs *is*

$$[\![\sigma]\!]_M = [\![\alpha s.\sigma]\!]_M$$

We can view the constructor $\_ \to \_$ of function types as a binary type constant with a fixed meaning. The interpretation of a function type is a set of total functions. Property **Fun** guarantees that the interpretations of function types exist in $\mathcal{U}$.

An *instance* of a type σ is formed by substituting types for the type variables in σ.

3.3 Terms

The primitive building blocks of terms are typed constants. A collection of constants is a signature.

Definition 9 (Signature, Constant). *A* signature Σ_Ω *over a type structure* Ω *is a set of constants. A* constant *is a pair* $c :: \sigma$, *where* $c \in$ Names *is a name and* $\sigma \in$ Types$_\Omega$ *is a type over* Ω.

There are four categories of terms over a signature: variables, constants, function applications, and λ-abstractions.

Definition 10 (Terms). *The set* Terms$_{\Sigma_\Omega}$ *of terms over a signature* Σ_Ω *is defined inductively:*

1. *If* $c :: \sigma \in \Sigma_\Omega$ *and* σ' *is an instance of* σ, *then* $c :: \sigma' \in$ Terms$_{\Sigma_\Omega}$
2. *If* $x \in$ Names *and* $\sigma \in$ Types$_\Omega$, *then* var $x :: \sigma \in$ Terms$_{\Sigma_\Omega}$. *A term of the form* var $x :: \sigma$ *is called a* variable.
3. *If* $t_1 :: \sigma_1 \to \sigma_2, t_2 :: \sigma_1 \in$ Terms$_{\Sigma_\Omega}$, *then* $(t_1 \ t_2) :: \sigma_2 \in$ Terms$_{\Sigma_\Omega}$. *A term of the form* $(t_1 \ t_2) :: \sigma_2$ *is called an* application.
4. *If* var $x :: \sigma_1, t :: \sigma_2 \in$ Terms$_{\Sigma_\Omega}$, *then* $(\lambda x.t) :: \sigma_1 \to \sigma_2 \in$ Terms$_{\Sigma_\Omega}$. *A term of the form* $(\lambda x.t) :: \sigma_1 \to \sigma_2$ *is called a* λ-abstraction.

In contrast to Z, all (syntactic) terms of HOL are well-typed by definition. An ill-typed construction is not considered part of the domain of semantic functions. thus, there is no distinction between value and meaning of a term like in the semantics of Z (c.f. Sections 2.2 and 2.4).

The semantics of terms is defined relative to a model of its signature. A model assigns each constant $c :: \sigma$ a dependently typed function that maps each $Xs \in \mathcal{U}^n$ to an element $[\![\sigma]\!]_M(Xs)$ of its type model.

Definition 11 (Model of a Signature). *Let Σ_Ω be a signature over a type structure Ω. A model M of Σ_Ω consists of a model of Ω and for each constant $c :: \sigma \in \Sigma_\Omega$ an element*

$$M(c :: \sigma) \in \prod_{Xs \in \mathcal{U}^n} [\![\sigma]\!]_M(Xs)$$

where n is the number of type variables in σ.

Like the meaning of types, the meaning of terms can be defined based on contexts. A *context* $\alpha s, xs$ consists of a type context αs and a list xs of distinct variables whose types contain only type variables of αs. The exact definitions of a term-in-context $\alpha s, xs.t$ and the meaning function $[\![\alpha s, xs.t]\!]_M$ are quite technical because they have to take simultaneous instantiations of type variables and variables into account (see [3, Section 15.3.2] for details). For our purposes, it suffices to summarize that the meaning of a λ-abstraction is a total function in $\mathcal{U}$, and that the meaning of an application is an application of the meaning of the first term to the meaning of the second term. Of course, type variables in the terms result in appropriately parameterized meanings.

3.4   Standard Structures

The definitions of type structures and signatures are very general. They do not require any specific atomic types or constants to exist. To come to a practically useful formalism, we impose some minimal structure on types and terms.

Definition 12 (Standard Type Structure). *A type structure Ω is standard if it contains the atomic types bool of truth-values and ind of individuals. A model M of Ω is standard if $M(bool) = 2$ and $M(ind) = \mathbb{I}$.*

Definition 13 (Standard Signature). *Let Ω be a standard type structure. A signature Σ_Ω is standard if it contains the following three constants:*

Implication $\Rightarrow :: bool \to bool \to bool$
Equality $= :: \sigma \to \sigma \to bool$
Select $\varepsilon :: (\sigma \to bool) \to \sigma$

A model M of Σ_Ω is standard if $M(\Rightarrow)$ is the standard implication function on 2, and, for all sets $X \in \mathcal{U}$, $M(=)(X)$ is the equality on X. For $X \in \mathcal{U}$, $M(\varepsilon)(X)$ is Hilbert's choice function on X, whose definition relies on the function ch given by the property **Choice** *of $\mathcal{U}$.*

From now on, we consider only standard structures and models.

Definition 14 (Theory). *A theory* thy $= (\Omega, \Sigma_\Omega, Ax_{\Sigma_\Omega})$ *comprises a type structure Ω, a signature Σ_Ω, and a set of terms $Ax_{\Sigma_\Omega} \subseteq Terms_{\Sigma_\Omega}$, the axioms of* thy.

The theory Min contains exactly the standard items and no axioms:

$$\text{Min} = \left(\begin{array}{c} \{(bool,0),(ind,0)\} \\ \left\{ \begin{array}{l} \Rightarrow :: bool \to bool \to bool \\ = :: \sigma \to \sigma \to bool \\ \varepsilon :: (\sigma \to bool) \to \sigma \end{array} \right\} \\ \varnothing \end{array} \right)$$

This theory has a unique standard model.

4   Relating the Type Models of Z and HOL

The language provided by the theory Min is not rich enough to relate to Z in a straight-forward way. In Section 4.1, we therefore extend Min by types and constants that provide a suitable basis to model the types and terms of Z. Section 4.2 defines a mapping of non-generic types of Z to types of the extended theory. Section 4.3 extends that mapping to the generic case.

4.1   A Definitional Extension of Min

In spite of being so small, the theory Min provides a suitable basis to define many interesting mathematical concepts. Only five axioms, which syntactically exhibit properties of the standard model of Min, suffice to build complex logical theories. Usually it is not necessary to extend a theory with arbitrary axioms. Arbitrary axiomatizations are usually avoided, because they are unsafe. Due to the power of the logic, innocent looking axioms may easily lead to inconsistent, and therefore useless theories. It is good practice in the HOL community to rely on *definitional* extensions only, which are safe because they preserve the existence of standard models. Thus, a theory constructed from Min only by definitional extensions is consistent. Implementations such as the HOL system and Isabelle/HOL support two forms of definitional extensions: constant definitions and type definitions.

A *constant definition* extends a theory *thy* by a new constant c and an axiom of the form $c = t$, where c does not appear in t. A technical condition on the type variables of t ensures that the resulting theory has a standard model if the theory *thy* has one. Intuitively, c is just a new name for the term t.

A *type definition* introduces a new type (ν, n) that is isomorphic to a set S of elements of some other type. An axiom asserting the existence of a bijection between S and the elements of the new type (ν, n) establishes that isomorphism. In addition to some technical conditions concerning polymorphism, we have to prove that S is non-empty to be sure that the type definition preserves the existence of standard models.

We use type and constant definitions to extend Min to the theory[3] Hol-Z, which is rich enough to establish a direct correspondence to Z.

Table 2 sketches the type structure and signature of Hol-Z. In addition to the standard elements, Hol-Z contains the type constants *unit*, *int*, $*$ and *set* that we need to model the types of Z. The atomic type *unit* contains exactly one element, which is denoted by $(\ )$. The model of the atomic type *int* is the set of integers. The type is defined by a quotient construction based on the type *nat* of the natural numbers, whose model is $\mathbb{I}$. The type $\sigma\, set$ is the type of sets over σ. Its model is the function that takes a model of σ to its power set. The model of $\sigma_1 * \sigma_2$ is the Cartesian product of the models of σ_1 and σ_2.

---

[3] There is nothing exotic in Hol-Z: it actually is a subtheory of the libraries of standard theories that come with systems such as HOL or Isabelle/HOL.

Table 2. The theory Hol-Z

$\Omega_{\text{Hol-Z}}$	$\Sigma_{\text{Hol-Z}}$
bool	$\Rightarrow, \wedge, \vee, \neg, \ldots$
unit	$()$
nat	*zero, succ, ...*
int	$0, +, -, *, \ldots$
$\alpha\,set$	$\{x.\,P\,x\}, \cup, \cap, \ldots$
$\sigma_1 * \sigma_2$	$(x,y), fst, snd$

Because Hol-Z extends Min only by type and constant definitions, it is consistent by construction.

4.2 Relating Non-Generic to Monomorphic Types

Let Γ be a set of given set names. The type structure $\Omega(\Gamma)$ is the extension of $\Omega_{\text{Hol-Z}}$ by atomic types whose names are the names in Γ.

$$\Omega(\Gamma) = \Omega_{\text{Hol-Z}} \cup \{\sigma : \Gamma \mid \sigma \neq Z^t \bullet (\sigma, 0)\}$$

Definition 15. *The function* $[\![\_]\!]^\tau : Z\text{Types}^\Gamma \longrightarrow \text{Types}_{\Omega(\Gamma)}$ *maps Z-types over* Γ *to HOL-types over* $\Omega(\Gamma)$. *We define it by induction on the structure of* $Z\text{Types}^\Gamma$.

$$[\![v]\!]^\tau = \begin{cases} int & \text{if } v = Z^t \\ v & \text{if } v \in \Gamma \setminus \{Z^t\} \end{cases} \tag{6}$$

$$[\![P^t\,\sigma]\!]^\tau = [\![\sigma]\!]^\tau\,set \tag{7}$$

$$[\![\sigma_1 \times_n^t \ldots \times_n^t \sigma_n]\!]^\tau = [\![\sigma_1]\!]^\tau * \ldots * [\![\sigma_n]\!]^\tau \tag{8}$$

$$[\![\{x_1 \mapsto \sigma_1, \ldots, x_n \mapsto \sigma_n\}]\!]^\tau = \begin{cases} unit & \text{if } n = 0 \\ [\![\sigma_{k_1}]\!]^\tau * \ldots * [\![\sigma_{k_n}]\!]^\tau & \text{if } n > 0 \end{cases} \tag{9}$$

where $\{x_1 \mapsto \sigma_1, \ldots, x_n \mapsto \sigma_n\} \in \text{Signature}^\Gamma$, and $x_{k_1} < \cdots < x_{k_n}$

The following proposition relates the semantics of a Z-type to the semantics of its counterpart in HOL. Under a few restrictions, an interpretation of given set names induces a type model such that the interpretations of Z-types and their images under $[\![\_]\!]^\tau$ are isomorphic.

Proposition 1. *For all sets of given set names* Γ *whose elements are distinct from the names of types in* $\Omega_{\text{Hol-Z}}$, *for all interpretations* Carrier_0 *of* Γ *with* $\text{ran Carrier}_0 \subseteq \mathcal{U}$, *and for all standard models* M *of* $\Omega_{\text{Hol-Z}}$, *the extension* $M' = M \cup \text{Carrier}_0$ *of* M *is a standard model of* $\Omega(\Gamma)$, *and for all* $\sigma \in Z\text{Types}^\Gamma$:

$$\text{Carrier}(\sigma) \cong [\![[\![\sigma]\!]^\tau]\!]_{M'}$$

Proof. The extended model M' interprets standard type constants like M does. It is therefore standard. The remaining proof is an induction on the structure of Z-types. The interesting cases are product types and schema signatures, which make the relation between the two interpretations an isomorphism instead of an equality.

We iterate the binary product type constructor $\_ * \_$ of HOL to model the countably many different type constructors of Z for Cartesian products. By the induction hypothesis, the set of nested pairs $[[[\sigma_1]]^\tau * \ldots * [[\sigma_n]]^\tau]]_{M'}$ is isomorphic to the set of n-tuples $\mathsf{Carrier}\,(\sigma_1 \times_n^t \ldots \times_n^t \sigma_n)$.

For schema signatures, we use the fixed order on Names (c.f. Section 2) and observe that for each fixed $n > 0$, the set of functions on Names with a *fixed* domain of size n is isomorphic to the n-fold Cartesian product of their range. For $n = 0$, the carrier of the empty signature contains exactly one element, which is the empty binding. It is isomorphic to $[[unit]]_{M'}$.   □

Proposition 1 does *not* entail that the type models of Z and HOL are isomorphic as a whole. The function $[[\_]]^\tau$ maps signatures with different domains but equal ranges to the same product types. Proposition 1 holds, because the carriers of these signatures are isomorphic:

$$\mathsf{Carrier}\,(\{x_1 \mapsto \sigma_1, \ldots, x_n \mapsto \sigma_n\}) \cong \mathsf{Carrier}\,(\{y_1 \mapsto \sigma_1, \ldots, y_n \mapsto \sigma_n\})$$

The function $[[\_]]^\tau$ is coarser than necessary on product types. It maps certain nested products and flat products of the same length to the same HOL-types. For example, nested products and triples of numbers are identified:

$$[[Z^t \times_2^t (Z^t \times_2^t Z^t)]]^\tau = int * (int * int) = [[Z^t \times_3^t Z^t \times_3^t Z^t]]^\tau$$

We could distinguish these types defining

$$[[\sigma_1 \times_n^t \ldots \times_n^t \sigma_n]]^\tau = [[\sigma_1]]^\tau * \ldots * [[\sigma_n]]^\tau * unit \qquad (10)$$

In (10), the type *unit* marks the end of a product of arity n. Both definitions, (8) and (10), yield isomorphic representations of product types. Given that $[[\_]]^\tau$ cannot distinguish the domains of signatures and must map certain signatures to the same representations, the alternative mapping (10) does not lead to a property stronger than Proposition 1.

The assumption $\mathsf{ran\,Carrier_0} \subseteq \mathcal{U}$ is crucial for Proposition 1. It rules out empty carriers as interpretations of types of Z. In Section 5.2, we will argue that this is not a strong restriction and that it may give rise to changing the semantics of Z to exclude empty carriers of types.

4.3   Generic Types and Polymorphism

For generic types, the situation is complicated by the fact that there are too many types in $\mathsf{GenTypes}^\Gamma$. A generic type $\gamma \in \mathsf{GenTypes}_n^\Gamma$ is an arbitrary total function mapping n power set types to a type. We can interpret the polymorphic types of HOL as functions mapping types to types, too, but these two sets of functions – generic types in Z and polymorphic types in HOL – differ in two respects. First, polymorphic types are more liberal, because a type variable may be instantiated by any type, not just by a power set type as in Z. In particular, they may be instantiated by polymorphic types. Second, polymorphic types are more restrictive than generic types, because their instances are all of a similar structure: they are all syntactically unifiable. This is not true for all elements of $\mathsf{GenTypes}_n^\Gamma$, because generic types are not defined as a case of the inductive definition of ZTypes^Γ, but they are defined as a set of functions over ZTypes^Γ (c.f. (5)). For example, the function $\bar{\gamma}$ on types with

$$\bar{\gamma}(\mathsf{P}^t(\mathsf{Z}^t \times_2^t \mathsf{Z}^t)) = \mathsf{Z}^t$$
$$\bar{\gamma}(\mathsf{P}^t \, \mathsf{Z}^t) = \mathsf{Z}^t \times_2^t \mathsf{Z}^t$$

is an element of $\mathsf{GenTypes}_1^\Gamma$ that has no polymorphic counterpart, because Z^t and $\mathsf{Z}^t \times_2^t \mathsf{Z}^t$ are not (syntactically) unifiable.

Fortunately, a type such as $\bar{\gamma}$ does not contribute to the semantics of Z, because there is no expression of such a type. We can safely restrict the generic types we map to types of HOL to an inductively generated subset of $\mathsf{GenTypes}^\Gamma$ that is rich enough to assign types to all expressions of Z.

Definition 16 (Polymorphic Z-types). *The set* $\mathsf{PolyTypes}^\Gamma$ *of polymorphic Z-types generalizes* ZTypes^Γ *by allowing type variables in the place of given set names.*

$$\mathsf{PolyTypes}_n^\Gamma = \{\alpha_1,\ldots,\alpha_n : \mathsf{TyVars}; \, \sigma : \mathsf{ZTypes}^{\Gamma \cup \{\alpha_1,\ldots,\alpha_n\}} \bullet \sigma\} \qquad (11)$$
$$\mathsf{PolyTypes}^\Gamma = \bigcup_{n \in \mathsf{N}} \mathsf{PolyTypes}_n^\Gamma \qquad (12)$$

We interpret the elements of $\mathsf{PolyTypes}_n^\Gamma$ as n-ary functions in their type variables.

The set of inductively generated Z-types is the subset of all generic types that we need to assign types to Z expressions.

Definition 17 (Inductively Generated Z-Types). *The set of* inductively generated Z-types *is the set of all ground instances of polymorphic Z-types.*

$$\mathsf{IndTypes}_n^\Gamma = \begin{cases} \mathsf{ZTypes}^\Gamma & \text{if } n = 0 \\ \{\bar{\sigma} : \mathsf{PolyTypes}_n^\Gamma; \, \sigma_1,\ldots,\sigma_n : \mathsf{PowTypes}_n^\Gamma & \text{if } n > 0 \\ \bullet \, (\sigma_1,\ldots,\sigma_n) \mapsto \bar{\sigma}(\sigma_1,\ldots,\sigma_n)\} \end{cases} \qquad (13)$$
$$\mathsf{IndTypes}^\Gamma = \bigcup_{n \in \mathsf{N}} \mathsf{IndTypes}_n^\Gamma \qquad (14)$$
$$\mathsf{IndTenv} = \mathsf{Names} \nrightarrow \mathsf{IndTypes}^\Gamma \qquad (15)$$

Proposition 2 (Z typing is inductive). *Let* Γ *be a set of given set names.*

1. For all $n \geq 1$:

$$\mathsf{IndTypes}_n^\Gamma \subseteq \mathsf{GenTypes}_n^\Gamma$$

2. *For all Z paragraphs $\mathcal{P}$ and all $\eta \in \mathsf{IndTenv}$, the semantics of $\mathcal{P}$ under η is an environment of inductively generated types:*

$$(\langle\!\langle \mathcal{P} \rangle\!\rangle^T \eta) \in \mathsf{IndTenv}$$

3. *The set of type environments* $\mathsf{IndTenv}$ *is sufficiently large to type all Z specifications.*

Proof. For statement 1, it suffices to observe that $\mathsf{IndTypes}_n^\Gamma$ is a set of total functions mapping power set types to types.

The proof of statement 2 is an induction on the structure of $\mathcal{P}$. The principal argument is that types are denoted only implicitly by expressions, and that the syntax of expressions is defined inductively. The interesting base case of the induction deals with generic parameters. The types of generic parameters are arbitrary new power set types, which correspond to the type variables in (11). The type of a generic paragraph is a function from power set types to types, which corresponds to the construction of $\mathsf{IndTypes}^\Gamma$.

Statement 3 is a corollary of statement 2. The typing of a specification is the composition of the typings of its paragraphs, applied to the empty environment. The empty environment is a member of $\mathsf{IndTenv}$. $\qquad\qquad\square$

Building on these preliminaries, we extend the correspondence between the types of Z and HOL to the generic case.

Proposition 3. *Under the assumptions of Proposition 1, it holds for all $n \in \mathbf{Z}$, $\hat{\sigma} \in \mathsf{IndTypes}_n^\Gamma$ that there exist $\bar{\sigma} \in \mathsf{PolyTypes}_n^\Gamma$, and $\sigma_1, \ldots, \sigma_n \in \mathsf{PowTypes}^\Gamma$ such that $\hat{\sigma} = \bar{\sigma}(\sigma_1, \ldots, \sigma_n)$ and*

$$\mathsf{Carrier}\,(\hat{\sigma}) \cong [\![[\![\bar{\sigma}]\!]^\tau]\!]_{M'} \left([\![[\![\sigma_1]\!]^\tau]\!]_{M'}, \ldots, [\![[\![\sigma_n]\!]^\tau]\!]_{M'}\right)$$

Proof. For $n = 0$, we have the statement of Proposition 1. For $n \geq 1$, the types $\bar{\sigma}$, and $\sigma_1, \ldots, \sigma_n$ exist by Definition 17. With $[\![\alpha]\!]^\tau = \alpha$, we know that $[\![\bar{\sigma}]\!]^\tau$ is a type in n type variables, whose meaning $[\![[\![\bar{\sigma}]\!]^\tau]\!]_{M'}$ is an n-ary function on $\mathcal{U}$ (c.f. Definition 8). For $i \in 1 .. n$, the HOL type $[\![\sigma_i]\!]^\tau$ is a set type, because $\sigma_i \in \mathsf{PowTypes}^\Gamma$. Thus, $[\![[\![\sigma_i]\!]^\tau]\!]_{M'} \in \mathcal{U}$ and the right-hand side of the relation is well-formed. It is isomorphic to $\mathsf{Carrier}\,(\hat{\sigma})$ by induction on the structure of $\bar{\sigma}$ and Case 1 of Definition 8, which fixes the interpretation of α_i to be $[\![[\![\sigma_i]\!]^\tau]\!]_{M'}$. $\qquad\qquad\square$

5 Relating Terms

The relation between types of Z and HOL established in the preceding section determines the relation between the terms[4] of the two languages to a large extent. It is unnecessary to elaborate that relation in full detail here, because the mapping of Z terms to HOL terms that is called for is exactly the shallow encoding $\mathcal{HOL\text{-}Z}$ of Z into HOL that we have presented elsewhere [6].

---

[4] We use the word "term" here to refer to terms of HOL, and to predicates, expressions, and schemas of Z, as well.

The HOL community distinguishes between deep and shallow encodings of formalisms into HOL. A *deep* encoding provides a suite of definitions that describe the syntactic and semantic domains of the encoded formalism, and semantic functions mapping syntactic constructions to their semantic counterparts. Thus, a deep encoding describes the syntactic and semantic entities of the language to be represented, using HOL as a meta-language. In particular, it will introduce types for constants, variables, and terms of the represented language. Similar uses of Z describe the semantics of other languages in Z. An example is Smith's definition of semantic models of Object-Z in Z [11].

A *shallow* encoding identifies a sublanguage of HOL that corresponds to the language to represent. The semantics of (the representing sublanguage of) HOL must coincide with the semantics of the represented language, because HOL is not used as a meta-language: the HOL terms do not describe the semantics of the represented language, but their semantics – as HOL terms – *is* the semantics of represented terms. In particular, variables are represented by variables. Therefore, the HOL semantics of variable binding and substitution must be compatible with similar concepts of the represented language. As a shallow encoding, $\mathcal{HOL}$-$\mathcal{Z}$ induces a relation between the semantics of Z and HOL.

On the background of the relation between types, and under the assumptions of Proposition 1, we can show that the semantic interpretation of terms in Z and their representations in HOL coincide (modulo isomorphism). Let us only review a few fine points of the encoding that are important to discuss the relation of the two semantic models in the following section.

5.1   Predicates and Boolean Terms

Predicates do not have a type in Z. Therefore, their interpretation is not directly influenced by the relation between type models. However, it is well-known that the usual operators of predicate logic are definable in HOL. The standard interpretation of *bool*, implication, and equality ensures that a monomorphic boolean term is interpreted as a function from the interpretation of its free variables to 2. That interpretation is the characteristic function of the corresponding predicate of Z interpreted by $\{\![\_]\!\}^{\mathcal{M}}$.

5.2   Definite Description, Empty Carriers, and the HOL Standard Model

The semantics of a definite description $(\mu S \bullet E)$ is defined only if it uniquely determines a value. If the value is not determined uniquely, the Z draft standard does not prescribe an interpretation. A total semantics of the description operator is impossible in the semantic model currently chosen by the Z standard, because it explicitly allows for *empty* carrier sets of given types [8, page 18]. The property **Inhab** of the HOL universe $\mathcal{U}$, in contrast, excludes empty carrier sets of types: each carrier set is inhabited, and the standard interpretation of Hilbert's choice function $(\varepsilon x :: \sigma.P)$ denotes an element of type σ regardless of the truth value of P. Therefore, we have to require $\operatorname{ran} \mathrm{Carrier}_0 \subseteq \mathcal{U}$ in Proposition 1. Totalizing the partial semantics of Z, we can establish a correspondence between the definite description of Z and Hilbert's choice function in

HOL. Their semantics coincide if the described value is uniquely determined. Otherwise, the value determined by the standard interpretation of ε – given by the choice element ch of Definition 4 – is an admissible interpretation of the corresponding μ-term.

5.3   Schemas

The $\mathcal{HOL}\text{-}\mathcal{Z}$ encoding represents schemas by predicates, i.e. schemas are functions mapping the Cartesian product type identified by (9) to the boolean values. Observing the isomorphism between boolean valued functions and sets, which is established by the set comprehension function $Collect : (\sigma \to bool) \to \sigma\, set$ and the membership test $\_ \in \_ : (\sigma\, set) \to (\sigma \to bool)$, the correspondence of that encoding of schemas to their semantics given by $([\_])^{\mathcal{M}}$ (c.f. Table 1) is obvious: the set of situations that a schema denotes under an environment is isomorphic to the set of tuples denoted by the corresponding HOL function.

Not surprisingly, there is a grain of salt in this argument: the mapping of types $[\![\_]\!]^\tau$ does not consider the domains of situations, which are the names of a schema's signature. Encoding schema references in $\mathcal{HOL}\text{-}\mathcal{Z}$ therefore must explicitly establish variable bindings by supplying appropriate parameters to the functions encoding schemas. Interestingly, the draft standard employs a similar mechanism in the semantic construction of schema references that introduce new local variables [8, Section 9.1]: type and meaning enrichment functions extend environments by the signature of a schema.

5.4   Genericity and Polymorphism

Using the polymorphic type model of Z that we have introduced in Section 4.3, we can establish an exact correspondence between generic constructs of Z and HOL functions in (polymorphic) set types: a generic constant $C[X]$ of type σ is represented by a function $C : \alpha\, set \to [\![\sigma]\!]^\tau$. This correspondence is exact, because the generic constructs are indeed *total* functions of their generic parameters, and generic actuals must be of an arbitrary power set type.

How to represent references to generic constants is not so obvious if the generic actuals are left implicit – which is often the case in practice. Consider an example, which was recently discussed on the Z/EVES mailing list [10]. Suppose we wish to prove the statement

$$\forall s : seq(seq\, X) \bullet \forall i : dom\, s \bullet s(i) \in seq\, X \qquad (16)$$

In the proof, we wish to apply the theorem

$$\forall s : seq\, X \bullet \forall i : dom\, s \bullet s(i) \in X \qquad (17)$$

The variable X is a generic parameter in both statements. We would expect (16) to be an immediate consequence of (17) by substituting $seq\, X$ for X. Whether this is true depends on the way in which implicit generic actuals are inferred. The Z standard [8, page 39] defines that inferred generic actuals are "the maximal sets of the appropriate type" – but what is the maximal set of the element type of a generic formal, such as X in (17)? We need that information to infer the generic actuals of dom in (17). There are two ways to approach the problem of inferring generic actuals in a generic context: we can treat generic formals as if they were maximal, or we can assume that generic formals have polymorphic types, and denote maximal sets polymorphically.

Let us first discuss the former alternative, which is implemented in Z/EVES. Treating generic formals as if they were maximal, we infer the generic actuals $[Z, X]$ for dom in (17), which yields

$$\forall s : \text{seq}\, X \bullet \forall i : \text{dom}[Z, X]\, s \bullet s(i) \in X \tag{18}$$

Substituting seq X for X in (18) yields

$$\forall s : \text{seq}(\text{seq}\, X) \bullet \forall i : \text{dom}[Z, \text{seq}\, X]\, s \bullet s(i) \in \text{seq}\, X \tag{19}$$

Inferring the generic actuals in (16) in the same manner, however, we find that $P(Z \times X)$ is the second generic actual to dom, because that is the maximal set of the type of $\text{seq}(\text{seq}\, X)$. Thus, to prove (16) from (17), we must show that dom does not crucially depend on its generic parameters.

The second alternative of inferring generic actuals assumes polymorphic types for generic formals. In this setting, the second generic formal of both applications of dom, in the instance of (17) and in (16), is the set $P(Z \times \tilde{X})$, where $\tilde{X}$ is the maximal set corresponding to X. Unfortunately, there is no way in Z to denote $\tilde{X}$, leaving the maximal set of the type of elements of a generic formal as a semantical concept only.

We can encode both alternatives equally well in $\mathcal{HOL}\text{-}Z$. For the first alternative of inferring implicit generic actuals, we can determine whether a variable is a generic formal and use it as a parameter to HOL functions encoding generic constants. The polymorphic term $\{(x :: \sigma).\, true\}$ uniformly denotes the maximal set of a (polymorphic) type σ. Thus, generic actuals that are maximal sets are encoded by (polymorphic instances of) that term. In the second alternative, the maximal set of the elements of a generic formal $(X :: \alpha\, set)$ is $\{(x :: \alpha).\, true\}$.

The preceding discussion illustrates that genericity (of Z) and polymorphism (of HOL) are strongly related but different concepts. Polymorphic terms are functions in types, i.e. maximal sets, whereas generic constructs are functions in sets, which need not be maximal. As a consequence, it is not always obvious which generic actuals to infer, whereas every polymorphic term has a most general type. Type variables are (at best) an implicit concept in Z, whereas they are part of the language of HOL. Therefore, some semantically relevant concepts have denotations in HOL but not in Z, where it is impossible to constrain generic formals to maximal sets.

6   Discussion

We have established a strong similarity between the semantic models of Z and the polymorphic variant of higher-order logic that is implemented in proof tools such as HOL [3] and Isabelle/HOL [9]. This research justifies the faithfulness of a shallow encoding of Z in HOL, such as $\mathcal{H}OL\text{-}\mathcal{Z}$ [6], at a more formal level than had been established before. It may also explain the apparent attractiveness of using proof tools for higher-order logic to reason about Z.

In a more general perspective, our work contributes to the ongoing discussion on the semantics of Z. One of the particular attractions of higher-order logic from a semantic point of view is its concise kernel language, which facilitates a thorough semantic analysis. Z, in contrast, is a very rich language, which is not easily given a complete and consistent semantics. Recent proposals to approach a semantics of Z [4, 14] identify a small kernel language and reduce the rest of the language to that kernel. As the example of HOL shows, this approach offers hope of producing an accessible and consistent semantics for the entire language.

The analysis of Section 5.2 reveals that the semantic model favored by the Committee Draft [8], which does not require types to be inhabited, is not fully compatible with the standard model of HOL. While another flavor of higher-order logic without that restriction on carrier sets is definable (it would use Russell's ι-operator instead of Hilbert's ε-operator [1]), it has turned out that the model $\mathcal{U}$ has advantages in practice, because many side conditions become unnecessary. Reinterpreting the traditional view on Z in this respect would change the semantics of pathological cases only. It would in no way affect the interpretation of specifications in practice, but it would lead to a less complex semantic model and would relieve tool constructors of dealing with rarely relevant cases. The discussion of generic constructs and polymorphism shows that the type system could be integrated more smoothly into the semantic model: Z is a strongly typed language and there is little motivation to give semantics to ill-typed terms. This is also true for the treatment of generic constructs: integrating polymorphism into the type language and considering generic parameters as typed entities would enable a more uniform treatment of all constructs of the language. Introducing a constant that denotes maximal sets would allow us to reconcile the different views on implicit generic actuals discussed in Section 5.4.

We do not maintain that Z and HOL are the same formalisms, or that HOL should be used as the semantic model of Z. But we feel that the semantic similarities of the two languages are so strong that it would be very promising to build a semantic model of Z in analogy to the one of HOL, and, in the course of doing so, build on nearly a century of research into higher-order logics.

Acknowledgements

Maritta Heisel convinced me to write this paper. Maritta, Ian Toyn, and Carsten Sühl commented on drafts. The constructive comments of the anonymous referees helped improve the presentation. My thanks to them all.

Thanks also to Martin Henson, Andrew Martin, Mark Saaltink, Ian Toyn, and Sam Valentine for inspiring discussions on various aspects of the semantics and the proof system of Z. The present work has emerged from the collaboration with Kolyang and Burkhart Wolff on $\mathcal{H}OL\text{-}\mathcal{Z}$. They and my colleagues of the project ESPRESS have influenced my view on Z and HOL.

References

1. P. B. Andrews. *An Introduction to Mathematical Logic and Type Theory: To Truth Through Proof.* Academic Press, 1986.
2. J. P. Bowen and M. J. C. Gordon. A shallow embedding of Z in HOL. *Information and Software Technology*, 37(5–6):269–276, May/June 1995.
3. M. J. C. Gordon and T. M. Melham, editors. *Introduction to HOL: A theorem proving environment for higher order logics.* Cambridge University Press, 1993.
4. M. C. Henson and S. Reeves. A logic for the schema calculus. In J. P. Bowen, A. Fett and M. G. Hinchey, editors, *ZUM'98: The Z Formal Specification Notation*, Lecture Notes in Computer Science, volume 1493, pages 172–191. Springer-Verlag, 1998. This volume.
5. R. B. Jones. ICL ProofPower. *BCS FACS FACTS* Series III 1(1):10–13, 1192.
6. Kolyang, T. Santen, and B. Wolff. A structure preserving encoding of Z in Isabelle/HOL. In J. von Wright, J. Grundy, and J. Harrison, editors, *Theorem Proving in Higher-Order Logics*, Lecture Notes in Computer Science, volume 1125, pages 283–298. Springer-Verlag, 1996.
7. A. Martin. Approaches to proof in Z – or – why effective proof tool support for Z is hard. Technical Report 97-34, Software Verification Research Centre, 1997.
8. J. Nicholls, editor. Z Notation – version 1.2. Draft ISO standard, 1995.
9. L. C. Paulson. *Isabelle – A Generic Theorem Prover.* Lecture Notes in Computer Science, volume 828. Springer-Verlag, 1994.
10. M. Saaltink. Inferring generic actuals in Z/EVES. The Z/EVES mailing list, May 1997. Email: zeves@ora.on.ca
11. G. P. Smith. *An Object-Oriented Approach to Formal Specification.* PhD thesis, University of Queensland, Australia, 1992.
12. J. M. Spivey. The *f*UZZ manual. Computing Science Consultancy, Oxford, UK, 1992.
13. J. M. Spivey. *The Z Notation – A Reference Manual.* Prentice Hall International Series in Computer Science, 2nd edition, 1992.
14. I. Toyn. Z notation – draft 0.7. Proposal to the ISO Z Standards Panel, December 1997.

HOL-Z in the UniForM-Workbench –
A Case Study in Tool Integration for Z[*]

C. Lüth[1], E. W. Karlsen[1], Kolyang[1], S. Westmeier[1], and B. Wolff[2]

[1] Bremen Institute for Safe Systems, FB 3, Universität Bremen
Postfach 330440, 28334 Bremen, Germany
Email: {cxl,ewk,kol,swm}@informatik.uni-bremen.de

[2] Universität Freiburg, Institut für Informatik, Germany
Email: wolff@informatik.uni-freiburg.de

Abstract. The UniForM-Workbench is an open tool-integration environment providing type-safe communication, a toolkit for graphical user-interfaces, version management and configuration management.

We demonstrate how to integrate several tools for the Z specification language into the workbench, obtaining an instantiation of the workbench suited as a software development environment for Z. In the core of the setting, we use the encoding HOL-Z of Z into Isabelle as semantic foundation and for formal reasoning with Z specifications. In addition to this, external tools like editors and small utilities are integrated, showing the integration of both self-developed and externally developed tools.

The resulting prototype demonstrates the viability of our approach to combine public domain tools into a generic software development environment using a strongly typed functional language.

1 Introduction

The need for tool integration has been widely recognised throughout software engineering. There is no single tool for all purposes. Moreover, we live in a highly distributed software production culture. Hence, it is likely to be impractical and unproductive to prescribe *ex cathedra* the particular tools to be used in a given development. Rather, it seems more advantageous to let software engineering teams employ the tools with which they are most comfortable, and combine the various tools into one integrated *Software Development Environment* (SDE).

In response to this need, a number of tool integration techniques have been developed. In the most simple approach, tools run independently, with the file system as a persistent store, and communication achieved by string-based "glueing" using Tcl [25], Expect [22] or Emacs Lisp. Unfortunately, this approach does not scale up to more sophisticated development environments, where features such as type-safe communication, persistent and distributed storage, version management and workflow management are required. In particular, this is the case for formal methods, where the semantic

---

[*] This work has been supported by the German Ministry for Education and Research (BMBF) as part of the project UniForM under grant No. FKZ 01 IS 521 B2.

integrity of the documents produced by the various formal method tools have to be maintained.

During the last decade, several attempts to meet this challenge were made based on environments for synthesising *tightly integrated* SDE's from the basis of abstract language specifications such as the Cornell Synthesizer Generator [30], Gandalf [9], PSG [1] or the Ipsen system [23]. These were not entirely satisfactory, due to either the development costs involved in requiring tools to be developed from scratch in a homogeneous language framework, or to the inapplicability of the language framework itself in the problem domain.

In the UniForM approach, tool integration is based on a *loosely coupled* architecture [21, 31] where prefabricated tools are integrated on top of a *tool integration framework*. The UniForM-Workbench, introduced in Sect. 2, is the implementation of this framework, which offers support for data, control and presentation integration. It is generic, and we will here introduce its instantiation to the Z specification language (Sect. 3), the Z-Workbench. The semantic cornerstone of this instantiation is the encoding of Z into the theorem prover Isabelle [26], called HOL-Z [18]. The encoding lends a semantic aspect to the integration, by providing type checking and the ultimate certification of the correctness of proof-scripts, allowing to maintain the semantic integrity of documents during the development process, and moreover allowing formal reasoning within Z specifications. HOL-Z and Isabelle will be the focus of Sect. 4. This is followed by the main section (Sect. 5) of our paper concerned with the data model of our Z-Workbench. We demonstrate the Z-Workbench at work with the canonical example at hand in Sect. 6.

2 The UniForM-Workbench

The design of the UniForM-Workbench [15] reflects the guidelines of the ECMA Reference Model [5] (see Fig. 1), which outlines the abstract functionality required to support the various dimensions of a tool integration process:

Data Integration addresses the issue of sharing and exchanging data between tools. It is mainly provided by the *repository manager*.

Control Integration is concerned with communication and inter-operation among and between tools and the integration framework. It is provided by the *subsystem interaction manager*.

Presentation Integration addresses the issue of tool appearance and user interaction, i.e. look-and-feel. It is provided by the *user interaction manager*.

Process Integration is concerned with the functions between tools of the environment and the end user, i.e. workflow management. It will be provided by the *development manager* (work in progress).

The ECMA reference model is also called the "ECMA Toaster Model", with the integration services in the rôle of the toaster and the integrated tools as slices of bread. In this integration framework SDE's are constructed by *encapsulating* existing development tools such as editors, model checkers and interactive proof tools. Figure 1 shows

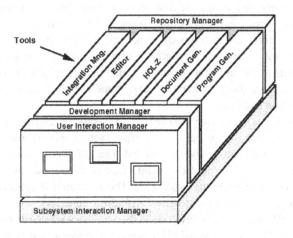

Fig. 1. ECMA Toaster Model

for example the instantiation used by the Z-Workbench with the various Z development tools.

The pure functional language Haskell [10, 27], extended with a higher order approach to concurrency [13] is used as a central integration language, i.e. as GlueWare[1] in this context. Each tool is encapsulated by wrapping Haskell interfaces around it using the integration manager. Section 5 will give an example of this process.

In the UniForM-Workbench, an SDE is viewed as a reactive, event driven system. Events in such an environment amount to user interactions of the user interaction manager, change notifications of the active repository manager, operating system events and individual tool events. The subsystem interaction manager [12] takes the rôle of the central control component in this reactive systems architecture. It is structured as a network of communicating agents called *interactors*, whose behaviour is expressed using composable event values in the style of Concurrent ML [29]. New events can be defined from the basis of existing ones, using the *guarded choice* operator that provides a choice between two events, or the *event-action* combinator that combines an event with some additional reactive behaviour. This way, integration can be expressed at a very high level of abstraction.

The repository manager [32] provides databases services for the persistent storage of objects, and their exchange between tools. It is implemented by a Haskell encapsulation of the Portable Common Tool Environment (PCTE) [6] standard, on top of which our own model to version and configuration management is implemented. The repository manager is an *active database*: changes to an object (i.e. committing a new version of an object) result in change notification events being sent to all other tools accessing the object.

---

[1] Thank you to Phil Trinder for coming up with this wonderful term!

In order to integrate one or more tool, one first develops a data model in terms of the extended entity-relationship model underlying PCTE. From this semi-formal model, the actual implementation in terms of Haskell data types and type classes is derived in a systematic way. During the integration process, each tool is set up to work with persistent objects of the repository manager, rather than the plain files of the file system. Alternatively, the repository manager can export and import objects from the repository into the file system and back.

The user interaction manager [14] provides Haskell-Tk, a strongly typed, fully concurrent and event driven graphical user interface system, with which graphical user interfaces for integrated tools can be constructed. The graph visualisation system daVinci [8] is used to provide a graphical user interface to the repository itself through the version and configuration graphs (see Fig. 2). The user can invoke services of the workbench using application menus associated with the graph.

The UniForM-Workbench obeys established industry standards such as the ECMA Reference Model, PCTE and Motif [7]. It has been implemented on the basis of public domain, off-the-shelf components supporting these standards. The repository manager for example is based on H-PCTE [4], whereas the user interaction manager integrates Tk [25] and the graph visualisation system daVinci. Moreover, the workbench offers a higher level of abstraction and uniformity than its underlying components, as well as additional utilities to support tool integration. The integration process is therefore much easier than if we had used these tools in their bare-bone form. One example is Haskell-Tk, which, as opposed to Tcl/Tk that it is based on, is strongly typed and fully concurrent. Another example is the repository manager, which provides version and configuration management on top of H-PCTE.

3   The Z-Workbench

The Z-Workbench is a Software Development Environment for Z built using the integration services provided by the UniForM-Workbench – in other words, an instantiation of the generic framework provided by the workbench to software development using Z. Its main component is the encoding of Z into Isabelle called HOL-Z [18], which provides a variety of services and the semantical underpinning of the integration.

HOL-Z reads Z specifications in the email format and type-checks them (i.e. it will reject specifications which do not type-check). One can then prove theorems within the specification, generate formatted documentation, or if the specification can be shown to be executable, generate program code. Thus, HOL-Z offers the following services:

- type check,
- symbolic theorem proving,
- documentation generation,
- and (currently under development) code generation.

Furthermore, a text editor (presently, the standard OpenWindows editor `textedit`) to edit specifications, and utilities such as the Unix tool `diff` which is used by the version management, are integrated.

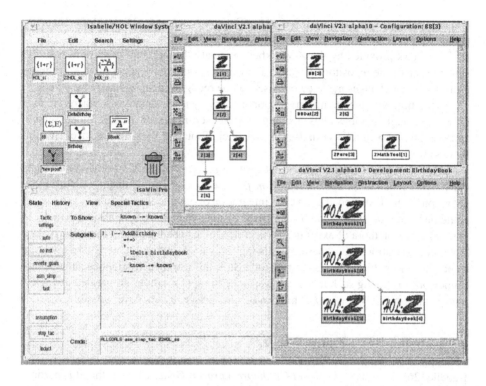

Fig. 2. Z-Workbench

A session with the Z-Workbench is pictured in Fig. 2. On the right, we can see daVinci visualisations of the development and configuration graphs, and on the left HOL-Z' graphical user interface. In the bottom right corner is the development graph of our running example BirthdayBook. The numbers [1],..., [4] denote the different versions; the edges of the graph denote the development relation, so e.g. version [4] is developed from version [2]. Actually, this development is currently taking place, as indicated by the brighter colour of version [4]. Its configuration graph, showing the objects comprising the development, is shown in the upper right corner. This configuration imports version Z[5] of the standard Z library, whose version graph is in turn shown to the left. The persistent objects taking part in the session are visualised in a brighter colour than objects that are not used by the session. These are also the objects which behind the scenes have been exported to the file system, in order to make them accessible to HOL-Z.

Integrating these tools into a Z-Workbench has numerous advantages over an implementation using stand alone tools working with a plain file system: all objects of the Z-Workbench, such as specifications and proofs, are versioned and permanently kept consistent in a distributed, multi-user environment. Not only Z specifications, but also tools and proofs are put under control of the version management system. Old versions are never deleted, only outdated, and can always be reverted to. Hence, a formal development is always kept consistent – if a specification is outdated, the development using the old, outdated specification is still available.

The views provided by the Z-Workbench are at all times kept consistent with the current state of the repository. Changes to the repository are broadcasted to all running tools, such that changes made by one user can be recognised immediately by others.

Interaction with the environment is on a query by navigation basis, where the user browses through the object base using graphical user interfaces such as folder, version and configuration graphs visualised by daVinci. Tools are then invoked from within these views.

Since it is based on the generic integration services of the UniForM-Workbench, the Z-Workbench is an *open integration framework* that can be extended with other development tools if needed. However, integration of other tools is not always as easy as could be hoped for, since it can be hampered by idiosyncrasies of prefabricated tools. In particular, the plethora of existing syntax styles for Z specifications (email, LATEX, box style) and deviations from these by existing tools may impose the need of converting a specification before it is passed to a tool. Still, the workbench provides an excellent framework for hiding such technicalities, since the specifications are treated as logical objects, and the conversions will happen behind the scenes whenever possible.

4   Isabelle, HOL-Z and Win-Z

Isabelle [26] is a *generic tactical LCF theorem prover*. *Generic* means that it is particularly suited for the encoding of different logics and formal methods, *tactical* means that it offers user-programmable proof support, and the *LCF design* means that the prover is centred around an abstract data type *theorems*, whose objects can only be constructed by applying the basic logical rules. The overall correctness of all formal activities is based on this (relatively small and well-investigated) logical engine.

As an implementation, the prover can be viewed as a collection of ML types modelling theorems, proofs and theories, and ML functions modelling the possible proof activities.

The encoding of Z into Isabelle, called HOL-Z, benefited in particular from Isabelle's genericity, while the LCF design allowed the implementation of a versatile graphical user interface not only for Isabelle itself, but also for other applications based on Isabelle, such as HOL-Z. We will now describe HOL-Z and the graphical interface in greater detail. Their combination will yield Win-Z, a tool with a graphical user interface for formal reasoning in Z specifications.

4.1   HOL-Z: Embedding Z into Isabelle

HOL-Z is an embedding of Z into Isabelle instantiated with Church's higher order logic (HOL), called Isabelle/HOL. Z schemas are represented as HOL formulas with specific operations modelling the binding structure of schemas explicitly in HOL. Thus, HOL-Z is a *shallow, structure preserving* embedding. Preservation of structure has the advantage that HOL-Z can be used for theorem proving in Z-specifications with realistic size. HOL-Z has been developed jointly with GMD FIRST Berlin, and is freely available at

```
http://www.informatik.uni-bremen.de/~agbkb/library/HOL-Z/
```

where further information can be found as well.

HOL-Z essentially consists of three parts:

- Isabelle Theories: An Isabelle theory, a collection of extensions to the Isabelle/HOL standard library, and the mathematical toolkit, the "library" of Z which consists itself of a collection of theories (relations, bags, sequences etc.);
- a loader for Z specifications;
- a collection of tactics to support proofs in Z specifications.

HOL-Z supports the email format as proposed in the Draft Standard for Z [24]. Thus, a schema is given in the email format; a loader converts it into a semantic representation where the corresponding schema is a boolean-valued function. This conversion process also type-checks the specification; specifications which do not type-check will be rejected.

The following schema known from the Birthday Book will be represented in the email input syntax as follows:

```
+-- BirthdayBook ---
          birthday : (Name -|-> Date);
          known : Pow Name
|---
          known = dom(birthday)
    ---
+-- AddBirthday   ---
        date? : Date;
        name? : Name;
        %Delta BirthdayBook
|---
        name? ~: known &
        birthday'= birthday Un {(name?, date?)}
    ---
```

The Z loader takes these schemas and produces two theorems, one for each schema, in Isabelle, the first of which is pretty printed as shown below:

```
+-- BirthdayBook ---
    birthday : (Naturals -|-> Date); known : Pow Name
|---
    known = dom(birthday)
    ---
```

A major advantage of HOL-Z over other embeddings is the preservation of the structure of the specification. For instance, *Z in HOL* [3] of Bowen and Gordon parses away the schema references, thus flattening the specification. *ProofPower* [11] represents schemas as sets of bindings which the schema operations work on. *Z-in-Isabelle* [19] of Kraan and Bauman makes the signatures of schemas globally visible causing the parser to expand schemas.

4.2 Win-Z: A Graphical User Interface for HOL-Z

Win-Z is the instantiation of a graphical user interface for the theorem prover Isabelle, called IsaWin [17], with HOL-Z. The theorem prover's objects – theorems, proofs, theories, sets of rewriting rules – are graphically represented. The operations on these objects making up the proof activity, are mostly affected by drag&drop, or to a lesser extent by activating buttons or menu entries. This gives the user access to nearly the full proof power of Isabelle without having to concern himself with ML and its syntax.

An interesting feature of IsaWin's system architecture is its versatility. Since it is implemented entirely in Standard ML "on top" of Isabelle, it makes use of Standard ML's powerful abstraction and modularisation concepts, in particular its parameterised modules, called *functors*. This way, to obtain a graphical user interface for an encoding or other application based on Isabelle, we merely need to instantiate the functor with different parameters.

The instantiation of IsaWin for HOL-Z, called Win-Z, contains *ZTheories* which are collections of schema declarations (sections) forming the context of a theorem, together with an environment, which contains extra-logical information about the type of schemas, to respect the define-before principle of Z. In Fig. 2, Win-Z can be seen on the left side.

5 The Integration

The development of integrated SDE's within the UniForM-Workbench starts out with a number of unintegrated, prefabricated development tools. In order to reach an integrated framework for Z development, issues regarding control, data and presentation integration must be addressed. Control integration means that the tool is given a Haskell abstract programming interface (API) so that it can be controlled by the subsystem interaction manager. Data integration means that it is set up to interface the development objects maintained by the repository manager, and presentation integration means that a graphical user interface along the guidelines of the Motif standard are wrapped around the tool, unless of course the tool already comes with such an interface.

The resulting SDE is organised according to the *Model-View-Controller paradigm* [20], with the repository manager in the rôle of the *Model*, the user interaction manager in the rôle of the *View* and the subsystem interaction manager in the rôle of the *Controller* [16]. We shall briefly demonstrate how integration is achieved using Haskell as an extensible scripting language.

5.1 Data Integration

The data model for the Z-Workbench is given in Fig. 3 as an extended Entity-Relationship diagram, which is then systematically converted into the actual Haskell modelling (see Sect. 2). Currently this is done manually, but there is ongoing work on a schema editor which will automate most of this work. The two most basic object types are *folders* and *versioned objects*. Folders are the basic structuring mechanism within the repository, comparable to directories in conventional file systems. Each folder may however be contained in a number of parent folders, and each folder may contain, in addition, a number of versioned objects. Versioned objects are the basic building blocks of the application. Each versioned object has two kinds of relationships: *dependency* and *development*. Dependency links model structural dependency, such as imports, and are given by all those links between the five subtypes of versioned objects marked ⓓ in Fig. 3. The development relationship defines *revisions* of an object, and can only exist between versioned objects of the same subtype. Dependency links will be essential to model change propagation: if a new revision of an object is created, the revisions of the objects depending on this object may have to be updated as well. Thus, if we create a new theory by editing an existing one, all proof scripts living in the old theory will have to be updated as well in order to live in the new theory.

Versioned objects come in five subtypes: *tools, theories, sessions, proof scripts* and *documentation*.

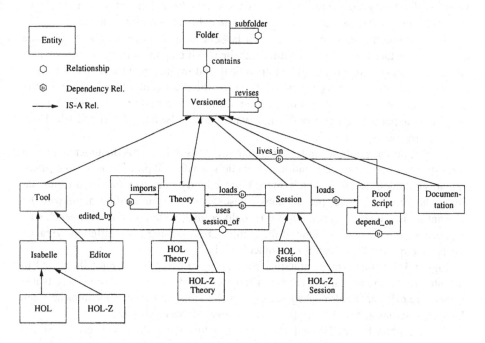

Fig. 3. Z-Workbench Data Model

The subset of tools considered here are either those based on Isabelle, such as plain Isabelle/HOL or the Z-encoding HOL-Z, or the OpenWindows text editor `textedit`. By modelling tools as versioned objects, the workbench is able to maintain and invoke different versions of the same tool. Tool revisions are used to represent new versions of the tool which are incompatible to existing developments; this is in particular relevant for Isabelle (and hence HOL-Z), where old tactical scripts will quite often not run on newer versions of Isabelle.

Theories represent specifications, type and datatype definitions and so forth. They come in subtypes corresponding to the different flavours of Isabelle; thus, there are HOL-Theories and Z-Theories, read by Isabelle/HOL and HOL-Z, respectively. Theories are edited externally (i.e. not within Isabelle itself). Theories in Isabelle are structured hierarchically, and hence come with an *import* relationship. Theories are *edited_by* the text editor.

Sessions represent the persistent state of a session with Isabelle/HOL or HOL-Z. Essentially this means that the user may save a session, and resume work later. When a session is resumed, the proof work being done up to that point is reconstructed. To maintain consistency of sessions, the distinction between checked and unchecked theories is important, since each session is reconstructed with the last checked version of the theory (which may be different from the last version of the theory, if it is unchecked). Every session is related (by the *is_session_of* link) to one specific Isabelle-based tool which it runs on. Further, every session may load several theories. The last checked versions of a theory are referenced by a session via the *loads* link, whereas a version of the same theory a user is currently working on may be referenced by the *uses* link.

Proof scripts are self-contained tactical Isabelle scripts. Since there is a multitude of objects and tactical operations within Isabelle making up these tactical scripts, modelling all of these in detail would be impractical, and we just treat them abstractly as a textual representation. Every proof script lives in the context of a theory, given by the *lives_in* link, and is loaded by one Isabelle session given by the *loads* link. A proof script may depend on other proof scripts which have to be loaded first and which are indicated by the *depend_on* link.

Finally, documentation can be generated out of a session. This documentation is a pretty-printed, typeset representation of Isabelle's or HOL-Z' proofs, theorems or theories; it is not documentation which can be freely edited by the user, or even documentation in the sense of literate specifications. These types of documentation, along with the relevant tools (Hypertext browsers etc.), could be integrated into our workbench easily, because there would be none of the complications arising from different syntactic formats hampering the integration of other Z tools.

Figure 3 is actually an abstraction from the more complicated modelling used in our integration. In particular, there are different types of sessions and proof scripts just as there are different kinds of theories and Isabelle tools; and the relationships between theories, sessions and proof scripts are on the level of these subtypes.

The workbench uses Haskell classes to structure the code and to generalise the API's. For example, the following class contains the operations and events modelling the *versioned objects* in Fig. 3:

```
class (RMIdObjectC vo) => RMVersionedObjectC vo where
    revise          :: vo -> IO vo
    getRevisions    :: vo -> IO [vo]
    getPredecessors :: vo -> IO [vo]
    revised         :: vo -> EV vo
```

The class provides (among others of course) a revise operation for creating new revisions, two computations for traversing the version tree (getRevisions, getPredecessors) together with a revised event that occurs whenever a versioned object has been revised. This class is instantiated as needed with theories, sessions and proof scripts.

5.2   Control Integration

All the development tools of the Z-Workbench happen to be interactive Unix tools. Even Win-Z, although it comes with a graphical user interface, can be squeezed into this category, since it is started and controlled from within a ML session.

The workbench provides a utility called Haskell-Expect [12] (inspired by expect [22]) for integrating such interactive Unix tools. It runs the Unix tool in the background, and lets the workbench take over communication with the tool by simulating the user dialogue. The encapsulation of Win-Z in Haskell comes quite straightforward in this setting, as we shall demonstrate by the following Haskell code fragment that starts up Win-Z loaded with a given session and theory:

```
startHolZ session theory = do {
  hz <- newExpect "holz" [];
  sync (match hz "^- ");
  sendCmd hz (load session theory);
  interactor (finished hz >>> do{sendCmd hz "quit();\n"; stop});
  return hz
} where load s t = "load " ++ show s ++ " " ++ t ++ ";\n"
```

An Expect tool is created first that starts up Win-Z as a ML session. We then wait until the ML interpreter responds with a prompt, as specified by the match event and responds by sending a command (sendCmd) that will start up Win-Z and load the given session and theory. The command is forwarded in the form of a string as specified by the function load. An interactor is finally spawned off to catch the events that occur when Win-Z finally returns control to the ML interpreter. The interactor responds by quitting the ML session before it terminates itself by calling stop.

The workbench is based on a higher order composable approach to event handling, where events are first class values. Base events can be combined into composite events using the guarded choice operator (e1 +> e2), and additional reactive behaviour can be glued onto existing events using the event-action combinator (e >>> a). The event that occurs when the session with Win-Z is over, consists for example of two base events:

```
finished hz = (match hz "^- ") +> (match hz "uncaught.*\n")
```

The first event occurs when the session has terminated normally, i.e. load has finished and the ML interpreter has generated a prompt and awaits user input. The second event should actually never occur, since it is generated when the session with Win-Z has ended abruptly with an uncaught exception.

The workbench can furthermore communicate with Win-Z running as a server, in order to request services of Win-Z or to inform Win-Z about some external event of relevance to the session (new theorems etc.). The way this is achieved has already been demonstrated: sendCmd is used to submit commands to the tool and match for looking for specific response patterns.

5.3 Presentation Integration

The need for presentation integration within the Z-Workbench is quite restricted since all tools come with a graphical user interface on their own. What remains is to develop the version and configuration graphs of the system, and provide the user with additional menus and user dialogues for calling and customising the services of the integrated workbench.

When the user requests the system to open up a new view such as a version graph, an initial view is built first, i.e. the repository is traversed and the appropriate visualisation commands are passed to the graph visualisation tool daVinci. A bunch of interactors are then associated with the graph to maintain consistency between the view and the underlying repository. An interactor for monitoring a single version looks like:

```
monitor g vo = interactor (
    revised vo >>>= (\rev -> do
        showRevision g vo rev
        monitor g rev
        redrawGraph g
        ))
```

The interactor reacts to the `revised` vo event, that occurs whenever a new revision of vo has been made, by showing the new revision link within the current version graph. It then spawns off a monitor for the new revision `rev` and redraws the graph. It actually is as simple as this, although the interactor is in reality set up to listen to a couple of events more.

Generating views, and maintaining the consistency of views, is one issue, tool invocation is another. The services of the workbench are invoked by using pull-down menus that are associated with the nodes within a view. For example, the version graph has a single interactor that listens to node selection events and menu invocation events:

```
controller g m o = interactor (
        nodeSelected g >>>= \o' -> become (controller g m o')
    +>  invoked m      >>>= \f -> f o
    )
```

The controller takes as parameter a handle to the current graph g, the application menu m and the selected object o. It responds to a node selection event by becoming an interactor that will apply commands to the new selection o' rather than the old one.

The second guard handles menu invocations. The application menu is set up to return the computation that defines the behaviour associated with the menu item. This computation is then applied to the object currently selected.

The missing link is the following piece of code that ensures that a new session with Win-Z is started whenever the user clicks the Revise button associated with a Win-Z session. The first line defines this button, and binds the function newHolZSession to it, which is defined below, such that this function is called whenever the button is pressed:

```
button [text "Revise", command (return newHolZSession)]
```

```
newHolZSession vo = do
    vo' <- revise vo
    (session,theory) <- exportSession vo'
    startHolZ session theory
```

A new revision is created first and all files of relevance to the Win-Z session are then exported to the file system. A new development using Win-Z is then started in the context of the given session and theory.

5.4 Experiences gained from the Prototype

The workbench provides, being based on Haskell extended with a higher order approach to concurrency, a high level of abstraction and expressive power that comes very close to the one of constructive formal specifications. There are several key features in achieving this.

First of all we benefit from Haskell's expressive power. In particular, classes are used to structure the code and to standardise the interfaces to the system. The sequential behaviour of the system is expressed in terms of IO computations that have a theoretical foundation in the monadic approach to IO. A more practical consequence is that we have an extensible language framework that can be enhanced with new computational paradigms on need. The innovative part of the system however is the approach to event handling that treats all events of the system, whether they are user interactions, data base change notifications, operating system signals or individual tool events in terms of first class composable values that entirely hide the source of the event. Tool integration can therefore be expressed in a style that comes close to a formal specification using process algebras. The difference though is that Haskell is executable – and highly efficiently compiled as well.

6 Proving in the Birthday Book

In this section we will use the classical birthday book example to demonstrate the look-and-feel for Win-Z and its interaction with the surrounding Z-Workbench. This will be done with a proof of a tiny property of *AddBirthday*, namely that the set of names known to the system will be different with the addition of a given new name.

First of all, we define a Z-theory *BB.zthy*, which is a Z paragraph containing the Z schemas defining the Birthday Book. The leading fragment of this paragraph has already been shown in Sect. 4.

We state our desired property as follows:

```
|-- AddBirthday =+=>
  +..
    %Delta BirthdayBook
  |---
    known ~= known'
  ---
```

We start with a Win-Z session where *BB.zthy* has already been loaded, and enter this goal. Figure 4 shows a screen-shot where the goal above has been refined with one tactical step making all the implicit free variables (the parameters of the schema) explicit by universally quantified variables.

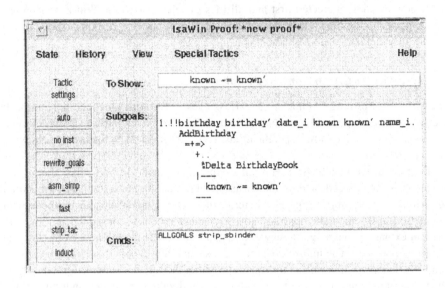

Fig. 4. Making implicit variables explicit

We now proceed by expanding the schema definitions for *AddBirthday* and *BirthdayBook*. Further, elementary simplification leads to the following proof state as shown in Fig. 5. At this point, we interrupt the development and save the session via the menu.

Now imagine another user goes to the version graph of the Win-Z session shown in Sect. 3. The workbench has meanwhile reacted to the change notifications of the repository manager, and has updated the version graph accordingly to show the new revision. The user clicks on the generated version, and the Z-Workbench will start Win-Z in exactly the state saved above.

After applying some minor tactics the goal is divided in small subgoals as shown in Fig. 6. The last three subgoals are proven automatically without user intervention by using Isabelle's decision procedures for sets. The first one involves some knowledge about domains. One therefore has to use the simplifier sets related to the Z mathematical toolkit. Fig. 7 shows the result of this simplification.

Here, a lemma about subsets and union is needed , stating that if *B* is not included in *A*, then *A* is not equal to the union of *A* and *B*:

$$not(B <= A) ==> A \text{ ~}= A \text{ Un } B$$

Using this lemma produces the proof state shown in Fig. 8. From here, Isabelle's decision procedure will do the rest. Again, the newly generated session can be saved, and

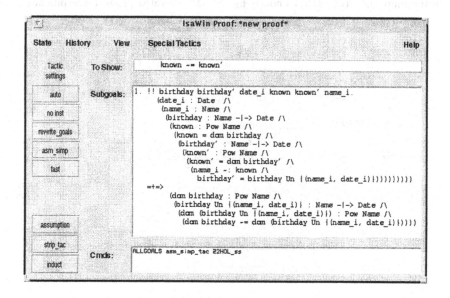

Fig. 5. After Schema Expansion and Simplification

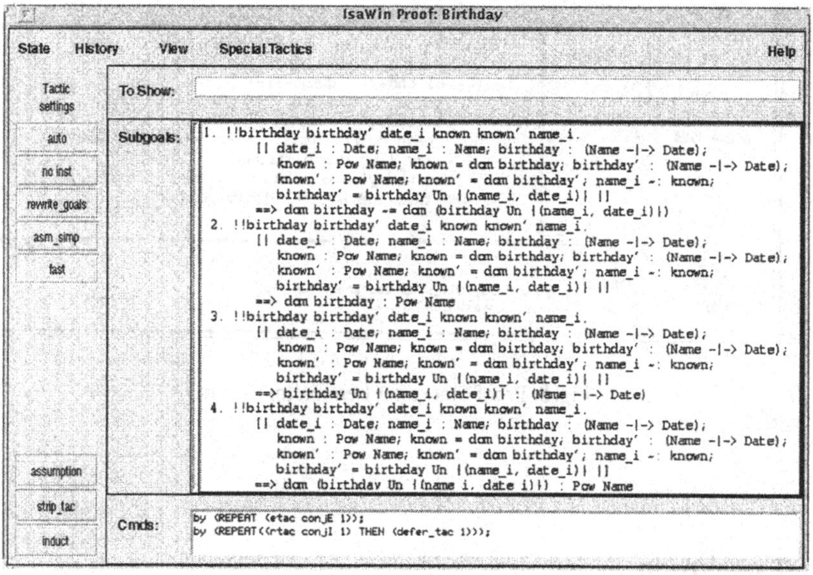

Fig. 6. Breaking up the Conjunction of the Conclusion

furthermore the proof script underlying the demonstrated proof development can be extracted.

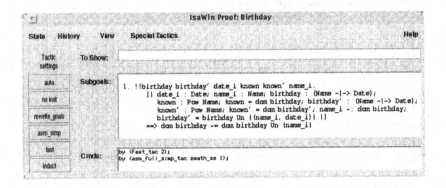

Fig. 7. Simplification with the Mathematical Toolkit

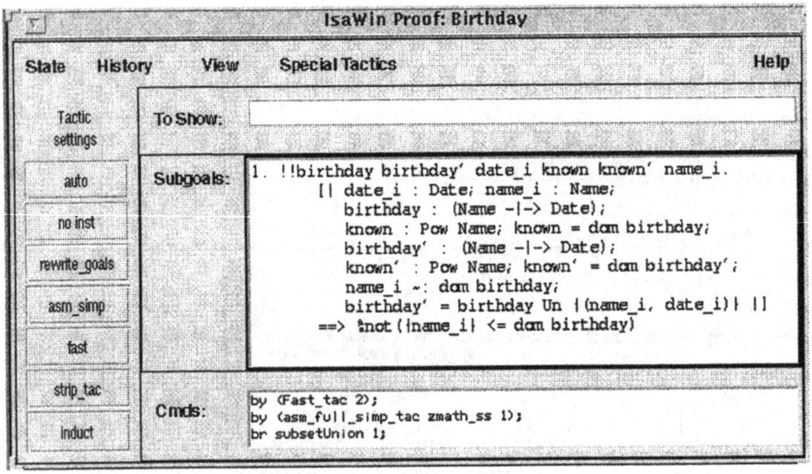

Fig. 8. Proof State after Lemma Introduction

7 Conclusion

We have seen an instantiation of the UniForM-Workbench for Z based on a prover environment called HOL-Z. The resulting prototype gives an impression of the power of the modular, generic and functional technology employed.

The modular aspect allows the development of the components of the workbench by different groups of developers and users. It is perfectly possible to use the pure encoding HOL-Z or its graphical interface Win-Z on its own. It is possible to use the GlueWare of the workbench for completely different tools, not necessarily connected to formal methods at all.[2] But it is the combination of these three that scales up a correctness-oriented, but notoriously difficult to use LCF-prover environment to a formal methods environment providing versioning (hence reproducibility) and maintaining the overall semantic integrity (this piece of code or this generated documentation belongs to this specific state of a Z-theory) even in a distributed, multi-user setting.

The pervasive generic aspect of our technology stresses this toolkit character of the workbench even more. The tools themselves are built from many components which are designed to be independent from each other and which can be *instantiated* for a particular application. For example, the graphical user interface for the theorem prover Isabelle can not only be instantiated to HOL-Z, but to any other application built using Isabelle, e.g. a system for transformational program development [17].

We are very happy with our decision to use strongly-typed, state-of-the-art functional programming languages for both the UniForM-Workbench and Win-Z. The combination of a purely functional language extended with a higher order approach to concurrency allows integration at a very high level of abstraction. Working with tool support for formal methods this has become a crucial aspect, since the technology allows us to experiment with new ideas without being slowed down by a large implementation and maintenance overhead.

7.1   Related Work

Other examples of integrated software developments geared towards formal methods are the Cogito [2] system, and KIV [28]. As tools, these are clearly superior to our workbench in terms of availability, user-friendliness and stability; but we believe they suffer from a system architecture which does not have a theorem prover as powerful and versatile as Isabelle at its heart, and which does not allow them to keep up with changes as good as our workbench, the modular design of which allows easy exchange of parts which are outdated or superseded by newer developments.

7.2   Future Work

With respect to the Z-Workbench, more tools supporting different documentation formats like LaTeX, RTF or HTML on the one hand and animators on the other would be desirable extensions to the existing prototype. The Win-Z component needs the integration of the code generator currently under development and more specialised tactical support.

Another line of extension is the integration of other Z-Tools (like animators or test-case generation tools) *not* based on Isabelle. Due to the variety of syntactical constructs of Z, this kind of integration requires conversions between the different formats. Although this may present a reliability problem to the integration in practice, the

---

[2] This has been done for the Hugs-Workbench [12, 16].

Z-Workbench can perform these conversions behind the scenes once they are implemented.

In our actual prototype, the granularity of data to be exchanged between different sessions is still rather coarse. For instance, the workbench has no access to the components of proof scripts. Proof scripts can be transferred to another session, but only *in toto*; this could be substantially enhanced if general merge techniques on proof scripts (as developed for specialised logic with the KIV system) were available. All these techniques could be combined with an active change propagation mode of the workbench – i.e. the workbench starts the logical engine in a batch mode, passes it a textually modified Z-theory, causes a re-evaluation of depending proof scripts with the aim to recertify as much as possible, and to save the resulting state of the logical engine in a session that is ready for further interactive development.

Last but not least a workspace model for the repository is currently being developed, extending our current model for version and configuration management. This will allow users of the workbench to work in isolation for a while, and later synchronize their work again.

References

1. R. Bahlke and G. Snelting. The PSG system: From formal language definitions to interactive programming environments. *ACM Transactions on Programming Languages and Systems*, October 1986.
2. A. Bloesch, E. Kazmierczak, P. Kearney, and O. Traynor. Cogito: A methodology and system for formal development. *International Journal of Software Engineering*, 4(3), 1995.
3. J. P. Bowen and M. J. C. Gordon. Z and HOL. In J. P. Bowen and J. A. Hall, editors, *Workshops in Computing*, Z Users Workshops, pages 141–167, Cambridge, UK, 1994. Springer-Verlag.
4. The H-PCTE Crew. H-PCTE vs. PCTE, version 2.8. Technical report, Universität Siegen, June 1996.
5. ECMA. Reference model for frameworks of software engineering environments. Technical Report TR/55, European Computer Manufacturers Association, June 1993.
6. ECMA. *Portable Common Tool Environment (PCTE) – Abstract Specification*. European Computer Manufacturers Association, 3 edition, December 1994. Standard ECMA-149.
7. Open Software Foundation. *OSF/Motif Series*. Prentice Hall, 1992.
8. M. Fröhlich and M. Werner. daVinci V2.0.3 online documentation. Universität Bremen, German, 1997. URL: http://www.informatik.uni-bremen.de/~davinci/
9. A.N. Habermann and D. Notkin. Gandalf: Software Development Environments. *IEEE Transactions on Software Engineering*, December 1985.
10. P. Hudak, S. L. Peyton Jones, and P. Wadler. Report on the programming language Haskell – a non strict purely functional language, version 1.2. *ACM SIGPLAN notices*, 27(5):1–162, 1992.
11. R. B. Jones. ICL ProofPower. *BCS FACS FACTS*, Series III 1(1):10–13, 1992.
12. E. W. Karlsen. Integrating interactive tools using concurrent Haskell and synchronous events. In *CLaPF'97: 2nd Latin-American Conference on Functional Programming*, September 1997.
13. E. W. Karlsen. The UniForM concurrency toolkit and its extensions to concurrent Haskell. In *GWFP'97: Glasgow Workshop on Functional Programming*, September 1997.

14. E. W. Karlsen. The UniForM user interaction manager. Draft technical report, FB 3, Universität Bremen, 1998.

15. E. W. Karlsen. The UniForM WorkBench – a higher order tool integration framework. In *International Workshop on Current Trends in Applied Formal Methods*, Boppard, Germany, 7–9 October 1998. URL: http://www.dfki.de/vse/fm-trends/

16. E. W. Karlsen and S. Westmeier. Using concurrent Haskell to develop views over an active repository. In *IFL'97: Implementation of Functional Languages*, September 1997.

17. Kolyang, C. Lüth, T. Meier, and B. Wolff. TAS and IsaWin: Generic interfaces for transformational program development and theorem proving. In M. Bidoit and M. Dauchet, editors, *TAPSOFT'97: Theory and Practice of Software Development*, Lecture Notes in Computer Science, volume 1214, pages 855–859. Springer-Verlag, 1997.

18. Kolyang, T. Santen, and B. Wolff. A structure preserving encoding of Z in Isabelle/HOL. In J. von Wright, J. Grundy, and J. Harrison, editors, *Theorem Proving in Higher Order Logics – 9th International Conference*, Lecture Notes in Computer Science, volume 1125, pages 283–298. Springer-Verlag, 1996.

19. I. Kraan and P. Baumann. Implementing Z in Isabelle. J. P. Bowen and M. Hinchey, editors, *ZUM'95: The Z Formal Specification Notation*, Lecture Notes in Computer Science, volume 967, pages 355–373. Springer-Verlag, 1995.

20. G. Krasner and S. Pope. A cookbook for using the model-view-controller user interface paradigm in Smalltalk-80. *Journal of Object Oriented Programming*, 1(3):26–49, 1988.

21. M. Lacroix and M. Vanhoedenaghe, editors. *Tool Integration in an Open Environment*, Lecture Notes in Computer Science, volume 387. Springer-Verlag, 1989.

22. D. Libes. expect: Scripts for controlling interactive processes. In *Computing Systems, Vol 4, No. 2*, Spring 1991.

23. Manfred Nagl, editor. *Building Tightly Integrated Software Development Environments: The IPSEN Approach*, Lecture Notes in Computer Science, volume 1170. Springer-Verlag, 1996.

24. J. Nicholls and the Z Standards Panel. Z notation, September 1995. URL: http://www.comlab.ox.ac.uk/oucl/groups/zstandards/

25. J. K. Ousterhout. *Tcl and the Tk Toolkit*. Addison Wesley, 1994.

26. L. C. Paulson. *Isabelle – A Generic Theorem Prover*. Lecture Notes in Computer Science, volume 828. Springer-Verlag, 1994.

27. S. Peyton Jones, A. Gordon, and S. Finne. Concurrent Haskell. In *Principles of Programming Languages '96 (POPL'96), Florida*, 1996.

28. W. Reif, G. Schellhorn, and K. Stenzel. Proving system correctness with KIV. In M. Bidoit and M. Dauchet, editors, *TAPSOFT'97, Theory and Practice of Software Development*, Lecture Notes in Computer Science, volume 1214, pages 859–862. Springer-Verlag, 1997.

29. J. H. Reppy. *Higher-Order Concurrency*. PhD thesis, Department of Computer Science, Cornell University, USA, 1992.

30. T. Reps. *Generating Language Based Environments*. PhD Thesis, Cornell University, USA. MIT Press, 1983.

31. D. Schefström and G. van den Broek. *Tool Integration*. John Wiley & Sons, 1993.

32. S. Westmeier. Verwaltung versionierter persistenter objekte in der UniForM WorkBench (UniForM OMS toolkit). Diplomarbeit, FB 3, Universität Bremen, Germany, January 1998.

Designing a Requirements Specification Language for Reactive Systems

(Abstract)

Nancy G. Leveson

MIT, Cambridge, Massachusetts, USA

Email: leveson@cs.washington.edu

Although I have been working in the area of safety analysis for 18 years, I only started designing modeling languages in 1990. Up to that time, I was satisfied with using existing languages. However, in 1990 I got an FAA research grant to build a system requirements specification for a real system, TCAS II (a collision avoidance system). When I tried to use some standard modeling languages, I found they were not adequate. Because we tried to make this exercise as realistic as possible, we could not simply specify the parts of the system that were easily modeled in a particular language, but needed to describe all the required behavior. In addition, our specification was continually reviewed by engineers, pilots, and certification officials, so we were able to determine which features were understandable and which were not. We ended up modifying the syntax (and some semantics) of a commercial language (Statecharts), and even then we were only half-satisfied with the results. The FAA officials and industry committee responsible for TCAS II liked our language, RSML (Requirements State Machine Language), and adopted it for the official TCAS II specification, which we helped them prepare.

In the process of modeling TCAS II, we learned many lessons about required features of a formal modeling language for control systems. Recently, we have taken those lessons learned and designed an entirely new language called SpecTRM-RL (Specification Tools and Requirements Methodology–Requirements Language), which is part of the larger SpecTRM environment for building safety-critical systems. SpecTRM is now a commercial product, with the tools to go into Beta test in a few months.

This talk will describe the lessons we learned during the TCAS specification exercise, how those lessons were incorporated into SpecTRM-RL, and what properties I believe a requirements specification language must have to be useful in a commercial environment. The emphasis will not be on SpecTRM-RL itself, but on some general lessons I have learned about designing usable, commercial requirements specification languages.

Analyzing a Real-Time Program with Z

Jonathan Jacky

Radiation Oncology, Box 356043
University of Washington, Seattle, WA 98195-6043, USA

Email: jon@radonc.washington.edu

Abstract. Real-time behavior of a multi-tasking program running on a pre-emptive priority-based operating system is analyzed. The operating system and a collection of application tasks are modelled in Z. Real-time is represented by an ordinary Z state variable. The model is adapted to a particular application by defining a state machine for each task and associating execution times with each state. The model is analyzed by exhaustive simulation with the SMV model checker. The state transitions described by Z operation schemas are implemented in the SMV programming language. Invariants, preconditions, and postconditions from the Z are translated to formulas in CTL, the SMV specification language. The SMV program is verified by checking these formulas. This detects coding errors in the SMV program and also reveals inconsistencies in the original Z where operation schemas are inconsistent with state invariants. The errors were corrected. Additional CTL formulas describe temporal properties that cannot be expressed directly in Z. The Z model is validated by checking an example SMV program with CTL formulas that confirm scheduling results from rate-monotonic analysis (RMA). Another application that does not satisfy the assumptions of RMA is analyzed, establishing that high-priority tasks cannot indefinitely delay low-priority tasks and real-time deadlines can be met.

1 Introduction

We wrote a control program for a radiation therapy machine, a safety-critical medical application [8, 11]. Our control program includes several concurrent tasks and meets real-time deadlines. It runs on a commercial off-the-shelf (COTS) real-time operating system.

We feel we should be able to answer questions such as these: Will each event be handled within its deadline? Is it possible for one high-priority task to indefinitely delay another low-priority task? In order to answer these questions, it is necessary to model the system as a collection of state transitions, and then analyze the model.

We chose ordinary Z [16] for our modelling notation. Many notations can describe state transitions; we use Z operation schemas for this. Moreover, Z state invariants provide essential information that cannot be expressed directly in notations that can only describe state transitions. The Z tool-kit provides the data types we need: sequences represent priority queues, relations (interpreted as finite state machines) represent the control structure of application tasks. Spivey modelled a multi-tasking operating system in Z [14]. However, he did not model the behavior of a complete system including application tasks, and did not model the passage of time or expiration of real-time deadlines.

We chose SMV (Symbolic Model Verifier) [3, 13], a model checker, for our analysis tool. It performs completely automatic analysis of state transition systems. It can investigate behaviors that emerge when a collection of Z operation schemas works together. To check a Z specification using SMV, one implements the Z in the programming language of the checker. One also provides properties to check expressed in CTL (Computation Tree Logic), the checker's specification language. The checker performs all possible executions of the program, in effect performing an exhaustive simulation of the system. The checker verifies each property or outputs a counterexample (a trace of an execution that violates the property). An earlier experiment with Z and SMV was reported in [10].

Other formal notations provide built-in constructs for representing real-time (several are reviewed in [2]), and there are special methods analyzing real-time scheduling [7, 12]. But sometimes the most general results can be obtained with the simplest notations and tools. Our results (Section 8, Table 2) show that ordinary Z and a general purpose model checker can support detailed analysis of a real-time program, providing quantitative answers to specific questions about performance.

2 Concurrency in Z

Before considering the tasking problem in detail, we represented our application in Z using the *interleaving* style proposed by Evans [4, 5]. All the data used by all tasks appears in the system state. All operations act on the same system state. The precondition of each operation schema is a guard: when the the precondition is satisfied, the operation is *enabled*. It is assumed that the underlying tasking system will provide *fairness*: every enabled operation will occur eventually. *Concurrency* becomes possible when more than one operation is enabled at the same time. In this situation it is assumed that all the enabled operations occur, but in nondeterministic order.

Up to a point, it is easy to design a multi-tasking system in Z using this style. One merely defines the state and the operations required by the application, taking care that the precondition of each operation causes it to become enabled when it is needed (examples based on our project appear in [8]).

However, difficulties can arise when the design is finally implemented on some real operating system. Operations are assigned to tasks which are scheduled by the operating system. It becomes necessary to write the code that is supposed to ensure fairness. For example, one task sets a semaphore to notify another task that new data are available. At this point, the operating system knows nothing of fairness. It deterministically selects the next task to run, based on task priorities assigned by the programmer. If this machinery is not coded carefully, the system might not meet the fairness assumption. For example, high-priority tasks might be able to delay a low-priority task indefinitely.

To ensure that each event is handled in time, we need to solve a real-time scheduling problem: in some worst case situation, the sum of the execution times of several operations must be less than some interval. But what is the worst case situation, and which operations must be counted? Several of our application tasks are not periodic and they interact, so the answers to these questions are not obvious. Schedulability tests such as rate-monotonic analysis are not applicable [7, 12]. A particular scheduling problem from our application is posed in Section 6 and analyzed in Section 8.

3   Operating system and application tasks

We inferred our model of the operating system from the vendor's manual [17]. Tasks may be *ready* (to run) or *pending* (waiting for an event). Each task has a priority; for each priority, there is a queue of ready tasks in first-in, first-out (FIFO) order. The task that runs is at the head of the highest priority queue. A task which becomes ready can *pre-empt* a lower-priority task. A task becomes pending when it calls a function that waits for an event which has not yet occurred, and becomes ready again when the event occurs.

In our application, tasks read from devices attached to the controlled equipment and also from interprocess communication channels connected to other application tasks. Tasks become pending when they attempt to read from a device or an inter-task communication channel where input is not available. Pending tasks can be made to *time out*: they abandon the read operation if input has not appeared when a timeout interval expires. Tasks can also be made to simply wait for a timeout, in order to schedule periodic operations and give low-priority tasks an opportunity to run.

4   Z Model

In this section we present a generic model of a multi-tasking program with real-time deadlines and timeouts running on a pre-emptive priority-based operating system, interacting with an environment that provides events. We call this a *model* not a specification because it represents an already existing system and is intended to support analyses of that system.

We abstract away the application data; our model only represents control structure, tasking, synchronization, and the passage of time. We specialize the model for our application in Section 5. The Z texts excerpted here [9] conform to the *Reference Manual* [16] and were type-checked [15].

4.1   Configuration

Our generic model can be specialized for any particular application by choosing values for the constants declared in this subsection (see Section 5).

An application consists of a set of *tasks*. Each task executes in several *phases*. The sets of phases and tasks are fixed, but their actual contents depend on the application (this is indicated by the three dots in the otherwise formal text below). A task can only wait for an event at the end of a phase. In order to model pre-emption and the passage of time, it is necessary to represent the internal structure of the phases. Each phase occupies a contiguous range of machine addresses or *program counter* (*PC*) values. When a task executes, the program counter advances through a phase. Actually, execution may take different paths through a phase, depending on the values of data which we do not model here. The length of each phase given here can be taken to be the longest (worst case) path through the phase.

$$PC == \mathbb{N}$$

$$TASK ::= t_1 \mid t_2 \mid t_3 \mid \ldots$$

$$PHASE ::= p_1 \mid p_2 \mid p_3 \mid p_4 \mid p_5 \mid \ldots$$

$$
\begin{array}{|l}
phs : PC \nrightarrow PHASE \\
start, end : PHASE \rightarrowtail PC \\
\hline
\forall ph : PHASE \bullet \\
\quad start\, ph < end\, ph \wedge \\
\quad (start\, ph) \ldots (end\, ph) \subseteq \operatorname{dom} phs \wedge \\
\quad phs(\!|(start\, ph) \ldots (end\, ph)|\!) = \{ph\}
\end{array}
$$

The control structure of each task is given by the finite state machine *next* (where states correspond to phases). After the program counter reaches the end of a phase, the task begins executing at the beginning of another phase, determined by which event has occurred. Some phases send *signals* to a *destination* task (this models semaphores and other intertask communication). Input data only remains available during a *hold* time, after this deadline expires the data is lost. A timeout *interval* is associated with each phase that can time out. The *len* function returns the length of any phase (in program counter units, which are the same as clock ticks). Our *len*, *interval*, and *hold* determine the real-time behavior of the application. The ability to express arbitrarily complex timing behavior by defining interacting state machines distinguishes our model from other schedulability tests [7, 12] and makes exhaustive simulation necessary.

$$TIME == \mathbb{N}$$

$$EVENT ::= signal \mid data \mid timeout \mid expire$$

$$
\begin{array}{|l}
dest : PHASE \nrightarrow TASK \\
len : PHASE \longrightarrow TIME \\
hold, interval : PHASE \nrightarrow TIME \\
next : PHASE \longrightarrow EVENT \nrightarrow PHASE \\
\hline
len = (\lambda ph : PHASE \bullet end\, ph - start\, ph) \\
\operatorname{dom} hold = \{ ph : PHASE \mid data \in \operatorname{dom}(next\, ph) \} \\
\operatorname{dom} interval = \{ ph : PHASE \mid timeout \in \operatorname{dom}(next\, ph) \}
\end{array}
$$

Each task has a *priority*. Assignment of phases to tasks is determined by the phase initially executed by each task (a phase may be executed by more than one task).

$$PRIORITY == \mathbb{N}$$

$$
\begin{array}{|l}
init : TASK \longrightarrow PHASE \\
pri : TASK \longrightarrow PRIORITY
\end{array}
$$

4.2   System state

The operating system stores each task's *context*, represented here by its program counter. Tasks that are *ready* to run wait in a *queue*, one for each priority. The other tasks are *pending*, blocked at the end of some phase, waiting for an event. New *events* appear in the environment. They may be handled soon after they occur, or they may remain *unhandled* while the pertinent tasks are ready but unable to run. A key invariant holds that no pending tasks wait for these unhandled events. The *clock* indicates real-time and a *timer* records when timeouts will expire for pending tasks. We also use the clock to model the expiration of real-time *deadlines*.

$$
\begin{array}{|l|}
\hline
\quad RTSys \\
\hline
context : TASK \rightarrow PC \\
ready, pending : \mathbb{P}\, TASK \\
queue : PRIORITY \rightarrow \text{iseq}\, TASK \\
clock : TIME \\
events, unhandled : TASK \leftrightarrow EVENT \\
timer, deadline : TASK \rightarrow\!\!\!\!\rightarrow TIME \\
\hline
\text{ran}\, context \subset \text{dom}\, phs \\
ready = TASK \setminus pending \\
\forall p : PRIORITY \bullet \text{ran}\,(queue\, p) = \{\, t : ready \mid pri\, t = p \,\} \\
\forall t : pending;\ ph : PHASE \mid ph = phs\,(context\, t) \bullet \\
\qquad context\, t = end\, ph \wedge \neg\ (\exists e : \text{dom}\,(next\, ph) \bullet (t,e) \in unhandled) \\
\forall t : \text{dom}\, deadline \bullet (t, data) \in unhandled \\
\forall t : \text{dom}\, timer \bullet t \in pending \wedge timeout \in \text{dom}\,(next\,(phs\,(context\, t))) \\
\forall t : \text{dom}\, timer \bullet clock \le timer\, t \\
\forall t : \text{dom}\, deadline \bullet clock \le deadline\, t \\
\hline
\end{array}
$$

The system is *Running* when there is at least one ready task. The task at the head of the highest priority queue is *current* (running). Redundant state components name the program counter, phase and priority of the current task.

$$
\begin{array}{|l|}
\hline
\quad Running \\
\hline
RTSys \\
pc : PC \\
phase : PHASE \\
current : TASK \\
priority : PRIORITY \\
\hline
ready \ne \varnothing \\
priority = max\,(pri(\!|ready|\!)) \\
current = head(queue\, priority) \\
pc = context\, current \\
phase = phs\, pc \\
\hline
\end{array}
$$

In the initial state each task begins at the start of its first phase. The system is *Waiting* when there are no ready tasks. In the *NoEvent* state there are no new events in the environment. In the *NoTimeout* state no timeouts or deadlines have expired.

$$Init \; \widehat{=} \; [Running \mid context = init \,\fatsemi\, start]$$

$$Waiting \; \widehat{=} \; [RTSys \mid ready = \varnothing]$$

$$NoEvent \; \widehat{=} \; [RTSys \mid events = \varnothing]$$

```
┌─ NoTimeout ─────────────────────────────────────────────
│ RTSys
├─────────
│ ∀t : dom timer • clock < timer t
│ ∀t : dom deadline • clock < deadline t
└─────────────────────────────────────────────────────────
```

4.3   Operations

There are thirteen state transitions, each modelled by a Z operation schema: *Wait*, *Compute*, *Continue*, *Switch*, *Block*, *Input*, *Timeout*, *Deadline*, *Expire*, *Defer*, *Enqueue*, *PreEmpt* and *Wakeup*. We call these *top-level* operations because none are included in the definitions of any other operations. The top-level operations define a state transition system which is complete and deterministic. Their preconditions are mutually exclusive and account for all states permitted by the invariant. Exactly one top-level operation is enabled in every possible state so the system cannot deadlock and we do not have to make any fairness assumptions.

Definitions of many top-level operations include these *building-block* operations: *Run*, *Phase*, *Pend*, *Event*, *Unhandled*, *Ready* and *Resume*. Building-block operations are not mutually exclusive; some top-level operations include more than one building block. A *Run* operation occurs when there is at least one ready task and no events or timeouts occur. *Phase* is the specialization of *Run* that occurs when the program counter reaches the end of the phase. *Pend* is the specialization of *Phase* that occurs when no events are available for the current task. *Event* occurs when an event is available. *Unhandled* is the specialization of *Event* that occurs when the event is not handled. *Ready* is the specialization of *Event* that occurs when a pending task is waiting for the event. *Resume* is the specialization of *Ready* that occurs when the task that handles the event is (or becomes) current.

The top-level *Wait* operation occurs when no tasks are ready and no events occur. *Compute*, *Continue*, *Switch* and *Block* are specializations of *Run*. *Compute* advances the program counter of the current task, but not to the end of the phase. *Continue* is the specialization of *Phase* that occurs when the event needed by the current task has already occurred. *Switch* and *Block* are specializations of *Pend* that occur when another task is ready, or when no more tasks are ready, respectively. *Input*, *Timeout* and *Deadline* model the occurrence of events in the environment. *Expire*, *Defer*, *Enqueue*,

PreEmpt and *Wakeup* are specializations of *Event*. *Expire* models the expiration of a real-time deadline. *Defer* occurs when no pending task is waiting to handle the event. *Enqueue* is the specialization of *Ready* that occurs when the newly ready task does not have a higher priority than the current task. *PreEmpt* and *Wakeup* are specializations of *Resume* that occur when the newly ready task has a higher priority than the current task, or when there is no current task, respectively.

The *Wait* and *Compute* operations are of interest because they model the passage of time by advancing *clock*. They are the only operations that do so. Other operations are considered to take negligible time.

The *Wait* operation occurs when nothing else can happen: no tasks are ready and no events occur. The clock advances, but not past any timeout or deadline. Nothing else changes (indicated by the three dots in the otherwise formal text below).

$$
\begin{array}{|l|}
\hline
\ \textit{Wait} \\
\ \Delta RTSys \\
\hline
\ \textit{Waiting} \\
\ \textit{NoEvent} \\
\ \textit{NoTimeout} \\
\\
\ \textit{clock}' > \textit{clock} \\
\\
\ \textit{context}' = \textit{context} \\
\ \textit{timer}' = \textit{timer} \wedge \textit{deadline}' = \textit{deadline} \wedge \textit{ready}' = \textit{ready} \wedge \ldots \\
\hline
\end{array}
$$

Compute advances the program counter of the current task, but not past the end of the phase. The clock advances also, at the rate of one tick for each program counter step. Nothing else changes. *Compute* includes the *Run* building-block.

$$Run \ \widehat{=}\ [\,\Delta RTSys;\ Running\ |\ NoEvent \wedge NoTimeout\,]$$

$$
\begin{array}{|l|}
\hline
\ \textit{Compute} \\
\ \textit{Run} \\
\ \textit{Running}' \\
\hline
\ pc < \textit{endphase} \\
\\
\ pc < pc' \leq \textit{endphase} \\
\ \textit{clock}' = \textit{clock} + (pc' - pc) \\
\\
\ \{\textit{current}\} \lhd \textit{context}' = \{\textit{current}\} \lhd \textit{context} \\
\ \textit{timer}' = \textit{timer} \wedge \textit{deadline}' = \textit{deadline} \wedge \textit{ready}' = \textit{ready} \wedge \ldots \\
\hline
\end{array}
$$

It is helpful to collect formulas from related operations together. Table 1 is similar to the mode transition tables of the SCR notation [1]. It summarizes the top-level operations *Wait, Compute, Continue, Switch* and *Block*, along with their building-blocks *Run, Phase* and *Pend*. The *Run* building block is included in all the operations that appear below it in the table. Likewise, *Pend* is included in all operations below it. The second column in the table shows that the preconditions are mutually exclusive and cover all states where there are no inputs, events, or timeouts. A second table in [9] summarizes the other operations, whose preconditions cover the rest of the state space. There are 246 lines of Z in the entire model[1]

Z operation	Precondition	Unchanged	Progress postcondition
Wait	*Waiting*, no input *NoEvent* ∧ *NoTimeout*	(All but *clock*)	$clock' > clock$
(Run)	*Running*, no input *NoEvent* ∧ *NoTimeout*		
Compute	$pc < endphase$	(All but *pc,clock*)	$pc' > pc$ $clock' = clock + (pc' - pc)$
Continue *(Phase)*	$pc = endphase$ $(\exists e : unhandled \dots)$	*ready* *pending* *queue* *current* *priority*	$Running'$ $e = (\mu e : unhandled \dots)$ $unhandled' = unhandled \setminus \{(current, e)\}$ $phase' = next\,phase\,e$ $pc' = start\,phase'$ $deadline' = deadline \setminus \{(current, \dots)\}$ $events' = events \cup \{(dest\,phase, signal)\}$
(Pend) *(Phase)*	$pc = endphase$ $\neg\,(\exists e : unhandled \dots)$	*unhandled* *context*	$ready' = ready \setminus \{current\}$ $pending' = pending \cup \{current\}$ $queue'\,priority = tail(queue\,priority)$ $timer' = timer \oplus \{\dots clock + interval\,phase\}$
Switch *(Pend)*	$ready \setminus \{current\} \neq \emptyset$		$Running'$ $priority' = max(pri(\!|ready'|\!))$ $current' = head(queue\,priority')$ $pc' = context\,current$ $current' \neq current$ $priority' \leq priority$
Block *(Pend)*	$ready = \{current\}$		$Waiting'$

Table 1. Task state transitions: *Wait* and *Run* operations

5   An application

We can specialize our model for any application by providing values for the constants declared in Section 4.1. This example is based on our radiation therapy control program [8, 11].

---

[1] Nonblank lines output by running the Fuzz tool -v option [15] on [9].

There are four tasks: a *watchdog*, an interlock scanner *intlk*, and two controller tasks *ctlr*1 and *ctlr*2. The watchdog runs at highest priority, the interlock scanner is next highest, and the two controller tasks are lowest, at the same low priority. The watchdog and interlock tasks each execute just one phase, *synch* and *scan*, respectively. The controller tasks both execute the *poll* and *read* phases, starting with *poll*.

$TASK ::= watchdog \mid intlk \mid ctlr1 \mid ctlr2$

$PHASE ::= synch \mid scan \mid poll \mid read$

$pri = \{watchdog \mapsto 3, intlk \mapsto 2, ctlr1 \mapsto 1, ctlr2 \mapsto 1\}$

$init == \{watchdog \mapsto synch, intlk \mapsto scan, ctlr1 \mapsto poll, ctlr2 \mapsto poll\}$

The *watchdog* task runs periodically: it pends at *synch* for the *timeout* event. The *intlk* task only runs when it is signalled by another task: it pends at *scan* for the *signal* event. The *ctlr*1 and *ctlr*2 tasks each pend at *poll* and *read*. If *data* appears, they execute the *read* phase. If no data appears, a *timeout* event will occur and they execute the *poll* phase again. At the end of its *synch* phase, the watchdog signals the *intlk* task, and at the end of their *read* phase, the two controller tasks signal the *intlk* task.

$next\,synch = \{timeout \mapsto synch\}$

$next\,scan = \{signal \mapsto scan\}$

$next\,poll = next\,read = \{data \mapsto read, timeout \mapsto poll\}$

$dest = \{synch \mapsto intlk, read \mapsto intlk\}$

$interval = \{synch \mapsto period, poll \mapsto sample, read \mapsto sample\}$

The watchdog task is periodic. The two controller tasks are recurrent: they run repeatedly, but not with any fixed period. Each of these tasks will pend for some variable amount of time until data appears (nondeterministically) or the timeout expires. They will become unsynchronized with each other and with the watchdog. The interlock task runs whenever it is signalled by the periodic watchdog or by either recurrent controller task, and the interlock task can pre-empt or delay the controller tasks.

6   A real-time scheduling problem

Real-time deadlines arise in our example (Section 5) because the information associated with a data event will be lost if the controller task does not begin to execute its read phase before the hold time expires. The controller task might miss the deadline because it cannot run while the higher priority watchdog and interlock tasks run. A controller task might also be delayed by the other controller task, which has the same priority.

Is it possible for a deadline to be missed? By applying reasoning similar to that of Liu and Layland [12], we can write some conditions which must be satisfied to prevent missing a deadline. The sum of the lengths of all the phases that might pre-empt a controller task must be less than the hold time. This includes the other controller task; moreover, the interlock task might run twice, signalled by both the watchdog task

and the other controller, so this condition is *len synch + len read + 2 ∗ len scan < hold*.
Also, the period of the watchdog task must be long enough to prevent it from pre-empting a controller task repeatedly: *len read + 2 ∗ len scan < period*. It seems obvious
that these conditions are necessary to prevent missing a deadline, but are they sufficient?
We should check our intuition with some analysis.

7   Analyzing the Z model using SMV

To analyze a Z model using the SMV model checker, one implements the Z in the SMV
programming language and provides properties to check in CTL, the SMV specification
language. The checker verifies each property or produces a counterexample (a trace of
an execution that violates the property).

7.1   Writing the SMV program

The SMV program is, in effect, a simulation of a multi-tasking application running on
a pre-emptive priority-based operating system. The Z texts presented in Section 4, originally considered a model of that system, now serve as the *specification* for the simulation program. The specification could be implemented in any programming language,
but there are two advantages to using SMV: the checker can verify that the program
implements the specification, and the checker performs all possible executions of the
program, achieving exhaustive simulation.

The SMV programming language [13] is much less expressive than Z. Its only data
types are small integers (including booleans and enumerations). Our specification cannot be implemented directly but must be simplified and made concrete.

To simplify, we abandon the generality of the model. We just implement one particular example, the application in Section 5. Now we only need one priority queue
that holds at most two controller tasks. The implementation is two-element array that
indicates whether the two positions in the queue hold *ctlr*1, *ctlr*2, or neither.

To make the model concrete we represent all state variables as integers (including
booleans and enumerations). The value of every variable must be kept small to limit
the size of the state space so exhaustive simulation will be feasible. Program counters,
clock and timers cannot be allowed to grow indefinitely. In our SMV program we reset
the program counter to zero at the beginning of each phase so the program counters
never grow larger than the length of the longest phase. Each phase is only a few units
long, just long enough to admit the possibility of being pre-empted by higher priority
tasks. We have a separate clock for each timeout and deadline, which remains at zero
except when its timeout or deadline is counting up (several might be counting at once).

We defined SMV symbols that implement redundant state components such as
current and predicates such as *Running*. This makes the SMV program shorter and
helps it resemble the Z model more closely, without enlarging the state space.

Most of the implementation is not difficult because our Z model is already expressed
in an operational style: the new value of every state variable after each transition appears
by itself on one side of an equation. These equations are translated to SMV assignments.
For each variable there is an SMV case statement. For each Z operation where that

variable changes value, there is a case branch that assigns the new value, guarded by that operation's precondition.

The checker itself provides input to our SMV program nondeterministically. When the *ctlr*1 or *ctlr*2 task is pending, the checker may (or may not) provide a *data* event to that task at each execution step. The checker explores all possible execution sequences: the one where the *data* event occurs on the first execution step after *ctlr*1 pends at *poll*, the one where the *data* event occurs on the second execution step, the one where the *data* event never occurs so the *timeout* event occurs instead, etc. As a result, the checker considers all possible interleavings of the tasks.

Our SMV program [9] (excluding CTL formulas that express properties to be checked) is 423 (nonblank, noncomment) lines long. Figure 1 shows excerpts that deal with *context watchdog*, *timer watchdog*, and *clock* (compare to the *Wait*, *Run* and *Compute* schemas in Section 4.3). We used the smallest values for lengths of phases and intervals that still reveal the properties of interest (Section 8). With these values, SMV reports that the program has 30062 reachable states in a space of more than 10^{23} states (2^{78}, or 78 state bits). SMV uses a data structure called a *binary decision diagram* (BDD) to represent the transition relation defined by a program [3]. It encodes the next-state relation implicitly defined by all thirteen top-level operation schemas described in Section 4.3. SMV reports that the BDD for our program contains 24594 nodes.

The checker's performance depends on the ordering of variable declarations in the program and on several command line parameters such as cache size [13]. We adjusted these by trial and error to achieve acceptable performance (on a Hewlett-Packard J282 workstation with a PA8000 processor running at 180 MHz). Most CTL formulas can be verified in a few minutes, using about ten megabytes of memory.

7.2 Refinement

The development of the SMV program can be easily (but tediously) formalized as a *refinement*. Refinement is a method for establishing formally that one (concrete) specification is an implementation of another (more abstract) specification. Here we use refinement to show how expressions in SMV and formulas in CTL can be identified with expressions and predicates in Z.

The concrete specification (below) closely resembles our SMV program: the set of *ready* tasks is represented by an array of booleans *cready*, the tasks themselves are the array indices *CTASK*1, and the priority queue for the two controller tasks is the two-element array *cqueue*, where the first element is the head of the queue. The invariant shows how the current task is selected, based on the priorities of the ready tasks. The corresponding predicates in *Running* are *priority* = *max*(*pri*(|*ready*|)) and *current* = *head*(*queue priority*).

$BOOLEAN == \{0,1\}$

$cnone == 0; cctlr1 == 1; cctlr2 == 2; cwatchdog == 3; cintlk == 4$

$CTASK == \{cnone, cctlr1, cctlr2, cwatchdog, cintlk\};$

$CTASK1 == CTASK \setminus \{cnone\}$

```
MODULE main

VAR
    context: array 1 .. 4 of {0,1,2,3,4}; -- program counter indexed by task
    tclock: {0,1,2,3,4,5,6,7};    -- clock for watchdog timer
    timer: boolean;               -- true if watchdog timer counting

DEFINE
    watchdog := 3;                -- index into context array
    lsynch := 1;                  -- watchdog task, len synch in the Z

    Running :=  ready[watchdog] | ready[intlk] | ready[ctlr1] | ready[ctlr2];
    preRun := Running & NoInput & NoEvent & NoTimeout;
    preWait := Waiting & NoInput & NoEvent & NoTimeout;
    preCompute := preRun & InPhase;

ASSIGN
    init(context[watchdog]) := 0;  -- program counter at start of phase
    init(timer) := 0;              -- watchdog timer is not counting
    init(tclock) := 0;             -- clock is reset

    next(context[watchdog]) := case
         preCompute & current = watchdog
            & context[watchdog] < lsynch: context[watchdog]+1; -- Compute
         preResumeWD: 0;                                        -- Resume
         1: context[watchdog];                                 -- else no change
    esac;

    next(tclock) := case
         preWait & timer & tclock < period: tclock + 1;    -- Wait, tick
         preCompute & timer & tclock < period: tclock + 1; -- Compute, tick
         preTimeoutWD: 0;                                  -- Timeout, reset
         1: tclock;                                        -- else no change
    esac;

    next(timer) := case
         prePend & current = watchdog: 1;                 -- (Pend), set
         preTimeoutWD: 0;                                 -- Timeout, reset
         1: timer;                                        -- else no change
    esac;
```

Fig. 1. Excerpts from SMV program

```
┌─ CRTSys ─────────────────────────────────────────────────
│ ccurrent : CTASK
│ cready : CTASK1 ⟶ BOOLEAN
│ cqueue : {1,2} ⟶ {none, cctlr1, cctlr2}
│ ...
├──────────────────────────────────────────────────────────
│ ccurrent = cwatchdog ⟺ cready cwatchdog = 1
│ ccurrent = cintlk ⟺ cready cwatchdog = 0 ∧ cready cintlk = 1
│ ccurrent = cqueue 1 ⟺ cready cwatchdog = 0 ∧ cready cintlk = 0
│ ...
└──────────────────────────────────────────────────────────
```

Now we can relate the two specifications. The function *abs* associates each concrete task with its abstract counterpart, and the abstraction schema *Abs* relates the concrete state *CRTSys* to the abstract state defined in *RTSys* and *Running*.

$$abs == \{cctlr1 \mapsto ctlr1, cctlr2 \mapsto ctlr2, cwatchdog \mapsto watchdog, cintlk \mapsto intlk\}$$

```
┌─ Abs ────────────────────────────────────────────────────
│ RTSys
│ Running
│ CRTSys
├──────────────────────────────────────────────────────────
│ ccurrent ≠ cnone ⟹ current = abs ccurrent
│ ready = {t : CTASK1 | cready t = 1 • abs t}
│
│ dom queue = {1,2,3}
│ queue 1 = (cqueue ↾ CTASK1) ⨾ abs
│ queue 2 = if cready cintlk = 1 then ⟨intlk⟩ else ⟨⟩
│ queue 3 = if cready cwatchdog = 1 then ⟨watchdog⟩ else ⟨⟩
│ ...
└──────────────────────────────────────────────────────────
```

We can define a concrete operation for each abstract operation. This fragment of the concrete *CPend* operation shows what happens when the controller task at the head of the priority queue becomes *pending*: the next array element advances to the head of the queue.

```
┌─ CPend ──────────────────────────────────────────────────
│ ΔCRTSys
├──────────────────────────────────────────────────────────
│ (ccurrent ∉ {cctlr1, cctlr2} ∧ cqueue' = cqueue) ∨
│ (ccurrent ∈ {cctlr1, cctlr2} ∧ cqueue' 1 = cqueue 2 ∧ cqueue' 2 = cnone)
│ ...
└──────────────────────────────────────────────────────────
```

The corresponding predicate in the abstract *Pend* operation is simply $queue'\,priority = tail(queue\,priority)$. The refinement laws in [16] can be used to check that *CPend* is a correct implementation of *Pend*, given the relations defined by *Abs*.

7.3   Analyzing the SMV program with CTL

Properties to check are expressed in CTL (Computation Tree Logic) [3]. CTL formulas are about SMV program *states* and *paths* (sequences of states that occur when the SMV program executes). CTL state formulas are like Z predicates. Path formulas provide temporal operators: if p is a state formula, G p means that condition p is true in all states on a path. F p means that p eventually becomes true. X p means that p is true in the next state. CTL also provides quantifiers: A (all paths) and E (some paths).

AG p expresses *safety*: p is invariant (is true on all paths, in all states). AG (*pre* -> AX *post*) means that if *pre* is true in a state, then *post* is true in the next state. These two CTL formulas correspond to predicates in Z state schemas and operation schemas, respectively. Other CTL formulas can express behaviors that emerge when sequences of operations are executed. EF p expresses *liveness*: p can occur, p is reachable (is true on some paths, eventually). AG AF p expresses that condition p is cyclic or recurrent (on all paths p is always true eventually, p occurs "infinitely often"). There are no built-in constructs corresponding to path formulas in ordinary Z, they can only be expressed after explicitly defining a next-state relation and sequences of states [6].

7.4   Verifying the SMV program

We verified our SMV program by the method of Atlee and Gannon [1]. For each Z operation, we wrote two kinds of CTL formulas: EF *pre* checks that the operation occurs and AG (*pre* -> AX *post*) checks that it has the intended effect. It is necessary to check both formulas; if the EF liveness property is false, the AG correctness property will be vacuously true.

These CTL formulas are a machine-checkable formal specification for the SMV program. At first the checker found counterexamples to several formulas, which we traced to trivial coding errors. After we corrected the errors, all formulas were verified. This is a machine-checked proof that the SMV program correctly implements its CTL specification. The close resemblance between the CTL formulas and their Z counterparts, supported by the refinement arguments of Section 7.2, suggest that the program correctly implements the Z specification as well.

We wrote 104 CTL formulas to verify the SMV program. The checker verified them in 24 minutes, using 10 megabytes.

7.5   Checking the Z specification

The preceding subsections establish that our SMV program is a correct implementation of the operation schemas in the Z specification. Therefore properties which are false in our program are not universally true in our specification. This means that checking our program can reveal errors in the Z. In particular, if a CTL property which is a translation of a (putative) Z invariant is not invariant in our SMV program, then the Z specification is inconsistent.

We translated the invariants of the *RTSys* and *Running* state schemas into CTL AG *inv* formulas. At first the checker found counterexamples to several formulas, revealing that the *RTSys* invariants were too strong[2]. After revising (weakening) the invariants to

---

[2] A reviewer of an early version of this paper also detected some of these errors.

those shown in Section 4.2, the checker verified all 34 of these formulas in one minute, using 9 megabytes.

Our SMV program is only one example implementation of our Z specification, so properties which are true in this program may not be universally true of our specification. There could be additional errors in our corrected Z specification which are not revealed by this example.

7.6 Validating the Z specification

We must show that the Z specification actually expresses the properties we intend. Checking the formula ! (EF *p*) causes the checker to generate a counterexample showing the execution sequence from the initial state to a state that satisfies *p* (see Table 2). This is a way of "running" the SMV program. Used in this way, the SMV program serves as a kind of animation of the Z specification. The counterexamples confirm that the intended behaviors occur.

If the Z specification is valid, our implementation should be able to reproduce examples of well-known results from real-time scheduling theory. Rate-monotonic analysis (RMA) applies in the special case where each task has a single phase, tasks do not signal each other, events occur on a strictly periodic schedule, and the deadline equals the period [7, 12]. A simple example with two tasks appears in [12]. We represented this example, and revised our SMV program to deliver events on a periodic schedule instead of nondeterministically. The program reproduced the results shown in Figures 2a, 2b, and 2c in [12] and discussed in the accompanying text.

8 Analyzing a real-time scheduling problem

In our application (Section 5), high-priority tasks must not be able to delay low-priority tasks indefinitely. All four tasks should be recurrent: each should execute repeatedly, though not necessarily with a fixed period. This property cannot be expressed directly in Z because each cycle involves the sequential execution of several operations. We wrote four CTL formulas to check recurrence: AG AF *current* = *watchdog* etc. The checker verified all four in less than two minutes, using 9 megabytes.

The application will miss a real-time deadline if a data event remains unhandled when its deadline expires. We checked ! (EF *p*) formulas which express that this condition is unreachable. To check this, it is necessary to assign values to the lengths of all the phases and intervals. We made the phases as short as possible, while still allowing for pre-emption: *len synch* = 1 and *len scan* = *len read* = *len poll* = 2. By trial and error, we found *period* = 10 (the watchdog task period) and *hold* = 12 (the data hold time) were the shortest intervals where the deadlines could always be met (the CTL formula was verified). Reducing the value of *period* or *hold* by one makes it possible for the deadline to be missed[3].

When the data hold time is reduced to 11, the checker takes two minutes and 10 megabytes to generate a counterexample of 57 states that shows how the deadline is

---

[3] We kept *sample* = 5 (the controller task read timeout period).

missed (Table 2): The read timeout for the *ctlr2* task expires (state 28), but then a data event occurs anyway (state 30). After *ctlr2* handles the timeout (state 40), it handles the data event also (state 43), and consequently signals the *intlk* task to run as well (state 47). All this delays *ctrl1* so it misses its deadline (state 57). We did not anticipate that a data event would appear after a read timeout. In fact this is unlikely, but the checker shows the consequences of the SMV program we actually wrote, not what we expected.

St.	Clk	Operation	Task	Comment
1		(*Init*)	*watchdog*	Initial state
⋮	⋮	⋮	⋮	⋮
28		*Timeout*	*intlk*	*timeout* event for *ctlr2* while *intlk* is current
29		*Enqueue*		*timeout* event queued for *ctlr2*
30		*Input*		*data* event for *ctlr2*
31		*Enqueue*		*data* event queued for *ctlr2*
32		*Switch*	*ctlr*1	*intlk* pends, *ctlr*1 becomes current
33		*Switch*	*ctlr*2	*ctlr*1 pends, *ctlr*2 becomes current
34		*PreEmpt*	*intlk*	*intlk* pre-empts *ctlr*2, handles signal from *ctlr*1
35		*Input*		*data* event for *ctlr*1
36	0	*Enqueue*		*data* event queued for *ctlr*1
37	1	*Compute*		*intlk* computes in *scan* phase
38	2	*Compute*		*intlk* computes in *scan* phase
39	2	*Switch*	*ctlr*2	*intlk* pends, *ctrl*2 becomes current
40	2	*Continue*		*ctrl*2 handles *timeout* event
41	3	*Compute*		*ctlr*2 computes in *poll* phase
42	4	*Compute*		*ctlr*2 computes in *poll* phase
43	4	*Continue*		*ctrl*2 handles *data* event
44	5	*Compute*		*ctlr*2 computes in *read* phase
45	6	*Compute*		*ctlr*2 computes in *read* phase
46	6	*Switch*	*ctlr*1	*ctlr*2 pends, *ctlr*1 becomes current
47	6	*PreEmpt*	*intlk*	*intlk* pre-empts *ctlr*1, handles signal from *ctlr*2
48	7	*Compute*		*intlk* computes in *scan* phase
49	8	*Compute*		*intlk* computes in *scan* phase
50	8	*Timeout*		*timeout* event for *watchdog*
51	8	*PreEmpt*	*watchdog*	*watchdog* pre-empts *intlk*, handles timeout
52	9	*Compute*		*watchdog* computes in *synch* phase
53	9	*Switch*	*intlk*	*watchdog* pends, *intlk* becomes current
54	9	*Defer*		*intlk* defers handling signal from *watchdog*
55	9	*Continue*		*intlk* handles signal from *watchdog*
56	10	*Compute*		*intlk* computes in *scan* phase
57	11	*Compute*		*ctlr*1 misses deadline

Table 2. Counterexample showing missed deadline

9 Conclusion

Ordinary Z and a general purpose model checker can support detailed analyses of a real-time program, providing quantitative answers to specific questions about performance. Exhaustive simulation with a model checker can be a practical alternative when other schedulability tests are not applicable. Our simulations used modest computing resources (two minutes, ten megabytes). Much larger simulations appear feasible.

The SMV programming language is so low-level that a formal specification at the level of Z operation schemas is a practical necessity. It would not be reasonable to write an SMV program by intuition and debug it by trial and error. Our program was automatically verified by checking CTL formulas based on the Z. The verification quickly revealed coding errors that could have been quite difficult to detect and correct.

SMV can be quite useful for checking and exploring Z specifications. It can investigate behaviors that emerge when sequences of operations are executed. By providing exhaustive simulation and counterexample generation, it combines some of the advantages of theorem proving and animation.

References

1. Joanne M. Atlee and John Gannon.   State-based model checking of event-driven system requirements. *IEEE Transactions on Software Engineering*, 19(1):24–40, January 1993.
2. Zhou Chaochen, C. A. R. Hoare, and Anders P. Ravn. A calculus of durations. *Information Processing Letters*, 40:269–276, 1991.
3. E. Clarke, O. Grumberg, and D. Long. Verification tools for finite-state concurrent systems. In J. W. de Bakker, W.-P. de Roever, and G. Rozenberg, editors, *A Decade of Concurrency*, pages 124–175. Lecture Notes in Computer Science, volume 803, Springer-Verlag, 1993.
4. Andy S. Evans. Specifying and verifying concurrent systems using Z. In Maurice Naftalin, Tim Denvir, and Miquel Bertran, editors, *FME '94: Industrial Benefit of Formal Methods*, pages 366–380. Lecture Notes in Computer Science, volume 873, Springer-Verlag, 1994.
5. Andy S. Evans. Visualizing concurrent Z specifications. In J. P. Bowen and J. A. Hall, editors, *Z User Workshop, Cambridge 1994*, Workshops in Computing, pages 269–281. Springer-Verlag, 1994.
6. Andy S. Evans. An improved recipe for specifying reactive systems in Z. In Jonathan P. Bowen, Michael G. Hinchey, and David Till, editors, *ZUM '97: The Z Formal Specification Notation*, pages 275–294. Lecture Notes in Computer Science, volume 1212, Springer-Verlag, 1997.
7. C. J. Fidge. Real-time schedulability tests for preemptive multitasking. *Real-Time Systems*, 14(1):61–93, 1998.
8. Jonathan Jacky. *The Way of Z: Practical Programming with Formal Methods*. Cambridge University Press, 1997.
9. Jonathan Jacky. Analyzing a real-time program with Z and SMV. Technical Report 98-06-01, Department of Radiation Oncology, University of Washington, Box 356043, Seattle, Washington 98195-6043, USA, June 1998.
10. Jonathan Jacky and Michael Patrick. Modelling, checking, and implementing a control program for a radiation therapy machine. In Rance Cleaveland and Daniel Jackson, editors, *AAS '97: Proc. 1st ACM SIGPLAN Workshop on Automated Analysis of Software*, pages 25–32, 1997.

11. Jonathan Jacky, Jonathan Unger, Michael Patrick, David Reid, and Ruedi Risler. Experience with Z developing a control program for a radiation therapy machine. In Jonathan P. Bowen, Michael G. Hinchey, and David Till, editors, *ZUM '97: The Z Formal Specification Notation*, pages 317–328. Lecture Notes in Computer Science, volume 1212, Springer-Verlag, 1997.

12. C. L. Liu and James W. Layland. Scheduling algorithms for multiprogramming in a hard-real-time environment. *Journal of the Association for Computing Machinery*, 20(1):46–61, 1973.

13. K. L. McMillan. The SMV system. Carnegie-Mellon University, USA, 2 February 1992. (Draft.)

14. J. M. Spivey. Specifying a real-time kernel. *IEEE Software*, 7(5):21–28, September 1990.

15. J. M. Spivey. *The ƒUZZ Manual*. Computing Science Consultancy, UK, January 1991. Second Printing.

16. J. M. Spivey. *The Z Notation: A Reference Manual*. Prentice Hall International Series in Computer Science, 2nd edition, 1992.

17. Wind River Systems, Inc., Alameda, California, USA. *VxWorks Programmer's Guide 5.3.1*, 1997.

Recursive Definitions in Z

R.D. Arthan

Lemma 1 Ltd.
2nd Floor, 31A Chain St., Reading, Berkshire, RG10 9NX, UK

Email: rda@lemma-one.com

Abstract. This paper considers some issues in the theory and practice of defining functions over recursive data types in Z. Principles justifying such definitions are formulated. Z free types are contrasted with the free algebras of universal algebra: the notions turn out to be related but not isomorphic.

1 Introduction

The consistency of a Z specification is a matter of some practical importance. Effort expended in reasoning about an inconsistent specification is wasted and implementation of an inconsistent specification is either impossible or trivial depending on one's point of view. The most widely used definitions of Z [8, 9] do consider the consistency of some Z paragraph forms, most notably the free type paragraph. This topic is further explored in [1, 7, 11].

In this paper, we consider approaches to proving the consistency of a particular class of axiomatic description, namely, axiomatic descriptions that define functions on a (typically recursive) free type. We consider principles allowing us to verify the consistency of such definitions. These principles are not themselves proposed for inclusion in the language definition, since, as we shall see, they are logical consequences of the usual axioms for a free type. Instead we present them to serve as rules of thumb for authors and readers of specifications and as guidelines for implementors of tools.

Z is founded on set theory. It is instructive to compare the Z approach to recursive definitions with what one might find in notations with different foundations. In this paper, we compare the Z approach with an approach based on universal algebra. It turns out that there is a broad overlap, but that there also non-trivial differences mainly arising from the extra expressiveness that set theory affords.

We make free use of the Z toolkit. Techniques for informal reasoning about the toolkit are discussed in several books, e.g., [13]; progress on one approach to automated proof for the Z toolkit is reported in [3].

The rest of this paper is structured as follows: Section 2 discusses the practical issues; Section 3 considers general principles for definition by recursion; Section 4 contrasts the theory for Z with concepts from universal algebra; finally, Section 5 gives some concluding remarks.

2   Recursive Definitions in Practice

The following free type definition will provide a running example throughout this section. BINTREE comprises binary trees with integer labels at each node and leaf. The definition may readily be seen to be consistent using the methods of [1, 9]. Some example members of BINTREE are shown in Figure 1.

$$\text{BINTREE} ::= \text{Leaf}\langle\!\langle \mathbb{Z} \rangle\!\rangle \mid \text{Node}\langle\!\langle \mathbb{Z} \times \text{BINTREE} \times \text{BINTREE} \rangle\!\rangle$$

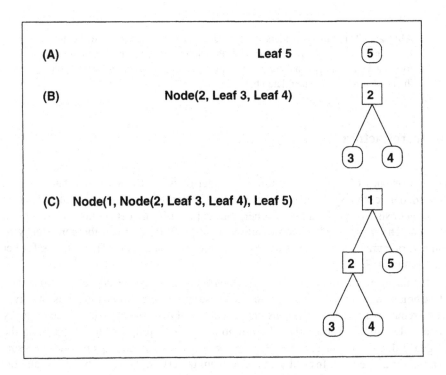

Fig. 1. Some Members of BINTREE

2.1   Definition by Cases

We will be concerned with the consistency of functions defined using axiomatic descriptions. The functions will have for their domain our sample free type BINTREE. Our notion of consistency is straightforward: an axiomatic description defining a function f is consistent if we can prove, without using the axiomatic description, that there exists a function g satisfying the same constraints that the axiomatic description places on f. We will sometimes call such a g a witness to the consistency of f. Approaches to verifying the consistency of Z specifications are discussed in more detail in earlier work of the present author [1] and in a forthcoming paper by Sam Valentine [12]

As a first example of a function defined on the set BINTREE, consider the following axiomatic description of a function intended to return the label at the root of a tree.

$$
\begin{array}{|l}
\text{labelOf} : \text{BINTREE} \to \mathbb{Z} \\
\hline
\forall i : \mathbb{Z} \bullet \text{labelOf}(\text{Leaf}\, i) = i \\
\forall i : \mathbb{Z};\ t_1, t_2 : \text{BINTREE} \bullet \text{labelOf}(\text{Node}(i, t_1, t_2)) = i
\end{array}
$$

We may ask whether this axiomatic description is consistent, i.e., whether a function enjoying the properties we require of labelOf actually exists. Well, by the usual axioms that characterise a free type[1], any tree t in BINTREE is either Leaf i for some i or Node(i, t_1, t_2) for some i, t_1 and t_2. Moreover, Leaf and Node are injections and their ranges are disjoint, so that there is exactly one i for which t has one or other of these forms. Taking labelOf t to be this i gives the desired function. More formally, with each of the constructor functions, we may associate a corresponding destructor function defined by:

$$
\text{destLeaf} == \text{Leaf}^{-1}
$$
$$
\text{destNode} == \text{Node}^{-1}
$$

We may then verify that these destructor functions are indeed functions and behave exactly as if they had been specified by the following axiomatic description:

$$
\begin{array}{|l}
\text{destLeaf} : \text{ran Leaf} \to \mathbb{Z} \\
\text{destNode} : \text{ran Node} \to (\mathbb{Z} \times \text{BINTREE} \times \text{BINTREE}) \\
\hline
\forall i : \mathbb{Z} \bullet \text{destLeaf}(\text{Leaf}\, i) = i \\
\forall i : \mathbb{Z};\ t_1, t_2 : \text{BINTREE} \bullet \text{destNode}(\text{Node}(i, t_1, t_2)) = (i, t_1, t_2)
\end{array}
$$

A witness to the existence of our function labelOf can then be defined explicitly by the formula:

$$
\text{destLeaf} \cup (\text{destNode} \, {}^{\circ}_{\circ} \, (\lambda i : \mathbb{Z};\ t_1, t_2 : \text{BINTREE} \bullet i))
$$

The use of destructor functions will enable us to justify most definitions of functions that pick apart the top level structure of an element of a free type. This pattern of definition may be called definition by cases; the principle of definition by cases, PDC, is a special case of the principle of definition by induction that we will now investigate.

2.2   Definition by Induction

The method of definition by cases is useful, but only gives us access to the top-level structure of an element of a free type. But we may need to dig deeper, e.g., to define a

---

[1] For a brief example and discussion of these axioms, see the proof of theorem 1 below. More leisurely expositions may be found in [1, 9].

function to count the non-leaf nodes in a tree. Intuitively, the count is 0 for a leaf, and, for a non-leaf node, the count is 1 more than the sum of the counts for the children. This suggests the following axiomatic description of our function nodeCount:

$$\text{nodeCount} : \text{BINTREE} \to \mathbb{N}$$

$$\forall i : \mathbb{Z} \bullet \text{nodeCount}(\text{Leaf}\,i) = 0$$
$$\forall i : \mathbb{Z};\ t_1, t_2 : \text{BINTREE}\bullet$$
$$\quad \text{nodeCount}(\text{Node}(i, t_1, t_2)) = 1 + \text{nodeCount}\,t_1 + \text{nodeCount}\,t_2$$

This definition is inductive, that is to say, the right-hand sides of the equations for nodeCount themselves involve uses of nodeCount. If we are given a concrete member of the free type, e.g., the tree C depicted in Figure 1, then we can use the two equations in the axiomatic description as rewrite rules to evaluate nodeCount C:

$$\begin{aligned}
\text{nodeCount}\,C &= \text{nodeCount}(\text{Node}(1, \text{Node}(2, \text{Leaf}\,3, \text{Leaf}\,4), \text{Leaf}\,5)) \\
&= 1 + \text{nodeCount}(\text{Node}(2, \text{Leaf}\,3, \text{Leaf}\,4) + \text{nodeCount}(\text{Leaf}\,5) \\
&= 1 + (1 + \text{nodeCount}(\text{Leaf}\,3) + \text{nodeCount}(\text{Leaf}\,4)) + 0 \\
&= 1 + (1 + 0 + 0) + 0 \\
&= 2
\end{aligned}$$

However, any attempt to use the second equation as a rewrite rule will fail, in general, to eliminate nodeCount from an expression of the form nodeCount u if u involves variables: e.g., without knowing the value of x, we cannot simplify nodeCount x.

How are we to know that our axiomatic description of nodeCount is consistent? Appealing to a general theorem we shall discuss later, we can use the following principle of definition by induction (PDI) for the free type BINTREE:

$$[Y] \vdash \forall\ e_1 : \mathbb{Z} \to Y;\ e_2 : (\mathbb{Z} \times Y \times Y) \to Y \bullet$$
$$\exists_1\ h : \text{BINTREE} \to Y \bullet$$
$$(\forall i : \mathbb{Z} \bullet h(\text{Leaf}\,i) = e_1\,i)$$
$$\wedge\ (\forall i : \mathbb{Z};\ t_1, t_2 : \text{BINTREE}\bullet h(\text{Node}\,(i, t_1, t_2)) = e_2(i, h\,t_1, h\,t_2)$$

The notation here means that the theorem PDI is generic in Y, i.e., we may instantiate Y to any set of any type. The theorem is concerned with the problem of defining a function $h : \text{BINTREE} \to Y$ satisfying the given equations. The functions e_1 and e_2 are the data of the problem: e_1 specifies how h is to behave on leaves; e_2 specifies how the results of applying h to the children of a node are to be combined to give the value of h at that node. The theorem asserts that every such problem has a unique solution.

For our node-counting function, we use $Y = \mathbb{N}$ and take the data e_1 and e_2 to be:

$$e_1 = (\lambda i : \mathbb{Z} \bullet 0)$$
$$e_2 = (\lambda i : \mathbb{Z};\ t_1, t_2 : \mathbb{N}\bullet 1 + t_1 + t_2)$$

Applying PDI, we can conclude that there exists a function $h : \mathsf{BINTREE} \to \mathbb{N}$ such that, for all integers, i, and trees, t_1 and t_2 the following equations hold:

$$h(\mathsf{Leaf}\,i) = e_1\,i = 0$$
$$h(\mathsf{Node}(i,t_1,t_2)) = e_2(i, h\,t_1, h\,t_2) = 1 + h\,t_1 + h\,t_2$$

These are precisely our requirements for nodeCount so this h supplies a witness to the consistency of our definition of nodeCount. As an exercise, the reader may wish to find the data functions e_1 and e_2 that give the height of a tree:

$\mathsf{height} : \mathsf{BINTREE} \to \mathbb{N}$

$\forall i : \mathbb{Z} \bullet \mathsf{height}(\mathsf{Leaf}\,i) = 0$

$\forall i : \mathbb{Z};\ t_1, t_2 : \mathsf{BINTREE} \bullet$

$\quad \mathsf{height}(\mathsf{Node}(i, t_1, t_2)) = 1 + max(\mathsf{height}\,t_1, \mathsf{height}\,t_2)$

2.3   Definition by Recursion

The principle of definition by induction, PDI is quite powerful, but has a limitation: in the function e_2, we can refer to the values of h on the children of a node, but we can't refer to the children themselves. As an example, assume we want a function which computes the sum over all non-leaf nodes in a tree of the node-heights weighted by the node-labels:

$\mathsf{heightSum} : \mathsf{BINTREE} \to \mathbb{Z}$

$\forall i : \mathbb{Z} \bullet \mathsf{heightSum}(\mathsf{Leaf}\,i) = 0$

$\forall i : \mathbb{Z};\ t_1, t_2 : \mathsf{BINTREE} \bullet$

$\quad \mathsf{heightSum}(\mathsf{Node}(i, t_1, t_2)) =$

$\quad i * \mathsf{height}(\mathsf{Node}(i, t_1, t_2)) + \mathsf{heightSum}\,t_1 + \mathsf{heightSum}\,t_2$

Here, since the function e_2 in PDI has no access to the values of the subtrees t_1 and t_2, PDI cannot be applied directly. Instead, we may appeal to the following principle of definition by recursion, PDR, which generalises PDI by making these subtrees available to the relevant data function in addition to the values of the recursive calls:

$$[Y] \vdash \forall\ d_1 : \mathbb{Z} \to Y;\ d_2 : \mathsf{BINTREE} \to (\mathbb{Z} \times Y \times Y) \to Y \bullet$$
$$\exists_1\ h : \mathsf{BINTREE} \to Y \bullet$$
$$(\forall i : \mathbb{Z} \bullet h(\mathsf{Leaf}\,i) = d_1\,i)$$
$$\wedge\ (\forall i : \mathbb{Z};\ t_1, t_2 : \mathsf{BINTREE} \bullet$$
$$h(\mathsf{Node}\,(i, t_1, t_2)) = d_2(\mathsf{Node}(i, t_1, t_2))(i, h\,t_1, h\,t_2))$$

Note that PDI is, essentially, the special case of PDR in which the function d_2 makes no use of its first argument; thus PDR implies PDI. As we shall see in the proof of theorem 1 one can also derive PDR from PDI, so the two principles are equivalent.

In order to justify our definition of heightSum, let us use PDR, with $Y = \mathbb{Z}$, and with d_1 and d_2 given by:

$$d_1 = (\lambda i : \mathbb{Z} \bullet 0)$$
$$d_2 = (\lambda b : \text{BINTREE} \bullet \lambda i : \mathbb{Z}; t_1, t_2 : \mathbb{N} \bullet i * \text{height } b + t_1 + t_2)$$

With this data, PDR delivers us a function h that is just what we need to justify the consistency of our axiomatic description of heightSum.

3   Theoretical Issues

3.1   PDR: The General Case

In Section 2, we have made several appeals to a general principle of definition by recursion (PDR). We now describe this principle in the general case. As the reader will see, the general principle is rather lengthy to describe.

So, let us consider a general free type definition. The free type definition has m nullary constructors, $\alpha_1, \ldots \alpha_m$ and n non-nullary constructors $\beta_1, \ldots \beta_n$. For simplicity, we assume that the nullary constructors are given first. Since the order of the branches in a free type is immaterial, this gives no real loss of generality. Our general free type definition thus has the form:

$$\mathcal{T} ::= \alpha_1 \mid \ldots \mid \alpha_m \mid \beta_1 \langle\!\langle E_1 \rangle\!\rangle \mid \ldots \mid \beta_n \langle\!\langle E_n \rangle\!\rangle$$

The type rules for Z require that each expression E_i be a set of elements of some type τ_i say. Here the type τ_i is some expression built up from ground types (and $\mathcal{T}$) using Cartesian product, power sets and schema type constructions. Since the elements of each set E_i have type τ_i, the soundness of the Z type system ensures that $E_i \in \mathbb{P}\tau_i$.

For example, consider the following type of trees, with leaves either empty or labelled with a sequence of binary trees (these trees being represented using the free type BINTREE discussed in Section 2), and with branches constructed using a schema type:

$$EG ::= \text{Empty} \mid \text{TreeList}\langle\!\langle \text{seq BINTREE} \rangle\!\rangle \mid \text{EGNode}\langle\!\langle [a, b : EG] \rangle\!\rangle$$

Remembering that sequences are partial functions on the integers and that functions are just sets of pairs, we see that in this example our metavariables, $\mathcal{T}$, m, n, etc., take the values shown in table 1.

Returning to the general case, PDR will be a theorem asserting the existence of solutions to problems of a certain kind. The theorem will have a generic parameter Y and will be constructed from the following components:

Data: the data comprise m elements of Y and n two-argument functions. The second argument of each function h_i ranges over the set, $\tau_i[Y/\mathcal{T}]$ obtained by substituting Y for each occurrence of $\mathcal{T}$ in the type τ_i:

$\mathcal{T}$	EG
m	1
n	2
α_1	Empty
β_1	TreeList
E_1	seq BINTREE
β_2	EGNode
E_2	$[a, b : \text{EG}]$
τ_1	$\mathbb{P}(\mathbb{Z} \times \text{BINTREE})$
τ_2	$[a, b : \text{EG}]$

Table 1. Metanotation for the Example

$$c_1, \ldots, c_m : Y$$
$$d_1 : \mathcal{T} \to \tau_1[Y/\mathcal{T}] \to Y$$
$$\vdots$$
$$d_n : \mathcal{T} \to \tau_n[Y/\mathcal{T}] \to Y$$

Solution: the solution is a function h:

$$h : \mathcal{T} \to Y$$

Condition: the condition comprises $m+n$ equations. The first m of these correspond to the data elements $c_1, \ldots c_m$ and are easy to state:

$$h\alpha_1 = c_1$$
$$\vdots$$
$$h\alpha_m = c_m$$

To state the remaining n equations, we need to represent the notion of a "recursive call" of the function h. To do this we need to use the structure of the types $\tau_1, \ldots \tau_n$. We think of an element of the type τ as an expression tree formed using tuples, bindings and set constructions. Some leaves of this expression tree correspond to recursive appearances of $\mathcal{T}$ in τ and are labelled with elements of $\mathcal{T}$. Other leaves of the expression tree corresponding to ground types, G, say are labelled with elements of G. We need to describe the function from τ to $\tau[Y/\mathcal{T}]$ that works by replacing each leaf label $t \in \mathcal{T}$ by ht and leaving other leaf labels as they are. The following function h_τ defined by induction over the structure of τ does the job:

$$h_{\mathcal{T}} x = hx \tag{1}$$

$$h_G y = y \tag{2}$$

$$h_{(\tau \times \ldots)}(x, \ldots) = (h_\tau x, \ldots) \tag{3}$$

$$h_{[a:\tau;\ \ldots]} \langle\!| \, a == x, \ldots, |\!\rangle = \langle\!| \, a == h_\tau x, \ldots, |\!\rangle \tag{4}$$

$$h_{(\mathbb{P}\tau)} A = h_\tau (|\!| A \, |) \tag{5}$$

Here the five clauses correspond to: (1) $\mathcal{T}$ itself, (2) some other ground type G, (3) a Cartesian product, (4) a schema type, and (5) a set type. The argument of h_τ in each clause represents a general element of τ, so the domain of h_τ is τ and, as $\operatorname{ran} h \subseteq Y$, the range of h_τ is contained in $\tau[Y/\mathcal{T}]$. The notation $\langle\!| \, a == x, b == y, \ldots \, |\!\rangle$ denotes a binding with a component a with value x, a component b of value y and so on.

To sum up, the above construction provides functions h_τ for each Z type τ; h_τ acts on an element, t, of τ by mapping h over the recursive appearances of members of $\mathcal{T}$ inside t. If a branch of the free type is not recursive (so that $\mathcal{T}$ does not appear in τ), the corresponding h_τ will be idτ. For example, for the types τ_1 and τ_2 that arise in the definition of EG, the functions h_{τ_1} and h_{τ_2} are as follows[2]:

$$h_{\tau_1} = (\lambda A : \mathbb{P}(\mathbb{Z} \times \mathsf{BINTREE}) \bullet (\lambda y : \mathbb{Z} \times \mathsf{BINTREE} \bullet y)(|\!| A \, |\!|))$$

$$= \operatorname{id} \mathbb{P}(\mathbb{Z} \times \mathsf{BINTREE})$$

$$h_{\tau_2} = (\lambda t : [a, b : \mathsf{EG}] \bullet \langle\!| \, a == h(t.a), t_2 == h(t.b) \, |\!\rangle)$$

Armed with h_τ, we can now give the remaining n equations to complete the condition of the PDR problem:

$$h(\beta_1 \, e_1) = d_1 \, (\beta_1 \, e_1) \, (h_{\tau_1} \, e_1)$$

$$\vdots$$

$$h(\beta_n \, e_n) = d_n \, (\beta_1 \, e_n) \, (h_{\tau_n} \, e_n)$$

To give the formal statement of PDR for the general case, we combine the above pieces in the form $\forall \, data \bullet \exists_1 \, solution \bullet conditions$:

$$[Y] \vdash \forall \; c_1, \ldots, c_m : Y;$$
$$d_1 : \mathcal{T} \to \tau_1[Y/\mathcal{T}] \to Y;$$
$$\vdots$$
$$d_n : \mathcal{T} \to \tau_n[Y/\mathcal{T}] \to Y \bullet$$
$$\exists_1 \, h : \mathcal{T} \to Y \bullet h\alpha_1 = c_1 \wedge$$
$$\vdots$$
$$h\alpha_m = c_m \wedge$$
$$(\forall e_1 : E_1 \bullet h(\beta_1 \, e_1) = d_1 \, (\beta_1 \, e_1) \, (h_{\tau_1} \, e_1)) \wedge$$
$$\vdots$$
$$(\forall e_n : E_n \bullet h(\beta_n \, e_n) = d_n \, (\beta_1 \, e_n) \, (h_{\tau_n} \, e_n))$$

---

[2] We have been slightly lax in giving equations to define the functions h_τ without making their domains explicit; a tool that automated the theory could either use λ-expressions for the functions, as we have done in this example, or introduce axiomatic descriptions for the functions that map h to h_τ and use those to abbreviate the predicates.

PDI is the special case of the above assertion PDR in which the functions d_i make no use of their first argument, in which case, we can reformulate the assertion to remove the first argument. Similarly, PDC is essentially the special case of PDR in which the d_i make no use of their second argument.

For example, using the relevant values for h_τ computed above, PDR for the free type EG is the following assertion:

$$
\begin{aligned}
&[Y] \vdash \forall \ c_1 : Y; \\
&\qquad\qquad d_1 : \text{EG} \to \mathbb{P}(\mathbb{Z} \times \text{BINTREE}) \to Y; \\
&\qquad\qquad d_2 : \text{EG} \to [a,b : Y] \to Y \\
&\quad \exists_1 \ h : \text{EG} \to Y \bullet \\
&\qquad\qquad h\,\text{Empty} = c_1 \ \wedge \\
&\qquad\qquad (\forall e_1 : \text{seq BINTREE} \bullet h(\text{TreeList}\,e_1) = d_1 \ (\text{TreeList}\,e_1)\,e_1) \ \wedge \\
&\qquad\qquad (\forall e_2 : [a,b : \text{EG}] \bullet h(\text{EGNode}\,e_2) = \\
&\qquad\qquad\qquad d_2 \ (\text{EGNode}\,e_2) \ \langle\!| \ a == h\,(e_2.a), b == h\,(e_2.b) \ |\rangle)
\end{aligned}
$$

At the price of complicating the description, our formulation of PDR is clearly amenable to some improvement. For example, the data functions for non-recursive branches (such as d_1 in the above example) have two arguments which contain the same information in the statement of the theorem; the extra argument can be removed. If the i-th branch of the free type is recursive, then the first argument of the function d_i is always $\beta\,e_i$, and arguably it would be better to use e_i instead. However, the latter proposal will usually make the declaration of d_i longer.

A further improvement that might be suggested would be to use $E_i[Y/\mathcal{T}]$ rather than $\tau_i[Y/\mathcal{T}]$ for the second domain of the data functions d_i. Typically, $E_i[Y/\mathcal{T}]$ will be a simpler expression than $\tau_i[Y/\mathcal{T}]$, as happens for d_1 in our example: the declaration would be shorter and clearer if we could use seq BINTREE in place of $\mathbb{P}(\mathbb{Z} \times \text{BINTREE})$. However, as we shall see in section 4, this suggestion does not work in general.

3.2   Proof of PDR and PDI

In this section, we present the main theoretical result of this document which states that the principle of definition by recursion (PDR) is a consequence of the usual axioms that characterise a free type as described in [1, 9]. Thus one can safely make free use of PDR once a free type definition is known to be consistent.

Theorem 1. PDR *and* PDI *are consequences of the usual axioms that characterise a free type.*

Proof: while no really creative work is required, the details of the proof are not entirely trivial. To state and prove the general result, it would probably be best to use the framework used in [1] to simplify the syntactic complications. For present purposes, we will proceed by example and just demonstrate the result for a particular free type. It is convenient to consider a free type with just one constructor, and so we will use the following free type FT representing trees with arbitrary finite unordered branching. Some elements of FT are shown in figure 2.

$$FT ::= k\langle\langle \mathbb{F}\, FT \rangle\rangle$$

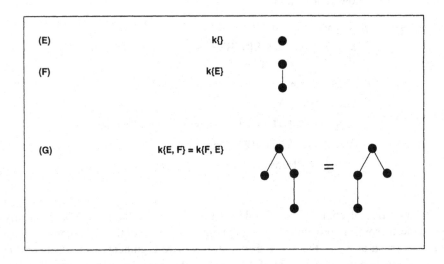

Fig. 2. Some Members of FT

The "usual axioms" for this free type amount to the following assertions: *(i)* the constructor function k is injective and surjective; and *(ii)* the following principle of proof by induction (PPI) holds:

$$\forall W : \mathbb{P}\, FT \bullet k(\!| \, \mathbb{F}\, W \, |\!) \subseteq W \Rightarrow W = FT$$

That is to say the only subset W of FT that is closed under formation of new trees from old is FT itself. This principle allows us to reason by structural induction over trees: to show that a property $P(x)$ holds for every $x \in$ FT, it suffices to show that if $A \in \mathbb{F}\, FT$ is such that $P(y)$ holds for every $y \in A$, then also $P(k(A))$ holds.

To prove the theorem, it is slightly easier and somewhat more informative to prove PDI first and then derive PDR from that. To demonstrate PDI for the free type FT, we must prove the following assertion (with generic parameter Y):

$$[Y] \vdash \forall e : \mathbb{P}\, Y \to Y \bullet \exists_1 h : FT \to Y \bullet \forall x : \mathbb{F}\, FT \bullet h(k(x)) = e(h(\!| \, x \, |\!)) \qquad (6)$$

The proof of (6) is similar to the proof of definition by induction for the natural numbers that one can find in elementary texts on set theory (e.g., [5]). Given Y and e as in the statement of the theorem, we consider partial approximations to the desired total function h, That is to say we consider functions $g : FT \to Y$ which satisfy $g(k(x)) = e(g(\!| \, x \, |\!))$ whenever both sides of that equation are defined. We show that any two such approximations g_1 and g_2 are compatible, i.e., their union is again a function. We then find that the union of all such approximations g turns out to be the desired total function h.

More formally, let us define a family J of subsets of FT as follows:

$$J = \{A : \mathbb{P}\,\text{FT} \mid \exists g : A \to Y \bullet \forall x : \mathbb{F}\,\text{FT} \bullet$$
$$\text{k}(x) \in A \Rightarrow x \subseteq A \wedge g(\text{k}(x)) = e(g(\!|\,x\,|\!))\}$$

We now make two claims about J:

Claim (A): Let $A_1, A_2 \in J$, and let $g_i : A_i \to Y$ be the functions whose existence is asserted by the definition of J $(i = 1, 2)$, then $(A_1 \cap A_2) \lhd g_1 = (A_1 \cap A_2) \lhd g_2$. That is to say, the functions g_1 and g_2 are *compatible*: their union $g_1 \cup g_2$ is also a function (from $A_1 \cup A_2$ to Y).

Claim (B): Let $A \in J$, and $x \in \mathbb{F}\,A$, then $(A \cup \{\text{k}(x)\}) \in J$. More precisely, if the set A is not closed under the constructor k, so that, for some finite subset x of A, $\text{k}(x) \notin A$, then we can extend a partial approximation $g : A \to Y$ to give a partial approximation $g' : (A \cup \{\text{k}(x)\}) \to Y$.

We will only sketch the proofs of these claims: *ad (A)*, one defines a set W by $W = \{y : \text{FT} \mid y \in A_1 \cap A_2 \Rightarrow g_1(y) = g_2(y)\}$, i.e., W is the set of points at which g_1 and g_2 agree, when they are both defined, and one then shows using PPI that $W = \text{FT}$; *ad (B)*, one defines the extension g' of g to agree with g on A and to take the value $e(g(\!|\,x\,|\!))$ on $\text{k}(x)$, and one then checks (using the injectivity of k) that this does indeed define a function on $A \cup \{\text{k}(x)\}$ with the necessary properties.

Taking $A_1 = A_2$ in claim *(A)*, we see that any two approximations g_1 and g_2 with common domain $A = A_1 = A_2$ are identical. In particular, if $A = \text{FT}$, the uniqueness part of (6) follows and it is only the existence of the function h that we have left to prove.

Let us now define $Q \subseteq \text{FT}$, and a function $q : Q \to Y$, by:

$$Q = \bigcup J$$

$$q = \bigcup \{g : \text{FT} \nrightarrow Y \mid \exists A : J \bullet g \in A \to Y \wedge$$
$$\forall x : \mathbb{F}\,\text{FT} \bullet \text{k}(x) \in A \Rightarrow x \in \mathbb{F}\,A \wedge h(\text{k}(x)) = e(h(\!|\,x\,|\!))\}$$

That q is indeed a function follows from claim *(A)*, which says that the functions whose union is formed in the definition of q are compatible. Note also that by the definitions of J, Q, and q, Q is indeed the domain of the function q.

We now make two further claims:

Claim(C) $Q \in J$.

Claim(D) $Q = \text{FT}$

Again we will only sketch the proofs: *ad (C)*, one checks that q will serve as a partial approximation to h on Q and so concludes that Q belongs to J; *ad (D)*, one uses claims *(B)* and *(C)* to show that Q is closed under the constructor k and concludes from PPI that $Q = \text{FT}$.

To complete the proof of (6), we deduce from claims *(C)* and *(D)* that $\text{FT} \in J$; then the definition of J furnishes us with a function $g : \text{FT} \to Y$ satisfying:

$$\forall x : \mathbb{F}\,\text{FT} \bullet \text{k}(x) \in \text{FT} \Rightarrow x \in \mathbb{F}\,\text{FT} \wedge g(\text{k}(x)) = e(g(\!|\,x\,|\!)) \tag{7}$$

(In fact, $g = q$, but we no longer need the details of our explicit construction of q.) As $k \in \mathbb{F}\,\mathsf{FT} \rightarrow \mathsf{FT}$, $k(x) \in \mathsf{FT}$ for any $x \in \mathbb{F}\,\mathsf{FT}$; so, taking $h = g$, (7) simplifies to:

$$\forall x : \mathbb{F}\,\mathsf{FT} \bullet h(\mathsf{k}(x)) = e(h(\!| \, x \, |\!))$$

Thus this choice of h has the properties we need to complete the proof of (6).

To derive PDR from PDI, what we have to do is prove the following, using (6) as an assumption:

$$[Y] \vdash \forall d : \mathsf{FT} \rightarrow \mathbb{P}\,Y \rightarrow Y \bullet \exists_1 h : \mathsf{FT} \rightarrow Y \bullet \\ \forall x : \mathbb{F}\,\mathsf{FT} \bullet h(\mathsf{k}x) = d(\mathsf{k}x)(h(\!| \, x \, |\!)) \tag{8}$$

So let us assume that (6) holds (as indeed it does, since we have just proved it). Assume that Y and d as above are given. We have to use (6) to construct a function h satisfying the above equation.

In the general case, one must account for the possibility that the free type defines an empty set (in which case both PDI and PDR may be seen to hold vacuously); for FT, we know that the free type is non-empty, and using (6) one can deduce that Y is also non-empty (otherwise the function d could not exist).

Given that FT and Y are not empty, let us choose elements $r_0 \in \mathsf{FT}$ and $y_0 \in Y$. Using these elements we define a function $e \in \mathbb{P}(\mathsf{FT} \times Y) \rightarrow \mathsf{FT} \times Y$ to which we can apply (6) as follows:

$$e(s) = \begin{cases} \mathsf{k}(\mathsf{first}(\!| \, s \, |\!)), d(\mathsf{k}(\mathsf{first}(\!| \, s \, |\!)))(\mathsf{second}(\!| \, s \, |\!)) & \text{if } \mathsf{first}(\!| \, s \, |\!) \text{ is finite} \\ (r_0, y_0) & \text{otherwise} \end{cases}$$

(Here the value of e is only relevant on sets s for which $\mathsf{first}(\!| \, s \, |\!)$ is finite; however, to apply (6) in the form in which we have stated it, we need e to be total on $\mathbb{P}(\mathsf{FT} \times Y)$, and so we have used r_0 and y_0 to extend the relevant parts of e to give a total function delivering an arbitrary fixed result on the irrelevant values of s.)

By (6), we know that there is a unique function $g \in \mathsf{FT} \rightarrow \mathsf{FT} \times Y$ such that:

$$\forall x : \mathbb{F}\,\mathsf{FT} \bullet g(\mathsf{k}(x)) = e(g(\!| \, x \, |\!))$$

We then define the desired function h by:

$$h = \mathsf{second} \circ g$$

One may now check using the various definitions that h satisfies the following equation, which completes the proof of the existence part of (8).

$$\forall x : \mathbb{F}\,\mathsf{FT} \bullet h(\mathsf{k}(x)) = d(\mathsf{k}x)(h(\!| \, x \, |\!))$$

The uniqueness part of (8) follows (with a little extra work) from the uniqueness of g. This completes the proof of our theorem in the special case of the free type FT. The proof in the general case is very similar in structure: using the terminology of [1], a monotonic operator ϕ would appear where the proof for FT has the finite set operator, $\mathbb{F}$; the type τ of this operator would appear in place of $\mathbb{P}$ where appropriate; and the use of relational image to map the function being defined over subtrees would be replaced by use of the operator $\hat{\tau}$ (cf. h_{τ} in the notation of section 3.1 above). The derivation of PDR from PDI in the general case involves some reasoning about the functorial properties of $\hat{\tau}$; to bypass this, it is not difficult to generalise the argument given above for PDI to deliver PDR directly. □

4   Comparison with Universal Algebra

Many people may have wondered why free types are called "free types". In this section, we shall explore the analogy that gives rise to the name, and find, perhaps surprisingly, that it is not as close as one might hope.

We will need some elementary ideas from universal algebra [4]. Universal algebra studies the features of algebraic systems such as rings, groups, fields, etc., that are independent of the fine details of the theory of rings, groups, fields, etc. Two basic concepts in universal algebra are signatures and structures:

A *signature* is a syntactic construct defining some typed operators, for example, the signature corresponding to the theory of groups might have a nullary operator, $e : G$, a unary operator $\_^{-1} : G \to G$ and a binary operator $\_ \bullet \_ : G \times G \to G$ giving the identity element, inverse operation and multiplication operation respectively.

A *structure* for a signature is a set provided with operations that implement the operators of the signature. The group of integers, for example, provides a structure for the signature described above taking $e = 0$, $x^{-1} = -x$ and $x \bullet y = x + y$.

We think of a signature as defining the set of all its structures. As an example, the following signature defines the set of all sets, X, equipped with a zero-element, Z and a function S from X to itself:

$$Z : X$$
$$S : X \to X$$

In describing structures for a given signature, we will use subscripts to distinguish different structures. Following this convention, an example of a structure for this signature might be to take $X_1 = \mathbb{N}$, $Z_1 = 0$ and $S_1 = succ$. Another might be to take $X_2 = \mathbb{Z}$, $Z_2 = 1$ and $S_2 = (\lambda i : \mathbb{Z} \bullet 2 * i)$. A function between two structures for the same signature is said to be a *morphism* if it commutes with the operations. For example, a function $f : X_1 \to X_2$ will be a morphism iff. $f\,0 = 1$ and $f(S_1\,i) = S_2(f\,i)$ for all i in X_1. One such morphism is the function that maps $i \in \mathbb{N}$ to $2^i \in \mathbb{Z}$, as one may readily check.

An isomorphism is a morphism that is also a bijection, and for many purposes isomorphic structures may be considered to be identical. Our example morphism from (X_1, Z_1, S_1) to (X_2, Z_2, S_2) is not a morphism, since it is not a surjection. However, if we take X_3 to be the set of non-negative powers of 2, take $Z_3 = 1$ and take $S_3 = (\lambda i : X_3 \bullet 2 * i)$, then mapping i to 2^i provides an isomorphism between (X_1, Z_1, S_1) and (X_3, Z_3, S_3) (which provides a discrete analogue of the principle that underlies slide-rules and log tables).

Subject to some restrictions on the types used in a signature, it turns out that any signature defines a non-empty set of structures and that the set of structures contains a distinguished class of structures called the *free algebras* for the signature. The characteristic property of a free algebra, A, is that for any other structure for the same signature, B, there exists a unique morphism from A to B. Any two free algebras for the same signature are isomorphic, and so we generally talk about "the" free algebra for a signature. For example the structure (X_1, Z_1, S_1) described above is the free algebra for its signature: this fact is essentially equivalent to a principle of definition by induction over the natural numbers (cf. the example morphisms given above).

We are concerned with the principles for definition by induction and recursion for a Z free type. The defining equations in these principles as exemplified in section 2 above are reminiscent of the equations that define a morphism in universal algebra. For example, PDI for the set of finite tree we used to illustrate the proof of theorem 1 contains the following equation:

$$h(k(x)) = e(h(\!| x |\!))$$

If k and e here were operators for two different structures for a suitable signature, the above equation would say that the function h is a morphism between the two structures. In this light, we might hope that PDI would correspond to the defining property of a free algebra.

So, given a Z free type definition, we can construct a corresponding signature whose operators are the constructors of the free type. Each non-nullary operator is assigned the type of a function from the domain of the corresponding constructor to the unknown X. For example, the following free type definition corresponds to the signature with operators Z and S mentioned above:

$$\text{Nat} ::= Z \,|\, S\langle\!\langle \text{Nat} \rangle\!\rangle$$

In the sequel, given a Z free type definition such as the above, we can conveniently borrow the terminology of universal algebra and say that a structure for the free type is a tuple (R, Z_0, S_0), where R is a set, $Z_0 \in R$ and $S_0 \in R \to R$.

For simple examples like the above, the analogy works quite well. However, the fact that one can write an arbitrary set-valued expression in a branch of a Z free type means that one can impose structural constraints[3]. that are not compatible with the usual methods of universal algebra. In the rest of this section, we will explore the somewhat unfortunate consequences of this aspect of free type definitions.

As a first observation on the technical problems that arise, we observe that the version of PDI or PDR that the theory of universal algebra delivers does not work so well for the signatures that can arise from Z free types. This relates to the question raised in the previous section of whether to use $\tau_i[Y/\mathcal{T}]$ or $E_i[Y/\mathcal{T}]$ in the statement of PDR or PDI. Consider for example the following type of unbalanced trees:

$$\text{UBT} ::= \text{Leaf}\langle\!\langle \mathbb{Z} \rangle\!\rangle \,|\, \text{Node}\langle\!\langle \{ i : \mathbb{Z};\ t_1, t_2 : \text{UBT} \,|\, t_1 \neq t_2 \} \rangle\!\rangle$$

---

[3] We do not have complete freedom however; in particular, the type and scope rules of Z prevent us from referring to the constructors of the free type inside the set-valued expressions that appear on the right-hand side of the definition.

For example, the trees depicted in Figure 1 may all be viewed as members of UBT. The definition of UBT is consistent and the version of PDI that universal algebra gives us would be the following theorem:

$$[Y] \vdash \forall \ d_1 : \mathbb{Z} \to Y;$$
$$d_2 : \{i : \mathbb{Z}; t_1, t_2 : Y \mid t_1 \neq t_2\} \to Y \bullet$$
$$\exists_1 \ h : \mathsf{UBT} \to Y \bullet (\forall e_1 : \mathbb{Z} \bullet h(\mathsf{Leaf}\, e_1) = d_1 \, e_1)$$
$$\wedge \ (\forall e_2 : \{i : \mathbb{Z}; t_1, t_2 : \mathsf{UBT} \mid t_1 \neq t_2\} \bullet$$
$$h(\mathsf{Node}\, e_2) = d_2 \, (e_2.1, h(e_2.2), h(e_2.3)))$$

In the notation of the previous section the above theorem uses $E_2[Y/\mathsf{UBT}]$ rather than $\tau_2[Y/\mathsf{UBT}]$ in the declaration of d_2; however, this is not strong enough to justify definitions that we might very well wish to make. For example, consider a function to count the non-leaf nodes in an unbalanced tree. This function, nodeCount say, ought to be defined just like the function of the same name in Section 2.2 using UBT instead of BINTREE. If we apply it to the tree B in Figure 1, we will compute:

$$\mathsf{nodeCountB} = 1 + \mathsf{nodeCount}(\mathsf{Leaf}\, 3) + \mathsf{nodeCount}(\mathsf{Leaf}\, 4)$$
$$= 1 + (1 + 1)$$
$$= 3$$

However, the data function d_2 required to carry out this computation is not a member of the set $\{i : \mathbb{Z}; t_1, t_2 : \mathbb{Z} \mid t_1 \neq t_2\} \to \mathbb{Z}$, because $1 = 1$.

We can draw two conclusions from the above example. Firstly, the form of PDR using $\tau_i[Y/T]$ as given in Section 3.1 is probably the one to use; secondly, we should be chary about drawing too much from the analogy of set-theoretic inductive definitions (i.e., Z free types) with universal algebra: the subjects are related but they are not isomorphic.

A deeper point at which the analogy breaks down highlights a potential misconception about the strength of PDR (or rather its equivalent PDI). In universal algebra terms, PDI should amount to the assertion that the type T in the statement of the theorem is the free algebra for its signature. Now, it is a fact of universal algebra that free algebras are unique up to isomorphism. The proof is elementary: if A and B are free algebras for the same signature, then there are unique morphisms $\alpha : A \to B$ and $\beta : B \to A$; now the composite $\alpha \, {}_9^{\circ} \, \beta$ is a morphism from A to itself, but so is $\mathsf{id}A$; so by the freeness of A, $\alpha \, {}_9^{\circ} \, \beta = \mathsf{id}A$, and similarly $\beta \, {}_9^{\circ} \, \alpha = \mathsf{id}B$; thus α and β are (mutually inverse) bijections and A and B are indeed isomorphic. It follows that PDI (or PDR) actually characterises the free algebra completely, and so, for example, other principles like the principle of proof by induction PPI[4] can be derived from it. Sadly, this reasoning does not transfer to Z free types, if we use our preferred formulation as in Section 3.1:

Theorem 2. *If we formulate* PDR *as in Section 3.1 (using* $\tau_i[Y/T]$ *rather than* $E_i[Y/T]$), *then* PDR *does not imply* PPI.

---

[4] See examples in the proof of theorems 1 and 2.

Proof: what we have to do is exhibit a set equipped with constructor functions for which PDR holds but PPI fails. To do this, let us consider the following free type definition:

$$\mathcal{D} ::= Z \mid S\langle\langle\{m : \mathcal{D} \mid \exists a,b : \mathcal{D} \bullet a \neq b\}\rangle\rangle$$

Here, the set expression $\{m : X \mid \exists a,b : X \bullet a \neq b\}$, is the empty set when X has less than 2 elements, and is equal to X otherwise. The free type definition $\mathcal{D}$ is therefore just like that for Nat in definition (9) above except that the "generative power" of the second branch is cut down to nothing when the free type is "small". PPI for a structure (R, Z_0, S_0) for $\mathcal{D}$ is the following assertion:

$$\forall A : \mathbb{P}R \bullet (Z_0 \in A \wedge \forall x : \{m : A \mid \exists a,b : A \bullet a \neq b\} \bullet S_0(x) \in A) \Rightarrow A = R$$

The only possible structure for $\mathcal{D}$ with PPI must have the carrier set R equal to the singleton set $\{Z_0\}$, because $\{m : A \mid \exists a,b : A \bullet a \neq b\}$ is empty if A is a singleton set.

Now, Nat has more than 1 element, so $\{m : \text{Nat} \mid \exists a,b : \text{Nat} \bullet a \neq b\} = \text{Nat}$. It follows that Nat, Z and S give a structure for $\mathcal{D}$, and, moreover, PDR holds for this structure, since the formal statement of PDR for this structure is equivalent to that for Nat. That is to say, the proposition:

$$\forall c_1 : Y; \ d_0 : \{m : \text{Nat} \mid \exists a,b : \text{Nat} \bullet a \neq b\} \times Y \to Y \bullet$$
$$\exists_1 h : \{m : \text{Nat} \mid \exists a,b : \text{Nat} \bullet a \neq b\} \to Y \bullet$$
$$h(Z) = c_1 \wedge$$
$$(\forall x : \{m : \text{Nat} \mid \exists a,b : \text{Nat} \bullet a \neq b\} \bullet h(S(x)) = d_0(x, h(x)))$$

is equivalent to:

$$\forall c_1 : Y; \ d_0 : \text{Nat} \times Y \to Y \bullet$$
$$\exists_1 h : \text{Nat} \to Y \bullet$$
$$h(Z) = c_1 \wedge (\forall x : \text{Nat} \bullet h(S(x)) = d_0(x, h(x)))$$

which is the formal statement of PDR for Nat. Thus, we have a structure for $\mathcal{D}$ which satisfies PDR but not PPI, since, as we have already remarked, a structure satisfying PPI has to have the carrier set equal to a singleton set. $\square$

In the proof of Theorem 2, the example involves a free type definition for which one of the branches is empty. It might be thought that this makes the example rather a special case which could be eliminated by an appropriate condition. However, there are more complex examples with PDR and not PPI which have no empty branches. Using an informal notation[5], one such is given by:

$$\mathcal{U} ::= u\langle\langle\{r : \mathbb{N} \leftrightarrow \mathcal{U} \mid \text{ran}\,r \text{ is finite} \wedge (\mathcal{U} \text{ is countable} \Rightarrow r \in \text{seq}\,\mathcal{U})\}\rangle\rangle$$

Here the least fixed point is the same as the countable set which is the least fixed point for the free type definition:

$$\mathcal{W} ::= w\langle\langle\text{seq}\,\mathcal{W}\rangle\rangle$$

---

[5] Formally, "X is finite" may be expressed in Z as "$X \in \mathbb{F}\,X$", and "X is countable" as "$\mathbb{N} \twoheadrightarrow X \neq \varnothing$".

However, a fixed point for $\mathcal{U}$ with PDR but not PPI is given by the uncountable set which is the least fixed point for the following free type definition (cf. Example 6 in Section 2 of [1]):

$$\mathcal{Q} ::= q\langle\!\langle \{r : \mathbb{N} \leftrightarrow \mathcal{Q} \mid \operatorname{ran} r \text{ is finite}\} \rangle\!\rangle$$

In the terminology of [1], the idea behind these examples is as follows. We start with some monotonic operator, ϕ say with a least fixed point satisfying PDR. We want to use ϕ to construct an example with PDR but not PPI, and to give some room for manoeuvre, we arrange for the carrier set R to be a "large" set in some sense to be defined. We then construct another monotonic operator ψ, such that $\psi(X) \subseteq (\phi(X))$, for all X. We do this in such a way that if X is a "small" subset of R, then $\psi(X)$ is a lot smaller than $\phi(X)$, whereas if X is a "large" subset of R, $\psi(X) = \phi(X)$. It then turns out that a least fixed point for ϕ with carrier set R say, may still have PDR with respect to ψ, since $\psi(R) = \phi(R)$, but R can contain "small" subsets which manage to be fixed points for ψ even though they are not fixed points for ϕ. In the case of $\mathcal{T}$ and $\mathcal{U}$ above "small" is interpreted as "no more than one element" and "countable" respectively.

Ultimately, the problem with formulating PDR as suggested by universal algebra, using $E_i[Y/\mathcal{T}]$, rather than $\tau_i[Y/\mathcal{T}]$ is that the resulting axiom involves application of the data functions d_i outside their domain of definition for bad cases like those we have just been looking at. Many of the free type definitions that arise in practice do not impose the structural constraints on the generative strengths of the constructors that give rise to this problem. In categorical language, these are the ones for which the operation mapping Y to $E_i[Y/\mathcal{T}]$ gives the objects part of a functor whose morphisms part is the operation h_τ discussed in Section 3.1 (see [2] for a more explicit account).

It may well be of benefit in developing conceptual and mechanised tools for working with Z free types to pay special attention to the functorial case[6] so as to exploit the additional properties it enjoys. This would let us use many of the practical techniques developed for other logical systems, e.g., see [6] for a treatment of recursive definitions in HOL. In particular, for functorial free type definitions, PDR actually entails all the other axioms and so may be used as a starting point for many lines of reasoning. It is perhaps unfortunate that this economy of axiomatisation is not available in the general case with which Z must deal.

5   Conclusions

The principles for defining functions over free types that we have articulated justify a useful class of definitions. The principles are intended to serve as rules of thumb for

---

[6] A possible line in this direction would be to adopt the approach of [10] which reports on an enrichment of the Z type system, extending the basic types of Z to allow finer distinctions to be made by a Z support tool, e.g., to distinguish sequences from other less structured functions. If one required the richer types to be functorial, then the methods of [10] might enable a tool to recognise and exploit the functorial case in a systematic way. An alternative approach would be to use some heuristic method to derive from each expression E_i a more convenient expression to use in place of $\tau_i[Y/\mathcal{T}]$. Care would be needed in designing such a mechanism to ensure that the resulting definitional principle is sufficient for all purposes.

the ordinary Z practitioner and to guide those constructing tools supporting mechanised reasoning in Z.

The foundation of Z in set theory means that the theory of recursion for Z is perhaps less widely known in the formal methods world than might be the case for a notation founded in domain theory or universal algebra. While there is a broad overlap, the approaches are not isomorphic. For many purposes, the set-theoretic approach is, I would claim, both simpler and more powerful.

Acknowledgements

Much of the work reported in this paper was undertaken while the author was working for International Computers Ltd. under contract to the UK Government's Communications and Electronics Security Group. I am indebted to Colin Champion of CESG for permission to publish the results and to the ZUM'98 referees for their sympathetic and helpful comments.

References

1. R. D. Arthan. On Free Type Definitions in Z. In J. E. Nicholls, editor, *Z User Workshop, York 1991*. Workshops in Computing, pages 40–58. Springer-Verlag, 1992.
2. R. D. Arthan. Recursive Data Types in Typed Set Theory. *Unpublished pre-print*, 1997.
3. R. D. Arthan. Mechanizing the Z Toolkit. In M. Mislova, editor, *Proceedings of the Oxford Workshop on Automated Formal Methods*. Elsevier Electronics Notes in Computer Science, To appear 1998.
4. P. M. Cohn. *Universal Algebra*. D. Reidel Publishing Company, 1981.
5. P. R. Halmos. *Naive Set Theory*. Springer-Verlag, 1974.
6. T. F. Melham. Automating Recursive Type Definitions in Higher Order Logic. In G. Birtwistle and P. A. Subrahmanyam, editors, *Current Trends in Hardware Verification and Automated Theorem Proving*. Springer-Verlag, 1989.
7. A. Smith. *On Recursive Free Types in Z*. RSRE Memorandum 91028. MOD PE, RSRE, UK, 1991.
8. J. M. Spivey. *The Z Notation: A Reference Manual*. Prentice Hall International Series in Computer Science, 1989.
9. J. M. Spivey. *The Z Notation: A Reference Manual, Second Edition*. Prentice Hall International Series in Computer Science, 1992.
10. J. M. Spivey. Richer Types for Z. *Formal Aspects of Computing*, 8(5):565–584, 1996.
11. J. M. Spivey. The Consistency Theorem for Free Type Definitions in Z (Short Communication). *Formal Aspects of Computing*, 8(3):369–376, 1996.
12. S. Valentine. Inconsistency and Undefinedness in Z – A Practical Guide. In J. P. Bowen, A. Fett, and M. G. Hinchey, editors, *ZUM'98: The Z Formal Specification Notation, Lecture Notes in Computer Science*, volume 1493, pages 233–249. Springer-Verlag, 1998. This volume.
13. J. C. P. Woodcock and J. Davies. *Using Z: Specification, Refinement and Proof*. Prentice Hall International Series in Computer Science, 1996.

A Logic for the Schema Calculus

Martin C. Henson[1] and Steve Reeves[2]

[1] Department of Computer Science, University of Essex, UK
Email: hensm@essex.ac.uk

[2] Department of Computer Science, University of Waikato, New Zealand
Email: stever@cs.waikato.ac.nz

Abstract. In this paper we introduce and investigate a logic for the schema calculus of Z. The schema calculus is arguably the reason for Z's popularity but so far no true calculus (a sound system of rules for reasoning about schema expressions) has been given. Presentations to date have either failed to provide a calculus (*e.g.* the draft standard [3]) or have fallen back on informal descriptions at a syntactic level (most text books *e.g.* [7]). Alongside the calculus, we introduce a derived equational logic; this enables us to formalise properly the informal notions of schema expression equality to be found in the literature.

1 Introduction

In this paper we provide, for the first time, a logic for the schema calculus of Z. This is constructed within a *specification logic* Z_C which we introduce in Section 2. Our calculus supports further logical development, for example an equational logic similar to that informally deployed in the literature. We illustrate its use in Section 5.

1.1 Background

The specification language Z has been developed over the last decade or so mainly in response to the needs of the practitioners who have used it. This is the source of its undoubted strength and popularity. Z's main technical innovation (which sets it apart from VDM, for example) is the concept of a *schema* and, additionally, a well designed set of operators for combining them. This language of schema expressions permits the user of Z to produce highly structured specifications and to employ very general organising principles, *e.g.* free promotion of operations (see [7] chapter 13).

This language of schema expressions has become known as the *schema calculus*. However, during the last seven or eight years, a period during which the need for a precise mathematical account of Z has been a major theme, there has been almost no success in making good this terminology: a *calculus* suggests that the language will be supported with *mathematical principles of reasoning* (*c.f.* the distinction between mere λ-notation and the λ-calculus). It is the aim of this paper to supply such a calculus; moreover, one which is able to support further mathematical development *e.g.* establishing an equational logic for schemas (as anticipated in the draft standard for Z [3] page 188).

The pictures of the language of schema expressions presented in the majority of text-books (*e.g.* [7]), and in more technical publications (*e.g.* the draft standard [3] and the reference manual [5]), are rather different, and it is worth exploring these two approaches in order to make clear our aims and purposes in this paper.

1.2   Schema expressions in the text books

The major difference between the majority of text books and the standard accounts is that schema expressions are taken to be *meta*-language in the former but *object*-language in the latter. In the text books a schema equation such as:

$$[D_0 \mid P_0] \wedge [D_1 \mid P_1] = [D_0 \sqcup D_1 \mid P_0 \wedge P_1]$$

defines schema conjunction. As a consequence Z's most important organising principles are relegated to the meta-language and become inaccessible to any putative logic for Z. Moreover, as definitions, these equations are *intensional* and *non-compositional*: they refer to syntactic subcomponents and their properties explicitly. Such definitions are at best mathematically awkward, and have no algebraic properties. The approach we take, on the other hand, will be *compositional*.

1.3   Schema expressions in the reference standards

The standard accounts [3, 5] make it perfectly clear that schema expressions belong to the *object* language. Consequently, the text book definitions must be established as *provable equalities*. But, since the standard does not provide a sufficiently complete logic for Z, these proof obligations cannot be discharged. In these circumstances the text book approach is the best that can be achieved. It, at least, provides an opportunity to say *something* about complex schema expressions (*e.g.* [7], pages 194–195, of which more below in Section 5), if only informally.

The rules in the draft standard which exist for schema expressions ([3], Section F.6.6, pages 207–208) are incomplete, too restrictive, or incorrect. The lacunæ are easy to spot. Less easy is the observation that of the following rules (which are derivable from rules (*SchBindMem*) and (*SAnd*)) the first is too limited and the conclusion of the second and third are not in general even well-formed.

$$\frac{\Gamma \vdash b \in S \quad \Gamma \vdash b \in T}{\Gamma \vdash b \in S \wedge T} \qquad \frac{\Gamma \vdash b \in S \wedge T}{\Gamma \vdash b \in S} \qquad \frac{\Gamma \vdash b \in S \wedge T}{\Gamma \vdash b \in T}$$

The problem here lies with rule (*SchBindMem*). This rule, incidentally, also makes the logic of the draft standard inconsistent, but the suggested repair (adding a proviso to that rule) only ensures that the derived elimination rules make *sense*. They remain, like the introduction rule, too restrictive and, most importantly, cannot be used to establish the equation for conjunction we introduced above. In this paper we show how this state-of-affairs can be remedied.

2   The specification logic Z_C

In this section we shall describe a simple specification logic which we call Z_C. It is based upon the notion of *schema type* which has been introduced in Z.

2.1   The language of Z_C

We begin with type names:

$$T \;::= \; \mathbb{N} \mid \mathbb{P}\, T \mid T \times T \mid [D_T]$$
$$D_T ::= \; \cdots l_i : T_i \cdots$$

Types of the form $[D_T]$ are called *schema types*, each component of which is a *prime* declaration; the order of these in a schema type is not important. The labels introduced must be distinct. Each type name denotes a type carrier, *i.e.* a set. The *proto-syntax*[1] of sets, in general, is given by:

$$C ::= \; \{z \in t \mid P\} \mid \mathbb{P}\, t \mid t \times t \mid \mathbb{N}^* \mid [D]$$
$$D ::= \; \cdots l_i \in t_i \cdots$$

Here, as we will soon see, the category t, of terms, includes C, sets, as a sub-category.

The carriers are picked out as T^* by:

$$T^* ::= \; \mathbb{N}^* \mid T^* \times T^* \mid \mathbb{P}\, T^* \mid [D^*]$$
$$D^* ::= \; \cdots l_i \in T_i^* \cdots$$

Sets of the form $[D^*]$ are called *schema carriers*. We shall write $[D_{T_0}] \sqsubseteq [D_{T_1}]$ when the set of prime declarations of D_{T_0} is a subset of that of D_{T_1}. Other meta-operations we shall need over schema types: $[D_{T_0}] - [D_{T_1}]$ is the schema type comprising all prime declarations of $[D_{T_0}]$ which do not occur in $[D_{T_1}]$. The schema type $[D_{T_0}] \sqcup [D_{T_1}]$ is the schema type comprising the union of the prime declarations in D_{T_0} and D_{T_1}. It is not defined when this union contains prime declarations $l : T_0$ and $l : T_1$ for which $T_0 \neq T_1$. Finally, we shall introduce meta-notational conventions which require substitution for labels. For this we need the *alphabet* operator, defined as follows: $\alpha[\cdots l_i : T_i \cdots] =_{df} \{\cdots l_i \cdots\}$ and then we shall write $[\alpha[D_T]/t.\alpha[D_T]]$ to represent the family of substitutions: $[\cdots][l_i/t.l_i][\cdots]$. All of these operations can clearly be extended to $[D^*]$ (remembering that : will change to $\in$ in the those cases). We will also extend α to members of $[D]$ in the obvious way.

The proto-syntax of formulæ is given by:

$$P ::= \; \bot \mid t = t \mid t \in t \mid \neg P \mid P \vee P \mid \exists z \in t \bullet P$$

The logic of Z_C is classical and so the remaining logical connectives and the universal quantifier can be defined in terms of the above in the usual manner.

The proto-syntax of terms is as follows:

$$t ::= \; x \mid n \mid C \mid t.l \mid (\!|\cdots l_i \Rrightarrow t_i \cdots|\!) \mid t.1 \mid t.2 \mid (t,t) \mid t \upharpoonright [D^*]$$

The last term formation operator will be unexpected, as it has had no history in Z so far as we can tell. We pronounce the symbol $\upharpoonright$ "filter" and its purpose is to permit the

---

[1] The categories of sets, propositions and terms, which we give in this section, overgenerate. The syntax of these is finally determined by the type assignment and propositionhood system which we introduce in Section 2.2 and describe in full in Appendix A.

restriction of bindings to a given schema type. These are crucial for characterising the membership conditions for schema expressions (*e.g.* the rules in Section 3.1).

To make our notation as readable and convenient as we can, we will henceforth allow C to range over all terms t which have type $\mathbb{P}\,T$ for any type T.

The subcategory of numerals is as expected:

$$n ::= 0 \mid succ\ n$$

The reader will have detected a notational shift in our presentation: we use a set membership relation and not a type assignment judgement in *declarations*. The usual reason for using the colon in declaration contexts in Z is that it permits a notational distinction between *defining* and *applied* occurrences. This is not without merit, but the embedding of the language within a *logic* has complicated matters. There should perhaps be some wider debate concerning this issue because there is *also* a distinction between "t has type *name* T" (written $t : T$) and "t is a member of the type *carrier* T^*" (usually written $t \in T$). This problem would disappear if we were not keen to preserve a valuable abuse of notation (see [5] page 24) in which we systematically fail to distinguish between type names and type carriers, an abuse it would be very tedious to do without. Perhaps we should preserve the standard notation and write $t \,\S\, T$ as a type judgement. We retain an open mind on this score.

2.2   Type assignment and propositionhood in Z_C

Sequents of the system have the form:

$$\Gamma \rhd_C t : T \qquad and \qquad \Gamma \rhd_C P\ prop$$

These state: "In the context Γ the proto-term t has the type T" and "In the context Γ the proto-proposition P is well-formed".

Γ is a *type assignment context* of types for free variables. Such contexts are understood to be *sets* and so are extended by taking a *union*, with the usual proviso that variables may occur at most once.

We give the entire system of rules in Appendix A. Here we illustrate the system by describing two typical rules.

$$\frac{\cdots \quad \Gamma \rhd_C t_i : T_i \quad \cdots}{\Gamma \rhd_C \langle\!|\cdots l_i \Rrightarrow t_i \cdots |\!\rangle : [\cdots l_i : T_i \cdots]} \ (C_\Rrightarrow) \qquad \frac{t : T_1 \quad T_0 \sqsubseteq T_1}{t \restriction T_0 : T_0} \ (C_\restriction)$$

The first of these assigns the relevant (schema) type to a binding with reference to the types of its component terms. The second is particularly important because it involves our innovation: the filtered terms. A term of schema type T_1 may be restricted to T_0 providing that T_0 is a subtype of T_1.

We will occasionally find it more convenient to write t^T when $\rhd t : T$, for closed t.

2.3   The logic of Z_C

The proto-judgements of the logic have the form $\Gamma \vdash_C P$ where a proto-context Γ has the form $\Gamma^-; \Gamma^+$, where Γ^- is a type assignment context (a context for the type system) and Γ^+ is a set of formulæ. These are well-formed according to the following rules.

$$\frac{}{\Gamma^- \ context} \qquad \frac{\Gamma^- \triangleright P \ prop \quad \Gamma \ context}{\Gamma^-; \ P, \Gamma^+ \ context}$$

Then a proto-judgement $\Gamma \vdash P$ is well-formed providing that $\Gamma, P \ context$.

The entire logic for Z_C is given in Appendix B. Here we draw the reader's attention to the rule which characterises filtered terms:

$$\frac{\Gamma \vdash t.l_i = t_i \quad \Gamma^- \triangleright t : T \quad [\cdots l_i : T_i \cdots] \sqsubseteq T}{\Gamma \vdash (t \restriction [\cdots l_i \in T_i \cdots]).l_i = t_i} \quad (\restriction^=)$$

As expected: a filtered term $t \restriction T_0$ agrees with t at every component of the sub-type T_0.

Many other rules are derivable *e.g.* transitivity and symmetry. We can usefully extend filtering to sets by means of:

$$C^{\mathbb{P} \, T_1} \restriction \mathbb{P} \, T_0 =_{df} \{z \in T_0 \mid \exists x \in T_1 \bullet x \in C \wedge z = x \restriction T_0\}$$

Then we have:

$$\frac{C : \mathbb{P} \, T_1 \quad T_0 \sqsubseteq T_1}{C \restriction \mathbb{P} \, T_0 : \mathbb{P} \, T_0} \quad (C_{\mathbb{P} \restriction})$$

and:

$$\frac{\Gamma \vdash t \in C \restriction \mathbb{P} \, T \quad \Gamma^-, x : T; \ \Gamma^+, x \in C, t = x \restriction T \vdash P}{\Gamma \vdash P} \quad (\in_{\restriction}^-)$$

which are rules we will need later. The latter follows by rules $(\{\}_I^-)$ and $(\exists^-)$.

Most importantly we have a syntactic consistency result for this system[2], which we state without proof (see [2] for the details).

Proposition 1. *If $\Gamma \vdash_C P$ when Γ context then $\Gamma^- \triangleright_C P$ prop* $\square$

Z_C is *consistent*: there is a trivial model for which Z_C is sound. In this model schema types are interpreted as suitable dependent function spaces over a small universe. Binding projection is then interpreted as dependent function application (see [2] for the details of a similar system).

3   The schema calculus

3.1   Basic schema calculus

We begin with basic schema expressions. These can be built directly on the logical structure of Z_C:

$$S ::= [D \mid P] \mid \neg t \mid t \vee t \mid \exists l \in T \bullet t$$

---

[2] Note that this result does *not* hold for the logic in [3]: *e.g.* consider the conjunction elimination rule we derived in Section 1.3

and the syntax of t is extended by adding the production $t ::= S$

Although l is a label (and it obviously makes no sense to *bind* a constant), there *is* a rationale for permitting the quantifier in the last case, but we must postpone the explanation until Section 3.2 below.

To make our notation as readable and convenient as we can, we will henceforth allow S to range over all terms t which have type $\mathbb{P}\,T$, where T is a schema type.

This basic language of schema expressions is interpreted into Z_C as follows:

$$
\begin{array}{lll}
(i) & [D \mid P] & =_{df} \{z \in [D] \mid P[\alpha[D]/z.\alpha[D]]\} \\
(ii) & \neg S & =_{df} \{z \in T \mid z \notin S\} \\
(iii) & S_0^{\mathbb{P}\,T_0} \vee S_1^{\mathbb{P}\,T_1} & =_{df} \{z \in T_0 \sqcup T_1 \mid z \restriction T_0 \in S_0 \vee z \restriction T_1 \in S_1\} \\
(iv) & \exists l \in T_1 \bullet S^{\mathbb{P}\,T_0} & =_{df} \{z \in (T_0 - [l \in T_1]) \mid P\} \\
where\ P & & =_{df} \exists x \in T_1 \bullet x \in S \wedge z = x \restriction (T_0 - [l \in T_1])
\end{array}
$$

In order to determine the terms over which S ranges we need some type rules for each of the above productions. We use the following, which are all derivable within the type system for Z_C:

$$
\frac{D : \mathbb{P}\,T \quad T \triangleright P\ prop}{[D \mid P] : \mathbb{P}\,T}\ (C_{[]}^S) \qquad
\frac{t : \mathbb{P}\,T}{\neg\,t : \mathbb{P}\,T}\ (C_\neg^S) \qquad
\frac{t_0 : \mathbb{P}\,T_0 \quad t_1 : \mathbb{P}\,T_1}{t_0 \vee t_1 : \mathbb{P}(T_0 \sqcup T_1)}\ (C_\vee^S)
$$

$$
\frac{l : T_1 \quad t : \mathbb{P}\,T_0}{\exists l \in T_1 \bullet t : \mathbb{P}[T_0 - [l \in T_1]]}\ (C_\exists^S)
$$

Within the logic the following rules are immediately induced:

$$
\frac{P[\alpha[D]/t.\alpha[D]] \quad t \in [D]}{t \in [D \mid P]}\ (S^+) \qquad
\frac{t \in [D \mid P]}{P[\alpha[D]/t.\alpha[D]]}\ (S_0^-) \qquad
\frac{t \in [D \mid P]}{t \in [D]}\ (S_l^-)
$$

Note that schemas are extensional, as a consequence of rule (*ext*).

Introduction and elimination rules for the more complex expressions are also derivable:

$$
\frac{t \notin S}{t \in \neg S}\ (\neg S^+) \qquad
\frac{t \in \neg S}{t \notin S}\ (\neg S^-)
$$

$$
\frac{\Gamma \vdash t \restriction T_0 \in S_0 \quad \Gamma^- \triangleright S_1 : \mathbb{P}\,T_1 \quad \Gamma^- \triangleright t : T_0 \sqcup T_1}{\Gamma \vdash t \in S_0 \vee S_1}\ (S_{\vee_0}^+)
$$

$$
\frac{\Gamma \vdash t \restriction T_1 \in S_1 \quad \Gamma^- \triangleright S_0 : \mathbb{P}\,T_0 \quad \Gamma^- \triangleright t : T_0 \sqcup T_1}{\Gamma \vdash t \in S_0 \vee S_1}\ (S_{\vee_1}^+)
$$

$$
\frac{t \in S_0 \vee S_1 \quad t \restriction T_0 \in S_0 \vdash P \quad t \restriction T_1 \in S_1 \vdash P \quad t : T_0 \sqcup T_1}{P}\ (S_\vee^-)
$$

$$
\frac{\Gamma \vdash t \in S \quad \Gamma^- \triangleright t : T_0}{\Gamma \vdash t \restriction (T_0 - [l \in T_1]) \in \exists l \in T_1 \bullet S}\ (S_\exists^+)
$$

$$
\frac{\Gamma \vdash t \in \exists l \in T_1 \bullet S \quad \Gamma^- \triangleright t : (T_0 - [l \in T_1]) \quad \Gamma' \vdash P}{\Gamma \vdash P}\ (S_\exists^-)
$$

where $\Gamma' =_{df} \Gamma^-, y : T_0; \Gamma^+, y \in S, y \upharpoonright (T_0 - [l \in T_1]) = t$.

There are also many congruence rules for equality which are derivable, *e.g.*:

$$\frac{\Gamma \vdash S_0 = S_1 \quad \Gamma^- \triangleright S_2 : \mathbb{P}\, T}{\Gamma \vdash S_0 \vee S_2 = S_1 \vee S_2} \ (sub_{\vee_0}) \qquad \frac{\Gamma \vdash S_1 = S_2 \quad \Gamma^- \triangleright S_0 : \mathbb{P}\, T}{\Gamma \vdash S_0 \vee S_1 = S_0 \vee S_2} \ (sub_{\vee_1})$$

Finally, we must mention schema renaming. This is simply a matter of permitting substitution for labels in the meta-language. We indicate this substitution with a left facing arrow to distinguish it from substitution for variables[3].

$$\frac{t \in S}{t[l_0 \leftarrow l_1] \in S[l_0 \leftarrow l_1]} \ (S_\leftarrow^+) \qquad \frac{t \in S[l_0 \leftarrow l_1]}{t[l_1 \leftarrow l_0] \in S} \ (S_\leftarrow^-)$$

3.2   Basic equational logic

All of the following rules, which allow equational reasoning on schemas expressions, are derived rules of the logic for Z_C. We give one example proof. Complete derivations of these rules from the logic for Z_C can be found in [2]. Note that they apply, as expected, only when the declarations range over type carriers.

$$\frac{\Gamma^- \triangleright [D^* \mid P] : \mathbb{P}\, [D^*]}{\Gamma \vdash \neg [D^* \mid P] = [D^* \mid \neg P]} \ (\neg^=)$$

$$\frac{\Gamma^- \triangleright [D_0^* \mid P_0] : \mathbb{P}\, T_0 \quad \Gamma^- \triangleright [D_1^* \mid P_1] : \mathbb{P}\, T_1}{\Gamma \vdash [D_0^* \mid P_0] \vee [D_1^* \mid P_1] = [D_0^* \sqcup D_1^* \mid P_0 \vee P_1]} \ (\vee^=)$$

Providing, of course, that $T_0 \sqcup T_1$ is defined.

Proof. We write D for $D_0^* \vee D_1^*$ in what follows. *Ad* $(\subseteq)$:
We proceed by rule $(S_\vee^-)$. Using rules (S_0^-), (S_1^-) and simple consequences of the assumptions, we obtain $P_0[\alpha[D]/t.\alpha[D]]$, $P_1[\alpha[D]/t.\alpha[D]]$, $t \upharpoonright [D_0^*] \in [D_0^*]$ and $t \upharpoonright [D_1^*] \in [D_1^*]$. From the latter pair, using $(S_\wedge^+)$ we have $t \in [D_0^* \sqcup D_1^*]$. From the former pair we obtain $(P_0 \vee P_1)[\alpha[D]/t.\alpha[D]]$, by rules $(\vee_0^+)$ and $(\vee_1^+)$ discharging the assumptions. It remains to apply rule (S^+) to this data to conclude that $t \in [D_0^* \sqcup D_1^* \mid P_0 \vee P_1]$ as required.
Ad $(\supseteq)$:
Suppose that $t \in [D \mid P_0 \vee P_1]$. Using rules (S_0^-), (S_1^-), and the facts that $D_0^* \sqsubseteq D$ and $D_1^* \sqsubseteq D$ we obtain: $(P_0 \vee P_1)[\alpha[D]/t.\alpha[D]]$, $t \upharpoonright D_0^* \in [D_0^*]$ and $t \upharpoonright D_1^* \in [D_1^*]$. Using rule $(\vee^-)$ on the disjunction above, we use simple consequences of each assumption to obtain $P_0[\alpha[D_0^*]/t \upharpoonright [D_0^*].\alpha[D_0^*]]$ and $P_1[\alpha[D_1^*]/t \upharpoonright [D_1^*].\alpha[D_1^*]]$. Combining these with the data above we have, by rule (S^+) (twice) $t \upharpoonright D_0^* \in [D_0^* \mid P_0]$ and $t \upharpoonright D_0^* \in [D_0^* \mid P_0]$. Using rules $(S_{\vee_0}^+)$ and $(S_{\vee_1}^+)$ we conclude, discharging the assumptions, that $t \in [D_0^* \mid P_0] \vee [D_1^* \mid P_1]$ as required. $\square$

---

[3] Note, for instance that $\langle\!\langle z \Rrightarrow x.z \rangle\!\rangle[x/t]$ is $\langle\!\langle z \Rrightarrow t.z \rangle\!\rangle$ (variable substitution) but $\langle\!\langle z \Rrightarrow x.z \mid \rangle\!\rangle[z \leftarrow v]$ is $\langle\!\langle v \Rrightarrow x.v \rangle\!\rangle$ (label renaming).

$$\frac{\Gamma^- \rhd [D^* \mid P] : \mathbb{P}\, T_1}{\Gamma \vdash \exists l \in T_0 \bullet [D^* \mid P] = [D^* - [l \in T_0] \mid \exists z \in T_0 \bullet P[l/z]]} \ (\exists^=)$$

Note that the right-hand side of the last equation expresses clearly the idea that quantification over a label l has the effect of *removing* (hiding not binding) l.

Finally, we have an equation relating general declarations over sets to declarations over types. This, by iteration, enables us to remove all non-type-carrier sets from the declarations of Z_C schema in the equational logic.

$$\frac{\Gamma^- \rhd [D; \, l \in C \mid P] : \mathbb{P}\, T_1 \quad \Gamma^- \rhd C : \mathbb{P}\, T_0}{\Gamma \vdash [D; \, l \in C \mid P] = [D; \, l \in T_0 \mid l \in C \wedge P]} \ (\in^=)$$

3.3 Schema conjunction

We would expect to define conjunction over schema by analogy with operations like set intersection and logical conjunction:

$$S_0 \wedge S_1 =_{df} \neg(\neg S_0 \vee \neg S_1)$$

Using rules $(C^S_\neg)$ and $(C^S_\vee)$ we obtain the following derived rule for type assignment:

$$\frac{\Gamma \rhd S_0 : \mathbb{P}\, T_0 \quad \Gamma \rhd S_1 : \mathbb{P}\, T_1}{\Gamma \rhd S_0 \wedge S_1 : \mathbb{P}(T_0 \sqcup T_1)} \ (C^S_\wedge)$$

The right-hand side can be shown to be equal to the following set:

$$\{y \in T_0 \sqcup T_1 \mid y \restriction T_0 \in S_0 \wedge y \restriction T_1 \in S_1\}$$

and, given this, the following rule follows by rules $(\wedge^+)$ (derived) and $(\{\}^+)$:

$$\frac{\Gamma \vdash t \restriction T_0 \in S_0 \quad \Gamma \vdash t \restriction T_1 \in S_1 \quad \Gamma^- \rhd t : T_0 \sqcup T_1}{\Gamma \vdash t \in S_0 \wedge S_1} \ (S^+_\wedge)$$

For the corresponding elimination rules we have the following rules, using rule $(\{\}^-)$ and (derived) rules $(\wedge^-_0)$ and $(\wedge^-_1)$:

$$\frac{\Gamma \vdash t \in S_0 \wedge S_1 \quad \Gamma^- \rhd S_0 : \mathbb{P}\, T_0 \quad \Gamma^- \rhd S_1 : \mathbb{P}\, T_1}{\Gamma \vdash t \restriction T_0 \in S_0} \ (S^-_{\wedge_0})$$

$$\frac{\Gamma \vdash t \in S_0 \wedge S_1 \quad \Gamma^- \rhd S_0 : \mathbb{P}\, T_0 \quad \Gamma^- \rhd S_1 : \mathbb{P}\, T_1}{\Gamma \vdash t \restriction T_1 \in S_1} \ (S^-_{\wedge_1})$$

With these in place we can prove the expected equation (see [7] pages 165–166):

$$\frac{\Gamma^- \rhd [D^*_0 \mid P_0] : \mathbb{P}\, T_0 \quad \Gamma^- \rhd [D^*_1 \mid P_1] : \mathbb{P}\, T_1}{\Gamma \vdash [D^*_0 \mid P_0] \wedge [D^*_1 \mid P_1] = [D^*_0 \sqcup D^*_1 \mid P_0 \wedge P_1]} \ (\wedge^=)$$

Finally we have substitution rules:

$$\frac{\Gamma \vdash S_0 = S_1 \quad \Gamma^- \rhd S_2 : \mathbb{P}\, T}{\Gamma \vdash S_0 \wedge S_2 = S_1 \wedge S_2} \qquad \frac{\Gamma \vdash S_0 = S_1 \quad \Gamma^- \rhd S_2 : \mathbb{P}\, T}{\Gamma \vdash S_2 \wedge S_0 = S_2 \wedge S_1}$$

Again, these follow easily from the corresponding rules for disjunction and negation schema.

3.4   Schema implication

Following the pattern given above for conjunction, we have the definition:

$$S_0 \Rightarrow S_1 =_{df} \neg S_0 \vee S_1$$

Using the rules $(C^S_\neg)$ and $(C^S_\vee)$ we obtain a derived rule for type assignment:

$$\frac{\Gamma \rhd S_0 : \mathbb{P}\, T_0 \quad \Gamma \rhd S_1 : \mathbb{P}\, T_1}{\Gamma \rhd S_0 \Rightarrow S_1 : \mathbb{P}(T_0 \sqcup T_1)}$$

The right-hand side of the definition can be shown to be equal to the set

$$\{ z \in T_0 \sqcup T_1 \mid z \upharpoonright T_0 \notin S_0 \vee z \upharpoonright T_1 \in S_1 \}$$

This leads to the following rules:

$$\frac{\Gamma, t \upharpoonright T_0 \in S_0 \vdash t \upharpoonright T_1 \in S_1 \quad \Gamma^- \rhd t : T_0 \sqcup T_1}{\Gamma \vdash t \in S_0 \Rightarrow S_1} \quad (S^+_\Rightarrow)$$

and:

$$\frac{\Gamma \vdash t \in S_0 \Rightarrow S_1 \quad \Gamma \vdash t \upharpoonright T_0 \in S_0 \quad \Gamma^- \rhd t : T_0 \sqcup T_1}{\Gamma \vdash t \upharpoonright T_1 \in S_1} \quad (S^-_\Rightarrow)$$

The expected relationship holds:

$$\frac{\Gamma^- \rhd [D^*_0 \mid P_0] : \mathbb{P}\, T_0 \quad \Gamma^- \rhd [D^*_1 \mid P_1] : \mathbb{P}\, T_1}{\Gamma \vdash [D^*_0 \mid P_0] \Rightarrow [D^*_1 \mid P_1] = [D^*_0 \sqcup D^*_1 \mid P_0 \Rightarrow P_1]}$$

Finally we have the substitution rules:

$$\frac{\Gamma \vdash S_0 = S_1 \quad \Gamma^- \rhd S_2 : \mathbb{P}\, T}{\Gamma \vdash S_0 \Rightarrow S_2 = S_1 \Rightarrow S_2} \qquad \frac{\Gamma \vdash S_0 = S_1 \quad \Gamma^- \rhd S_2 : \mathbb{P}\, T}{\Gamma \vdash S_2 \Rightarrow S_0 = S_2 \Rightarrow S_1}$$

3.5   Schema inclusion

Schema inclusion can be defined in terms of schema conjunction.

$$[D^*_0; \, [D^*_1 \mid P_1] \mid P_0] =_{df} [D^*_0 \sqcup D^*_1 \mid P_0] \wedge [D^*_1 \mid P_1]$$

The rules are then easily calculated as special cases of those for schema conjunction. First the typing rule:

$$\frac{\Gamma \triangleright [D_0^* \sqcup D_1^* \mid P_0] : \mathbb{P}(T_0 \sqcup T_1) \quad \Gamma \triangleright [D_1^* \mid P_1] : \mathbb{P}\, T_1}{\Gamma \triangleright [D_0^*; [D_1^* \mid P_1] \mid P_0] : \mathbb{P}(T_0 \sqcup T_1)}$$

The introduction rule is:

$$\frac{\Gamma \vdash t \in [D_0^* \sqcup D_1^* \mid P_0] \quad \Gamma \vdash t \restriction T_1 \in [D_1^* \mid P_1]}{\Gamma \vdash t \in [D_0^*; [D_1^* \mid P_1] \mid P_0]}$$

The elimination rules are:

$$\frac{\Gamma \vdash t \in [D_0^*; [D_1^* \mid P_1] \mid P_0]}{\Gamma \vdash t \in [D_0^* \sqcup D_1^* \mid P_0]}$$

and:

$$\frac{\Gamma^- \triangleright [D_1^* \mid P_1] : \mathbb{P}\, T_1 \quad \Gamma \vdash t \in [D_0^*; [D_1^* \mid P_1] \mid P_1]}{\Gamma \vdash t \restriction T_1 \in [D_1^* \mid P_1]}$$

Finally, we have the expected equational law:

$$\frac{\Gamma^- \triangleright [D_0^* \mid P_0] : \mathbb{P}\, T_0 \quad \Gamma^- \triangleright [D_1^* \mid P_1] : \mathbb{P}\, T_1}{\Gamma \vdash [D_0^*; [D_1^* \mid P_1] \mid P_0] = [D_0^* \sqcup D_1^* \mid P_0 \wedge P_1]} \ (inc^=)$$

3.6   Schema restriction

In view of our filtering operation on terms which we have extended to sets, we can give a pleasant definition[4]:

$$S_0^{\mathbb{P}\, T_0} \restriction S_1^{\mathbb{P}\, T_1} =_{df} S_0 \mathbin{\rfloor} \mathbb{P}\, T_1 \wedge S_1$$

when $T_1 \sqsubseteq T_0$ It is, then, easy to see that this collapses to our extension of filtered terms to sets when the schema S_1 is just a schema *type*.

The rules are then just a special case of those for conjunction. Using rules $(C_\wedge^S)$ and $(C_{\mathbb{P} \restriction})$ we obtain the type rule:

$$\frac{\Gamma \triangleright S_0 : \mathbb{P}\, T_0 \quad \Gamma \triangleright S_1 : \mathbb{P}\, T_1 \quad T_1 \sqsubseteq T_0}{\Gamma \triangleright S_0 \restriction S_1 : \mathbb{P}\, T_1}$$

The introduction and elimination rules are then as follows:

$$\frac{\Gamma \vdash t \in S_0 \quad \Gamma \vdash t \restriction T_1 \in S_1 \quad T_1 \sqsubseteq T_0}{\Gamma \vdash t \restriction T_1 \in S_0 \restriction S_1} \ (S_\restriction^+)$$

This follows by rules $(S_\wedge^+)$, noting that $T_1 = T_1 \sqcup T_1$ and $T_0 = T_0 \sqcup T_1$.

$$\frac{\Gamma \vdash t \in S_0 \restriction S_1}{\Gamma \vdash t \in S_0 \restriction T_1} \ (S_{\restriction_0}^-) \qquad \frac{\Gamma \vdash t \in S_0 \restriction S_1}{\Gamma \vdash t \in S_1} \ (S_{\restriction_1}^-)$$

---

[4] This is deliberately weaker than the standard definition (see [5] page 34) which permits T_1 to introduce new components. The interested reader will have no difficulty in extending our definition to the standard, if that is considered necessary.

These follow directly from the rules $(S_{\wedge_0}^+)$ and $(S_{\wedge_1})$ noting that $t^T = t \upharpoonright T$.

The substitution rules are:

$$\frac{\Gamma \vdash S_0 = S_1 \quad \Gamma^- \rhd S_2 : \mathbb{P}\, T}{\Gamma \vdash S_0 \upharpoonright S_2 = S_1 \upharpoonright S_2} \qquad \frac{\Gamma \vdash S_0 = S_1 \quad \Gamma^- \rhd S_2 : \mathbb{P}\, T}{\Gamma \vdash S_2 \upharpoonright S_0 = S_2 \upharpoonright S_1}$$

3.7   Schema level hiding

We should provide a form of schema-level hiding: $\exists S_1 \bullet S_0$ (see *e.g.* [5] page 76). In view of earlier infrastructure we can define this easily using schema conjunction and restriction:

$$\exists S_1^{\mathbb{P}\, T_1} \bullet S_0^{\mathbb{P}\, T_0} =_{df} (S_0 \wedge S_1) \upharpoonright \mathbb{P}(T_0 - T_1)$$

Using rules $(C_\wedge^S)$, $(C_{\mathbb{P}\upharpoonright})$, noting that $T_1 \sqsubseteq T_0$, we obtain:

$$\frac{\Gamma \rhd S_0 : \mathbb{P}\, T_0 \quad \Gamma \rhd S_1 : \mathbb{P}\, T_1 \quad T_1 \sqsubseteq T_0}{\Gamma \rhd \exists S_1 \bullet S_0 : \mathbb{P}(T_0 - T_1)}$$

The introduction rule is calculated using rules $(S_\upharpoonright^+)$, $(S_\wedge^+)$.

$$\frac{\Gamma \vdash t \in S_0 \quad \Gamma \vdash t \upharpoonright T_1 \in S_1 \quad T_1 \sqsubseteq T_0}{\Gamma \vdash t \upharpoonright (T_0 - T_1) \in \exists S_1 \bullet S_0}$$

The elimination rule is obtained using rule $(\in_\upharpoonright^-)$:

$$\frac{\Gamma \vdash t \in \exists S_1 \bullet S_0 \quad \Gamma' \vdash P \quad \Gamma^- \rhd t : T_0 - T_1}{\Gamma \vdash P}$$

where $\Gamma' =_{df} \Gamma^-, x : T_0; \Gamma^+, x \in S_0, x \upharpoonright T_1 \in S_1, x \upharpoonright (T_0 - T_1) = t$.

There is a useful equational rule for schema level hiding. This may be compared with the syntactic characterisation of (a simpler form of) schema existential quantification which is given in [7] (page 178).

Let $\alpha[D_1^*] = \{\cdots l_i \cdots\}$ and $\sigma = [\cdots l_i \cdots / \cdots z_i \cdots]$ where the z_i are fresh variables.

$$\frac{\Gamma^- \rhd [D_0^* \mid P_0] : \mathbb{P}\, T_0 \quad \Gamma^- \rhd [D_1^* \mid P_1] : \mathbb{P}\, T_1}{\Gamma \vdash \exists [D_1^* \mid P_1] \bullet [D_0^* \mid P_0] = [D_0^* - D_1^* \mid \exists D_1^* \sigma \bullet (P_0 \wedge P_1)\sigma]}$$

The substitution rules are:

$$\frac{\Gamma \vdash S_0 = S_1 \quad \Gamma^- \rhd S_2 : \mathbb{P}\, T}{\Gamma \vdash \exists S_2 \bullet S_0 = \exists S_2 \bullet S_1} \qquad \frac{\Gamma \vdash S_0 = S_1 \quad \Gamma^- \rhd S_2 : \mathbb{P}\, T}{\Gamma \vdash \exists S_0 \bullet S_2 = \exists S_1 \bullet S_2}$$

3.8   Some useful generalisations

It turns out that when it comes to *using* the schema calculus, rather more general rules, which are common strategies for combining several of the above rules, are needed. In this section we review a few that will be useful in our extended example at the end of the paper.

The following two rules are used together for reasoning about general conjunction schemas.

$$\frac{\Gamma \vdash [D_0] \subseteq [D_1] \quad \Gamma^- \triangleright [D_0 \mid P_0] : \mathbb{P} \, T_0 \quad \Gamma^- \triangleright [D_1 \mid P_1] : \mathbb{P} \, T_1}{\Gamma \vdash [D_0 \mid P_0] \wedge [D_1 \mid P_1] = [D_0 \mid P_0] \wedge [D_0 \mid P_1]} \ (\wedge^{res})$$

This is easily proved using (*sub*), the rule ($\in^=$) for moving sets out of the declaration in favour of types and the standard version of the conjunction rule ($\wedge^=$). A more general form of the rule for conjunction is:

$$\frac{\Gamma^- \triangleright [D_0; D \mid P_0] : \mathbb{P} \, T_0 \quad \Gamma^- \triangleright [D_1; D \mid P_1] : \mathbb{P} \, T_1}{\Gamma \vdash [D_0; D \mid P_0] \wedge [D_1; D \mid P_1] = [D_0; D_1; D \mid P_0 \wedge P_1]} \ (\wedge^=_{gen})$$

subject to the condition $\alpha D_0 \cap \alpha D_1 = \{\}$. The proof of this uses the rules ($\in^=$), (*sub*) and ($\wedge^=$).

There is a version of this pair for disjunction too, proved in similar ways:

$$\frac{\Gamma \vdash [D_0] \supseteq [D_1] \quad \Gamma^- \triangleright [D_0 \mid P_0] : \mathbb{P} \, T_0 \quad \Gamma^- \triangleright [D_1 \mid P_1] : \mathbb{P} \, T_1}{\Gamma \vdash [D_0 \mid P_0] \vee [D_1 \mid P_1] = [D_0 \mid P_0] \vee [D_0 \mid P_1]} \ (\vee^{exp})$$

$$\frac{\Gamma^- \triangleright [D_0; D \mid P_0] : \mathbb{P} \, T_0 \quad \Gamma^- \triangleright [D_1; D \mid P_1] : \mathbb{P} \, T_1}{\Gamma \vdash [D_0; D \mid P_0] \vee [D_1; D \mid P_1] = [D_0; D_1; D \mid P_0 \vee P_1]} \ (\vee^=_{gen})$$

A final generalisation, for existential hiding, that we shall need for our example is:

$$\frac{\Gamma^- \vdash [D; l \in T_0 \mid P] : \mathbb{P} \, T_1}{\Gamma \vdash \exists l \in T_0 \bullet [D; l \in T_0 \mid P] = [D \mid \exists z \in T_0 \bullet P[l/z]]} \ (\exists^=_{gen})$$

which is proved using (*sub*), ($\in^=$) and ($\exists^=$).

4 The language of Z

We do not have the space at our disposal in this paper to outline the interpretation of Z into Z_C in full generality. In this section we will simply develop just enough extra infrastructure to enable us to demonstrate our logic for the schema calculus when we turn to the examination of an example in Section 5.

First we consider the use in Z of Δ-schemas. These appear in the context of operation schema to indicate initial and final states. We note that, in recent years, schema have come to play a far more active role than their original structuring one. This greater role presupposes that they represent specifications of collections rather than of individuals. This perspective offers us the opportunity to interpret the Z idiom ΔS by the declaration $z, z' \in S$ in our core logic Z_C[5]. This turns out to have a desirable technical side effect: we can represent the Z idiom ΞS by the schema $[z, z \in S \mid z = z']$. As a

---

[5] This interpretation is *uniform* providing that the labels z and z' do not occur elsewhere.

result the *type* of the equality is preserved naturally, without the complications which, in some accounts, accompany discussion of the θ operator, in particular those concerning the equation $\theta S = \theta S'$ (in which S' does *not* denote the schema expression S'). Indeed this approach can be employed whenever the θ operation is normally required. It is a natural corollary of adding schema as sets in Z that the θ operation is not required in the core logic Z_C and that its use in Z can always be interpreted in the manner illustrated.

The following schematic equations are sufficient for our requirements in this paper.

$$[\cdots \Delta S \cdots \mid P] =_{df} [\cdots z, z' \in S \cdots \mid P\sigma]$$

where the substitution is:

$$\sigma =_{df} [\alpha S/z.\alpha S][\alpha S'/z'.\alpha S][\theta S/z][\theta S'/z']$$

Then:

$$[\cdots \Xi S \cdots \mid P] =_{df} [\cdots \Delta S \cdots \mid P \wedge \theta S = \theta S']$$

as expected.

5   Example

Here we consider a reasonably complex example from the literature. This uses the technique of *promotion* (see [7] chapter 13). The example is taken from this chapter (*ibid.* pages 194–195) and the earlier chapter which introduces the schema operators (*ibid.* chapter 12, pages 170–175) and concerns the promotion of an operation over a local state to an operation over a global state. This is Z at its very best: providing a general organising strategy which structures a specification. First we present the example as it stands in the book[6].

First we have the Box Office itself:

```
┌─ BoxOffice ──────────────────────────
│ seating ∈ ℙ Seat
│ sold ∈ Seat ↦ Customer
├──────────────────────────────────────
│ dom sold ⊆ seating
└──────────────────────────────────────
```

Purchasing a ticket can succeed or fail. The prototype for a successful purchase is given by:

```
┌─ Purchase₀ ──────────────────────────
│ ΔBoxOffice
│ s? ∈ Seat
│ c? ∈ Customer
├──────────────────────────────────────
│ s? ∈ seating \ dom sold
│ sold' = sold ∪ {s? ↦ c?}
│ seating = seating'
└──────────────────────────────────────
```

---

[6] Apart from our use of '∈' instead of ':', as explained in Section 2.

and success is specified to be:

$$Success =_{df} [r! \in Response \mid r! = \text{okay}]$$

If, on the other hand, the seat requested by the customer is not available, we have:

$$
\begin{array}{l}
\underline{\quad NotAvailable \underline{\hspace{6cm}}} \\
\quad \Xi BoxOffice \\
\quad \underline{\hspace{2.5cm}} \\
\quad s? \notin seating \setminus sold \\
\underline{\hspace{8cm}}
\end{array}
$$

and failure is captured by means of:

$$Failure =_{df} [r! \in Response \mid r! = \text{sorry}]$$

The specification for purchasing a ticket is now composed from these individual specifications:

$$Purchase =_{df} (Purchase_0 \wedge Success) \vee (NotAvailable \wedge Failure)$$

The equational logic can now be deployed in order to investigate this new composite specification:

By rule $(\wedge_{gen}^{=})$, we have $Purchase_0 \wedge Success =$

$$
\begin{array}{l}
\underline{\quad PandS \underline{\hspace{6cm}}} \\
\quad \Delta BoxOffice \\
\quad s? \in Seat \\
\quad c? \in Customer \\
\quad r! \in Response \\
\quad \underline{\hspace{4cm}} \\
\quad s? \in seating \setminus \text{dom}\, sold \\
\quad sold' = sold \cup \{s? \mapsto c?\} \\
\quad seating' = seating \\
\quad r! = \text{okay} \\
\underline{\hspace{8cm}}
\end{array}
$$

Similarly, using rule $(\wedge_{gen}^{=})$, we have $NotAvailable \wedge Failure =$

$$
\begin{array}{l}
\underline{\quad NandF \underline{\hspace{6cm}}} \\
\quad \Xi BoxOffice \\
\quad s? \in Seat \\
\quad r! \in Response \\
\quad \underline{\hspace{4cm}} \\
\quad s? \notin seating \setminus \text{dom}\, sold \\
\quad r! = \text{sorry} \\
\underline{\hspace{8cm}}
\end{array}
$$

By rules $(sub_{\vee_0})$ and $(sub_{\vee_1})$ we now have $Purchase = PandS \vee NandF$. $NandF$ is, by the definition of Ξ-schemas, equivalently:

$\begin{array}{|l}
\underline{\quad NandF \rule{4cm}{0pt}} \\
\Delta BoxOffice \\
s? \in Seat \\
r! \in Response \\
\hline
s? \notin seating \setminus \operatorname{dom} sold \\
r! = \text{sorry} \\
\theta BoxOffice = \theta BoxOffice' \\
\end{array}$

Finally, we use the general rule for disjunction to obtain $Purchase =$

$\begin{array}{|l}
\hline
\Delta BoxOffice \\
s? \in Seat \\
c? \in Customer \\
r! \in Response \\
\hline
(s? \in seating \setminus \operatorname{dom} sold \land \\
\quad sold' = sold \cup \{s? \mapsto c?\} \land \\
\quad seating' = seating \land \\
\quad r! = \text{okay}) \\
\quad \lor \\
(s? \notin seating \setminus \operatorname{dom} sold \land r! = \text{sorry} \land \\
\quad \theta BoxOffice = \theta BoxOffice') \\
\hline
\end{array}$

We promote this local operation of purchasing a ticket to be a global one by conjoining it with the promotion schema:

$\begin{array}{|l}
\underline{\quad Promote \rule{4cm}{0pt}} \\
\Delta GlobalBoxOffice \\
\Delta BoxOffice \\
p? \in Performance \\
\hline
p? \in \operatorname{dom} booking \\
\theta BoxOffice = booking\, p? \\
\theta BoxOffice' = booking'\, p? \\
\{p?\} \lessdot booking' = \{p?\} \lessdot booking \\
announced' = announced \\
\end{array}$

where we have:

$\begin{array}{|l}
\underline{\quad GlobalBoxOffice \rule{3cm}{0pt}} \\
announced \in \mathbb{P}\, Performance \\
booking \in Performance \nrightarrow BoxOffice \\
\hline
\operatorname{dom} booking \subseteq announced \\
\end{array}$

We then hide the components of the local state

$$GlobalPurchase_0 =_{df} \exists \Delta BoxOffice \bullet (Purchase \land Promote)$$

We then have, by rule $(\wedge_{gen}^{=})$ $Purchase \wedge Promote =$

$$
\begin{array}{|l}
\underline{\quad PandP\ \rule[0pt]{280pt}{0.4pt}} \\[4pt]
\Delta GlobalBoxOffice \\
\Delta BoxOffice \\
s? \in Seat \\
c? \in Customer \\
p? \in Performance \\
r! \in Response \\
\hline
p? \in \mathrm{dom}\, booking \\
\theta BoxOffice = booking\ p? \\
\theta BoxOffice' = booking'\ p? \\
\{p?\} \lhd booking' = \{p?\} \lhd booking \\
announced' = announced \\
((s? \in seating \setminus \mathrm{dom}\, sold\ \wedge \\
\quad sold' = sold \cup \{s? \mapsto c?\}\ \wedge \\
\quad seating' = seating\ \wedge \\
\quad r! = \mathrm{okay}) \\
\quad \vee \\
\ (s? \notin seating \setminus \mathrm{dom}\, sold\ \wedge\ r! = \mathrm{sorry}\ \wedge \\
\quad \theta BoxOffice = \theta BoxOffice'))
\end{array}
$$

Then we have: $\exists \Delta BoxOffice \bullet (Purchase \wedge Promote) = (sub_{\exists})$
$\exists \Delta BoxOffice \bullet PandP = (\exists_{gen}^{=})$

$$
\begin{array}{|l}
\underline{\quad GlobalPurchase_1\ \rule[0pt]{260pt}{0.4pt}} \\[4pt]
\Delta GlobalBoxOffice \\
s? \in Seat \\
c? \in Customer \\
p? \in Performance \\
r! \in Response \\
\hline
\exists z, z' \in BoxOffice \bullet \\
\qquad (p? \in \mathrm{dom}\, booking \\
\qquad z = booking\ p? \\
\qquad z' = booking'\ p? \\
\qquad \{p?\} \lhd booking' = \{p?\} \lhd booking \\
\qquad announced' = announced \\
\qquad ((s? \in z.seating \setminus \mathrm{dom}\, z.sold\ \wedge \\
\qquad\quad z'.sold = z.sold \cup \{s? \mapsto c?\}\ \wedge \\
\qquad\quad z'.seating = z.seating\ \wedge \\
\qquad\quad r! = \mathrm{okay}) \\
\qquad\quad \vee \\
\qquad\ (s? \notin z.seating \setminus \mathrm{dom}\, z.sold\ \wedge\ r! = \mathrm{sorry}\ \wedge \\
\qquad\quad z = z'))
\end{array}
$$

Use of the one-point rule on both z and z' in the predicate part of this schema gives, by substitution:

┌─ *GlobalPurchase* ──────────────────────────────────
│ Δ *GlobalBoxOffice*
│ $s? \in Seat$
│ $c? \in Customer$
│ $p? \in Performance$
│ $r! \in Response$
├──
│ $p? \in \mathrm{dom}\, booking$
│ $\{p?\} \lhd booking' = \{p?\} \lhd booking$
│ $announced' = announced$
│ $((s? \in booking\ p?.seating \setminus \mathrm{dom}\, booking\ p?.sold\ \wedge$
│ $\quad booking'\ p?.sold = booking\ p?.sold \cup \{s? \mapsto c?\}\ \wedge$
│ $\quad booking'\ p?.seating = booking\ p?.seating\ \wedge$
│ $\quad r! = \mathrm{okay})$
│ $\vee$
│ $(s? \notin booking\ p?.seating \setminus \mathrm{dom}\, booking\ p?.sold\ \wedge\ r! = \mathrm{sorry}\ \wedge$
│ $\quad booking\ p? = booking'\ p?))$
└──

Note that this is not quite the same as the corresponding result on page 195 of [7] since that version contains some errors. It might be argued that these would have been detected if the schema in question had been properly type-checked. But that, alone, is far too weak. Firstly, there is no guarantee that incorrect equational reasoning will yield a type incorrect schema. Secondly, type-checking cannot identify the nature of the errors. The schema in question could be made to type-check by modifying misused applied occurrences or by declaring missing defining occurrences of schema components, but only the former is the correct strategy. Identifying the correct approach requires more than type-checking. The advantage of obtaining the result by means of an equational logic is that, not only is the schema type-checked (see proposition 1 above), it is also guaranteed to be correct.

6   Conclusions and future work

We have provided, for the first time, a schema logic for the schema expressions of Z: a schema calculus. In this paper we are not able to develop this in full and there is very much more to be said on the subject; this we will make good in a fuller version of the paper. In particular we will describe those schema operations designed to encourage the modular design of operations, for example, schema composition and piping. Here we can only sketch the trajectory: If we restrict ourselves to composition along a single pair of complementary labels (for expository purposes) we can follow the approach of, for example, [1] and define:

$$S_0 \mathbin{;}_{(l',l):T} S_1 =_{df} \exists v \in T \bullet (S_0[l' \leftarrow v] \wedge S_1[l \leftarrow v])$$

In general the data indexing the operator, that is the set of complementary pairs of labels and their types, can be calculated from the *type* of the component schema. We can define a similar operation over types, as follows:

$$T_0;_{(l,l'):T} T_1 =_{df} \exists v \in T \bullet (T_0[l'/v] \sqcup T_1[l/v])$$

and then, for example, we can easily derive the following type assignment rule:

$$\frac{S_0 : \mathbb{P}\, T_0 \quad S_1 : \mathbb{P}\, T_1}{S_0;_{(l',l):T} S_1 : \mathbb{P}(T_0;_{(l,l'):T} T_1)}$$

and the corresponding introduction and elimination rules.

With the schema calculus in place we were able to begin the task of developing higher level reasoning systems, in particular an equational logic. Now that this much is in place, it is possible to contemplate the development of more complex modes of reasoning which will permit reasoning at a usefully high level. The few rules we introduce in Section 3.8 begin this process.

Naturally, our system lends itself to mechanisation and an implementation of Z_C, extended to the schema calculus we have presented here, is currently under construction in Isabelle [4, 6].

We are also involved in a wider project which is looking at alternative foundations for Z, specifically based on intensional set theory and constructive logic. The purpose of this is to investigate alternative means for integrating program development with specification. In the context of this project, the schema calculus we have introduced here is of particular significance: associated with the various rules are mechanisms for combining programs, and this allows the schema calculus to play the dual role of organising specifications and, additionally, methodically constructing implementations.

Acknowledgements

We would like to thank the University of Waikato, the Royal Society of Great Britain and the EPSRC (grant number GR/L57913) for supporting the work reported here. We would also like to thank Stephen Brien and the four anonymous referees who provided useful feedback on the original submission.

References

1. A. Diller. *Z: An Introduction to Formal Methods*. John Wiley & Sons, 2nd edition, 1994.
2. M. C. Henson and S. Reeves. Revising Z: Semantics and logic. Submitted to *Formal Aspects of Computer Science*, 1998.
3. J. Nicholls, editor. *Z Notation: Version 1.2*. Z Standards Panel, 1995.
4. L. C. Paulson. *Isabelle: A Generic Theorem Prover*, volume 828 of *Lecture Notes in Computer Science*. Springer-Verlag, 1994.
5. J. M. Spivey. *The Z Notation: A Reference Manual*. Prentice Hall International Series in Computer Science, 2nd edition, 1992.
6. N. Völker. Private communication, 1998.
7. J. Woodcock and J. Davies. *Using Z: Specification, Refinement and Proof*. Prentice Hall International Series in Computer Science, 1996.

A   Type assignment and propositionhood for Z_C

For clarity we shall omit the entailment symbol and all components of contexts which are irrelevant to, or which remain unchanged by, any rule.

$$\frac{}{\bot\ prop}\ (C_\bot) \qquad \frac{t_0 : T \quad t_1 : T}{t_0 = t_1\ prop}\ (C_=) \qquad \frac{t : T \quad C : \mathbb{P}\,T}{t \in C\ prop}\ (C_\in) \qquad \frac{P\ prop}{\neg\,P\ prop}\ (C_\neg)$$

$$\frac{P_0\ prop \quad P_1\ prop}{P_0 \vee P_1\ prop}\ (C_\vee) \qquad \frac{C : \mathbb{P}\,T \quad z : T \triangleright P\ prop}{\exists z \in C \bullet P\ prop}\ (C_\exists) \qquad \frac{}{x : T \triangleright x : T}\ (C_x)$$

$$\frac{}{0 : \mathbb{N}}\ (C_0) \qquad \frac{n : \mathbb{N}}{succ\ n : \mathbb{N}}\ (C_s) \qquad \frac{C : \mathbb{P}\,T}{\mathbb{P}\,C : \mathbb{P}\mathbb{P}\,T}\ (C_\mathbb{P})$$

$$\frac{C : \mathbb{P}\,T \quad z : T \triangleright P\ prop}{\{z \in C \mid P\} : \mathbb{P}\,T}\ (C_{\{\}}) \qquad \frac{C_0 : \mathbb{P}\,T_0 \quad C_1 : \mathbb{P}\,T_1}{C_0 \times C_1 : \mathbb{P}(T_0 \times T_1)}\ (C_\times)$$

$$\frac{}{\mathbb{N} : \mathbb{P}\mathbb{N}}\ (C_\mathbb{N}) \qquad \frac{\cdots\ C : \mathbb{P}\,T\ \cdots}{[\cdots l \in C \cdots] : \mathbb{P}[\cdots l : T \cdots]}\ (C_{[]}) \qquad \frac{t : [\cdots l_i : T \cdots]}{t.l_i : T}\ (C_.)$$

$$\frac{\cdots\ t_i : T_i\ \cdots}{\langle\!\lvert \cdots l_i \Rightarrow t_i \cdots \rvert\!\rangle : [\cdots l_i : T_i \cdots]}\ (C_\Rightarrow) \qquad \frac{t : T_0 \times T_1}{t.1 : T_0}\ (C_1) \qquad \frac{t : T_0 \times T_1}{t.2 : T_1}\ (C_2)$$

$$\frac{t_0 : T_0 \quad t_1 : T_1}{(t_0, t_1) : T_0 \times T_1}\ (C_{()}) \qquad \frac{t : T_1 \quad T_0 \sqsubseteq T_1}{t \upharpoonright T_0 : T_0}\ (C_\upharpoonright)$$

B   The logic of Z_C

We again omit all data which remain unchanged by a rule.

$$\frac{\Gamma \vdash P_0 \quad \Gamma^- \triangleright P_1\ prop}{\Gamma \vdash P_0 \vee P_1}\ (\vee_0^+) \qquad \frac{\Gamma \vdash P_1 \quad \Gamma^- \triangleright P_0\ prop}{\Gamma \vdash P_0 \vee P_1}\ (\vee_1^+)$$

$$\frac{P_0 \vee P_1 \quad P_0 \vdash P_2 \quad P_1 \vdash P_2}{P_2}\ (\vee^-) \qquad \frac{\Gamma, P \vdash \bot \quad \Gamma^- \triangleright P\ prop}{\Gamma \vdash \neg P}\ (\neg^+)$$

$$\frac{\neg\neg P}{P}\ (\neg^-) \qquad \frac{P \quad \neg P}{\bot}\ (\bot^+)$$

$$\frac{\Gamma \vdash \bot \quad \Gamma^- \triangleright P\ prop}{\Gamma \vdash P}\ (\bot^-) \qquad \frac{P[z/t] \quad t \in C}{\exists z \in C \bullet P}\ (\exists^+)$$

$$\frac{\Gamma \vdash \exists z \in C \bullet P_0 \quad \Gamma^- \triangleright C : \mathbb{P}\,T \quad \Gamma^-, y : T;\ \Gamma^+, P_0[z/y] \vdash P_1}{P_1}\ (\exists^-)$$

$$\frac{\Gamma, P \ context}{\Gamma, P \vdash P} \ (ass) \qquad \frac{\Gamma^- \vartriangleright t : T}{\Gamma \vdash t = t} \ (ref) \qquad \frac{t = t' \quad P[z/t]}{P[z/t']} \ (sub) \qquad \frac{}{0 \neq succ \ 0}$$

$$\frac{\Gamma^- \vartriangleright \langle\!| \cdots l_i \Rrightarrow t_i \cdots |\!\rangle : T}{\Gamma \vdash \langle\!| \cdots l_i \Rrightarrow t_i \cdots |\!\rangle.l_i = t_i} \ (\Rrightarrow^{=_0}) \qquad \frac{\Gamma^- \vartriangleright t : [\cdots l_i : T_i \cdots]}{\Gamma \vdash \langle\!| \cdots l_i \Rrightarrow t.l_i \cdots |\!\rangle = t} \ (\Rrightarrow^{=_1})$$

$$\frac{\Gamma^- \vartriangleright (t, t') : T}{\Gamma \vdash (t, t').1 = t} \ (()^=_0) \qquad \frac{\Gamma^- \vartriangleright (t, t') : T}{\Gamma \vdash (t, t').2 = t'} \ (()^=_1) \qquad \frac{\Gamma^- \vdash t : T_0 \times T_1}{\Gamma \vdash (t.1, t.2) = t} \ (()^=_2)$$

$$\frac{P[z/t] \quad t \in C}{t \in \{z \in C \mid P\}} \ (\{\}^+) \qquad \frac{t \in \{z \in C \mid P\}}{t \in C} \ (\{\}^-_0) \qquad \frac{t \in \{z \in C \mid P\}}{P[z/t]} \ (\{\}^-_1)$$

$$\frac{\Gamma, z \in C_0 \vdash z \in C_1 \quad \Gamma^- \vartriangleright z \in C_0 \ prop}{\Gamma \vdash C_0 \in \mathbb{P} \, C_1} \ (\mathbb{P}^+) \qquad \frac{C_0 \in \mathbb{P} \, C_1 \quad t \in C_0}{t \in C_1} \ (\mathbb{P}^-)$$

$$\frac{t_0 \in C_0 \quad t_1 \in C_1}{(t_0, t_1) \in C_0 \times C_1} \ (\times^+) \qquad \frac{t \in C_0 \times C_1}{t.1 \in C_0} \ (\times^-_0) \qquad \frac{t \in C_0 \times C_1}{t.2 \in C_1} \ (\times^-_1)$$

$$\frac{\cdots \quad t_i \in C_i \quad \cdots}{\langle\!| \cdots l_i \Rrightarrow t_i \cdots |\!\rangle \in [\cdots l_i \in C_i \cdots]} \ (\![]^+) \qquad \frac{t \in [\cdots l_i \in C_i \cdots]}{t.l_i \in C_i} \ (\![]^-)$$

$$\frac{\Gamma \vdash C_0 \equiv C_1 \quad \Gamma^- \vartriangleright C_0 : \mathbb{P} \, T}{\Gamma \vdash C_0 = C_1} \ (ext)$$

$$\frac{\Gamma \vdash t.l_i = t_i \quad \Gamma^- \vartriangleright t : T \quad [\cdots l_i : T_i \cdots] \sqsubseteq T}{\Gamma \vdash (t \restriction [\cdots l_i \in T_i \cdots]).l_i = t_i} \ (\restriction^=)$$

Definition 1. *If, for some context* Γ, $\Gamma^- \vartriangleright C_0 : \mathbb{P} \, T$ *then:*

$$\Gamma \vdash C_0 \equiv C_1 \ =_{df} \ \Gamma \vdash (\forall z \in C_0 \bullet z \in C_1) \wedge (\forall z \in C_1 \bullet z \in C_0)$$

As usual, we can derive rules for $\wedge$ and $\Rightarrow$ from the above system and we use such rules as necessary without further comment.

Combining Specification Techniques for Processes, Data and Time

(Abstract)

Ernst-Rüdiger Olderog

Fachbereich Informatik, Universität Oldenburg
Postfach 2503, D-26111 Oldenburg, Germany
Email: olderog@informatik.uni-oldenburg.de

Complex computing systems exhibit various behavioural aspects, for example communication between components, state transformation inside components, and real-time constraints on the communications and state changes. Formal specification techniques for such systems have to be able to describe all these aspects.

Unfortunately, a single specification technique that is well suited for all these aspects is not available. Instead one finds various specialised techniques that are very good at describing individual aspects of system behaviour. This observation has led to research into the combination and semantic integration of specification techniques.

In this talk we discuss the combination of techniques for the specification of processes, data and time. This will be done more specifically by looking at CSP, Z and the Duration Calculus [1, 2]. The emphasis is on a smooth integration of the underlying semantic models.

References

1. M. R. Hansen, Zhou Chaochen, Duration Calculus: Logical foundations. *Formal Aspects of Computing*, 9:283–330, 1997.
2. Zhou Chaochen, C. A. R. Hoare, A. P. Ravn. A calculus of durations. *Information Processing Letters*, 40:269–276, 1991.

Innovations in the Notation of Standard Z

Ian Toyn

Department of Computer Science, University of York, UK

Tel: +44 1904 433386   Fax: +44 1904 432708

Email: ian@cs.york.ac.uk

Abstract. The second Committee Draft of the ISO standard "Z Notation" is expected to be published soon after the ZUM'98 proceedings. This paper provides an overview of Standard Z from the perspective of the differences between its notation and that of Spivey's *de facto* standard "The Z Notation: A Reference Manual". Its aim is to make the differences be more widely known and hence enable wider exploitation of the improvements, by both specifiers and tool builders. The differences reported are those for which the author perceives there to be consensus within the Z panel. As the second Committee Draft is not yet finished, beware that this consensus could yet change.

1   Introduction

This paper compares the notation that is expected to be defined by the second Committee Draft (CD) of the ISO standard "Z Notation" [26] with that of Spivey's "The Z Notation: A Reference Manual" [15, 16]. Spivey's book [16] is referred to below as "ZRM".

ZRM was a huge step forward at the time of its first publication. Many syntax and type-checking tools for Z have been based on it, and it has become a *de facto* standard. It is an excellent work that has certainly served the Z community well, but it is not perfect, there being several issues that it did not adequately address. Such inadequacies are inevitably resolved by different users in different ways. Standardization aims to provide widely acceptable solutions to the problems, so that diverse dialects can be avoided.

The ISO standardization process recognizes that standards documents evolve through four identifiable phases in becoming acceptable. *Working Drafts* are ones reviewed by panel members. *Committee Drafts* are ones on which the panel invites the public to comment. *Draft International Standards* are ones which the panel believe to be acceptable. An *International Standard* is one that has been accepted. The process involves deadlines to ensure progress. The Z panel issued its first CD in September 1995. The second CD is expected soon; the final CD must appear by September 1999.

Highlights of the first CD [14] include the results of much work by Stephen Brien, Jim Woodcock and others on how to define formally the meaning of the Z notation. Ideas on how to resolve some of the inadequacies in the Z notation were evident. The second CD will address comments on the first CD, as well as incorporating several rationalizations and enhancements of the language that have been developed since the first CD was prepared. The panel have tried to be faithful to the spirit of both the first CD and the ZRM, preferring the more widely read ZRM where there is a conflict.

Some of the innovations arise from cleaning up the syntax. For example, ZRM syntax treats schemas distinctly from expressions, disguising the simple view of a schema as just an expression whose type is power set of bindings. Removing such irregularities from the syntax results in a better notation for specification. Motivation for such changes came partly from those doing formal proofs, where the ability to substitute any formula by any equivalent formula had been hindered by those syntactic irregularities. Interestingly, Spivey anticipated the problem in ZRM:

> "I have also felt unable to include a system of formal inference rules for deriving theorems about specifications. ... the practical usefulness of inference rules seems to depend crucially on making them interact smoothly, and we have not yet gained enough experience to do this."

The author of this paper is a member of the Z panel, with a particular responsibility for the syntax in the second CD. That makes him an appropriate person to write this paper, though most of the ideas can be attributed to other members of the Z panel. Some historical remarks are included below as a way of acknowledging where some of the ideas were discussed in writing. Users of Z should refer to the latest available draft rather than to those older documents for further up-to-date details of Standard Z. Indeed, no commitment to the inclusion in the standard of the innovations presented in this paper should be inferred, though attempts have been made to avoid presenting anything that is still contentious. There are other likely innovations that are not presented here, e.g. some in the toolkit, as they are still somewhat contentious.

The Z panel has taken into account other work from the history of Z besides ZRM. Amongst the important early works are Sufrin's Z Handbook [20], Hayes' Case Studies [9], and King *et al*'s Grammar [12]. The formal reasoning experiences gained with ProofPower [6], Zola [8] and CADiZ [22, 25] have had some influence. Most users of Z regard ZRM as their *de facto* standard, and so that is the most suitable point of comparison for this paper.

The rest of this paper is in three parts. First, the inadequacies of ZRM are identified and Standard Z's solutions are outlined. Second, the incompatibilities arising from those solutions between ZRM and Standard Z notations are discussed, with guidance being offered on how to detect and resolve instances of them. Third, some subtle changes are explained where, although existing ZRM notation still has the same meaning, the interpretation of the notation to give that meaning has changed. There is lots more that could be said about the Standard document and its history, but this paper avoids doing so.

2   Improvements

This section presents improvements in Standard Z that address inadequacies in ZRM.

2.1 Sections

Specifications are rarely written in terms of the Z base language. Even pedagogic examples usually refer to the definitions of the mathematical toolkit. Real specifications are constructed from libraries or toolkits of operations relevant to particular application domains. It should be possible to reuse toolkits by reference, without having to duplicate them into every specification that uses them. This is an issue that ZRM ignores.

Standard Z provides probably the simplest possible solution to the toolkit reuse problem, in the form of its section notation. A Z section contains a sequence of paragraphs, just like a ZRM specification. It also has a header which gives this section its name and lists the names of those other sections that are parents of this one.

> section *myspec* parents *toolkit*
> *paragraph*$_1$
> $\vdots$
> *paragraph*$_n$

Such a section, in combination with its ancestral sections, is what comprises a specification in Standard Z. At any point in a specification, the environment of global declarations comprises those already declared in the current section and all declarations of all sections named as parents of the current one. For example, consider a specification comprising four sections from which just the headers are as follows.

> section *A*
> section *B* parents *A*
> section *C* parents *A*
> section *D* parents *B*, *C*

The parents relation can be depicted as a directed acyclic graph.

Within sections *B* and *C*, the declarations of section *A* may be used. Within section *D*, the declarations of sections *A*, *B* and *C* may be used.

Global redeclaration is not permitted, either within a section or across related sections. Unlike other proposals for module-like facilities, a section cannot hide any of its paragraphs – it is not an encapsulation mechanism. For backwards compatibility, a single sequence of paragraphs with no section header is accepted as a single section with *toolkit* as its sole parent.

The mechanics of exactly how parents are brought together is unspecified. Parents might be separate documents, or chapters or appendices in the same document. A tool might use a relation between section names and file names.

Historical remarks. Sections were proposed in [2].

2.2 Mutually-recursive Free Types

ZRM presents a free type as an abbreviation for a given type followed by axiomatic constraints to ensure that its constants are elements of the given type, that its constructors are injections producing members of the given type, that the elements and the values returned by the injections are all distinct from each other, and that all values of the type are either elements or returned by an injection. Unfortunately, it does not consider mutually-recursive free types.

Standard Z permits mutually-recursive free types to be written, separated by & symbols within a single paragraph. Mutually-recursive free types are especially useful in defining the syntax of languages, as illustrated by the following fragment.

$$
\begin{aligned}
&dec ::= Dec\langle\!\langle name \times exp \rangle\!\rangle \\
&\& \\
&exp ::= Let\langle\!\langle seq\ dec \times exp \rangle\!\rangle \\
&\qquad\ |\ Num\langle\!\langle \mathbb{N} \rangle\!\rangle
\end{aligned}
$$

In this example, a declaration *dec* involves an expression *exp*, and an *exp* can involve local declarations. A larger example would be mutual recursion between predicates and expressions in Z.

The second CD will present a transformation of mutually-recursive free types to given types and axiomatic constraints. Its definition of the membership, totality, injectivity and disjointness axioms follow the same pattern as before, the only change being in the induction axiom which involves all of the mutually-recursive types simultaneously.

Historical remarks. The & notation was suggested in [1]. The transformation was defined in [23, 5].

2.3 Operators

An operator is a name with special lexical status, for example an infix operator appears between its operands. ZRM notation allows the use of various operators. A use of an operator has to be preceded by its definition. Its definition ought to be preceded by an introduction of a template for the operator, to indicate that the name will be defined and used in, for example, infix position. Without the information provided by the template, it is not possible to parse the operator's definition and uses. Although ZRM says what kinds of templates it permits operators to have, no notation is specified for the introduction of operator templates. It presumes that all the operators defined in its toolkit are already known to the reader and hence recognizable, and leaves each tool to implement its own distinct notation for templates.

Standard Z has a notation called an operator template paragraph that serves to introduce new operators. Here are some examples from the toolkit.

relation $(\_ \neq \_)$
function 30 leftassoc $(\_ \cup \_)$
generic 5 rightassoc $(\_ \leftrightarrow \_)$
function 90 $(\_ ^{-1})$
function 90 $(\_ (\!| \_ |\!))$
relation (disjoint $\_$)

Each of these lines begins with an operator's category and ends with a parenthesized pattern. In between, as appropriate for the operator, is precedence and associativity information. An operator's category determines how applications of the operator are parsed: an application of a relation operator is parsed as a relational predicate; an application of a function operator is parsed as a function application expression; an application of a generic operator is parsed as a generic instantiation expression. When applications of operators are nested, so that one operator application appears as an operand in another operator application, the intended nesting can be made explicit using parentheses. Alternatively, if no parentheses are used, the precedence and associativity information determines how the applications are nested: applications of operators with higher precedence bind more tightly than ones of lower precedence; nested applications of infix operators with the same precedence associate either to the left or right as declared (all operators sharing the same precedence must have the same associativity).

Standard Z notation permits a wider variety of operators to be introduced than ZRM notation. The following table summarizes what is permitted.

	ZRM	Standard Z
Category	relation, function, generic	relation, function, generic
Precedence	infix functions 1..6, others fixed by syntax	functions and generics $a..b$, relations fixed by syntax
Associativity	left or right, fixed by syntax	left or right, user-defined
Arity	1..2	1..n, operands and symbols alternate

The range of precedences $a..b$ has yet to be decided. When it is, the precedences of toolkit operators will be renumbered in that range, maintaining their order. The generalization to arbitrary arity is subject to the restriction that operands and symbols must alternate, meaning that two operands cannot be consecutive without an intervening symbol, and two symbols cannot be consecutive without an intervening operand. An example of the latter restriction would be the consecutive symbols *else if* (within the obvious operator), whereas writing them as a single symbol *elsif* would be permitted. ZRM is more restrictive than suggested by the above table: relations and generics cannot be postfix, functions cannot be declared to be prefix (they just are by default), and there are no "nofix" (bracketing) operators. Standard Z permits more than suggested by the table: it permits sequence arguments distinct from normal value arguments, as in the following examples of sequence extension brackets and bag extension brackets.

function $(\langle ,, \rangle)$
function $([\![,,]\!])$

Standard Z defines relational image brackets and sequence brackets in the toolkit, whereas ZRM had to make special cases for them in the base syntax.

Chaining of relations in Standard Z is exactly as permitted by ZRM, i.e. only infix binary relations may be chained; a chain may not commence with a prefix relation, nor end with a postfix relation, nor can tertiary or higher relations appear in a chain. Technically these would all be possible, but they would never be good stylistically.

Function and relation operators that are generic invariably have their generic arguments left implicit, but if those arguments are explicit then they appear in square brackets, whether in ZRM or Standard Z (unlike in the first CD).

Having introduced the template of an operator, the notation for defining and using an operator is similar to that of ZRM, as illustrated by the maplet example below. The definition has as its left-hand side the pattern without the parentheses. Applications of an operator are written with expressions in place of _ operand markers, and comma-separated lists of zero-or-more expressions in place of ,, operand markers. References to an operator without applying it to any arguments are written as the pattern enclosed in parentheses.

function 10 leftassoc $(\_ \mapsto \_)$

$$
\begin{array}{l}
=[X, Y]======================= \\
\quad \_ \mapsto \_ : X \times Y \to X \times Y \\
\hline
\quad \forall x : X; \; y : Y \bullet \\
\qquad x \mapsto y = (x, y)
\end{array}
$$

Note that the shapes of paragraph outlines are not prescribed by Standard Z, allowing use of outlines that uniformly reflect not just the extent but also the genericity and scope of the declared names.

Some further improvements on ZRM are that an operator name may be the name of an element or injection of a free type, may be the name of a **let** definition, and may be selected from a binding.

Historical remarks. A sketch of the notation for operators was suggested in [1]. A detailed proposal was included in [17]. That was then revised in the light of experience such as that reported in [4, 21].

2.4 Conjectures

ZRM presents many laws, but without formalizing their syntax as part of Z. Their presentation is pseudo-formal, none of their variables being declared. Proof tools typically provide sequents, which are a notation suitable for expressing not only laws, but also conjectures, theorems, goals, lemmas and axioms. Of these, conjectures are the starting point for proofs, and are sometimes hand-written within specifications. Different proof tools use different syntaxes for sequents, so it is not appropriate to standardize their syntax. However, standardizing a simpler syntax specifically for conjectures is possible and worthwhile, as this allows them to be written within specifications in a form that potentially eases their interchange between tools and allows them to be subjected to type-checking.

Standard Z's notation for a (generic) conjecture involves a ⊢ symbol followed by a single predicate. The following examples formalize a couple of laws from ZRM.

$$\vdash \forall a : \mathbb{Z} \bullet a..a = \{a\}$$
$$[X] \vdash \forall A : \mathbb{P}_1 \, \mathbb{P} X; \ S : \mathbb{P} X \bullet S \setminus \bigcup A = \bigcap \{T : A \bullet S \setminus T\}$$

This simple syntax is chosen as it is likely to conform to the syntax of a sequent, or at least be translatable to a sequent, whatever proof tool is used. A conjecture is valid if its predicate can be shown to be implied by the properties of the specification, without itself contributing to those properties. The following conjecture is an example of an invalid one, but the specification of which it is a part remains well-formed nevertheless.

$$\vdash 42 \in \{1, 2, 3\}$$

Historical remarks. Some motivation for conjectures was given in [1].

2.5   Binding Extensions and Tuple Selections

The Z base language provides both labelled and unlabelled product types, called schema types and Cartesian product types respectively. One would expect to find notations for construction and selection operations on values of each of these types, but ZRM offers only a selection operation for values of schema type, and only a construction operation for values of Cartesian product type. Standard Z also offers notations for the other two operations. The following table summarizes the notations.

	ZRM		Standard Z	
	Constructors	Selectors	Constructors	Selectors
Tuples	(x, y, z)		(x, y, z)	*triple*.3
Bindings		*binding*.*name*	$(\!\| x == 1, y == 42 \|\!)$	*binding*.*name*

ZRM explains bindings using the notation $\langle p_1 \Rrightarrow x_1, \ ..., \ p_n \Rrightarrow x_n \rangle$ (pages 26 and 62), but does not permit use of this as Z notation. ZRM notation is used largely for producing abstract specifications of systems, where the emphasis is on the use of schemas and constraints on them rather than particular bindings, those being more specific and concrete. However, Z can be used in other ways and in other contexts, for example, the author has used it in reasoning about a relational database, where the rows of a table were modelled by the bindings of a schema. Standard Z's notation for the construction of bindings from explicit component values is called a binding extension expression. The syntax of a binding extension expression conforms to the template

$$(\!\| i_1 == e_1, \ ..., \ i_n == e_n \|\!)$$

where the subscripts distinguish different names i and their associated expressions e, and $n \geq 0$. Bindings can arise in ZRM either by theta expressions or as members of schemas. It is particularly useful to have binding extension notation during proofs, where showing the truth of predicates such as $\theta S = \theta S\,'$ involves consideration of the underlying binding values. An example of such a proof appears in the next subsection.

Standard Z's notation for the selection of components from tuples is called a tuple selection expression. The syntax of a tuple selection expression conforms to the template

$$e.b$$

where the expression e denotes a tuple and b is a base ten positive number literal in the range up to the arity of the tuple. These conditions are verifiable by type-checking. ZRM notation provides *first* and *second* selectors for pairs in the toolkit, but no selectors for larger tuples. Standard Z retains *first* and *second* in the toolkit for backwards compatibility.

Historical remarks. These changes were proposed in [1], with the particular notation for binding extensions being decided subsequently [18].

2.6   Schemas as Expressions

An expression has a value of a particular type. A schema has a value – it is a set of bindings – but in ZRM the syntax permits only references to named schemas, not general schema expressions, to be used as expressions. Instead, ZRM has a separate category of schema expressions, that may appear only in named horizontal schema definition paragraphs. This distinction between schema expressions and other expressions also prohibits an expression whose type is that of a set of bindings from being used within a schema expression.

This syntactic restriction is an obstacle to formal reasoning. The replacement of a name by its defining expression is a typical substitution-of-equals-for-equals logical inference, but that is precluded by the syntactic restriction. Without that particular inference rule, it is not clear how to replace a reference to a schema by the mathematics of its definition, and hence to reason further. More generally, all formulae arising from logical inferences should be expressible in the concrete syntax, and so irregularities in the concrete syntax should be eradicated.

In Standard Z, the syntactic category of schema expressions has been merged into that of expressions. So an arbitrary schema expression may appear as an inclusion declaration, as a predicate, as an operand to θ, or as an expression, i.e. wherever a schema reference could appear in ZRM notation. The type system ensures that a schema is used only where an expression whose type is that of a set of bindings is permissible, and that only an expression whose type is that of a set of bindings is used where a schema is required. Tutorials on Z can now give a much simpler description of schemas, e.g. this taken from [11].

> "A schema is any value whose type is a set of bindings. In addition to its ordinary use as a set, a schema may be used in three special, and important ways: (i) as a declaration; (ii) as a predicate and (iii) as an operand of certain special operators (called the schema calculus operators) which construct new schemas from old in various convenient ways."

The following example illustrates use of schema expressions as inclusion declarations and as operands to θ.

$$\begin{array}{|l}\hline S \underline{\hspace{6cm}} \\ \hline x : \mathbb{Z} \\ y : \mathbb{N} \\ \hline \end{array} \qquad \begin{array}{|l}\hline \Delta Sx \underline{\hspace{5cm}} \\ \hline S; \, S' \\ \hline \theta(S \setminus (x)) = \theta(S \setminus (x))' \\ \hline \end{array}$$

The ΔSx schema can be interpreted as defining a change to the state represented by schema S in which only the x component's value can change. The conjecture that the value of component y is left unchanged by ΔSx can now be stated and proved. In this proof, schema expressions can be seen being used as predicates.

$\vdash \forall S; \, S' \bullet \Delta Sx \Rightarrow y = y'$

$\qquad\qquad\qquad\qquad\qquad\qquad\qquad\qquad\qquad$ [*expansion of ΔSx*]

$\vdash \forall S; \, S' \bullet [S; \, S' \mid \theta(S \setminus (x)) = \theta(S \setminus (x))'] \Rightarrow y = y'$

$\qquad\qquad\qquad\qquad\qquad\qquad\qquad\qquad\qquad$ [*expansion of thetas*]

$\vdash \forall S; \, S' \bullet [S; \, S' \mid \langle\!| \, y == y \, |\!\rangle = \langle\!| \, y == y' \, |\!\rangle] \Rightarrow y = y'$

$\qquad\qquad\qquad\qquad\qquad\qquad$ [*absorption of binding extensions*]

$\vdash \forall S; \, S' \bullet [S; \, S' \mid y = y'] \Rightarrow y = y'$

$\qquad\qquad\qquad\qquad\qquad\qquad$ [*absorption of schema predicate*]

$\vdash \forall S; \, S' \bullet y = y' \Rightarrow y = y'$

$\qquad\qquad\qquad\qquad\qquad\qquad$ [*absorption of implication*]

$\vdash \forall S; \, S' \bullet true$

$\qquad\qquad\qquad\qquad\qquad$ [*absorption of universal quantification*]

$\vdash true$

Historical remarks. A proposal to allow general use of expressions as schemas was made to the Z panel in [11]. An argument for merging schema expressions with expressions was published to the wider community in [29].

2.7 Empty Schemas

An empty schema is a schema with no declarations. One can arise in ZRM notation *via* the hiding of all declarations from a schema.

$\qquad Schema \mathrel{\widehat{=}} [x, y : \mathbb{Z} \mid x \neq y] \setminus (x, y)$

This should simplify to the following equivalent paragraph, but ZRM does not permit this to be written.

$\qquad Schema \mathrel{\widehat{=}} [\; \mid \exists x, y : \mathbb{Z} \bullet x \neq y]$

Standard Z does permit the list of declarations in a schema text to be empty. Empty schemas are surprisingly useful. If the type of S is that of an empty schema, then S must have one of only two possible values, according to whether the constraint in the schema is *true* or *false*.

$$S \in \mathbb{P}\ [\,] \Rightarrow S = [\ |\ true] \lor S = [\ |\ false]$$

When an empty schema is used as a predicate, if its predicate part is *true*, the whole schema predicate is *true*,

⊢ [| *true*]

[*expansion of schema predicate*]

⊢ θ[| *true*] ∈ [| *true*]

[*expansion of empty schema*]

⊢ θ[| *true*] ∈ {⟨|⟩}

[*expansion of theta*]

⊢ ⟨|⟩ ∈ {⟨|⟩}

[*expansion of membership*]

⊢ *true*

else if its predicate part is *false*, the whole schema predicate is *false*.

⊢ [| *false*]

[*expansion of schema predicate*]

⊢ θ[| *false*] ∈ [| *false*]

[*expansion of empty schema*]

⊢ θ[| *false*] ∈ {}

[*expansion of theta (unnecessary)*]

⊢ ⟨|⟩ ∈ {}

[*expansion of membership*]

⊢ *false*

The two possible values of an empty schema can be seen from the above to be isomorphic to the Booleans. The following definitions would thus make sense, though they do not appear within Standard Z's toolkit.

False == [| *false*]
True == [| *true*]
Boolean == {*False, True*}

Z has never provided a *Boolean* type because when writing abstract specifications it is relatively poor style: it is better to use relations and test for membership of those relations. However, Z can also be used in other circumstances. For example, the author was once involved in a project that involved translation of another notation to Z, where that other notation did not share Z's syntactic distinction between predicates and expressions. Wherever a predicate *p* was used as a Boolean-valued expression, empty schemas enabled the straightforward translation to [| *p*]. Another example is refinement toward code, where the code will use a Boolean data type. The definition of *Boolean* given above is superior to the occasionally used free type *Boolean* ::= *False* | *True* because the definition as schemas allows use as predicates.

To summarize: Standard Z adds notation for empty schemas; Booleans are rarely appropriate for use in abstract specifications and are not defined by Standard Z, but if needed, the definition given above is recommended.

Historical remarks. Empty schemas and their isomorphism with Booleans were discussed in [27].

2.8   Loose Generics

ZRM informally requires that generic definitions not be loose:

> "A restriction must be obeyed by the definitions of generic constants for them to be mathematically sound: the definition must uniquely determine the value of the constant for each possible value of the formal parameters. ... [This] places a proof obligation on the author of a specification..."

That proof obligation is rarely discharged by authors, but fortunately the semantics of Standard Z allow the restriction to be relaxed. An example of a useful loose generic definition is the following choice function (suggested by Rob Arthan). It is loose in the sense that it avoids specifying which component of the given pair is returned by the function.

$$
\begin{array}{l}
\quad\![X]\!= \\
\mid\; pick\_from\_pair : X \times X \to X \\
\mid\!\!\rule{3cm}{0.4pt} \\
\mid\; \forall x,y : X \times X \bullet pick\_from\_pair(x,y) \in \{x,y\}
\end{array}
$$

In combination with global constraints (which can now be generic), loose generics provide a kind of *ad hoc* overloading mechanism without any additional notation. For example, different instantiations of the generic definition *pick_from_pair* can be constrained to behave differently.

$$
\begin{array}{l}
\mid\; pick\_from\_pair[\mathbb{N}] = first \\
\mid\; pick\_from\_pair[\mathbb{R}] = second
\end{array}
$$

This paragraph outline reflects Standard Z's view of a global constraint as being an axiomatic paragraph with an empty schema.

Although there is consensus within the Z panel for loose generics, the overloading that they enable has been little used as yet. There is potential for obfuscation, so use loose generics with care.

Historical remarks. The consistency of loose generics is discussed in [31]. The desirability of allowing generic constraints was suggested in [1].

2.9   Local Constant Declarations

ZRM's restriction to the global level on the use of == in non-generic declarations is an unnecessary irregularity. Standard Z has removed this restriction, allowing use of == in schema texts. A declaration $i == e$ is equivalent to the declaration $i : \{e\}$. Also, the merging of schemas with expressions has made the $\hat{=}$ symbol redundant: the == symbol can be used wherever $\hat{=}$ could be used.

When used in quantified predicates or definite description (or let) expressions, local constant declarations provide a neat notation for expressing substitutions.

$$\exists x == 42; \, y == 1998 \bullet p$$
$$\mu x == 42; \, y == 1998 \bullet e$$
$$\text{let}\, x == 42; \, y == 1998 \bullet e$$

This generalization makes **let** notation redundant, but it is retained for backwards compatibility with ZRM (though only the expression form is retained, as explained in Section 3.4).

Historical remarks. Local constant declarations were first suggested in [27].

2.10 Axiom-parts as Predicates

ZRM permits newline or semicolon to separate outermost conjuncts in an Axiom-part. Standard Z removes the unnecessary irregularity that distinguishes Axiom-parts from other predicates by permitting newline or semicolon between any predicates to mean conjunction, and giving newline and semicolon very low precedences, so that any such new uses of newline and semicolon must be parenthesized.

2.11 Soft Newlines

Newlines serve two different purposes in Z: so-called hard newlines separate declarations and conjuncts; so-called soft newlines merely break up long formulae onto multiple lines without themselves having any semantic significance. In ZRM notation, newlines are soft if they are adjacent to an infix operator. In Standard Z, newlines are also soft if they follow a prefix operator or precede a postfix operator. This improvement recognizes the other circumstances where the next line must contain a continuation of the same formula. A particular case that was not breakable in ZRM is the application expression

very_long_function_expression very_long_argument_expression

which in Standard Z, with the addition of parentheses, can be broken.

very_long_function_expression (
    very_long_argument_expression)

Historical remarks. These additional soft newlines were suggested in [13].

2.12 Lexis of Words

In the ZRM syntax, Word is a terminal symbol. There is some informal description of a Word being made up of letters, digits, underscores and other symbols, but it is imprecise about what those are and how they can be put together. Standard Z gives a formal definition of Word, referring to the symbols of the Unicode standard [7]. It is a very flexible definition, and largely compatible with traditional practice. See the latest draft for details.

Historical remarks. A proposal [19] is to be submitted to the Unicode standards panel for the addition of those Z symbols that are currently absent from Unicode.

2.13   Toolkit

The major inadequacy in ZRM's toolkit is the omission of a definition of the numeric operations. This omission is resolved in Standard Z as follows. The integers $\mathbb{Z}$ have been replaced as the basis for numeric operations by the set called "arithmos" and denoted $\mathbb{A}$, representing an unrestricted concept of number. $\mathbb{A}$ is introduced in the prelude section, along with $\mathbb{N}$, 0, *succ*, and addition and multiplication of naturals, which provide a basis for the semantics of natural number literals in the Z base language. The prelude section is written in Z like any other section, but is regarded as part of the Z base language for the purpose of the semantic definition; it is an implicit parent of every other section.

The properties of the real numbers $\mathbb{R}$ are defined in the toolkit, together with subsets the rationals $\mathbb{Q}$, the positive rationals $\mathbb{Q}_+$, the integers $\mathbb{Z}$, the natural numbers $\mathbb{N}$, and the positive integers $\mathbb{N}_1$. Having these sets as subsets of $\mathbb{A}$ and making the numeric operations be partial functions on $\mathbb{A}$ avoids having either to introduce distinct names for the operations on different subsets or to introduce an overload resolution mechanism into Z. (The *ad hoc* overloading introduced by loose generics is inappropriate in this context.) Moreover, their definitions could be widened in future to cope with other kinds of numbers. The numeric functions and relations declared in ZRM Section 4.4, except *succ*, have had their domains widened to apply to the real numbers where appropriate, while retaining their ZRM meanings for integers.

The opportunity will be taken to revise the toolkit in other ways. The meanings of most definitions will remain unchanged, though the domains of some will be widened. Some new definitions might be introduced, and some old ones that have been little used may be moved to sections separate from the toolkit. Many changes have been suggested, but few have been widely discussed yet, and so it is inappropriate to detail them here. One that deserves consideration is the re-formulation of definitions in the style recommended in [31].

Historical remarks. Work on the definition of numbers is reported in [28, 3, 10, 24, 30]. Recent development of the Standard Z toolkit [30] has been done in the context of the CADiZ tool [25] to ensure conformance with the syntax and type rules of Standard Z.

3   Incompatibilities

This section lists backwards incompatibilities between ZRM and Standard Z arising from the improvements discussed in the previous section. For each incompatibility is given an explanation of *what* it is, a rationale for *why* it exists, and some notes on *how* instances of it can be detected and rectified.

3.1   Singleton Sets

What? The notation $\{i\}$ where i is the name of a schema is parsed differently: ZRM parses it as a set comprehension, whereas Standard Z parses it as a singleton set extension. (In ZRM, the set extension (set display) containing a single schema reference is written $\{(i)\}$.)

Why? Standard Z permits any schema-valued expression to be written wherever ZRM permits only a schema reference, so the potential ambiguity between singleton set extensions and set comprehensions is broadened to expressions matching the pattern $\{e\}$. Since e can contain parentheses, the ambiguity cannot be resolved in the way ZRM resolves it. (Where e is not a schema name, both parse $\{e\}$ as a set extension.)

How? The type of the ZRM set comprehension $\{i\}$ is that of a set of bindings, whereas the type of the Standard Z set extension $\{i\}$ is that of a set of sets of bindings, so a type-checking tool will detect and report most instances of this incompatibility. The Standard Z coercion to a set comprehension is to write $\{i \mid true\}$. The value of the set comprehension is just i, and that equivalence holds in ZRM notation too, so another translation from ZRM to Standard Z is just to drop the set brackets.

Historical remarks. The original disambiguation by parentheses was said to be "against normal mathematical usage" in [1], and hence the change is desirable anyway.

3.2   Decorated References to Schemas

What? Any decoration on a reference to a schema must be separated from the schema name.

Why? The merging of schemas and expressions has included the merging of the namespaces of schema names and other names, so a schema can now be defined with a decoration within its name. For each expression comprising a name with a decoration, there are two possible intentions and hence interpretations: either the name refers to a schema declaration in the environment and the decoration is to be applied to the components of that schema, or the decorated name refers to a schema declaration in the environment whose name is itself decorated. Standard Z must be able to express either intention, whereas ZRM-compliant specifications have only the former possibility.

How? Standard Z distinguishes the two intentions by the presence or absence of separation between the name and decoration. That separation can be either white space or parentheses around the name. For example, consider the parentheses in the following.

$$S == [x : \mathbb{N}]$$

$$S' == [x : \mathbb{N}]$$

$$T == (S)' \wedge S'$$

The expression $(S)'$ is a reference to schema S with its components decorated, giving $[x' : \mathbb{N}]$, whereas the expression S' is a reference to the schema S'. The decoration expression $(S)'$ could equally have been written $S\ '$. Separation is needed to get the ZRM interpretation, but ZRM-compliant specifications might not have that separation. If there is no white space, then a type-checking tool will report that the decorated schema name is not declared.

This backwards incompatibility could be avoided by transforming undeclared decorated references to decoration expressions, distributing the minimum number of strokes from the references to the decoration expressions to give a type correct result. However, reliance on this transformation in new specifications would make those specifications less clear for readers, and the transformation would complicate both tools and the standard. Use of separation in decoration expressions should be at least encouraged.

Historical remarks. There is discussion of this in [1].

3.3 Decorated References to Generic Schemas

What? The decoration and instantiation on a reference to a generic schema must be reversed, for example, $S'[\mathbb{N}]$ must be changed to $S[\mathbb{N}]'$.

Why? ZRM notation treats both the decoration and the instantiation as part of a schema reference, requiring them to be written in that order. Standard Z requires the instantiation to be on the reference, but the decoration could be on any schema, and so the decoration must follow the instantiation.

How? A syntax checking tool will recognize a decoration expression, and will then be able to recognize an instantiation list (that being distinct from a schema construction expression, and can appear only in different contexts to generic parameter lists), but will be unable to recognize their juxtaposition, so a syntax error is guaranteed. The decoration and the instantiation must be reversed.

3.4 "let" on Predicates

What? The **let** notation introduced in ZRM (second edition) cannot be used as a predicate in Standard Z.

Why? In ZRM notation, in a context where a predicate is expected, a **let** with a schema name after its • can be parsed as either a **let** expression used as a predicate or as a **let** predicate with a schema name used as a predicate, but both have the same meaning. In Standard Z, any schema expression can be used after the •, and so there can be free variables in that part, leading to different meanings depending on whether the let is taken to be an expression or a predicate. So Standard Z cannot have both **let** expressions and **let** predicates. Neither is needed, thanks to local constant declarations. The expression form is retained, as it allows some uses of μ, which is less familiar to non-specialists than $\exists$, to be avoided.

How? A syntax checking tool will detect some uses of **let** on predicates, but might mistake some uses of **let** on relational predicates as **let** on the leading expression. Each use of **let** on a predicate should be replaced by $\exists$ (or by $\exists_1$ or $\forall$ since all mean the same given that the quantified declarations are all $==$ declarations).

3.5   Renaming on Theta Expressions

What? The square-bracketed renaming notation on theta expressions, that was introduced in 2nd edition ZRM, is parsed differently in Standard Z.

Why? The Z Standard's merging of the syntaxes of schemas and expressions has resulted in a single schema renaming production that permits renaming of any expression, with the type constraint that the expression be a schema. The renaming production has lower precedence than that of θ, so $\theta S[new/old, ...]$ is parsed as $(\theta S)[new/old, ...]$.

How? Since θS is a binding not a schema and renaming is permitted only of a schema not a binding, the renaming of θS will always be detected as a type error. The ZRM notation $\theta S[new/old]$ denotes the binding $(\!|\, old == new \,|\!)$. (It is interesting to note that the effect of the notation is not to rename the name on the left of the $==$ but rather to substitute for the value on the right.) That same binding can be built in Standard Z using the notation **let** $old == new \bullet \theta S$ (which with the addition of surrounding parentheses would be valid ZRM notation too).

3.6   Underlined Infix Relations

What? The underlining notation for infix relational operators, introduced in ZRM second edition, cannot be used in Standard Z.

Why? In ZRM notation, there is no way of introducing new operator notation, so instead each use of an identifier as an infix relation can be underlined to make clear that it is being used as an infix symbol. In Standard Z, operator template paragraphs provide a way of introducing new operator notation, so there is no need to mark uses of it as such. Moreover, the underlining notation has not caught on, and it does not help with operators other than infix relations.

How? A syntax checking tool will detect all uses of underlining notation. Each underlined infix relational operator should be declared in an earlier operator template paragraph.

3.7   Operator Precedences

What? Table 1 enumerates the relative precedences of the predicate and expression notations in ZRM and Standard Z, from lowest at the top to highest at the bottom, revealing some differences. Schema expression notations of ZRM are omitted, as they appear in separate contexts. The relative precedences of ZRM's schema calculus operations are, from lowest to highest, $\gg, \,_9^\circ, \,\backslash, \,\upharpoonright, \Leftrightarrow, \Rightarrow, \vee, \wedge, \text{pre}, \neg$.

Why? Operator templates cause several rows of the table to appear to be different, but in fact the only change in relative precedence caused by them is that between *juxtaposed function applications* and *postfix functions*. The merging of schema expressions with expressions is the cause of most of the differences. Many schema expressions use the same operators as quantified or logical predicates. In Standard Z, one of these schemas used as a predicate is equivalent to the corresponding predicate involving the operand schemas used as predicates. By using the same precedences, that ambiguity can be resolved arbitrarily. The remaining schema operators ($\gg$, $\S$, $\backslash$, $\upharpoonright$, pre) are given precedences adjacent to those of other expression-forming (functional) operators, and hence bind more tightly than they do in ZRM. The ZRM column omits some operators (namely *newline*, $==$, *decoration*, and *renaming*) because ZRM notation permits their use in only restricted contexts.

How? Type errors are likely as a result of unintended parses, but are not guaranteed.

3.8   Theta Expressions

What? Standard Z requires the types of components in the operand schema to be the same as the types of the same names in the current environment, unlike ZRM.

Why? Mismatching types is likely to be indicative of a mistake, and, in those cases where it isn't, binding extensions provide an alternative notation.

How? A type-checker will detect and report all such problems.

3.9   Lexis of Words

What? The lexis of words has changed, resulting in, for example, λx being lexed as a single word.

Why? ZRM viewed λ as a symbol and x as a letter, whereas Standard Z inherits Unicode's classification of both of them being letters.

How? Wherever two words are parsed as one, or one word is parsed as two, syntax or type errors are likely to result. White space should be inserted, e.g. λ x, or the single word renamed, as appropriate to conform to Standard Z.

4   Subtle Changes

This section discusses some subtle changes in the interpretation of certain notations that nevertheless leave the semantics of ZRM notation unchanged.

4.1   Quantified Expressions

ZRM notation's requirement that a schema quantification should quantify only names that are declared within the schema after the $\bullet$ is relaxed in Standard Z, for consistency with the scope rules of quantified predicates. For example, the expression $\forall x : A \bullet [y : A]$ is erroneous in ZRM but acceptable in Standard Z.

ZRM	Standard Z
	newline
•	•
;	;
:	: ==
⇔	⇔
⇒	⇒
∨	∨
∧	∧
¬	¬
pre	
prefix and infix relations	*relational predicates*
if then else	*if then else*
	>>
	$^o_9$
	\
	⌈
	pre
infix generics	*Operator...*
×	*...templates...*
infix functions	*...with...*
ℙ	*... × ℙ etc...*
prefix generics	*...at...*
(– _)	*...same...*
(_ (| _ |))	*...precedence.*
juxtaposed function application	*juxtaposed function application*
postfix functions	
	decoration
	renaming
selection	*selection*
θ	θ

Table 1. Operator precedences.

4.2   Preconditions

ZRM notation has pre predicates and pre schema expressions. Standard Z has only pre expressions. ZRM pre predicates are parsed as expressions, and those expressions are treated as schema predicates, giving a backwards-compatible effect.

4.3   Schema Instantiation

References to generic schemas no longer have to be given explicit instantiations, so long as the instantiations can be determined from the context. On the other hand, a reference to a generic schema in a theta expression is now permitted to have an explicit instantiation.

Historical remarks. This was noted in [1].

4.4   Precedence of lambda and mu

ZRM notation requires all λ and μ expressions to be parenthesized. Standard Z gives them precedences, so that parentheses can often be omitted. Parentheses are still required in the case of a μ expression whose • part is omitted.

5   Conclusions

Several innovations in Standard Z relative to ZRM have been presented. These are at the cost of some backwards incompatibilities. Those incompatibilities have been explained and justified, and advice has been given on how to detect and resolve instances of them in existing Z specifications. Although several pages of this paper have been devoted to the incompatibilities, they are all relatively minor things compared to the improvements.

It is hoped that the innovations presented resolve satisfactorily the known inadequacies in the notation of ZRM, and that this paper will assist their adoption into practice. However, no guarantee can be given that these innovations will appear in a future Z standard. Inevitably, the second CD will not be the last word on Z – the Z panel has already discussed some other issues, without coming to agreements yet.

Acknowledgements

Thanks are of course due to those members of the Z panel who have originated the ideas presented in this paper. The historical remarks inevitably do not tell the whole story. The first CD acknowledges some more of the contributions that were made before I joined the panel.

Specific comments on earlier drafts of this paper were received from Rob Arthan, David Duffy, Steve King, John Nicholls, Mike Spivey, Susan Stepney, Sam Valentine and referees.

References

1. R. D. Arthan. Issues for Z concrete syntax, February 1992. URL:
   http://www.lemma-one.com/zstan_docs/wrk036.ps.
2. R. D. Arthan. Modularity for Z, September 1995. URL:
   ftp://www.comlab.ox.ac.uk/pub/Zforum/ZSTAN/papers/z-182.ps.
3. R. D. Arthan. Arithmetic for Z, February 1996. URL:
   ftp://www.comlab.ox.ac.uk/pub/Zforum/ZSTAN/papers/z-188.ps.
4. R. D. Arthan. Note on operator templates. ICL, UK, March 1996.
5. R. D. Arthan. Axioms for mutually recursive free type definitions. URL:
   http://www.lemma-one.com/zstan_docs/z-225.ps, July 1997.
6. R. D. Arthan. The ProofPower Web pages, November 1997. URL:
   http://www.lemma-one.demon.co.uk/ProofPower/.
7. Unicode consortium, editor. *ISO/IEC 10646 Unicode: worldwide character encoding.* ISO
   CD 13568, 1996.
8. W. Harwood, editor. *A Zola Tutorial.* Imperial Software Technology, UK, October 1995.
9. I. Hayes, editor. *Specification Case Studies.* Prentice Hall International Series in Computer
   Science, 1987.
10. I. Hayes. Numbers in the base standard. SVRC, Queensland, Australia, November 1996.
11. R. B. Jones. Proposal to allow general use of expressions as schemas in Z. ICL, UK, 1992.
12. S. King, I. H. Sørensen, and J. C. P. Woodcock. Z: Grammar and concrete and abstract
    syntaxes. Technical Monograph PRG-68, Programming Research Group, Oxford University
    Computing Laboratory, UK, 1988.
13. P. Lupton. Newline and free form. IBM UK Labs Ltd, Hursley Park, Winchester, UK,
    October 1992.
14. J. E. Nicholls, editor. *Z Notation – First Committee Draft.* ISO, September 1995.
15. J. M. Spivey. *The Z Notation: A Reference Manual.* Prentice Hall International Series in
    Computer Science, 1st edition, 1989.
16. J. M. Spivey. *The Z Notation: A Reference Manual.* Prentice Hall International Series in
    Computer Science, 2nd edition, 1992.
17. P. Steggles and W. Harwood. Z standard syntax (proposed). Z Standards Panel – Document
    173, March 1995.
18. S. Stepney. Lexis and concrete syntax issues. Z Standards Panel – Document 191, March
    1996.
19. S. Stepney. Proposal to add the ISO standard Z character set to Unicode ISO/IEC 10646. Z
    Standards Panel – Document 234, March 1998.
20. B. Sufrin, editor. *Z Handbook.* Programming Research Group, Oxford University Computing
    Laboratory, UK, March 1986.
21. I. Toyn. Comments on operator templates. Department of Computer Science, University of
    York, UK, January 1995.
22. I. Toyn. Formal reasoning in the Z notation using CADiZ. In N. A. Merriam, editor, *2nd
    International Workshop on User Interface Design for Theorem Proving Systems,* July 1996.
23. I. Toyn. Free types – by semantic transformation, June 1997. URL:
    ftp://ftp.cs.york.ac.uk/hise_reports/cadiz/scratch/freetypes2.ps.
24. I. Toyn. Numbers in Z, January 1997. URL:
    ftp://ftp.cs.york.ac.uk/hise_reports/cadiz/ZSTAN/numbers2.ps.
25. I. Toyn. CADiZ Web pages, February 1998. URL:
    http://www.cs.york.ac.uk/~ian/cadiz/.
26. I. Toyn, editor. *Z Notation – Second Committee Draft.* ISO, to appear 1998.

27. S. H. Valentine. Some detailed proposals for the Z standard. Z Standards Panel – Document 136, January 1993.

28. S. H. Valentine. An algebraic introduction of real numbers into Z. In H. Habrias, editor, *Proc. 7th International Conference on Putting into Practice Methods and Tools for Information System Design: Z Twenty Years On – What is its Future?*, pages 183–204, France, 10–12 October 1995. IRIN, Université de Nantes.

29. S. H. Valentine. Equal rights for schemas in Z. In J. P. Bowen and M. G. Hinchey, editors, *ZUM'95: The Z Formal Specification Notation*, volume 967 of *Lecture Notes in Computer Science*, pages 183–202. Springer-Verlag, 1995.

30. S. H. Valentine. The place of numbers in Z – a discussion paper. Z Standards Panel – Document 223, January 1997.

31. S. H. Valentine. Inconsistency and undefinedness in Z – a practical guide. In J. P. Bowen, A. Fett, and M. G. Hinchey, editors, *ZUM'98: The Z Formal Specification Notation*, volume 1493 of *Lecture Notes in Computer Science*, pages 233–249. Springer-Verlag, September 1998. In this volume.

Comparing Extended Z with a Heterogeneous Notation for Reasoning about Time and Space

Richard F. Paige

Department of Computer Science, York University
Toronto, Ontario, Canada, M3J 1P3

Email: paige@cs.yorku.ca

Abstract. We contrast using a notation extension with using a combination of notations. Specifically, we compare the use of an extended dialect of Z [10] with a combination of Z and predicative programming notation [6] for algorithm refinement and for reasoning about time and space constraints on systems. We discuss the difficulty of using extended notations versus using heterogeneous notations, and consider when we might prefer to extend or combine notations. We conclude that there exist situations where a heterogeneous notation can be more appropriate to use than an extended notation.

1 Introduction

Notation extension, the process of adding new syntactic or semantic features to a language, is an important topic in formal method and software engineering research. Notations have been extended for a variety of reasons: in order to generalize the notation; in order to use concepts available in other languages that have proven to be useful in practice; or, to compare notations in a systematic manner. Notation extension has also been used for notation *development*, the process for which starts with a concise kernel language, that over time is developed into a general-purpose language.

An alternative approach to extension is to construct *heterogeneous notations*. A heterogeneous notation is manufactured from two or more distinct languages, combining the syntax and semantics of each in some manner so as to produce a new language. Heterogeneous notations are used to write *heterogeneous specifications*, which are compositions of partial specifications written in two or more different notations [9]. A specifier might prefer to use a heterogeneous notation rather than extend a notation for a number of reasons: e.g., to keep individual notations simple; or to be able to write specifications in the most suitable specialized language [5, 9, 13].

In this paper, we are interested in contrasting the use of an extended Z dialect with the use of a heterogeneous notation composed from Z and predicative notation [6]. We do this so as to make a preliminary attempt to determine if there exist situations where heterogeneous notations are *useful*, for writing more understandable (or possibly more concise) specifications, and for producing simpler, more understandable refinement proofs than are possible with extended notations. To this end, we will carry out two case studies in applying an extended language and a heterogeneous notation. The case studies will be as follows.

- *Timing study:* the Z notation, extended with a notion of time [3], will be applied in specification, refinement, and proof of timing constraints. Its use will be contrasted with an application of Z combined with predicative programming [6] – which has a built-in notion of timing.
- *Space study:* the Z notation, extended with a simple notion of space, will be applied in specification, refinement, and proof of space constraints. Its use will be contrasted with an application of Z combined with predicative programming that has built-in notations for space [7].

The applications of the extended notations and heterogeneous notations are not meant to be illustrative of all of the features of the individual approaches; the reader is directed to the references for further examples [3, 9]. Rather, the case studies are intended to demonstrate how heterogeneous notations and extended notations can be used, and how the use of heterogeneous notations can compare to use of extended notations. It is also important to note that our comparisons are given in terms of *existing* and very specific notations, and in terms of eliminating limitations of these notations.

The organization of this paper will be as follows.

- In Section 2, we outline the predicative programming method. We also explain our definition of heterogeneous notations, and how heterogeneous specifications are to be formally manipulated, based on the approach of [9].
- In Section 3, we compare the use of Z extended with reasoning about time with the use of a heterogeneous notation combining Z and predicative programming. We carry out a refinement case study in order to compare the two approaches.
- In Section 4, we compare the use of Z extended with reasoning about space with the use of a heterogeneous notation combining Z and predicative programming. Again, we carry out a refinement case study in order to compare the two approaches.
- In Section 5, we discuss our findings, and attempt to suggest why using a heterogeneous approach may be preferable to an extension approach, and vice versa.

2 Notation and Approaches to Extension and Heterogeneity

2.1 Predicative programming

Predicative programming is due to Hehner [6]. It is a program design calculus like Morgan's refinement calculus [8], but unlike the latter treats programs as specifications. In this approach, programs and specifications are predicates on pre- and post-state (final values of variables are annotated with a prime; initial values of variables are undecorated). The weakest predicate specification is $\top$ ("true"), and the strongest specification is $\bot$ ("false"). Refinement is just boolean implication.

Definition 1. *A predicative specification P on prestate σ and post-state σ' is refined by a specification Q if $\forall \sigma, \sigma' \cdot (P \Leftarrow Q)$.*

The refinement relation enjoys various properties that allow specifications to be refined by parts, steps, and cases. Since refinement is just implication, carrying out a refinement is equivalent to carrying out a logical proof. Therefore, the refinement rules of predicative programming are laws of boolean logic; see [6] for a complete list.

Predicative specifications can be combined using the familiar operators of boolean theory, along with all the usual program combinators (e.g., '.' is the sequencing combinator), as well as combinators for parallelism and communication through channels. Predicative programming also has a **frame** construct equivalent to that of [8]. The specification **frame** $w \cdot P$ means that predicate P can change variables w, but no other variables; if the state consists of variables w and ρ, then **frame** $w \cdot P$ is equivalent to $(P \wedge \rho' = \rho)$.

One particular novelty with predicative programming is that *recursive* programs can be developed rather than iterative programs, using recursive refinement rules. It has been suggested that this simplifies the process of developing certain programs [6], since in particular it eliminates the need to construct invariants *before* developing loops.

Predicative specifications do not express constraints on termination. Instead, specifications can include reference to time variables, t and t', which can be used to place time bounds on any implementation. Furthermore, predicative specifications may include constraints on space that must be met by any implementation. Space constraints are expressed through references to a space variable s, which represents the current space usage of a specification, and a maximum space variable m, which represents the maximum usage. Detailed examples of using space and time variables can be found in [6, 7]. In general, non-trivial space usage arises with recursive implementations and programs, so in the case studies that use predicative programming, we typically use recursive refinement techniques, which are very useful in proving space bounds [7].

As an example of a predicative specification, the following specification requires reversal of the order of items in a list L, taking no more than $\#L$ div 2 units of time (where $\#L$ is list length, and one unit is the time for a recursive call).

$$\#L' = \#L \wedge \forall n : 0, .. \#L \cdot L'(n) = L(\#L - n - 1) \wedge t' \leq t + \#L \text{ div } 2$$

2.2   Approach to extension

In the two case studies using extended notations in Sections 3 and 4, we use standard Z notation [10], extended to specifying and reasoning about *timing constraints* and *space usage constraints*. We now outline the approaches to extension that we will use.

For the timing case study in Section 3, we use the real-time Z extension described in [3]; alternatives are listed in the references [1, 2]. In this approach, Z specifications are extended with fresh variables t and t', which express the time when a computation starts and when a computation finishes. In [3], constraints placed on t and t' can be sets of times; without loss of generality, we will only place deterministic constraints on computation time, in order to keep the examples of manageable size.

In order to reason about time in specifications, all specifications will include the schema $\Delta Time$, as follows ($\mathbb{N}_1$ is all non-zero naturals).

$$\Delta Time \mathrel{\widehat{=}} [\, t, t' : \mathbb{N}_1 \mid t' \geq t \,]$$

The extension in [3] modifies refinement rules from [12] to include constraints on time. These constraints express how long the primitive commands in a simple programming language will take – for example, time constraints for evaluating the truth of guards, or for branching back to the top of a loop after an executing the loop body. The rules include references to a schema-valued function, *age*, which returns instantiations of time-change schemas specifying the passage of a specific amount of time. The primitive time-change schema, *ChangeTime*, which we use in the case study is

$$ChangeTime \mathrel{\widehat{=}} \left[\Delta Time;\; \Xi ProgVar;\; d : \mathbb{N}_1 \mid t' - t = d\right]$$

where *d* is an amount of time that some program will take, while *ProgVar* is a schema of program variables of interest. The *age* function is defined as follows.

$$
\begin{array}{|l}
age : \mathbb{N}_1 \to ChangeTime \\
\hline
\forall t : \mathbb{N}_1 \cdot age(t).d = t
\end{array}
$$

Without loss of generality, we will use only two timing constraints: an assignment takes one unit of time (for the store to memory); and a branch back to the top of a **do** loop takes one unit of time. All other commands take no time. We will use the same constraints in both the extension example and the heterogeneous example. This set of timing constraints is unrealistic for some problems, but it is sufficient for the case studies herein. These timing constraints mean that the effect of an assignment statement $x := E$ is defined by the operation schema *AssignEtoX* (where *x* can be many variables).

$$AssignEtoX \mathrel{\widehat{=}} \left[x, x' : T;\; \Xi AllElse;\; \Delta Time \mid x' = E \wedge t' - t = 1\right]$$

(where *AllElse* is all variables in scope, excepting those in *x*). We use $x := E$ as syntax for the schema *AssignEtoX* when using Z.

The refinement rules from [3] are low-level, in that from them it is possible to derive 'short-cut' rules that make the approach more practical (involving shorter proof steps). Thus, the complexity of proofs in the extended Z method that we use can be reduced. In order to be consistent in the comparisons, we use low-level laws in applying the heterogeneous method. In this manner, we have a common basis for comparison.

The extension of Z to reason about space is much simpler; in fact, for the most part standard Z specifications can be written (with inclusion of some extra schema details and syntax). To reason about space, we declare a state schema $\Delta Space$, which defines instances of two new variables: *s*, the current space usage of a program executing a specification; and *m*, the maximum space usage of a program executing a specification.

$$\Delta Space \mathrel{\widehat{=}} \left[m, m', s, s' : \mathbb{N} \mid m \geq s \wedge m' \geq s' \wedge m' \geq m\right]$$

$\Delta Space$ is to be included in any specifications for which we want to reason about space usage. Non-trivial space usage only results with specifications that are to be implemented by recursive programs. So in the space case studies, we write specifications as procedures, with Z specifications for bodies. These specifications will be implemented using recursive calls to the original procedure. We will write procedure interfaces using the notation of [8], and base the development of recursive programs on [8] as well (though modified to Z).

The refinement rules that we use for reasoning about space in Z are unchanged from those in [12], since space usage is represented by two variables. In order to calculate space bounds, in proofs we preface a recursive call to a procedure by $s := s + 1$ and $m := max\{m, s + 1\}$. On return from a recursive call, we decrease space usage by $s := s - 1$. With such rules, bounds on space can be proven with respect to a specification and implementation.

2.3   Approach to heterogeneity

We aim to compare the use of an extended version of Z with a heterogeneous notation constructed from Z and predicative programming. Since we are interested in formally reasoning about heterogeneous specifications composed from Z specifications and predicative specifications, we need to give the heterogeneous notation a formal semantics.

The approach to formally defining the meaning of heterogeneous notations that we use is from [9]. Translations are defined between formal notations of interest. The translations provide the mechanisms by which a heterogeneous specification can be given a formal semantics using a homogeneous specification, via mapping the original specification into a single-notation formulation[1]. A set of notations and translations between them, which is to be used to give a formal semantics to heterogeneous specifications, is called a *heterogeneous basis*. The small heterogeneous basis that we use in this paper consists of the Z notation and the predicative notation. It is derived from a much larger basis given in [9], which includes Z and predicative notation, as well as a number of other formal and informal notations. We require only one translation in the basis, a mapping from Z to predicative notation. See [9] for mappings from predicative notation to Z, and for other translations.

To translate from a Z schema $Op \mathrel{\widehat{=}} [\, \Delta S;\ i?:I;\ o!:O \mid P\,]$ to a predicative specification, we use the translation *ZToPP*, defined as follows.

$$ZToPP(Op) \mathrel{\widehat{=}} \mathbf{frame}\ w \cdot ((\exists w' \cdot P) \Rightarrow P)$$

The frame w consists of the variables in S and the operation outputs. Inputs $i?$ are mapped to state variables or to parameters (if the resulting specification is to be encompassed in a procedure or function). The existential quantifier is necessary in the translation to extract the precondition of the operation. We assume that any schema property for S has been expanded and included in the predicate P of Op. Though *ZToPP* is written as a total function, we require that for any Op, $P \neq true$, because predicative programming cannot describe terminating yet arbitrary computations [5].

To include time variables in the result of the translation *ZToPP*, the most we can say in the resulting predicative specification is that time does not decrease. This results in conjoining the predicate term $t' \geq t$ in the result of *ZToPP*.

In the heterogeneous method, we extend Z's definition of *max* to apply to empty sets of integers (we use the standard function *max* when applying pure Z). This is done so as to be able to develop equivalent programs using the extended and the heterogeneous methods. *max* applied to an empty set gives $-\infty$, which is smaller than any integer; ∞, correspondingly, is larger than any integer and $-\infty$. A full axiomatic definition of

---

[1] This notation need not be the same as the languages used for writing specifications.

max and 'extended' integers is beyond the scope and space constraints of this paper (but one can be found in [6]). We define $\mathbb{Z}_\infty$, the *extended integers*, as $\mathbb{Z} \cup \{\infty, -\infty\}$. The definition of *max* on sets of extended integers is

$$max : \mathbb{P}\,\mathbb{Z}_\infty \twoheadrightarrow \mathbb{Z}_\infty$$

$$max\{\,\} = -\infty$$
$$\forall S : \mathbb{P}_1\,\mathbb{Z}_\infty;\ m : \mathbb{Z}_\infty \bullet$$
$$\quad (max\,S = m) \Leftrightarrow (m \in S \wedge \forall n : S \bullet n \le m)$$

2.3.1 Semantics of heterogeneous specifications The translation *ZToPP* can be used to formally define the semantics of compositions of Z specifications and predicative specifications, by translating heterogeneous specifications into a homogeneous specification. In this paper, heterogeneous specifications are given a semantics in terms of predicative notation. Details of how the translation process operates over combinators are in [9]. Informally, *ZToPP* applies partwise over predicative combinators. Therefore, we always write Z specifications under the assumption that we can translate them into predicative notation. While we have checked that translation is possible for the specifications in this paper, we do not show the checking in the case studies.

As an example, consider the semantics of the specification $(j = n) \Rightarrow Op$, where $j = n$ is a predicative specification, $\Rightarrow$ is boolean implication, and *Op* is the schema

$$Op \,\widehat{=}\, \left[L, L' : \text{seq}\,\mathbb{N};\ r, r' : \mathbb{N} \mid L' = L \wedge r' = max\{r, max\{i : j..n - 1 \bullet Li\}\} \right]$$

The semantics of this heterogeneous specification is

$$(j = n) \Rightarrow \mathbf{frame}\ r, L \cdot (L' = L \wedge r' = max\{r, max\{i : j..n - 1 \bullet Li\}\})$$

This can be refined by the specification **ok**, which does nothing.

Some rules for refining heterogeneous specifications composed from Z and predicates were given in [9]. A useful rule that we will need in the timing case study is the following. Informally, the rule states the conditions to be checked in order to refine a schema by a predicative specification.

Rule 1. For a prestate σ and post-state σ', a Z schema with property P is refined by a predicative specification Q if

$$\forall \sigma, \sigma' \cdot ((\exists \sigma' \cdot P) \Rightarrow P) \Leftarrow Q$$

We introduce one new rule here, for the purposes of simplifying the process of refinement of heterogeneous specifications. It generalizes the *substitution rule* from [6].

Rule 2. Let x be a variable and E an expression, where '.' is predicative sequencing. If S is a schema with property P, then

$$(x := E.\,S) = S'[E/x]$$

where S' is the same as S except with property $(\exists \sigma' \cdot P) \Rightarrow P$. Read $S'[E/x]$ as "substitute E for x in the property of schema S'".

Informally, Rule 2 means that we can apply the predicative substitution rule when using Z schemas in refinements. The property of S' changes under the substitution due to the translation of Z into predicative notation: the existential quantification in the property is necessary because the predicative notation can express miraculous computations, while Z cannot.

In order to be able to use Z and predicative notations together, we must also be able to parse specification compositions. This means that we have to eliminate any syntactic ambiguity that arises by combining the two notations. For this reason, we do the following when writing heterogeneous specifications.

- We use standard Z notation for types, e.g., $\mathbb{Z}, \mathbb{N}$, and to describe ranges.
- Refinement in Z follows the approach of Wordsworth [12], and the refinement relation will be written as $\sqsubseteq$. Refinement of Z will be to the guarded command language of Dijkstra.
- We use Morgan's notation for writing procedures that have Z specification bodies [8]. Procedure syntax will be necessary for reasoning about space usage [7].

3   Reasoning about Time

Existing refinement methods, such as those presented in [6, 8, 12], provide the means for rigorously developing correct programs from specifications. In critical applications, correctness may also be measured in terms of performing actions at the right time. Therefore, it is necessary to reason about timing, too.

In this section, we compare the use of Z, extended with refinement rules for timing, with the use of Z combined with predicative programming. The comparison is done in the context of a small case study. We first outline the problem for the case study, then develop a solution using extended Z, and thereafter Z combined with predicates.

3.1   The problem

The very simple problem that we consider is taken from [3]; we choose it because it is small enough to allow comparisons of two separate solutions in the space available. We want to calculate the maximum r of a non-empty list of integers L in time that is proportional (within a constant factor) to the length, n, of the list.

3.2   Using extended Z

We start the example by specifying the state of the system. The system state contains three variables: the list L, the result r, and a counter variable j.

$$State \cong \left[L : 0..n-1 \to \mathbb{N}; \; j : \mathbb{N}; \; r : \mathbb{Z} \mid j \leq n \right]$$

The problem, S, that we want to solve, is therefore

```
┌─ S ──────────────────────────────────────────────────
│ ΔState; ΔTime
├───────────────────────────────────────────────────────
│ L' = L
│ r' = max{i : 0..n − 1 • Li}
│ t' − t = 2n − 1
└───────────────────────────────────────────────────────
```

The time constraint, $t' - t = 2n - 1$, requires that any implementation of this specification takes $2n - 1$ units of time to execute.

We implement the problem S using the real-time refinement rules of [3]. The first step is to refine S into a sequence of two schemas, where the first initializes j and r (taking one unit of time). We show that $S \sqsubseteq A_1; A_2$, where

```
┌─ A₁ ─────────────────────┐        ┌─ A₂ ──────────────────────────────
│ ΔState; ΔTime            │        │ ΔState; ΔTime
├──────────────────────────┤        ├────────────────────────────────────
│ j' = 1 ∧ r' = L0         │        │ j = 1 ∧ r = L0 ∧ L' = L
│ L' = L                   │        │ r' = max{r, max{i : j..n − 1 • Li}}
│ t' − t = 1               │        │ t' − t = 2(n − 1)
└──────────────────────────┘        └────────────────────────────────────
```

To show that $S \sqsubseteq A_1; A_2$, the following obligations must be discharged.

$$\text{pre}\,S \vdash \text{pre}\,A_1 \tag{1}$$

$$\text{pre}\,S \wedge A_1 \vdash (\text{pre}\,A_2)' \tag{2}$$

$$\text{pre}\,S \wedge A_1 \wedge A_2' \vdash S[\_''/\_'] \tag{3}$$

In (1), it is shown that the sequence precondition can be established by the precondition of S. In (2), we show that the precondition of the second step in the sequence, A_2, can be established by A_1 in a precondition of S. In the final step, we show that the sequence establishes the problem. (The priming notations are described in [12]. The notation $S[\_''/\_']$ means "substitute doubly primed variables for primed variables in S".) Steps (1) and (2) are straightforward (because $\text{pre}\,S$ and $\text{pre}\,A_1$ are *true*). The last step, (3), is the liveness condition, and it is also straightforward once we substitute primed values of variables from A_1 for unprimed values of variables in A_2, and see that this entails S.

A_1 is a schema expression for an assignment statement $r, j := L0, 1$ which takes one unit of time and needs no further refinement. The next step is to refine A_2. We see that A_2 determines the maximum of L for all elements except the first; therefore, it needs to be implemented by a loop which takes time $2(n - 1)$. An invariant for a loop that implements A_2 is as follows.

```
┌─ Inv ─────────────────────────────────────────────────
│ ΔState; ΔTime
├───────────────────────────────────────────────────────
│ r' = max{i : 0..j' − 1 • L'i}
│ L' = L
│ t' − t = 2(j' − 1)
└───────────────────────────────────────────────────────
```

A loop variant is $n - j$. The time constraint in the invariant is $t' - t = 2(j' - 1)$, since this is the time that has been taken by the loop after $j' - 1$ iterations. We claim that $A_2 \sqsubseteq \mathbf{do}\, j < n \rightarrow A_3\ \mathbf{od}$, where

$$
\begin{array}{|l}
\hline
\_A_3\ \underline{\hspace{8cm}} \\
\quad \Delta State;\ \Delta Time \\
\hline
\quad L' = L \\
\quad j' = j + 1 \\
\quad r' = max\{r, Lj\} \\
\quad t' - t = 1 \\
\hline
\end{array}
$$

To show this, we must verify the following proof obligations (where $B = j < n$). The first obligations require showing that the invariant is properly initialized (4), and that the invariant and guard B together establish the loop body (5). Showing these two steps is straightforward.

$$pre A_2 \wedge \mathbf{skip} \vdash Inv \tag{4}$$

$$Inv \wedge pre A_2 \wedge (age(T(\mathbf{do})) \wedge B')' \vdash (pre A_3)'' \tag{5}$$

where $T(\mathbf{do})$ is the time required to evaluate the guard and conditionally branch, and $T(\mathbf{od})$ is the time for the branch-back. In our example, these values are 0 and 1 respectively. Thus, $age(T(\mathbf{do}))$ and $age(T(\mathbf{od}))$ are

$$
\begin{array}{|l}
\hline
\_age(T(\mathbf{od}))\ \underline{\hspace{4cm}} \\
\quad \Delta Time;\ \Xi State \\
\hline
\quad t' - t = 1 \\
\hline
\end{array}
\qquad
\begin{array}{|l}
\hline
\_age(T(\mathbf{do}))\ \underline{\hspace{4cm}} \\
\quad \Delta Time;\ \Xi State \\
\hline
\quad t' = t \\
\hline
\end{array}
$$

In our example, only the branch-back takes non-zero time. But the refinement rules of [3] require us to include the time constraints for branch *into* the loop as well, in order for the proof to discharge.

The next two proof steps are as follows.

$$pre A_2 \wedge (Inv \, ^\circ_9 \, age(T(\mathbf{do}))) \wedge \neg B' \vdash A_2 \tag{6}$$

$$pre A_2 \wedge Inv \wedge (age(T(\mathbf{do})) \wedge B')' \wedge (A_3 \, ^\circ_9 \, age(T(\mathbf{od})))'' \vdash Inv[\_'''/\_'] \tag{7}$$

Step (6) is straightforward, by the definition of *max* and of ranges. The final step, (7), showing that the invariant is maintained by the loop ('body liveness'), is more complex. The left hand side of the proof resolves to the conjunction of the following two schemas.

$$
\begin{array}{|l}
\hline
\quad \Delta State;\ \Delta Time \\
\hline
\quad j = 1 \wedge r = L0 \\
\quad r' = max\{i : 0..j' - 1 \bullet L'i\} \\
\quad L' = L \wedge L'' = L' \\
\quad j'' = j' \wedge t'' = t' \wedge r'' = r' \\
\quad t' - t = 2(j' - 1) \\
\quad j'' \leq n \\
\hline
\end{array}
\qquad
\begin{array}{|l}
\hline
\quad \Delta State;\ \Delta Time \\
\hline
\quad L''' = L'' \\
\quad j''' = j'' + 1 \\
\quad r''' = max\{r'', L''(j'')\} \\
\quad t''' - t'' = 2 \\
\hline
\end{array}
$$

while the right hand side resolves to

$$
\begin{array}{|l|}
\hline
\Delta State;\ \Delta Time \\
\hline
L''' = L \\
j''' \leq n \\
r''' = max\{i : 0..j''' - 1 \bullet L'''(i)\} \\
t''' - t = 2(j''' - 1) \\
\hline
\end{array}
$$

and the proof obligation is then straightforward to discharge, by substitution and simple comparison.

In order to complete the proof, it is necessary to discharge termination obligations. We must therefore show that

$$pre\,A_2 \wedge Inv \wedge (age(T(\mathbf{do})) \wedge B')' \vdash n - j' > 0 \tag{8}$$

$$pre\,A_2 \wedge Inv \wedge (age(T(\mathbf{do})) \wedge B')' \wedge (A_3 \,{}^{\circ}_{9}\, age(T(\mathbf{od})))'' \vdash n - j''' < n - j' \tag{9}$$

Both obligations follow directly from the conjuncts in their hypotheses, which relate j'' to j' and j''' to j'.

Finally, we note that A_3 is a schema expression for the simultaneous assignment $j, r := j + 1, max\{r, Lj\}$, and so the calculation is complete.

3.3   Using the heterogeneous method

We now use the combination of Z and predicative programming. Predicative programming has techniques for dealing with timing constraints built-in. We propose to specify the state-based aspects of our system using Z, and the timing aspects using predicative programming. The predicative refinement rules, extended to heterogeneous specifications, will be used to refine the heterogeneous specification to an implementation that meets the time constraints.

The approach to constructing and manipulating heterogeneous specifications that we use was outlined in Section 2.3. We use predicative refinement rules on heterogeneous specifications taken from [9]. These refinement rules are syntactically very similar to standard predicative refinement rules, and they provably maintain the key properties of predicative refinement, e.g., the ability to refine specifications by parts and steps [9]. It is these properties that can make the heterogeneous approach to proving time constraints very attractive.

The problem specification in the heterogeneous case is very similar to that for the extended Z setting. The system state is

$$State \mathrel{\widehat{=}} \left[L : 0..n - 1 \to \mathbb{N};\ j : \mathbb{N};\ r : \mathbb{Z}_\infty \mid j \leq n \right]$$

We do not include time constraints in the Z schema. Instead, time constraints are expressed as predicates. The initial problem specification is $S \wedge Time$, where

$$S \mathrel{\widehat{=}} \left[\Delta State \mid L' = L \wedge r' = max\{j : 0..n - 1 \bullet Lj\} \right]$$

and *Time* $\cong t' - t = 2n - 1$. In the refinement, we assume that an assignment statement and a tail-recursive call (equivalent to a loop branch-back) take one unit of time each, and that no other operations take any time.

The refinement proceeds as follows. Since we have composed S and *Time* via a predicative combinator, we use predicative refinement to implement the specification. We do this in two steps, as is standard in predicative refinement. We first refine the heterogeneous specification into code, ignoring all timing issues. Then, once complete, we prove that the time constraints written in the initial specification are satisfied by the implementation. We prove this last step by reusing the refinement tree of the first part, considering only time variables. Then, due to refinement by parts over predicative combinators, the composition of the timing and correctness proofs satisfies the original (timed) specification.

The refinement without time is straightforward. The first step is:

$$S \Leftarrow j, r := 1, L0. \; S1$$

where $S1$ is a Z schema, defined as follows.

$$S1 \cong \left[\Delta State \mid L' = L \wedge r' = max\{r, max\{i : j..n - 1 \bullet Li\}\} \right]$$

This is trivial to prove using Rule 2. Note that the value of r is not constrained in the schema; it will be constrained by the recursive refinement. If we were developing a looping program, the value of r would have to be constrained. We next refine $S1$ into a two-branch **if** statement, using the *refinement by cases* rule of [6].

$$S1 \Leftarrow \textbf{if } j = n \textbf{ then ok else } (j \neq n \Rightarrow S1)$$

(**ok** is the empty program that does nothing.) To prove the **then** branch, we use Rule 1, and in the process substitute n for j in the property of $S1$, so as to show that $S1[n/j]$ reduces to the schema that changes no variables. In doing this, we follow Section 2.3.1 and define the meaning of $j = n \Rightarrow S1$ as a predicate (which is justifiable in this case, because $S1$ is expressible in predicative notation). Substituting n for j gives us

$$
\begin{array}{l}
\underline{S1[n/j]} \\
\quad \Delta State \\
\hline
L' = L \\
r' = max\{r, max\{i : n..n - 1 \bullet Li\}\}
\end{array}
$$

The last line of the schema reduces to $r' = max\{r, -\infty\}$, which simplifies to $r' = r$. This schema can be implemented by **ok**. To prove the **else** branch, we apply the boolean laws of specialization and discharge, which prove the obligation in two lines. We omit the details.

The proof continues by refining the **else** branch.

$$(j \neq n \Rightarrow S1) \Leftarrow j, r := j + 1, max\{r, Lj\}. \; S1 \tag{10}$$

This refinement says that we implement $j \neq n \Rightarrow S1$ by first setting r to the maximum of the previous value of r and the value of Lj, and simultaneously increase j by 1. Then we behave like schema $S1$ again. This style of recursive refinement is a standard technique in predicative programming; it is done in lieu of developing looping programs with invariants (though in fact an invariant is present, but it is buried within the proof step).

To verify that this proof step is correct, we apply Rule 2 to the right-hand-side of (10), and show that it implies $(j \neq n) \Rightarrow S1$, by Rule 1. Applying Rule 2 to the right-hand-side of (10) gives the anonymous schema

$$
\begin{array}{|l}
\hline
\Delta State \\
\hline
L' = L \\
r' = max\{max\{r, Lj\}, max\{i : j + 1..n - 1 \bullet Li\}\} \\
\hline
\end{array}
$$

By definition of *max* and ranges, this simplifies to

$$\left[\Delta State \mid L' = L \wedge r' = max\{r, max\{i : j..n - 1 \bullet Li\}\} \right]$$

which is $S1$, and so the refinement holds by specialization.

Now for the timing proof. Since predicative refinement can be done by parts (and since S and *Time* are composed predicatively), we can prove that the timing constraints placed on the initial specification are maintained by the implementation, separate from the correctness proof. This requires us to show

$$Time \Leftarrow j, r, t := 1, L0, t + 1 \, . \, U \tag{11}$$

$$U \Leftarrow \text{if } j = n \text{ then ok else } Q \tag{12}$$

$$Q \Leftarrow j, r, t := j + 1, max\{r, Lj\}, t + 1 \, . \, t := t + 1 \, . \, U \tag{13}$$

for suitable timing predicates U and Q. Notice that the timing proof structure reuses the structure of the correctness proof.

We conjecture that

$$U = (j = n \Rightarrow t' = t) \wedge (j < n \Rightarrow t' = t + 2(n - j))$$
$$Q = j < n \Rightarrow t' = t + 2(n - j)$$

and now verify the steps. The proof of time is done in the predicative notation only; therefore, standard predicative rules apply. The proof of step (11) is straightforward by the substitution rule of [6]. Step (12) is also straightforward, applying the law of refinement by cases. The third step, (13), is the most complicated. (13) simplifies to, after three applications of the substitution rule

$$Q \Leftarrow (j + 1 = n \Rightarrow t' = t + 2) \wedge$$
$$(j + 1 < n \Rightarrow t' = t + 2 + 2(n - j - 1))$$

which, by further simplification, is true. We conclude that the timing constraint *Time* is satisfied by the implementation. By monotonicity, $S \wedge Time$ is implemented, and satisfies its time bound.

We discuss the heterogeneous development, and compare it with the extended Z development, in Section 5.

4 Reasoning about Space

Many formal notations and methods have been constructed or extended so as to be able to reason about time for the purposes of developing real-time and reactive systems. There has been less work done on formal reasoning about space and space usage in formal notations and methods. One reason for this might be that space usage is typically a quantity associated with executing a specification, whereas formal notations are typically used for writing specifications that need not be immediately executable.

In this section, we compare Z extended with space variables with a heterogeneous combination of Z and predicative programming. We apply the two techniques to a simple problem, an abstraction of the Towers of Hanoi, to demonstrate some non-trivial space reasoning. We might expect different results than with a comparison in terms of time, mainly because reasoning about space (and extending notations to space) is much simpler than time, and only requires use of conventions.

4.1 The problem

The problem we want to solve is an abstraction of the Towers of Hanoi. We ignore the issue of putting disks on pegs, and instead concentrate on the issue of space use. The standard (exponential) solution to this problem is doubly recursive. Let x be the number of disks. The system state is $State \mathrel{\widehat{=}} [x : \mathbb{N}]$. A solution to our abstraction of the Towers of Hanoi problem is given in the guarded command language procedure *tower*.

$$\textbf{procedure } tower \mathrel{\widehat{=}} \textbf{if } x > 0 \to$$
$$x := x - 1; \; tower; \; x := x + 1;$$
$$MoveDisk;$$
$$x := x - 1; \; tower; \; x := x + 1$$
$$[] \; x = 0 \to \textbf{skip fi}$$

Procedure *MoveDisk* carries out the moving of disks from peg to peg (we leave its functionality unspecified, since it will not affect space calculations). To move the pile of disks, if there is at least one disk, first, ignore the bottom disk, remove the remaining pile, then reconsider all disks. Now move one disk (the one we previously ignored); then, again ignore the bottom disks, move the remaining pile, then reconsider all disks. If there are no disks, do nothing.

We assume that a recursive call to a procedure costs one unit of space (for holding a return address), and that *MoveDisk* and all other statements require no further space.

In proving bounds on space use, we will prove that the proposed solution satisfies a proposed space bound, i.e., a posit-and-prove approach.

4.2 Using the heterogeneous method

We first want to use the heterogeneous method to prove a bound on the maximum space used by the program *tower*. We specify the goal of the space calculation in Z.

$$TowerSpace \mathrel{\widehat{=}} [\Delta State; \; \Delta Space \mid m' = max\{m, s + x\}]$$

That is, we intend to show that the recursive procedure *tower* satisfies the space bound *TowerSpace*. To prove this, we start with specification *tower*, and in it replace the recursive calls to *tower* with calls to *TowerSpace*, performing the translation from Z to predicative notation behind-the-scenes. In doing so, we prefix the calls with changes in variables s and m; on returns from calls, we reset variables s and m. From this specification, we propose that (with some simplification)

$$TowerSpace \Leftarrow \textbf{if } x > 0 \textbf{ then}$$
$$(x, s, m := x - 1, s + 1, max\{m, s + 1\}.$$
$$TowerSpace. \ TowerSpace.$$
$$x, s := x + 1, s - 1)$$
$$\textbf{else ok}$$

(*max* is predicative programming is a function of two arguments.) The proposed refinement is constructed directly from *tower*. Note that this is a heterogeneous specification, composing Z specification *TowerSpace* with predicative specifications using predicative combinators.

We verify the refinement by cases. The **else** branch is straightforward, and simply requires us to show that

$$TowerSpace \Leftarrow x = 0 \wedge (x' = x \wedge s' = s \wedge m' = m)$$

With the assumption that $m \geq s$ in $\Delta Space$, this implication is clearly *true*. For the **then** branch, we first simplify the body. The first two statements in the sequence of the **then** branch simplify to (by applying the substitution rule from [6], as well as *ZToPP*)

$$m' = max\{m, max\{s + 1, s + x\}\} \wedge x' = x - 1 \wedge s' = s + 1$$

The second two statements in sequence simplify to

$$m' = max\{m, max\{s, s + x\}\} \wedge s' = s \wedge x' = x$$

The sequence of these two specifications, followed by the simultaneous assignment $s, x := s - 1, x + 1$, is the assignment

$$m := max\{m, max\{s + 1, s + x\}\}$$

In order to complete the proof, we therefore must show that

$$TowerSpace \Leftarrow x > 0 \wedge m := max\{m, max\{s + 1, s + x\}\}$$

which is equivalent to showing that

$$TowerSpace \Leftarrow x > 0 \wedge m := max\{m, s + x\}$$

We therefore must prove that

$$(m \geq s \Rightarrow m' = max\{m, s + x\} \wedge x' = x \wedge s' = s) \Leftarrow x > 0 \wedge m := max\{m, s + x\}$$

By expanding the assignment statement with its predicative semantics, and by applying the one-point rule three times, this reduces to *true*, and the proof is done.

4.3 Using Z

We now prove that the space bound is satisfied using the extended Z notation. We again use a *posit-and-prove* approach. We have a proposed solution to the Towers of Hanoi abstraction. We next specify a procedure *recSpace* that calculates the maximum space required for an implementation of *tower*. The body of *recSpace* is a Z schema.

$$\textbf{procedure } recSpace \mathrel{\widehat{=}}$$
$$\left[\Delta State;\ \Delta Space \mid m' = max\{m, s + x\} \wedge s' = s \wedge x' = x\right]$$

We will prove that *recSpace* is implemented by a recursive program. We claim that

$$recSpace \sqsubseteq \textbf{if } x > 0 \rightarrow x, s, m := x - 1, s + 1, max\{m, s + 1\};$$
$$recSpace;\ recSpace;$$
$$x, s := x + 1, s - 1$$
$$[]\ x = 0 \rightarrow \textbf{skip fi}$$

The proposed refinement is obtained from *tower*, where each call to *recSpace* is prefixed with $s, m := s + 1, max\{m, s + 1\}$. The call to *MoveDisk* is removed since it will not affect space use. We prove the refinement by first simplifying the $x > 0$ branch of the guarded command. For each occurrence of *recSpace*, we substitute the schema definition of its body, and simplify. The first two statements in the sequence of the $x > 0$ branch is equivalent to the schema

$$
\begin{array}{l}
\hline
\Delta State;\ \Delta Space \\
\hline
m' = max\{m, max\{s + 1, s + x\}\} \\
x' = x - 1 \\
s' = s + 1 \\
\hline
\end{array}
$$

The second two statements in sequence simplify to the anonymous schema

$$\left[\Delta State;\ \Delta Space \mid m' = max\{m, max\{s, s + x\}\} \wedge s' = s \wedge x' = x\right]$$

The sequence of these two anonymous schemas and the schema for the simultaneous assignment $s, x := s - 1, x + 1$ is then

$$\left[\Delta State;\ \Delta Space \mid m' = max\{m, max\{s + 1, s + x\}\} \wedge s' = s \wedge x' = x\right]$$

which is equivalent to $m := max\{m, max\{s + 1, s + x\}\}$. Therefore, we want to prove that

$$recspace \sqsubseteq \textbf{if } x > 0 \rightarrow m := max\{m, max\{s + 1, s + x\}\}$$
$$[]\ x = 0 \rightarrow \textbf{skip}$$
$$\textbf{fi}$$

To prove the **if** branch, we must show that

$$recspace \sqsubseteq x > 0 \wedge m' = max\{m, max\{s+1, s+x\}\}$$

To do so, we assume that $m \geq s$. Then, since $x > 0 \Rightarrow s + x \geq s + 1$, the proof goes through. To prove the **else** branch, we take a similar approach to proving

$$recspace \sqsubseteq x = 0 \wedge \mathbf{skip}$$

and by assuming $m \geq s$, we see that $s + x = s$, and because $x = 0$, the proof also goes through. So we have shown that the maximum space bound on the implementation of *tower* is $max\{m, s + x\}$.

5 Discussion and Comparison

We can compare the use of extended Z with a heterogeneous combination of Z and predicative programming in a number of different ways, such as in terms of conciseness of the specifications, or in terms of the simplicity of the refinement rules of each method. Many forms of comparison are subjective. We therefore compare the two methods in terms of complexity of the method steps, i.e., refinement rules, *and* in terms of the complexity of the proofs.

With the extended Z method from [3], two changes must be made from standard Z in order to reason about time: specifications must include references to time variables and timing constraints; and, real-time refinement rules must be constructed from standard rules. The main extension with respect to the refinement rules is to introduce time constraints for programming language statements. The *structure* of refinements itself is not changed; one must still show safety and liveness conditions in order to prove correct refinements. However, the individual refinement rules are made more complicated (and longer, since we have to deal with larger specifications) by the addition of new terms, e.g., *age* schemas. As well, the refinement rules require some 'place-holder' terms, e.g., $age(T(\mathbf{do}))$, in order to properly discharge the proofs, even though the specific programming language entities that they describe require no time. Such placeholders, while certainly necessary for the proof, are unintuitive, and make proofs longer than is necessary. Specialization of the refinement rules would seem to be necessary in order to simplify the rules in cases where trivial time bounds are present.

Finally, we mention that the requirement to use refinement rules that contain both timing and state-based constructs simultaneously can make the process of proof in the extended method more complicated than in the heterogeneous method. It does not seem to be possible to separate proof of timing from proof of correctness when using the extended Z method, because this will require use of the schema calculus: a specification of behaviour will have to be (schema) conjoined with a specification of time constraints. Refinement is not in general monotonic over the schema calculus conjunction combinator [11], and so separating proof of correctness from proof of timing is not generally possible.

In the heterogeneous method applied to timing, the refinement rules that are used are simple, generalized rules from [6]. For those rules that are added in order to carry out the proof of partial correctness (but not the proof of timing) – e.g., refinement of a Z schema by a predicate – the additions are small and used in the same manner as existing predicative refinement rules. The added rules are straightforward and for the most part syntactic generalizations of the refinement rules from [6], with minimal restrictions on their use. Importantly, with the heterogeneous method, proofs of correctness and timing can be separated, due to monotonicity properties. This lets us carry out the proof of timing in predicative notation.

If we were to look solely at using extended Z or the heterogeneous approach for writing specifications (with time), we would find many similarities. The initial specifications that we wrote when applying extended Z and the heterogeneous approach were similar in size and complexity. However, the specifications that were *constructed* during the refinement were more complex with extended Z. With the heterogeneous approach, the specifications that were constructed were no more complex than what occurs when writing standard predicative specification, which may be important, in particular, when doing automated proof.

Differences between using the two approaches is less clear when we consider space reasoning. In applying Z method, refinement rules do not have to be changed in order to reason about space, because we treat space as new state components. However, specifications are made modestly larger because of the need to add procedure interfaces to proposed solutions. This is due to the fact that non-trivial space behaviour arises only with recursive procedures. In the heterogeneous approach, we can avoid adding procedure interfaces because of the capability of using recursive refinement techniques [6] on heterogeneous specifications, which negates the requirement to explicitly introduce recursive procedures.

In the heterogeneous method, one new refinement rule must be introduced, for refining Z schemas by predicative specifications. This rule is a simple generalization of standard predicative refinement. But in the extended Z method, refinement as described in [12] suffices for proof of space bounds. Therefore, we might conclude that the extension with respect to space favours the extended Z approach rather than the heterogeneous approach, at least in terms of complexity or any requirements to adapt proof rules to heterogeneous notations. When we look at the proofs of space bounds, in both the extended Z and the heterogeneous case, we see that the proofs are of similar complexity, and take similar steps. Therefore, we might also conclude that the two approaches are too similar in their application to make any overall distinction. Part of the reason for this similarity is due to the fact that extension or notation integration for reasoning about space is much more straightforward than for time: detailed new proof rules do not have to be constructed, and existing proof rules do not generally have to be modified.

In general, then, we found that using the extension of Z to reason about time was more complex and intrusive than using the heterogeneous combination of Z and predicative programming. This intrusiveness manifested itself in terms of both writing specifications, and in terms of proof. On the other hand, we found that using the extension of Z to reason about space was no more complex than using a heterogeneous combination of Z and predicative programming. This was primarily an artifact of reasoning about space constraints, which is simpler to do than reasoning about time constraints, because there are fewer ways to effect a change in space use within a program.

This suggests that whether we should prefer an extension approach over a heterogeneous approach will depend on the task to which we want to apply the method. The timing case study has shown that a heterogeneous approach can be simpler to use than an extension approach. But the space case study has also shown that in some situations – e.g., when reasoning about a system artifact that does not broadly require changes in refinement rules – an extension approach can be just as straightforward to use as a heterogeneous approach.

As an alternative to adding Z to predicative programming for proving time and space bounds, we might consider the reverse situation: where we take predicative programming and add Z notations to it. We could then use the resulting heterogeneous notation to reason about time, space, and refinement. But predicative programming already has built-in mechanisms for reasoning about time and space, and is a wide-spectrum design calculus with a simpler notion of refinement – boolean implication – than Z. Therefore, for this purpose (reasoning about time, space, and refinement), it seems to be redundant to add Z to predicative programming; there of course may be other valid reasons for the addition.

6 Conclusions

We have briefly compared the use of an extension approach to formal methods with a heterogeneous approach to formal methods. Applying Z, extended with specification and reasoning for time and space, and comparing it with applications of Z combined with predicative programming, has been carried out on small examples. We found that the heterogeneous combination of Z and predicative programming was easy to use for timing specification and reasoning, resulting in shorter proofs than was the case with extended Z. And we found that the extension and heterogeneous approaches were similar in complexity for specifying and reasoning about space usage. We therefore can conclude that there exists a situation where heterogeneous notations are useful – and are more useful than an extended notation.

More work remains to be done on comparing extension and heterogeneity. We have only carried out a small pair of case studies here. It seems likely that there will be special cases of applications for which our conclusions will not hold, and discovering such special cases will be of interest, especially with respect to determining fundamental system properties for which extension is simpler to use than heterogeneity (or vice versa). As well, it would be useful to attempt other case studies, beyond time and space. Extension with respect to semantics, e.g., such as is done in [5], would be interesting to study and compare as well.

Acknowledgements. Thanks to Rick Hehner, Jonathan Ostroff, and Phil Brooke for their comments. Special thanks to the anonymous referees for their detailed suggestions, which have improved the quality and presentation of the paper. This work was supported with the help of the National Science and Engineering Research Council of Canada.

References

1. P. Baumann and K. Lerner. A Framework for the Specification of Reactive and Concurrent Systems in Z. In P.S. Thiagarajan (ed.), *Foundations of Software Technology and Theoretical Computer Science*, Lecture Notes in Computer Science, volume 1026, Springer-Verlag, 1995.

2. J.-M. Bruel, A. Benzekri, and Y. Raymaud. Z and the Specification of Real-time Systems. In *Proc. 7th Int. Conf. on Putting into Practice Methods and Tools for Information System Design*, IRIN, 1995.

3. C.J. Fidge. Real-time Refinement. In M. Naftalin, T. Denvir and M. Bertran (eds.), *FME '93: Industrial Strength Formal Methods*, Lecture Notes in Computer Science, volume 670, Springer-Verlag, 1993.

4. J. Grundy. Predicative Programming – A Survey. In D. Bjørner, M. Broy and I.V. Pottosin (eds.), *Formal Methods in Programming and Their Applications*, Lecture Notes in Computer Science, volume 735, Springer-Verlag, 1993.

5. E.C.R. Hehner and A.J. Malton. Termination Conventions and Comparative Semantics, *Acta Informatica*, 25 (1988).

6. E.C.R. Hehner. *A Practical Theory of Programming*, Springer-Verlag, 1993.

7. E.C.R. Hehner. Formalization of Time and Space, submitted.

8. C.C. Morgan. *Programming from Specifications*, Prentice Hall International Series in Computer Science, Second Edition, 1994.

9. R.F. Paige. A Meta-Method for Formal Method Integration. In J. Fitzgerald, C.B. Jones and P. Lucas (eds.), *FME '97: Industrial Applications and Strengthened Foundations of Formal Methods*, Lecture Notes in Computer Science, volume 1313, Springer-Verlag, 1997.

10. J.M. Spivey. *The Z Notation: A Reference Manual*, Prentice Hall International Series in Computer Science, 1989.

11. N. Ward. Adding specification constructors to the refinement calculus. In M. Naftalin, T. Denvir and M. Bertran (eds.), *FME '93: Industrial Strength Formal Methods*, Lecture Notes in Computer Science, volume 670, Springer-Verlag, 1993.

12. J.B. Wordsworth. *Software Development with Z*, Addison-Wesley, 1992.

13. P. Zave and M. Jackson. Where do operations come from? An approach to multiparadigm specification, *IEEE Transactions on Software Engineering*, 12(7), July 1996.

Inconsistency and Undefinedness in Z –
A Practical Guide

Samuel H. Valentine

Department of Computer Science, University of York, UK

Tel: +44 1904 432778   Fax: +44 1904 432708
Email: sam@cs.york.ac.uk

Abstract. Consistency is essential for a Z specification to have any useful meaning. We give some sufficient conditions and stylistic guidelines for achieving it and for proving that this has been done. We also describe the Z interpretation of "undefined" expressions, and relate this to rules of proof. The paper is mainly tutorial; experience has shown that these issues have caused confusion.

1   Introduction

The status of undefined terms in Z seems to be a "frequently asked question" from those learning to use or to carry out proofs in Z. Functions in Z are, in general, not total, and the application of a function outside its domain gives rise to a term whose value is not defined. The question as to what this means in theory and in practice deserves a clear response.

The different but related question of consistency of Z specifications seems to be, rather, a question not asked frequently enough, since it is a proof obligation on all specifications, and even cursory observation is enough to show that the obligation is not always discharged.

2   Preliminaries

The mention of "proof" presupposes that we have proof rules. Those used in the development of this paper are given in [12]. Similar rules are given in [3, 4] for instance. In general a "common sense" idea of proof rules will be adequate except as clarified here.

Throughout this discussion we assume that any specification under consideration is syntactically correct and is type correct. There are several good tools available to check these properties. Any text which is not correct in both these respects is considered to be meaningless.

We also are ignoring the general problem of validation, which is the correspondence between the meaning of the specification, assuming it has a meaning, with the intentions of the author or sponsor. This is the most difficult problem, because unlike the other issues it cannot be solved solely by examination of the specification's text, but requires reference to the proposed environment of use, with all the complexities which that may entail.

The formal material of this paper is written in Draft Standard Z (see [13, 14]). One of the innovations in the Standard, compared with the notation of [11], is the ability to declare a new "section", which allows a specification to be divided into separate parts linked only by an explicit statement, for each section, of its "parents". The meaning of each section depends only on the meaning of its own paragraphs and those of its parents.

Other innovations of the forthcoming Standard, some of which are used below, are:

a) a syntax for conjectures;

b) template declarers to describe:

   i) generic infix operators, using "generic",

   ii) infix relations, using "relation", and

   iii) functions with their binding powers, using "function";

c) the ability to declare with == in all declaration positions, rather than just at top level;

d) a general permission for the declaration part of a schema text to be empty;

e) permission for generic definitions to be loose.

Nevertheless all the significant points of the paper apply equally to the Z of [11], except the generalisation to loose generics, as explained below.

3   What is consistency, and why is it important?

We can show the importance of consistency by a simple example.

section *thePope*

$Person ::= SamValentine \mid thePope$

$$
\begin{array}{|l}
\hline
x : \mathbb{N} \\
\hline
x = 2 + 2 \\
\end{array}
$$

$$
\begin{array}{|l}
\hline
y : \mathbb{N} \\
\hline
y = x \\
y = 5 \\
\end{array}
$$

Then having stated the defining paragraphs, we pose a conjecture:

$\vdash \quad SamValentine = thePope$

The original theorem on which this result is based is apparently due to G. H. Hardy (see [6]), where the proof proceeds by analysis of the cardinality of the set $\{Sam\text{-}Valentine, thePope\}$, which is 2, which can be shown to be equal to 1, so the two members of the set are equal. More seriously, all formal proof systems agree that any conjecture with a false antecedent is a theorem, so if, as here, we can show that $2 + 2 = 5$, we can prove anything at all.

The point of this example is that something similar could easily arise by accident. The specification looks valid when considered bit by bit. If any one of the predicates, $x = 2 + 2, y = x, y = 5$ were omitted, the opportunity for paradox would vanish.

This leads us to the conclusion that we must have criteria to establish that proposed specifications are not self-contradictory, and we must accept a proof obligation on all specifications that they fulfil those criteria. Otherwise what we write may be nonsense.

4   How can we ensure consistency?

4.1   Consistency and satisfiability

Z is a notation for describing an assignment of values to names in typed set theory. This in turn can be described in untyped set theory, (see [10, 14]). By the word "assignment" we mean a tuple of name-value pairs, where each declared name is represented once.

Each paragraph of a Z section can declare new names, or establish constraints, or both. The meaning of a section is the set of assignments of values to names which satisfy all the constraints. If the set of all assignments contains more than one member, we say the section is satisfiable, and loose. If there is exactly one assignment, we say the section is uniquely satisfiable. If the set of assignments is empty, the section is unsatisfiable.

It is the intention of the designers of the proof rules for Z that those rules should be sound with respect to the meaning. This means that the theory formed by taking as axiomatic all the constraints in a satisfiable section should be consistent. If a section is not satisfiable, but we take all its constraints as axioms, then using the proof rules we may be able to prove a conjecture equivalent to *false*. This is what we did in the example above. The proof rules allow as a theorem any conjecture whose antecedent is false, so from one falsehood we can derive all falsehoods, and this is what we mean by an inconsistent theory. On the other hand, provided our system is sound, a satisfiable section has a proof theory which is consistent.

4.2   Extensions and conservative extensions

We can establish sufficient conditions for consistency using the notion of "extensions" and "conservative extensions". A theory, T2, is an extension of another, T1, if the set of names in T1 is a subset of the set of names in T2 and the set of theorems of T1 is a subset of the set of theorems of T2. A theory, T2, is a conservative extension of another, T1, if the set of theorems of T1 is equal to the set of theorems of T2 which refer only to the names in T1.

In a consistent theory, not all conjectures are theorems. In an inconsistent theory, all conjectures are theorems. Therefore, a conservative extension of a consistent theory is itself consistent.

Applying this to Z specifications, first we make the assumption of "definition before use". The most desirable rule is that there must exist an ordering of the paragraphs which places the definition of each variable before its use; there must not be any circularity in the pattern of paragraph cross-reference. Here we are supposing that any necessary paragraph re-ordering to achieve this has been done. Now we can take the paragraphs within a section one by one, considering each in the context of its predecessors.

Next we observe that the empty (and parentless) section is satisfiable, since its meaning is the set containing the empty assignment. Provided our system is sound, the empty section is therefore consistent.

Each paragraph either declares new names, or establishes new constraints, or both. Within each section, however, neither names nor constraints can be removed. Therefore the theory formed by a sequence of paragraphs within a section is an extension of that formed by any well-typed subsequence of them, and therefore if any sequence of paragraphs within a section is consistent, any well-typed subsequence of them is also consistent.

Since the number of paragraphs in a specification is finite, we can show (by induction) that a necessary and sufficient condition for consistency is that the theory formed by each well-typed subsequence of paragraphs within each section is a conservative extension of that formed by some smaller well-typed subsequence.

Similarly, a necessary and sufficient condition for consistency is that the theory formed by each initial sequence of paragraphs is a conservative extension of that formed by some smaller initial sequence.

In particular, consistency will be ensured if the theory of each initial sequence is a conservative extension of that formed by the sequence obtained by deleting its last paragraph. A sufficient condition for consistency is that every paragraph forms part of a conservative extension in that sense.

4.3 Axiomatic and abbreviation definitions

To be part of a conservative extension of its predecessors means that for each paragraph, any theorem which can be derived from it either:
a) contains references to variables introduced in this paragraph; or
b) is a theorem without use of this paragraph.

For each sort of paragraph where it makes syntactic sense to do so, it will form part of a conservative extension if the conjecture, formed by prefixing the paragraph with an $\exists$ symbol and then making the appropriate adjustments to rectify the syntax, is a theorem. (Compare [5].)

In the case of an axiomatic definition, this means adding the $\exists$ symbol and then separating the declaration part from the constraint part with a $\bullet$ symbol.

In the case of a global constraint, the existential quantification over an empty declaration part may be elided, and the resulting conjecture has the same form as the proposed constraint. If this is a theorem, the proposed constraint is redundant; otherwise the extension is not conservative. So global constraints are not conservative except in the trivial case that they tell us nothing new.

In the case of abbreviation definitions using the $==$ symbol, the existential quantification is guaranteed to be true provided the expression on its right-hand side has some value. As we shall see below, this is always the case provided its type is not empty. In particular, since power-set types are never empty, an abbreviation definition of a set always forms part of a conservative extension, and preserves consistency, without further question.

In the case of the example above, for the second paragraph we pose the conjecture
$$\vdash \qquad \exists x : \mathbb{N} \bullet x = 2 + 2$$

Since this is a theorem, that paragraph creates a conservative extension, so we make that definition,

$$\begin{array}{|l}
x : \mathbb{N} \\
\hline
x = 2 + 2
\end{array}$$

and in that context, go on to the next conjecture to check, which is

$$\vdash \quad \exists y : \mathbb{N} \bullet y = x \wedge y = 5$$

This conjecture is not a theorem. So we have found the problem; the final paragraph, namely

$$\begin{array}{|l}
y : \mathbb{N} \\
\hline
y = x \\
y = 5
\end{array}$$

has not been shown to be consistent with its predecessors.

The notion of conservative extension provides a stylistic guide when defining several new variables axiomatically. If a single paragraph does not represent a conservative extension on its predecessors, but several paragraphs can be merged to achieve this effect, it is probably good style to do so; and if it is possible to split a proposed definition into several separate axiomatic definitions, each of which represents a conservative extension on its predecessors, it is probably good style to do so.

4.4   Free types

In the above discussion, we have used properties of numbers. Numbers are expressible in terms of free types, and it is the rules for consistency in the latter which we next explore.

In the first example, we assumed that the free type definition

$$Person ::= SamValentine \mid thePope$$

was consistent, but on what grounds?

The definition of such a free type is equivalent, (see [11]), to the given set introduction

$$[Person]$$

which creates no problem as such, since we can always assume that a given set exists, together with the constraints

$$\begin{array}{|l}
SamValentine, thePope : Person \\
\hline
\neg\, SamValentine = thePope \\
Person = \{SamValentine, thePope\}
\end{array}$$

which do not form part of a conservative extension. So how can we establish that there is a set with precisely two members?

To answer this, we need to consider the model of Z within some other theory, such as Zermelo-Fraenkel theory. Then it becomes easy using the axioms of empty set and of union (using the nomenclature of [2]) to prove that such a set exists.

The general issue here is quite complex, but fortunately has been well explored in the literature. See for example [1, 9].

In the non-recursive case, a free type definition can always be built up from existing elements. The existence of a model then follows from the axiom of union.

The interesting case is where there is recursion. Let's start with an example where we get it wrong.

section *Russell* parents *toolkit*

For instance, suppose we have the definition

$$S ::= cons\langle\langle \mathbb{P}\,S\rangle\rangle$$

The properties of the free type imply that *cons* is a total injection from $\mathbb{P}\,S$ to S. If we then declare

$$|\quad H == \{x : S \mid \neg\; \exists t : \mathbb{P}\,S \bullet x \in t \wedge cons\; t = x\}$$

we can prove that

$$\vdash\qquad cons\; H \in H \Leftrightarrow \neg\; cons\; H \in H$$

So what are the general criteria for doing it right? They are stated in [1] and then in [11]. (NB This is one of the things which Spivey changed between editions, so ignore his first edition on this point.)

We recall that the axioms generated by a free type definition can be summed up in the words "no confusion and no junk" or at slightly greater length:

a) everything which looks as if it is defined, is defined;

b) things which look as if they are different, are different;

c) if you've got all the starting values, and all the steps, you've got the lot.

The second of these principles gives rise to the formal statements that the free type functions are injections, and their ranges are disjoint. The last is the principle of induction.

It is the induction principle which guides the consistency rule. In the non-recursive case, consistency is trivial and the induction rule reduces to the statement that the simple free type constants and the ranges of the constructors together cover the whole of the free type.

For the recursive case, a sufficient consistency requirement is that each set given as the domain of a constructor function should be a monotonic and finitary function of the free type being defined.

a) A function is monotonic if the subset relation between any pair of its argument values is preserved by application of the function. Thus in this case any element which can be introduced by any number of uses of the recursive definition remains there as the recursion depth increases.

b) A function is finitary if its value is equal to the union of the application of itself to all the finite subsets of its argument. Thus in this case any element introduced by the recursive definition gets introduced by a finite number of uses of the recursion.

The definition given makes monotonicity a consequence of finitariness, but it helps to clarify the ideas if we take them separately.

The power-set function is not finitary, and the example above shows the consequences of allowing that to be used within the constructor function.

An example of a non-monotonic definition would be

$$trapped ::= unit \mid successor\langle\langle\{t : trapped \mid \forall x, y : trapped \bullet x = y\}\rangle\rangle$$

which clearly contains *unit*, but if it contains *successor unit* then it doesn't, but if it doesn't, it does.

Just to finish with a positive example, we can see that a definition such as:

$$numtree ::= leaf\langle\langle\mathbb{N}\rangle\rangle \mid node\langle\langle\mathbb{N} \times numtree \times numtree\rangle\rangle$$

is monotonic and finitary (proved by structural induction), and so can be used to create a consistent recursive free type.

As a postscript on this discussion, we could mention the possibility of mutually recursive free types. These are not given in [11], but they can be provided under conditions which are a simple extrapolation of those for simple free types, and it is proposed to include them in Standard Z (see [13, 14]). The rules for disjointness and injectivity continue for each of the constituent free types separately, and there is a single induction principle for all the types taken together.

4.5   Given sets

The discussion of free types above guides us as to the consistency or otherwise of given sets and their uses. It is always legitimate to assume that a given set exists, and that it may have members, but if there are any axioms which constrain those members we need to look more carefully.

In practice, the best way of showing that the uses of a given set are consistent may be to replace it and its associated axiomatic uses with a free type declaration. If this can be done and the resulting definition and enclosing section shown to be consistent, all is well. If not, the proof of consistency needs to be more direct, using the ideas described in [1, 9] for instance.

4.6   Axiomatic definitions and explicit definitions

Many axiomatic definitions of functions and relations are given in the "Mathematical Tool-kit" of [11]. The definitions are claimed to be consistent, but are not there formally proved to be so. (It seems that they all are; see [8] for instance.)

Let's look at the form of these definitions, with particular reference to functions. Take as an example "number range" as defined by Spivey.

section *numRange* parents *toolkit*

$$\_\,.\,.\_ : \mathbb{Z} \times \mathbb{Z} \to \mathbb{P}\mathbb{Z}$$

$$\forall a, b : \mathbb{Z} \bullet a\,.\,.\,b = \{k : \mathbb{Z} \mid a \leq k \leq b\}$$

which is consistent provided

$$\vdash \quad \exists \_..\_ : \mathbb{Z} \times \mathbb{Z} \to \mathbb{PZ} \bullet \forall a,b : \mathbb{Z} \bullet a..b = \{k : \mathbb{Z} \mid a \le k \le b\}$$

which is a conjecture we can begin to prove by providing an explicit description of the object in question, for example as:

$$(\_..\_) = \lambda a,b : \mathbb{Z} \bullet \{k : \mathbb{Z} \mid a \le k \wedge k \le b\}$$

so we might just as well have written

$$\mid \quad \_..\_ == \lambda a,b : \mathbb{Z} \bullet \{k : \mathbb{Z} \mid a \le k \wedge k \le b\}$$

in the first place.

We may wish to prove that this object is a total function, but that is optional, depending on whether we need to know that explicitly. We can use the function anyway, confident in the knowledge that the making of its definition introduced no inconsistency.

It might be argued that skilled specifiers know what they are doing, and therefore one should concentrate on familiar idioms, leaving all thoughts of formal proof till later. As a counter-example, consider the following definition of "pairwise concatenation", taken from [15];

section *pwcat* parents *seqkit*

function 50 leftassoc (_ *pwcat* _)

$$\begin{array}{l} \underline{\quad[X]\quad} \\ \_ pwcat \_ : \operatorname{seq}(\operatorname{seq}X) \times \operatorname{seq}(\operatorname{seq}X) \nrightarrow \operatorname{seq}(\operatorname{seq}X) \\ \hline \forall s,t : \operatorname{seq}(\operatorname{seq}X) \mid \#s = \#t \bullet \\ \quad \forall i : \operatorname{dom}s \bullet (s\ pwcat\ t)i = (s\ i) \frown (t\ i) \end{array}$$

This is consistent, but not uniquely satisfiable. It almost certainly does not correspond with the authors' intentions, since it specifies neither the domain of the function itself, nor the domain of the result. Use of the style recommended here would give us:

$$\begin{array}{l} \underline{\quad[X]\quad} \\ \_ pwcat \_ == \\ \quad \lambda s,t : \operatorname{seq}(\operatorname{seq}X) \mid \#s = \#t \bullet \lambda i : \operatorname{dom}s \bullet (s\ i) \frown (t\ i) \end{array}$$

which is briefer, just as clear, uniquely satisfiable, and probably means what the authors of the original version meant to express.

4.7   The recursive case

Whereas this is attractive, simple and brief for non-recursive definitions, the question arises as to how it compares in the recursive case, where the direct replacement with a lambda-expression is not possible.

A general recursive axiomatic definition of a total function can be represented as

$$\begin{array}{|l}
\hline
f : X \rightarrow Y \\
\hline
p(x,f) \\
\end{array}$$

where $p(x,f)$ is some predicate constraining the declared function. We can express this explicitly as

$$| \quad f == \bigcap \{g : X \rightarrow Y \mid p(x,g)\}$$

which is correct, but may not make things easy to prove. Alternatively, we can write

$$| \quad f == \bigcap \{g : X \nrightarrow Y \mid p'(x,g)\}$$

where p' differs from p in including explicit constraints that arguments given to g are in its domain, or even

$$| \quad f == \bigcap \{g : X \leftrightarrow Y \mid p''(x,g)\}$$

where p'' differs from p' in being formulated without assuming that g is a function.

Any of these forms may be used to prove the consistency of the original axiomatic definition, but they may be seen as less legible, and therefore as not suitable for replacing it. If the function in the axiomatic definition is not total, however, these alternative forms become relatively more attractive.

4.8 Loose definition – an example

We have seen that axiomatic forms of definition require non-trivial consistency proofs, and we are recommending that where there is a straightforward explicit form of definition, it may be preferable to use it.

One case where this cannot be done is where the definition is loose, that is, it does not fully constrain the object it describes.

It is important to allow this, because a specification has a history. There may be a long succession of drafts through all the phases of the program development process. At some stage and in some order the specification should be "tightened", as well as verified as consistent, validated and implemented. But at earlier stages it may be useful to capitalise on the controlled vagueness of the axiomatic method. The axiomatic form is the only one which allows us to leave unspecified those choices which are not relevant to the requirement.

To tighten the specification is in general to make a non-conservative extension, so consistency proofs may need to be repeated. Consistency proofs for axiomatic definitions may take the form of providing explicit objects which satisfy the axioms, which may be viewed as a sort of "trial tightening", but this does not mean that those are the objects which will eventually be used.

The "looseness" we are here discussing is analogous to, but not the same as, non-determinism in operation schemas. The difference is that looseness refers to the many different ways of satisfying the whole section, whereas non-determinism in an operation schema refers only to the elements of that schema, where the relation between the precondition values and the postcondition values is not functional. Similarly, tightening is analogous to what is done in the refinement process and could be considered perhaps as another form of refinement, along with operation refinement and data refinement, although it is formally different from both.

As an example of a loose specification, consider the "monotonic integer square root". Its verbal statement is:

a) Provide a square root function which is a total function on the natural numbers, with natural number range;

b) Where the argument is a perfect square, the result must be exact;

c) The function must be monotonically non-decreasing.

Formally:

section *sqrtBit* parents *toolkit*

$$sqrt : \mathbb{N} \rightarrow \mathbb{N}$$

$$\forall r : \mathbb{N} \bullet sqrt(r * r) = r$$
$$\forall x, y : \mathbb{N} \mid x < y \bullet sqrt\, x \leq sqrt\, y$$

Now it is provably true from this definition that
$$sqrt\, 4 = 2 \wedge sqrt\, 9 = 3$$
and possible, but not provable, that
$$sqrt\, 5 = 2 \wedge sqrt\, 8 = 2$$
but it is possible, but again not provable, that
$$sqrt\, 5 = 3 \wedge sqrt\, 8 = 3$$
but the conjecture that
$$sqrt\, 5 = 3 \wedge sqrt\, 8 = 2$$
is certainly false, in that its negation is a theorem.
We can be sure that
$$sqrt\, 5 = sqrt\, 5$$
so *sqrt* 5 certainly has a value, which we know a lot about, but we cannot pin it down explicitly and unambiguously.

To prove consistency of this definition, we could exemplify with a specific function, such as

$$sqrt = \lambda x : \mathbb{N} \bullet max\{r : \mathbb{N} \mid r * r \leq x\}$$

but having done the proof, we discard the exemplifying function, as being only one of many. The implementor is then allowed to tighten in some other way, and it would be wrong for the specifier to remove that liberty if it is not necessary to do so.

So we see, for appropriate loose specifications, axiomatic definitions are the only way.

5   Why do we need to allow for undefinedness?

So far our discussions have been couched in terms of expressions with definite values, and predicates which are clearly either true or false. Things are not always so clear-cut, however.

section *undefinedness* parents *numkit*

Consider the definition

$$\begin{array}{|l} total, count, average : \mathbb{N} \\ \hline \neg\, count = 0 \Rightarrow average = total \,\mathrm{div}\, count \end{array}$$

This looks entirely reasonable. There seems to be no problem with dividing by zero, because we have checked for that first.

With an operational logic, and in programming languages, that would indeed be the case. The check that count is non-zero would act as a guard on the division, and the question of the result of dividing by zero need never arise. It would not matter if a division by zero would cause an infinite loop or a complete abandonment of the process of computation, since the attempt will not be made.

Z is not a programming language, however, and its logic is mathematical, not operational. The proof rules allow us to transform the above predicate through the following successive stages:

$$\begin{array}{|l} \\ \hline count = 0 \vee average = total \,\mathrm{div}\, count \end{array}$$

$$\begin{array}{|l} \\ \hline average = total \,\mathrm{div}\, count \vee count = 0 \end{array}$$

where we have commuted the operands to the disjunction, which is not generally valid in operational terms.

But this begins to make it clear that we must give some value to the division in all cases, even though if the divisor is zero the predicate will be true anyway, so the actual value doesn't matter.

5.1   Undefinedness – partial functions and mu-expressions

Dividing by zero is a special case of applying a partial function outside its domain. In Z we have the general identity

$$\forall f : \mathbb{P}(X \times Y); \; x : X \bullet f\, x = (\mu y : Y \mid (x, y) \in f)$$

so the question of undefined partial function applications can be seen as equivalent to that of undefined μ-expressions.

A μ-expression is considered to be well-formed if it corresponds to a choice from a set which has exactly one member. This can fail to happen because either:

a) the set is empty, corresponding to the application of a partial function outside its domain;

b) the set has several members, corresponding to the use, as a function, of a relation which is not functional at the point of application.

The former is the case of the greater practical importance. The solution found for that case will be used in the other case too.

So we have generalised the problem of division by zero to that of the meaning of improper μ-expressions. We henceforth treat all undefinedness issues as interchangeable.

Let us add one detail to our motivation, however. Since we want to support a mathematical logic, we must have a value for "undefined" expressions. On the other hand, we do not necessarily need to have a means in the notation for expressing the property of being undefined. In cases where we want to know that, we must establish it explicitly.

6   What do undefined expressions and predicates mean?

Various mechanisms have been suggested for dealing with undefinedness. In particular, these include either or both of:

a) a special "bottom" value, distinct from all well-defined values, which is the value of undefined expressions (one or possibly more for each type);

b) a third predicate value, neither true nor false, corresponding to "don't know" (see [7] for example).

The solution which has been chosen for Z, as recorded by Spivey and continued in the Standard, is to dispense with both these complications. The rules are the following:

a) Every predicate is either true or false (though sometimes we don't know which).

b) Every expression has a value (though sometimes we don't know what it is) provided it is of non-empty type.

Some of the motivation for this approach and clarification of how it works out in practice is given by considering two rules of inference which it is found useful to have in the proof system, namely the "axiom of reflexivity" and the "carrier" rule.

6.1   The axiom of reflexivity

The axiom of reflexivity states that any predicate of the form

expression = *expression*

where the two expressions are textually identical, is unconditionally true.

This is a very useful rule, and although it is seldom needed where the two operands are known to be undefined, its utility would be greatly decreased if establishing definedness was required before the rule could be used.

So we need the property of reflexivity for equality of undefined expressions, even if they seldom actually are undefined when we use the property. In the case of division by zero, we want to be sure that

$\forall x : \mathbb{N} \bullet x \operatorname{div} 0 = x \operatorname{div} 0$

Now we said above that every expression must have some value, although sometimes we don't know what it is. In a well-formed specification, we make sure that this result is never used, so that actual value chosen doesn't matter. So if we consistently take $x \operatorname{div} 0$ to be 42, all will be well. Furthermore, if we consistently take $x \operatorname{div} 0$ to be 37, it will still work. But if we take $x \operatorname{div} 0$ to be sometimes 37, sometimes 42, for the same value of x, we lose reflexivity. So the selected value of the type taken to represent the value of undefined expressions must be the same every time. The proof rules will not allow us to discover what the value is, but we can assume that it is stable.

In the case of division, we can choose a value and solve the problem, but in general there may be lots of undefined expressions in a specification. We need to have at least one consistent choice of value for each type. (It doesn't matter whether the value chosen is the same for all expressions of the type, or varies according to the nature of the undefined expression.)

6.2   The carrier rule, and empty types

We have said that the value of any expression can be assumed to be a member of its type, provided that the type is not empty. The proof rule which allows us to make use of this fact may be called the "carrier" rule. This rule is useful in discharging the side-conditions of other rules.

Power-set types are never empty, so in the (common) case where some expression is of power-set type, we can use the carrier rule without hesitation. In other cases, however, it might be empty, and the carrier axiom can only be applied if it explicitly stipulates that the type concerned has a member.

A possible partial solution to this difficulty might be to demand that types are never empty, but this cannot be a complete answer:

a) it would be possible to stipulate that given sets must be non-empty, although this would be a break with Z tradition;

b) the rules given for consistency of a free type do not guarantee that the type is non-empty, although they could be extended to cover this;

c) it is not rare to instantiate a generic object with an empty set, so to demand non-emptiness here would be a radical change.

6.3   Undefined expressions in a loose context

section *undefinedLoose* parents *seqkit*

The fact that an undefined expression always has some meaning has the consequence that it cannot be used to create a "covert" constraint.

As a simple example, if we have

$$\begin{array}{|l} x, y : \mathbb{N} \\ \hline y = (\mu z : \mathbb{N} \mid x = 3 \wedge z = 4) \end{array}$$

the conjecture
$$\vdash \qquad x = 3$$
is not a theorem.

If the value of x happens to be 3, the constraint part of the μ-expression can be satisfied uniquely by making $z = 4$. The μ-expression is defined to have the meaning given by that assignment, so $y = 4$ in that case too.

If the value of x is not equal to 3, the constraint part of the μ-expression cannot be satisfied by any assignment to z. The μ-expression is defined to have an unknown value of the right type. The specification is still satisfiable, however, so we cannot draw any inference about the value of x.

This state of affairs often appears where we are applying a function to an argument without being sure that it is in the domain of the function. Since the application unconditionally means something, it does not constrain the argument to be in the domain. As an example, if we have

$$\begin{array}{|l}
s : \mathbb{P}\,\mathbb{N} \\
\hline
\#s = 3
\end{array}$$

we have not thereby guaranteed that s is finite, since the function application might have the value 3 even if s is infinite. We must add a constraint such as $s \in \mathbb{F}\,s$ to be sure that it isn't.

7   Generic definitions

Generic definitions are made in terms of generic parameters. When a generic definition is used, each of its generic parameters can be instantiated by any set, and the resultant object is formed by replacing the generic parameters with their instantiations. Within a generic definition, the generic parameter is treated as a type.

7.1   Satisfiability of generic definitions

Suppose we define

$$\begin{array}{|l}
=[X]=\!\!=\!\!=\!\!=\!\!=\!\!=\!\!=\!\!=\!\!=\!\!=\!\!=\!\!= \\
sub1 : \mathbb{P}\,X \\
\hline
\exists x, y : X \bullet x \in sub1 \wedge \neg\, y \in sub1
\end{array}$$

The object $sub1$ is defined as being a non-empty proper subset of its generic parameter.

If the generic instantiation is a set with only one member, or with none, whatever value we give to $sub1$ the predicate part of its definition must be false,

We can set up the generic consistency check as a generic conjecture:

$[X]$
$\vdash \quad \exists sub1 : \mathbb{P}\,X \bullet \exists x, y : X \bullet x \in sub1 \wedge \neg\, y \in sub1$

which will not be a theorem, since it is not true for all values of the generic parameter.

If we wanted to allow the use of this object where the parameter had at least two members, we could make that an antecedent of the conjecture, and having proved it, check that proviso when using the object. We may prefer not to need to do that, however.

When considering questions of consistency and meaning of generic definitions, we have, logically, a choice:

a) we can allow anything to be included in the definition, then check for consistency when we use it;

b) we can check that all possible uses of the definition are consistent.

In practice, the former approach would remove much of the usefulness of generic definitions. We want to state and prove theorems about generic objects, create families of related definitions, and build up theories about them. The preferred approach is therefore the latter: to establish consistency for all possible uses.

7.2   Loose generic definitions

This brings us to a difference between the rules given by Spivey and the forthcoming Standard. Spivey stipulates that generics should always have a unique model (see [10] pages 85–86 and [11] page 40). We here agree that there should always be a model, but the current draft of the Standard [13, 14] permits generics to be loose.

Suppose for example we define

$$
\begin{array}{|l}
\hline \!\![X]\!\!=\!=\!=\!=\!=\!=\!=\!=\!=\!=\!=\!=\!=\!=\!=\!=\!= \\
\quad sub : \mathbb{P}\,X \\
\hline
\end{array}
$$

The object *sub* is defined as being any subset of its generic parameter.

We can set up the generic consistency check as a generic conjecture:

$[X]$
$\vdash \qquad \exists\, sub : \mathbb{P}\,X \bullet true$

which we can show to be a theorem.

This definition is loose. We can say only that the value of *sub* is one of the specified values, and although we cannot establish which one, we can be sure that it is a particular fixed one for each instantiation of X, so that reflexivity is preserved.

Having made this definition, we can (non-conservatively) constrain it by giving *sub* a value for particular instantiations, as for instance

$$
\begin{array}{|l}
\hline \rule{0pt}{2ex}\\[-1.5ex]
\rule{4cm}{0.4pt}\\
sub[S] = someSet \\
sub[T] = someOtherSet \\
\hline
\end{array}
$$

thus introducing a form of overloading into Z. The full implications of this relaxation have not yet been much explored or exploited in the Z literature.

7.3   Global generic element definitions

There are some cases where it is immediately apparent that the use of a generic parameter is in general unsatisfiable because of the possibility that it might be empty.

Let us first define a concept we call "elementary use" of a type, defined as being either
a) the type itself, or
b) a Cartesian product or schema, any one of whose components is an elementary use of the type.
A type is empty if and only if elementary uses of it are empty. Power-set types are not elementary uses.

There is no problem in allowing the direct declaration of variables using elementary uses of generic types in quantifications, comprehensions and so on, since if the type is empty, the quantification can unconditionally be seen to be false (if existential) or true (if universal), or the comprehension to be empty, and there is no need to assign a value to the variable.

On the other hand, elementary use of a generic parameter as the type of a declarand (at top level) in a generic paragraph must be in general unsatisfiable. Checking whether there is such a use can easily be done as a small enhancement to a type-checker. It might be helpful if type-checkers routinely did this. Thus with the example given in [11] page 40, where Spivey says: " the following definition would not be allowed ..."

$$
\begin{array}{|l}
\hline
[X] \\
\hline
left, right : X \\
\hline
left \neq right \\
\hline
\end{array}
$$

we agree in banning this example, but suggest it could be eliminated by the type-checker, rather than treating it as a semantic issue.

8   Conclusions

We have shown why consistency is important, and have given some guidelines as to ways of achieving it and proving that it has been achieved. We have also described the Z approach to undefinedness, and shown how this is related to rules of inference which Z provers need.

Acknowledgements

Thanks are due to Rob Arthan, David Duffy, Steve King, Susan Stepney, Ian Toyn, and to the referees, for helpful comments and criticisms. This paper is part of the work of the Dependable Computing Systems Centre at the University of York.

References

1. R. D. Arthan. On free type definitions in Z. In J. E. Nicholls, editor, *Z User Workshop, York 1991*. Springer-Verlag, Workshops in Computing, pages 40–58, 1992.
2. H. B. Enderton. *Elements of Set Theory*. Academic Press, 1977.
3. J. G. Hall and A. P. Martin. W reconstructed. In J. P. Bowen, M. G. Hinchey and D. Till, editors, *ZUM '97: The Z Formal Specification Notation*. Springer-Verlag, Lecture Notes in Computer Science, volume 1212, pages 115–134, 1997.
4. W. T. Harwood. Proof rules for Balzac. Technical Report WTH/P7/001, Imperial Software Technology, UK, 1991.
5. J. G. Hall, J. A. McDermid and I. Toyn. Model conjectures for Z specifications. In H. Habrias, editor, *Z Twenty Years On – What is its Future?* IRIN, Université de Nantes, France, pages 41–51, October 1995.
6. Sir Harold Jeffreys. *Scientific Inference*. Cambridge University Press, second edition, 1957.

7. C. B. Jones. *Systematic Software Development using VDM*. Prentice Hall Internationa Series in Computer Science, 1986.
8. M. Saaltink. Z and Eves. In J. E. Nicholls, editor, *Z User Workshop, York 1991*. Springer-Verlag, Workshops in Computing, pages 223–242, 1992.
9. A. Smith. On recursive free types in Z. In J. E. Nicholls, editor, *Z User Workshop, York 1991*. Springer-Verlag, Workshops in Computing, pages 3–39, 1992. December 1991.
10. J. M. Spivey. *Understanding Z*. Cambridge University Press, 1988.
11. J. M. Spivey. *The Z Notation: A Reference Manual*. Prentice Hall, second edition, 1992.
12. I. Toyn. CADiZ Web pages, 1998. URL: http://www.cs.york.ac.uk/~ian/cadiz/
13. I. Toyn. Innovations in standard Z. In J. P. Bowen, A. Fett and M. G. Hinchey, editors, *ZUM'98: The Z Formal Specification Notation*. Springer-Verlag, Lecture Notes in Computer Science, volume 1493, pages 193–213, 1998. In this volume.
14. I. Toyn, editor. *Z Notation*. ISO, to appear 1998.
15. J. C. P. Woodcock and J. Davies. *Using Z – Specification, Refinement and Proof*. Prentice Hall International Series in Computer Science, 1996.

Compositional Specification of Controllers for Batch Process Operations

K. Lano[1], P. Kan[1], and A. Sanchez[2]

[1] Dept. of Computing, Imperial College
180 Queens Gate, London SW7 2BZ, UK

[2] Dept. de Ingenieria Electrica, CINVESTAV-Guadalajara. Apdo. Postal 31-438
Guadalajara 45090, Jalisco, Mexico

Abstract. This paper describes a combination of techniques from control engineering and formal methods in order to specify and implement control systems for batch process operations. It extends previous work by providing a non-trivial specification for the top-level polling loop of a control system, and defining composition techniques for controllers.

Batch process operations are common in industrial practice. Automated manufacturing systems and chemical processing are two examples. Common features of these operations enable us to provide a generic method for the formalisation of controllers for a large class of such systems, using B and procedural controller synthesis.

We give examples from case studies to illustrate the techniques.

1 Introduction

Operational aspects of batch process systems (i.e. chemical, pharmaceutical) are typically studied in disciplines such as control science, operations research and mechanical, electrical and chemical engineering. These disciplines focus on the design of processing devices and ways of operating and controlling them where automation frequently plays a key role. A recently proposed paradigm, Procedural Control Theory (PCT) [20, 21], for the synthesis of control devices at a high level (i.e. abstract design of behavioural specifications), termed *procedural controllers*, has demonstrated its applicability in process systems [3]. PCT builds upon standard control engineering methods. Based on a model of the process to be controlled and a theoretical framework to support the synthesis activities, "control laws" are designed for making the event-driven process behave in an expected and safe manner (e.g. rejecting unexpected perturbances, following state trajectories). In PCT the control law thus synthesised takes the form of a finite state machine (FSM) that can be used as a provably correct specification of the process behaviour (i.e. the logic) to be achieved by the automation system. This FSM can be used as a basis of a B specification and implementation of a controller for the batch process system.

2 Generic Process Modelling

Instead of using models of a specific process and hardware configuration (e.g., particular arrangements of valves, pumps, sensors, etc.) it is beneficial to carry out procedural controller synthesis and B development from more generic models, with adaption to specific plants being performed by suitable software interfaces which translate events specific to the actual system into generic events. For example, a generic command "open route from tank 1 to tank 2" could be translated into a sequence of commands to open particular valves. This improves the maintainability of the system and its robustness in the face of physical configuration changes to the plant.

Batch process systems have many common features. At the most basic level they can be considered as a set of processing objects (e.g. vessels) linked by interconnections (piping). The physicochemical processes carried out in the processing objects (e.g. a chemical reaction) assign attributes to the processing objet, such as temperature , presence of agitation, liquid level, etc. The processing object notion can also be relevant for discrete part processing. A vessel can be *full* or *empty* or in some intermediate state, and an interconnection between two vessels can either be open or closed, and if it is open then there may be a flow through the interconnection. These states are the essential minimum needed for the specification and design of a control algorithm: we know that a connection for a flow into vessel X should only be opened if X is not full, for example.

Generic control responses include:

- stop flow from vessel X to vessel Y if Y becomes full or X becomes empty;
- start flow from vessel X to vessel Y if Y becomes not full, during automated transfer from X to Y, if X is not empty;
- start flow from vessel X to vessel Y if X becomes not empty, during automated transfer from X to Y, if Y is not full.

Other attributes of vessels, such as temperature, the presence of agitation, etc., will also be of significance in specific systems. This model is also relevant for discrete parts manufacturing processes such as the production cell [16], which at the most abstract level can be viewed as managing the transfer of components from one processing unit to another, or from a robot arm/crane to a processing unit [17].

3   Structuring control architectures

Control structures in batch processes are of a hierarchical nature because of the complexity of process operations involved. Typical arrangements include the use of *phases* as ordered sets of elementary actions achieving an operational goal (e.g. opening and closing valves to transfer liquid), *operations* as ordered sets of phases changing the state of the material being processed and *procedures* as ordered sets of operations satisfying a production goal [7].

The possible roles of B in specifying and implementing such processes include:

1. Specification of the operation processing (eg: in the pasteurisation case study [19], how the phases for feeding and discharging milk must be alternated)
2. Specification of phases. That is, responses to individual process events. We refer to this level of specifications as the "high level controller".

3. Response cycle specification: given an interval of time in which a set of input events can be detected and processed (eg: the interval between two polling activities), what control outputs should be issued by the software in response to this set of events? We refer to this level of specification as the "outer controller".

The response cycle will typically be implemented by polling the physical system components in a particular order, and reacting to changes in the states of these components in this order, using the responses defined in the high level controller specification. We must show that this implementation meets the specification of the sampling cycle responses.

Temporal logic can be used to express requirements in a clear manner. A procedural controller and B specifications can then be generated from the temporal logic theories and other information about the system.

The processing model of reactive systems used here is that in which intervals of environment (input) and system (internal or output) events strictly alternate, initiated by an environment event interval. An environment event interval is a time interval in which only environment events happen. These events can be considered as being added to a set or list to be processed. In the following system response interval a response is computed and output events (commands to actuators) are generated [4].

Therefore, the temporal logic specification of responses are formulae of the form:

$$att = val_1 \land \bigcirc att = val_2 \Rightarrow \bigcirc \alpha$$

"If *att* changes in value from val_1 to val_2 (indicating the occurrence of some environment event in the current interval) then in the next (response) interval the response action α will occur." Figure 1 shows this pattern.

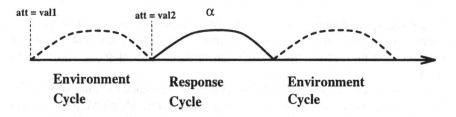

att = val1   att = val2 α

**Environment   Response   Environment
Cycle   Cycle   Cycle**

Fig. 1. Environment and Response Cycles

This can be directly compared with the specification of the response cycle in B, which will have the form

$cycle(new\_att1,\ new\_att2,\ \dots\ )\ =$
       PRE *"change of state is valid"*
       THEN
            IF $att\ =\ val_1\ \land\ new\_att\ =\ val_2$
            THEN
                α
            ELSE ...

new_att here represents ○*att* in the temporal logic specification.

The generic structure of a control system design in B using our approach, and its relationship to data and control flow diagram structures, is shown in Figure 2. In specific

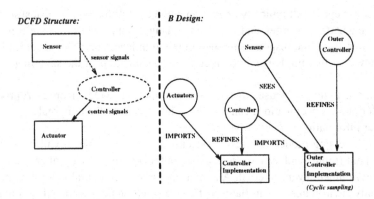

Fig. 2. Generic Control System Structure

systems further machines may be used as intermediaries between the outer controller and high level controller.

4   Development Method

4.1   Abstract Specification

The abstract specification stage is primarily concerned with the extraction and representation of requirements from the user documentation. Both diagrammatic (finite state machines, data and control flow diagrams) and mathematical (temporal logic) notations are used.

The processes and components of the system are identified from the informal user requirements specification. Operations and phases are also identified, for example in the pasteurisation plant case study, a requirement specification given by the process engineer is that the process must be initialised by the milk intake operation [19].

A data and control flow diagram (DCFD) can be used to represent the conceptual architecture of the system and the events which are sent between the controller and the components. The DCFD of the pasteurisation plant controller is shown in Figure 3. In this diagram the *Actuators* component performs a translation of commands from the generic *open_MilkInRoute*, etc. issued by the control system, to the specific sequences of valve and pump commands used in a particular physical configuration.

Temporal logic, specifically the Object Calculus [5] can be used to express the informal requirements in a transparent way. An object calculus theory consists of a set of *type symbols, constant symbols, attributes* (representing time-varying data) and *actions* (which may change that data). Axioms are usually of the following forms:

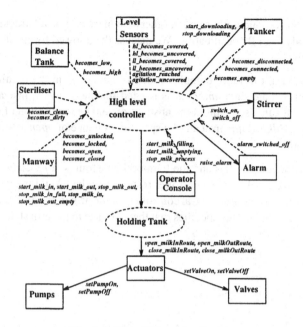

Fig. 3. DCFD of Pasteurisation Plant

1. Initial state specification, of the form $BEG \Rightarrow att = value$. These yield the initialisation of the high level controller.
2. Specification of responses to environment events, of the form $att = val_1 \wedge \bigcirc att = val_2 \Rightarrow \bigcirc action$. These yield the specification of event detection and responses in the outer controller.
3. Specification that an action *only* should take place under certain conditions: *action* $\Rightarrow$ *Condition*. These yield the B preconditions of operations in the high level controller.
4. Specification of the effect of an action on data: *action* $\Rightarrow \bigcirc att = E$. These yield the B definitions of operations in the high level controller.

For example, in the pasteurisation plant there is an informal specification that an alarm is raised if sensor 1.80 (manway sensor) is deenergised whilst there is fluid in the holding tank or sensor 1.63 (connection sensor for tanker) is deenergised during filling. This can be formalised as:

$$
\begin{aligned}
alarm = off \; \wedge \\
((manway = closed \; \wedge \; \bigcirc manway = open \; \wedge \\
\bigcirc low\_level\_sensor = covered) \; \vee \\
(tanker = connected \; \wedge \; \bigcirc tanker = disconnected \; \wedge \\
\bigcirc htank = milk\_filling)) \; \Rightarrow \\
\bigcirc raise\_alarm
\end{aligned}
$$

It is possible to decompose an object calculus theory into several sub-theories, as is done for the steam boiler in [10], for example. Care is needed that the composition techniques used correspond to those of B, otherwise there will be a 'structural clash' in the step from analysis to B specification. We discuss the allowed forms of composition in Section 5 below.

Analysis may result in more complex models than stated in the requirements (for example, an intermediate state *unlocked* is needed for the manway, instead of simply *open* and *closed*). It can also result in the abstraction and generalisation of events (such as an action *open_MilkInRoute* instead of a specific sequence of *open* actions on particular valves and pumps).

From the component models and the temporal constraints, a *procedural controller* can be synthesised, describing the controller responses to be taken for each input event [11, 21]. An extract from the procedural controller for the arm in the production cell case study is shown in Figure 4. This specifies that the response to the arm state transitioning

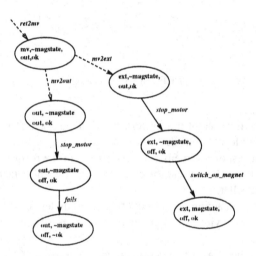

Fig. 4. Procedural Controller Extract

from a "moving" *mv* to an "extended" *ext* position with the magnet off ($\neg$ *magstate*) is to stop the arm motor and then switch on the arm magnet. The response to a transition to the "out of position" *out* state is to stop the motor and set the *ok* flag to false.

B machines are defined for each component. These represent the controllers *record* of the state of this component at the termination of the most recent response cycle, rather than the current state of these components (which is notified to the controller via polling or interrupts, for instance). The operations of the machine represent the actions that can take place to change the state of the component, and are given the same name as these events. So for example, the *Alarm* machine has operations *raise_alarm* and *alarm_switched_off* which set the value of a variable *alarm_state* of the enumerated type {*on, off*}.

4.2   High Level Controller Specification

The specification of the high level controller is carried out using PCT. Based on a discrete-event model of the process to be controlled and stated operational goals (including safety and production requirements), the processing logic, or high level controller, satisfying such requirements is synthesised. The result is a finite state machine (FSM) that is mathematically guaranteed to model the processing sequential behaviour required to meet the specifications and thus can be used as a provably correct specification in B. The FSM states are interpreted as process states whilst transitions are either events generated by the process (depicted by dashed line arrows) or control commands being issued by the controller to the process (continuous line arrows). The use of PCT in the development of reactive systems was investigated initially in [11].

The procedural controller is used to give the specification of the high-level controller operations. These operations correspond to the events to which the controller must react. For example, the specification of the *tanker_becomes_disconnected* operation is:

```
tanker_becomes_disconnected =
        PRE tanker_state /= tanker_disconnected
        THEN
          IF tanker_state = tanker_downloading & alarm_state = off
          THEN
            raise_alarm ||
            stop_milk_in
          END  ||
          set_tanker_state(tanker_disconnected)
        END;
```

The correspondence between a procedural controller, object calculus and the two levels of specification in B is shown in Figure 5. Notice that invariants of the B machines therefore refer *only* to the states established by response intervals (and the initial state). The intermediate states at the end of environment intervals are not part of the statespace of the B machines. In the object calculus a B invariant *Inv* would be expressed by the formulae

$$BEG \;\Rightarrow\; \bigcirc^n Inv$$

for each even $n \in \mathbb{N}$.

Invariants of the high level controller express:

1. Expected properties of the model
2. Safety properties of the system (such as if the manway is open, and the low level sensor is covered, the alarm must be on)

Proof in B can then be used to verify these properties or detect errors in the model or the requirements.

Animation in B can also be used to check conformance of the specification of the controller to the expected behaviour. Consistency and completeness checks on the temporal axioms are aided by the explicit nature of the B specification and by the validation checks provided by B.

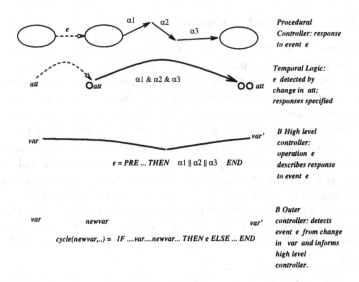

Fig. 5. Correspondences Between Specifications

Implementation of this level of specification is a direct process: the structure of the implementation of the high level controller follows the structure of the specification very closely, and hence is relatively easy to prove correct. As an example, the robot arm high level controller implementation (108 lines of B code) in the production cell case study produced only 17 proof obligations, of which 15 were proved automatically.

The implementation of the above operation has the form:

```
tanker_becomes_disconnected =
      VAR ts, as
      IN
        ts <-- get_tanker_state;
        as <-- get_alarm_state;
        IF ts = tanker_downloading & as = off
        THEN
          raise_alarm;
          stop_milk_in
        END;
        set_tanker_state(tanker_disconnected)
      END;
```

4.3 Outer Controller Specification

The outer controller describes how environment events are actually detected by the software and communicated (in some order) to the high level controller. A number of strategies can be used, such as buffered messages (used in the steam boiler specification [10]) or polling of sensors at regular intervals.

Here we will describe the use of a polling approach, whereby an operation *cycle* specifies the response cycle of the system. The parameters of the operation represent the values of sensors read at the end of the preceding environment cycle.

We assume that the polling is sufficiently frequent that each individual component can only undergo a *single* state transition in its FSM in each cycle. Several components may undergo state transitions in the cycle, however (for example, the manway could be opened in the same cycle that the tanker runs out of milk, in the pasteurisation plant case study).

Again, there are several levels of abstraction at which the response cycle can be specified. A fully detailed definition, giving the expected effect of the operation on each system component can be derived from the high level controller by 'inverting' its logic. Specifically, the form of *cycle* in this case is:

```
cycle(new_att1, new_att2, ... )  =
    PRE "change of state is valid"
    THEN
        change_component_1(new_att1, ...) ||
        change_component_2(new_att1, ...) ||
            ⋮
        change_component_n(new_att1, ...)
    END
```

where *change_component_i* identifies what the new state of component C_i of the system should be, given the environment events deduced to have occurred by comparing the old state of the sensors of the system (at the end of the previous response cycle) and the new values input in *new_att1*, etc. (representing the values at the end of the environment cycle just completed).

An alternative approach is to use the concept of 'mode' of the controller software, and to specify the effect of the *cycle* operation only in terms of the changes it causes to this mode. The resulting specification is usually smaller than in the first approach, and therefore easier to animate and prove. The use of controller modes is a frequent feature of reactive systems (for example the steam boiler [1]) and is also compatible with the use of finite state *safety models* in standards such as DEF-STAN 00-55 [18]. The ISA standard also advocates generic state-transition models for processes [7].

In this case the *cycle* operation specification consists of a set of clauses of the form:

```
IF mode = state1
THEN
    "compute next mode"
END
```

which can either be combined with || or made into nested conditionals.

The modes can be constructed so as to abstract from actuator states. For example, the outer controller specification of the press in the production cell case study has the form:

```
MACHINE PressOuter
SEES RobotTypes, Bool_TYPE
SETS
```

```
      PressMode = { waiting4get, waiting4put, ready, idle, returning, forging,
                    forged, alarmed }
VARIABLES
  lower, middle, upper, blank, pstate, arm1pos, arm2pos
INVARIANT
  (pstate = waiting4get  =>  lower = absent & middle = present &
                            upper = absent & blank = absent) &  ....
INITIALISATION ....
OPERATIONS

  press_cycle(nlower,nmiddle,nupper,nblank,narm1pos,narm2pos) =
  PRE nlower: ExtBoolean & nmiddle: ExtBoolean &
      nupper: ExtBoolean & nblank: ExtBoolean &
      narm1pos: ArmPosition & narm2pos: ArmPosition
  THEN
    arm1pos := narm1pos || arm2pos := narm2pos ||
    lower := nlower || upper := nupper ||
    middle := nmiddle || blank := nblank ||
    IF (nlower = error or nmiddle = error or nupper = error) or
       (nlower = present & nupper = present) or .... or
       (pstate : {idle, waiting4put, waiting4get, ready} &
          (middle /= nmiddle or upper /= nupper or
           lower /= nlower)) or
       (pstate: {idle, ready, forging, forged, returning} &
        blank /= nblank) or ....
    THEN
      pstate := alarmed
    ELSE
      IF pstate = waiting4get
      THEN /* All three position sensors remain unchanged */
        IF nblank = blank   /* No get */
        THEN skip
        ELSE
          IF nblank = present & blank = absent
          THEN pstate := ready  /* gets */
          ELSE pstate := alarmed
          END
        END
      ELSE
        IF pstate = waiting4put
        THEN ...
        END
      END
    END
  END

END
```

The state *forging* represents the press moving up loaded, the state *forged* represents the press moving down loaded, and *returning* represents the press moving up unloaded. In the other states the motor is off.

5   Compositionality

It is preferable to specify controllers for separate parts of a system in distinct B machines and refine these to executable systems in separate B developments, where possible. The controller structure significantly determines how flexible the plant operation can be. Industrial practice tends to impose conservative modes of operation to diminish the risk of accidents. From a theoretical point of view, this is a topic of current research [22]. In a B specification controllers must reflect the architecture given in the requirement specifications where conflicts of operations are solved in advance.

Controllers can be decomposed into:

1. *horizontal* composition of controllers: events e are copied (by the sampling operation) to two separate control algorithms S_1 and S_2, which compute their reactions independently. This requires that S_1 and S_2 control disjoint sets of actuators, and that the timing of their responses relative to each other is not critical.
2. *vertical* composition of controllers: events e are dealt with first by a overseer controller S which deals with certain interactions between components, and are then forwarded to subordinate controllers responsible for managing the individual behaviour of subcomponents.

In the case of the flexible production cell [14], the control of the feed belt motor and reader can be managed independently of the control of the main part of the production cell in the first way. The control of the cranes and processing units can be managed in the second way, by an overall cell controller.

If there are no shared actuators between two control systems S_1 and S_2, these can be separately specified and their response cycle specifications, say *cycle_S₁* and *cycle_S₂*, combined via || to give an overall specification of the response cycle of the complete system:

```
cycle(new_att1, ... )   =
    PRE ...
    THEN
        cycle_S1(new_att1, ...) ||
        cycle_S2(...)
    END
```

Their implementations can be combined via ; . This approach works well in the case of the fault tolerant production cell, since each controller (for the arms, the presses, belts, etc.) is of manageable size and has a set of actuators disjoint from those of other components. It works less well when several processes share the same plant machinery, as is the case in the pasteurisation plant (cleaning, flushing and milk processes all operate on the input holding tank).

If there are shared actuators, then the required changes for these must be combined into a single clause in the operation body of the *cycle* specification.

Alternatively, the two control systems can be more closely integrated by adding new states to the controller. In the case of the pasteurisation system, control code for the cleaning operations on the tank would be most naturally added in this way, resulting in new states for the holding tank, and new actuator actions to start and complete cleaning and flushing phases. This however raises the complexity of the controller.

6 Flexibility

B seems most suitable for control systems where dynamic reconfiguration of processing objects is not required. That is, where the components of the system are fixed in their relationships with each other. The steam boiler and pasteurisation plants are examples of such systems. In the flexible production cell either a configuration with one crane and two processing units, or two cranes and four processing units must be controlled.

It is possible to deal with such situations by describing the control of an unspecified *set* of objects (cranes, processing units, etc.) in a single machine. This uses the standard techniques for coding up object-oriented designs in B [9]. Each event response operation e of these machines now carries an additional parameter a which represents the particular object to which the event is being sent. For example, part of the *Crane* controller from [14] is:

```
MACHINE Crane(maxcr)
....
VARIABLES
    cranes, cranepos, cranestat, craneload, cranegrip,
    cranehome, cranemagnet
INVARIANT
    cranes <: CRANE &
    cranepos: cranes --> POSITIONS &
    cranestat: cranes --> CraneStatus &
    craneload: cranes --> BOOL &
    ....
OPERATIONS
    pickup_from(cc,pu) =
        PRE cc: cranes & pu: PICKUPPOS &
            cranestat(cc) = free &
            craneload(cc) = FALSE & cranegrip(cc) = up
        THEN
            cranepos(cc) := pu ||
            move_to(cc,xcoord(pu),ycoord(pu)) ||
            cranestat(cc) := moving_to_pickup
        END;

    ....

END
```

Using this approach, we were able to use the same controller specifications for both the one-crane and two-crane versions of the flexible production cell. Only the outer controller which detected events on the basis of sensor readings needed to be different for the two versions, because the set of sensors in the two cases are different.

7 Comparison with other Approaches

B does not support a pure object-oriented approach, whereby a decomposition of the controller based on the separate cases of the control invariant into separate subclasses is performed, with objects of these separate subclasses being dynamically swapped when the mode of the controller changes (the State pattern of [6]). This produces more elegant control code, but a more complex and harder to verify implementation. In contrast the code produced using B does not essentially use pointers or dynamic memory allocation, and is very close in its structure to the B implementation and specification, hence facilitating verification and test case generation.

An alternative approach to the development of event-driven systems is that of Abrial [2]. This approach corresponds to transformations on state-machine models of a system, and provides a more abstract view of a system in general than our approach. However it requires more work in the selection and proof of refinement steps.

8 Conclusion

We have given an overview of a method combining control engineering techniques (procedural controller synthesis) and formal methods (B specification) for the development of controllers for discrete event systems, and specifically for batch processing systems such as chemical plants or manufacturing cells.

The advantage of this combination is that while procedural control theory gives a systematic means of synthesising the control logic for a particular system, from temporal constraints and component models, it is limited to a very simple form of state-transition system, without timed or parameterised transitions. B on the other hand can be used to express more complex data structures (such as schedules, in the flexible production cell case study [15]) and can also provide a verified path to an executable implementation. The 'outer controller' layer in a B development provides a way of specifying *how* events become known to the procedural controller (expressed in the high level controller implementation).

B was felt to be particularly suitable because of its extensive tool support and its implementation-oriented character. However limitations in the available forms of B structuring (e.g., it is not possible to have shared write access to modules) does lead to restrictions in the possible ways of structuring control systems (when two controllers share actuators, they must be combined outside of the B development environment).

Detailed guidelines for the development of such B specifications and implementations have been given [8, 15]. Several case studies have been carried out using the guidelines: gas burner ignition system [11]; fault tolerant production cell control system [13]; measure tank control system [12]; pasteurisation plant control system [8, 19]; steam boiler control system [1, 10]; flexible real-time production cell [14, 17].

Of these the pasteurisation plant was the largest, with a final executable of 5,600 lines of C code. The system specified represents about 10% of the complete control task for a single pasteurisation unit consisting of holding tank, balance tank, steriliser, discharge tank and ancillary equipment [19].

Further work is in progress to decompose controllers into separate machines for each separate control phase, and to minimise proof complexity.

References

1. J.-R. Abrial, E. Börger and H. Langmaack, editors, *Formal Methods for Industrial Applications: Specifying and Programming the Steam Boiler Control*, Lecture Notes in Computer Science, volume 1165, Springer-Verlag, 1996.
2. J.-R. Abrial and L. Mussat, *Specification and Design of a Transmission Protocol by Successive Refinements using B*, 1997.
3. N. Alsop, L. Camillocci, A. Sanchez and S. Macchietto, *Synthesis of Procedural Controllers – Application to a batch plant*, Computers and Chemical Engineering, 20:S1481–S1486, 1996.
4. M. Butler, E. Sekerinski and K. Sere, *An Action System Approach to the Steam Boiler Problem*, in [1], pages 129–148, 1996.
5. J. Fiadeiro and T. Maibaum, *Temporal Theories as Modularisation Units for Concurrent System Specification*, Formal Aspects of Computing 4(3):239–272, 1992.
6. E. Gamma, R. Helm, R. Johnson and J. Vlissides. *Design Patterns: Elements of Reusable Object-oriented Software*. Addison-Wesley, 1994.
7. International Society for Measurement and Control, *Batch Control Models and Terminology*, ISA-S88.01-1995, 1995.
8. P. Kan, *Specification and Implementation of Reactive Systems with B*, MSc thesis, Imperial College, London, UK, 1997.
9. K. Lano, P. Wheeler and H. Haughton, *Integrating Formal and Structured Methods in Object Oriented System Development*. In S. Goldsack and S. Kent, editors, *Formal Methods and Object Technology*, Springer-Verlag, 1996.
10. K. Lano, J. Bicarregui, T. Maibaum and J. Fiadeiro, *Composition of Reactive System Components*. In G. T. Leavens and M. Sitaraman, editors, *Proc. Foundations of Component-based Systems Workshop*, Zurich, Switzerland, 26 September 1997. European Software Engineering Conference. URL: http://www.cs.iastate.edu/~leavens/FoCBS/
11. K. Lano and A. Sanchez, *Design of Reactive Control Systems for Event-driven Operations*, In J. Fitzgerald, C. B. Jones and P. Lucas, editors, *FME '97: Industrial Applications and Strengthened Foundations of Formal Methods*. Lecture Notes in Computer Science, volume 1313, Springer-Verlag, 1997.
12. K. Lano and A. Sanchez, *Formal Development of Event-Driven Controllers for Process Manufacturing Systems*, in *Industrial Strength Formal Methods*, M. G. Hinchey and J. P. Bowen, editors, Academic Press International Series in Formal Methods, 1998. To appear.
13. K. Lano, *Design of Fault Tolerant Production Cell*, ROOS Project Internal Report, Department of Computing, Imperial College, London, UK, 1997.
14. K. Lano and P. Kan, *Design of Flexible Production Cell*, ROOS Project Internal Report, Department of Computing, Imperial College, London, UK, 1998.
15. K. Lano, P. Kan and J. Bicarregui, *Combining Scheduling Theory and Formal Methods in the Development of a Flexible Manufacturing System*, submitted to *Theory and Formal Methods '98* conference, 1998.
16. C. Lewerentz and T. Lindner, editors, *Case Study "Production Cell": A comparative study in formal software development*, FZI Publication 1/94, University of Karlsruhe, Germany, 1994. Also in Lecture Notes in Computer Science, volume 891, Springer-Verlag, 1996.
17. A. Lötzbeyer and R. Mühlfeld, *Task Description of a Flexible Production Cell with Real Time Properties*, FZI, Karlsruhe, Germany, 1996.
18. Ministry of Defence, *The Procurement of Safety Critical Software in Defence Equipment*, DEF-STAN 00-55, Issue 1, Part 2. Room 5150, Kentigern House, 65 Brown St., Glasgow G2 8EX, UK, 1997.

19. PRESTO P4 Project, *Integrated Design of Control and Automation Systems*, PRESTO Document 200197A11, Centre for Process Systems Engineering, Imperial College, London, UK, 1997.
20. G. E. Rotstein, A. Sanchez and S. Macchietto, *Procedural Control of Discrete Event Systems*. Submitted to *International Journal of Control*, 1998.
21. A. Sanchez, *Formal Specification and Synthesis of Procedural Controllers for Process Systems*. Lecture Notes in Control and Information Sciences, volume 212, Springer-Verlag, 1996.
22. A. Sanchez, G. Rotstein, N. Alsop and S. Macchietto, *Synthesis of Procedural Controllers for Chemical Processes*. Submitted to *AIChEJ*, 1998.

Testing Refinements by Refining Tests

John Derrick and Eerke Boiten

Computing Laboratory, University of Kent, Canterbury CT2 7NF, UK

Email: J.Derrick@ukc.ac.uk

Abstract. One of the potential benefits of formal methods is that they offer the possibility of reducing the costs of testing. A specification acts as both the benchmark against which any implementation is tested, and also as the means by which tests are generated. There has therefore been interest in developing test generation techniques from *formal* specifications, and a number of different methods have been derived for state based languages such as Z, B and VDM. However, in addition to deriving tests from a formal specification, we might wish to refine the specification further before its implementation.

The purpose of this paper is to explore the relationship between testing and refinement. As our model for test generation we use a DNF partition analysis for operations written in Z, which produces a number of disjoint test cases for each operation. In this paper we discuss how the partition analysis of an operation alters upon refinement, and we develop techniques that allow us to refine abstract tests in order to generate test cases for a refinement. To do so we use (and extend existing) methods for calculating the weakest data refinement of a specification.

1 Introduction

Testing and specifications are intrinsically interlinked. Specifications act as the benchmark against which any implementation is tested, and they also provide a means by which to generate the tests themselves. The advent and use of formal methods does not change this. Although the aim of formal methods is to move some of the effort spent on error detection to more effort spent on correct construction, even a fully verified formal development will at some stage be tested against the original specification. Indeed, the use of formal methods offers a promise of reduced overall development cost by automating part of the testing process.

There has therefore been interest in developing techniques by which test case generation and test case scheduling can be automatically (or semi-automatically) generated from formal specifications. Different paradigms have developed different ways to do this, and techniques for state based languages such as Z [17], B [1] and VDM [12] have been developed, see for example [4, 5, 8, 11, 14, 18].

There are many aspects to the provision of formal support for the testing process. In this paper we shall be concerned with the issue of test case generation from individual operations. The attraction of using an abstract formal specification as the basis to generate the tests (as opposed to an informal specification of even an implementation) is that it concisely captures the essential behaviour required: any correct implementation should pass all the tests derived from this specification, and yet the tests will be as abstract as possible, ensuring their number is kept low.

One elegant and simple method for generating and sequencing tests from state based languages has been developed by Dick and Faivre [8]. The basic technique of test generation consists of a partition analysis, which reduces the specification of each operation into its Disjunctive Normal Form (DNF). The approach was based on VDM, but has been applied to Z in [11, 15] and B in [20], and benefits from tool support, which is described in [8, 20]. [11] describes an industrial application of the method to an aircraft control system.

However, in addition to deriving tests from a formal specification, we might wish to develop or refine the specification further before its implementation. Indeed we can view any implementation as a refinement of the original specification. The conditions under which a development is a correct refinement are encapsulated into two refinement rules: downward and upward simulations [22]. To verify a refinement the simulations use a retrieve relation which relates the concrete to abstract states.

The purpose of this paper is to explore the relationship between testing and refinement. In particular, we aim to develop techniques whereby we can reuse abstract tests to develop tests for a concrete specification or implementation. As our model for test generation we use the DNF partition analysis for operations written in Z as discussed in [11], although it should be noted that the methods are applicable to other testing scenarios and state based languages such as B and VDM.

Dick and Faivre did not consider further refinements of the abstract specification, however, they posed the open question: *does refining a specification create a super-set of the partitions of the previous level?* We will answer this question in the negative. We will then go onto answer the question: *how do we generate tests for a refinement based on the tests derived from the abstract specification?* We do so by developing a means to calculate concrete tests based upon methods that generate the weakest (i.e. most general) refinement of an abstract operation. We do this first for refinements which are downward simulations, and we discuss the properties of the constructed tests, and in particular whether they capture all the requirements and whether they are disjoint. We next develop similar results for upward simulations, however, here we first have to derive techniques to calculate the weakest upward simulation of an operation. In each case the results simplify if the retrieve relation used in the refinement is a surjective function from concrete to abstract state spaces.

The structure of the paper is as follows. Section 2 introduces the method of DNF partition analysis, and Section 3 provides some background material on refinement in Z. Sections 4 and 5 form the heart of the paper where we develop the theory of testing refinements by refining tests, and discuss relevant properties. Section 4 looks at downward simulations and Section 5 considers upward simulations. We conclude in Section 6.

2   Testing

Testing is an indispensable part of the software construction and maintenance process, irrespective of whether or not the development of a system has involved the use of formal methods and verification. Therefore there has been considerable interest in the use of formal methods to *support* the testing process as opposed to viewing formal methods as an *alternative* to the testing process [4, 5, 8, 11, 18, 19].

Different formal paradigms have associated methods for aiding this test generation process in an automatic, semi-automatic or manual fashion. For example, there has been considerable research on testing specifications in the context of process algebras [2, 3, 6, 10]. There has also been analogous work for state based languages such as Z, B and VDM. The approach we consider here is that of Dick and Faivre [8], which describes a means to automate test generation and sequencing from VDM specifications, and has also been applied to Z specifications in [11, 15]. For example, [11] describes application of this methodology to a portion of the Cabin Intercommunication Data System for the Airbus A330/340 aircraft. An alternative approach to testing is discussed in [18] which derives a testing methodology suitable for the construction of tests from OSI Managed Object specifications [21], and manual approaches to test generation have also been considered in [4, 14].

Dick and Faivre consider the complete testing activity from test generation from individual operations, through the scheduling of tests, to the verification of test results. The basic technique of test case generation consists of a partition analysis, which reduces the specification of each operation into its Disjunctive Normal Form (DNF). Each element in the DNF represents an individual test case for the operation. The partition then serves as a basis for the construction of a finite state automaton (FSA) which is then used to derive test suites (i.e., a structured sequence of test cases).

In this paper we are concerned with the use of DNFs to provide a suitable partition analysis of operations, and we aim to show how this partition alters upon refinement.

As an example of the methodology let us consider the specification of a cinema box office (adapted from [16, 22]). The Kurbel box office allows customers to book tickets in advance by telephone. When a customer calls, if there is an available ticket then the customer's name is simply recorded. When a customer whose name has been recorded arrives at the box office, a ticket is allocated. The Kurbel is specified as follows:

$$\begin{array}{l} \underline{Kurbel} \\ kpool : \mathbb{P}\,Ticket \\ bkd : \mathbb{P}\,Name \end{array}$$

$$\begin{array}{l} \underline{KInit} \\ Kurbel' \\ \hline bkd' = \varnothing \end{array}$$

$$\begin{array}{l} \underline{KBook} \\ \Delta Kurbel \\ name? : Name \\ \hline name? \notin bkd \\ \#bkd < \#kpool \\ bkd' = bkd \cup \{name?\} \\ kpool' = kpool \end{array}$$

$$\begin{array}{l} \underline{KArrive} \\ \Delta Kurbel \\ name? : Name \\ t! : Ticket \\ \hline name? \in bkd \\ bkd' = bkd \setminus \{name?\} \\ t! \in kpool \\ kpool' = kpool \setminus \{t!\} \end{array}$$

The state variable *kpool* denotes the pool of tickets and *bkd* denotes the set of names of customers who have booked a ticket. The operation *KBook* records a booking provided that there are currently less bookings than tickets. The operation *KArrive* allocates a ticket to a customer who has a booking. In order to test an implementation of the box office we generate test cases for each operation in the specification.

We do this by transforming each operation into a DNF. Each schema in this DNF then represents a single test case. Each test case will be disjoint, allowing them all to be treated separately. The transformation into test cases for *KBook* and *KArrive* is thus given by (to simplify the presentation we just consider tests for a single fixed input *name?* throughout the paper):

$KBook = KBook$

$KArrive = \bigvee_{t \in kpool} KA_t$ where

$$
\begin{array}{|l}
\hline
\_KA_t \underline{\hspace{6cm}} \\
\Delta Kurbel \\
name? : Name \\
t! : Ticket \\
\hline
name? \in bkd \\
bkd' = bkd \setminus \{name?\} \\
t! = t \\
kpool' = kpool \setminus \{t!\} \\
\hline
\end{array}
$$

We have used a distributed disjunction ($\bigvee$) here, which although nonstandard Z, can be defined in the obvious manner (for example, by $\exists t : kpool \bullet KA_t$). Similarly, the equality sign between schemas should be viewed as schema equivalence. We retain $\bigvee$ and = for the sake of clarity.

From this we see that *KBook* is already in DNF, and thus represents a single atomic test case in itself. However, *KArrive* has a number of test cases, each one representing a different possible choice of allocated ticket. This structuring of test cases as DNFs has two important properties: coverage and disjointness; that is, *KArrive* equals the disjunction of its test cases (coverage) and these tests are disjoint. In general we say that a collection of tests $\{AOp_i\}_i$ covers an operation AOp acting on state space $Astate$ if

$$AOp = \bigvee_i AOp_i$$

and that the tests are disjoint, if, for all $i \neq j$

$$\neg \exists Astate; Astate' \bullet AOp_i \wedge AOp_j$$

It is easy to see that $\{KA_t\}_{t \in kpool}$ form a disjoint covering of *KArrive*.

Note that there are many possible decompositions of an operation into DNF, and not every decomposition will produce test cases considering single elements $t \in kpool$. For example, if *kpool* was infinite some of the test cases would contain infinite partitions of *kpool* representing the various test cases we are interested in. It is by this means that a finite state machine can be obtained from a specification with infinite state. See [8] for a discussion of this point.

3 Refinement

In addition to deriving tests from a formal specification, we might wish to *refine* the specification further before its implementation. Such a refinement might typically weaken the precondition of an operation, remove some non-determinism or even alter the state space of the specification. The conditions under which a development is a correct refinement are encapsulated into two rules: downward and upward simulations [22]. These refinement rules are known to be sound and jointly complete, that is any upward or downward simulation is a valid refinement, and any refinement can be proved correct by application of appropriate upward and downward simulations [9, 23]. (Downward and upward simulations are sometimes also known as forward and backward simulations respectively.)

The downward simulation rules are more straightforward, and form the usual presentation of refinement (e.g., as in [17]), however, upward simulations are occasionally necessary, for example when the resolution of non-determinism has been postponed [22]. Let us consider an abstract specification with state space *Astate* and initialisation schema *Ainit* being refined by a concrete specification with state space *Cstate* and initialisation schema *Cinit*.

Definition 1. *Downward simulation*
The concrete specification is a downward simulation of the abstract if there is a retrieve relation Ret such that every abstract operation AOp is recast into a concrete operation COp and the following hold.

DS.1 $\forall Astate; Cstate \bullet pre\,AOp \land Ret \implies pre\,COp$
DS.2 $\forall Astate; Cstate; Cstate' \bullet Ret \land pre\,AOp \land COp \implies \exists Astate' \bullet Ret' \land AOp$
DS.3 $\forall Cstate' \bullet Cinit \implies \exists Astate' \bullet Ainit \land Ret$

Definition 2. *Upward simulation*
The concrete specification is an upward simulation of the abstract if there is a retrieve relation Ret such that every abstract operation AOp is recast into a concrete operation COp and the following hold.

US.1 $\forall Cstate \bullet (\forall Astate \bullet Ret \implies pre\,AOp) \implies pre\,COp$
US.2 $\forall Astate'; Cstate; Cstate' \bullet (\forall Astate \bullet Ret \implies pre\,AOp) \implies (COp \land Ret' \implies \exists Astate \bullet Ret \land AOp)$
US.3 $\forall Astate'; Cstate' \bullet Cinit \land Ret' \implies Ainit$

As an example, consider the specification of the Marlowe box office. Like the Kurbel, the Marlowe box office allows customers to book tickets in advance by telephone. However, the procedure is different from that used at the Kurbel. When a customer calls, if there is an available ticket then one is allocated and put to one side for the caller. When the customer arrives, they are presented with this ticket.

┌─*Marlowe*─────────────
│ $mpool : \mathbb{P}\ Ticket$
│ $tkt : Name \rightarrowtail Ticket$
└───────────────────────

┌─*MInit*───────────────
│ *Marlowe'*
├───────────────────────
│ $tkt = \varnothing$
└───────────────────────

$$
\begin{array}{l}
\underline{MBook}\underline{\hspace{4cm}} \\
\Delta Marlowe \\
name? : Name \\
\hline
name? \notin \mathrm{dom}\,tkt \\
mpool \neq \varnothing \\
\exists t : mpool \bullet \\
\quad mpool' = mpool \setminus \{t\} \\
\quad tkt' = tkt \cup \{name? \mapsto t\}
\end{array}
\qquad
\begin{array}{l}
\underline{MArrive}\underline{\hspace{4cm}} \\
\Delta Marlowe \\
name? : Name \\
t! : Ticket \\
\hline
name? \in \mathrm{dom}\,tkt \\
t! = tkt(name?) \\
tkt' = \{name?\} \lhd tkt \\
mpool' = mpool
\end{array}
$$

The contrast between the Marlowe and the Kurbel box offices is the point of allocation of tickets (at booking time *vs* at collection time). However, at this level of abstraction the customer cannot tell that the Kurbel is behaving differently to the Marlowe, and this can be demonstrated by showing (see [22]) that the Marlowe is a downward simulation of the Kurbel where the retrieve relation is given by

$$
\begin{array}{l}
\underline{Ret}\underline{\hspace{6cm}} \\
Kurbel \\
Marlowe \\
\hline
bkd = \mathrm{dom}\,tkt \\
kpool = mpool \cup \mathrm{ran}\,tkt \\
mpool \cap \mathrm{ran}\,tkt = \varnothing
\end{array}
$$

In fact, the Kurbel specification is also a refinement of the Marlowe, but this must be shown using an upward simulation (i.e., it is *not* a downwards simulation), where we use the same retrieve relation as before. Therefore the Marlowe and Kurbel have identical observational behaviour, and so the tests for one specification should be able to be applied to the other. In order to do this and to be able to reuse abstract tests to test a refinement we have to be able to translate the state spaces of each test case, and we will use the retrieve relation to do this. This will involve us *calculating* refinements, a process that we now describe.

3.1   Calculating Downward Simulations

Given an abstract specification, a concrete state space and a retrieve relation between the concrete and abstract state spaces, it is possible to calculate the weakest (most general) description of the concrete operations [13, 22]. Let *Astate* and *Cstate* be the abstract and concrete state spaces, *Ret* the retrieve relation and *AOp* an abstract operation. We calculate* the weakest refinement *COp* of *AOp* by

$$
COp \mathrel{\widehat{=}} (\exists Astate \bullet \mathrm{pre}\,AOp \land Ret) \land \\
(\forall Astate \bullet \mathrm{pre}\,AOp \land Ret \Rightarrow \exists Astate' \bullet AOp \land Ret')
$$

---

* We use calculate in the sense that *COp* is described by a formula in terms of known components. One might also say that *COp* is specified instead of calculated, and that the specification of *COp* is the starting point for its calculation through a series of simplification steps.

In general, if it is not known whether *Ret* defines a refinement, it is necessary to check the applicability. This is summarised in the following theorem (for a proof, see [13]) which shows that *COp* is the weakest refinement of *AOp*, provided that one exists.

Theorem 1. *Let us denote a downward simulation by* $\sqsubseteq_{DS}$. *Suppose that AOp specifies an operation over the abstract state space Astate. Let Cstate be a concrete state space, and Ret a retrieve relation between concrete and abstract. Let COp be defined as above. Then for every operation X*

$$AOp \sqsubseteq_{DS} X \text{ iff } pre\,AOp \wedge Ret \Rightarrow pre\,COp \text{ and } COp \sqsubseteq_{DS} X$$

We are interested in cases when it is known that *Ret* defines a refinement since *we are generating tests for an existing development*, therefore we know that applicability ($pre\,AOp \wedge Ret \Rightarrow pre\,COp$) holds. In these circumstances *COp* describes our most general concrete refinement of the operation *AOp*.

The calculation can be simplified considerably ([13, 22]) when the retrieve relation defines a surjective (partial) function from *Cstate* to *Astate*, and we find that the following suffices for *COp*.

$$COp \triangleq \exists Astate;\ Astate' \bullet Ret \wedge AOp \wedge Ret'$$

For example, the retrieve relation from Marlowe to Kurbel could in fact be used to calculate the book and arrive operations in Marlowe. The retrieve relation is functional since both *kpool* and *bkd* are uniquely determined by *Ret*, however, *Ret* is not surjective (states where $\#bkd > \#kpool$ are not in the range of *Ret*). We can in fact make it surjective without altering the specification by adding the state invariant $\#bkd \leq \#kpool$ to Kurbel, the simplified method of calculation can then be used.

In fact it can be shown [7] that the complex formula given in Theorem 1 can *always* be replaced by the simplified version $\exists Astate;\ Astate' \bullet Ret \wedge AOp \wedge Ret'$. We will therefore use this simplified version subsequently.

The method described in [13, 22] calculates the weakest downward simulation. We shall derive similar results for upward simulations in Section 5.1 below.

3.2   Generating Tests

The technique we develop for generating tests for a refinement is very simple. Given an abstract specification with operation *AOp* and a covering disjoint set of tests $\{AOp_i\}_i$; a concrete specification with operation *COp* which refines *AOp*, and a retrieve relation *Ret*, we generate a set of tests $\{COp_i\}_i$ where each test COp_i is the weakest refinement calculated from *Ret* and AOp_i. The remainder of the paper discusses the two cases of downward and upward simulations separately, and each case is subdivided according as to whether *Ret* is a surjective function or not. In each case we explore the two questions:

- do the tests $\{COp_i\}_i$ cover *COp*;
- are the tests $\{COp_i\}_i$ disjoint.

4   Refining Tests 1: Downward Simulations

Downward simulations are perhaps the most common form of state based refinement: we saw an example above where the Marlowe box office was a downward simulation of the Kurbel box office. How do the test cases of the operations in the two specifications compare, and in particular *does refining a specification create a super-set of the partitions of the previous level?* [8]. To answer this question let us derive the test cases for the Marlowe operations:

$$MArrive = MArrive$$
$$MBook = \bigvee_{t \in mpool} MB_t \text{ where}$$

$$
\begin{array}{l}
\underline{\quad MB_t \rule{5cm}{0.4pt}} \\
\Delta Marlowe \\
name? : Name \\
\underline{\rule{4cm}{0.4pt}} \\
name? \notin \mathrm{dom}\, tkt \\
mpool \neq \varnothing \\
mpool' = mpool \setminus \{t\} \\
tkt' = tkt \cup \{name? \mapsto t\} \\
\end{array}
$$

and document the results in the following table.

	Kurbel	Marlowe
Book	$KBook$	$\bigvee_{t \in mpool} MB_t$
Arrive	$\bigvee_{t \in kpool} KA_t$	$MArrive$

From this table we see that for the book operation one test ($KBook$) becomes $\#mpool$ tests (MB_t) upon refinement, whereas for the arrive operation a collection of $\#kpool$ tests become one. This clearly answers the question of Dick and Faivre in the negative in the first instance - we do not in general create a super-set of the partition upon refinement. Let us see how calculating the tests effects coverage and disjointness in general.

4.1   Functional Surjective Retrieve Relation

We first consider the particular case when the retrieve relation used is a surjective function from concrete to abstract. Given an operation AOp with $AOp = \bigvee_i AOp_i$ being its disjoint set of tests, and a retrieve relation Ret which is a surjective function, the concrete tests are given by

$$COp_i \cong \exists Astate; Astate' \bullet Ret \land AOp_i \land Ret'$$

These will in some way represent test cases for the original concrete operation COp, and in fact we have the following result.

Theorem 2. *Let AOp be an abstract operation with $AOp = \bigvee_i AOp_i$ being its disjoint set of tests. Let COp be a downward simulation of AOp. Let Ret be the retrieve relation. Let COp_i be the concrete tests given above. Then*

$$\bigvee_i COp_i \sqsubseteq_{DS} COp$$

and if COp is the weakest downward simulation of AOp then $COp = \bigvee_i COp_i$.

Proof. The proof is simple, and follows from:

$$
\begin{aligned}
\bigvee_i COp_i &= \bigvee_i (\exists Astate; \; Astate' \bullet Ret \wedge AOp_i \wedge Ret') \\
&= \exists Astate; \; Astate' \bullet \bigvee_i (Ret \wedge AOp_i \wedge Ret') \\
&= \exists Astate; \; Astate' \bullet Ret \wedge \bigvee_i AOp_i \wedge Ret' \\
&= \exists Astate; \; Astate' \bullet Ret \wedge AOp \wedge Ret' \\
&\sqsubseteq_{DS} COp
\end{aligned}
$$

□

    The practical consequences of this is that we can use abstract tests together with the retrieve relation to calculate tests for a refinement.

Example 1. Calculating tests for a refinement.

Consider the following two specifications which describe *Staff* entering and leaving the box office. The first is specified using a set

```
┌─SSystem──────────────────
│ s : ℙ Staff
├──────────────────────────
│ #s ≤ maxentry
└──────────────────────────
```

```
┌─SInit────────────────────
│ SSystem'
├──────────────────────────
│ s' = ∅
└──────────────────────────
```

```
┌─SEnter───────────────────
│ ΔSSystem
│ p? : Staff
├──────────────────────────
│ #s < maxentry
│ p? ∉ s
│ s' = s ∪ {p?}
└──────────────────────────
```

```
┌─SLeave───────────────────
│ ΔSSystem
│ p? : Staff
├──────────────────────────
│ p? ∈ s
│ s' = s \ {p?}
└──────────────────────────
```

The second description uses a list (an injective sequence)

```
┌─LSystem──────────────────
│ l : iseq Staff
├──────────────────────────
│ #l ≤ maxentry
└──────────────────────────
```

```
┌─LInit────────────────────
│ LSystem'
├──────────────────────────
│ l' = ⟨⟩
└──────────────────────────
```

```
┌─LEnter───────────────────
│ ΔLSystem
│ p? : Staff
├──────────────────────────
│ #l < maxentry
│ p? ∉ ran l
│ l' = l ⌢ ⟨p?⟩
└──────────────────────────
```

```
┌─LLeave───────────────────
│ ΔLSystem
│ p? : Staff
├──────────────────────────
│ p? ∈ ran l
│ l' = l ↾ (Staff \ {p?})
└──────────────────────────
```

The second specification is a refinement of the first (see [22]), where the retrieve relation is given by

$$
\begin{array}{|l}
\hline
\_Ret \underline{\hspace{3cm}} \\
LSystem \\
SSystem \\
\hline
s = \mathrm{ran}\, l \\
\hline
\end{array}
$$

This is a total surjective function from concrete (list) to abstract (set). The test cases of *SEnter* are just *SEnter* itself, however, calculating the weakest refinement $\exists SSystem$; $SSystem' \bullet Ret \wedge SEnter \wedge Ret'$ to give the concrete test cases produces:

$$
\begin{array}{|l}
\hline
\_LEnter \underline{\hspace{3cm}} \\
\Delta LSystem \\
p? : Staff \\
\hline
\#l < maxentry \\
p? \notin \mathrm{ran}\, l \\
\mathrm{ran}\, l' = \mathrm{ran}\, l \cup \{p?\} \\
\hline
\end{array}
$$

The partition of this into DNF will produce a collection of tests $\{LEnter_i\}_i$, one for each possible choice of l' satisfying $\mathrm{ran}\, l' = \mathrm{ran}\, l \cup \{p?\}$ We can see that $\bigvee_i LEnter_i \sqsubseteq_{DS} LEnter$, but since *LEnter* is not the weakest refinement of *SEnter* the calculated tests contain additional tests not included in the concrete operation.

However, in this case we can construct an exact covering by taking the individual tests to be $LEnter_i \wedge LEnter$. Indeed this is a general strategy which works whenever the concrete operation has failed to be the weakest refinement because it has resolved more non-determinism than formally necessary.   □

Note that from this example we can see that after calculating the concrete tests, further partition analysis might be necessary to put them into DNF.

So much for coverage, what about disjointness? For a functional surjective retrieve relation disjoint abstract tests will generate disjoint concrete tests.

Theorem 3. *Let* $\{AOp_i\}_i$ *be disjoint test cases, Ret a functional surjective retrieve relation and* $\{COp_i\}_i$ *calculated from* $\{AOp_i\}_i$. *Then* $\{COp_i\}_i$ *are disjoint.*

Proof. Suppose that $\{COp_i\}_i$ were not disjoint. Then for some i and j

$$\exists Cstate; \ Cstate' \bullet COp_i \wedge COp_j$$

Thus there exists states *Cstate* and *Cstate'* for which

$$\exists Astate; \ Astate' \bullet Ret \wedge AOp_i \wedge Ret', \quad \text{and}$$
$$\exists Astate; \ Astate' \bullet Ret \wedge AOp_j \wedge Ret'$$

For these states *Cstate* and *Cstate'*, there are unique states *Astate* and *Astate'* such that $Ret \wedge Ret'$. Therefore

$$\exists Astate; \ Astate' \bullet AOp_i \wedge AOp_j$$

and so $\{AOp_i\}_i$ are not disjoint.   □

Note that disjointness is not the same as inequality (two tests with false predicates are considered disjoint).

Example 2. Refined tests are disjoint.

If we consider the operation *KArrive* in the Kurbel box office and its set of tests $\{KA_t\}_{t\in kpool}$. These are disjoint and we produce a set of disjoint concrete tests

$$
\begin{array}{|l}
\underline{MA_t}\underline{} \\
\quad \Delta Marlowe \\
\quad name? : Name \\
\quad t! : Ticket \\
\hline
\quad name? \in \mathrm{dom}\, tkt \\
\quad t! = t = tkt(name?) \\
\quad tkt' = \{name?\} \lhd tkt \\
\quad mpool' = mpool \\
\end{array}
$$

All but one of these tests are false (*tkt* is a function, so *tkt(name?)* must be a unique *t*). Therefore the set of concrete tests $\{MA_t\}$ reduces to the single test *MArrive*.   □

4.2   General Retrieve Relation

We now consider the general case. Recall that to generate tests from abstract test cases $\{AOp_i\}_i$ we can still use the simplified formula

$$COp_i \mathrel{\widehat{=}} \exists Astate;\ Astate' \bullet Ret \wedge AOp_i \wedge Ret'$$

Therefore in this general case the covering theorem still holds. However, disjointness in general fails as the proof needed functionality of the retrieve relation. This can be seen from the following example.

Example 3. Refined tests are not disjoint in general.

Consider the two specifications which describe staff entering and leaving the box office. Suppose that we modify the second specification so that *LEnter* is now

$$
\begin{array}{|l}
\underline{LEnter}\underline{} \\
\quad \Delta LSystem \\
\quad p? : Staff \\
\hline
\quad \#l < maxentry \\
\quad p? \notin \mathrm{ran}\, l \\
\quad \mathrm{ran}\, l' = \mathrm{ran}\, l \cup \{p?\} \\
\end{array}
$$

SSystem is now a refinement of this specification with the same retrieve relation as before. However, viewed this way round the retrieve relation is not functional: each set *s* has many (abstract) representations as a list with $s = \mathrm{ran}\, l$.

The DNF for *LEnter* contains many tests (one for each permutation of l with $p?$ inserted into it); for example, two such tests would be

$LEnter_1$
$\Delta LSystem$
$p? : Staff$
$\#l < maxentry$
$p? \notin \operatorname{ran} l$
$l' = l \frown \langle p? \rangle$

$LEnter_2$
$\Delta LSystem$
$p? : Staff$
$\#l < maxentry$
$p? \notin \operatorname{ran} l$
$l' = \langle p? \rangle \frown l$

Calculating the refined tests for each one of these abstract tests produces

$SEnter$
$\Delta SSystem$
$p? : Staff$
$\#s < maxentry$
$p? \notin s$
$s' = s \cup \{p?\}$

in every case. So *all* the abstract tests were mapped onto the same concrete test, which are therefore not disjoint.   □

5   Refining Tests 2: Upward Simulations

Some valid refinements can not be proved correct with a downwards simulation, and for these we need to use an upwards simulation. An example of this was provided above where we commented that the Kurbel box office was a refinement of the Marlowe box office, but this could only be verified using an upward simulation (see [22] for details). The previous section has discussed how to derive tests from refinements which were downward simulations, we now do the same for upward simulations, and to do so we will need to derive a method for calculating the weakest upward simulation of an abstract operation.

Let us first, however, comment upon the partitioning. We found that refining a specification doesn't create a super-set of the partitions of the previous level for refinements that were downward simulations. The same can be seen to be true for refinements that are upward simulations. From the table of tests for the Kurbel and Marlowe specifications given at the start of Section 4 we find that under an upward simulation, one abstract test (*MArrive*) becomes $\#kpool$ tests (KA_t) upon refinement, and a collection of $\#mpool$ tests (MB_t) become one. There is thus, in general, no relationship between the size of the partitioning before and after refinement for both upward and downward simulations.

We will now turn to the problem of calculating the weakest upward simulation, which will allow us to derive concrete tests from abstract ones.

5.1   Calculating Upward Simulations

The methodology given in [13, 22] calculates the most general downward simulation of an abstract operation with respect to a retrieve relation between the abstract and concrete state spaces. We do the same here for upward simulations.

In a manner similar to downward simulations, the refinement rules for upward simulations simplify considerably for a retrieve relation which is a total function from concrete to abstract. In this case it is easy to show that the correctness condition US.2

$$\forall Astate'; Cstate; Cstate' \bullet$$
$$(\forall Astate \bullet Ret \implies \text{pre}\, AOp) \implies (COp \wedge Ret' \implies \exists Astate \bullet Ret \wedge AOp)$$

reduces to

$$\forall Cstate; Cstate' \bullet (\forall Astate \bullet Ret \implies \text{pre}\, AOp) \wedge$$
$$(COp \implies \exists Astate; Astate' \bullet Ret \wedge AOp \wedge Ret')$$

Then, if the retrieve relation is additionally surjective, the weakest refinement of AOp will again be given by

$$COp \mathrel{\widehat{=}} \exists Astate; Astate' \bullet Ret \wedge AOp \wedge Ret'$$

a formula that is identical to the downward simulation case.

Turning to the general situation (i.e. an arbitrary retrieve relation), the following will define the weakest refinement of AOp

$$COp \mathrel{\widehat{=}}$$
$$(\forall Astate \bullet Ret \implies \text{pre}\, AOp) \wedge \forall Astate' \bullet (Ret' \implies \exists Astate \bullet Ret \wedge AOp)$$

For an arbitrary relation R we would still have to check applicability

$$\forall Cstate \bullet (\forall Astate \bullet R \implies \text{pre}\, AOp) \implies \text{pre}\, COp$$

However, if we know that the retrieve relation does indeed define an upward simulation it is not necessary to check this.

Theorem 4. *Let us denote an upward simulation by* $\sqsubseteq_{US}$. *Suppose that AOp specifies an operation over the abstract state space Astate. Let Cstate be a concrete state space, and Ret a retrieve relation between concrete and abstract. Let COp be defined as above. Then for every operation X*

$$AOp \sqsubseteq_{US} X \text{ iff } (\forall Astate \bullet Ret \implies \text{pre}\, AOp) \implies \text{pre}\, COp \text{ and } COp \sqsubseteq_{US} X$$

Proof
To show that the above definition of COp does refine AOp we need to show that

$$\forall Astate'; Cstate; Cstate' \bullet$$
$$(\forall Astate \bullet Ret \implies \text{pre}\, AOp) \implies (COp \wedge Ret' \implies \exists Astate \bullet Ret \wedge AOp)$$

which reduces to showing that

$\forall Astate'; Cstate; Cstate' \bullet$
$(Ret' \implies \exists Astate \bullet Ret \land AOp) \land Ret' \implies (Ret' \implies \exists Astate \bullet Ret \land AOp)$

which can easily seen to be true.

To show that COp defines the most general refinement of AOp, let us suppose that in addition $AOp \sqsubseteq_{US} X$, we will show that $COp \sqsubseteq_{US} X$. Furthermore, let us suppose that the refinement $AOp \sqsubseteq_{US} COp$ is verified by a retrieve relation R_1 and that of $AOp \sqsubseteq_{US} X$ by a retrieve relation R_2. Let us denote the state space of COp by C_1 and that of X by C_2. We abbreviate $Astate$ to A.

We first consider applicability. We know that

$$\forall C_2 \bullet (\forall A \bullet R_2 \implies preAOp) \implies preX \qquad (\alpha)$$
$$\forall C_1 \bullet (\forall A \bullet R_1 \implies preAOp) \implies preCOp \qquad (\beta)$$

and we need to show that for some retrieve relation R

$$\forall C_2 \bullet (\forall C_1 \bullet R \implies preCOp) \implies preX$$

First let us define R as $\exists A \bullet R_1 \land R_2$. Now suppose that for a given concrete state C_2, $(\forall C_1 \bullet R \implies preCOp)$ holds. First note that if C_2 is not in the domain of R_2, then by α, $preX$ holds at that state. Next suppose that $C_2 \in dom R_2$ and $(C_2, C_1) \notin R$, and consider a state A then $(C_2, A) \in R_2$ implies that $(A, C_1) \notin R_1$. Then by β, α and the definition of COp, $preX$ holds at state C_2. The case when $(C_2, C_1) \in R$ is similar.

To show correctness holds, we have to show that (see figure below)

$$\forall C_2 \bullet (\forall C_1 \bullet R \implies preCOp) \implies \forall C_1'; C_2' \bullet (X \land R' \implies \exists C_1 \bullet R \land COp)$$

given that we know

$$\forall C_2 \bullet (\forall A \bullet R_2 \implies preAOp) \implies \forall A'; C_2' \bullet (X \land R_2' \implies \exists A \bullet R_2 \land AOp)$$

Given that $(\forall C_1 \bullet R \implies preCOp)$ implies that $(\forall A \bullet R_2 \implies preAOp)$, by correctness of $AOp \sqsubseteq_{US} X$ we have

$$\forall A'; C_2' \bullet (X \land R_2' \implies \exists A \bullet R_2 \land AOp)$$

Now suppose that given any C_1'; C_2', $X \land R'$ implies that $\exists C_1 \bullet R \land COp$. Now if $X \land R'$ then there exists A' with $(C_2, C_2') \in X$, $(C_2', A') \in R_2$, $(A', C_1') \in R_1$. Thus there exists A with $AOp \land R_2$. By definition of COp there exists C_1 with $(C_1, C_1') \in COp$ and $(A, C_1) \in R$. That is $\exists C_1 \bullet R \land COp$ as required.

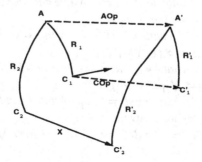

5.2   Generating Tests

The preceding theorem means that to generate concrete tests from the abstract test cases $\{AOp_i\}_i$ we can use the formula

$$COp_i \cong$$
$$(\forall Astate \bullet Ret \Longrightarrow pre\,AOp_i) \land \forall Astate' \bullet (Ret' \Longrightarrow \exists Astate \bullet Ret \land AOp_i)$$

Since we know that *Ret* defines a refinement (no need to check applicability), each COp_i is a refinement of AOp_i.

Example 4. Calculating concrete tests from an upward simulation.

Considering the Kurbel specification as an upward simulation of the Marlowe specification we can generate test cases for the Kurbel operations from the abstract test cases of the Marlowe operations. Considered in this direction the retrieve relation is not functional, so we have to use the general formulae given above.

Calculation shows that the abstract *MArrive* test case produces a number of concrete test cases $\{KA_t\}_t$, one for each $t \in kpool$. Similarly, we can calculate concrete tests for the book operation via its test cases $\{MB_t\}_t$, upon refinement these produce one concrete test *KBook* for the Kurbel specification.   □

Having shown how to calculate tests we now consider their properties of coverage and disjointness in turn.

We begin with coverage, where we have the following result.

Theorem 5. *Let AOp be an abstract operation with $AOp = \bigvee_i AOp_i$ being its disjoint set of tests. Let COp be an upward simulation of AOp. Let Ret be the retrieve relation. Let COp_i be the concrete tests given above. Then*

$$\bigvee_i COp_i \sqsubseteq_{US} COp$$

and if COp is the weakest upward simulation of AOp then $COp = \bigvee_i COp_i$.

Proof

Let us first observe the following:

$$\bigvee_i COp_i$$
$$= \bigvee_i((\forall Astate \bullet Ret \Longrightarrow pre\,AOp_i) \land$$
$$\forall Astate' \bullet (Ret' \Longrightarrow \exists Astate \bullet Ret \land AOp_i))$$
$$\Longrightarrow \bigvee_i(\forall Astate \bullet Ret \Longrightarrow pre\,AOp_i) \land$$
$$\bigvee_i(\forall Astate' \bullet (Ret' \Longrightarrow \exists Astate \bullet Ret \land AOp_i))$$
$$\Longrightarrow (\forall Astate \bullet \bigvee_i(Ret \Longrightarrow pre\,AOp_i)) \land$$
$$(\forall Astate' \bullet \bigvee_i(Ret' \Longrightarrow \exists Astate \bullet Ret \land AOp_i))$$
$$= (\forall Astate \bullet (Ret \Longrightarrow \bigvee_i pre\,AOp_i)) \land$$
$$(\forall Astate' \bullet Ret' \Longrightarrow \bigvee_i(\exists Astate \bullet Ret \land AOp_i))$$
$$= (\forall Astate \bullet (Ret \Longrightarrow pre \bigvee_i AOp_i)) \land$$
$$(\forall Astate' \bullet Ret' \Longrightarrow (\exists Astate \bullet Ret \land \bigvee_i AOp_i))$$
$$\sqsubseteq_{US} COp$$

Therefore

$$\bigvee_i COp_i \sqsubseteq_{US} COp$$

If COp was in fact the weakest refinement of AOp then we need to show that equality holds between COp and $\bigvee_i COp_i$. This will follow from the fact that

$$(\forall Astate \bullet (Ret \implies \mathrm{pre} \bigvee_i AOp_i)) \wedge$$
$$(\forall Astate' \bullet Ret' \implies (\exists Astate \bullet Ret \wedge \bigvee_i AOp_i))$$
$$\sqsubseteq_{US} \bigvee_i COp_i$$

which is easily shown.   □

   Therefore the covering properties for upward simulations are the same as for downward simulations.

   The disjointness properties are also pleasingly symmetric. When the retrieve relation is a surjective function, the formulae for calculating tests is the same as for downward simulations. Therefore, as was the case then, disjoint abstract disjoint tests will produce disjoint concrete tests. However, in general we again find that refined tests are not disjoint.

Example 5. Refined tests are not disjoint in general.

To see this it suffices to consider again the refinement of the Marlowe specification. The retrieve relation is not functional, since the predicates in *Ret* do not define the abstract space uniquely (in particular, $kpool = mpool \cup \mathrm{ran}\,tkt$ allows many choices of *mpool* and *tkt* for a given *kpool*).

   Each abstract test (MB_i) of *MBook* (and there are #*mpool* of them) is mapped onto the same concrete test (*KBook*). Therefore the refined concrete tests are not disjoint whereas the abstract ones were.   □

6   Conclusions

We have provided a means to calculate concrete tests from abstract ones for both upward and downward simulations. For retrieve relations which are surjective functions the calculations simplified considerably, and in this case the formulae for upward and downward simulations coincide.

   We can use this as a basis for a methodology to determine the correct concrete test calculation. Given abstract and concrete state spaces, a retrieve relation and an abstract operation, we proceed as follows:

1. Determine whether *Ret* is a surjective function. If it is, then the concrete tests are given by

$$COp_i \,\hat{=}\, \exists Astate; \, Astate' \bullet Ret \wedge AOp_i \wedge Ret'$$

2. If *Ret* is not a surjective function we determine whether it defines a downward or upward simulation. We do this by determining if

$$\text{pre} AOp \land Ret \Rightarrow \text{pre} COp$$

If this is the case, then the refinement is a downward simulation, and therefore the concrete tests are still given by

$$COp_i \cong \exists Astate; \ Astate' \bullet Ret \land AOp_i \land Ret'$$

3. If *Ret* does not define a downward simulation, then the refinement must be an upward simulation. In this case the concrete tests are given by

$$COp_i \cong (\forall Astate \bullet Ret \Longrightarrow \text{pre} AOp_i) \land$$
$$\forall Astate' \bullet (Ret' \Longrightarrow \exists Astate \bullet Ret \land AOp_i)$$

4. In all cases, check whether *COp* was in fact the weakest refinement, we do this by determining if

$$\bigvee_i COp_i = COp$$

If this is the case then the set of covering test cases is $\{COp_i\}_i$, if not we may wish to restrict the set of concrete tests further by taking the tests to be $\{COp_i \land COp\}_i$.

Since refining *AOp* might weaken its precondition, note that it may be necessary to perform further partition analysis in order to place the concrete tests into DNF.

If *COp* is the weakest refinement of *AOp* then the set of tests $\{COp_i\}_i$ cover *COp*. If *Ret* is functional then the concrete tests will be disjoint whenever the abstract tests are disjoint.

In this paper we have just considered the partition analysis for the individual operations to produce a number of test cases derived by conversion of an operation into disjunctive normal form. Further work on this methodology would also consider the partition analysis of the system state and the scheduling of tests to see how these change under refinement.

The partition analysis of the system state again transforms the state into a disjunctive normal form, which is then used to construct a finite state automaton from the specification. The state space changes under refinement and a new partition will be obtained for the concrete state space. We would expect that refinements have a similar effect on the state space to those found for the partition analysis of the operations. This needs to be confirmed.

In addition, we would like to determine whether we can use the retrieve relation to calculate a new FSA for the concrete specification from the abstract one using similar techniques to those above. The scheduling of tests for the concrete specification, which involves finding paths through the FSA which cover all the required tests, would also have to be investigated in light of our discussion of refinement.

References

1. J.-R. Abrial. *The B-Book: Assigning programs to meanings.* Cambridge University Press, 1996.

2. E. Brinksma. A theory for the derivation of tests. In S. Aggarwal and K. Sabnani, editors, *Protocol Specification, Testing and Verification, VIII*, pages 63–74, Atlantic City, USA, June 1988. North-Holland.

3. E. Brinksma, G. Scollo, and C. Steenbergen. Process specification, their implementation and their tests. In B. Sarikaya and G. v. Bochmann, editors, *Protocol Specification, Testing and Verification, VI*, pages 349–360, Montreal, Canada, June 1986. North-Holland.

4. D. Carrington and P. Stocks. A tale of two paradigms: Formal methods and software testing. In J. P. Bowen and J. A. Hall, editors, *Z User Workshop, Cambridge 1994*, pages 51–68, June 1994.

5. E. Cusack and C. Wezeman. Deriving tests for objects specified in Z. In J. P. Bowen and J. E. Nicholls, editors, *Z User Workshop, London 1992*, Workshops in Computing, pages 180–195. Springer-Verlag, 1993.

6. R. de Nicola and M. Hennessy. Testing equivalences for processes. *Theoretical Computer Science*, 34(3):83–133, 1984.

7. J. Derrick and E.A. Boiten. Calculating and verifying refinements of state based specifications. Submitted of publication, 1998.

8. Jeremy Dick and Alain Faivre. Automating the generation and sequencing of test cases from model-based specifications. In J. C. P. Woodcock and P. G. Larsen, editors, *FME'93: Industrial-Strength Formal Methods*, volume 670 of *Lecture Notes in Computer Science*, pages 268–284. Formal Methods Europe, Springer-Verlag, 1993.

9. J. He. Process refinement. In J. McDermid, editor, *The Theory and Practice of Refinement*. Butterworths, 1989.

10. L. Heerink and J. Tretmans. Refusal testing for classes of transition systems with inputs and outputs. In T. Mizuno, N. Shiratori, T. Higashino, and A. Togashi, editors, *FORTE/PSTV XVII'97*. Chapman and Hall, November 1997.

11. H.-M. Horcher. Improving software tests using Z specifications. In J. P. Bowen and M. G. Hinchey, editors, *ZUM'95: The Z Formal Specification Notation*, volume 967 of *Lecture Note in Computer Science*, pages 152–166. Springer-Verlag, 1995.

12. C. B. Jones. *Systematic Software Development using VDM*. Prentice Hall International Series in Computer Science, 1989.

13. M. B. Josephs. The data refinement calculator for Z specifications. *Information Processing Letters*, 27:29–33, February 1988.

14. G. T. Scullard. Test case selection using VDM. In R. Bloomfield, L. Marshall, and R. Jones, editors, *VDM '88: VDM – The Way Ahead*, volume 328 of *Lecture Notes in Computer Science*, pages 178–186. Springer-Verlag, 1988.

15. H. Singh, M. Conrad, and S. Sadeghipour. Test case design based on Z and the classification-tree method. In M. G. Hinchey and Shaoying Liu, editors, *First IEEE International Conference on Formal Engineering Methods (ICFEM '97)*, pages 81–90, Hiroshima, Japan, November 1997. IEEE Computer Society Press.

16. G. Smith and J. Derrick. Refinement and verification of concurrent systems specified in Object-Z and CSP. In M. G. Hinchey and Shaoying Liu, editors, *First IEEE International Conference on Formal Engineering Methods (ICFEM '97)*, pages 293–302, Hiroshima, Japan, November 1997. IEEE Computer Society Press.

17. J. M. Spivey. *The Z Notation: A Reference Manual*. Prentice Hall International Series in Computer Science, 1989.

18. S. Stepney. Testing as abstraction. In J. P. Bowen and M. G. Hinchey, editors, *ZUM'95: The Z Formal Specification Notation*, volume 967 of *Lecture Note in Computer Science*, pages 137–151. Springer-Verlag, 1995.

19. P. Stocks and D. Carrington. Deriving software test cases from formal specifications. In *6th Australian Software Engineering Conference*, pages 327–340, July 1991.

20. L. van Aertryck, M. Benveniste, and D. Le Metayer. Casting: A formally based software test generation method. In M. G. Hinchey and Shaoying Liu, editors, *First IEEE International Conference on Formal Engineering Methods (ICFEM '97)*, pages 101–110, Hiroshima, Japan, November 1997. IEEE Computer Society Press.

21. C. Wezeman and A. J. Judge. Z for managed objects. In J. P. Bowen and J. A. Hall, editors, *Z User Workshop, Cambridge 1994*, Workshops in Computing, pages 108–119. Springer-Verlag, 1994.

22. J. C. P. Woodcock and J. Davies. *Using Z: Specification, Refinement, and Proof*. Prentice Hall International Series in Computer Science, 1996.

23. J. C. P. Woodcock and C. C. Morgan. Refinement of state-based concurrent systems. In D. Bjørner, C. A. R. Hoare, and H. Langmaack, editors, *VDM '90: VDM and Z – Formal Methods in Software Development*, volume 428 of *Lecture Note in Computer Science*, pages 340–351. Springer-Verlag, 1990.

More Powerful Z Data Refinement: Pushing the State of the Art in Industrial Refinement

Susan Stepney[1], David Cooper[1], and Jim Woodcock[2]

[1] Logica UK Ltd
Betjeman House, 104 Hills Road, Cambridge CB2 1LQ, UK
Email: stepneys@logica.com & cooperd@logica.com

[2] Oxford University Computing Laboratory
Wolfson Building, Parks Road, Oxford OX1 3QD, UK
Email: Jim.Woodcock@comlab.ox.ac.uk

Abstract. We have recently completed the specification and full refinement proof of a large, industrial scale application. The application was security critical, and the modelling and proof was done to increase the client's assurance that the implemented system had no design flaws with security implications. Here we describe the application, and then discuss an essential lesson to learn concerning large proof contracts: that one must forge a path between mathematical formality on the one hand and practical achievement of results on the other. We present a number of examples of such decision points, explaining the considerations that must be made in each case.

In the course of our refinement work, we discovered that the traditional Z data refinement proof obligations [8, section 5.6], were not sufficient to prove our refinement. In particular, these obligations assume the use of a 'forward' (or 'downward') simulation. Here we present a more widely applicable set of Z data refinement proof obligations that we developed for and used on our project. These obligations allow both 'forward' and 'backward' simulations, and also allow non-trivial initialisation, finalisation, and input/output refinement.

1 Introduction

Over the past few years we have been working with the NatWest Development Team proving the correctness of Smartcard applications for electronic commerce. Here we describe one of those applications. We have modelled the abstract behaviour of the product, modelled its more concrete top level design, and have rigorously proved the correctness of the refinement from one to the other. All work was done in Z.

In the first half of this paper, we describe the application and the form of the design step modelled (Section 2), and discuss a number of lessons learnt during the proof process (Section 3). These lessons centre around the tension between mathematical formality and the need to achieve a demonstrable benefit to the project.

In the second half of this paper (Sections 4–7), we focus on one particular lesson: the importance of a sufficiently rich refinement theory. We discovered that the traditional Z data refinement proof obligations [8, section 5.6] (hereafter we refer to these as 'the Spivey rules') were not sufficient to prove our refinement, because they make some simplifications, and assume the use of a 'forward' (or 'downward') simulation. We had to remove some of these simplifications, and we required the use of a 'backward' simulation. We present a more widely applicable set of Z data refinement proof obligations that we developed for and used on our project. These obligations allow both 'forward' and 'backward' simulations, and also allow non-trivial initialisation, finalisation, and input/output refinement.

2 The application

NatWest Development Team had a product under development that was deeply security critical. They were developing a Smartcard application to handle electronic commerce, and they wanted to be sure that these cards would not contain any bugs in implementation or design that would allow them to be subverted once in the field. They called in Logica to develop formal models of the system and the security policy, and to prove that the system design met all the security properties required.

The system consists of a number of *electronic purses* that carry financial value, each hosted on a Smartcard. The purses interact with each other, via a communication device, to exchange value. Once released into the field, each purse is on its own, and has to ensure the security of all its transactions without recourse to a central controller. All the security measures have to be implemented on the card, with no real-time external audit logging or monitoring.

These cards are to be sold to members of the public to enable them to carry out fully electronic financial transactions with other individuals, with banks, retailers, etc. Insecurities could allow people to forge the value on their purses, and so obtain goods for free, thereby severely impacting the commercial viability of the project.

The task of the formal methods team was to model the system to ensure it behaved sensibly, and prove that the system design accurately reflected the behaviour specified.

2.1 Models

We developed two key models. We wrote an *abstract* model, describing the world of purses and the exchange of value through atomic transactions. This model expressed the security properties that the cards must preserve.

We wrote a *concrete* model, mirroring the design of the purses, which exchange value using a protocol of messages.

We rigorously proved that the concrete model is a *refinement* of the abstract.

Abstract model: The abstract model is small, simple, and easy to understand, running to approximately 20 pages of Z and natural language commentary.

The key operation is to transfer a chosen amount of value from one purse to another, modelled as an atomic action to decrement the value in the paying purse and increment the value in the receiving purse (Figure 1). This operation (and all the others, too) preserves the two key system security properties:

– no value may be created in the system

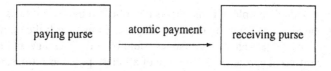

Fig. 1. An atomic transaction in the abstract model.

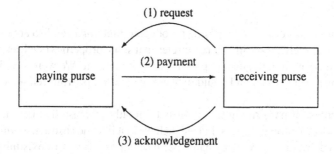

Fig. 2. Part of the *n*-step protocol used to implement the atomic transaction in the concrete model.

– all value is accounted in the system (no value is lost)

The simplicity of the abstract model allows these properties to be expressed in a way that the client can easily see are as they desired them to be. 20 pages of Z may sound a lot for such a simple operation, but the abstract model also includes a number of other operations around the periphery of this central behaviour, such as card locking and query operations.

Concrete model: The concrete model is more complicated, reflecting the real system design. The key changes from the abstract are:

– transactions are no longer atomic, but instead follow an *n*-step protocol (Figure 2)
– the communication medium is insecure and unreliable
– transaction logging is added to handle lost messages
– no global properties: each purse has to be implementable in isolation

This model is approximately 60 pages long, including Z and natural language commentary. Once again, there are a number of periphery operations and state components in addition to those to model the central operation of value transfer.

The basic protocol is:

1. communication device ascertains the transaction to perform
2. receiving purse requests the transfer of an amount from the paying purse
3. paying purse sends that amount to the receiving purse
4. receiving purse sends an acknowledgement of receipt to the paying purse

The protocol, although simple in principle, is complicated by several facts. The protocol can be stopped at any point by removal of power from a card; the communication medium could lose a message; a wire tapper could record a message and play it back to the same or different card later. In the face of all these possible actions, the protocol must correctly implement the atomic transfer of value as specified in the abstract model.

2.2   Proofs

All the security properties of the abstract model are *functional*, and so are preserved by refinement. It is well known in security circles that some properties (such as information flow properties) are not, in general, preserved by refinement. We were saved from such complications in this case, and could concentrate just on proving refinement between the models.

The purpose of performing the proof is to greatly increase the assurance that the chosen design (the protocol) does, indeed, behave just like the abstract, atomic transfers. We chose to do rigorous proofs by hand, because our experience of existing proof tools is that current tools are not yet appropriate for a task of this size. We did, however, type-check the statements of the proof obligations and many of the proof steps using a combination of fuzz [7] and Formaliser [2] [9]. As part of the development process, all proofs were also independently checked by external evaluators.

The proofs of the refinement obligations and the proofs of some model consistency obligations take approximately 200 pages. In addition, we produced approximately 100 pages of formal derivation in support of the underlying theory.

3   Between the devil and the deep blue sea

In developing the models and the proofs we were caught between opposing forces. On the one hand, we had a real product that was to hit the streets. We were proving properties because the client wanted to be sure the design was secure, not because they were a fan of obscure mathematical theories. We had to get the job done. On the other hand, proofs would give us no added assurance if they were faked, rushed, or so inelegant that no one would be able to check them.

The formal aspects of the development therefore plotted a course between perfect mathematical formality on one side and pragmatic 'just do it' on the other. Our course weaved from side to side as different concerns appeared. At each stage we focused on attacking the weakest part of the formal argument. Sometimes it was lack of faith in the questions we were asking, which forced us toward greater mathematical formality in search of an underlying theory to support our decisions. At other times it was the need to press on and cover more of the purse functionality, forcing us to 'just do' the proofs any way we could.

It is important to see this process as a continual trade off. There is no point in having a very sound underlying mathematical theory, but then no time or money to apply it to the product. Equally, there is no point in proving a theorem about the product when you have no understanding of whether it is an appropriate theorem to be proving.

There were a number of specific examples of this trade off, discussed below.

3.1 New proof rules needed

One of the early problems with the development forced us in the direction of formality to solve it.

We had developed an abstract model, with a single atomic transaction, and a concrete model with the protocol steps. Intuitively it appeared that the concrete should be a refinement of the abstract, but all our attempts to prove refinement using the Spivey rules failed. Looking at why the proof failed showed that there was a serious obstacle, not just an inability to push symbols around. The problem centred on when non-determinism was resolved: the concrete protocol resolved the non-determinism inherent in the system later than did the abstract atomic transaction. The rules of refinement that we were trying to use allow non-determinism to be resolved *earlier* in the concrete, but not later. (See Section 4.2 for more detail.)

We made some brief attempts to 'just do it' anyway, trying to modify the models to resolve the non-determinism differently, and even trying to prove something other than refinement. But it became clear that a more fundamental look at the proof rules held better hope for a solution.

There is a larger, more general theory of refinement, of which the Spivey rules are a specific instance, the forward proof rules. The more general theory includes another set of rules, the backward proof rules, which cater for the form of non-determinism resolution we needed. We needed to recast these rules from their relational form into the Z world of schemas, state transitions, inputs and outputs. (We have subsequently published a simplified form of these newly derived Z backwards rules in [12]. See Section 6 for more details of the derivation of the full proof rules we derived, including input-output refinement.)

Armed with an early version of the new rules, we were able to carry out our proofs successfully. However, as we did so, we found the new rules seemed too good, making our proofs too easy. We started investigating toy examples, and found we could prove refinement of patently non-refining systems! Rushing back in the direction of mathematical formality, we discovered that yes, indeed, these early proof rules were unsound, and some other aspects that we had originally thought unnecessary (because they were unnecessary in the forward rules) needed to be brought in. Some more working to put all the proof rules on a sound footing, doing all the derivations in detail, gave us the confidence to go back to our models, knowing that we were now working in the right context.

So, the path we took in this case was

1. 'just did it' with the theory we had until the theory (the proof rules available to us at the time) failed us
2. moved toward formality to find a larger, more general theory that included some new tools (backward rules) to help
3. used the new rules until doubt arose
4. investigated the problems (toy examples), then went back to correct
5. tightening of the theory
6. use the new theory with confidence

3.2　Problems with generic proofs

Sometimes doing things elegantly costs too much.

We had first modelled and proved a reduced version of the system, and were now expanding it to incorporate the full richness of the actual system. As we added one particular feature, we noticed that it had a similar mathematical structure to a feature already modelled and proved. The existing feature used integer addition as a binary operator, and the new feature used *max*, but the proofs seemed to rely only on properties of addition that are shared by *max* (such as commutativity).

Rather than just blindly re-doing all the proofs with the new feature, we decided to generalise the existing proof, and then separately instantiate it, once for addition and once for *max*. This should have cut down on the amount of work (one set of proofs rather than two) and made it easier for the evaluators to understand (understand one general proof, rather than two 'similar' ones).

As most people who have worked on automated theorem provers probably know, generalising proofs is much harder than it looks. For example, addition has an inverse, and we had used subtraction to simplify our original proof, even though it was not necessary to do so. To generalise the proof so that it was also applicable to an operator like *max* without an inverse was possible, but made the proof more complicated.

In other places we made use of properties of addition that are shared by *max*, but not by all binary operators. Thus we had to decide what the key property was so that the scope of the generality of the proof could be defined.

All this meant our general proof was becoming significantly longer than the original, and very obscure. There seemed to be no intuitive peg on which to hang our understanding — we could read the proof only as a series of meaningless symbols.

Although we saw no theoretical reason why a general proof would not be possible, we abandoned the attempt. We needed a proof of both features: we had one already for addition, and our work on the general proof had shown how the proof of the *max* feature would go. We therefore pressed ahead on a specific proof for the second feature, finishing it in less time than it would have taken us to finish the general proof and two instantiations. Furthermore, we found the proofs actually easier to understand as specifics than as instantiations of the general proof.

We believe it would have been possible to complete the general proof. It may well be possible to complete it more elegantly, and produce instantiations that are intuitively understandable. But in this case we could gain the benefit from the proof (increased assurance) for less effort by doing two, similar, repeated proofs.

Our weaving path was

1. do a specific proof
2. notice the scope for generality and elegance, and start a general proof
3. abandon general proof when cost grows too large
4. use the experience gained doing the general proof to 'just do' two specific proofs

3.3　No need to justify a working strategy

Even if you think there may be a better solution around the corner, if you have a solution that works, that may be good enough. This is a lesson hardest to accept if you are an

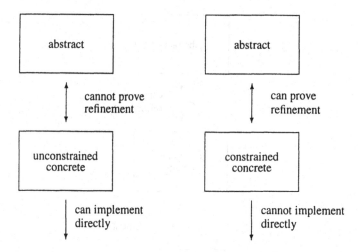

Fig. 3. We found that we could implement, but not prove, or that we could prove, but not implement.

academic at heart. The nature of academic research encourages reworking and revisiting solutions to find different insights. But in an industrial context, the benefit of such further work may not be worth the cost.

We had been using our backward proof rules to prove the refinement of the abstract model by the concrete model. We were successful with some proofs, but there were always some proofs at which we failed. We modified the models, often making the failed proofs possible, but then invalidating the previously successful ones.

The problem centred on the use of the backward proof rules. In the more conventional forward Spivey proof rules you attempt to show that there is a reasonable abstract state that an operation can take you *to*, given that you have an abstract state to start from and a concrete operation that occurs. In the backward rules, you instead attempt to show that there is a reasonable abstract state that an operation can take you *from*, given that you have an abstract state to go to and a concrete operation that occurs. This requires you to reason about the properties of a previous state.

Our model makes such reasoning difficult, because as the protocol progresses information that is no longer needed is lost from the state, and it is precisely this information that is needed in order to construct the prior abstract state. We could not include this extra information in the concrete model because it relates to global properties of a number of purses, which cannot be implemented by a set of independent purses.

However, we knew that these global properties *do* hold: the protocol forces them to hold. It is just that a model that expresses them explicitly cannot be implemented appropriately. If these constraints are in the concrete model, the refinement can be proved, but the model does not match the implementation. If these constraints are *not* in the concrete model, the model matches the implementation, but we cannot prove the refinement (Figure 3).

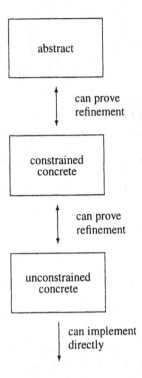

Fig. 4. We proved the refinement in two steps.

The solution was to add the constraints in an intermediate model, and then do an additional refinement to remove them (Figure 4) from the final model.

This second refinement could be performed using the conventional forward rules. This we did, and succeeded in proving both refinements. This issue drove the entire structure of the development.

This approach raised a question: does there exist a single refinement that could do the job of these two? Although this question is interesting, as far as our project in hand was concerned *it was irrelevant*. We had a solution that worked (an intermediate model, with two refinements) that was mathematically sound. Whether or not two refinements are *necessary*, in this case two refinements are certainly *sufficient*. We ignored the forces pulling us toward mathematical elegance, and pressed on using a solution that worked, even though we did not have a theoretical justification for its necessity.

3.4 Rework repaid in easier understanding

In contrast to the previous two examples, we also found that sometimes reworking a successful solution more elegantly and generally can be worthwhile.

We developed our models and proofs in two phases: once concentrating on just the key central functionality, and then again covering all the functionality. Having done some parts of the derivations repeatedly for different but similar operations, when we came to the rework we extracted the similar parts, generalised, and defined a number of useful lemmas. These we used to simplify some of the derivations for the new operations.

While generalising the derivations, we noticed that those operations that aborted the current transaction did not fit into the mould of the generalised derivation. However, if the aborting part were extracted, the remaining piece of the operation did fit. This restructuring made the general derivation more widely applicable, and significantly simplified the proofs of the aborting operations.

So here our path was:

1. develop complete models and proof for a subset of the system (just do it)
2. identify commonalities (mathematical elegance)
3. generalise
4. expand with additional functionality

3.5 Hand-proof delivered the goods

Given a client who wants to "increase assurance through formal methods", one has to use the tools to hand and supply the greatest possible increase in assurance at acceptable cost. It is not necessary to have every mathematical *i* dotted and *t* crossed before you can help real projects.

We decided to do all our proofs by hand, with no machine checking of the proof steps (although we did type-check all the mathematical statements). There are a number of good Z theorem provers/checkers around, such as Z/Eves [6], ProofPower [5], and CADiZ [11], but we believe the extra cost of doing proof at the level of rigour enforced by a theorem prover/checker far outweighs the benefits of greater assurance in this case. We have done some small scale investigations of the cost of using CADiZ and Z/Eves for our proofs that support this view.

However, it is likely that if a set of proofs need to be maintained in the face of continuing changes to a model, tool support may become more important.

3.6 Presentation is important

Having a mathematically correct proof is insufficient if it is presented too badly to be read and understood by a reviewer.

Part of the development process imposed by the client includes detailed external evaluation of the formal models and proofs. These evaluators have to be able to read a proof and both understand it intuitively and check it line by line for correctness. To ensure readability we developed a number of presentation styles.

We started all proofs with a clear, mathematical statement of the theorem to be proved, expressed in the conventional *hypothesis* ⊢ *conclusion* style, where *hypothesis* is a declaration and *conclusion* is a predicate. This rigour ensured that we knew clearly what was to be proved, and often prompted us to ask why we were proving this. We also described the theorem in English, explaining what property was being proved, and explaining why it was reasonable to believe that it was true.

Many proofs were broken down into a number of subsections, and in these cases we stated the subtheorems themselves formally and, where possible, intuitively justified them. To make it easy to follow this nesting of proofs, when a subtheorem was proved, we added an end marker □ labelled with the section number, to help bracket the subproof. For example,

3.1 theorem ...
    proof steps, leading to two things to prove ...
    3.1.1 first sub-theorem
        proof of first sub-theorem
        □ 3.1.1
    3.1.2 second sub-theorem
        proof of second sub-theorem
        □ 3.1.2
    tidy up of whole proof ...
    □ 3.1

Lemmas that were of a more general applicability were extracted into an appendix, so they could be read in isolation.

We wrote the proofs themselves in one of two styles: either rigorously step by step, with each step labelled with an inference rule; or more free-flowing English with the key points expressed mathematically.

We used the rigorous presentation when symbol manipulation was most important, which often occurred when large schemas were being restructured and manipulated to extract some key component. This was the predominant style, and we used it whenever we were in doubt of the validity of our arguments.

The more free-flowing presentation was appropriate when there was little doubt of the validity of the argument, but the details would be long and cumbersome.

A formalist would demand all arguments to be presented step-by-step, with each step labelled. But with limited resources, it is sometimes better to tighten up the rigour of some other part (such as the derivation of the proof rules themselves) than spend the precious resource expanding "some set-theoretic manipulations can show ..." in detail.

4   A closer look at the need for new proof rules

As explained earlier (Section 3.1), in the course of our refinement work it became apparent to us that the traditional Z data refinement proof obligations [8, section 5.6] were insufficient for our purpose. We were forced back to first principles, to derive suitable new proof obligations.

Here we present the two sets of Z data refinement proof obligations we derived for our work, each of which are more more widely applicable than the Spivey rules. These new rules cover both 'forward' and 'backward' simulations, allow non-trivial initialisation and finalisation steps, and provide the ability to perform input/output refinement.

In the following sections we describe which assumptions used to derive the traditional rules we relaxed, and the new proof obligations we derived[1].

4.1 Traditional Z data refinement proof obligations – recap

The traditional Z data refinement proof obligations are given in [8, section 5.6]. To recap, they comprise the three following proof obligations:

initialisation: for each concrete initial state, there must be a corresponding abstract initial state.

$$CInit \vdash \exists A' \bullet AInit \wedge R'$$

applicability: whenever it is possible to perform the abstract operation AOp, it must be possible to perform the concrete operation COp on the corresponding concrete state (also known as 'widening the precondition').

$$R; \text{pre } AOp \vdash \text{pre } COp$$

correctness: for any abstract state A within the precondition of AOp, corresponding to a before state C (which, by applicability, is within the precondition of COp), then, corresponding to any C' reachable from C by COp, there must be an abstract state A' related to A by AOp.

$$R; COp \mid \text{pre } AOp \vdash \exists A' \bullet AOp \wedge R'$$

4.2 Resolution of non-determinism

The Spivey rules are applicable when the concrete model resolves any remaining non-determinism sooner (or at the same point as) the abstract model. However, it is possible to develop models where concrete non-determinism is resolved later than the abstract non-determinism.

For example, consider the case of two booking offices [12, section 17.3]. The Apollo theatre, when you book a ticket, chooses a particular ticket to give you, and when you arrive at the theatre, gives you that ticket. It non-deterministically chooses which particular ticket you get *early* in the process. The Phoenix cinema, on the other hand, when you book a ticket, merely notes that yet another ticket has been booked; only when you arrive at the cinema does it choose which particular ticket to give you. It non-deterministically chooses which particular ticket you get *late* in the process. These two systems are behaviourally equivalent — so each is a refinement of the other — but with the Spivey rules we can prove only that (early) Apollo refines (late) Phoenix, not that Phoenix refines Apollo.

Our own application was another, much larger, example of later resolution. We had an abstract transaction that atomically either succeeded or failed, straight away. The concrete model implemented the transaction as an n-step protocol, and whether the transaction succeeded or failed could not be determined until late in the protocol.

---

[1] We use Standard Z [13] syntax in our small illustrative examples, and note where this differs from the Z Reference Manual [8] syntax.

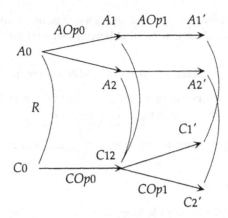

Fig. 5. A case not provable by the Spivey rules: non-determinism resolved later in the concrete than in the abstract.

In all such later-resolution cases, the Spivey rules *cannot* prove the refinement. To see why this is, consider Figure 5. This shows a non-deterministic abstract operation AOp_0, followed by a deterministic one AOp_1. In our application, AOp_0 is the initial atomic transaction that non-deterministically succeeds or aborts, and AOp_1 is essentially 'nothing happening', ΞA. AOp_0 is refined by a deterministic concrete operation COp_0, and AOp_1 is refined by a non-deterministic concrete operation COp_1. In our application, COp_0 is the first always successful *request* step of the protocol, and COp_1 is the later *payment* step that either succeeds or aborts.

By the time both operations have been performed, the non-determinism has been resolved both concretely and abstractly, and so the retrieve relation relates A_1' and C_1', and separately relates A_2' and C_2'. Because the first operation can result in one of two abstract states, A_1 and A_2, but only a single concrete state, C_{12}, the retrieve relation has to relate C_{12} to both A_1 and A_2.

Now consider what happens when the Spivey rule for correctness is applied to the second operation, AOp_1 and COp_1:

> *for any abstract state A within the precondition of AOp* (here consider the state A_1), *corresponding to a before state C* (which is C_{12}) *then, corresponding to any C' reachable from C by COp* (let's consider C_2'), *there must be an abstract state A' related to A by AOp.*

But there is *no* such state A' that retrieves from state C_2' whilst being reachable from state A_1 by the abstract operation. The proof fails.

It turns out that the Spivey rules are *sufficient* — anything they can prove is indeed a refinement — but not *necessary* — there are some cases of refinement that cannot be proved using them. We discovered that our own application fell into this second class, and so we needed to understand refinement better in order to derive refinement proof obligations that were sufficient for our case.

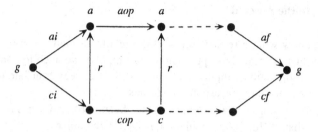

Fig. 6. A relational view of refinement (after [3]). The global-to-global relation $g \leftrightarrow g$ can be implemented abstractly, by initialisation *ai*, operation(s) *aop* and finalisation *af*. The corresponding concrete relation, defined by *ci*, *cop*, and *cf*, refines the abstract precisely when it is a subset of the abstract relation.

5   What is refinement?

There are some specifications that we intuitively feel *are* refinements, but which we cannot prove using the Spivey rules as they stand. So, what *is* a refinement?

5.1   A relational model

[3] give a *relational* definition of refinement. A 'global-to-global' relation can be *implemented* by moving into some abstract world (by a process called initialisation), performing a sequence of abstract operations, then moving back into the global world (called finalisation). If another implementation (via a concrete world) defines a relation that is a subset of the one obtained via the abstract world, then the concrete implementation *refines* the abstract one. (We refer the reader to the original paper for precise definitions of these terms, sketched in Figure 6.)

This subsetting requirement formally captures the notion of "refining away non-determinism". The [3] definitions require all the various global, abstract and concrete operations to be *total*, so there is no danger of subsetting all the way to the empty set.

We can now ask the question, "what is a refinement?" independent of the particular choice of refinement proof obligations. Refinement, in this relational world, is simply subsetting.

Reasoning over the whole global relation, which itself is defined in terms of sequences of operations ('programs' in the terminology of [3]) is difficult. It is much more tractable to reason over individual operations, and [3] give *two* different sufficient conditions for a collection of concrete operations to be a refinement of a collection of abstract operations in this relational world. The Spivey rules are derived from one of these conditions, that for 'forward simulation'. However, the other condition, for 'backward simulation', is the one appropriate for proving refinements with a later resolution of non-determinism.

5.2   Casting to the Z world

Now that we know what a refinement is in the relational model (expressed in terms of total operations, with no concept of inputs or outputs), we need to convert to the Z world (of partial operations, inputs, and outputs), and thereby translate the relational refinement obligations into corresponding Z ones.

Making certain simplifying assumptions (see Section 6), and translating one of the [3] conditions, that of 'forward' simulation, results in the Spivey rules. If we make the same simplifying assumptions, and translate the other 'backward' simulation condition, we get the analogous 'backward' Z refinement rules. (We have since published these simplified backward rules in [12, section 17.3].) If, further, we relax some of the simplifying assumptions, we get the more powerful refinement rules (see Section 6) that we found necessary for our particular application.

The new (simplified) backward rules allow us to prove that the situation in Figure 5 is indeed a refinement. Formally, we have to show:

$$COp; R' \vdash \exists A \bullet R \wedge AOp$$

Informally:

> for any abstract state A' (consider state A'_2) corresponding to the after state C' (which is state C'_2) reached from C (which here is state C_{12}) by the concrete operation, there must be an abstract state A (there is! — it is state A_2) that both corresponds to C and is related to A' by the abstract operation.

6   Relaxing the simplifying assumptions

Now that we have the wider theory from [3] available to us, we can see some of the *other* assumptions (beyond the choice of forward simulation) that go into deriving the Spivey rules, and consider relaxing those assumptions, too. The proof obligations that result from relaxing some of these assumptions are given in Section 7.

6.1   Computational model

The wider theoretical model of [3] is purely relational; it has no concept of inputs or outputs. When moving to a Z model, the relational state needs to be provided with some internal structure, to give it a Z-like state along with (sequences of) inputs and outputs.

A *computational model* is then imposed, determining restrictions on how these input and output sequences can be used in operations. We choose a natural one (others are possible): each operation consumes the head of the input sequence, and appends an output to the output sequence (see Figure 7). Furthermore, we require the operation itself to depend only on this input and output (and the state): it is independent of the 'past outputs' and 'future inputs' sequences.

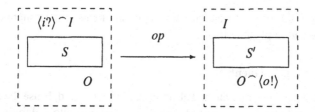

Fig. 7. Embedding a Z-like state S, input sequence I and output sequence O in the relational state, and imposing a computational model on the behaviour of I and O.

6.2 Observability and Finalisation

It is well known that the refinements of a specification provable using the Spivey rules depend on what parts of the state are 'observed' by outputs. For example, if a *Stack* specification includes no operation such as *Top* to observe the state, then bizarre specifications — such as ones that randomly change the values, or throw them away altogether — can be proved to be refinements. In the trivial case where all outputs are indistinguishable then any specification can refine any other (with identically named operations), by chosing the chaotic retrieve[2] $R == [A; C \mid true]$.

In [3]'s relational model, the *finalisation* process captures what is observable. When deriving the Spivey rules, the only part of the relational state that is finalised is the output sequence. This is why, with those rules, the outputs provide the only way of observing the state.

In an abstract model, state is usually present because it is felt to be needed to capture the required abstract properties. It is certainly possible to have a 'large' abstract state that is not observed, in order to ease the statement of these properties. (For example, consider a 'Parity' specification that keeps the entire sequence of input bits in the abstract state, but where only the parity of this sequence is observed.) Providing 'observation' operations that merely observe the state may well pollute the model, especially if these operations do not map naturally onto any concrete operation. In such cases, a cleaner model may be possible by finalising (part of) the state to the relevant global state, and thus observing it directly.

In our own application, our abstract state includes a component, *sink*, that records the quantity of the value that has become unavailable to the rest of the system. A property of *sink* is quoted as a security requirement: the total value still available to the system, plus that in the *sink*, is required to be constant. The concrete model, following the actual implementation, has the corresponding information distributed amongst the collection of automonous purses, in various log files. The retrieve relation relates all these log files in a subtle way to the abstract *sink*. We showed that the distributed log files implement the abstract *sink*, and thereby satisfy the required security property. There is a concrete operation that observes the contents of a single purse's log file, but we did not wish to clutter our model with a concrete operation that corresponds to observing all the log files simultaneously, which would correspond to observing the abstract *sink*. So, instead of observing this component with an output, we finalise the

---

[2] In Standard Z [13] notation, schemas are introduced using '==', rather than '$\hat{=}$'.

sink component of the abstract state, and the *log* components of the concrete state, and discharge a finalisation proof obligation.

6.3   Input/output refinement

With the Spivey rules, the concrete and abstract (and global) models use the *same* input and output state; only the Z-state part of the relational state is allowed to differ. Initialisation of the inputs (how the inputs in the abstract or concrete model are related to the global ones) is a trivial identity, and the input initialisation proof obligation vanishes, leaving only the state initialisation rule. Similarly, finalisation of the outputs is a trivial identity, and finalisation of the state throws it all away, and so the entire finalisation proof obligation disappears.

As explained above, we relaxed the assumption about finalising the state to nothing, to allow non-trivial state finalisation. We also relaxed the assumption that the inputs and outputs are the same in all models, allowing the concrete and abstract inputs and outputs to differ (from each other, and from the global ones, too). So now we can refine our input and output data types from more abstract to more concrete representations, in the same way that we have always been able to refine state. This requires an additional definition of how inputs are initialised and how outputs are finalised.

In the relational world, the retrieve relates the entire abstract and concrete state (including inputs and outputs as well as the Z-like state). With the Spivey rules, where the input and output parts are the same in the concrete and abstract models, there is no need to retrieve them (the retrieve is just the identity). Relaxing this assumption of equality, we now have to provide a part of the retrieve relation to map concrete inputs and outputs to abstract ones.

We choose to require that the complete retrieve be written as three independent parts: one between inputs, one between outputs, and one between Z-states. This does restrict the kinds of refinements that are provable. For example, anything observed by finalisation abstractly has to be observed by finalisation concretely; the requirement of independence of the retrieves means that we cannot move the observation into an output. However, we found that the resulting proof obligations, even with this restriction, are sufficiently powerful to enable us to prove our own application, and so any more general rules would have been overly complicated.

As an example of output refinement, consider a global model of traffic lights where the output is the current colour state, represented as an element of an enumerated (free) type; the abstract model could use natural numbers to represent these colours, and the concrete model could say how these numbers are represented as a sequence of bits.

$$LIGHT ::= red \mid amber \mid green$$
$$aLight == \{0, 1, 2\}$$
$$cLight == \{\langle 0, 0 \rangle, \langle 0, 1 \rangle, \langle 1, 0 \rangle\}$$

The global model talks in terms of global outputs $g! : LIGHT$, the abstract model in terms of $a! : aLight$, and the concrete model in terms of $c! : cLight$.

The abstract output finalisation defines how the abstract numbers represent the global colours:

$$\begin{array}{|l|}
\hline
\_AFin_! _____ \\
\; a! : aLight \\
\; g! : LIGHT \\
\hline
\; g! = red \Rightarrow a! = 0 \\
\; g! = amber \Rightarrow a! = 1 \\
\; g! = green \Rightarrow a! = 2 \\
\hline
\end{array}$$

We can write this schema equivalently as[3]:

$$AFin_! == \{ \langle\!\langle g! == red, a! == 0 \rangle\!\rangle, \langle\!\langle g! == amber, a! == 1 \rangle\!\rangle,$$
$$\langle\!\langle g! == green, a! == 2 \rangle\!\rangle \}$$

The concrete output finalisation defines how the concrete bit-streams represent the global colours:

$$CFin_! == \{ \langle\!\langle g! == red, c! == \langle 0,0 \rangle \rangle\!\rangle, \langle\!\langle g! == amber, c! == \langle 0,1 \rangle \rangle\!\rangle,$$
$$\langle\!\langle g! == green, c! == \langle 1,0 \rangle \rangle\!\rangle \}$$

The output retrieve defines how the concrete bit-streams represent the abstract numbers:

$$R_! == \{ \langle\!\langle a! == 0, c! == \langle 0,0 \rangle \rangle\!\rangle, \langle\!\langle a! == 1, c! == \langle 0,1 \rangle \rangle\!\rangle,$$
$$\langle\!\langle a! == 2, c! == \langle 1,0 \rangle \rangle\!\rangle \}$$

We find we need to include the output retrieve in each operation proof, and do a new output finalisation proof, in order to demonstrate refinement (see Section 7).

We need to be a little careful about interpreting outputs when we have a non-trivial finalisation. It is not the raw output itself (a bit-stream in the above example) that is observed, but rather that output *as viewed through finalisation*. So when interpreting the above specification, we do not 'observe' $\langle 0,0 \rangle$, we actually 'observe' *red*. In this example, this does not cause too much of a problem, because there is a bijection between each of the global, abstract and concrete outputs. However, it is possible to write specifications that 'confuse' or 'merge' apparently different abstract (or concrete) outputs to the *same* global one. For example, consider the case where the 'Parity' specification mentioned in Section 6.2 is modified so that the abstract state (a sequence of bits) is apparently 'observed' by an abstract output comprising just this sequence, but where the abstract output is *finalised* to a global output comprising just the parity of the sequence. Then in fact only the parity has truly been observed (as can be demonstrated by refining the specification to a concrete one that outputs just the parity). So, when reading a specification the output finalisation has to be read along with the operation definition to understand precisely what is being observed.

Similar remarks apply to input initialisation.

In our own application, we performed input refinement. The abstract operation inputs a simple *go* to perform the transaction; the various steps in the concrete protocol input differing protocol messages.

---

[3] by using Standard Z's [13] explicit binding construction notation

6.4 State initialisation

With the Spivey rules, there is no Z-like state component in the global state, so state initialisation is independent of the global state. We relax this constraint and allow the global state to have a non-trivial Z-like component, and initialisation to depend on this value of the global state. This allows initial states to be set up with particular state values.

It is possible to model such initialisation by putting the system into some initial state unconstrained by the global state, then performing a state transition, using some special input, to 'initialise' it. But this is rather clumsy, and can pollute the model with a state component to capture whether the state has been initialised yet. More general initialisation permits cleaner models.

Also, having a specific initialisation allows the before global state to be related to the final global state, which means it is possible to express 'global-to-global' properties, for example, that a certain quantity is preserved.

In our own application, we found we needed to perform an initialisation based on the global state, because the actual devices entered the modelled world already having particular values for some of their components (for example, unique identification number).

6.5 Totalisation

The wider theory is cast in terms of *total* operations. When moving to a Z world, we have to decide how to treat Z's partial operations. We do this by choosing a totalisation: we assume the operation is chaotic outside its precondition, and moreover, that there is some 'bottom' state (representing a broken system), which is itself propagated appropriately chaotically to ensure that broken systems stay broken. (We require initialisation and finalisation to be total.)

Such a choice of operation totalisation corresponds to one common interpretation of the meaning of a Z operation outside its precondition: that 'anything can happen'. It also explains why refinement allows widening the precondition: it is simply a reduction of non-determinism, from completely chaotic to something rather less chaotic.

This chaotic totalisation corresponds to replacing a partial operation relation $op : X \leftrightarrow X$ with its totalised counterpart $\overset{\bullet}{op} = (X^{\perp} \times X^{\perp}) \oplus op$, where $X^{\perp}$ is the set X augmented with an extra 'bottom' state. Other totalisations are possible, for example:

$$\overset{\bullet}{op} = (X^{\perp} \times \{\perp\}) \oplus op$$

$$\overset{\bullet}{op} = \operatorname{id} X^{\perp} \oplus op$$

Other totalisations correspond to other interpretations of the meaning of a Z operation outside its precondition, and result in different sets of refinement proof obligations. The most common is the 'firing condition' interpretation [4] [10], that *nothing* can happen outside the precondition.

So, the choice of a particular set of refinement proof obligations determines how a Z 'state and operations'-style specification should be interpreted.

In our own application, the traditional 'anything can happen' totalisation was appropriate for our model, so we did not need to derive more exotic rules.

7 Resulting data refinement proof obligations

The simplifying assumptions used to derive the Spivey rules from the relational refinement model are:

- The global relational state comprises only inputs and outputs. There is no Z-like state to initialise from, so state initialisation does not consider it, or finalise to, so state finalisation "throws it all away".
- The global, abstract, and concrete inputs and outputs are the same: the input initialisation, the output finalisation, and the respective retrieves, are the identity relation.
- Totalisation gives 'anything can happen' outside the precondition.
- The 'forward simulation' choice is made.

We have relaxed these assumptions in the following ways, to derive more widely applicable Z data refinement proof obligations:

- The global state can have a Z-like state component, and so the initial state can be related to the global one.
- State finalisation need not 'throw it all away'; state components can be observed without using outputs.
- Abstract and concrete inputs and outputs can differ, and are related by an appropriate retrieve; so i/o can be refined.
- Totalisation gives 'anything can happen' outside the precondition (as for the Spivey rules). The more widely applicable initialisation and finalisation steps are required to be total.
- Both the 'forward' and 'backward' choices are made.

These more relaxed choices lead to the more widely applicable Z data refinement proof obligations, given in sections 7.2 (forward rules) and 7.3 (backward rules).

7.1 Notation

In this section we introduce the various schemas used to define the refinement proof obligations in the following sections.

We use schemas to capture the global state G, global inputs $G_?$ and global outputs $G_!$. (We choose to bundle up our inputs and outputs each into a schema, to avoid polluting the description with their explicit types.)

The abstract model has abstract state A, inputs $A_?$ and outputs $A_!$. We initialise from the global to the abstract state with

$$AInit == [G; A' \mid \ldots]$$

We initialise from global inputs to abstract inputs with

$$AInit_? == [G_?; A_? \mid \ldots]$$

The abstract operation is

$$AOp == [\Delta A; A_?; A_! \mid \ldots]$$

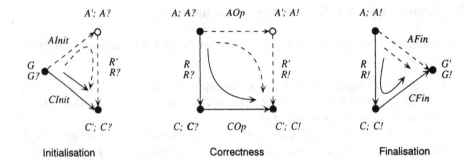

Fig. 8. The more powerful forward rules. The solid lines and states represent the hypothesised conditions; the dashed lines and circled states have to be proved to exist.

and the abstract state finalisation and output finalisations are

$$AFin == [A; G' | \ldots]$$
$$AFin_! == [A_!; G_! | \ldots]$$

The concrete model has concrete state C, inputs $C_?$ and outputs $C_!$. The corresponding concrete initialisations, operation, and finalisations are

$$CInit == [G; C' | \ldots]$$
$$CInit_? == [G_?; C_? | \ldots]$$
$$COp == [\Delta C; C_?; C_! | \ldots]$$
$$CFin == [C; G' | \ldots]$$
$$CFin_! == [C_!; G_! | \ldots]$$

The concrete and abstract states, inputs and outputs are related by the retrieve relations:

$$R == [A; C | \ldots]$$
$$R_? == [A_?; C_? | \ldots]$$
$$R_! == [A_!; C_! | \ldots]$$

7.2 Forward rules

The forward rules are sketched in Figure 8.

initialisation: for each concrete initial state obtained from some global state (and there must always be at least one), there must be a corresponding abstract initial state obtained from the same global state.

$$G \vdash \text{pre } CInit$$
$$CInit \vdash \exists A' \bullet AInit \wedge R'$$

For each concrete input obtained from some global input (and there must always be at least one), there must be a corresponding abstract input obtained from the same global input.

$G \vdash$ pre $CInit_?$

$CInit_? \vdash \exists A_? \bullet AInit_? \wedge R_?$

applicability: whenever it is possible to perform the abstract operation AOp, it must be possible to perform the concrete operation COp on the corresponding concrete state and concrete input.

$R; R_? \mid$ pre $AOp \vdash$ pre COp

correctness: whenever it is possible to perform the abstract operation, and the corresponding concrete operation can result in state C' and output $C_!$, then it must be possible to find an abstract state A' and output $A_!$, corresponding to that C' and $C_!$, that is the result of performing the abstract operation.

$R; R_?; COp \mid$ pre $AOp \vdash \exists A'; A_! \bullet AOp \wedge R' \wedge R_!$

finalisation: for each concrete state that corresponds to some abstract state, where the concrete state finalises to global state G (and it must finalise), the corresponding abstract state must finalise to the same global state.

$R \vdash$ pre $CFin$

$R; CFin \vdash AFin$

For each concrete output that corresponds to some abstract output, where the concrete output finalises to global output $G_!$ (and it must finalise), the corresponding abstract output must finalise to the same global output.

$R_! \vdash$ pre $CFin_!$

$R_!; CFin_! \vdash AFin_!$

7.3 Backward rules

The backward rules are sketched in Figure 9.

initialisation: for each concrete initial state obtained from some global state, that has a corresponding abstract state, that abstract state must be obtainable from the same global state.

$G \vdash$ pre $CInit$

$CInit; R' \vdash AInit$

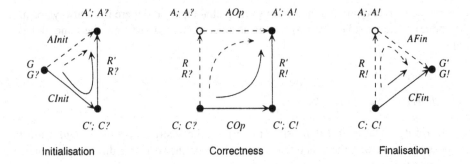

Fig. 9. The more powerful backward rules. The solid lines and states represent the hypothesised conditions; the dashed lines and circled states have to be proved to exist.

For each concrete input obtained from some global input, that has a corresponding abstract input, that abstract input must be obtainable from the same global input.

$G_? \vdash$ pre *CInit*?

CInit?; $R_? \vdash$ *AInit*?

applicability: whenever it is possible to perform the abstract operation from all the abstract states and inputs corresponding to a chosen concrete state and input, then it must be possible to perform the concrete operation.

$C; C_? \mid (\forall A; A_? \mid R \wedge R_? \bullet$ pre *AOp*$) \vdash$ pre *COp*

correctness: for any abstract state A' corresponding to the after state C' reached from C by the concrete operation, there must be an abstract state A that both corresponds to C and is related to A' by the abstract operation.

$C; C_? \mid (\forall A; A_? \mid R \wedge R_? \bullet$ pre *AOp*$)$
$\qquad \vdash \forall R'; R_! \mid COp \bullet \exists A; A_? \bullet R \wedge R_? \wedge AOp$

When *AOp* is a *total* operation, this obligation reduces to

$COp; R'; R_! \vdash \exists A; A_? \bullet R \wedge R_? \wedge AOp$

finalisation: for each concrete state that finalises to a global state G, there must be a corresponding abstract state that finalises to the same global state.

$R \vdash$ pre *CFin*

CFin $\vdash \exists A \bullet R \wedge AFin$

For each concrete output that finalises to a global output $G_!$, there must be a corresponding abstract output that finalises to the same global output.

$R_! \vdash$ pre *CFin*!

CFin! $\vdash \exists A_! \bullet R_! \wedge AFin_!$

8 Summary

We have been able to prove the correctness of the refinement of a real industrial product, working to real development time scales. In the process, we uncovered a security flaw in one part of the system design, and identified the corrections needed.

In the process of showing that it is possible to do Z refinement on an industrial scale and in an industrial context, we have learnt some lessons about how such a development can usefully be carried out. These lessons centre around the tension between two forces: the force driving one toward greater mathematical and aesthetic precision; and the other the desire to 'just do it' and achieve something useful for the project.

It is not possible to say that it is always better to follow the line of formality, or to say that it is always better to be strictly pragmatic. In some cases one decision must be made, and in other cases another. The guiding principle is usually the question of addressing the weakest link. Asking the question: "If I had only a week to complete this project, will I give greater assurance of correctness if I get this part more mathematically justified, or if I do proofs for more of the system, or if I present this more neatly, or ..."

A realistic assessment of this question will sometimes force you to get the maths right (no assurance is achieved if you don't know that your proof techniques work) and will sometimes force you to use the inelegant tools you have (no assurance is achieved if you prove nothing about the actual system in hand).

We achieved a very high level of rigour in our proofs. The proofs are far more detailed than typical proofs done in general mathematics. Despite this the formal methods activity was never on the critical path of the development. The formal methods component was usually ahead of schedule, and never caused a delay in development.

The success of this project has lead the client to do formal development, at the same level of rigour, on further products they are developing.

The proofs are also built on very sound theory: we investigated the foundations of the proof rules in great detail.

As a byproduct of doing these proofs, we have also improved the foundations of Z refinement rules. We have explained how the traditional Z data refinement proof obligations are the result of making certain simplifying assumptions, and embedding the Z world of state, inputs and outputs in a relational model. Different assumptions lead to different refinement rules; for our own application, we had to relax certain assumptions that go into deriving the Spivey rules in order to prove that our particular concrete specification was indeed a refinement on the abstract. We have presented here the actual proof obligations we discharged in our own application.

Other teams may well find they have to relax different assumptions, provide different computational models, or different totalisation embeddings, in order to prove their own refinements. ([1] will provide a detailed description of the precise derivations, in order that others may derive their own appropriate refinement proof obligations.)

Acknowledgements

The work described in the paper took place as part of a development funded by the NatWest Development Team.

Part of the refinement work was carried out by Eoin McDonnell.

References

1. David Cooper, Susan Stepney, and Jim Woodcock. *Refinement: Theory and Practice*. In preparation.

2. Mike Flynn, Tim Hoverd, and David Brazier. Formaliser – An interactive support tool for Z. In John E. Nicholls, editor, *Z User Workshop, Oxford 1989*, Workshops in Computing, pages 128–141. Springer-Verlag, 1990.

3. He Jifeng, C. A. R. Hoare, and Jeff W. Sanders. Data refinement refined (resumé). In B. Robinet and R. Wilhelm, editors, *ESOP'86*, Lecture Notes in Computer Science, volume 213, pages 187–196. Springer-Verlag, 1986.

4. Mark B. Josephs. Specifying reactive systems in Z. Technical Report TR-19-91, Programming Research Group, Oxford University Computing Laboratory, UK, 1991.

5. D.J. King and R.D. Arthan. Development of Practical Verification Tools. *The ICL Systems Journal*, 11(1), May 1996.

6. Irwin Meisels and Mark Saaltink. *The Z/EVES Reference Manual*, Technical Report TR-97-5493-03c. ORA, 267 Richmond Road, Suite 100, Ottawa, Ontario, K1Z 6X3, Canada, June 1997. URL: http://www.ora.on.ca/z-eves/

7. J. Michael Spivey. *The ƒUZZ Manual*. Computer Science Consultancy, UK, 2nd edition, 1992. URL: ftp://ftp.comlab.ox.ac.uk/pub/Zforum/fuzz

8. J. Michael Spivey. *The Z Notation: A Reference Manual*. Prentice Hall International Series in Computer Science, 2nd edition, 1992.

9. Susan Stepney. Formaliser Home Page. URL:
http://public.logica.com/~formaliser/

10. Ben Strulo. How firing conditions help inheritance. In Jonathan P. Bowen and Michael G. Hinchey, editors, *ZUM'95: The Z Formal Specification Notation*, Lecture Notes in Computer Science, volume 967, pages 264–275. Springer-Verlag, 1995.

11. Ian Toyn. Formal reasoning in the Z notation using CADiZ. In N. A. Merriam, editor, *2nd International Workshop on User Interface Design for Theorem Proving Systems*. Department of Computer Science, University of York, July 1996. URL:
http://www.cs.york.ac.uk/~ian/cadiz/home.html

12. Jim Woodcock and Jim Davies. *Using Z: Specification, Refinement, and Proof*. Prentice Hall International Series in Computer Science, 1996.

13. Z Notation version 1.2. Committee Draft Standard: CD13568. ISO panel JTC1/SC22/WG19, BSI panel IST/5/-/19/2, September 1995. URL:
http://www.comlab.ox.ac.uk/oucl/groups/zstandards/

Network Topology and a Case Study in TCOZ

Brendan Mahony[1,*] and Jin Song Dong[2]

[1] Information Technology Division
Defence Science and Technology Organisation (DSTO), Australia
Email: Brendan.Mahony@dsto.defence.gov.au

[2] Mathematical and Information Sciences
Commonwealth Scientific and Industrial Research Organisation (CSIRO), Australia
Email: jinsong.dong@cmis.csiro.au

Abstract. Object-Z is strong in modeling the data and operations of complex systems. However, it is weak in specifying real-time and concurrent systems. Timed Communicating Object-Z (TCOZ) extends the Object-Z notation with Timed CSP constructs. TCOZ is particularly well suited for specifying complex systems whose components have their own thread of control. This paper demonstrates expressiveness of the TCOZ notation through a case study on specifying a multi-lift system that operates in real-time.

1 Introduction

Many formal specification and design notations have tended to concentrate either on data modeling and algorithmic concerns (eg. Z, VDM, etc.) or else on process control concerns (eg. CSP, CCS, StateCharts, etc.). Parallel and distributed systems often have intricate system states and process control structures involving concurrency and real-time interactions. To formalise such systems, it is necessary to have a notation which is able to capture both the data/algorithmic issues and the process behaviour issues in a smoothly integrated, but also highly structured and modular, manner.

Timed Communicating Object Z (TCOZ) [17] builds on the respective strengths of the Object-Z and Timed CSP notations in order to provide a single notation for modeling both the state and timed process aspects of complex systems. The notion of blending Object-Z with CSP has been suggested by Fischer, Smith and Derick [10, 24]. TCOZ is novel in that it includes timing primitives; properly separates process control and data/algorithm issues; fully integrates notions of refinement from both languages; supports the modeling of true multi-threaded concurrency; and distinguishes the notion of active and passive objects.

The basic TCOZ notation has been briefly described in an introductory paper by these authors [17] and this paper further enhances the TCOZ notation with a new network topology operator which simplifies the description of complex networks of communicating processes. However the main purpose of this paper is to demonstrate the

---

* This paper was written during the first author's visit to the CSIRO Mathematical and Information Sciences Division as part of the DSTO/CSIRO Fellowship Programme.

expressiveness of TCOZ through a case study in the specification of a real-time multi-lift system. The lift system is chosen because it is a standard case study, having been treated in a large number of specification notations including Object-Z and CSP. Developing a TCOZ version of the lift case study puts us in a good position to make qualitative assessments of the relative merits of TCOZ.

It is assumed that the reader has some familiarity with both Object-Z [7] and CSP, since the mechanics of blending the two notations is considered only briefly in Section 2. The network topology operator is introduced in Section 3 The TCOZ specification of the lift case study is presented and evaluated in Section 4 and the features of TCOZ compared to similar languages in Section 5.

2   Aspects of TCOZ

TCOZ is essentially just a blending of Object-Z and Timed CSP [21], for the most part preserving them as proper sub-languages of the blended notation. The essence of this blending is the identification of Object-Z operation specification schemas with terminating CSP processes. Thus operation schemas and CSP processes occupy the same syntactic category, operation schema expressions may appear wherever processes may appear in CSP and CSP process definitions may appear wherever operation definitions may appear in Object-Z. The primary specification structuring device in TCOZ is the Object-Z classing mechanism. In this section we briefly consider the aspects of TCOZ which help to bring the two notations together. A detailed introduction to TCOZ and its Timed CSP and Object-Z features may be found elsewhere [17].

2.1   Declaring channels

CSP channels are given an independent, first class role in TCOZ. This allows the communications and control topology of a network of objects to be designed orthogonally to their class structure. In order to support the role of CSP channels, the state schema convention is extended to allow the declaration of communication channels. If c is to be used as a communication channel by any of the operations of a class, then it must be declared in the state schema to be of type **chan**. Channels are type heterogeneous and may carry communications of any type. Contrary to the conventions adopted for internal state variables, channels are viewed as shared rather then as encapsulated entities. This is an essential consequence of their role as communications interfaces *between* objects.

2.2   A model of time

In TCOZ, all timing information is represented as real valued measurements in *seconds*. Describing time and other physical quantities in terms of standard units of measurement is an important aspect of ensuring the completeness and soundness of specifications of real-time, reactive, and hybrid systems. In order to support the use of standard units of measurement, extensions to the Z typing system suggested by Hayes and Mahony [11] are adopted. Under this convention, time quantities are represented by the type $\mathbb{R}s$, where $\mathbb{R}$ represents the real numbers and s is the SI symbol for the standard unit of time.

2.3   Guards and preconditions

A CSP operator, the state-guard, is used to *block* or *enable* execution of an operation on the basis of an object's local state. For example, the operation $[a \geq 0] \bullet [\Delta(a) \mid a \geq 0 \wedge a' = \sqrt{a}]$ will replace the state variable a with its square root if a is positive otherwise it will *deadlock*, that is be blocked from executing. The blocking or enabling of this operation is achieved by the state guard $[a \geq 0] \bullet \_$ and not by the precondition $a \geq 0$ within the operation schema. If the operation schema alone is invoked with a negative, it will *diverge* rather than block. The difference between deadlock and divergence is that a divergence may be refined away by making an operation more robust, whilst a deadlock can never be refined away.

An additional function of state guards is as a substitute for CSP's indexed external choice operator. The process $[n : \mathbb{N} \mid 0 \leq n \leq 5] \bullet c?n \rightarrow P(n)$ may input any value of n between 0 and 5 (from channel c) as chosen by its environment. CSP's indexed internal choice is replaced by the operation schema and sequential composition. The process $[n! : \mathbb{N} \mid 0 \leq n! \leq 5]; c!n \rightarrow P(n)$ may output any value of n between 0 and 5 according to its own designs.

2.4   Active and passive objects

Active objects have their own thread of control, while passive objects are controlled by other objects in a system. In TCOZ, an identifier MAIN (non-terminating process) is used to determine the behaviour of active objects of a given class [4]. The MAIN process is required to have neither input nor output parameters. If ob_1 and ob_2 are active objects of the class C, then the independent parallel composition behaviour of the two objects can be represented as $ob_1 \mid\mid\mid ob_2$, which means $ob_1.\text{MAIN} \mid\mid\mid ob_2.\text{MAIN}$

2.5   Semantics of TCOZ

A separate paper details the blended state/event process model which forms the basis for the TCOZ semantics [16]. In brief, a schema expression describes a relationship on or between process state/s, whilst a process expression describes the overall behaviour or evolution of a process. The semantic model for Z schemas consists of sets of variable *bindings*, mappings from variable names to values. One semantic model for Timed CSP processes consists of sets of tuples consisting of a *trace* (a sequence of time stamped events), a *refusal* (a record what and when events are refused by the process), and a *divergence* (a record of if and when the process diverged). The trace/refusal pair is called a *failure* and the overall model the failures/divergences model. The basic approach taken in the TCOZ semantics is to adopt this Timed CSP semantic model and to provide an interpretation of the Z semantic model in terms of failures and divergences, though two additions are required to make this possible. Firstly, a variable binding is added to represent the initial values of all the process attributes. Secondly, a new class of

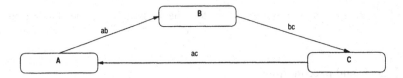

Fig. 1. Two dimensional communication topology

events, referred to as *update* events, is introduced to represent changes to the process attributes. The resulting model is called the state/failures/divergences model. The state of the process at any given time is the initial state updated by all of the updates that have occurred up to that time. If an event trace terminates (that is if a $\checkmark$ event occurs), then the state at the time of termination is called the *final* state.

The process model of an operation schema consists of all initial states and update traces (terminated with a $\checkmark$) such that the initial state and the final state satisfy the relation described by the schema. If no legal final state exists for a given initial state, the operation diverges immediately. Active classes are given a CSP semantics. Passive classes are treated as libraries of definition.

3 Complex network topologies

The syntactic structure of the CSP synchronisation operator is convenient only in the case of pipe-line like communication topologies. Expressing more complex communication topologies generally results in unacceptably complicated expressions. For example, consider the communication topology shown in Figure 1, processes A and B communicate privately through the channel ab, processes A and C communicate privately through the channel ac, and processes B and C communicate privately through the channel bc. One CSP expression for such a network communication system is

$$(A[bc'/bc]\,|[\,ab,ac\,]|\,(B[ac'/ac]\,|[\,bc\,]|\,C[ab'/ab]) \setminus ab,ac,bc)[ab,ac,bc/ab',ac',bc'].$$

The hiding and renaming is necessary in order to cover cases such as C being able to communicate on channel ab.

The above expression not only suffers from syntactic clutter, but also serves to obscure the inherently simple network topology described so elegantly by Figure 1. We believe that network topologies can be better described by adopting a notation inspired by the graph-based approach embodying in Figure 1.

A *network topology abstraction* is is an expression of the form

$$(\,\|\,\, v_1, v_2, v_3 \dots \bullet v_1 \xleftarrow{ch_{12}} v_2;\; v_2 \xleftarrow{ch_{23}} v_3;\; v_3 \xleftarrow{ch_{13}} v_1;\; \dots).$$

The variables $v_1, v_2, v_3, \dots$ are called the *formal network parameters* and the network connections

$$v_1 \xleftarrow{ch_{12}} v_2;\; v_2 \xleftarrow{ch_{23}} v_3;\; v_3 \xleftarrow{ch_{13}} v_1;\; \dots$$

are called the *formal network topology*. It describes a finite graph in which each edge or *network connection* describes a single local channel connection between processes which have the role of graph nodes. Multiple connections between processes and connections between multiple processes over a single channel are represented by multiple connection expressions. In the latter case the channel becomes a party line between the various participating processes.

A network topology abstraction describes a *network constructor*, that is a function which builds a process network using its process arguments as nodes. The above network topology describes the following constructor.

$$\lambda v_1, v_2, v_3, \ldots \bullet$$
$$(v_1[ch'_{23}/ch_{23}, \ldots] \| [ch_{12}, ch_{13}, \ldots] \|$$
$$(v_2[ch'_{13}/ch_{13}, \ldots] \| [ch_{23}, \ldots] \|$$
$$(v_3[ch'_{12}/ch_{12}, \ldots] \| [\ldots] \|$$
$$\vdots$$
$$)$$
$$)$$
$$\backslash ch_{12}, ch_{13}, ch_{23}, \ldots)[ch_{12}/ch'_{12}, ch_{13}/ch'_{13}, ch_{23}/ch'_{23}, \ldots]$$

Once again the hiding and renaming is necessary to ensure the privacy of the specified network connections.

The system in Figure 1 can be described by applying a suitable network topology abstraction to the processes *A*, *B*, and *C*.

$$(\| v_1, v_2, v_3 \bullet v_1 \xleftrightarrow{ab} v_2; \ v_2 \xleftrightarrow{bc} v_3; \ v_3 \xleftrightarrow{ac} v_1)(A, B, C)$$

The processes A, B, C are the *actual network parameters*. When the actual network parameters are all process names, the syntactic conventions are relaxed to allow the formal network topology to act in the guise of a process operator. For example, the network topology of Figure 1 may be described by the lax usage

$$\| (A \xleftrightarrow{ab} B; \ B \xleftrightarrow{bc} C; \ C \xleftrightarrow{ca} A).$$

Such usage is considered acceptable since the names representing the actual parameter can serve the dual purpose of also identifying the formal parameters. Other forms of lax usage allow network connections with common nodes to be run together, for example

$$\| (A \xleftrightarrow{ab} B \xleftrightarrow{bc} C \xleftrightarrow{ca} A),$$

and multiple channels above the arrow, for example

$$\| (A \xleftrightarrow{ab_1, ab_2} B).$$

We believe this TCOZ network topology convention to be a good candidate to be included in the basic CSP notation itself.

4   The lift case study

The multi-lift system is a standard example used to demonstrate the expressive power of various specification techniques in modeling concurrent reactive systems. People are familiar with the user requirement of a lift system, so they can concentrate on the modeling notations. However, the lift case study is not a trivial example because of the complexity caused by inherent concurrent interaction in the system [25]. We chose the specification of the lift system as the TCOZ case study also because both CSP and Object-Z have been applied to the lift system allowing a comparison to be drawn. The CSP 'lift' model [22] describes the sequences of events for the lift system well, however, it struggles to deal with the data aspects of the lift system. Furthermore, the CSP model has a flat and in places awkward structure and the communications interfaces between the lift system components (i.e. floor-buttons and lifts) are not clearly documented. The Object-Z 'lift' model [6] (a single-lift system is also modelled in Z [8]) demonstrates the power of modeling the state change of the lift system in a structured way. However, it is complicated by the need to represent process state as data and it uses a complex, centralised control-model because of the Object-Z's single thread semantics. Neither the CSP or Object-Z model addresses the real-time issues for the lift system.

Our goal for the TCOZ specification of the lift system is to provide a true multi-threaded model that captures both the data structures and the real-time reactive behaviour of the lift system.

4.1   System overview

A lift system for a building consists of multiple lifts each providing transport between the various floors of the building as dictated by the pressing of a range of service-request buttons. Inside each lift there is a panel of buttons, one for requesting travel to each of the building's floors. The panel buttons of any lift must be in one-to-one correspondence with the floor numbers. In general there are two service-request buttons on each floor, for upward and downward travel respectively, though on the first floor and the top floor there is only one button. Any service-request button can be pushed at any time. Once pushed the button is said to be *on* and it remains on until the requested service is provided. Pressing an internal button requests the lift to visit the corresponding floor. Pressing an external button requests a lift to visit the floor with the desired direction of travel. The lift controller has a queue which stores all current (external) floor requests. When a request arrives from a floor, the system will put the request at the end of the external request queue. When a lift becomes available, the controller will assign the first request of the queue to the lift for service. When visiting a floor, a lift door operates in the order of open-door, wait, then close-door. This normal process can be interrupted by a customer crossing the door as detected by some sensors.

Furthermore, the following timing properties must be captured in the model:

- lift travel time between two consequent floors is a constant, however there is a constant time delay for acceleration and braking;
- without interrupts, the lift door should be kept at the 'open' state for a fixed time period before closing.

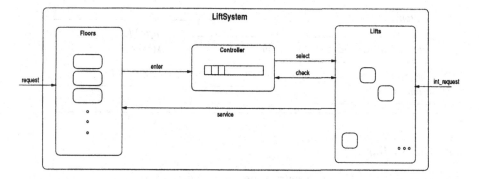

Fig. 2. Lift system communication diagram

4.2 Specification structure

The lift specification is developed in a bottom-up manner, beginning with models of basic (passive) component objects, such as 'buttons', which are then used to develop more complex (active) component objects such as 'floors' (requests), 'lifts' and a 'controller'. Then the lift system is modeled as a composite active object which allows the component objects to interact through their channels.

Figure 2 illustrates the communication interfaces between lift system components. There are three major components, the service-request panels on each floor, the lifts themselves, and the central controller which mediates service requests from the floors. External requests received by a floor on the *request* channel cause the floor's corresponding service button to be lit and the request is communicated to the controller on the *enter* channel. The button remains lit until a confirmation is received on the *service* channel. Requests received by the controller on the *enter* channel are enqueued and sent to idle lifts on the *select* channel on a first-in-first-out basis. Whenever a lift receives an internal request on the *int_request* channel, the corresponding button is lit and the requested entered into its itinerary. While the lift has local requests pending, it services them in strict order according to its current movement direction, reversing direction at the extreme floors. The behaviour of the active lifts is monitored on the *check* channel and if a request can be serviced en route it is dispatched to the lift in question and dequeued. Once the lift becomes idle, it may accept an external request on the *select* channel, move to the requested floor, and send a confirmation to the floor panel on the *service* channel.

4.3 Buttons

A basic component of the lift system is the button panel. Buttons have a common behaviour; they can be pushed 'On' by people and turned 'Off' by the system.

ButtonStatus ::= *On* | *Off*

Buttons are modeled using a simple passive class which records their current state and provides operations for turning them on and off.

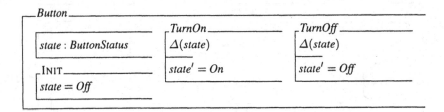

4.4 The building

Our model of the building concentrates on the behaviour of the service-request panels on each floor.

Floor panels Floors may be divided into two classes, those from which it is possible to travel upward and those from which is possible to travel downward. The *TopFloor* is a floor from which only downward travel is possible,

$$
\begin{array}{l}
\underline{\quad TopFloor\underline{\hspace{6cm}}} \\
\qquad \begin{array}{l}
\underline{\quad\quad\quad\quad\quad\quad\quad\quad\quad} \quad\quad \underline{\quad INIT\underline{\hspace{3cm}}} \\
downbutton : Button_{\textcircled{C}} \quad\quad\quad downbutton.\text{INIT} \\
num : \mathbb{N} \\
request, enter, service : \textbf{chan}
\end{array} \\
\\
PressDown \,\widehat{=}\, request?(num, Down) \rightarrow \\
\qquad [downbutton.state = Off] \bullet downbutton.TurnOn;\ enter!(num, Down) \rightarrow \text{SKIP} \\
\qquad [downbutton.state = On] \bullet \text{SKIP} \\
DownOff \,\widehat{=}\, service?(num, Down) \rightarrow downbutton.TurnOff \\
\text{MAIN} \,\widehat{=}\, \mu\,T \bullet (PressDown\ \Box\ DownOff);\ T
\end{array}
$$

and the *BottomFloor* is a floor from which only upward travel is possible.

$$
\begin{array}{l}
\underline{\quad BottomFloor\underline{\hspace{6cm}}} \\
\qquad \begin{array}{l}
\underline{\quad\quad\quad\quad\quad\quad\quad\quad\quad} \quad\quad \underline{\quad INIT\underline{\hspace{3cm}}} \\
upbutton : Button_{\textcircled{C}} \quad\quad\quad upbutton.\text{INIT} \\
num : \mathbb{N} \\
request, enter, service : \textbf{chan}
\end{array} \\
\\
PressUp \,\widehat{=}\, request?(num, Up) \rightarrow \\
\qquad [upbutton.state = Off] \bullet upbutton.TurnOn);\ enter!(num, Up) \rightarrow \text{SKIP} \\
\qquad [upbutton.state = On] \bullet \text{SKIP} \\
UpOff \,\widehat{=}\, service?(num, Up) \rightarrow upbutton.TurnOff \\
\text{MAIN} \,\widehat{=}\, \mu\,B \bullet (PressUp\ \Box\ UpOff);\ B
\end{array}
$$

A *MiddleFloor* is a floor from which both upward and downward travel is possible. Object-Z's class inheritance features are used to allow both upward and downward travel for the *MiddleFloor* class.

```
┌─MiddleFloor──────────────────────────────────────────────
│ TopFloor, BottomFloor
│ ┌──────────────────────────────────────────────────────
│ │ downbutton ≠ upbutton
│ ├──────────────────────────────────────────────────────
│ MAIN ≙ μM • (PressDown □ DownOff □ PressUp □ UpOff); M
└──────────────────────────────────────────────────────────
```

The subscript '$_©$' (object containment [3]) indicates that the button objects are contained in their corresponding floor object.

As a floor can be either top-floor or bottom-floor or middle-floor, the general type of a floor is defined as a class-union [2].

$$Floor ≙ TopFloor ∪ BottomFloor ∪ MiddleFloor$$

The building The building is modeled as an aggregate of active floor objects. Individual floors do not communicate with each other, but rather with the central controller and with the lifts. Thus the MAIN processes of the individual floor objects are combined using asynchronous composition, $_-|||_-$.

```
┌─Building─────────────────────────────────────────────────
│ ┌──────────────────────────────────────────────────────
│ │ floors : seq Floor_©
│ ├──────────────────────────────────────────────────────
│ │ ∀i : dom floors • floors(i).num = i
│ │ floors(1) ∈ BottomFloor ∧ floors(#floors) ∈ TopFloor
│ │ ∀i : (2..(#floors − 1)) • floors(i) ∈ MiddleFloor
│ ├──────────────────────────────────────────────────────
│ MAIN ≙ |||fl : dom floors • floors(fl)
└──────────────────────────────────────────────────────────
```

4.5 Lifts

A lift consists of four parts as depicted in Figure 3, a door for allowing access to and from the lift, a shaft for transporting the lift, an internal queue for determining the lift itinerary, and a controller for coordinating the behaviour of the other components. This division structures the specification in such a way as to limit the complexity of the individual components and to highlight the potential for concurrency.

Lift door control The lift door controller is treated as a separate class so as to ensure a clear description of its timing and safety properties. Under this limited aim, the class may be described entirely within the Timed CSP idiom.

The controller interfaces on a channel *servo* with a servomechanism that activates the door to open or close and on a channel *sensor* to determine when the door is open, closed, or blocked from closing. The messages that may be set on these channels are then

$$DoorMess ::= ToOpen | Opened | ToClose | Closed | Interrupt.$$

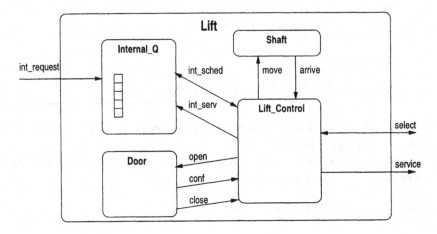

Fig. 3. Internal lift communication diagram

The timing property of the door is that once it is open, it must remain open for time period ($t_o : \mathbb{R}$s). before closing. The safety property is that if the closing of the door is blocked (as indicated by receipt of an *Interrupt* message) the door must be reopened.

The door cycle is initiated by receipt of an *open* signal from the lift controller and completed by sending a *close* signal. As soon as the door is open, a *conf* signal must be sent to the lift controller so as to indicate fulfillment of a service request.

Door

> *open, conf, close, servo, sensor* : **chan**
>
> ---
>
> *OpenDoor* $\widehat{=}$ *servo*!(*self, ToOpen*) $\rightarrow$ *sensor*?(*self, Opened*) $\rightarrow$ SKIP
> *CloseDoor* $\widehat{=}$ *servo*!(*self, ToClose*) $\rightarrow$ *sensor*?(*self, Closed*) $\rightarrow$ SKIP
> *CycleDoor* $\widehat{=}$ *OpenDoor*; *conf* $\rightarrow$
>   ($\mu CD \bullet$ WAIT t_o; *CloseDoor* $\triangledown${*sensor*?(*self, Interrupt*)} *OpenDoor*; *CD*)
> MAIN $\widehat{=}$ $\mu D \bullet$ *open* $\rightarrow$ *CycleDoor*; *close* $\rightarrow$ *D*

In the *CycleDoor* process we make use of the CSP interrupt primitive which allows an exception handling behaviour to be triggered by the occurrence of an unusual event. The normal door cycle follows the order of open-door, wait t_o, then close-door. This normal cycle can be interrupted and re-started by the event which detects a message *Interrupt* from the channel *sensor*. This message acts as an interrupt on the normal cycle and control is returned to the start of the normal cycle.

Moving the lift The essentially analog nature of the movement of the lift presents something of a modeling problem. The technique used throughout this specification has been to abstract real-world interactions as CSP events (eg the *request* and *int_request*) channels, but the movement betweens floors is by its nature a time-consuming process. We thus adopt the common technique of delimiting the period of movement by start and finish events. The start event of the movement process is a communication to the lift-shaft apparatus of the number of floors to be moved. The finish event is a communication from the lift-shaft apparatus that the lift has arrived at the destination floor. The timing properties of lift movement are described by two time constants.

$\bar{\imath} : \mathbb{R}s$	[time to move one floor Up or Down]
$delay : \mathbb{R}s$	[acceleration and braking delay]

The normal time to pass from one floor to another is $\bar{\imath}$ for each floor travelled plus a delay of *delay* caused by initial acceleration and final braking of the lift.

___Shaft_____

$move, arrive :$ **chan**

$\text{MAIN} \cong \mu S \bullet [n : \mathbb{N} \mid n \neq 0] \bullet move?n \rightarrow \text{WAIT} \mid n \mid * \bar{\imath} + delay; \; arrive \rightarrow S$

Such event based models are highly abstract and perhaps are less satisfying when applied to the complex process of moving the lift, than when applied to the more event-like process of pressing a button. However, the channel based interfaces of TCOZ processes mean that such models must be used. In their favour it must be pointed out that from the point of view of the lift controller the matters of essential interest are precisely when the movement commences and when it finishes.

Lift itinerary The itinerary of the lift is determined by the requests made by passengers using the internal floor-request panel and those dispatched from the central control. For the purposes of limiting design complexity a separate class is defined to determine the lift's internal service itinerary.

This internal queue makes use of a *panel* of buttons to communicate with passengers and to maintain a record of the floor-requests pending. A dependent state variable [5] *irs* records the set of destinations that have been selected by the passengers at any given time. This set may in turn be split into those destinations above a given floor, *ups*, and those below, *dns*. Floor services are requested on the *int_request* channel and confirmed on the *int_serv* channel. Scheduling services are requested by passing the current floor and movement direction on the *int_sched* channel.

$MoveDirection ::= Up \mid Down$

The operations of the controller are: turning the panel buttons on and off, in response to service requests and confirmations; and determining the next destination for the lift itinerary. The next destination is the first requested destination in the current direction of movement, reversing at either extremity of movement. A scheduling request is only serviced if there are pending floor-service requests.

Internal_Q

$panel : seq Button_{©}$
$int\_request, int\_sched, int\_serv :$ **chan**
Δ
$irs : \mathbb{F}\,\mathbb{N};\ ups, dns : \mathbb{N} \nrightarrow \mathbb{F}\,\mathbb{N}$

$irs = \{f : \mathrm{dom}\,panel \mid panel(f).state = On\}$
$ups = \lambda fl : \mathrm{dom}\,panel \bullet \{n : irs \mid n \geq fl\}$
$dns = \lambda fl : \mathrm{dom}\,panel \bullet \{n : irs \mid n \leq fl\}$

NextUp

$fl?, dest! : \mathrm{dom}\,panel$

$(ups(fl?) \neq \varnothing \wedge dest! = min\,ups(fl?))$
$\vee$
$(ups(fl?) = \varnothing \wedge dns(fl?) \neq \varnothing \wedge$
$dest! = max\,dns(fl?))$

NextDown

$fl?, dest! : \mathrm{dom}\,panel$

$(dns(fl?) \neq \varnothing \wedge dest! = max\,dns(fl?))$
$\vee$
$(dns(fl?) = \varnothing \wedge ups(fl?) \neq \varnothing \wedge$
$dest! = min\,ups(fl?))$

$Next \mathrel{\widehat{=}} [md? : MoveDirection \mid md? = Up] \wedge NextUp \vee$
$\qquad [md? : MoveDirection \mid md? = Down] \wedge NextDown$

$\textsc{Main} \mathrel{\widehat{=}} \mu\,IQ \bullet$
$\qquad [fl : \mathrm{dom}\,panel] \bullet int\_request?(self, fl) \to panel(fl).TurnOn;\ IQ\ \square$
$\qquad [fl : \mathrm{dom}\,panel] \bullet int\_serv?fl \to panel(fl).TurnOff;\ IQ\ \square$
$\qquad [fl : \mathrm{dom}\,panel;\ md? : MoveDirection \mid irs \neq \varnothing] \bullet$
$\qquad\qquad int\_sched?(fl, md) \to Next;\ int\_sched!dest \to IQ$

Lift controller The lift controller keeps record of the current floor and movement direction and provides the interface between the lift environment and the other lift components. The lift controller exhibits three modes of behaviour.

The lift begins at rest awaiting either a passenger destination request or a dispatch from the central controller. Any passengers inside the lift are given a period of time $(t_p : \mathbb{R}s)$ to make an internal request before the lift accepts any external requests.

The controller determines that an internal request is pending through the willingness of the internal queue to perform a scheduling transaction. Once the queue has indicated the next destination the central controller is checked to see if there is an external request from an intermediate floor. If so the lift services the external request first. If not it services the internal request: the new direction is calculated and set; the lift is moved to the new floor and the door is opened; the internal queue and the central controller are notified; and then once the door is closed, the lift returns to the rest mode.

If, after waiting t_p, an external request becomes available before any internal request: the new move direction is set; the lift is moved to the new floor and the door is opened; the floor service-request panel is notified; and then, once the door is closed, control is returned to the rest mode.

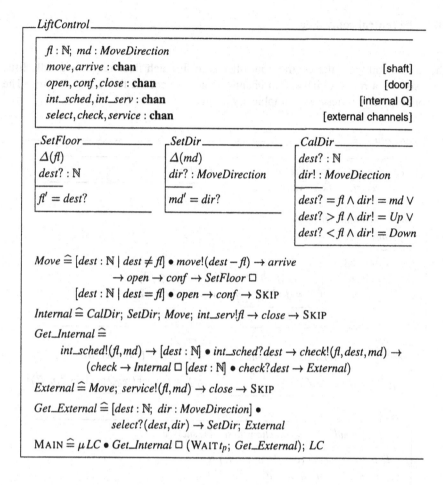

__LiftControl_____

$fl : \mathbb{N};\ md : MoveDirection$
$move, arrive : \textbf{chan}$ [shaft]
$open, conf, close : \textbf{chan}$ [door]
$int\_sched, int\_serv : \textbf{chan}$ [internal Q]
$select, check, service : \textbf{chan}$ [external channels]

__SetFloor__   __SetDir__   __CalDir__
$\Delta(fl)$ $\Delta(md)$ $dest? : \mathbb{N}$
$dest? : \mathbb{N}$ $dir? : MoveDirection$ $dir! : MoveDiection$

$fl' = dest?$ $md' = dir?$ $dest? = fl \wedge dir! = md\ \vee$
                                      $dest? > fl \wedge dir! = Up\ \vee$
                                      $dest? < fl \wedge dir! = Down$

$Move \cong [dest : \mathbb{N} \mid dest \neq fl] \bullet move!(dest - fl) \to arrive$
$\qquad\qquad \to open \to conf \to SetFloor\ \Box$
$\qquad [dest : \mathbb{N} \mid dest = fl] \bullet open \to conf \to \textsc{Skip}$

$Internal \cong CalDir;\ SetDir;\ Move;\ int\_serv!fl \to close \to \textsc{Skip}$

$Get\_Internal \cong$
$\qquad int\_sched!(fl, md) \to [dest : \mathbb{N}] \bullet int\_sched?dest \to check!(fl, dest, md) \to$
$\qquad (check \to Internal\ \Box\ [dest : \mathbb{N}] \bullet check?dest \to External)$

$External \cong Move;\ service!(fl, md) \to close \to \textsc{Skip}$

$Get\_External \cong [dest : \mathbb{N};\ dir : MoveDirection] \bullet$
$\qquad\qquad select?(dest, dir) \to SetDir;\ External$

$\textsc{Main} \cong \mu LC \bullet Get\_Internal\ \Box\ (\textsc{Wait}\, t_p;\ Get\_External);\ LC$

_____

The bank of lifts Each lift consists of a door, a shaft, and a controller.

__Lift_____

$iq : Internal\_Q_{©};\ lc : LiftControl_{©};\ s : Shaft_{©};\ d : Door_{©}$

$\textsc{Main} \cong {\parallel} (lc \xleftarrow{move, arrive} s;\ lc \xleftarrow{open, close, conf} d;\ lc \xleftarrow{int\_sched, int\_serv} iq)$

_____

The collection of all the lifts in the system is modeled as an aggregate of the individual lifts acting autonomously.

__Lifts_____

$lifts : \mathbb{P} Lift_{©}$

$\textsc{Main} \cong {\parallel\parallel\parallel}\, l : lifts$

_____

4.6   The central controller

The responsibility of the central controller is to dispatch floor requests to idle lifts. It consists of a request queue with channels that connect the floors and the lifts. The network topology is described graphically in Figure 2.

$\boxed{\begin{array}{l}
\underline{Controller}\underline{\hspace{11cm}} \\[4pt]
\boxed{\begin{array}{l}
reqQ : seq(\mathbb{N} \times MoveDirection) \\
enter, select, check, service : \mathbf{chan} \\
\Delta \\
req : \mathbb{N} \leftrightarrow MoveDirection \\
ups, dns : \mathbb{N} \times \mathbb{N} \to \mathbb{P}\,\mathbb{N} \\
\hline
req = \mathrm{ran}\, reqQ \\
\forall f_1, f_2 : \mathbb{N} \bullet ups(f_1, f_2) = \{f : \mathbb{N} \mid f\ \underline{req}\ Up \wedge f_1 \le f \le f2\} \\
\qquad\qquad dns(f_1, f_2) = \{f : \mathbb{N} \mid f\ \underline{req}\ Down \wedge f_1 \le f \le f2\}
\end{array}}
\quad
\boxed{\begin{array}{l}
\underline{\text{INIT}}\underline{\hspace{2cm}} \\
reqQ = \langle\,\rangle
\end{array}} \\[6pt]

\boxed{\begin{array}{l}
\underline{Join}\underline{\hspace{3cm}} \\
\Delta(reqQ) \\
req? : (\mathbb{N} \times MoveDirection)\ \mathbf{on}\ enter \\
\hline
reqQ' = reqQ \frown \langle req?\rangle
\end{array}}
\quad
\boxed{\begin{array}{l}
\underline{Remove}\underline{\hspace{3cm}} \\
\Delta(reqQ) \\
(dest?, md?) : \mathbb{N} \times MoveDirection \\
\hline
reqQ' = \mathrm{squash}(reqQ \rhd \{(dest?, md?)\})
\end{array}} \\[6pt]

\boxed{\begin{array}{l}
\underline{Find}\underline{\hspace{9cm}} \\
fl?, d? : \mathbb{N};\ md? : MoveDirection;\ dest! : \mathbb{N};\ suc! : \mathbb{B} \\
\hline
md? = Up \wedge suc! = (ups(fl?, d?) \ne \varnothing) \wedge \\
suc! \Rightarrow dest! = \min ups(fl?, d?) \\
\vee \\
md? = Down \wedge suc! = (dns(fl?, d?) \ne \varnothing) \wedge \\
suc! \Rightarrow dest! = \min dns(fl?, d?)
\end{array}} \\[6pt]

Dispatch \mathrel{\widehat{=}} \\
\quad [(dest, md) : \mathbb{N} \times MoveDirection \mid reqQ \ne \langle\,\rangle \wedge (dest, md) = \mathrm{head}\, reqQ] \bullet \\
\qquad select!(dest, md) \to Remove \\
CheckServ \mathrel{\widehat{=}} [fl, d : \mathbb{N};\ md : MoveDirection] \bullet check?(fl, d, md) \to Find; \\
\qquad\qquad ([suc] \bullet check!dest \to Remove \,\square\, [\neg\, suc] \bullet check \to \textsc{Skip}) \\
\textsc{Main} \mathrel{\widehat{=}} \mu\, C \bullet (Join \,\square\, Dispatch \,\square\, CheckServ);\ C
\end{array}}$

The controller receives requests from the floors and enters them into the *reqQ* queue (*Join* operation). In the ordinary case these requests are dispatched in first-in-first-out manner (*Dispatch* operation) as idle lifts become available, but if in the course of servicing internal requests a lift can visit a floor whilst moving in the floor required direction, the request is removed from the queue (*CheckServ* operation).

4.7   The lift system

The lift system consists of the floors of the building, the bank of lifts and the central controller. The number of floor-service buttons in each lift must be exactly the number of floors in the building.

```
┌─LiftSystem────────────────────────────────────────────────
│ ┌─────────────────────────────────────────────────────────
│ │ bd : Building; ls : Lifts; contr : Controller
│ ├─────────────────────────────────────────────────────────
│ │ ∀ l : ls.lifts • #l.iq.panel = #bd.floors
│ │
│ │ MAIN ≘ ‖ (bd ←^enter→ contr ←^select,check→ ls ←^service→ bd)
└─┴─────────────────────────────────────────────────────────
```

The lift system behaviour MAIN describes the communication channels between the independent concurrently executing system components: the lifts, the floors, and the controller. The floors communicate service requests to the controller through the *enter* channel, the controller dispatches these requests to the lifts through the *select* and *check* channels, and the lifts indicate successful servicing of requests to the floors through the *service* channel.

4.8   Discussion

The application of TCOZ to the multi-lift system has been convincingly successful, despite the relatively modest real-time aspects of the specification. The powerful combination of object-oriented structuring, data modeling, and process modeling features available in TCOZ has allowed the clean presentation of an ambitiously detailed (when compared to versions described in other languages) treatment of the multi-lift system. This strongly supports our claims that TCOZ represents a highly scalable and reusable method for describing real-time and concurrent systems. As an example, consider modifying the specification so as to allow 'opportunistic' servicing of requests entered after a lift starts moving. The modular nature of the specification immediately draws attention to the *Shaft* class which controls the movement of the lift between floors. The interface of this class needs to be expanded to include events to indicate the lift is approaching the next floor and to stop the lift at the next floor. Armed with these additional controls the *LiftControl* class can easily be modified to react opportunistically to new service requests.

One surprise in the development of the TCOZ lift was the degree to which the process model idiom came to dominate. The starting point of the development had been a data oriented standard Object-Z specification [6]. Rather than being a simple matter of adding real-time and concurrent features to the existing specification it soon became clear that much of its 'data' was in fact being used to represent 'process' behaviour which could be more elegantly represented using the CSP process modeling features of TCOZ. The final approach adopted was to model the system primarily as a network of communicating processes and to make use of Object-Z's data modeling features to simplify and structure the specification by abstracting away from algorithmic specifics and reusing common data components such as buttons.

A perceived weakness of the TCOZ approach was identified in its handling of the interface between TCOZ processes and the real world. Although the abstraction of button presses as communications on external channels is reasonably acceptable, the inability to describe 'continuously' changing aspects of the system such as 'lift position' is particularly disturbing. Whilst modeling the moving process by start and finish events provides an adequate interface to the TCOZ specification it goes no way at all toward ensuring that lift shaft satisfies our informal intuitions as to its behaviour. The specification is thus strictly speaking not of a system for moving people between floors of a building, but rather simply a description of a method of controlling such a system in a satisfactory manner.

One advantage of choosing the lift system to exercise the TCOZ language is the availability of existing lift specifications in both CSP [22] and Object-Z [6]. Apart from the ability of TCOZ to describe timing aspects not addressed by either of these specifications, such as the correct behaviour of the door opening cycle, TCOZ represents an improvement in expressibility, modularity, and reusability over both existing specifications.

The CSP 'lift' model [22] is similar in spirit to the TCOZ lift presented here, except that it does not consider the door cycle nor the movement of the lift. However, in contrast to the highly modular approach of the TCOZ specification, the CSP version is forced to adopt a quite flat structure because the only structuring facility available is the process definition. The channel interface declarations and the network topology operator provide valuable information to the reader of the TCOZ specification regarding the source and destination of communications, which is not available to the reader of the CSP specification. Although some attempt is made to structure the CSP specification document through the use of section headings to distinguish system components, the essentially global nature of all process definitions and communication channels makes it difficult to comprehend individual process definitions without extensive reference to the rest of the specification. The standard CSP synchronisation operator ($_- \parallel _-$) is a particular point of weakness as it offers no visual feedback as to the interface between network components. The use of the network topology operator (and associated diagrams) is a particular strength of the TCOZ specification.

The weaknesses in CSP's treatment of data and algorithms not only adds syntactic clutter to the CSP lift, but also appears to influence the structure of the specification. In particular, the difficulty in abstracting various calculations away from the specific direction of travel results in a 'split' specification, with many features being repeated for both the 'up' and 'down' directions of travel. For example, the specification of a single lift [22, p 26] includes subprocesses $Lift(f, up)$ and $Lift(f, down)$ which differ primarily in the method of calculating the next floor on the itinerary. In contrast the TCOZ version abstracts this calculation into the *Next* operation of the *Internal_Q* class allowing the description of the lift's gross behaviour to be independent of the direction of travel, even despite using a more complex method of determining the itinerary. Although a specification of this form is possible in CSP, the lack of strong, modular data modeling facilities acts as a strong disincentive to this form of abstraction.

The Object-Z 'lift' model [6] provided a structured and reusable model and was able to describe the sequence of state changes of the overall lift system. However, Object-

Z's rudimentary operational semantics forces the specification to include extra data for describing process state and all system components to be viewed passively (except the lift system class) which leads to a complex, centralised control-model. The lift components, such as the shaft and the door, were abstractively modeled as internal state components (rather than component objects) of the lift. The system class *LiftSystem* [6, pages 146–147] became very complex (and lengthy) because the global ordering of synchronisations between lifts, floor requests and request queue must be explicitly determined. In the TCOZ model only the local ordering of these events need be specified, the global ordering is implicit in the CSP event synchronisation model. In addition, the TCOZ model gives the freedom of viewing the lift system components as active entities allowing a more natural, modular, and reusable description of the lift system.

5   Related work

The expressiveness of the integrated notation TCOZ (Timed CSP + Object-Z) has been demonstrated through the lift case study in Section 4. The basis for the successful blending of the two notations is the duality between state transition semantics and event semantics. This has long been recognised [12, 14, 19] and has undoubtedly helped shape the development of Object-Z's behavioural semantics. Perhaps the most mature formalism based on this duality is Butler's blending of CSP with Back's Action Systems [1]. An important lesson from this work is the need to distinguish strongly between the notions of guard and precondition in the state-transition view. The failure to do so in Object-Z has made it impossible to reconcile algorithmic refinement with the default behavioural semantics, greatly reducing the value of refinement in Object-Z. The adoption of a distinct notion of state guards in TCOZ makes possible a full blending of Z-style algorithm and CSP-style process refinement.

The notion of blending the untimed CSP and Object-Z has been proposed independently by Fischer [9] and Smith [23]. Both take the approach of identifying the notion of channel with that of operation and operation invocations with atomic communications of both inputs and outputs. The latter prevents the modeling of timing and concurrency at the operation level and complicates the CSP semantics through the mixing of elements of external (inputs) and internal (outputs) choice in a single event. The former is undesirable from a theoretical standpoint because it confuses communications interfaces which are essentially process related attributes with algorithmic structures which are essentially data related attributes. An object's communications interface should be determined by high-level considerations of the overall system structure, whilst the operational interface should be determined by consideration of the internal data structures. The purpose of the class envelope is to resolve such tensions locally, not to propagate them up and down the design hierarchy. The practical consequences of the identification of channel and operation is the promotion of both high degrees of coupling between classes and unnatural class structures. Neither formalism makes a complete distinction between preconditions, guards, and operations and consequently refinement issues are complicated in both. Smith adopts a semantics which is unable to model process divergence and as a consequence must identify preconditions with guards, making process and algorithmic refinement incompatible. The semantics adopted by Fischer does allow a distinction between guards and preconditions, but guards are tightly coupled with operations so that the same operation may not be used in differing circumstances as is the *Remove* operation in the *Controller* class on p.321. Moreover, a convention is introduced whereby when an operation guard is not explicitly defined the precondition is used by default, thus complicating both the understanding of the process behaviour and the refinement of the operation. Issues, such as real-time and the distinction between active and passive objects, are not addressed by either formalism.

More generally, the need for specification notations capable of addressing both data/algorithmic issues and process control issues is now widely recognised. Several notations now exist aimed at bridging this divide. These fall essentially into two classes, those that adopt a process-algebra/event-based style (LOTOS, ESTEREL, RAISE) and those that adopt a transition system style (UNITY, Action Systems, TLA). Since it is closest in spirit to TCOZ, we briefly consider the relationship between TCOZ and the real-time extension to LOTOS, E-LOTOS [13].

The LOTOS specification language is very similar in approach to TCOZ, blending CSP-like process primitives with an algebraic-style data-specification language. E-LOTOS [13] is a recently developed real-time extension to LOTOS. The process and real-time primitives of E-LOTOS are influenced by Timed-CSP, therefore these aspects of E-LOTOS are similar to TCOZ. The primary difference lies in the data modeling and structuring aspects of the two formalisms. The data modeling language of E-LOTUS is equational algebra based, whilst TCOZ is model based. The module construct of E-LOTOS is similar to the class construct of TCOZ in that it can encapsulate states and operations. Modules can be reused via the *imports* mechanism which is similar to the class inheritance. However E-LOTOS modules cannot be instantiated as a type, while TCOZ classes can. Therefore, the notions of object and composition of objects (aggregation) are missing from E-LOTOS. In TCOZ this adds another dimension of potential for reuse of specifications. E-LOTOS's subtyping is a simple record-type extension mechanism which is less powerful than the TCOZ's polymorphic typing (inheritance hierarchy and class union).

6   Conclusions and further work

Timed CSP and Object-Z complement each other not only in their expressive capabilities, but also in their underlying semantics. In addition, the object oriented flavour of Object-Z provides an ideal foundation for promoting modularity and separation of concerns in system design. The combination of the two, TCOZ, treats data and algorithmic concerns in the Object-Z style and treats process control and communication concerns in the CSP style. Timing concerns are distributed according to their status as relating to algorithm or control. The notion of active and passive objects are clearly distinguished in TCOZ model.

This powerful modeling combination, TCOZ, has been successfully applied to a comprehensive case study on specifying a real-time multi-lift system. In comparison to the CSP model [22] and the standard Object-Z model [6] of the lift system, the TCOZ model not only captures the complex system state and behaviour, but also captured the true concurrent real-time interactions between various system components of the lift system. The lift case study also provides feedback to the development of TCOZ. For example, the development of the modeling notation for complex network topologies is motivated by the lift case study. A particular weakness of the language has been identified in its ability interface with 'real-world' aspects of a system. This clearly limits the applicability of the notation to the software aspects of a system. Future work will be directed toward improving its capabilities in this direction so as to integrate it into a more holistic approach to real-time and embedded systems design. One promising approach is to enhance TCOZ with features of the Timed Refinement Calculus [15, 18] which allow convincing descriptions of continuously varying real-world observables.

TCOZ preserves in large part both the syntax and semantics of the individual notations and hence can potentially benefit from the large body of experience developed in the use of and tool support for the individual notations and their parents, such as verification and refinement techniques and tools, model checkers, etc.. Additional planned work includes developing refinement rules for the TCOZ specification language based on existing Z and CSP refinement systems. Schneider has described a system for capturing and verifying abstract temporal requirements of Timed CSP processes [20], it is hoped that this might also form a valuable addition to the TCOZ notation.

Acknowledgements

We would like to thank John Colton, Ian Hayes, Keith Gallagher and anonymous referees for many useful comments. This work is supported in part by the DSTO/CSIRO Fellowship programme.

References

1. R. J. R. Back and J. von Wright. Refinement calculus, part II: Parallel and reactive programs. In J. W. de Bakker, W.-P. de Roever, and G. Rozenberg, editors, *Stepwise Refinement of Distributed Systems: Models, Formalism, Correctness*, volume 430 of *Lecture Notes in Computer Science*, pages 42–66. Springer-Verlag, 1990.
2. J.S. Dong. Living with free type and class union. In *Proc. 1995 Asia-Pacific Software Engineering Conference (APSEC'95)*, pages 304–312. IEEE Computer Society Press, December 1995.
3. J.S. Dong and R. Duke. The geometry of object containment. *Object-Oriented Systems*, 2(1):41–63, March 1995.
4. J.S. Dong and B. Mahony. Active Objects in TCOZ. In *Proc. 2nd IEEE International Conference on Formal Engineering Methods (ICFEM'98)*. IEEE Computer Society Press, December 1998. To appear.
5. J.S. Dong, G. Rose, and R. Duke. The role of secondary attributes in formal object modelling. In A. Stoyenko, editor, *Proc. 1st IEEE International Conference on Engineering Complex Computer Systems (ICECCS'95)*, pages 31–38, Florida, USA, November 1995. IEEE Computer Society Press.
6. J.S. Dong, L. Zucconi, and R. Duke. Specifying parallel and distributed systems in Object-Z. In G. Agha and S. Russo, editors, *Proc. 2nd International Workshop on Software Engineering for Parallel and Distributed Systems*, pages 140–149, Boston, Massachusetts, USA, 1997. IEEE Computer Society Press.

7. R. Duke, G. Rose, and G. Smith. Object-Z: a specification language advocated for the description of standards. *Computer Standards and Interfaces*, 17:511–533, 1995.
8. A. Evans. Specifying & verifying concurrent systems using Z. In M. Naftalin, T. Denvir, and M. Bertran, editors, *FME '94: Industrial Benefit of Formal Methods*, volume 873 of *Lecture Notes in COmputer SCience*, pages 366–400. Springer-Verlag, 1994.
9. C. Fischer. CSP-OZ: A combination of Object-Z and CSP. In H. Bowmann and J. Derrick, editors, *Formal Methods for Open Object-Based Distributed Systems (FMOODS '97)*, volume 2, pages 423–438. Chapman & Hall, 1997.
10. C. Fisher and G. Smith. Combining CSP and Object-Z: Finite or Infinite Trace Semantics? In *IFIP International Conference on Formal Description Techniques and Protocal Specification, Testing and Verification*, pages 503–518. Chapman & Hall, November 1997.
11. I. J. Hayes and B. P. Mahony. Using units of measurement in formal specifications. *Formal Aspects of Computing*, 7(3), 1995.
12. He Jifeng. Process simulation and refinement. *Formal Aspects of Computing*, 1(3):229–241, 1989.
13. ISO. SC21/WG7 Working Draft on Enhancements to LOTOS. ISO Working Group 7, December 1997.
14. M. B. Josephs. A state-based approach to communicating processes. *Distributed Computing*, 3:9–18, 1988.
15. B. P. Mahony. Networks of predicate transformers. Technical Report 95-05, Software Verification Research Centre, Department of Computer Science, The University of Queensland, St. Lucia, Queensland 4072, Australia, February 1995.
16. B. P. Mahony and J.S. Dong. The semantics of TCOZ. Technical Report 97-24, Mathematical and Information Sciences, Commonwealth Scientific and Industrial Research Organisation (CSIRO), Australia, 1997.
17. B. P. Mahony and J.S. Dong. Blending Object-Z and Timed CSP: An introduction to TCOZ. In *Proc. 20th International Conference on Software Engineering (ICSE'98)*, pages 95–104. IEEE Computer Society Press, April 1998.
18. B. P. Mahony and I. J. Hayes. A case-study in timed refinement: A mine pump. *IEEE Transactions on Software Engineering*, 18(9):817–826, 1992.
19. C. C. Morgan. Of wp and CSP. In W. H. J. Feijen et al., editors, *Beauty is our Business: A Birthday Salute to Edsger W. Dijkstra*, pages 319–326. Springer-Verlag, 1989.
20. S. Schneider. *Correctness and Communication in Real-Time Systems*. PhD thesis, Oxford University Computing Laboratory, Programming Research Group, 1990. Available as Technical Monograph PRG-84.
21. S. Schneider and J. Davies. A brief history of Timed CSP. *Theoretical Computer Science*, 138, 1995.
22. M. D. Schwartz and N. M. Delisle. Specifying a lift control system with CSP. In *Proc. 4th IEEE International Workshop on Software Specification and Design (IWSSD'87)*, pages 21–27, Monterey, California, April 1987. IEEE Computer Society Press.
23. G. Smith. A semantic integration of Object-Z and CSP for the specification of concurrent systems. In J. Fitzgerald, C. B. Jones, and P. Lucas, editors, *FME '97: Industrial Applications and Strengthened Foundations of Formal Methods*, volume 1313 of *Lecture Notes in Computer Science*. Springer-Verlag, 1997.
24. G. Smith and J. Derick. Refinement and verification of concurrent systems specified in Object-Z and CSP. In *Proc. IEEE International Conference on Formal Engineering Methods (ICFEM'97)*, pages 293–302, Hiroshima, Japan, November 1997. IEEE Computer Society Press.
25. J. C. P. Woodcock, S. King, and I. H. Sørensen. Mathematics for specification and design: The problem with lifts. In *Proc. 4th IEEE International Workshop on Software Specification and Design (IWSSD'87)*, pages 265–268. IEEE Computer Society Press, 1987.

Object-Oriented Specification of Hybrid Systems Using UML^h and ZimOO

Viktor Friesen[1], André Nordwig[1], and Matthias Weber[2]

[1] Technische Universität Berlin, FB 13, Sekr. FR 5-6
Franklinstraße 28/29, D-10587 Berlin, Germany
Tel: +49-30-314-23859
Email: {friesen,nordwig}@cs.tu-berlin.de

[2] Daimler-Benz AG, Research and Technology
Alt-Moabit 96a, D-10559 Berlin
Tel: +49-30-39982-248
Email: Weber@DBAG.Bln.DaimlerBenz.Com

Abstract. In this paper, we present an object-oriented approach to the specification of hybrid systems using a combination of a graphical design notation and a formal specification language. In particular, we use UML^h, a variant of UML for hybrid systems, to graphically describe the objects and associations of hybrid system models, and we use ZimOO, a variant of Object-Z for hybrid systems, for the precise and complete specification of hybrid systems. We introduce the main concepts of UML^h and ZimOO, describe a support tool, and look at their application for the design of a steam-boiler system.

1 Introduction

Hybrid systems are networks of components with discrete and continuous behavior. Typical examples of hybrid systems are physical processes along with their discrete controllers. In this paper, we present an object-oriented approach to the specification of hybrid systems using a combination of a graphical design notation and a formal specification language.

We use a graphical notation for modeling the objects and associations of hybrid systems, which is based on UML (*Unified Modeling Language* [26]). This notation is called *UML^h (hybrid UML)*. UML is becoming a quasi standard in the OOD of discrete systems. It standardizes and integrates many popular notations of OOD, including class diagrams, use-case diagrams, collaboration diagrams, and Statecharts. UML^h is still limited to class diagrams, but it is planned to extend it, adapting and integrating other UML concepts for hybrid systems. Furthermore, initial work has been done to develop a design methodology based on UML^h [17].

The main extension of UML^h w.r.t. UML concerns the class diagrams. UML provides only one general notation for a class. As different specification means are needed to describe discrete or continuous behavior (a method is really something quite different from a differential equation), we are convinced that – even at the design level – different notations are needed for discrete and continuous classes. UML^h therefore provides notations for three different kinds of classes: discrete, continuous, and hybrid[1].

In combination with UML^h we use ZimOO, a variant of Object-Z for hybrid systems, for the precise and complete specification of hybrid systems. The present status of ZimOO is described in [14]. In this paper, we use ZimOO as the target language for UML^h; in fact, ZimOO itself was used as a basis for the development of UML^h. However, UML^h could, in principle, also be used in combination with other object-oriented (specification or simulation) languages for hybrid system modeling.

Before turning to the detailed description of UML^h and ZimOO and their application, we would like to make some more general remarks about hybrid system modeling and analysis, and explain how our approach fits into the global process of simulation development for hybrid systems.

As hybrid systems are often involved in safety-critical applications, their analysis plays an important role in current research. Three major analysis strategies can be identified: verification, testing, and simulation. Recently, numerous formalisms have been developed for the precise specification of the behavior of hybrid systems; typical examples are Hybrid Automata [2], Extended Duration Calculus [6], and Hybrid CSP [19]. Most of these formalisms are designed to support formal verification. But there is a fundamental problem with the formal verification of hybrid systems: the majority of such systems are not analytically tractable, only for some special types of (in)equation systems do there exist closed solutions and are algorithms known specifying how these solutions can be found. Hence, formal verification can succeed only for a few special types of problems. On the other hand, systematic testing of a hybrid system using physical prototypes or even a real environment is very expensive. Moreover, errors found during unit or integration testing are very expensive to fix. In the case of safety-critical systems, the resources needed for (regression) testing may account for more than 2/3 of the overall development budget. Simulation is therefore an essential analysis method for hybrid systems, especially if it can help to identify errors at an early stage.

The complexity of applications involving hybrid systems continues to grow rapidly. Powerful structuring means are therefore needed to describe such systems. This is one of the reasons why recently proposed simulation languages like Omola [3], Dymola [9], Smile [20], or Modelica [10] all incorporate object-oriented structuring concepts. Another advantage of the object-oriented paradigm is the adequacy of modeling physical components as objects, which leads to model components that are more reusable. The software engineering group at the TU Berlin has proposed an integrated approach to the development of object-oriented simulations of hybrid systems [4]. The main idea behind this approach is to adapt the conventional software-development process to the simulation development. Here we distinguish three main activities: design, model specification, and implementation (Figure 1). The results of these activities are a set of structure diagrams in UML^h, a precise and complete description of the behavioral model (ZimOO specification), and a model in an executable simulation language (Smile model description), respectively. For the last two phases, we use the object-oriented specification language ZimOO [13] and the simulation language Smile [20]. The interplay

---

[1] UML^h also supports so-called *abstract* classes, which are a generalization of the three "concrete" kinds of classes. This notion will be explained later.

between these last two development phases was described in [4]. Hence, in this paper, we concentrate on the first two phases.

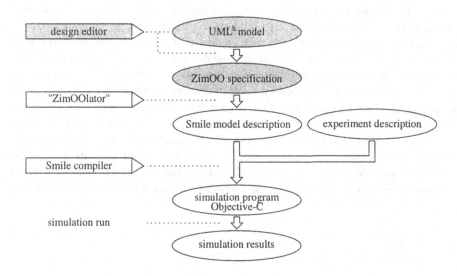

Fig. 1. Structure of object-oriented simulation development

The paper is organized as follows. In Section 2, we introduce the UML^h notation, explaining in particular the different kinds of classes and the relations between them. Section 3 introduces the specification language ZimOO and explains basic aspects of its formal semantics. In Section 4, we demonstrate the applicability of the proposed approach by specifying a small section of a steam-boiler system [1]. A graphical editor for UML^h and ZimOO specifications is described in Section 5. Some concluding remarks are given in Section 6.

2   UML^h – A Graphical Design Notation for Hybrid Systems

Object-oriented design languages and methods are becoming increasingly important. They prove very helpful in managing the high complexity of the software-development process. Although practically every OOD book contains numerous descriptive examples urging the reader to view the real world as a collection of objects, a closer look at conventional OOD notations reveals that, while they are very well suited for object-oriented software development, they are only of limited suitability for the development of technical systems with discrete behavior, and they are completely inadequate when dealing with physical systems exhibiting continuous behavior. The reason for this deficiency is quite simple: the object descriptions are based on two key concepts – *attributes* describing the state of the object, and *methods (operations)* allowing this state to be updated at certain discrete points in time. It is obvious that neither the continuous behavior of physical components nor the "continuous communication" between such components can be properly described using these concepts.

At the beginning of our project, there was no suitable graphical notation for hybrid systems. A new notation, UML^h, was therefore developed. As mentioned above, this notation is based on the Unified Modeling Language (UML) [26], thus ensuring compatibility with well-known methods. This modeling language comes with a wide variety of concepts for building complex discrete applications. Since hybrid systems are also characterized by a high complexity it is advantageous to work in these concepts into UML^h. At this stage we concentrate on the class diagrams which are a reasonable foundation for further extensions such as collaboration diagrams or Statecharts. The requirements for such a notation were obtained by abstraction from specification languages for hybrid systems. The main purpose of the language to developed is to support early phases of hybrid system's development. So it should be abstract enought to identify key components of the system without the need of exact specifications of their behaviors. Later, it should be possible to enrich the model by setting up constraints on its artifacts. So a smooth transition from UML^h to ZimOO becomes possible. The results of the above mentioned analysis are the language concepts discussed in the following subsections.

2.1 Classes

To begin with, we should point out some semantic differences between conventional discrete artifacts and hybrid ones. This is important because we use a taxonomy similar to that of discrete models.

As in conventional object-oriented models, the *class* is the key concept of UML^h. A class defines the structure and behavior of a set of *objects*. In hybrid systems, both are found: discrete objects and objects characterized by continuous behavior. We therefore distinguish between discrete, continuous, and hybrid classes. This is a special interpretation of the stereotypes in UML. There it is used to informally distinguish different types of classes. The latter have a special semantics; they model hybrid objects, which serve to combine discrete and continuous objects. Figure 2 shows the graphical representations of these classes.

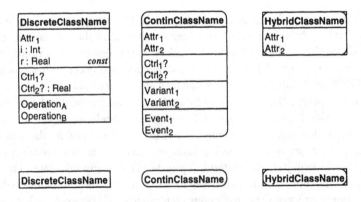

Fig. 2. Notation of classes (top: expanded, bottom: collapsed)

Nontrivial classes may have large extensions, so it is useful to give a collapsed representation as shown at the bottom of Figure 2.

Discrete classes can be used to model discrete behavior, which is typically found in controllers. They are represented by rectangles, including a *name* and sets of *attributes*, *control variables*, and *operations*. *Names* are used to identify the classes throughout the model; they have a global scope.

The set of *attributes* together with their appropriate types defines the state space of the class. Each attribute may be complemented by an *extension* **const** or **state**, indicating whether the attribute's value is constant or not. Owing to the communication mechanism between objects, which is discussed later, there is no need for read permissions. Thus, all system objects have read access to the attributes.

The *control variables* are part of the class interface. They provide ports that are used for an asynchronous exchange of values between objects. The receiving "inner" discrete object has only read access to the control variables. Their values are changed by other "outer" objects. Control variables are used for modeling sensor coupling between continuous and discrete components. It is important to separate control variables from state variables, otherwise external events could potentially violate the class invariant. Control variables are decorated by the suffix "?"; this is influenced by Z and ZimOO, which is based on the Z notation. But there is an important semantic difference. As discussed below, there is no need to provide parameters for operations of discrete classes. Instead, the control variables are implicit parameters for all operations of the object. Moreover, as explained below, control variables serve to trigger operations.

Operations change the state of a discrete object by changing the values of its state variables. In our approach, discrete objects are independent parallel components that can be externally controlled by *control variables* only, operations are therefore called from the object itself. As soon as the precondition of an operation is met, it is executed immediately. Obviously, such preconditions depend essentially on the values of the control variables.

Continuous classes can be used to model components with continuous behavior. The rounded corners of their shapes illustrate the smooth state trajectory. A continuous class is described by a (global) *name* and sets of *attributes*, *control variables*, *variants*, and (internal) *events*.

In continuous classes, *attributes* and *control variables* play the same sort of role as in discrete classes. The attributes define the state space of the class, the control variables being interpreted as ports which can be used to pass information to a continuous object in order to influence its behavior. Thus, control variables can be viewed here as interfaces to actuators.

Variants can be viewed as higher-level states of a continuous class. They should be used to describe a finite partitioning of the set of valuations of the attributes and the control variables. An example of such a partition are the three different submodels (ice, liquid, steam) for water, depending on the temperature.

It is often necessary to model jumps (discontinuities) in the otherwise continuous trajectories of state variables. Thus, *events*, which may effect such jumps, are also provided in the last section of the continuous class shape.

Hybrid classes are used for coupling discrete and continuous classes. Hybrid objects link control variables to their associated attributes. This requires a referencing scheme for all the objects involved. These object references appear as attributes of hybrid classes. It also requires the conversion of continuous to discrete values and vice versa. Here we use the semantics of actuators and sensor coupling introduced in ZimOO [14].

A hybrid class is represented by a mixed box shape symbolizing its "hybrid" character.

Abstract classes are intended to support the early stages of design. They are used for structuring the overall system in manageable components. Their introduction can be motivated as follows.

If a system has to be decomposed, there is often uncertainty about the proper classification of the identified artifacts. As a rule, an immediate classification at this stage is impossible because of the lack of knowledge about the nature of associated components. Thus, the identified components are modeled as *abstract classes*. Their only property is a unique *name*.

In later design phases, depending on the specific context, all abstract classes are replaced by one of the three class types mentioned above. The system model is therefore in a consistent valid state throughout the design process.

The diagram below shows the notation of abstract classes. The broken corners indicate the temporary nature of this nonconcrete kind of class.

[AbstractClassName]

2.2 Relations

Relations are used to model the cooperation between identified components. The current version of UML^h supports three kinds of relations: association, inheritance, and aggregation.

Associations are used to substructure the hybrid system at an early stage. First, a relation between classes can be identified using a very general name. Then, depending on its specific context, this will be implemented as inheritance or aggregation in later design phases. In UML^h, then, associations are temporary design artifacts.

As in conventional object-oriented models, they are represented by a line drawn between the relevant classes. Decorations like cardinalities or names specify their semantics. Currently, only binary associations are used. Figure 3 gives an example in which two up to five valves cooperate with one controller.

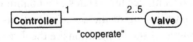

Fig. 3. Association

Inheritance is used to structure the model hierarchically as in conventional object-oriented models. This kind of relation is illustrated by a long hollow-tipped arrow pointing from the subclass to the superclass (Figure 4).

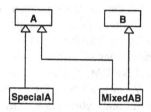

Fig. 4. Inheritance

It is useful to allow multiple inheritance because e.g. physical properties encapsulated by continuous classes could be reused by inheritance without referencing separate objects to create a new class behavior. Owing to the different semantics of the classes introduced above, only classes of the same kind can have inheritance relations. Because of their abstract nature, only abstract classes can be used in inheritance relations with all other classes.

Aggregation is used to model containment relations between objects. Though using the same notation (Figure 5) as conventional object-oriented design notations, this relation has a different quality in UML[h] because there is no communication in the sense of operation calls. Aggregation is used instead to symbolize the coupling between corresponding control variables and attributes of the classes involved.

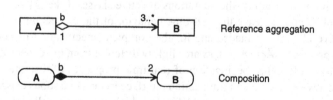

Fig. 5. Aggregation

In this context, it is necessary to allow both kind of aggregations, i.e. reference aggregation and composition. While discrete and hybrid objects use reference aggregation due to their self-sufficient character, continuous classes use composition instead. This is obvious since the coupling of continuous objects decisively influences their individual behaviors.

3   ZimOO – A Formal Specification Language for Hybrid Systems

The main motivation for the development of ZimOO was the need to describe models for the dynamic simulation of complex energy systems in a readable and abstract but formal style. Investigation of the models to be simulated shows that nearly all of them are hybrid in nature. Hence, the application domain of ZimOO has changed from dynamic simulation models to the more general area of hybrid systems [23, 24].

The present status of ZimOO is described in [14]. ZimOO is an extended subset of Object-Z [7] allowing descriptions of discrete and continuous features of a system in a common formalism. Like UML^h, ZimOO supports three different kinds of classes: discrete (as in Object-Z, enriched by a few constructs for the specification of real-time properties), continuous, and hybrid classes. In ZimOO, discrete classes can inherit only from discrete classes, continuous only from continuous classes, and hybrid only from hybrid classes. Hybrid classes are created by introducing discrete and continuous object-valued variables. The information interchange between discrete and continuous objects is realized by *control variables* which transfer data from the discrete to the continuous world and vice versa.

A clear distinction between discrete and continuous classes is important in order to treat the different aspects of a system adequately. This enables the system to be structured better, and suitable well-known formalisms can be used to describe, analyze, and refine the different parts of the system. Hybrid classes form the bridge between the continuous and the discrete world.

A ZimOO specification consists of two parts: a *Z-part* containing the definitions of auxiliary functions and predicates which can be used in the discrete, continuous, and hybrid classes that constitute the *model part* of the specification.

3.1   Discrete Classes

Discrete ZimOO classes serve to specify discrete components of hybrid systems. ZimOO distinguishes between *passive* and *active* discrete classes. The former are equivalent to Object-Z classes (with value semantics). They are used primarily to structure the state space and to decompose the operations of active classes. Like classes in Object-Z, passive ZimOO classes leave the real-time behavior of the objects unspecified. Obviously, passive classes are inadequate for the complete specification of controllers of continuous processes. *Active classes* are slightly different from the Object-Z classes. In particular, they allow the specification of real-time properties of discrete components and provide a well-defined communication interface to the continuous classes. The rest of this paper focuses on active discrete classes, which are simply called *discrete*.

To illustrate the differences between discrete ZimOO and Object-Z classes we use the following example. The class *Controller* is a specification of a simple two-point switch. The constants θ_{min} and θ_{max} and the state variable *switch* are introduced in an axiomatic definition and a state schema, like in Object-Z. Operations in discrete ZimOO classes do not contain any input variables; they are replaced by *control variables* collected in the *PORT* schema of a class. The control variables are viewed not as data placeholders belonging to a single operation, but as signal channels belonging to the whole class. Thus, *all* operations depend on the same set of control variables. The *PORT* schema of *Controller* declares the control variable *val?*. The operations in ZimOO correspond to the operations in Object-Z, extended by Fidge's duration specification [11, 12]. (Fidge's notation assumes a distinguished variable Δ_t denoting the execution duration of an operation. Its value can be constrained in the operation's axiomatic part.) The intuitive meaning of the controller is very simple. At every time point in the underlying discrete time domain, the control variable *val?* represents some value, which is "continuously" updated from the outside. If *val?* falls below θ_{min}, *On* is immediately executed, and *switch* is set to 1. The execution lasts one time unit. If *val?* exceeds θ_{max}, *Off* is executed, setting *switch* to 0.

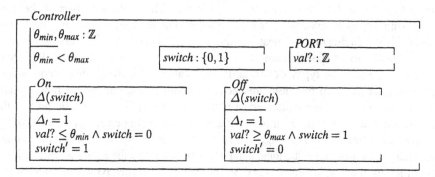

The behavior of discrete classes is generally triggered by control variables in the following way. If the precondition of one of the operations is fulfilled, this operation is *immediately* executed. If several operations are enabled, the choice is nondeterministic (it being assumed that one operation at most can be in execution at the same time point). The "suspended" operations are not queued, and the preconditions of all operations are checked again once the execution of an operation terminates. The execution duration of an operation may be zero (this is actually the default duration when Δ_t does not occur in an operation).

In addition to specifying of operation durations with Δ_t, ZimOO provides the Π-operator, allowing the minimal time distance between two executions of the same operation to be specified. This constraint can be expressed by placing a conjunction such as $\Pi(op_1) \wedge \ldots \wedge \Pi(op_n)$ in the class just below the last operation. An example of the use of the Π-operator can be found in the *HeatController* specification in Sec. 4 (Figure 9). The formal semantics of discrete classes is described in [14].

3.2 Continuous Classes

Continuous ZimOO classes are normally used to describe the continuous environment of discrete components, i.e. the processes controlled by them. Continuous classes are a real extension of Object-Z with a similar class structure but a completely different semantics. Let us first consider a small specification describing the temperature curve in a heated room [25].

┌─ *Temperature* ───┐
│   │
│ ┌─────────────────────┐   ┌──────────────────────────────┐ │
│ │   │   │ $\theta : CONT$ │ │
│ │ $h_{on}, h_{off} : \mathbb{R}$ │ $heat? : STEP\{0,1\}$ │ │
│ │ $K_{on}, K_{off} : \mathbb{R}_{>0}$ ├──────────────────────┤ │
│ ├─────────────────────┤   │ $\dot{\theta} =_{co}$ $heat? \cdot K_{on} \cdot (h_{on} - \theta) +$ │ │
│ │ $h_{off} < h_{on}$ │   │ $(1 - heat?) \cdot K_{off} \cdot (h_{off} - \theta)$ │ │
│ └─────────────────────┘   └──────────────────────────────┘ │
└──┘

The real-valued constants h_{on}, h_{off}, K_{on}, K_{off} defined in the axiomatic schema are parameters of possible behaviors. The semantics of axiomatic definitions in continuous ZimOO classes match their semantics in Object-Z. The declaration part of the state schema introduces the state variable θ (denoting the current temperature) and the control variable *heat?* (indicating the heat supply switch). Because control variables can be used in the invariant specification of a continuous class, they are declared directly in the state schema. The types *CONT* and *STEP* can be intuitively understood as sets of continuous and step functions, respectively defined on a continuous time domain (the formal semantics are explained in more detail later). The axiomatic part of the state schema describes the invariant of the class. Depending on the value of *heat?*, θ behaves according to $\dot{\theta} = K_{on} \cdot (h_{on} - \theta)$ or $\dot{\theta} = K_{off} \cdot (h_{off} - \theta)$. The user-defined binary predicate $=_{co}$ states that if the local behavior represented by the right-hand side of $=_{co}$ is continuous, then the left-hand side describes defined local behavior (*local behavior* is modeled by an *environment-based value* defined below). This means, for our example, that if *heat?* does not jump, then the derivative of θ exists and fulfills one of the two differential equations. In jump points of *heat?*, which according to the semantics of *STEP* can occur only in isolation, the value of θ is uniquely determined by the continuity of θ.

In addition to axiomatic definitions and state schemas, ZimOO provides special syntactic constructs for *variants* and *events*. *Variants* can be viewed as high-level states of the model. An example of variants are the meta-states *High*, *Low*, and *Off* in the *HeatSource* specification in Sec. 4 (Figure 7). *Events* allow an explicit naming of behavioral discontinuities, their syntax resembling that of discrete operations. Neither variants nor events contribute to the expression power of ZimOO; both are merely syntactic sugar.

The formal semantics of continuous classes is based strongly on the Continuous Environment-Based Logic (CEL) described in [15]. CEL can be motivated as follows. When specifying continuous systems, special operators known from the calculus, like derivation or limit, are needed. Since these operators are defined not upon a single value but upon a whole function, the variables in continuous system specifications are usually also interpreted as functions of the form *Time* → $\mathbb{R}$. Thus, continuous systems are normally specified not by describing the state invariant of the system, but by predicates constraining the behavior functions, which is not in keeping with the Z specification style. In CEL, the variables are interpreted as *environment-based values* allowing the specification of continuous behavior in a style appropriate to Z.

To motivate the structure of the environment-based values *Val_E*, we consider the following problem. Let $f : \mathbb{R} \to \mathbb{R}$ be a function and $t \in \mathbb{R}$. Which information about

f is necessary and sufficient to decide the following questions: Is f continuous at t? Does the limit (derivative) of f at t exist and, if so, what is its value? On the one hand, we obviously do not have to know the values of f on whole $\mathbb{R}$. On the other hand, it is not enough to know only the value of f at t, i.e. $f(t)$. The knowledge of f in every ε-environment of t is sufficient, but there is no concrete ε-environment for which it is really necessary. So, roughly speaking, we can represent the local behavior of f around t by the collection of *all* functions matching pairwise on some ε-environment of t.

To formalize this idea, we define the set of *basic functions*, which play the role of f in the above motivation, as follows.

$$\mathbf{BF} == \mathbb{R} \nrightarrow \mathbb{R}$$

Since in CEL, we want to be able to define limit, derivation, continuity, and other similar *environment-based notions* as total functions and predicates on Val_E, and because such functions do not always yield a defined value when defined conventionally, we allow basic functions to be partial. Next, we define the equivalence relation $\sim$ on $\mathbf{BF} \times \mathbb{R}$. $(f_1, t_1) \sim (f_2, t_2)$ states that f_1 and f_2 behave equally in an ε-environment of t_1 and t_2, respectively. ((a, b) stands for an open real-valued interval bounded by a and b. $\mathbb{R}_{>0}$ denotes the positive real numbers. The application of the auxiliary function *Shift* on (f, x) shifts to the right the basic function f for the value of x.)

$$
\begin{array}{|l}
\_\sim\_ : (\mathbf{BF} \times \mathbb{R}) \leftrightarrow (\mathbf{BF} \times \mathbb{R}) \\
\hline
\forall f_1, f_2 : \mathbf{BF};\ t_1, t_2 : \mathbb{R} \bullet (f_1, t_1) \sim (f_2, t_2) \Leftrightarrow \\
\quad \exists \varepsilon : \mathbb{R}_{>0} \bullet (t_1 - \varepsilon, t_1 + \varepsilon) \lhd f_1 = Shift((t_2 - \varepsilon, t_2 + \varepsilon) \lhd f_2, t_1 - t_2)
\end{array}
$$

An *environment-based value* is represented by a function mapping each time point $t \in \mathbb{R}$ to a set of all basic functions matching pairwise on some ε-environment of t. We model the local behavior by *all* functions and for *all* points of time in order to avoid different representations for the same local behavior. An environment-based value contains less information than a definition of a function on any nonempty interval and more than a conventional point-based value.

$$
\begin{aligned}
Val_E == \{ ev : \mathbb{R} \rightarrow \mathbb{P}_1 \mathbf{BF} \mid (\forall t_1, t_2 : \mathbb{R} \bullet \forall f_1 : ev(t_1);\ f_2 : ev(t_2) \bullet \\
(f_1, t_1) \sim (f_2, t_2) \wedge \\
(\forall f : \mathbf{BF} \bullet (f, t_1) \sim (f_1, t_1) \Rightarrow f \in ev(t_1))) \}
\end{aligned}
$$

All state and control variables in continuous ZimOO classes are interpreted as elements of Val_E. The formulas in the axiomatic part of the state schema are therefore CEL-formulas (no further consideration is given to CEL here, the interested reader is referred to [15]). The types $CONT$ and $STEP$ used in *Temperature* are defined as subsets of Val_E, and the derivation operator as an element of $Val_E \rightarrow Val_E$ in the ZimOO toolkit [14]. Additionally, this toolkit contains lots of other helpful functions and predicates known from the calculus.

3.3 Hybrid Classes

Hybrid classes are used to combine discrete and continuous objects to specify hybrid systems. Thus, hybrid classes usually consist of a state schema introducing object-valued variables. We adapt the specifications of *Controller* in 3.1 and *Temperature* in

3.2 to specify a simple thermostat system [25]. *Thermostat* aggregates an object of *Temperature* and an object of *Controller*. The discrete control variable *val?* of *Controller* is connected to the temperature θ by the sensor $\rightsquigarrow$. The control variable *heat?* gets its value from *switch* via the actuator $\rightsquigarrow$. The sensors and actuators, which are part of the ZimOO toolkit, behave like conversion functions from Val_E to discrete values ($\mathbb{Z}$, in our example) and vice versa. Their precise semantics depends on the chosen discrete time model, which is a parameter of a ZimOO specification. The user is free to define different conversion rules for sensors and actuators.

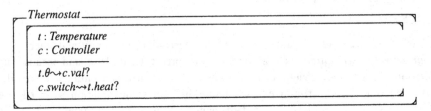

4 An Example

To demonstrate the applicability of our method, we used UML^h to develop part of the steam-boiler system, a well-known benchmark in the area of real-time systems [1]. This example has already been dealt with in some of our previous papers. In [5], correct control of the steam-boiler system was developed based on the given parameters of the environment. In [16], we showed how these parameters can be determined by simulation (here we already used a loose notation for object-oriented design). In this section, we show how UML^h supports the design of hybrid systems and the transition from design to a formal specification in ZimOO.

At the highest level of abstraction, a steam-boiler system consists of three components: the steam boiler itself, the heat source, and the control unit. We know that the control unit has to be a discrete class, but the three other classes are still abstract.

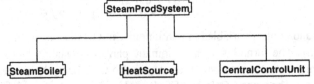

In the next design step, we decided to model the heat source by a continuous class and fix its attributes and model variants (Figure 6). The constants $grad_{on}$ and $grad_{off}$ denote the increase and decrease of the heat power dQ, *min* and *max* denoting the minimum and maximum heat power, respectively. The control variables *switch?* and *mode?* can be viewed as instructions to the heat source; depending on their values, it switches to one of the variants *High*, *Low*, or *Off*. In the same design step, we decided that the central controller should contain a special heat controller (Figure 6).

To complete the design of the heat source, we now have to specify the behavior of the introduced classes and their components. Figure 7 shows the corresponding ZimOO

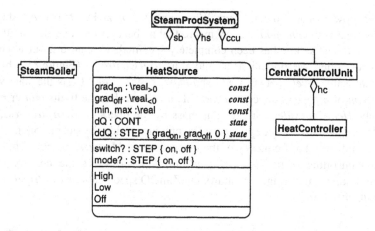

Fig. 6. Refinement of the heater subsystem

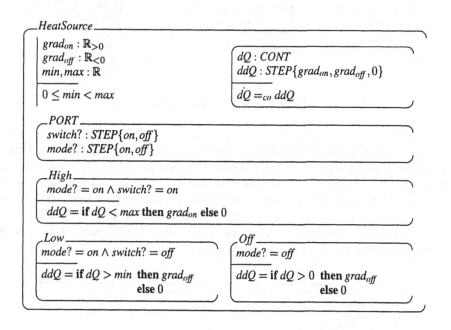

Fig. 7. ZimOO specification of the heat source

specification containing this additional information (i.e. the precise specification of behavior equations). The differential equation $\dot{dQ} =_{co} ddQ$ states that ddQ is the gradient of dQ ($=_{co}$ means that the differential equation holds whenever ddQ is continuous). The ZimOO specification describes in detail the relation between the control variables and the model variants. If *mode?* and *switch?* are both *on*, the system tries to supply as much heat power as possible, i.e. *max*. When *mode?* is *on* and *switch?* is *off*, the power supply decreases to *min*. *mode?* = *off* means that no heat power is needed at all.

Once the heat source has been completely specified, we can turn our attention to the heat controller. We model it as a child of a *StripeController* (Figure 8), which tries to keep the value *level?* between *min* and *max*: if *req?* = *on*, it sets the state variable *switch* to *on* or *off* when the control variable *level?* reaches the limits *min* or *max*, respectively. *HeatController* enriches this class by the operation *MeasurePress*, which computes a qualitative value (*press*) for the pressure inside the steam boiler. The constant *rate* indicates the frequency of the invocations of *MeasurePressure*. Thus, in addition to controlling the heat source, *HeatController* performs some measurements for the central control unit. Figure 9 shows the ZimOO specifications of *StripeController* and *HeatController*.

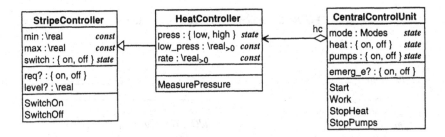

Fig. 8. Model of the *HeatController*

Now we can specify in ZimOO the part of the steam-boiler system developed here. The ZimOO class *SteamProdSystem* is a ZimOO refinement of the UML^h diagram from Figure 6. The actuator $\leadsto$ connects the variable *heat* of the central control unit (not refined here) to the control variable *mode?* of the heat source. Similarly, *switch* of the heat controller is connected to *switch?* of the heat source. The control variable *level?* of the heat controller measures the pressure of the steam-boiler vessel (*sb.ve*), which owing to lack of space is not further specified here.

___SteamProdSystem___

hs : *HeatSource*
sb : *SteamBoiler*
ccu : *CentralControlUnit*

ccu.heat $\leadsto$ hs.mode?
ccu.hc.switch $\leadsto$ hs.switch?
sb.ve.P_s $\leadsto$ ccu.hc.level?

· · ·

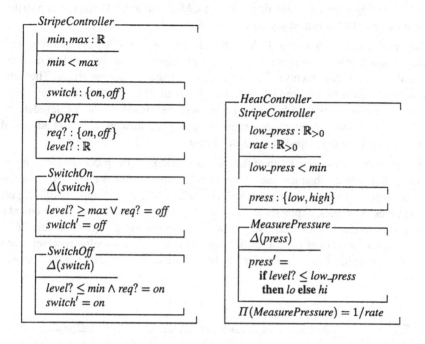

Fig. 9. ZimOO specification of *StripeController* and *HeatController*

For the sake of completeness, we add the following diagram showing the complete class structure of the entire system:

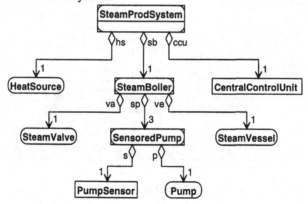

5   A Prototypical Design Editor

To verify the usability of our method, it is necessary to provide tools that support it. A graphical editor has therefore been developed by the Software Engineering group at the TU Berlin. In nature, it is somewhere between a design editor implementing UML[h] and an environment for producing ZimOO specifications. It also has advanced coupling features providing a smooth transition between UML[h] and ZimOO since it is possible to express all ZimOO constructs within the editor.

The development of this tool follows the object-oriented paradigm. Starting with the identification of basic requirements for the functionalities in the problem domain, we considered the requirements for the application's graphical user interface. Then, the components of the editor were identified and designed. It is worth mentioning that a systematic approach was used here. Beginning with the design of the metamodel, the other components (view concept, controller concept, data management, and advanced functionalities) were developed on a stepwise basis.

Figure 10 shows a screen dump of the interface. It depicts the process of refining an association between an abstract class *SteamVessel* and a continuous class *VesselThermDyn* by an aggregation using popup control. This release of the tool supports TEX-export functionalities. Complex expressions can thus be used to describe textual elements, which is very useful in technical and physical applications (e.g. "\real" means "$\mathbb{R}$"). Some frequently used ones have already been translated into an analog representation (e.g. "\pi" is visualized as "π"). Another useful feature is the support for subscripts and indices.

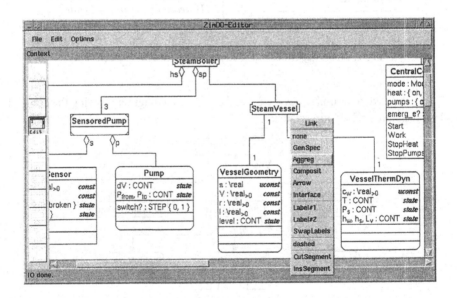

Fig. 10. Screenshot

To derive ZimOO specifications from the UML[h] model, there is an internal text editor to specify the behavior of the classes using ZimOO statements. This enables us, for instance, to set up constraints for attributes introduced earlier. Thus, the tool's runtime metamodel contains all the information on the classes' behavior, which allows automated export of ZimOO schemas.

Another export filter implements the conversion of the runtime metamodel to POST-SCRIPT. To illustrate the tool's functionality, we used it to generate all the figures and ZimOO specifications in this paper.

Through the introduction of conventional object-oriented classes in the metamodel it was possible to document the whole development process using the tool itself[2]. This procedure provided a lot of hints for the tool's design. The development process can therefore be seen as an instance of bootstrapping.

To ensure portability and further support, the tool was implemented in Java using the Java Development Kit 1.1 [21]. This decision involves a lot of features. For example, an automated documentation via javadoc can be used which produces a hypertext glossary. Furthermore, Java comes with automatic memory management. There is thus no need to explicitly implement it. The lack of performance of the Java virtual machine was made up for by elaborate visualization algorithms.

6   Comparison to related work and conclusions

We are not aware of any other extensions of UML for hybrid system design. Similarly, we are not aware of hybrid specification languages based on ObjectZ. VDM++ [8, 22] is an object oriented extension of VDM which offers powerful features for discrete real-time specification and some basic means for hybrid specification. In particular, it offers the concept of real-valued *time variables*, whose behavior can be specified by assumptions about the hybrid environment. However, continuous objects and means to specify complex dependencies between time variables are not provided in VDM++. Furthermore, VDM++ does not provide a crisp semantic foundation for hybrid system specification comparable to the continuous environment-based logic (CEL) of ZimOO. In summary, in comparison to ZimOO, VDM++ is oriented more towards discrete real-time system and does not offer adequate means to specify complex hybrid systems.

In this paper, we presented an object-oriented approach to the specification of hybrid systems using the graphical design notation UML^h, a variant of UML for hybrid systems, and the formal specification language ZimOO, a variant of Object-Z for hybrid systems. Though UML^h and ZimOO are still under development, we have demonstrated that they can already be used to design hybrid systems such as the steam-boiler benchmark. Further work on UML^h and its tool support will include: various extensions to its class diagrams, hybrid Statecharts, and collaboration diagrams for hybrid systems. Further work on ZimOO will include the development of compilers that translate ZimOO subsets into object-oriented simulation languages.

---

[2] In other words, we have swallowed our own medicine.

References

1. J.-R. Abrial, E. Börger, and H. Langmaack, editors. *Formal Methods for Industrial Applications: Specifying and Programming the Steam Boiler Control*, volume 1165 of *Lecture Notes in Computer Science*. Springer-Verlag, 1996.
2. R. Alur, C. Courcoubetis, T. A. Henzinger, and P.-H. Ho. Hybrid automata: An algorithmic approach to the specification and verification of hybrid systems. In Grossman et al. [18], pages 209–229.
3. M. Andersson. *Object-Oriented Modelling and Simulation of Hybrid Systems*. PhD thesis, Lund Institute of Technology, Denmark, December 1994.
4. M. Biersack, V. Friesen, S. Jähnichen, M. Klose, and M. Simons. Towards an architecture for simulation environments. In *Proc. Summer Computer Simulation Conference*. The Society for Computer Simulation (SCSC'95), 1995.
5. R. Büssow and M. Weber. A steam-boiler control specification with Statecharts and Z. In Abrial et al. [1], pages 109–128.
6. Z. Chaochen, A. P. Ravn, and M. R. Hansen. An extended duration calculus for hybrid real-time systems. In Grossman et al. [18], pages 36–59.
7. R. Duke, P. King, G. A. Rose, and G. Smith. The Object-Z specification language. In T. Korson, V. Vaishnavi, and B. Meyer, editors, *Technology of Object-Oriented Languages and Systems: TOOLS 5*, pages 465–483. Prentice Hall, 1991.
8. E. H. Dürr and N. Plat (editor). VDM^{++} Language Reference Manual. Afrodite (ESPRIT-III project number 6500) document AFRO/CG/ED/LRM/V11, Cap Volmac, August 1995.
9. H. Elmqvist, F. E. Cellier, and M. Otter. Object-oriented modeling of hybrid systems. In *ESS'93, European Simulation Symposium*, Delft, October 25–28 1993.
10. H. Elmqvist and S. E. Mattsson. Modelica – The next generation modeling language: An international design effort. In *Proc. 1st World Congress on System Simulation (WCSS'97)*, Singapore, August 1997.
11. C. Fidge. Real-time refinement. In J. Woodcock and P. G. Larsen, editors, *FME'93: Industrial-Strength Formal Methods: First International Symposium of Formal Methods Europe*, volume 670 of *Lecture Notes in Computer Science*, pages 314–331. Springer-Verlag, 1993.
12. C. Fidge. Adding real time to formal program development. In M. Naftalin, T. Denvir, and M. Bertran, editors, *FME'94: Industrial Benefit of Formal Methods: Second International Symposium of Formal Methods Europe*, volume 873 of *Lecture Notes in Computer Science*, pages 618–638. Springer-Verlag, 1994.
13. V. Friesen. An exercise in hybrid system specification using an extension of Z. In A. Bouajjani and O. Maler, editors, *Second European Workshop on Real-Time and Hybrid Systems*, pages 311–316, 1995.
14. V. Friesen. *Objektorientierte Spezifikation hybrider Systeme*. PhD thesis, Technical University of Berlin, 1997.
15. V. Friesen. A logic for the specification of continuous systems. In *Hybrid Systems: Computation and Control*, Lecture Notes in Computer Science. Springer-Verlag, 1998. To appear.
16. V. Friesen, S. Jähnichen, and M. Weber. Specification of software controlling a discrete-continuous environment. In *19th International Conference on Software Engineering (ICSE-19)*. IEEE Computer Society, 1997.
17. V. Friesen, A. Nordwig, and M. Weber. Toward an object-oriented design methodology for hybrid systems. Submitted to *Colloquium on Object Technology and System Re-Engineering*, Oxford, 1998.
18. R. Grossman, A. Nerode, H. Rischel, and A. Ravn, editors. *Hybrid Systems*, volume 736 of *Lecture Notes in Computer Science*. Springer-Verlag, 1993.

19. He Jifeng. From CSP to hybrid systems. In A. W. Roscoe, editor, *A Classical Mind, Essays in Honour of C. A. R. Hoare*, pages 171–189. Prentice Hall International Series in Computer Science, 1994.

20. M. Kloas, V. Friesen, and M. Simons. Smile – A simulation environment for energy systems. In A. Sydow, editor, *Proc. 5th International IMACS-Symposium on Systems Analysis and Simulation (SAS'95)*, pages 503–506. Gordon and Breach Publishers, 1995.

21. Doug Kramer. *JDK 1.1.1 Documentation*. Sun Microsystems, Inc., USA, 1997.

22. K. Lano. *Formal Object-Oriented Development*. Springer-Verlag, London, 1995.

23. O. Maler, Z. Manna, and A. Pnueli. From timed to hybrid systems. In J. W. de Bakker, K. Huizing, W.-P. de Roever, and G. Rozenberg, editors, *Real Time: Theory in Practice*, volume 600 of *Lecture Notes in Computer Science*, pages 446–484. Springer-Verlag, 1992.

24. Z. Manna and A. Pnueli. Verifying hybrid systems. In Grossman et al. [18], pages 4–35.

25. X. Nicollin, A. Olivero, J. Sifakis, and S. Yovine. An approach to the description and analysis of hybrid systems. In Grossman et al. [18], pages 149–178.

26. Rational Software Corporation. *Unified Modeling Language, Version 1.1*, 1 September 1997.

Translating the OMT Dynamic Model into Object-Z[*]

S. Dupuy, Y. Ledru, and M. Chabre-Peccoud

Laboratoire Logiciels, Systèmes et Réseaux, IMAG
B.P. 72, 38402, Saint Martin d'Hères Cedex, France

Tel: +04 76 82 72 57   Fax: +04 76 82 72 87
Email: Sophie.Dupuy@imag.fr

Abstract. Object models and formal notations offer complementary advantages for information systems analysis and design. In this paper, we consider the mapping of OMT notations into Object-Z formal specifications for the OMT dynamic model. This allows to better specify the OMT semantics and some of the consistency rules between the object model and the dynamic one. We propose a constructive way to develop a formal specification. Our work develops a systematic translation process in order to produce formal specifications with good readability and traceability quality. Such proposals should help to implement CASEs integrating multi-modelling processes (natural, graphical, formal) producing better system specifications tools.

1   Introduction

Industrial object-oriented methods for information system analysis and design (e.g. OMT Object Modeling Technique [15]) are semi-formal methods based on graphical models (data, functional models ...). These models have the advantage of offering a synthetic view of the system which allows communication with customers. But their notations are ambiguous and result in a lack of precision in the specifications. This lack of precise semantics leads to difficulties to interpret models and to construct complete tools. On the contrary, formal methods are based on mathematical notations. They have specified notations which permit proofs construction and refinement towards executable code. While their use allows to increase system quality, these methods are not most used in practice and their application field is generally limited to safety-critical systems. There are numerous reasons why formal methods do not enter the general practice [16]. One of them is that they are often perceived as a revolution in system development leading to change the usual tools, methods and processes. Semi-formal and formal methods seem

Several proposals have been done in order to combine semi-formal and formal methods. They include the translation of structured methods [13, 14] and object-oriented methods like OMT [6, 11], Fusion [7], or UML [8]. These object-oriented methods present two specific characteristics. On the one hand, some aspects of their semantics, like inheritance or encapsulation of data and operations, are difficult to express with a formalism such as Z which offers poor support for these object oriented concerns.

---

[*] This work was partially funded by the Rhône-Alpes region through the Emergence programme.

On the other hand, a specification is expressed with several models, e.g. an object, a functional, and a dynamic model in OMT. For a given formal language, some of these models are easier to express than others. For example, Z covers more easily the object and functional models while a language for reactive systems, like STATECHARTS[1] is better suited for the dynamic model.

As a consequence, most translation schemes for object-oriented methods do not cover the full semantics or all models.

Our work consists of deriving Object-Z specifications from OMT notations. Our long-term goal is to propose an integrated approach for specification which combines semi-formal techniques with formal and natural language annotations. Translating OMT into a formal language contributes to this goal in several ways.

- It determines the semantics of OMT constructs.
- It produces a specification skeleton to be filled in later by formal annotations. The challenge here is to have a readable skeleton that allows traceability between the semi-formal and the formal description.
- It helps locate the limits of the notation: the holes in the skeleton correspond to aspects that OMT cannot express, e.g. integrity constraints on the object model. These aspects are usually expressed in natural language as complements to the specification. They may also take the form of formal annotations.

As already mentioned, OMT is composed of three models: the object, dynamic and functional models. The object model describes the static structure of the system studied. The dynamic model shows objects evolution and the functional model represents information flows between the actors of the system.

In a previous work [3], we have proposed a translation scheme for the object model. Object-Z was chosen as a target for the translation process because a first attempt had shown the limits of Z to express inheritance and encapsulation. This previous work has shown the feasibility of the approach: the full object model has been covered, the semantics of some OMT constructs (like aggregation) has been detailed (see also Section 3.2), and a readable skeleton is produced by the translation schema.

This paper studies the translation of the dynamic model of OMT into Object-Z [2]. As mentioned earlier, translating all models into a single formal language is not easy, and it seems reasonable to combine a language designed for transformational aspects (here Object-Z) with a language for reactive systems (e.g. Statecharts or CSP). But while such languages are well-suited to express the semantics of the dynamic model alone, it turns the resulting translation into a multi-language description. This makes it more difficult to express the consistency between the models and explains our choice to try to express all models in a single language. Moreover, originally our choice of Object-Z was also motivated by the possibility to describe behavioural aspects with class history invariants. Unfortunately, this language feature is not supported by the current Object-Z tools, and was finally not used in our translation schema.

The remainder of the paper is organized as follows. First we present the OMT dynamic model formalism and the case study which is specified in this paper. Next the translation from OMT dynamic model into Object-Z specifications is described: the main concepts (state and transition) of the OMT dynamic model and more complex notions, like state generalization, are studied. Then we compare our approach with related work. Finally we give a summary and discuss future investigations.

2   Context

2.1   The OMT dynamic model

The OMT dynamic model aims to describe the evolution constraints of objects. It is based on the Statecharts formalism [9]. The dynamic model formalism is also called state diagram.

A state diagram represents the local behaviour of the objects of a class. State diagrams are based on the notions of state and transitions between these states.

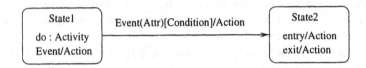

Fig. 1. State Diagram Style

The state of an object is an abstraction of the value of this object at a particular time. It is a function of the values of the attributes and the links of this object. In a state, an object can realize some operations which do not modify its state. These operations can be activities or actions. An activity is an operation that takes time to complete. It is represented by the keyword *do*. An action is an instantaneous operation. Actions can be performed at the entry (*entry*), at the exit (*exit*) of the state or when an event happens (/).

A transition represents the change from a state to another one. It is associated to an event that triggers it, a condition and an action to execute. An event is something happening instantaneously at a point in time. It is a mean to transmit information from an object to another one. So it can have attributes. In particular the moment when it occurs characterizes it explicitly. Events are collected in classes. A condition is a boolean function on the object values or on the values of other objects. In particular a condition can refer to the states of other objects.

State diagrams can also be structured by generalization or aggregation. Generalization is a form of state generalization: a state is specialized in a subdiagram. Aggregation corresponds to a state decomposition in which the global state is an aggregate of all its substates.

2.2   Case study: Railway level crossing

To illustrate these notions, the OMT object and dynamic models of a railway level crossing will be presented in Section 3.

A railway level crossing is made up of several devices that warn car riders and prevent them to cross the railway track when a train approaches (see Figure 2). These are a sound signal, flashing red lights, and a gate. Actually, these devices appear on both sides of the track, but it is assumed that both sides exhibit the same behaviour (the fault-tolerant aspects of the problem are not considered here).

When a train enters the train detection area, coming from either direction, the lights and the sound signal start while the gate begins its closing process. When all trains have exited the train detection area, the gates open and when they have reached the upright position, the lights and the sound signal stop.

It is assumed that when a train enters the train detection area, a *TrainArrival* event is issued, and similarly, a *TrainRemoval* event signals the exit of a train.

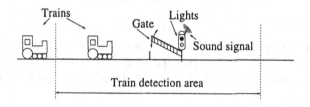

Fig. 2. Level Crossing

3   Translation from the OMT dynamic model to Object-Z

This part presents the translation of some concepts of the OMT dynamic model into Object-Z. It particularly insists on the link between the object and dynamic models and shows how the consistency between these models can be expressed in Object-Z.

First, the translation of the two mains concepts of the OMT dynamic model (state and transition) are defined. It is illustrated by the simplified version of the level crossing example introduced in the previous part. Secondly more complex concepts (like state specialisation) are studied on a more complete version of the level crossing.

3.1   State and transition

The expression of state diagrams in Object-Z completes the Object-Z specification skeletons which are obtained from the translation of the object model.

From a static point of view, the level crossing described above can be represented in the OMT object model by the class *LevelCrossing* (Figure 3). It has the attributes *nbTrain* which represents the number of trains present in the detection area, *light*, *soundsignal* and *gate*. Four operations *PermitCrossing*, *ForbidCrossing*, *AddTrain* and *RemoveTrain* can be performed.

This OMT class can be expressed in Object-Z by a class [3]. An Object-Z class is mainly composed of a state schema, an initial state schema and operation schemata. In the state schema, the attributes of the OMT class are declared like secondary variables i.e. variables implicitly included in the Δ of the class operations. Each OMT class operation gives rise to a skeleton of Object-Z operation. The *LevelCrossing* class is

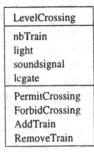

Fig. 3. The Level Crossing Class

represented by an Object-Z *LevelCrossing* class which has for attributes *nbTrain*, *light*, *lcgate* and *soundsignal*. The Object-Z specification allows to define the type of the attributes. For example, *light* has an enumerated type which has two values *ON* and *OFF*.

$$SIGNAL ::= ON \mid OFF$$
$$LCGATE ::= OPENED \mid CLOSED$$

```
__LevelCrossing_____
  _Δ_____

   nbTrain : ℕ
   light : SIGNAL
   lcgate : LCGATE
   soundsignal : SIGNAL
  _____

  __PermitCrossing_____
  _____

  ...
_____
```

The class skeleton obtained is completed by the class behaviour described in the OMT state diagram. The *LevelCrossing* state diagram (Figure 4) expresses the fact that a level crossing can be in two states *Permitted* and *Forbidden* which represent the right to cross the tracks. If a train arrives in the detection area corresponding to the level crossing, the state becomes *Forbidden*. The event *TrainArrival* triggers the actions *ForbidCrossing*, which switches the signals (the light, the sound signal and the gate) on, and *AddTrain* which increases the number of trains present in the detection area. When all trains have left the detection area (event *TrainRemoval* and condition *nbTrain* = 1), the crossing is *Permitted*.

In OMT, the **state** of an object is an abstraction of the value of this object during an interval. It is defined by the values of the attributes or/and of the links with other objects. So it is represented in Object-Z by a secondary variable. Its type is an enumerated type that is composed of the possible states of the object. For the level crossing example, the state is represented by a variable *state* in the class *LevelCrossing*. The type *LCState*

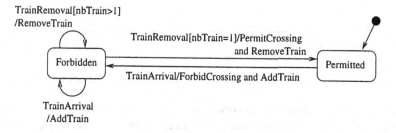

Fig. 4. The Level Crossing State Diagram

contains two values *Permitted* and *Forbidden* which correspond to the two states of *LevelCrossing*.

$$LCState ::= Forbidden \mid Permitted$$

In addition to the direct translation, the Object-Z specification can add information not included in the original OMT description. In particular the links between the state and the attributes of the class can be made explicit. For instance, the state is *Permitted* if the light of the level crossing is off, if the sound signal is off and if the level crossing gate is opened.

$$state = Permitted \Leftrightarrow light = OFF \wedge lcgate = OPENED \wedge soundsignal = OFF$$

There is also a link between the state *Permitted* and the number of trains present in the detection area:

$$state = Permitted \Leftrightarrow nbTrain = 0$$

These constraints are added in the predicates of the class state schema. The initial state can also be defined in the initial state schema.

$$SIGNAL ::= ON \mid OFF$$
$$LCGATE ::= OPENED \mid CLOSED$$
$$LCState ::= Forbidden \mid Permitted$$

LevelCrossing _____
△ _____

$nbTrain : \mathbb{N}$
$light : SIGNAL$
$lcgate : LCGATE$
$soundsignal : SIGNAL$
$state : LCState$

_____

$state = Permitted \Leftrightarrow$
    $(light = OFF \wedge lcgate = OPENED \wedge soundsignal = OFF)$
$state = Permitted \Leftrightarrow (nbTrain = 0)$
$state = Forbidden \Leftrightarrow$
    $light = ON \vee lcgate = CLOSED \vee soundsignal = ON$

```
┌─INIT──────────────────────────────────────────────
│ ┌──────────────────────────────────────────────
│ │ state = Permitted
│ └──────────────────────────────────────────────
│ ...
└──────────────────────────────────────────────────
```

The second concept studied is **transition**. A transition can be composed of an event, a condition and an action. An event can be seen as an operation call or as an external stimulus. So two different ways to represent an event are proposed. If it is an operation call, the event gives rise to an operation in the Object-Z class. If it is an external stimulus, it is described by a class. OMT specifies that events can be grouped in classes and that they have for explicit attribute the moment when they occur. So a class *Event* which is a generalized class for all possible events is created. It has for attribute the moment of the event. The specific attributes of an event are represented in its class. For example, the event *TrainArrival* gives rise to a class *TrainArrival* that inherits from the class *Event* and that has for specific attributes the arriving train.

$[MOMENT, TRAIN]$

```
┌─EVENT─────────────────         ┌─TrainArrival──────────
│ ┌─m──────────────             │ EVENT
│ │ oment : MOMENT               │ ┌─t──────────────
│ └──────────────────           │ │ rain : TRAIN
└──────────────────────         │ └──────────────────
                                 └──────────────────────
```

At the class level, an event is an input of an operation modifying the state. For instance, the event which triggers the transition from *Forbidden* to *Permitted* is an input of the operation *ModifyStateForbiddenPermitted*. The type of the event is specified in the precondition of the operation ($ev? \in TrainRemoval$) and the state change is characterized by the modification of the attribute *state* ($state = Forbidden \land state' = Permitted$).

```
┌─ModifyStateForbiddenPermitted────────────────────────
│ ev? :↓ EVENT
├──────────────────────────────────────────────────────
│ ev? ∈ TrainRemoval ∧ state = Forbidden ∧ state' = Permitted
└──────────────────────────────────────────────────────
```

A transition can also call an action (e.g. *AddTrain*). This action should be declared in the object model as an operation. So in Object-Z, the operation corresponding to an action has been translated from the object model. It remains to express that this action is called on a transition.

The whole information composing the transition is gathered in a transition operation which makes the conjunction of the operations representing the state change and the action, with a precondition corresponding to the transition condition. For example, the transition from *Forbidden* to *Permitted* is composed of the event *TrainRemoval*, which is the input of *ModifyStateForbiddenPermitted*, a condition ($nbTrain = 1$) which is a precondition of the transition and the operations *PermitCrossing* and *AddTrain*. It is represented by an operation which is the conjunction of the operations *ModifyState-ForbiddenPermitted, PermitCrossing, AddTrain* with the precondition Formatting added by JPB

$$TransitionForbiddenPermitted \,\widehat{=}$$
$$\quad ModifyStateForbiddenPermitted \wedge [\, nbTrain = 1 \,] \wedge$$
$$\quad RemoveTrain \wedge PermitCrossing$$

The same rule can be used for all the transitions of the *LevelCrossing* state diagram. Then the transitions are gathered in an operation *ConsumeEvent* which should execute the operation corresponding to the event received. For this, the non-deterministic choice operator ($[]$) is used: it chooses what operation to execute if the preconditions of several operations are satisfied. In OMT, the choice must always be deterministic because several transitions from a state cannot be triggered on the same event. For the *LevelCrossing* class, *ConsumeEvent* groups the operations of transitions *TransitionForbiddenPermitted, TransitionPermittedForbidden* and *TransitionStayForbidden*.

$$ConsumeEvent \,\widehat{=}$$
$$\quad TransitionForbiddenPermitted \;[]\; TransitionPermittedForbidden$$
$$\quad []\; TransitionStayForbidden$$

Finally, the intermediate operations are hidden and only the operation of event consumption and the class operations are kept visible. This is expressed by adding to the class the list of the visible features preceded by the visibility symbol ($\upharpoonright$).

$$\upharpoonright (ConsumeEvent, PermitCrossing, ForbidCrossing, AddTrain, RemoveTrain)$$

To summarize, the following Object-Z class is obtained from the translation of the state diagram:

LevelCrossing
$\upharpoonright (ConsumeEvent, PermitCrossing, ForbidCrossing, AddTrain,$
$RemoveTrain)$

Δ

$nbTrain : \mathbb{N}$
$light : SIGNAL$
$lcgate : LCGATE$
$soundsignal : SIGNAL$
$state : LCState$

$state = Permitted \Leftrightarrow$
$\quad light = OFF \wedge lcgate = OPENED \wedge soundsignal = OFF$
$state = Permitted \Leftrightarrow nbTrain = 0$
$state = Forbidden \Leftrightarrow$
$\quad light = ON \vee lcgate = CLOSED \vee soundsignal = ON$

INIT

$state = Permitted$

```
_ModifyStateForbiddenPermitted_____
 ev? :↓ EVENT
────────────────────────────────────────────────────────────
 ev? ∈ TrainRemoval ∧ state = Forbidden ∧ state' = Permitted
```

```
_ModifyStatePermittedForbidden_____
 ev? :↓ EVENT
────────────────────────────────────────────────────────────
 ev? ∈ TrainArrival ∧ state = Permitted ∧ state' = Forbidden
```

```
_StayStateForbidden1_____
 ev? :↓ EVENT
────────────────────────────────────────────────────────────
 ev? ∈ TrainRemoval ∧ state = Forbidden ∧ state' = Forbidden
```

```
_StayStateForbidden2_____
 ev? :↓ EVENT
────────────────────────────────────────────────────────────
 ev? ∈ TrainArrival ∧ state = Forbidden ∧ state' = Forbidden
```

```
_ForbidCrossing_____
 light' = ON ∧ lcgate' = CLOSED ∧ soundsignal' = ON
```

```
_PermitCrossing_____
 light' = OFF ∧ lcgate' = OPENED ∧ soundsignal' = OFF
```

```
_AddTrain_____      _RemoveTrain_____
 nbTrain' = nbTrain + 1               nbTrain' = nbTrain − 1
```

$TransitionStayForbidden \ \widehat{=}$
  $(StayStateForbidden1 \wedge [nbTrain > 1] \wedge RemoveTrain)\ []$
  $(StayStateForbidden2 \wedge AddTrain)$

$TransitionForbiddenPermitted \ \widehat{=}$
  $ModifyStateForbiddenPermitted \wedge [nbTrain = 1] \wedge$
  $PermitCrossing \wedge RemoveTrain$

$TransitionPermittedForbidden \ \widehat{=}$
  $ModifyStatePermittedForbidden \wedge ForbidCrossing \wedge AddTrain$

$ConsumeEvent \ \widehat{=}\ TransitionForbiddenPermitted\ []$
  $TransitionPermittedForbidden\ []\ TransitionStayForbidden$

3.2 State Diagram Stucturing

The previous example was kept simple in order to illustrate the translation of the main concepts of the OMT dynamic model. In this section, more complex concepts are studied. A first study relies on state specialization. A second point of interest is the link between some concepts of the object model and their implications on the behaviour. This link motivates our choice of a single language for all the models.

The level crossing example is now completed in a more realistic way. From a static point of view, the level crossing is now an aggregate of a light, a sound signal, and a gate (see Figure 5).

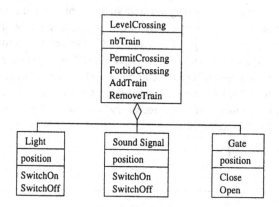

Fig. 5. Object model

The semantics of OMT aggregation is not precisely defined: the existential dependency between the aggregate object and its components is not mandatory. In the case study, the components of the aggregate are independent of the level crossing: for example, a light can exist without being associated to a level crossing. So each component has its own evolution which does not refer to the behaviour of the other objects of the aggregate. So aggregation can simply be represented in Object-Z by the inclusion of the component object in the aggregate object. Classes of the aggregate are translated into Object-Z classes and each object of *LevelCrossing* included objects of the classes *Light*, *SoundSignal* and *Gate*.

```
┌─ LevelCrossing ────────────────────────────────────────
│ ┌─ △ ───────────────────────────────────────────
│ │ nbTrain : N
│ │ light : Light
│ │ gate : Gate
│ │ soundsignal : SoundSignal
│ │ ...
│ └──────────────────────────────────────────────
│ ...
└────────────────────────────────────────────────────
```

We start by presenting the local behaviour of the level crossing components. Since each component is independent, their behaviour can be described independently of the other objects.

The light and the sound signal have the same state diagram. They have two states *ON* and *OFF*. The transitions are triggered the events *SwitchOn* and *SwitchOff*:

Fig. 6. The Light and SoundSignal State Diagram

This diagram is translated into Object-Z specifications according to the above rules. The state is translated into a secondary variable state. In this case, it corresponds exactly to the attribute *position*. This redundancy is due to the systematic translation of the state. But the constraint *state = position* can be added to define the link between *state* and *position*. The two events *SwitchOn* and *SwitchOff* are operation calls. Then the operations *SwitchOn* and *SwitchOff* are completed. They simply modify the state. The transitions are represented by these operations since no particular constraint is added to the transitions. A *ConsumeEvent* is not necessary because *SwitchOn* and *SwitchOff* can be called directly from other objects.

$SIGNAL ::= ON \mid OFF$

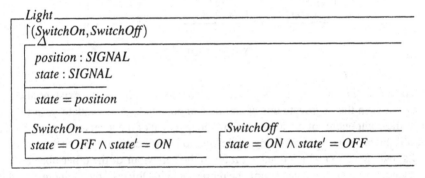

The gate has a more complex evolution. It can be *Opened* when the high position is reached, *Closed* when the low position is reached and *in process* when it proceeds from a position to the other one. The events *HighPositionReached* and *LowPositionReached* are internal events of the gate.

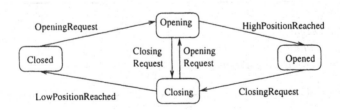

Fig. 7. The Gate State Diagram

The translation rules presented in the last section are applied to this state diagram. The *Gate* state diagram has only transitions with an event. So it is not necessary to create operations to combine transitions with actions or conditions.

$POSITION ::= High \mid Low$
$GateState ::= Closed \mid Closing \mid Opened \mid Opening$

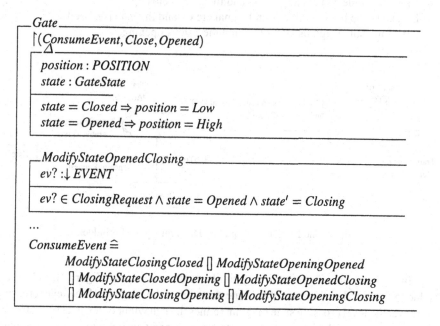

Viewing the level crossing like an aggregate restricts the behaviour of the *LevelCrossing* objects. Moreover the evolution of a level crossing depends on the behaviour of its components. The level crossing behaviour can be seen as a parallel composition of the local behaviour of its components with some restrictions.

Now the transition from *Forbidden* to *Permitted* relies on the states of the light, of the sound signal and of the gate. But a level crossing also influences the evolution of its components by sending them events. For instance, on the transition from *Permitted* to *Forbidden*, a closing request is sent to the gate, and the light and the sound signal are switched on.

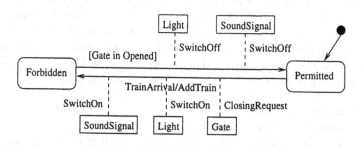

Fig. 8. The Level Crossing State Diagram

Unlike the specification of Figure 4, the closure and the opening of the level crossing are not instantaneous: it depends on the time to close the gate. This induces to specialize the state *Forbidden* by a subdiagram which has three substates:

- Closing : some signals are not on and the gate is closing.
- Blocked : the light and the sound signal are on and the gate is closed.
- Opening : some signals are not on and the gate is opening.

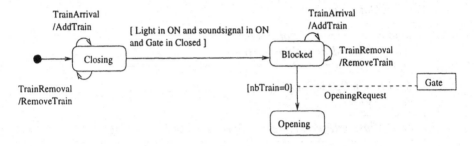

Fig. 9. The Level Crossing State Diagram – State Forbidden

This subdiagram (Figure 9) is very similar to that of the gate (Figure 7). In fact, this is due to the fact that the state of the gate determines the substate of the level crossing. Moreover the level crossing state diagram refines the behaviour of the gate by restricting the transitions from the intermediate states *Opening* and *Closing*. This means that when the gate starts to open, the opening must terminate (idem for the closure).

First, the main level crossing state diagram is translated into Object-Z. The state is now defined according to the state of the level crossing components. For example:

state = Permitted ⇔ light.state = OFF ∧ gate.state = Opened ∧
    soundsignal.state = OFF

The transition from *Permitted* to *Forbidden* follows the rules expressed above for events and actions: an operation of state change *ModifyStatePermittedForbidden* has for input *TrainArrival*, the action called *AddTrain* is an operation of the class.

Events sent to other objects remain to be expressed. If the event is an operation call, the transition operation simply performs the operation. If the event is an external stimulus, the transition performs the operation of event consumption of the target class with the type of the event as precondition. For example, the transition from *Permitted* to *Forbidden* is a conjunction of the operations *ModifyStatePermittedForbidden*, *AddTrain*, *SwitchOn* of the light and sound signal class, and *ConsumeEvent* of the gate class with the precondition that the input of *ConsumeEvent* is *ClosingRequest*.

TransitionPermittedForbidden ≙
    ModifyStatePermittedForbidden
        ∧ ([*ev?* :↓ *EVENT* | *ev?* ∈ *ClosingRequest*] ∧*gate.ConsumeEvent*)
        ∧ *light.SwitchOn* ∧ *soundsignal.SwitchOn* ∧*AddTrain*

The other transition of the *LevelCrossing* state diagram is from *Forbidden* to *Permitted*. It is triggered when the condition on the state of the light, the sound signal and the gate is satisfied. There is no event to make the state change. So the operation *ModifyStateForbiddenPermitted* should not have an input event. But in Object-Z, the non-determinist choice operator $[]$ of *ConsumeEvent* requires to have the same inputs and outputs for all operations linked by it. So *ModifyStateForbiddenPermitted* must have an input event which is considered like an internal event ($ev? \in Internal$) sent when the condition is satisfied.

LevelCrossing

$\lceil (ConsumeEvent, AddTrain...)$

Δ

$nbTrain : \mathbb{N}$
$light : Light$
$gate : Gate$
$soundsignal : SoundSignal$
$state : LCState$

$state = Permitted \Leftrightarrow$
$light.state = OFF \wedge gate.state = Opened \wedge soundsignal.state = OFF$
$...$

INIT

$state = Permitted$

ModifyStatePermittedForbidden

$ev? :\downarrow EVENT$

$ev? \in TrainArrival \wedge state = Permitted \wedge state' = Forbidden$

AddTrain

$nbTrain' = nbTrain + 1$

$...$

$TransitionPermittedForbidden \mathrel{\widehat{=}}$
$\quad ModifyStatePermittedForbidden \wedge light.SwitchOn \wedge$
$\quad ([ev? :\downarrow EVENT \mid ev? \in ClosingRequest] \wedge gate.ConsumeEvent)$
$\quad \wedge soundsignal.SwitchOn \wedge AddTrain$
$ConsumeEvent \mathrel{\widehat{=}}$
$\quad TransitionForbiddenPermitted [] TransitionPermittedForbidden$

The next step is to express the subdiagram of *Forbidden* in Object-Z. Like the other diagrams, the substate gives rise to a secondary variable. The type of this variable is an enumerated type which elements are the states of the diagram and a *Void* element, necessary to express the link between the substates and their superstate.

$LCSubForbidden ::= Closing \mid Blocked \mid Opening \mid Void$

The superstate is linked to its substates by a predicate which expresses that being in the superstate is equivalent to being in one of its substates.

$$state = Forbidden \Leftrightarrow$$
$$substateForbidden \in \{Closing, Blocked, Opening\}$$

It is also specified that if the state is not *Forbidden*, the substate is *Void*:

$$\neg\,(state = Forbidden) \Leftrightarrow substateForbidden = Void$$

The initial state of the subdiagram has also to be specified. This means that each time the level crossing enters in *Forbidden*, the substate is *Closing*. So all transitions arriving in *Forbidden* must specify that they arrive in *Closing* too. Only the operation *ModifyStatePermittedForbidden* has to evolve:

```
┌─ModifyStatePermittedForbidden──────────────────────────
│  ev? :↓ EVENT
├─────────────────────────────────────────────────────────
│  ev? ∈ TrainArrival ∧ state = Permitted ∧ substateForbidden′ = Closing
│  state′ = Forbidden
└─────────────────────────────────────────────────────────
```

The transitions of the subdiagram into Object-Z remain to be translated following the rules presented above. Each transition can give rise to:

- an operation of state change
- an operation for each action called on the transition
- an operation to represent sending events to others class
- an operation TransitionXY which makes the conjunction of all elements of the transition
- a condition which is a precondition of TransitionXY

For example, the transition from *Blocked* to *Opening* is represented by the following Object-Z operation:

$$TransitionBlockedOpening \mathrel{\widehat{=}}$$
$$\quad ModifyStateBlockedOpening \wedge$$
$$\quad ([\,ev? :\downarrow EVENT \mid ev? \in OpeningRequest \wedge nbTrain = 0\,]$$
$$\quad \wedge\, gate.ConsumeEvent)$$

The transitions of the subdiagram are considered like transitions that do not modify the superstate. So the operations representing these transitions are grouped in a single operation. For instance, the transitions of the subdiagram of *Forbidden* are gathered in the *TransitionStayForbidden* operation.

$$TransitionStayForbidden \mathrel{\widehat{=}}$$
$$\quad TransitionStayClosing\,[]\,TransitionClosingBlocked\,[]$$
$$\quad TransitionStayBlocked\,[]\,TransitionBlockedOpening$$

Then the operation *TransitionStayForbidden* is added to the choices of the *ConsumeEvent* operation.

ConsumeEvent $\hat{=}$
    TransitionForbiddenPermitted [] *TransitionPermittedForbidden* []
    TransitionStayForbidden

4   Related work

Many works have proposed to combine semi-formal and formal methods. As mentioned earlier, several research teams have addressed non object-oriented methods, like structured methods [13, 14]. Classical model based methods like Z, B or VDM offer a good support to express their main concepts. But the introduction of the object paradigm increases the difficulty. At the moment, most works deal with integrating formal methods with object-oriented methods. But many works [6–8] only deal with the static aspects of object modelling. In fact only five other works have studied the problem of integrating the dynamic model of OMT into formal specifications:

- [5, 12] translate Statecharts in B. More precisely, Facon *et al.* [5, 6] are interested in translating all OMT models into B.
- [4] translates the OMT models in Lotos: algebraic specifications are used to expressed the object model and a process algebra describes the behaviour.
- in [10, 11] Lano illustrates the use of object-oriented formal languages (Z++ and VDM++) for the integration with semi-formal methods.

But all these works differ from our approach in some of the following aspects:

- some works have not studied the links between the static and dynamic models. Consistency between the models only relies on the static semantics of the target language, while we try to explicit additional consistency properties.
- structuring primitives of the Statecharts (nesting and composition) are not treated by all the other works. In this work, we address nested Statecharts and parallel composition (behaviour of an aggregate which components evolve in parallel).
- most works do not differentiate between different categories of events: events only correspond to operation calls. This is not completely in accordance with the OMT semantics that proposed to group events into a hierarchy of classes having a *Event* class as root. In [5], two types of events are distinguished (operation call and external event), but only operation call is covered.
- [11] introduces a specific development process. This approach is a restriction of the initial OMT method, and could introduce a drawback for industrial integration.

These comments are summarized in the following table:

	link static/dynamic		structuring		event	specific
	static sem.	other link	nesting	comp.		process
B [5]	yes	yes	no	no	2 types	no
B [12]	yes	no	no	yes	operation call	no
Lotos [4]	yes	no	no	yes	gate	no
Z++ [10]	yes	no	yes	yes	operation call	no
VDM++ [10, 11]	yes	no	yes	yes	operation call	yes [11]
Object-Z	yes	yes	yes	to deepen	3 types	no

5 Conclusion

5.1 Summary of the work

This article has proposed a way to translate the OMT dynamic model into Object-Z. Most concepts of the dynamic model can be taken into account with this approach.

We have shown how states, substates, and transitions can be translated into Object-Z. Events, conditions and actions associated to transitions have also been covered.

Parallelism of state machines has been handled as the parallel composition of object behaviours (see Figure 8). For parallel composition occurring inside a single object, interleaving the object actions can provide a solution as soon as strong synchronization is not required between the parallel tasks.

Actions may also take place on entry and exit of a state (see Figure 1). These cases boil down to distribute these actions into all incoming or outgoing transitions respectively. Also, taking into account an Event/Action pair within a state (see *State*1 in Figure 1) corresponds to add a transition from this state to itself labelled with the Event/Action pair.

Activities are the only uncovered concept in the dynamic model. The translation of this construct requires further investigation in order to understand its semantics which may exhibit a notion of duration or a repetitive character.

This work goes into the direction of our original objectives (see Section 1):

- It makes the semantics of OMT more precise. In particular, the notion of event has been further detailed. Events have been classified into three categories: external events which are handled by *ConsumeEvent*, operation calls (e.g. *SwitchOn*), and internal events. Internal events are necessary to fire transitions which only exhibit a condition (e.g. *Permitted* to *Forbidden* in Figure 9).

  It must be noted that, in this approach, events are sent to a specific object instead of being implicitly broadcasted. If an object wants to broadcast an event, it has to send it explicitly to all other objects. In other words, this event mechanism does not support implicit invocation. Further work might investigate the specification of such implicit mechanisms. Once again, this precises the OMT semantics.

  As far as internal events are concerned, the sender of such events has not been described. Actually, internal events occur after state changes. But they may rely on a state change in another object. Such state changes must be tracked and turned into the generation of internal events. This can result in a transformation of the operation specifications where every (or targeted) state changes are explicitly associated to the generation of the internal event. It may also correspond to implementation level mechanisms, as can be found in active databases, or reactive objects (e.g. JavaBeans components).

– We have tried to make the resulting Object-Z specifications readable by proposing a systematic translation which facilitates the traceability from the dynamic model. Nevertheless Object-Z specifications become rapidly big and difficult to read because Object-Z does not always provide the flexibility of Z schemata.

– The translation scheme also helps to locate the limits of the OMT notations. These correspond to *holes* in the skeleton that must be filled in as further annotations. Here these holes include building precise correspondence between the states of the object and its attributes and links to other objects; giving a precise type to the notion of event and making explicit the distribution scheme of events (broadcast or targeted invocation).

5.2   The choice of a single formal language

This approach has deliberately taken the choice of a single formal language as the target of the translation process. Actually, the choice of Object-Z instead of classical languages for reactive systems even brings benefits for the translation of the dynamic model because classical languages for reactive systems are able to express complex behaviours, but can hardly handle complex data. In OMT, events may correspond to complex classes, conditions may refer to elaborated data structures and actions can manipulate all data defined in the object model. In our translation scheme, such references to complex data types and structures are easily handled in the operation schemata which model transitions.

Nevertheless, the main motivation for the choice of a single language is to express the consistency between the object and dynamic model. The consistency between the models is first checked by verifying that the names used in the dynamic model are introduced in the object model. This is achieved by the classical type-checking algorithm of the Object-Z tools. Further consistency may be checked by proving the satisfiability of the Z schemata, i.e. showing that there exists a state which satisfies the invariant and that all operations are implementable.

Other proof obligations are specific to the approach, and additional work should be done to define these more precisely. For example, it seems that OMT requires a dynamic diagram to be deterministic. This impulses to prove that the preconditions of all transitions existing from a state are mutually exclusive. One may also further investigate the consistency between the behaviour of an aggregate object and the behaviour of its components. Here, the behaviour of the level crossing constrains the behaviour of the gate, which corresponds to some refinement relation.

5.3   Perspectives

This work demonstrates that it is possible to integrate semi-formal and formal methods. Further work is necessary to express the three OMT models into Object-Z. But if, when starting this work, the choice of OMT was obvious as one of the most used object-oriented methods, now the semi-formal method studied should evolve to UML (Unified Modeling language [17]) as it might replace OMT especially in the CASE environments.

We discuss here only the dynamic aspects of the changes from OMT to UML. UML has four pertinent diagrams (sequence, collaboration, activity and state diagrams) to represent the behaviour. Activity and state diagrams are based on automata which have been inspired from the OMT dynamic model. But in UML, state diagrams have a more elaborated semantics than in OMT as through the i-Logix company, Harel and his team contributed with expertise in the definition, semantics and use of executable behaviour within UML. Sequence, collaboration and activity diagrams can be used during requirements capture or during design. So on the one hand, they are suitable for validation, but they are difficult to express formally; on the other hand, they are (with state diagram) pertinent for verification. A first step in our further work should consist in studying the adaptability of our work to the UML state diagram. Then we will have to take into account the other diagrams to complete the formal specification of the behaviour.

This work should be supported by a tool which would permit to check the usability of the translation proposals and to check consistency between the models. It is actually obvious that the introduction of CASE's to manage specification results has favoured the development of semi-formal methods. The formal approach might become a more common practice when CASE's will integrate it with the semi-formal one and with a real cooperation with natural language and document processing, especially managing modifications and consistency between the three types of information models. The prototyping of our translation proposals will be a step toward such tools.

References

1. R. Buessow and M. Weber. BW: A steam-boiler control specification with Statecharts and Z. In J.-R. Abrial, E. Börger, and H. Langmaack, editors, *Formal Methods for Industrial Applications: Specifying and Programming the Steam Boiler Control*, volume 1165 of *Lecture Notes in Computer Science*, pages 109–128. Springer-Verlag, 1996.
2. R. Duke, P. Kin, G. Rose, and G. Smith. The Object-Z specification langage: Version 1. Technical Report 91-1, Software Verification Research Centre, Department of Computer Science, University of Queensland, Australia, April 1991.
3. S. Dupuy, Y. Ledru, and M. Chabre-Peccoud. Integrating OMT and Object-Z. In A. Evans and K. Lano, editors, *Proc. BCS FACS/EROS ROOM Workshop*, London, UK, June 1997. Department of Computing, Imperial College. Technical Report GR/K67311-2.
4. E.Wand, H.Richter, and B.Cheng. Formalizing and integrating the dynamic model within OMT. In *Proc. 19th International Conference on Software Engineering*, Boston, USA, May 1997.
5. P. Facon, R. Laleau, and H.P. Nguyen. Dérivation de spécifications formelles B à partir de spécifications semi-formelles de systèmes d'information. In H. Habrias, editor, *Proc. 1st Conference on the B Method*, Nantes, France, November 1996.
6. P. Facon, R. Laleau, and H.P. Nguyen. Mapping object diagrams into B specifications. In A. Bryant and L. Semmens, editors, *Method Integration Workshop*, Electronic Workshops in Computing. Springer-Verlag, March 1996.
7. R. France and J.-M. Bruel. Using formal techniques to strengthen informal object-oriented modeling techniques: The FuZE experience. Technical report, Department of Computer Science and Engineering, Florida Atlantic University, Boca Raton, USA, 1997.

8. R. France, J.-M. Bruel, M. Larrondo-Petrie, and M. Shroff. Exploring the semantics of UML type structures with Z. In H. Bowman and J. Derrick, editors, *Proc. 2nd IFIP Conference on Formal Methods for Open Object-Based Distributed Systems (FMOODS)*, pages 247–260. Chapman and Hall, 1997.

9. D. Harel. Statecharts: A visual formalism for complex systems. *Science of Computer Programming*, 8(3):231–274, 1987.

10. K. Lano. *Formal Object-Oriented Development*. FACIT. Springer-Verlag, 1995.

11. K. Lano and S. Goldsack. Integrated formal and object-oriented methods: The VDM++ approach. In A. Bryant and L. Semmens, editors, *Method Integration Workshop*, Electronic Workshops in Computing. Springer-Verlag, March 1996.

12. K. Lano, H. Houghton, and P. Wheeler. *Integrating Formal and Structured Methods in Object-Oriented System Development*, chapter 7. Springer-Verlag, 1996.

13. F. Polack, M. Whiston, and K. Mander. The SAZ project: Integrating SSADM and Z. In J. C. P. Woodcock and P. G. Larsen, editors, *FME '93: Industrial-Strength Formal Methods*, volume 670 of *Lecture Notes in Computer Science*, pages 541–557. Springer-Verlag, 1993.

14. G.P. Randell. Translating data flow diagrams into Z (and vice versa). Technical Report 90019, Royal Signals and Radar Establishement, Malvern, UK, October 1990.

15. J. Rumbaugh, M. Blaha, M. Premerlani, F. Eddy, and W. Lorensen. *Object-Oriented Modeling and Design*. Prentice Hall International, 1991.

16. H. Saiedian. An invitation to formal methods. *IEEE Computer*, 24(4):16–30, April 1996.

17. The UML Group. *UML Notation Guide, Version 1.1*, September 1997. URL: http://www.rational.com/uml/documentation.html.

Select Z Bibliography

Jonathan P. Bowen

The University of Reading, Department of Computer Science
Whiteknights, PO Box 225, Reading, Berks RG6 6AY, UK

Email: J.P.Bowen@reading.ac.uk
URL: http://www.cs.reading.ac.uk/people/jpb/

Abstract. This bibliography contains a list of references concerned with the formal Z notation that are either available as published papers, books, selected technical reports, or on-line. Some references on the related B-Method are also included. The bibliography is in alphabetical order by author name(s).

Introduction

The list of references presented here is maintained in electronic form, in BIBTEX bibliography database format, which is compatible with the widely used LATEX document preparation system [408]. It is intended to keep the bibliography up to date and to issue it to coincide with the regular International Conference of Z Users (aka Z User Meeting – ZUM). The latest version of BIBTEX source file used for this bibliography [1] is available as a searchable on-line database on the World Wide Web under the following Uniform Resource Location (URL):

$$\text{http://www.comlab.ox.ac.uk/archive/z/bib.html}$$

Hyperlinks to on-line versions of publications and related resources are included where known. This bibliography has been regularly maintained for Z User Meeting proceedings in the past (e.g., see [79]). For an alternative annotated Z bibliography, see [89] and Appendix C *Literature Guide* of [77].

To add new references concerned with Z to this list, please send details to Jonathan Bowen (contact details above), preferably via electronic mail. It is helpful if you can give as much information as possible so the entry could be included as a reference in future papers concerning Z.

Acknowledgements

Ruaridh Macdonald of RSRE, Malvern, UK initiated the idea of a Z bibliography and helped maintain it for several years. Joan Arnold at the Oxford University Computing Laboratory, UK has previously assisted in maintaining the bibliography as part of her work as secretary to the European ESPRIT **ProCoS-WG** Working Group (no. 8694) on 'Provably Correct Systems'. Thank you to everybody who has submitted entries over the years. The excellent on-line UK Bath Information and Data Service (BIDS) bibliographic database (see under http://www.bids.ac.uk/) has been used for some of the more recent entries, enabling abstracts to be included on-line.

References

1. Z bibliography. URL: http://www.comlab.ox.ac.uk/archive/z/bib.html, 1990 onwards.

   This bibliography is maintained in BIBTEX database source format accessible in searchable form on the World Wide Web. To add entries, please send as complete information as possible to Jonathan Bowen on J.P.Bowen@reading.ac.uk.

2. G. D. Abowd. Agents: Communicating interactive processes. In D. Diaper, D. Gilmore, G. Cockton, and B. Shackel, editors, *Human-Computer Interaction: INTERACT'90*, pages 143–148. Elsevier Science Publishers (North-Holland), 1990.

3. G. D. Abowd. *Formal Aspects of Human-Computer Interaction*. DPhil thesis, Oxford University Computing Laboratory, Wolfson Building, Parks Road, Oxford, UK, 1991.

4. G. D. Abowd, R. Allen, and D. Garlan. Using style to understand descriptions of software architectures. *ACM Software Engineering Notes*, 18(5):9–20, December 1993.

5. G. D. Abowd, R. Allen, and D. Garlan. Formalizing style to understand descriptions of software architecture. *ACM Transactions on Software Engineering and Methodology (TOSEM)*, 4(4):319–364, October 1995.

   The formal model is described using the Z specification language.

6. J.-R. Abrial. Data semantics. In J. W. Klimbie and K. L. Koffeman, editors, *IFIP TC2 Working Conference on Data Base Management*, pages 1–59. Elsevier Science Publishers (North-Holland), April 1974.

   A seminal paper for the formal Z notation, as noted in [303].

7. J.-R. Abrial. The B tool. In Bloomfield et al. [54], pages 86–87.

8. J.-R. Abrial. The B method for large software, specification, design and coding (abstract). In Prehn and Toetenel [531], pages 398–405.

9. J.-R. Abrial. *The B-Book: Assigning Programs to Meanings*. Cambridge University Press, 1996.

   This book is a reference manual for the B-Method developed by Jean-Raymond Abrial, also the originator of the Z notation. B is designed for tool-assisted software development whereas Z is designed mainly for specification.

   Contents: Mathematical reasoning; Set notation; Mathematical objects; Introduction to abstract machines; Formal definition of abstract machines; Theory of abstract machines; Constructing large abstract machines; Example of abstract machines; Sequencing and loop; Programming examples; Refinement; Constructing large software systems; Example of refinement;

   Appendices: Summary of the most current notations; Syntax; Definitions; Visibility rules; Rules and axioms; Proof obligations.

10. J.-R. Abrial, E. Börger, and H. Langmaack, editors. *Formal Methods for Industrial Applications: Specifying and Programming the Steam Boiler*, volume 1165 of *Lecture Notes in Computer Science*. Springer-Verlag, 1996.

    A comparative collection of formal methods case studies. See [126, 565].

11. J.-R. Abrial, S. A. Schuman, and B. Meyer. Specification language. In R. M. McKeag and A. M. Macnaghten, editors, *On the Construction of Programs: An Advanced Course*, pages 343–410. Cambridge University Press, 1980.

12. J.-R. Abrial and I. H. Sørensen. KWIC-index generation. In J. Staunstrup, editor, *Program Specification: Proceedings of a Workshop*, volume 134 of *Lecture Notes in Computer Science*, pages 88–95. Springer-Verlag, 1981.

13. K. Achatz and W. Schulte. A formal OO method inspired by Fusion and Object-Z. In Bowen et al. [101], pages 92–111.

14. M. Ainsworth, A. H. Cruickshank, P. J. L. Wallis, and L. J. Groves. Viewpoint specification and Z. *Information and Software Technology*, 36(1):43–51, 1994.

15. A. J. Alencar and J. A. Goguen. OOZE: An object-oriented Z environment. In P. America, editor, *Proc. ECOOP'91 European Conference on Object-Oriented Programming*, volume 512 of *Lecture Notes in Computer Science*, pages 180–199. Springer-Verlag, 1991.

16. M. A. Ardis, J. A. Chaves, L. J. Jagadeesan, P. Mataga, C. Puchol, M. G. Staskauskas, and J. von Olnhausen. A framework for evaluating specification methods for reactive systems experience report. *IEEE Transactions on Software Engineering*, 22(6):378–389, June 1996. Several different methods, including Modechart, VFSM, ESTEREL, Basic LOTOS, Z, SDL, and C, are applied to a problem encountered in the design of software for AT&T's 5ESS telephone switching system.

17. D. B. Arnold, D. A. Duce, and G. J. Reynolds. An approach to the formal specification of configurable models of graphics systems. In G. Maréchal, editor, *Proc. EUROGRAPH-ICS'87, European Computer Graphics Conference and Exhibition*, pages 439–463. Elsevier Science Publishers (North-Holland), 1987.
The paper describes a general framework for the formal specification of modular graphics systems, illustrated by an example taken from the Graphical Kernel System (GKS) standard.

18. D. B. Arnold and G. J. Reynolds. Configuring graphics systems components. *IEE/BCS Software Engineering Journal*, 3(6):248–256, November 1988.

19. R. D. Arthan. Formal specification of a proof tool. In Prehn and Toetenel [530], pages 356–370.

20. R. D. Arthan. On free type definitions in Z. In Nicholls [506], pages 40–58.

21. R. D. Arthan. Recursive definitions in Z. In Bowen et al. [85], pages 154–171.

22. K. Ashoo. The Genesis Z tool – an overview. *BCS-FACS FACTS*, Series II, 3(1):11–13, May 1992.

23. S. Atkinson and D. Scholefield. Transformational vs reactive refinement in real-time systems. *Information Processing Letters*, 55(4):201–210, 1995.

24. S. Aujla, A. Bryant, and L. Semmens. A rigorous review technique: Using formal notations within conventional development methods. In Katsolakos [393], pages 247–255.

25. P. B. Austin, K. A. Murray, and A. J. Wellings. File system caching in large point-to-point networks. *IEE/BCS Software Engineering Journal*, 7(1):65–80, January 1992.

26. S. Austin and G. I. Parkin. Formal methods: A survey. Technical report, National Physical Laboratory, Queens Road, Teddington, Middlesex, TW11 0LW, UK, March 1993.

27. C. Bailes and R. Duke. The ecology of class refinement. In Morris and Shaw [487], pages 185–196.

28. M. Bailey. Formal specification using Z. In *Proc. Software Engineering anniversary meeting (SEAS)*, page 99, 1987.

29. J. Bainbridge, R. W. Whitty, and J. B. Wordsworth. Obtaining structural metrics of Z specifications for systems development. In Nicholls [504], pages 269–281.

30. J.-P. Banâtre. About programming environments. In J.-P. Banâtre, S. B. Jones, and D. de Métayer, editors, *Prospects for Functional Programming in Software Engineering*, chapter 1, pages 1–22. Springer-Verlag, 1991.

31. P. Bancroft and I. J. Hayes. A formal semantics for a language with type extension. In Bowen and Hinchey [99], pages 299–314.

32. R. Barden and S. Stepney. Support for using Z. In Bowen and Nicholls [102], pages 255–280.

33. R. Barden, S. Stepney, and D. Cooper. The use of Z. In Nicholls [506], pages 99–124.

34. R. Barden, S. Stepney, and D. Cooper. *Z in Practice*. BCS Practitioner Series. Prentice Hall, 1994.

35. G. Barrett. Formal methods applied to a floating-point number system. *IEEE Transactions on Software Engineering*, 15(5):611–621, May 1989.

   A formalization of the IEEE standard for binary floating-point arithmetic in Z is presented. The formal specification is refined into four components. The procedures presented form the basis for the floating-point unit of the Inmos IMS T800 Transputer. This work resulted in a joint UK Queen's Award for Technological Achievement for Inmos Ltd and the Oxford University Computing Laboratory in 1990. It was estimated that the approach saved a year in development time compared to traditional methods.

36. L. M. Barroca, J. S. Fitzgerald, and L. Spencer. The architectural specification of an avionic subsystem. In France and Gerhart [265], pages 17–29.

37. L. M. Barroca and J. A. McDermid. Formal methods: Use and relevance for the development of safety-critical systems. *The Computer Journal*, 35(6):579–599, December 1992.

38. B. W. Bates, J.-M. Bruel, R. B. France, and M. M. Larrondo-Petrie. Guidelines for formalizing Fusion object-oriented analysis models. In P. Constantopoulos, J. Mylopoulos, and Y. Vassiliou, editors, *Advanced Information Systems Engineering*, volume 1080 of *Lecture Notes in Computer Science*, pages 222–233. Springer-Verlag, 1996.

39. P. Baumann. Z and natural semantics. In Bowen and Hall [91], pages 168–184.

40. P. Baumann and K. Lermer. A framework for the specification of reactive and concurrent systems in Z. In P. S. Thiagarajan, editor, *Foundations of Software Technology and Theoretical Computer Science*, volume 1026 of *Lecture Notes in Computer Science*, pages 62–79. Springer-Verlag, 1995.

41. P. Baumann and K. Lermer. Specifying parallel and distributed real-time systems in Z. In *Proc. 4th International Workshop on Parallel and Distributed Real-Time Systems, Hawaii*, pages 216–222, April 1996.

42. M. Benjamin. A message passing system: An example of combining CSP and Z. In Nicholls [502], pages 221–228.

43. M. Benveniste. Writing operational semantics in Z: A structural approach. In Prehn and Toetenel [530], pages 164–188.

44. S. Bera. Structuring for the VDM specification language. In Bloomfield et al. [54], pages 2–25.

45. P. Bernard and G. Laffitte. The French population census for 1990. In Bowen and Hinchey [99], pages 334–352.

46. D. Bert, editor. *B'98: Recent Developments in the Use of the B Method*, volume 1393 of *Lecture Notes in Computer Science*. Springer-Verlag, 1998.

   Proceedings of the 2nd B Conference, Montpellier, France, 22–24 April 1998.

47. J. Bicarregui, J. Dick, and E. Woods. Supporting the length of formal development: From diagrams to VDM to B to C. In Habrias [303], pages 63–75.

48. J. Bicarregui, J. Dick, and E. Woods. Quantitative analysis of formal methods. In Gaudel and Woodcock [280], pages 60–73.

49. J. Bicarregui and B. Ritchie. Invariants, frames and postconditions: A comparison of the VDM and B notations. *IEEE Transactions on Software Engineering*, 21(2):79–89, February 1995.

50. P. G. Bishop, editor. *Fault Avoidance*, chapter 3, pages 56–140. Applied Science. Elsevier Science Publishers, 1990.

   Section 3.88 (pages 94–96) provides an overview of Z. Other sections describe related techniques.

51. D. Bjørner, C. A. R. Hoare, and H. Langmaack, editors. *VDM and Z – Formal Methods in Software Development*, volume 428 of *Lecture Notes in Computer Science*. VDM-Europe, Springer-Verlag, 1990.

The 3rd VDM-Europe Symposium was held at Kiel, Germany, 17–21 April 1990. A significant number of papers concerned with Z were presented [138, 231, 277, 194, 294, 308, 399, 562, 607, 660, 692].

52. A. Bloesch, E. Kazmierczak, P. Kearney, and O. Traynor. Cogito: A methodology and system for formal software-development. *International Journal of Software Engineering and Knowledge Engineering*, 5(4):599–617, 1995.

53. B. Bloom, A. Cheng, and A. Dsouza. Using a Protean language to enhance expressiveness in specification. *IEEE Transactions on Software Engineering*, 23(4):224–234, 1997.

54. R. Bloomfield, L. Marshall, and R. Jones, editors. *VDM – The Way Ahead*, volume 328 of *Lecture Notes in Computer Science*. VDM-Europe, Springer-Verlag, 1988.
   The 2nd VDM-Europe Symposium was held at Dublin, Ireland, 11–16 September 1988. See [7, 44].

55. E. A. Boiten, H. Bowman, J. Derrick, and M. Steen. Issues in multiparadigm viewpoint specification. In A. Finkelstein and G. Spanoudakis, editors, *SIGSOFT '96 International Workshop on Multiple Perspectives in Software Development (Viewpoints '96)*, pages 162–166. ACM, 1996.

56. E. A. Boiten, H. Bowman, J. Derrick, and M. Steen. Viewpoint consistency in Z and LOTOS: A case study. In Fitzgerald et al. [260], pages 644–664.
   The 4th FME Symposium was held at Graz, Austria, 15–19 September 1997. See the Z-related paper [56].

57. E. A. Boiten, J. Derrick, H. Bowman, and M. Steen. Unification and multiple views of data in Z. In J. C. van Vliet, editor, *Proc. Computing Science in the Netherlands*, pages 73–85, November 1995.

58. E. A. Boiten, J. Derrick, H. Bowman, and M. Steen. Consistency and refinement for partial specifications in Z. In Gaudel and Woodcock [280], pages 287–306.

59. E. A. Boiten, J. Derrick, H. Bowman, and M. Steen. Coupling schemas: Data refinement and view(point) composition. In D. J. Duke and A. S. Evans, editors, *Northern Formal Methods Workshop*, Electronic Workshops In Computing. Springer-Verlag, 1997.

60. E. Börger and S. Mazzanti. A practical method for rigorously controllable hardware design. In Bowen et al. [101], pages 151–187.

61. J. Bosch and S. Mitchell, editors. *Object-Oriented Technology: ECOOP'97 Workshop Reader*, volume 1357 of *Lecture Notes in Computer Science*. Springer-Verlag, 1997.
   See Z-related papers [152, 243, 264].

62. A. Boswell. Specification and validation of a security policy model. In Woodcock and Larsen [689], pages 42–51.
   The 1st FME Symposium was held at Odense, Denmark, 19–23 April 1993. Z-related papers include [103, 165, 254, 372, 447, 526].

63. A. Boswell. Specification and validation of a security policy model. *IEEE Transactions on Software Engineering*, 21(2):99–106, February 1995.
   This paper describes the development of a formal security model in Z for the NATO Air Command and Control System (ACCS): a large, distributed, multilevel-secure system. The model was subject to manual validation, and some of the issues and lessons in both writing and validating the model are discussed.

64. L. Bottaci and J. Jones. *Formal Specification Using Z: A Modelling Approach*. International Thomson Publishing, London, 1995.

65. J. P. Bowen. Formal specification and documentation of microprocessor instruction sets. *Microprocessing and Microprogramming*, 21(1–5):223–230, August 1987.

66. J. P. Bowen. The formal specification of a microprocessor instruction set. Technical Monograph PRG-60, Oxford University Computing Laboratory, Wolfson Building, Parks Road, Oxford, UK, January 1987.
   The Z notation is used to define the Motorola M6800 8-bit microprocessor instruction set.

67. J. P. Bowen, editor. *Proc. Z Users Meeting, 1 Wellington Square, Oxford*, Wolfson Building, Parks Road, Oxford, UK, December 1987. Oxford University Computing Laboratory.
    Proceedings of the 2nd Z User Meeting, Department of External Studies, Rewley House, Oxford, UK, Friday 8 December 1987. Note that there were no written proceedings for the 1st Z User Meeting, held in Oxford, December 1986.

68. J. P. Bowen. Formal specification in Z as a design and documentation tool. In *Proc. 2nd IEE/BCS Conference on Software Engineering*, number 290 in Conference Publication, pages 164–168. IEE/BCS, July 1988.

69. J. P. Bowen, editor. *Proc. Third Annual Z Users Meeting*, Wolfson Building, Parks Road, Oxford, UK, December 1988. Oxford University Computing Laboratory.
    Proceedings of the 3rd Z User Meeting, Department of External Studies, Rewley House, Oxford, UK, Friday 16 December 1988. Issued with *A Miscellany of Handy Techniques* by R. Macdonald, *Practical Experience of Formal Specification: A programming interface for communications* by J. B. Wordsworth, and a number of posters.

70. J. P. Bowen. Formal specification of window systems. Technical Monograph PRG-74, Oxford University Computing Laboratory, Wolfson Building, Parks Road, Oxford, UK, June 1989.
    Three window systems, X from MIT, WM from Carnegie-Mellon University and the Blit from AT&T Bell Laboratories are covered.

71. J. P. Bowen. POS: Formal specification of a UNIX tool. *IEE/BCS Software Engineering Journal*, 4(1):67–72, January 1989.

72. J. P. Bowen. Formal specification of the ProCoS/safemos instruction set. *Microprocessors and Microsystems*, 14(10):631–643, December 1990.
    This article is part of a special feature on *Formal aspects of microprocessor design*, edited by H. S. M. Zedan. See also [574].

73. J. P. Bowen. X: Why Z? *Computer Graphics Forum*, 11(4):221–234, October 1992.
    This paper asks whether window management systems would not be better specified through a formal methodology and gives examples in Z of the X Window System.

74. J. P. Bowen. Formal methods in safety-critical standards. In Katsolakos [393], pages 168–177.

75. J. P. Bowen. Report on Z User Meeting, London 1992. *BCS-FACS FACTS*, Series III, 1(3):7–8, Summer 1993.
    Other versions of this report appeared as follows:
    – Z User Meetings, *Safety Systems: The Safety-Critical Systems Club Newsletter*, 3(1):13, September 1993.
    – Z User Group activities, *JFIT News*, 46:5, September 1993.
    – Report on Z User Meeting, *Information and Software Technology*, 35(10):613, October 1993.
    – Z User Meeting Activities, *High Integrity Systems*, 1(1):93–94, 1994.

76. J. P. Bowen. Glossary of Z notation. *Information and Software Technology*, 37(5–6):333–334, May–June 1995.

77. J. P. Bowen. *Formal Specification and Documentation Using Z: A Case Study Approach.* International Thomson Computer Press, 1996.
    Contents: Foreword; Preface; Part I: Introduction – Chapter 1: Formal Specification using Z, Chapter 2: Industrial Use of Formal Methods, Chapter 3: A Brief Introduction to Z; Part II: Network Services – Chapter 4: Documentation using Z, Chapter 5: A File Storage Service; Part III: UNIX Software – Chapter 6: A Text Formatting Tool, Chapter 7: An Event-based Input System; Part IV: Instruction Sets – Chapter 8: Machine Words, Chapter 9: The Transputer Instruction Set; Part V: Graphics – Chapter 10: Basic Graphical Concepts, Chapter 11: Raster-Op Functions; Part VI: Window Systems – Chapter 12: The ITC 'WM'

Window Manager, Chapter 13: Blit Windows, Chapter 14: The X Window System, Chapter 15: Formal Specification of Existing Systems; Appendices – A: Information on Z, B: Z Glossary, C: Literature Guide.

78. J. P. Bowen. Comp.specification.z and Z FORUM frequently asked questions. In Bowen et al. [101], pages 425–433.

79. J. P. Bowen. Select Z bibliography. In Bowen et al. [101], pages 391–424.

80. J. P. Bowen. Comp.specification.z and Z FORUM frequently asked questions. In Bowen et al. [85], pages 407–415.

81. J. P. Bowen. Select Z bibliography. In Bowen et al. [85], pages 367–406.

82. J. P. Bowen, P. T. Breuer, and K. C. Lano. A compendium of formal techniques for software maintenance. *IEE/BCS Software Engineering Journal*, 8(5):253–262, September 1993.

83. J. P. Bowen, P. T. Breuer, and K. C. Lano. Formal specifications in software maintenance: From code to Z^{++} and back again. *Information and Software Technology*, 35(11/12):679–690, November/December 1993.

84. J. P. Bowen and D. Chippington. Z on the Web using Java. In Bowen et al. [85], pages 66–80.

85. J. P. Bowen, A. Fett, and M. G. Hinchey, editors. *ZUM'98: The Z Formal Specification Notation, 11th International Conference of Z Users, Berlin, Germany, 24–26 September 1998*, volume 1493 of *Lecture Notes in Computer Science*. Springer-Verlag, 1998.
Proceedings of the 11th Z User Meeting, Technical University of Berlin, Germany. For individual papers presented at the main conference, see [21, 84, 149, 188, 242, 259, 269, 301, 342, 375, 425, 429, 440, 443, 489, 516, 517, 564, 598, 615, 624, 651, 659]. The proceedings also includes as appendices this bibliography [81] and a section answering *Frequently Asked Questions* [80].

86. J. P. Bowen, R. B. Gimson, and S. Topp-Jørgensen. The specification of network services. Technical Monograph PRG-61, Oxford University Computing Laboratory, Wolfson Building, Parks Road, Oxford, UK, August 1987.

87. J. P. Bowen, R. B. Gimson, and S. Topp-Jørgensen. Specifying system implementations in Z. Technical Monograph PRG-63, Oxford University Computing Laboratory, Wolfson Building, Parks Road, Oxford, UK, February 1988.

88. J. P. Bowen and M. J. C. Gordon. Z and HOL. In Bowen and Hall [91], pages 141–167.

89. J. P. Bowen and M. J. C. Gordon. A shallow embedding of Z in HOL. *Information and Software Technology*, 37(5–6):269–276, May–June 1995.
Revised version of [88].

90. J. P. Bowen and M. J. C. Gordon. A shallow embedding of Z in HOL. *Information and Software Technology*, 37(5–6):269–276, 1995.

91. J. P. Bowen and J. A. Hall, editors. *Z User Workshop, Cambridge 1994*, Workshops in Computing. Springer-Verlag, 1994.
Proceedings of the 8th Z User Meeting, St. John's College, Cambridge, UK. Published in collaboration with the British Computer Society. For individual papers, see [39, 88, 110, 137, 139, 198, 246, 248, 275, 309, 312, 317, 321, 409, 449, 524, 591, 668, 688, 694]. The proceedings also includes an *Introduction and Opening Remarks*, a *Select Z Bibliography* and a section answering *Frequently Asked Questions*.

92. J. P. Bowen, He Jifeng, R. W. S. Hale, and J. M. J. Herbert. Towards verified systems: The SAFEMOS project. In C. J. Mitchell and V. Stavridou, editors, *The Mathematics of Dependable Systems*, volume 55 of *The Institute of Mathematics and its Applications Conference Series*, pages 23–48. Oxford University Press, 1995.

93. J. P. Bowen and M. G. Hinchey. Formal methods and safety-critical standards. *IEEE Computer*, 27(8):68–71, August 1994.

94. J. P. Bowen and M. G. Hinchey. Seven more myths of formal methods: Dispelling industrial prejudices. In Naftalin et al. [490], pages 105–117.

95. J. P. Bowen and M. G. Hinchey. Editorial. *Information and Software Technology*, 37(5–6):258–259, May–June 1995.
A special issue on Z. See [76, 96, 89, 105, 276, 424, 446, 451, 654].

96. J. P. Bowen and M. G. Hinchey. Report on Z User Meeting (ZUM'94). *Information and Software Technology*, 37(5–6):335–336, May–June 1995.

97. J. P. Bowen and M. G. Hinchey. Seven more myths of formal methods. *IEEE Software*, 12(4):34–41, July 1995.
This article deals with further myths in addition to those presented in [307]. Previous versions issued as:
   – Technical Report PRG-TR-7-94, Oxford University Computing Laboratory, June 1994.
   – Technical Report 357, University of Cambridge, Computer Laboratory, January 1995.

98. J. P. Bowen and M. G. Hinchey. Ten commandments of formal methods. *IEEE Computer*, 28(4):56–63, April 1995.
Previously issued as: Technical Report 350, University of Cambridge, Computer Laboratory, September 1994.

99. J. P. Bowen and M. G. Hinchey, editors. *ZUM'95: The Z Formal Specification Notation, 9th International Conference of Z Users, Limerick, Ireland, September 7–9, 1995, Proceedings*, volume 967 of *Lecture Notes in Computer Science*. Springer-Verlag, 1995.
Proceedings of the 9th Z User Meeting, University of Limerick, Ireland. For individual papers presented at the main conference, see [31, 45, 120, 144, 180, 193, 213, 245, 266, 284, 292, 311, 353, 357, 376, 407, 432, 436, 441, 463, 520, 543, 552, 592, 611, 628, 658, 665].
Some papers formed part of an associated Educational Issues Session organized by Neville Dean [143, 181, 300, 465, 521, 673]. The proceedings also includes as appendices a *Select Z Bibliography* and a section answering *Frequently Asked Questions*.

100. J. P. Bowen and M. G. Hinchey. Formal models and the specification process. In A. B. Tucker, Jr., editor, *The Computer Science and Engineering Handbook*, chapter 107, pages 2302–2322. CRC Press, 1997. Section X, Software Engineering.

101. J. P. Bowen, M. G. Hinchey, and D. Till, editors. *ZUM'97: The Z Formal Specification Notation, 10th International Conference of Z Users, Reading, UK, 3–4 April 1997*, volume 1212 of *Lecture Notes in Computer Science*. Springer-Verlag, 1997.
Proceedings of the 10th Z User Meeting, The University of Reading, UK. For individual papers presented at the main conference, see [13, 60, 130, 148, 191, 201, 249, 310, 306, 339, 340, 345, 377, 402, 406, 416, 412, 554, 623]. The proceedings also includes as appendices a *Select Z Bibliography* [79] and a section answering *Frequently Asked Questions* [78].

102. J. P. Bowen and J. E. Nicholls, editors. *Z User Workshop, London 1992*, Workshops in Computing. Springer-Verlag, 1993.
Proceedings of the 7th Z User Meeting, DTI Offices, London, UK. Published in collaboration with the British Computer Society. For individual papers, see [32, 108, 160, 167, 176, 174, 225, 335, 371, 403, 421, 434, 452, 507, 513, 532, 550, 638, 656]. The proceedings also includes an *Introduction and Opening Remarks*, a *Select Z Bibliography* and a section answering *Frequently Asked Questions*.

103. J. P. Bowen and V. Stavridou. The industrial take-up of formal methods in safety-critical and other areas: A perspective. In Woodcock and Larsen [689], pages 183–195.

104. J. P. Bowen and V. Stavridou. Safety-critical systems, formal methods and standards. *IEE/BCS Software Engineering Journal*, 8(4):189–209, July 1993.
A survey on the use of formal methods, including B and Z, for safety-critical systems. Winner of the 1994 IEE Charles Babbage Premium award. A previous version is also available as Oxford University Computing Laboratory Technical Report PRG-TR-5-92.

105. J. P. Bowen, S. Stepney, and R. Barden. Annotated Z bibliography. *Information and Software Technology*, 37(5–6):317–332, May–June 1995.
See also *Literature Guide*, Appendix C, pages 239–251 of [77].

106. H. Bowman and J. Derrick. Modelling distributed systems using Z. In K. M. George, editor, *ACM Symposium on Applied Computing*, pages 147–151. ACM Press, February 1995.

107. H. Bowman, J. Derrick, P. Linington, and M. Steen. FDTs for ODP. *Computer Standards & Interfaces*, 17(5–6):457–479, September 1995.

108. A. Bradley. Requirements for Defence Standard 00-55. In Bowen and Nicholls [102], pages 93–94.

109. P. T. Breuer. Z! in progress: Maintaining Z specifications. In Nicholls [504], pages 295–318.

110. P. T. Breuer and J. P. Bowen. Towards correct executable semantics for Z. In Bowen and Hall [91], pages 185–209.

111. S. M. Brien. The development of Z. In D. J. Andrews, J. F. Groote, and C. A. Middelburg, editors, *Semantics of Specification Languages (SoSL)*, Workshops in Computing, pages 1–14. Springer-Verlag, 1994.

112. S. M. Brien and J. E. Nicholls. Z base standard. Technical Monograph PRG-107, Oxford University Computing Laboratory, Wolfson Building, Parks Road, Oxford, UK, November 1992. Accepted for standardization under ISO/IEC JTC1/SC22.
This is the first publicly available version of the proposed ISO Z Standard. The latest draft is Version 1.2, September 1995. See also [604] for a widely used Z reference manual.

113. C. Britton, M. Loomes, and R. Mitchell. Formal specification as constructive diagrams. *Microprocessing and Microprogramming*, 37(1–5):175–178, January 1993.

114. M. Brossard-Guerlus and F. Klay. Introducing formal specification in an industrial context: An experiment in Z. In Habrias [303], pages 229–242.

115. D. J. Brown and J. P. Bowen. The Event Queue: An extensible input system for UNIX workstations. In *Proc. European Unix Users Group Conference*, pages 29–52, Helsinki, Finland, 12–14 May 1987.

116. D. Brownbridge. Using Z to develop a CASE toolset. In Nicholls [502], pages 142–149.

117. J.-M. Bruel, A. Benzekri, and Y. Raymaud. Z and the specification of real-time systems. In Habrias [303], pages 77–91.

118. A. Bryant. Structured methodologies and formal notations: Developing a framework for synthesis and investigation. In Nicholls [502], pages 229–241.

119. A. Bryant and A. S. Evans. Formalizing the Object Management Group's Core Object Model. *Computer Standards & Interfaces*, 17(5–6):481–489, September 1995.

120. A. Bryant, A. S. Evans, L. Semmens, R. Milovanovic, S. Stockman, M. Norris, and C. Selley. Using Z to rigorously review a specification of a network management system. In Bowen and Hinchey [99], pages 423–433.

121. A. Bryant and L. Semmens, editors. *Methods Integration*, Electronic Workshops in Computing. Springer-Verlag, 1996.
Proceedings of the Methods Integration Workshop, University of Leeds, UK, 25–26 March 1996. See [241, 267, 347, 352, 391, 415, 539].

122. G. R. Buckberry. ZED: A Z notation editor and syntax analyser. *BCS-FACS FACTS*, Series II, 2(3):13–23, November 1991.

123. A. Burns and I. W. Morrison. A formal description of the structure attribute model for tool interfacing. *IEE/BCS Software Engineering Journal*, 4(2):74–78, March 1989.

124. A. Burns and A. J. Wellings. Occam's priority model and deadline scheduling. In *Proc. 7th Occam User Group Meeting, Grenoble*, 1987.

125. J. S. Busby and D. Hutchison. The practical integration of manufacturing applications. *Software Practice and Experience*, 22(2):183–207, 1992.

126. R. Büssow and M. Weber. A steam-boiler control specification with Statecharts and Z. In Abrial et al. [10], pages 109–128.

127. P. Butcher. A behavioural semantics for Linda-2. *IEE/BCS Software Engineering Journal*, 6(4):196–204, July 1991.

128. G. Butler, P. Grogono, and F. Khendek. A Z specification of use cases: A preliminary report. In *Proc. Asia-Pacific Software Engineering Conference / International Computer Science Conference (APSEC'97/ICSC'97)*, pages 505–506, Hong Kong, 2–5 December 1997. IEEE Computer Society Press.

129. M. J. Butler. Service extension at the specification level. In Nicholls [504], pages 319–336.

130. M. J. Butler. An approach to the design of distributed systems with B AMN. In Bowen et al. [101], pages 223–241.

131. S. Butler and R. Duke. Defining composition operators for object interaction. *Object Oriented Systems*, 5(1):1–16, 1998.

132. J. Campin, N. Paton, and M. H. Williams. Specifying active database systems in an object-oriented framework. *International Journal of Software Engineering and Knowledge Engineering*, 7(1):101–123, 1997.

133. D. Carrington. ZOOM workshop report. In Nicholls [506], pages 352–364.
     This paper records the activities of a workshop on Z and object-oriented methods held in August 1992 at Oxford. A comprehensive bibliography is included.

134. D. Carrington, D. J. Duke, R. Duke, P. King, G. A. Rose, and G. Smith. Object-Z: An object-oriented extension to Z. In S. Vuong, editor, *Formal Description Techniques, II (FORTE'89)*, pages 281–296. Elsevier Science Publishers (North-Holland), 1990.

135. D. Carrington, D. J. Duke, I. J. Hayes, and J. Welsh. Deriving modular designs from formal specifications. *ACM Software Engineering Notes*, 18(5):89–98, December 1993.

136. D. Carrington and G. Smith. Extending Z for object-oriented specifications. In *Proc. 5th Australian Software Engineering Conference (ASWEC'90)*, pages 9–14, Australia, 1990. IREE.

137. D. Carrington and P. Stocks. A tale of two paradigms: Formal methods and software testing. In Bowen and Hall [91], pages 51–68.
     Also available as Technical Report 94-4, Department of Computer Science, University of Queensland, Australia, 1994.

138. P. Chalin and P. Grogono. Z specification of an object manager. In Bjørner et al. [51], pages 41–71.

139. D. K. C. Chan and P. W. Trinder. An object-oriented data model supporting multi-methods, multiple inheritance, and static type checking: A specification in Z. In Bowen and Hall [91], pages 297–315.

140. W. Chantatub and M. Holcombe. Software testing strategies for software requirements and design. In *Proc. EuroSTAR'94*, pages 40/1–40/29, 3000-2 Hartley Road, Jacksonville, Florida 32257, USA, 1994. Software Quality Engineering.
     The paper describes how to construct a detailed Z specification using traditional software engineering techniques (ERDs, DFDs, etc.) in a top down manner. It introduces a number of notational devices to help with the management of large Z specifications. Some issues about proving consistency between levels are also addressed.

141. J. Y. Chauvet. Le cas "legislation viellesse": Etude de cas. In Habrias [303], pages 243–264.

142. C. M. Chung, T. K. Shih, and C. C. Wang. Object-oriented software testing and metric in Z specification. *Information Sciences*, 98(1–4):175–202, 1997.

143. P. Ciaccia and P. Ciancarini. A course on formal methods in software engineering: Matching requirements with design. In Bowen and Hinchey [99], pages 482–496.

144. P. Ciaccia, P. Ciancarini, and W. Penzo. A formal approach to software design: The Clepsydra methodology. In Bowen and Hinchey [99], pages 5–24.

145. P. Ciaccia, P. Ciancarini, and W. Penzo. Formal requirements and design specifications: The Clepsydra methodology. *International Journal of Software Engineering and Knowledge Engineering*, 7(1):1–42, 1997.

146. P. Ciancarini, S. Cimato, and C. Mascolo. Engineering formal requirements: An analysis and testing method for Z documents. *Annals of Software Engineering*, 3:189–219, 1997.

147. P. Ciancarini and C. Mascolo. Analyzing the dynamics of a Z specification. In J. Calmet and C. Limongelli, editors, *Proc. 4th International Symposium on Design and Implementation of Symbolic Computation Systems (DISCO'96)*, volume 1128 of *Lecture Notes in Computer Science*, pages 138–149. Springer-Verlag, 1996.

148. P. Ciancarini and C. Mascolo. Analysing and refining an architectural style. In Bowen et al. [101], pages 349–368.

149. P. Ciancarini, C. Mascolo, and F. Vitali. Visualizing Z notation in HTML documents. In Bowen et al. [85], pages 81–95.

150. P. Ciancarini, A. Rizzi, and F. Vitali. An extensible rendering engine for XML and HTML. *Computer Networks and ISDN Systems*, 30(1–7):225–237, 1998.

151. B. Cohen. Justification of formal methods for system specifications & A rejustification of formal notations. *IEE/BCS Software Engineering Journal*, 4(1):26–38, January 1989.

152. B. Cohen. Set theory as a semantic framework for object-oriented modeling. In Bosch and Mitchell [61].

153. B. Cohen and D. Mannering. The rigorous specification and verification of the safety aspects of a real-time system. In *Proc. COMPASS '90*, Gaithersburg, USA, 1990.

154. D. L. Coleman and A. L. Baker. Synthesizing structured analysis and object-based formal specifications. *Annals of Software Engineering*, 3:221–253, 1997.

155. B. P. Collins, J. E. Nicholls, and I. H. Sørensen. Introducing formal methods: The CICS experience with Z. In B. Neumann et al., editors, *Mathematical Structures for Software Engineering*. Oxford University Press, 1991.

156. J. Cooke. Editorial – formal methods: What? why? and when? *The Computer Journal*, 35(5):417–418, October 1992.

   An editorial introduction to two special issues on *Formal Methods*. See also [37, 157, 471, 570, 685] for papers relevant to Z.

157. J. Cooke. Formal methods – mathematics, theory, recipes or what? *The Computer Journal*, 35(5):419–423, October 1992.

158. A. C. Coombes, L. Barroca, J. S. Fitzgerald, J. A. McDermid, L. Spencer, and A. Saeed. Formal specification of an aerospace system: The attitude monitor. In Hinchey and Bowen [348], pages 307–332.

159. A. C. Coombes and J. A. McDermid. A tool for defining the architecture of Z specifications. In Nicholls [504], pages 77–92.

160. A. C. Coombes and J. A. McDermid. Using diagrams to give a formal specification of timing constraints in Z. In Bowen and Nicholls [102], pages 119–130.

161. D. Cooper. Educating management in Z. In Nicholls [502], pages 192–194.

162. V. A. O. Cordeiro, A. C. A. Sampaio, and S. L. Meira. From MooZ to Eiffel – a rigorous approach to system development. In Naftalin et al. [490], pages 306–325.

163. S. Craggs and J. B. Wordsworth. Hursley Lab wins another Queen's Award & Hursley and Oxford – a marriage of minds & Z stands for quality. *Developments, IBM Hursley Park*, 8:1–2, 21 April 1992.

164. I. Craig. *The Formal Specification of Advanced AI Architectures*. AI Series. Ellis Horwood, September 1991.

   This book contains two rather large (and relatively complete) specifications of Artificial Intelligence (AI) systems using Z. The architectures are the blackboard and Cassandra architectures. As well as showing that formal specification *can* be used in AI at the architecture level, the book is intended as a case-studies book, and also contains introductory material on Z (for AI people). The book assumes a knowledge of Z, so for non-AI people its primary use is for the presentation of the large specifications. The blackboard specification, with explanatory text, is around 100 pages.

165. D. Craigen, S. L. Gerhart, and T. J. Ralston. Formal methods reality check: Industrial usage. In Woodcock and Larsen [689], pages 250–267.
The 1st FME Symposium was held at Odense, Denmark, 19–23 April 1993. Z-related papers include [103, 165, 254, 372, 447, 526].

166. D. Craigen, S. L. Gerhart, and T. J. Ralston. An international survey of industrial applications of formal methods. Technical Report NIST GCR 93/626-V1 & 2, Atomic Energy Control Board of Canada, US National Institute of Standards and Technology, and US Naval Research Laboratories, 1993.
Volume 1: Purpose, Approach, Analysis and Conclusions; Volume 2: Case Studies. Order numbers: PB93-178556/AS & PB93-178564/AS; National Technical Information Service, 5285 Port Royal Road, Springfield, VA 22161, USA.

167. D. Craigen, S. L. Gerhart, and T. J. Ralston. An international survey of industrial applications of formal methods. In Bowen and Nicholls [102], pages 1–5.

168. D. Craigen, S. L. Gerhart, and T. J. Ralston. Formal methods reality check: Industrial usage. *IEEE Transactions on Software Engineering*, 21(2):90–98, February 1995.
Revised version of [165].

169. D. Craigen, S. L. Gerhart, and T. J. Ralston. Formal methods technology transfer: Impediments and innovation. In Hinchey and Bowen [348], pages 399–419.

170. D. Craigen, S. Kromodimoeljo, I. Meisels, W. Pase, and M. Saaltink. EVES: An overview. In Prehn and Toetenel [530], pages 389–405.

171. J. Crowcroft and M. d'Inverno. Languages and formal methods. In J. Crowcroft, editor, *Open Distributed Systems*, pages 99–137. UCL Press, London, 1996.

172. E. Cusack. Inheritance in object oriented Z. In P. America, editor, *Proc. ECOOP'91 European Conference on Object-Oriented Programming*, volume 512 of *Lecture Notes in Computer Science*, pages 167–179. Springer-Verlag, 1991.

173. E. Cusack. Object oriented modelling in Z for open distributed systems. In J. de Meer, editor, *Proc. International Workshop on ODP*. Elsevier Science Publishers (North-Holland), 1992.

174. E. Cusack. Using Z in communications engineering. In Bowen and Nicholls [102], pages 196–202.

175. E. Cusack and M. Lai. Object oriented specification in LOTOS and Z (or my cat really is object oriented!). In J. W. de Bakker, W. P. de Roever, and G. Rozenberg, editors, *REX/FOOL School/Workshop on Foundations of Object-Oriented Languages*, volume 489 of *Lecture Notes in Computer Science*, pages 179–202. Springer-Verlag, 1990.

176. E. Cusack and C. D. Wezeman. Deriving tests for objects specified in Z. In Bowen and Nicholls [102], pages 180–195.

177. R. S. M. de Barros. Deriving relational database programs from formal specifications. In Naftalin et al. [490], pages 703–723.

178. R. S. M. de Barros and D. J. Harper. Formal development of relational database applications. In D. J. Harper and M. C. Norrie, editors, *Specifications of Database Systems, Glasgow 1991*, Workshops in Computing, pages 21–43. Springer-Verlag, 1992.

179. R. S. M. de Barros and D. J. Harper. A method for the specification of relational database applications. In Nicholls [506], pages 261–286.

180. P. D. de Lima Machado and S. L. Meira. On the use of formal specifications in the design and simulation of artificial neural nets. In Bowen and Hinchey [99], pages 63–82.

181. N. Dean. Mental models of Z: I – sets and logic. In Bowen and Hinchey [99], pages 498–507.

182. N. Dean. *The Essence of Discrete Mathematics*. The Essence of Computing Series. Prentice Hall, 1997.
An introductory book using a Z-like notation.

183. N. Dean and M. G. Hinchey. Introducing formal methods through rôle-playing. *ACM SIGCSE Bulletin*, 27(1):302–306, March 1995.

184. A. M. Dearden and M. D. Harrison. A software engineering model for case memory systems. *The Computer Journal*, 40(4):167–182, 1997.

185. B. Dehbonei and F. Mejia. Formal methods in the railways signalling industry. In Naftalin et al. [490], pages 26–34.

186. N. Delisle and D. Garlan. Formally specifying electronic instruments. In *Proc. 5th International Workshop on Software Specification and Design*. IEEE Computer Society, May 1989. Also published in *ACM SIGSOFT Software Engineering Notes*, 14(3).

187. N. Delisle and D. Garlan. A formal specification of an oscilloscope. *IEEE Software*, 7(5):29–36, September 1990.
Unlike most work on the application of formal methods, this research uses formal methods to gain insight into system architecture. The context for this case study is electronic instrument design.

188. J. Derrick and E. A. Boiten. Testing refinements by refining tests. In Bowen et al. [85], pages 265–283.

189. J. Derrick, E. A. Boiten, H. Bowman, and M. Steen. Supporting ODP – translating LOTOS to Z. In E. Najm and J.-B. Stefani, editors, *Proc. 1st IFIP International Workshop on Formal Methods for Open Object-based Distributed Systems*, pages 399–406. Chapman & Hall, March 1996.

190. J. Derrick, E. A. Boiten, H. Bowman, and M. Steen. Translating LOTOS to Object-Z. In D. J. Duke and A. S. Evans, editors, *Northern Formal Methods Workshop*, Electronic Workshops In Computing. Springer-Verlag, 1997.

191. J. Derrick, E. A. Boiten, H. Bowman, and M. Steen. Weak refinement in Z. In Bowen et al. [101], pages 369–388.

192. J. Derrick, H. Bowman, and M. Steen. Maintaining cross viewpoint consistency using Z. In K. Raymond and L. Armstrong, editors, *IFIP TC6 International Conference on Open Distributed Processing*, pages 413–424. Chapman & Hall, February 1995.

193. J. Derrick, H. Bowman, and M. Steen. Viewpoints and objects. In Bowen and Hinchey [99], pages 449–468.

194. R. Di Giovanni and P. L. Iachini. HOOD and Z for the development of complex systems. In Bjørner et al. [51], pages 262–289.

195. A. J. J. Dick, P. J. Krause, and J. Cozens. Computer aided transformation of Z into Prolog. In Nicholls [502], pages 71–85.

196. A. Diller. Z and Hoare logics. In Nicholls [506], pages 59–76.

197. A. Diller. *Z: An Introduction to Formal Methods*. John Wiley & Sons, 2nd edition, 1994.
This book offers a comprehensive tutorial to Z from the practical viewpoint. Many natural deduction style proofs are presented and exercises are included. Z as defined in the 2nd edition of *The Z Notation* [604] is used throughout.
Contents: Tutorial introduction; Methods of reasoning; Case studies; Specification animation; Reference manual; Answers to exercises; Glossaries of terms and symbols; Bibliography.

198. A. Diller and R. Docherty. Z and abstract machine notation: A comparison. In Bowen and Hall [91], pages 250–263.

199. M. d'Inverno and J. Crowcroft. Design, specification and implementation of a real time conferencing system. In *Proc. 10th Annual Joint Conference of IEEE INFOCOM'91*, pages 1114–1125, New York, USA, 1991.

200. M. d'Inverno, M. Fisher, A. Lomuscio, M. Luck, M. de Rijke, M. Ryan, and M. Wooldridge. Formalisms for multi-agent systems. *Knowledge Engineering Review*, 12(3):315–321, 1997.
Includes a discussion of the appropriateness of Z for multi-agent systems.

201. M. d'Inverno and M. J. Hu. A Z specification of the soft-link hypertext model. In Bowen et al. [101], pages 297–316.

202. M. d'Inverno, G. R. Justo, and P. Howells. A formal framework for specifying design methodologies. In H. El-Rewini and B. D. Shriver, editors, *Proc. 29th Annual Hawaii International Conference on System Sciences*, pages 741–750. IEEE Computer Society Press, 1996.

203. M. d'Inverno, G. R. Justo, and P. Howells. A formal framework for specifying design methodologies. *Software Process: Improvement and Practice*, 2(3):181–195, 1996.

204. M. d'Inverno, D. Kinny, and M. Luck. Interaction protocols in Agentis. In *Proc. 3rd International Conference on Multi-Agent Systems (ICMAS'98)*, Paris, France, 1998.

205. M. d'Inverno, D. Kinny, M. Luck, and M. Wooldridge. A formal specification of dMARS. In M. Singh, A. Rao, and M. Wooldridge, editors, *Intelligent Agents IV: Proc. 4th International Workshop on Agent Theories, Architectures and Languages*, volume 1365 of *Lecture Notes in Computer Science*, pages 155–176. Springer-Verlag, 1998.

206. M. d'Inverno and M. Luck. A formal view of social dependence networks. In C. Zhang and D. Lukose, editors, *Distributed Artificial Intelligence Architecture and Modelling: Proc. 1st Australian Workshop on Distributed Artificial Intelligence*, volume 1087 of *Lecture Notes in Artificial Intelligence*, pages 115–129. Springer-Verlag, 1996.

207. M. d'Inverno and M. Luck. Formalising the contract net as a goal directed system. In W. Van de Velde and J.W. Perram, editors, *Agents Breaking Away: Proc. 7th European Workshop on Modelling Autonomous Agents in a Multi Agent World, Lecture Notes in Artificial Intelligence*, volume 1038, pages 72–85. Springer-Verlag, 1996.

208. M. d'Inverno and M. Luck. Understanding autonomous interaction. In W. Wahlster, editor, *Proc. 13th European Conference on Artificial Intelligence (ECAI'96)*, pages 529–533. John Wiley & Sons, 1996.

209. M. d'Inverno and M. Luck. Development and application of an formal agent framework. In Hinchey and Liu [350], pages 222–231.

210. M. d'Inverno and M. Luck. Making and breaking engagements: An operational analysis of agent relationships. In C. Zhang and D. Lukose, editors, *Multi-Agent Systems Methodologies and Applications: Proc. 2nd Australian Workshop on Distributed Artificial Intelligence, Lecture Notes in Artificial Intelligence*, volume 1286, pages 48–62. Springer-Verlag, 1997.

211. M. d'Inverno and M. Luck. A formal specification of AgentSpeak(L). *Logic and Computation*, 8(3), 1998.

212. M. d'Inverno, M. Luck, and M. Wooldridge. Cooperation structures. In *Proc. 15th International Joint Conference on Artificial Intelligence*, pages 600–605, Nagoya, Japan, 1997.

213. M. d'Inverno and M. Priestley. Structuring specification in Z to build a unifying framework for hypertext systems. In Bowen and Hinchey [99], pages 83–102.

214. M. d'Inverno, M. Priestley, and M. Luck. A formal framework for hypertext systems. *IEE Proceedings – Software Engineering*, 144(3):175–184, June 1997.

215. A. J. Dix. *Formal Methods for Interactive Systems*. Computers and People Series. Academic Press, 1991.

216. A. J. Dix, J. Finlay, G. D. Abowd, and R. Beale. *Human-Computer Interaction*. Prentice Hall International, 1993.

217. R. F. Docherty. Translation from Z to AMN. In Habrias [303], pages 205–228.

218. C. J. Dodge. *A Fast Fourier Transform Accelerator for a Transputer System*. PhD thesis, University of Aberdeen, Department of Biomedical Physics, Foresterhill, Aberdeen AB9 2ZD, UK, 1993.
     The design includes a detailed Z specification.

219. C. J. Dodge, P. G. B. Ross, A. R. Allen, and P. E. Undrill. Formal methods in the design of an FFT accelerator for a Transputer based image processing system. *Medical and Biological Engineering and Computing*, 29:91, 1991.

220. C. J. Dodge, P. E. Undrill, A. R. Allen, and P. G. B. Ross. Application of Z in digital hardware design. *IEE Proceedings – Computers and Digital Techniques*, 143(1):79–86, 1996.

221. V. Doma and R. Nicholl. EZ: A system for automatic prototyping of Z specifications. In Prehn and Toetenel [530], pages 189–203.

222. J. S. Dong and R. Duke. An object-oriented approach to the formal specification of ODP trader. In *Proc. IFIP TC6/WG6.1 International Conference on Open Distributed Processing*, pages 341–352, September 1993.

223. J. S. Dong, R. Duke, and G. Rose. An object-oriented denotational semantics of a small programming language. *Object Oriented Systems*, 4(1):29–52, 1997.

224. J. S. Dong, R. Duke, and G. A. Rose. An object-oriented approach to the semantics of programming languages. In *Proc. 17th Australian Computer Science Conference (ACSC-17)*, pages 767–775, January 1994.

225. C. Draper. Practical experiences of Z and SSADM. In Bowen and Nicholls [102], pages 240–251.

226. D. A. Duce, D. J. Duke, P. J. W. ten Hagen, I. Herman, and G. J. Reynolds. Formal methods in the development of PREMO. *Computer Standards & Interfaces*, 17(5–6):491–509, September 1995.

227. D. A. Duce, D. J. Duke, P. J. W. ten Hagen, and G. J. Reynolds. PREMO – an initial approach to a formal definition. *Computer Graphics Forum*, 13(3):C–393–C–406, 1994.
   PREMO (Presentation Environments for Multimedia Objects) is a work item proposal by the ISO/IEC JTC11/SC24 committee, which is responsible for international standardization in the area of computer graphics and image processing.

228. D. J. Duke. Structuring Z specifications. *Australian Computer Science Communications*, 12(1):1–10, 1991. Proc. 14th Australian Computer Science Conference.

229. D. J. Duke. Enhancing the structures of Z specifications. In Nicholls [506], pages 329–351.

230. D. J. Duke. *Object-Oriented Formal Specification*. PhD thesis, Department of Computer Science, University of Queensland, St. Lucia 4072, Australia, 1992.

231. D. J. Duke and R. Duke. Towards a semantics for Object-Z. In Bjørner et al. [51], pages 244–261.

232. D. J. Duke and M. D. Harrison. Event model of human-system interaction. *IEE/BCS Software Engineering Journal*, 10(1):3–12, January 1995.

233. D. J. Duke and M. D. Harrison. Mapping user requirements to implementations. *IEE/BCS Software Engineering Journal*, 10(1):13–20, January 1995.

234. R. Duke and D. J. Duke. Aspects of object-oriented formal specification. In *Proc. 5th Australian Software Engineering Conference (ASWEC'90)*, pages 21–26, Australia, 1990. IREE.

235. R. Duke, I. J. Hayes, P. King, and G. A. Rose. Protocol specification and verification using Z. In S. Aggarwal and K. Sabnani, editors, *Protocol Specification, Testing, and Verification VIII*, pages 33–46. Elsevier Science Publishers (North-Holland), 1988.

236. R. Duke, P. King, G. A. Rose, and G. Smith. The Object-Z specification language. In T. Korson, V. Vaishnavi, and B. Meyer, editors, *Technology of Object-Oriented Languages and Systems: TOOLS 5*, pages 465–483. Prentice Hall, 1991.

237. R. Duke, P. King, G. A. Rose, and G. Smith. The Object-Z specification language: Version 1. Technical Report 91-1, Department of Computer Science, University of Queensland, St. Lucia 4072, Australia, April 1991.
   The most complete (and currently the standard) reference on Object-Z. It has been reprinted by ISO JTC1 WG7 as document number 372. A condensed version of this report was published as [236].

238. R. Duke, G. Rose, and G. Smith. Object-Z: A specification language advocated for the description of standards. *Computer Standards & Interfaces*, 17(5–6):511–533, September 1995.

239. R. Duke, G. A. Rose, and A. Lee. Object-oriented protocol specification. In L. Logrippo, R. L. Probert, and H. Ural, editors, *Protocol Specification, Testing, and Verification X*, pages 325–338. Elsevier Science Publishers (North-Holland), 1990.

240. R. Duke and G. Smith. Temporal logic and Z specifications. *Australian Computer Journal*, 21(2):62–69, May 1989.

241. L. Dunckley and A. Smith. Improving access of the commercial software developer to formal methods: Integrating MERISE with Z. In Bryant and Semmens [121].

242. S. Dupuy, Y. Ledru, and M. Chabre-Peccoud. Translating the OMT dynamic model into Object-Z. In Bowen et al. [85], pages 347–366.

243. J. Ebert and R. Süttenbach. Integration of Z-based semantics of OO-notations. In Bosch and Mitchell [61].

244. D. Edmond. *Information Modeling: Specification and Implementation*. Prentice Hall, 1992.

245. D. Edmond. Refining database systems. In Bowen and Hinchey [99], pages 25–44.

246. M. Engel. Specifying real-time systems with Z and the Duration Calculus. In Bowen and Hall [91], pages 282–294.

247. A. S. Evans. Specifying & verifying concurrent systems using Z. In Naftalin et al. [490], pages 366–400.

248. A. S. Evans. Visualising concurrent Z specifications. In Bowen and Hall [91], pages 269–281.

249. A. S. Evans. An improved recipe for specifying reactive systems in Z. In Bowen et al. [101], pages 275–294.

250. P. C. Fencott, A. J. Galloway, M. A. Lockyer, S. J. O'Brien, and S. Pearson. Formalising the semantics of Ward/Mellor SA/RT essential models using a process algebra. In Naftalin et al. [490], pages 681–702.

251. N. E. Fenton and D. Mole. A note on the use of Z for flowgraph transformation. *Information and Software Technology*, 30(7):432–437, 1988.

252. E. Fergus and D. C. Ince. Z specifications and modal logic. In P. A. V. Hall, editor, *Proc. Software Engineering 90*, volume 1 of *British Computer Society Conference Series*. Cambridge University Press, 1990.

253. C. J. Fidge. Specification and verification of real-time behaviour using Z and RTL. In J. Vytopil, editor, *Formal Techniques in Real-Time and Fault-Tolerant Systems*, Lecture Notes in Computer Science, pages 393–410. Springer-Verlag, 1992.

254. C. J. Fidge. Real-time refinement. In Woodcock and Larsen [689], pages 314–331.

255. C. J. Fidge. Adding real time to formal program development. In Naftalin et al. [490], pages 618–638.

256. C. J. Fidge. Proof obligations for real-time refinement. In Till [646], pages 279–305.

257. C. J. Fidge, M. Utting, P. Kearney, and I. J. Hayes. Integrating real-time scheduling theory and program refinement. In Gaudel and Woodcock [280], pages 327–346.

258. K. Finney. Mathematical notation in formal specification: Too difficult for the masses? *IEEE Transactions on Software Engineering*, 22(2):158–159, February 1996.

259. C. Fischer. How to combine Z with a process algebra. In Bowen et al. [85], pages 5–23.

260. J. Fitzgerald, C. B. Jones, and P. Lucas, editors. *FME'97: Industrial Application and Strengthened Foundations of Formal Methods*, volume 1313 of *Lecture Notes in Computer Science*. Formal Methods Europe, Springer-Verlag, 1997.
    The 4th FME Symposium was held at Graz, Austria, 15–19 September 1997. See the Z-related paper [56].

261. M. Flynn, T. Hoverd, and D. Brazier. Formaliser – an interactive support tool for Z. In Nicholls [502], pages 128–141.

262. I. Fogg, B. Hicks, A. Lister, T. Mansfield, and K. Raymond. A comparison of LOTOS and Z for specifying distributed systems. *Australian Computer Science Communications*, 12(1):88–96, February 1990.

263. D. C. Fowler, P. A. Swatman, and P. M. C. Swatman. Implementing EDI in the public sector: Including formality for enhanced control. In *Proc. 7th International Conference on Electronic Data Interchange*, June 1993.

264. R. B. France and J.-M. Bruel. Integrated informal object-oriented and formal modeling techniques. In Bosch and Mitchell [61].

265. R. B. France and S. L. Gerhart, editors. *Proc. Workshop on Industrial-strength Formal Specification Techniques*. IEEE Computer Society Press, 1995.

266. R. B. France and M. M. Larrondo-Petrie. A two-dimensional view of integrated formal and informal specification techniques. In Bowen and Hinchey [99], pages 434–448.

267. R. B. France, J. Wu, M. M. Larondo-Petrie, and J.-M. Bruel. A tale of two case studies: Using integrated methods to support rigorous requirements specification. In Bryant and Semmens [121].
    Includes a study of an integrated Object-Oriented Analysis (OOA) method (Fusion) and formal specification technique (Z) used to create requirements models that are graphical and analyzable.

268. V. Friesen. An exercise in hybrid system specification using an extension of Z. In A. Bouajjani and O. Maler, editors, *Proc. 2nd European Workshop on Real-Time and Hybrid Systems*, pages 311–316, 1995.

269. V. Friesen, A. Nordwig, and M. Weber. Object-oriented specification of hybrid systems using UML[h] and ZimOO. In Bowen et al. [85], pages 328–346.

270. N. E. Fuchs. Specifications are (preferably) executable. *IEE/BCS Software Engineering Journal*, 7(5):323–334, September 1992.

271. A. J. Galloway and H. Habrias. Formalising the semantics of GRAFCET function charts using Z. Rapport de Recherche IRIN - 131, Université de Nantes, Institut de Recherche en Informatique de Nantes, France, 1996.

272. A. J. Galloway and H. Habrias. Integrating NIAM, JSD, CCS and Z. Rapport de Recherche IRIN - 130, Université de Nantes, Institut de Recherche en Informatique de Nantes, France, 1996.

273. P. H. B. Gardiner, P. J. Lupton, and J. C. P. Woodcock. A simpler semantics for Z. In Nicholls [504], pages 3–11.

274. D. Garlan. The role of reusable frameworks. *ACM SIGSOFT Software Engineering Notes*, 15(4):42–44, September 1990.

275. D. Garlan. Integrating formal methods into a professional master of software engineering program. In Bowen and Hall [91], pages 71–85.

276. D. Garlan. Making formal methods effective for professional software engineers. *Information and Software Technology*, 37(5–6):261–268, May–June 1995.
    Revised version of [275].

277. D. Garlan and N. Delisle. Formal specifications as reusable frameworks. In Bjørner et al. [51], pages 150–163.

278. D. Garlan and N. Delisle. Formal specification of an architecture for a family of instrumentation systems. In Hinchey and Bowen [348], pages 55–72.

279. D. Garlan and D. Notkin. Formalizing design spaces: Implicit invocation mechanisms. In Prehn and Toetenel [530], pages 31–45.

280. M.-C. Gaudel and J. C. P. Woodcock, editors. *FME'96: Industrial Benefit and Advances in Formal Methods*, volume 1051 of *Lecture Notes in Computer Science*. Formal Methods Europe, Springer-Verlag, 1996.
    The 3rd FME Symposium was held at Oxford, UK, 18–22 October 1996. The proceedings includes Z-related papers [58, 257, 392, 664] and B-related papers [48, 351, 663].

281. S. L. Gerhart. Applications of formal methods: Developing virtuoso software. *IEEE Software*, 7(5):6–10, September 1990.
This is an introduction to a special issue on Formal Methods with an emphasis on Z in particular. It was published in conjunction with special Formal Methods issues of *IEEE Transactions on Software Engineering* and *IEEE Computer*. See also [187, 307, 491, 602, 672].

282. S. L. Gerhart, D. Craigen, and T. J. Ralston. Observations on industrial practice using formal methods. In *Proc. 15th International Conference on Software Engineering (ICSE), Baltimore, Maryland, USA*, May 1993.

283. S. L. Gerhart, D. Craigen, and T. J. Ralston. Experience with formal methods in critical systems. *IEEE Software*, 11(1):21–28, January 1994.
Several commercial and exploratory cases in which Z features heavily are briefly presented on page 24. See also [404].

284. D. M. Germán and D. D. Cowan. Experiments with the Z Interchange Format and SGML. In Bowen and Hinchey [99], pages 224–233.

285. S. Gilmore. Correctness-oriented approaches to software development. Technical Report ECS-LFCS-91-147 (also CST-76-91), Department of Computer Science, University of Edinburgh, Edinburgh EH9 3JZ, UK, 1991.
This PhD thesis provides a critical evaluation of Z, VDM and algebraic specifications.

286. R. B. Gimson. The formal documentation of a Block Storage Service. Technical Monograph PRG-62, Oxford University Computing Laboratory, Wolfson Building, Parks Road, Oxford, UK, August 1987.

287. R. B. Gimson and C. C. Morgan. Ease of use through proper specification. In D. A. Duce, editor, *Distributed Computing Systems Programme*. Peter Peregrinus, London, 1984.

288. R. B. Gimson and C. C. Morgan. The Distributed Computing Software project. Technical Monograph PRG-50, Oxford University Computing Laboratory, Wolfson Building, Parks Road, Oxford, UK, July 1985.

289. J. Ginbayashi. Analysis of business processes specified in Z against an E-R data model. Technical Monograph PRG-103, Oxford University Computing Laboratory, Wolfson Building, Parks Road, Oxford, UK, December 1992.

290. H. S. Gonzalez. A symbolic representation of transcendental logic using Z language and its role in knowledge base systems. In F. J. Cantu, R. Soto, J. Liebowitz, and E. Sucar, editors, *Proc. 4th World Congress of Expert Systems: Application of Advanced Information Technologies*, volume 1&2, pages 383–387, Mexico City, 16–20 March 1998. Scholium International Inc.

291. H. S. Goodman. From Z specifications to Haskell porgrams: A three-pronged approach. In Habrias [303], pages 167–182.

292. H. S. Goodman. The Z-into-Haskell tool-kit: An illustrative case study. In Bowen and Hinchey [99], pages 374–388.

293. R. Goodwin. Formalizing properties of agents. *Journal of Logic and Computation*, 5(6):763–781, 1995.

294. R. Gotzhein. Specifying open distributed systems with Z. In Bjørner et al. [51], pages 319–339.

295. W. K. Grassmann and J.-P. Tremblay. *The Formal Specification of Requirements in Z*, chapter 8, pages 441–480. Prentice Hall, 1996.

296. A. M. Gravell. Minimisation in formal specification and design. In Nicholls [502], pages 32–45.

297. A. M. Gravell. What is a good formal specification? In Nicholls [504], pages 137–150.

298. A. M. Gravell and P. Henderson. Executing formal specifications need not be harmful. *IEE/BCS Software Engineering Journal*, 11(2):104–110, March 1996.

299. A. M. Gravell and C. H. Pratten. Formal methods and open systems. *Software—Concepts and Tools*, 16(4):183–188, 1995.

300. D. Gries. Equational logic: A great pedagogical tool for teaching a skill in logic. In Bowen and Hinchey [99], pages 508–509.

301. K. Grimm. Industrial requirements for the efficient development of reliable embedded systems. In Bowen et al. [85], pages 1–4. Extended abstract.

302. H. Habrias. Z, chapter 10, pages 267–290. Méthodologies du Logiciel. Masson, Paris, 1993.

303. H. Habrias, editor. *Z Twenty Years on – What is its Future?*, Université de Nantes, France, 1995. IRIN (Institut de Recherche en Informatique de Nantes).
    Proceedings of the 7th International Conference on *Putting into Practice Methods and Tools for Information System Design*, Nantes, France, 10–12 October 1995. This conference considered the future of Z, about twenty years after a seminal paper relating to Z [6]. See [47, 114, 117, 141, 217, 291, 313, 332, 427, 500, 519, 529, 583, 625, 657].

304. H. Habrias, S. Dunne, and W. J. Stoddart. From natural language to Z specification. In J. E. Labarre, editor, *Proc. Conference on Information Systems and Global Competitiveness*, pages 126–145, Toronto, Canada, 28–30 September 1995. International Association for Computer Information Systems.

305. F. Halasz and M. Schwartz. The Dexter hypertext reference model. In *Proc. NIST Hypertext Standardization Workshop*, Gaithersburg, USA, January 1990.

306. J. Hall and A. Martin. *W* reconstructed. In Bowen et al. [101], pages 116–134.

307. J. A. Hall. Seven myths of formal methods. *IEEE Software*, 7(5):11–19, September 1990.
    Formal methods are difficult, expensive, and not widely useful, detractors say. Using a case study and other real-world examples, this article challenges such common myths. See also [97].

308. J. A. Hall. Using Z as a specification calculus for object-oriented systems. In Bjørner et al. [51], pages 290–318.

309. J. A. Hall. Specifying and interpreting class hierarchies in Z. In Bowen and Hall [91], pages 120–138.

310. J. A. Hall. Taking Z seriously. In Bowen et al. [101], pages 89–91. Extended abstract.

311. J. A. Hall, D. L. Parnas, N. Plat, J. Rushby, and C. T. Sennett. The future of industrial formal methods. In Bowen and Hinchey [99], pages 238–242.
    Position statements for a panel session moderated by T. King.

312. J. G. Hall and J. A. McDermid. Towards a Z method: Axiomatic specification in Z. In Bowen and Hall [91], pages 213–229.

313. J. G. Hall, J. A. McDermid, and I. Toyn. Model conjectures for Z specifications. In Habrias [303], pages 41–51.

314. P. A. V. Hall. Towards testing with respect to formal specification. In *Proc. 2nd IEE/BCS Conference on Software Engineering*, number 290 in Conference Publication, pages 159–163. IEE/BCS, July 1988.

315. U. Hamer and J. Peleska. Z applied to the A330/340 CICS cabin communication system. In Hinchey and Bowen [348], pages 253–284.

316. V. Hamilton. The use of Z within a safety-critical software system. In Hinchey and Bowen [348], pages 357–374.

317. J. A. R. Hammond. Producing Z specifications from object-oriented analysis. In Bowen and Hall [91], pages 316–336.

318. J. A. R. Hammond. Z. In J. J. Marciniak, editor, *Encyclopedia of Software Engineering*, volume 2, pages 1452–1453. John Wiley & Sons, 1994.

319. M. D. Harrison. Engineering human-error tolerant software. In Nicholls [506], pages 191–204.

320. A. Harry. *Formal Methods Fact File: VDM and Z*. John Wiley & Sons, 1996.
Contents: Why do we need formal methods?; Background material; Formal specification styles; Introduction to model-based languages; VDM; The Z notation; Formal semantics; Tool support; The future of formal methods.

321. W. Hasselbring. Animation of Object-Z specifications with a set-oriented prototyping language. In Bowen and Hall [91], pages 337–356.

322. W. Hasselbring. Prototyping parallel algorithms in a set-oriented language. Dissertation, Department of Computer Science, University of Dortmund, Hamburg, Germany, 1994.
This dissertation presents the design and implementation of an approach to prototyping parallel algorithms with ProSet-Linda. The presented approach to designing and implementing ProSet-Linda relies on the use of the formal specification language Object-Z and the prototyping language ProSet itself.

323. H. P. Haughton. Using Z to model and analyse safety and liveness properties of communication protocols. *Information and Software Technology*, 33(8):575–580, October 1991.

324. I. J. Hayes. Applying formal specification to software development in industry. *IEEE Transactions on Software Engineering*, 11(2):169–178, February 1985.

325. I. J. Hayes. Specification directed module testing. *IEEE Transactions on Software Engineering*, 12(1):124–133, January 1986.

326. I. J. Hayes. Using mathematics to specify software. In *Proc. First Australian Software Engineering Conference*. Institution of Engineers, Australia, May 1986.

327. I. J. Hayes. A generalisation of bags in Z. In Nicholls [502], pages 113–127.

328. I. J. Hayes. Interpretations of Z schema operators. In Nicholls [504], pages 12–26.

329. I. J. Hayes. Multi-relations in Z: A cross between multi-sets and binary relations. *Acta Informatica*, 29(1):33–62, February 1992.

330. I. J. Hayes. VDM and Z: A comparative case study. *Formal Aspects of Computing*, 4(1):76–99, 1992.

331. I. J. Hayes, editor. *Specification Case Studies*. Prentice Hall International Series in Computer Science, 2nd edition, 1993.
This is a revised edition of the first ever book on Z, originally published in 1987; it contains substantial changes to every chapter. The notation has been revised to be consistent with *The Z Notation: A Reference Manual* by Mike Spivey [604]. The CAVIAR chapter has been extensively changed to make use of a form of modularization.
Divided into four sections, the first provides tutorial examples of specifications, the second is devoted to the area of software engineering, the third covers distributed computing, analyzing the role of mathematical specification, and the fourth part covers the IBM CICS transaction processing system. Appendices include comprehensive glossaries of the Z mathematical and schema notation. The book will be of interest to the professional software engineer involved in designing and specifying large software projects.
The other contributors are W. Flinn, R. B. Gimson, S. King, C. C. Morgan, I. H. Sørensen and B. A. Sufrin.

332. I. J. Hayes. Specification models. In Habrias [303], pages 1–10.

333. I. J. Hayes and C. B. Jones. Specifications are not (necessarily) executable. *IEE/BCS Software Engineering Journal*, 4(6):330–338, November 1989.

334. I. J. Hayes, C. B. Jones, and J. E. Nicholls. Understanding the differences between VDM and Z. *FACS Europe*, Series I, 1(1):7–30, Autumn 1993.
Also available as Technical Report UMCS-93-8-1, Department of Computer Science, University of Manchester, UK, 1993.

335. I. J. Hayes and L. Wildman. Towards libraries for Z. In Bowen and Nicholls [102], pages 9–36.

336. He Jifeng, C. A. R. Hoare, M. Fränzle, M. Müller-Ulm, E.-R. Olderog, M. Schenke, A. P. Ravn, and H. Rischel. Provably correct systems. In H. Langmaack, W.-P. de Roever, and J. Vytopil, editors, *Formal Techniques in Real Time and Fault Tolerant Systems*, volume 863 of *Lecture Notes in Computer Science*, pages 288–335. Springer-Verlag, 1994.

337. He Jifeng, C. A. R. Hoare, and J. W. Sanders. Data refinement refined. In B. Robinet and R. Wilhelm, editors, *Proc. ESOP 86*, volume 213 of *Lecture Notes in Computer Science*, pages 187–196. Springer-Verlag, 1986.

338. D. Heath, D. Allum, and L. Dunckley. *Introductory Logic and Formal Methods*. A. Waller, Henley-on-Thames, UK, 1994.

339. C. Heitmeyer. Formal methods: Panacea or academic poppycock? In Bowen et al. [101], pages 3–9.

340. S. Helke, T. Neustupny, and T. Santen. Automating test case generation from Z specifications with Isabelle. In Bowen et al. [101], pages 52–71.

341. P. Hennessey, M. T. Ibrahim, and A. M. Fedorec. Formal specification, object oriented design, and implementation of an ephemeral logger for database systems. In R. Wagner and H. Thoma, editors, *Database and Expert System Applications*, volume 1134 of *Lecture Notes in Computer Science*, pages 333–355. Springer-Verlag, 1996.

342. M. C. Henson and S. Reeves. A logic for the schema calculus. In Bowen et al. [85], pages 172–191.

343. B. Hepworth. ZIP: A unification initiative for Z standards, methods and tools. In Nicholls [502], pages 253–259.

344. B. Hepworth and D. Simpson. The ZIP project. In Nicholls [504], pages 129–133.

345. M. A. Hewitt, C. M. O'Halloran, and C. T. Sennett. Experiences with PiZA, an animator for Z. In Bowen et al. [101], pages 37–51.

346. M. G. Hinchey. Formal methods for system specification: An ounce of prevention is worth a pound of cure. *IEEE Potentials Magazine*, 12(3):50–52, October 1993.

347. M. G. Hinchey. JSD $\hat{=}$ ΔCSP ⊕ TLZ – a case study. In Bryant and Semmens [121].

348. M. G. Hinchey and J. P. Bowen, editors. *Applications of Formal Methods*. Prentice Hall International Series in Computer Science, 1995.
A collection on industrial examples of the use of formal methods. Chapters relevant to Z include [158, 169, 278, 315, 316, 349, 450].

349. M. G. Hinchey and J. P. Bowen. Applications of formal methods FAQ. In *Applications of Formal Methods* [348], pages 1–15.

350. M. G. Hinchey and Shaoying Liu, editors. *Formal Engineering Methods: Proc. 1st International Conference on Formal Engineering Methods (ICFEM'97)*, Hiroshima, Japan, 12–14 November 1997. IEEE Computer Society Press.
See Z-related papers [209, 566, 644].

351. J. Hoare, J. Dick, D. Neilson, and I. H. Sørensen. Applying the B technologies to CICS. In Gaudel and Woodcock [280], pages 74–84.

352. S. Hooker, M. A. Lockyer, and P. C. Fencott. CASE support for methods integration: Implementation of a translation from a structured to a formal notation. In Bryant and Semmens [121].
The work presented takes the Z specification of the Semantic Function and implements it in the functional programming language, ML.

353. H.-M. Hörcher. Improving software tests using Z specifications. In Bowen and Hinchey [99], pages 152–166.

354. I. S. C. Houston and M. Josephs. Specifying distributed CICS in Z: Accessing local and remote resources (short communication). *Formal Aspects of Computing*, 6(6):569–579, 1994.

355. I. S. C. Houston and M. B. Josephs. A formal description of the OMG's Core Object Model and the meaning of compatible extension. *Computer Standards & Interfaces*, 17(5–6):553–558, September 1995.

356. I. S. C. Houston and S. King. CICS project report: Experiences and results from the use of Z in IBM. In Prehn and Toetenel [530], pages 588–596.

357. A. P. Hughes and A. A. Donnelly. An algebraic proof in VDM♣. In Bowen and Hinchey [99], pages 114–133.

358. A. D. Hutcheon and A. J. Wellings. Specifying restrictions on imperative programming languages for use in a distributed embedded environment. *IEE/BCS Software Engineering Journal*, 5(2):93–104, March 1990.

359. P. L. Iachini. Operation schema iterations. In Nicholls [504], pages 50–57.

360. M. Imperato. *An Introduction to Z*. Chartwell-Bratt, 1991.
    Contents: Introduction; Set theory; Logic; Building Z specifications; Relations; Functions; Sequences; Bags; Advanced Z; Case study: a simple banking system.

361. D. C. Ince. Z and system specification. In D. C. Ince and D. Andrews, editors, *The Software Life Cycle*, chapter 12, pages 260–277. Butterworths, 1990.

362. D. C. Ince. *An Introduction to Discrete Mathematics, Formal System Specification and Z*. Oxford Applied Mathematics and Computing Science Series. Oxford University Press, 2nd edition, 1993.

363. INMOS Limited. Specification of instruction set & Specification of floating point unit instructions. In *Transputer Instruction Set – A compiler writer's guide*, pages 127–161. Prentice Hall, 1988.
    Appendices F and G use a Z-like notation to give a specification of the instruction set of the IMS T212 and T414 Transputers, and the T800 floating-point Transputer.

364. ISO/IEC. It – security techniques – hash-functions – part 3: Dedicated hash-functions. International Standard ISO/IEC DIS 10118-3, International Standards Organization, 1997. Contains a Z specification of the hash functions. This is believed to be the first published ISO standard which contains a complete specification in Z.

365. A. Jack. It's hard to explain, but Z is much clearer than English. *Financial Times*, page 22, 21 April 1992.

366. D. Jackson. Abstract model checking of infinite specifications. In Naftalin et al. [490], pages 519–531.

367. D. Jackson. Structuring Z specifications with views. *ACM Transactions on Software Engineering and Methodology (TOSEM)*, 4(4):365–389, October 1995.

368. D. Jackson and C. A. Damon. Elements of style: Analyzing a software design feature with a counterexample detector. *IEEE Transactions on Software Engineering*, 22(7):484–495, July 1996.
    Nitpick, a specification checker, is applied to the design of a style mechanism for a word processor, using a subset of Z.

369. D. Jackson and M. Jackson. Problem decomposition for reuse. *IEE/BCS Software Engineering Journal*, 11(1):19–30, January 1996.
    An approach to software development based on the idea of *problem frames* and of structuring Z specifications as *views*.

370. J. Jacky. Formal specifications for a clinical cyclotron control system. *ACM SIGSOFT Software Engineering Notes*, 15(4):45–54, September 1990.

371. J. Jacky. Formal specification and development of control system input/output. In Bowen and Nicholls [102], pages 95–108.

372. J. Jacky. Specifying a safety-critical control system in Z. In Woodcock and Larsen [689], pages 388–402.
    The 1st FME Symposium was held at Odense, Denmark, 19–23 April 1993. Z-related papers include [103, 165, 254, 372, 447, 526].

373. J. Jacky. Specifying a safety-critical control system in Z. *IEEE Transactions on Software Engineering*, 21(2):99–106, February 1995.
Revised version of [372].

374. J. Jacky. *The Way of Z: Practical Programming with Formal Methods*. Cambridge University Press, 1997.

375. J. Jacky. Modelling a real-time program in Z. In Bowen et al. [85], pages 136–153.

376. J. Jacky and J. Unger. From Z to code: A graphical user interface for a radiation therapy machine. In Bowen and Hinchey [99], pages 315–333.

377. J. Jacky, J. Unger, M. Patrick, and R. Risler. Experience with Z developing a control program for a radiation therapy machine. In Bowen et al. [101], pages 317–328.

378. J. Jacob. The varieties of refinements. In Morris and Shaw [487], pages 441–455.

379. C. W. Johnson. Using Z to support the design of interactive safety-critical systems. *IEE/BCS Software Engineering Journal*, 10(2):49–60, March 1995.

380. C. W. Johnson. Literate specification: Using design rationale to support formal methods in the development of human-machine interfaces. *Human-Computer Interaction*, 11(4):291–320, 1996.

381. D. R. Johnson and H. Kilov. Can a flat notation be used to specify an OO system: using Z to describe RM-ODP constraints. In E. Najm and J.-B. Stefani, editors, *Proc. 1st IFIP International Workshop on Formal Methods for Open Object-based Distributed Systems*, pages 391–398. Chapman & Hall, March 1996.

382. D. R. Johnson and H. Kilov. An approach to an RM-ODP toolkit in Z. In G. T. Leavens and M. Sitaraman, editors, *Proc. Foundations of Component-based Systems Workshop*, Zurich, Switzerland, 26 September 1997. European Software Engineering Conference.

383. M. Johnson and P. Sanders. From Z specifications to functional implementations. In Nicholls [502], pages 86–112.

384. P. Johnson. Using Z to specify CICS. In *Proc. Software Engineering anniversary meeting (SEAS)*, page 303, 1987.

385. C. B. Jones. Interference revisited. In Nicholls [504], pages 58–73.

386. C. B. Jones, R. C. Shaw, and T. Denvir, editors. *5th Refinement Workshop*, Workshop in Computing. Springer-Verlag, 1992.
The workshop was held at Lloyd's Register, London, UK, 8–10 January 1992. See [573].

387. R. B. Jones. ICL ProofPower. *BCS-FACS FACTS*, Series III, 1(1):10–13, Winter 1992.

388. D. Jordan, J. A. McDermid, and I. Toyn. CADiZ – computer aided design in Z. In Nicholls [504], pages 93–104.

389. M. B. Josephs. The data refinement calculator for Z specifications. *Information Processing Letters*, 27(1):29–33, 1988.

390. M. B. Josephs. A state-based approach to communicating processes. *Distributed Computing*, 3:9–18, 1988.
A theoretical paper on combining features of CSP and Z.

391. V. Kasurinen and K. Sere. Data modelling in ZIM. In Bryant and Semmens [121].

392. V. Kasurinen and K. Sere. Integrating action systems and Z in a medical system specification. In Gaudel and Woodcock [280], pages 105–119.

393. T. Katsolakos, editor. *Proc. 1993 Software Engineering Standards Symposium (SESS'93)*, Brighton, UK, 30 August – 3 September 1993. IEEE Computer Society Press.
See Z-related papers [24, 74, 423].

394. H. Kilov. Information modeling and Object Z: Specifying generic reusable associations. In O. Etzion and A. Segev, editors, *Proc. NGITS-93 (Next Generation Information Technology and Systems)*, pages 182–191, June 1993.

395. H. Kilov and J. Ross. Declarative specifications of collective behavior: Generic reusable frameworks. In H. Kilov and W. Harvey, editors, *Proc. Workshop on Specification of Behavioral Semantics in Object-Oriented Information Modeling*, pages 71–75, Washington DC, USA, 1993. OOPSLA.

396. H. Kilov and J. Ross. Appendix A: A more formal approach. In *Information Modeling: An Object-Oriented Approach* [397], pages 199–207.

397. H. Kilov and J. Ross. *Information Modeling: An Object-Oriented Approach*. Object-Oriented Series. Prentice Hall, 1994.

398. P. King. Printing Z and Object-Z LaTeX documents. Department of Computer Science, University of Queensland, May 1990.

   A description of a Z style option 'oz.sty', an extended version of Mike Spivey's original 'zed.sty' [601], for use with the LaTeX document preparation system [408]. It is particularly useful for printing Object-Z documents [134, 231].

399. S. King. Z and the refinement calculus. In Bjørner et al. [51], pages 164–188.

   Also published as Technical Monograph PRG-79, Oxford University Computing Laboratory, UK, February 1990.

400. S. King and I. H. Sørensen. Specification and design of a library system. In McDermid [457].

401. S. King, I. H. Sørensen, and J. C. P. Woodcock. Z: Grammar and concrete and abstract syntaxes. Technical Monograph PRG-68, Oxford University Computing Laboratory, Wolfson Building, Parks Road, Oxford, UK, 1988.

402. J. C. Knight and S. S. Brilliant. Preliminary evaluation of a formal approach to user interface specification. In Bowen et al. [101], pages 329–346.

403. J. C. Knight and D. M. Kienzle. Preliminary experience using Z to specify a safety-critical system. In Bowen and Nicholls [102], pages 109–118.

404. J. C. Knight and B. Littlewood. Critical task of writing dependable software. *IEEE Software*, 11(1):16–20, January 1994.

   Guest editors' introduction to a special issue of *IEEE Software* on *Safety-Critical Systems*. A short section on formal methods mentions several Z books on page 18. See also [283].

405. R. D. Knott and P. J. Krause. The implementation of Z specifications using program transformation systems: The SuZan project. In C. Rattray and R. G. Clark, editors, *The Unified Computation Laboratory*, volume 35 of *IMA Conference Series*, pages 207–220, Oxford, UK, 1992. Clarendon Press.

406. I. Kraan. Using the rippling heuristic in set membership proofs. In Bowen et al. [101], pages 135–147.

407. I. Kraan and P. Baumann. Implementing Z in Isabelle. In Bowen and Hinchey [99], pages 355–373.

408. L. Lamport. *LaTeX User's Guide & Reference Manual: A document preparation system*. Addison-Wesley Publishing Company, 2nd edition, 1993.

   Z specifications may be produced using the document preparation system LaTeX together with a special LaTeX style option. The most widely used style files are fuzz.sty [603], zed.sty [601] and oz.sty [398].

409. L. Lamport. TLZ. In Bowen and Hall [91], pages 267–268. Abstract.

410. K. C. Lano. Z^{++}, an object-orientated extension to Z. In Nicholls [504], pages 151–172.

411. K. C. Lano. Refinement in object-oriented specification languages. In Till [646], pages 236–259.

412. K. C. Lano. Specifying reactive systems in B AMN. In Bowen et al. [101], pages 242–274.

413. K. C. Lano and P. T. Breuer. From programs to Z specifications. In Nicholls [502], pages 46–70.

414. K. C. Lano, P. T. Breuer, and H. P. Haughton. Reverse engineering COBOL via formal methods. *Software Maintenance: Research and Practice*, 5:13–35, 1993.

   Also published in a shortened form as Chapter 16 in [662].

415. K. C. Lano and S. Goldsack. Integrated formal and object-oriented methods: The VDM^{++} approach. In Bryant and Semmens [121].

Structure Diagrams are formalized in terms of TLZ [409], a combination of the Z notation and the simple temporal logic of Lamport's TLA, with changes in state being a function of the events in the RPT+ formalization.

416. K. C. Lano, S. Goldsack, J. Bicarregui, and S. Kent. Integrating VDM++ and real-time system design. In Bowen et al. [101], pages 188–219.

417. K. C. Lano and H. P. Haughton. An algebraic semantics for the specification language Z^{++}. In *Proc. Algebraic Methodology and Software Technology Conference (AMAST '91)*. Springer-Verlag, 1992.

418. K. C. Lano and H. P. Haughton. Reasoning and refinement in object-oriented specification languages. In O. L. Madsen, editor, *ECOOP '92: European Conference on Object-Oriented Programming*, volume 615 of *Lecture Notes in Computer Science*, pages 78–97. Springer-Verlag, 1992.

419. K. C. Lano and H. P. Haughton. *The Z^{++} Manual*. Lloyd's Register of Shipping, 29 Wellesley Road, Croydon CRO 2AJ, UK, 1992.

420. K. C. Lano and H. P. Haughton, editors. *Object Oriented Specification Case Studies*. Object Oriented Series. Prentice Hall International, 1993.

Contents: Chapters introducing object oriented methods, object oriented formal specification and the links between formal and structured object-oriented techniques; seven case studies in particular object oriented formal methods, including:

The Unix Filing System: A MooZ Specification; An Object-Z Specification of a Mobile Phone System; Object-oriented Specification in VDM^{++}; Specifying a Concept-recognition System in Z^{++}; Specification in OOZE; Refinement in Fresco; SmallVDM: An Environment for Formal Specification and Prototyping in Smalltalk.

A glossary, index and bibliography are also included. The contributors are some of the leading figures in the area, including the developers of the above methods and languages: Silvio Meira, Gordon Rose, Roger Duke, Antonio Alencar, Joseph Goguen, Alan Wills, Cassio Souza dos Santos, Ana Cavalcanti.

421. K. C. Lano and H. P. Haughton. Reuse and adaptation of Z specifications. In Bowen and Nicholls [102], pages 62–90.

422. K. C. Lano and H. P. Haughton. *Reverse Engineering and Software Maintenance: A Practical Approach*. International Series in Software Engineering. McGraw Hill, 1993.

423. K. C. Lano and H. P. Haughton. Standards and techniques for object-oriented formal specification. In Katsolakos [393], pages 237–246.

424. K. C. Lano and H. P. Haughton. Formal development in B Abstract Machine Notation. *Information and Software Technology*, 37(5–6):303–316, May–June 1995.

425. K. C. Lano, P. Kan, and A. Sanchez. Compositional specification of controllers for batch process operations. In Bowen et al. [85], pages 250–264.

426. G. Laycock. Formal specification and testing: A case study. *Software Testing, Verification and Reliability*, 2(1):7–23, May 1992.

427. Y. Ledru and Y. Chiaramella. Integrating and teaching Z and CSP. In Habrias [303], pages 131–147.

428. J. Lee and J. I. Pan. A rule-based approach to producing Z specifications from Jackson System Development. *International Journal of Intelligent Systems*, 13(7):587–611, 1998.

429. N. Leveson. Designing a requirements specification language for reactive systems. In Bowen et al. [85], page 135. Abstract.

430. D. Lightfoot. *Formal Specification using Z*. Macmillan, 1991.

Contents: Introduction; Sets in Z; Using sets to describe a system – a simple example; Logic: propositional calculus; Example of a Z specification document; Logic: predicate calculus; Relations; Functions; A seat allocation system; Sequences; An example of sequences

– the aircraft example again; Extending a specification; Collected notation; Books on formal specification; Hints on creating specifications; Solutions to exercises. Also available in French.

431. P. A. Lindsay. On transferring VDM verification techniques to Z. In Naftalin et al. [490], pages 190–213.
     Also available as Technical Report 94-10, Department of Computer Science, University of Queensland, Australia, 1994.

432. B. Liskov and J. M. Wing. Specifications and their use in defining subtypes. In Bowen and Hinchey [99], pages 246–263.

433. R. L. London and K. R. Milsted. Specifying reusable components using Z: Realistic sets and dictionaries. *ACM SIGSOFT Software Engineering Notes*, 14(3):120–127, May 1989.

434. M. Love. Animating Z specifications in SQL*Forms3.0. In Bowen and Nicholls [102], pages 294–306.

435. M. Luck and M. d'Inverno. A formal framework for agency and autonomy. In *Proc. 1st International Conference on Multi-Agent Systems*, pages 254–260. AAAI Press / MIT Press, 1995.

436. M. Luck and M. d'Inverno. Structuring a Z specification to provide a formal framework for autonomous agent systems. In Bowen and Hinchey [99], pages 47–62.

437. M. Luck and M. d'Inverno. Engagement and cooperation in motivated agent modelling. In C. Zhang and D. Lukose, editors, *Distributed Artificial Intelligence Architecture and Modelling: Proc. 1st Australian Workshop on Distributed Artificial Intelligence*, volume 1087 of *Lecture Notes in Artificial Intelligence*, pages 70–84. Springer-Verlag, 1996.

438. M. Luck, N. Griffiths, and M. d'Inverno. From agent theory to agent construction: A case study. In J. P. Müller, M. Wooldridge, and N. Jennings, editors, *Intelligent Agents III: Proc. 3rd International Workshop on Agent Theories, Architectures and Languages, Lecture Notes in Artificial Intelligence, 1193*, pages 49–63. Springer-Verlag, 1997.

439. P. J. Lupton. Promoting forward simulation. In Nicholls [504], pages 27–49.

440. C. Lüth, E. W. Karlsen, Kolyang, S. Westmeier, and B. Wolff. Hol-Z in the UniForM-workbench – a case study in tool integration for Z. In Bowen et al. [85], pages 116–134.

441. A. MacDonald and D. Carrington. Structuring Z specifications: Some choices. In Bowen and Hinchey [99], pages 203–223.

442. R. Macdonald. Z usage and abusage. Report no. 91003, RSRE, Ministry of Defence, Malvern, Worcestershire, UK, February 1991.
     This paper presents a miscellany of observations drawn from experience of using Z, shows a variety of techniques for expressing certain class of idea concisely and clearly, and alerts the reader to certain pitfalls which may trap the unwary.

443. B. Mahony and J. S. Dong. Adding timed concurrent processes to Object-Z: A case study in TCOZ. In Bowen et al. [85], pages 308–327.

444. B. P. Mahony and I. J. Hayes. A case-study in timed refinement: A central heater. In Morris and Shaw [487], pages 138–149.

445. B. P. Mahony and I. J. Hayes. A case-study in timed refinement: A mine pump. *IEEE Transactions on Software Engineering*, 18(9):817–826, September 1992.

446. K. C. Mander and F. Polack. Rigorous specification using structured systems analysis and Z. *Information and Software Technology*, 37(5–6):285–291, May–June 1995.
     Revised version of [524].

447. A. Martin. Encoding W: A logic for Z in 2OBJ. In Woodcock and Larsen [689], pages 462–481.

448. A. Martin. *Machine-Assisted Theorem-Proving for Software Engineering*. DPhil thesis, Oxford University Computing Laboratory, Wolfson Building, Parks Road, Oxford, UK, 1995.

449. P. Mataga and P. Zave. Formal specification of telephone features. In Bowen and Hall [91], pages 29–50.

450. P. Mataga and P. Zave. Multiparadigm specification of an AT&T switching system. In Hinchey and Bowen [348], pages 375–398.

451. P. Mataga and P. Zave. Using Z to specify telephone features. *Information and Software Technology*, 37(5–6):277–283, May–June 1995.
Revised version of [449].

452. I. Maung and J. R. Howse. Introducing Hyper-Z – a new approach to object orientation in Z. In Bowen and Nicholls [102], pages 149–165.

453. M. D. May. Use of formal methods by a silicon manufacturer. In C. A. R. Hoare, editor, *Developments in Concurrency and Communication*, University of Texas at Austin Year of Programming Series, chapter 4, pages 107–129. Addison-Wesley Publishing Company, 1990.

454. M. D. May, G. Barrett, and D. E. Shepherd. Designing chips that work. In C. A. R. Hoare and M. J. C. Gordon, editors, *Mechanized Reasoning and Hardware Design*, pages 3–19. Prentice Hall International Series in Computer Science, 1992.

455. M. D. May and D. E. Shepherd. Verification of the IMS T800 microprocessor. In *Proc. Electronic Design Automation*, pages 605–615, London, UK, September 1987.

456. J. A. McDermid. Special section on Z. *IEE/BCS Software Engineering Journal*, 4(1):25–72, January 1989.
A special issue on Z, introduced and edited by Prof. J. A. McDermid. See also [71, 151, 600, 681].

457. J. A. McDermid, editor. *The Theory and Practice of Refinement: Approaches to the Formal Development of Large-Scale Software Systems*. Butterworth Scientific, 1989.
This book contains papers from the 1st Refinement Workshop held at the University of York, UK, 7–8 January 1988. Z-related papers include [400, 496].

458. J. A. McDermid. Formal methods: Use and relevance for the development of safety critical systems. In P. A. Bennett, editor, *Safety Aspects of Computer Control*. Butterworth-Heinemann, Oxford, UK, 1993.
This paper discusses a number of formal methods and summarizes strengths and weaknesses in safety critical applications; a major safety-related example is presented in Z.

459. M. A. McMorran and J. E. Nicholls. Z user manual. Technical Report TR12.274, IBM United Kingdom Laboratories Ltd, Hursley Park, Winchester, Hampshire SO21 2JN, UK, July 1989.

460. M. A. McMorran and S. Powell. *Z Guide for Beginners*. Blackwell Scientific, 1993.

461. S. L. Meira and A. L. C. Cavalcanti. Modular object-oriented Z specifications. In Nicholls [504], pages 173–192.

462. B. Meyer. On formalism in specifications. *IEEE Software*, 2(1):6–26, January 1985.

463. E. Mikk. Compilation of Z specifications into C for automatic test result evaluation. In Bowen and Hinchey [99], pages 167–180.

464. L. Mikušiak, M. Adamy, and T. Seidmann. Publishing formal specifications in Z notation on the WWW. In M. Bidoit and M. Dauchet, editors, *TAPSOFT'97: Theory and Practice of Software Development*, volume 1214 of *Lecture Notes in Computer Science*, pages 871–874. Springer-Verlag, 1997.

465. L. Mikušiak, V. Vojtek, J. Hasaralejko, and J. Hanzelová. Z browser – tool for visualization of Z specifications. In Bowen and Hinchey [99], pages 510–523.

466. C. Minkowitz, D. Rann, and J. H. Turner. A C++ library for implementing specifications. In France and Gerhart [265], pages 61–75.

467. R. Mitchell, M. Loomes, and J. Howse. Structuring formal specifications: A lesson re-learned. *Microprocessors and Microsystems*, 18(10):593–599, 1994.

468. V. B. Mišić and S. Moser. Formal approach to metamodeling: A generic object-oriented perspective. In D. W. Embley and R. C. Goldstein, editors, *Proc. 16th Conference on Conceptual Modeling (ER'97)*, pages 243–256, Los Angeles, USA, November 1997.

469. V. B. Mišić and S. Moser. From formal metamodels to metrics: An object-oriented approach. In J. Chen, M. Li, C. Mingins, and B. Meyer, editors, *Proc. 24th Conference on Technology of Object-Oriented Languages and Systems (TOOLS Asia)*, pages 413–422, Beijing, China, September 1997.

470. V. B. Mišić and D. Velašević. Formal specifications in software development: An overview. *Yugoslav Journal for Operations Research*, 7(1):79–96, January 1997.

471. V. B. Mišić, D. Velašević, and B. Lazarević. Formal specification of a data dictionary for an extended ER data model. *The Computer Journal*, 35(6):611–622, December 1992.

472. J. D. Moffett and M. S. Sloman. A case study representing a model: To Z or not to Z? In Nicholls [504], pages 254–268.

473. B. Q. Monahan. Book review. *Formal Aspects of Computing*, 1(1):137–142, January–March 1989.
    A review of *Understanding z: A Specification Language and Its Formal Semantics* by Mike Spivey [599].

474. B. Q. Monahan and R. C. Shaw. Model-based specifications. In J. A. McDermid, editor, *Software Engineer's Reference Book*, chapter 21. Butterworth-Heinemann, Oxford, UK, 1991.
    This chapter contains a case study in Z, followed by a discussion of the respective trade-offs in specification between Z and VDM.

475. C. C. Morgan. Data refinement using miracles. *Information Processing Letters*, 26(5):243–246, January 1988.

476. C. C. Morgan. Procedures, parameters, and abstraction: Separate concerns. *Science of Computer Programming*, 11(1), October 1988.

477. C. C. Morgan. The specification statement. *ACM Transactions on Programming Languages and Systems (TOPLAS)*, 10(3), July 1988.

478. C. C. Morgan. Types and invariants in the refinement calculus. In *Proc. Mathematics of Program Construction Conference*, Twente, The Netherlands, June 1989.

479. C. C. Morgan. *Programming from Specifications*. Prentice Hall International Series in Computer Science, 2nd edition, 1994.
    This book presents a rigorous treatment of most elementary program development techniques, including iteration, recursion, procedures, parameters, modules and data refinement.

480. C. C. Morgan and K. A. Robinson. Specification statements and refinement. *IBM Journal of Research and Development*, 31(5), September 1987.

481. C. C. Morgan and J. W. Sanders. Laws of the logical calculi. Technical Monograph PRG-78, Oxford University Computing Laboratory, Wolfson Building, Parks Road, Oxford, UK, September 1989.
    This document records some important laws of classical predicate logic. It is designed as a reservoir to be tapped by *users* of logic, in system development.

482. C. C. Morgan and B. A. Sufrin. Specification of the Unix filing system. *IEEE Transactions on Software Engineering*, 10(2):128–142, March 1984.

483. C. C. Morgan and T. Vickers, editors. *On the Refinement Calculus*. Formal Approaches to Computing and Information Technology series (FACIT). Springer-Verlag, 1994.
    This book collects together the work accomplished at the Oxford University Computing Laboratory on the refinement calculus: the rigorous development, from state-based assertional specification, of executable imperative code.

484. C. C. Morgan and J. C. P. Woodcock. What is a specification? In D. Craigen and K. Summerskill, editors, *Formal Methods for Trustworthy Computer Systems (FM89)*, Workshops in Computing, pages 38–43. Springer-Verlag, 1990.

485. C. C. Morgan and J. C. P. Woodcock, editors. *3rd Refinement Workshop*, Workshops in Computing. Springer-Verlag, 1991.
The workshop was held at the IBM Laboratories, Hursley Park, UK, 9–11 January 1990. See [572].

486. I. Morrey, J. Siddiqi, R. Hibberd, and G. Buckberry. A toolset to support the construction and animation of formal specifications. *Journal of Systems and Software*, 41(3):147–160, 1998.

487. J. M. Morris and R. C. Shaw, editors. *4th Refinement Workshop*, Workshops in Computing. Springer-Verlag, 1991.
The workshop was held at Cambridge, UK, 9–11 January 1991. For Z related papers, see [27, 378, 444, 675, 683, 671].

488. S. Moser and V. B. Mišić. Measuring class coupling and cohesion: A formal metamodel approach. In *Proc. 4th Asia Pacific Software Engineering Conference APSEC'97*, Hong Kong, December 1997.

489. L. Murray, D. Carrington, I. MacColl, J. McDonald, and P. Strooper. Formal derivation of finite state machines for class testing. In Bowen et al. [85], pages 42–59.

490. M. Naftalin, T. Denvir, and M. Bertran, editors. *FME'94: Industrial Benefit of Formal Methods*, volume 873 of *Lecture Notes in Computer Science*. Formal Methods Europe, Springer-Verlag, 1994.
The 2nd FME Symposium was held at Barcelona, Spain, 24–28 October 1994. Z-related papers include [94, 162, 177, 247, 250, 255, 366, 431, 514]. B-related papers include [185, 546, 627].

491. K. T. Narayana and S. Dharap. Formal specification of a look manager. *IEEE Transactions on Software Engineering*, 16(9):1089–1103, September 1990.
A formal specification of the look manager of a dialog system is presented in Z. This deals with the presentation of visual aspects of objects and the editing of those visual aspects.

492. K. T. Narayana and S. Dharap. Invariant properties in a dialog system. *ACM SIGSOFT Software Engineering Notes*, 15(4):67–79, September 1990.

493. T. C. Nash. Using Z to describe large systems. In Nicholls [502], pages 150–178.

494. Ph. W. Nehlig and D. A. Duce. GKS-9x: The design output primitive, an approach to specification. *Computer Graphics Forum*, 13(3):C–381–C–392, 1994.

495. M. Neil, G. Ostrolenk, M. Tobin, and M. Southworth. Lessons from using Z to specify a software tool. *IEEE Transactions on Software Engineering*, 24(1):15–23, 1998.

496. D. S. Neilson. Hierarchical refinement of a Z specification. In McDermid [457].

497. D. S. Neilson. From Z to C: Illustration of a rigorous development method. Technical Monograph PRG-101, Oxford University Computing Laboratory, Wolfson Building, Parks Road, Oxford, UK, 1990.

498. D. S. Neilson. Machine support for Z: The zedB tool. In Nicholls [504], pages 105–128.

499. D. S. Neilson and D. Prasad. zedB: A proof tool for Z built on B. In Nicholls [506], pages 243–258.

500. K. Nguyen and R. Duke. A formal analysis method for conceptual modelling of information systems. In Habrias [303], pages 93–110.

501. J. E. Nicholls. Working with formal methods. *Journal of Information Technology*, 2(2):67–71, June 1987.

502. J. E. Nicholls, editor. *Z User Workshop, Oxford 1989*, Workshops in Computing. Springer-Verlag, 1990.
Proceedings of the 4th Z User Meeting, Wolfson College & Rewley House, Oxford, UK, 14–15 December 1989. Published in collaboration with the British Computer Society. For the opening address see [515]. For individual papers, see [42, 116, 118, 161, 195, 261, 296, 327, 343, 383, 413, 493, 522, 588, 608, 669].

503. J. E. Nicholls. A survey of Z courses in the UK. In *Z User Workshop, Oxford 1990* [504], pages 343–350.

504. J. E. Nicholls, editor. *Z User Workshop, Oxford 1990*, Workshops in Computing. Springer-Verlag, 1991.
   Proceedings of the 5th Z User Meeting, Lady Margaret Hall, Oxford, UK, 17–18 December 1990. Published in collaboration with the British Computer Society. For individual papers, see [29, 109, 129, 159, 273, 297, 328, 344, 359, 385, 388, 410, 461, 472, 498, 503, 512, 534, 569, 670, 697]. The proceedings also includes an *Introduction and Opening Remarks*, a *Selected Z Bibliography*, a selection of posters and information on Z tools.

505. J. E. Nicholls. Domains of application for formal methods. In *Z User Workshop, York 1991* [506], pages 145–156.

506. J. E. Nicholls, editor. *Z User Workshop, York 1991*, Workshops in Computing. Springer-Verlag, 1992.
   Proceedings of the 6th Z User Meeting, York, UK. Published in collaboration with the British Computer Society. For individual papers, see [20, 33, 179, 133, 196, 229, 319, 499, 505, 525, 553, 589, 639, 655, 686, 702].

507. J. E. Nicholls. Plain guide to the Z base standard. In Bowen and Nicholls [102], pages 52–61.

508. J. E. Nicholls et al. Z in the development process. Technical Report PRG-TR-1-89, Oxford University Computing Laboratory, Wolfson Building, Parks Road, Oxford, UK, June 1989. Proceedings of a discussion workshop held on 15 December 1988 in Oxford, UK, with contributions by Peter Collins, David Cooper, Anthony Hall, Patrick Hall, Brian Hepworth, Ben Potter and Andrew Ricketts.

509. C. J. Nix and B. P. Collins. The use of software engineering, including the Z notation, in the development of CICS. *Quality Assurance*, 14(3):103–110, September 1988.

510. A. Norcliffe and G. Slater. *Mathematics for Software Construction*. Series in Mathematics and its Applications. Ellis Horwood, 1991.
   Contents: Why mathematics; Getting started: sets and logic; Developing ideas: schemas; Functions; Functions in action; A real problem from start to finish: a drinks machine; Sequences; Relations; Generating programs from specifications: refinement; The role of proof; More examples of specifications; Concluding remarks; Answers to exercises.

511. A. Norcliffe and S. Valentine. Z readers video course. PAVIC Publications, 1992. Sheffield Hallam University, 33 Collegiate Crescent, Sheffield S10 2BP, UK.
   Video-based Training Course on the Z Specification Language. The course consists of 5 videos, each of approximately one hour duration, together with supporting texts and case studies.

512. A. Norcliffe and S. H. Valentine. A video-based training course in reading Z specifications. In Nicholls [504], pages 337–342.

513. G. Normington. Cleanroom and Z. In Bowen and Nicholls [102], pages 281–293.

514. C. O' Halloran. Evaluation semantics in Z. In Naftalin et al. [490], pages 502–518.

515. B. Oakley. The state of use of formal methods. In Nicholls [502], pages 1–5.
   A record of the opening address at ZUM'89.

516. E.-R. Olderog. Combining specification techniques for processes, data and time. In Bowen et al. [85], page 192. Abstract.

517. R. Paige. Comparing extended Z with a heterogeneous notation for reasoning about time and space. In Bowen et al. [85], pages 214–232.

518. C. E. Parker. Z tools catalogue. ZIP project report ZIP/BAe/90/020, British Aerospace, Software Technology Department, Warton PR4 1AX, UK, May 1991.

519. H. Parker, F. Polack, and K. C. Mander. The industrial trial of SAZ: Reflections on the use of an integrated specification method. In Habrias [303], pages 111–129.

520. D. L. Parnas. Language-free mathematical models for software design. In Bowen and Hinchey [99], pages 3–4. Extended abstract.

521. D. L. Parnas. Teaching programming as engineering. In Bowen and Hinchey [99], pages 471–481.

522. M. Phillips. CICS/ESA 3.1 experiences. In Nicholls [502], pages 179–185.
    Z was used to specify 37,000 lines out of 268,000 lines of code in the IBM CICS/ESA 3.1 release. The initial development benefit from using Z was assessed as being a 9% improvement in the *total development cost* of the release, based on the reduction of programmer days fixing problems.

523. M. Pilling, A. Burns, and K. Raymond. Formal specifications and proofs of inheritance protocols for real-time scheduling. *IEE/BCS Software Engineering Journal*, 5(5):263–279, September 1990.

524. F. Polack and K. C. Mander. Software quality assurance using the SAZ method. In Bowen and Hall [91], pages 230–249.

525. F. Polack, M. Whiston, and P. Hitchcock. Structured analysis – a draft method for writing Z specifications. In Nicholls [506], pages 261–286.

526. F. Polack, M. Whiston, and K. C. Mander. The SAZ project: Integrating SSADM and Z. In Woodcock and Larsen [689], pages 541–557.

527. B. F. Potter, J. E. Sinclair, and D. Till. *An Introduction to Formal Specification and Z*. Prentice Hall International Series in Computer Science, 2nd edition, 1996.
    Contents: Formal specification in the context of software engineering; An informal introduction to logic and set theory; A first specification; The Z notation: the mathematical language, relations and functions, schemas and specification structure; A first specification; Formal reasoning; From specification to program: data and operation refinement, operation decomposition; From theory to practice.

528. B. F. Potter and D. Till. The specification in Z of gateway functions within a communications network. In *Proc. IFIP WG10.3 Conference on Distributed Processing*. Elsevier Science Publishers (North-Holland), October 1987.

529. C. H. Pratten. An introduction to proving AMN specifications with PVS and the AMN-PROOF tool. In Habrias [303], pages 149–165.

530. S. Prehn and W. J. Toetenel, editors. *VDM'91: Formal Software Development Methods*, volume 551 of *Lecture Notes in Computer Science*. Springer-Verlag, 1991. Volume 1: Conference Contributions.
    The 4th VDM-Europe Symposium was held at Noordwijkerhout, The Netherlands, 21–25 October 1991. Papers with relevance to Z include [19, 43, 170, 221, 279, 356, 661, 674, 701]. See also [531].

531. S. Prehn and W. J. Toetenel, editors. *VDM'91: Formal Software Development Methods*, volume 552 of *Lecture Notes in Computer Science*. Springer-Verlag, 1991. Volume 2: Tutorials.
    Papers with relevance to Z include [8, 684]. See also [530].

532. G.-H. B. Rafsanjani and S. J. Colwill. From Object-Z to C^{++}: A structural mapping. In Bowen and Nicholls [102], pages 166–179.

533. RAISE Language Group. *The RAISE Specification Language*. BCS Practitioner Series. Prentice Hall International, 1992.

534. G. P. Randell. Data flow diagrams and Z. In Nicholls [504], pages 216–227.

535. D. Rann, J. Turner, and J. Whitworth. *Z: A Beginner's Guide*. Chapman & Hall, London, 1994.

536. B. Ratcliff. *Introducing Specification Using Z: A Practical Case Study Approach*. International Series in Software Engineering. McGraw-Hill, 1994.

537. A. P. Ravn, H. Rischel, and V. Stavridou. Provably correct safety critical software. In *Proc. IFAC Safety of Computer Controlled Systems 1990 (SAFECOMP'90)*. Pergamon Press, 1990.

538. M. Rawson. OOPSLA'93: Workshop on formal specification of object-oriented systems – position paper. In H. Kilov and W. Harvey, editors, *Proc. Workshop on Specification of Behavioral Semantics in Object-Oriented Information Modeling*, pages 125–135, Washington DC, USA, 1993. OOPSLA.

539. M. Rawson and P. Allen. Synthesis – an integrated, object-oriented method and tool for requirements specification in Z. In Bryant and Semmens [121].

540. T. J. Read. Formal specification of reusable Ada software packages. In A. Burns, editor, *Proc. Towards Ada 9X Conference*, pages 98–117, 1991.

541. J. N. Reed. Semantics-based tools for a specification support environment. In *Mathematical Foundations of Programming Language Semantics*, volume 298 of *Lecture Notes in Computer Science*. Springer-Verlag, 1988.

542. J. N. Reed and J. E. Sinclair. An algorithm for type-checking Z: A Z specification. Technical Monograph PRG-81, Oxford University Computing Laboratory, Wolfson Building, Parks Road, Oxford, UK, March 1990.

543. C. Reilly. Exploring specifications with Mathematica. In Bowen and Hinchey [99], pages 408–420.

544. N. R. Reizer, G. D. Abowd, B. C. Meyers, and P. R. H. Place. Using formal methods for requirements specification of a proposed POSIX standard. In *Proc. IEEE International Conference on Requirements Engineering (ICRE'94)*, April 1994.

545. G. J. Reynolds. Yet another approach to the formal specification of a configurable graphics system. In *Proc. Eurographics Association Formal Methods in Computer Graphics*, June 1991.

546. B. Ritchie, J. Bicarregui, and H. P. Haughton. Experiences in using the abstract machine notation in a GKS case study. In Naftalin et al. [490], pages 93–104.

547. K. A. Robinson. Refining Z specifications to programs. In *Proc. Australian Software Engineering Conference*, pages 87–97, 1987.

548. G. A. Rose. Object-Z. In Stepney et al. [613], pages 59–77.

549. G. A. Rose and P. Robinson. A case study in formal specifications. In *Proc. First Australian Software Engineering Conference*, May 1986.

550. A. R. Ruddle. Formal methods in the specification of real-time, safety-critical control systems. In Bowen and Nicholls [102], pages 131–146.

551. P. Rudkin. Modelling information objects in Z. In J. de Meer, editor, *Proc. International Workshop on ODP*. Elsevier Science Publishers (North-Holland), 1992.

552. J. Rushby. Mechanizing formal methods: Challenges and opportunities. In Bowen and Hinchey [99], pages 105–113.

553. M. Saaltink. Z and Eves. In Nicholls [506], pages 223–242.

554. M. Saaltink. The Z/EVES system. In Bowen et al. [101], pages 72–85.

555. H. Saiedian. Mathematics of computing. *Journal of Computer Science Education*, 3(3):203–221, 1992.

556. H. Saiedian. Information systems and the engineering paradigm: Integrating the formal methods technology into the development process. *International Journal of Computing and Information Technology*, 2(4):277–290, 1994.

557. H. Saiedian. An invitation to formal methods. *IEEE Computer*, 29(4):16–30, 1996. This article includes an introduction to and commentaries by Jonathan P. Bowen, Ricky W. Butler, David L. Dill, Robert L. Glass, David Gries, J. Anthony Hall, Michael G. Hinchey, C. Michael Holloway, Daniel Jackson, Cliff B. Jones, Michael J. Lutz, David L. Parnas, John Rushby, Jeannette Wing, and Pamela Zave in a virtual roundtable on formal methods.

558. H. Saiedian. Formal methods in information systems engineering. In R. Thayer and M. Dorfman, editors, *Software Requirements Engineering*, pages 336–349. IEEE Computer Society Press, 1997.

559. H. Saiedian. Information systems design is an engineering process. In A. Kent, editor, *Encyclopedia of Information Science*, volume 60, pages 120–133. Marcel Dekker, New York, USA, 1997.

560. H. Saiedian and M. G. Hinchey. Issues surrounding the transferring of formal methods technology into the actual workplace. In *Proc. International Workshop on Formal Methods Application in Software Engineering Practice*, pages 69–76, Seattle, USA, April 1995. 17th International Conference on Software Engineering, IEEE Computer Society Press.

561. H. Saiedian and M. G. Hinchey. Challenges in the successful transfer of formal methods technology into industrial applications. *Information and Software Technology*, 38(5):313–321, May 1996.

562. A. C. A. Sampaio and S. L. Meira. Modular extensions to Z. In Bjørner et al. [51], pages 211–232.

563. P. Sanders, M. Johnson, and R. Tinker. From Z specifications to functional implementations. *British Telecom Technology Journal*, 7(4), October 1989.

564. T. Santen. On the semantic relation of Z and HOL. In Bowen et al. [85], pages 96–115.

565. M. Schenke and A. P. Ravn. Refinement from a control problem to programs. In Abrial et al. [10], pages 403–427.

566. D. Scholz and C. Petersohn. Towards a formal semantics for an integrated SA/RT & Z specification language. In Hinchey and Liu [350], pages 28–37.

567. S. A. Schuman and D. H. Pitt. Object-oriented subsystem specification. In L. G. L. T. Meertens, editor, *Program Specification and Transformation*, pages 313–341. Elsevier Science Publishers (North-Holland), 1987.

568. S. A. Schuman, D. H. Pitt, and P. J. Byers. Object-oriented process specification. In C. Rattray, editor, *Specification and Verification of Concurrent Systems*, pages 21–70. Springer-Verlag, 1990.

569. L. T. Semmens and P. M. Allen. Using Yourdon and Z: An approach to formal specification. In Nicholls [504], pages 228–253.

570. L. T. Semmens, R. B. France, and T. W. G. Docker. Integrated structured analysis and formal specification techniques. *The Computer Journal*, 35(6):600–610, December 1992.

571. C. T. Sennett. Formal specification and implementation. In C. T. Sennett, editor, *High-Integrity Software*, Computer Systems Series. Pitman, 1989.

572. C. T. Sennett. Using refinement to convince: Lessons learned from a case study. In Morgan and Woodcock [485], pages 172–197.

573. C. T. Sennett. Demonstrating the compliance of Ada programs with Z specifications. In Jones et al. [386].

574. D. E. Shepherd. Verified microcode design. *Microprocessors and Microsystems*, 14(10):623–630, December 1990.
This article is part of a special feature on *Formal aspects of microprocessor design*, edited by H. S. M. Zedan. See also [72].

575. D. E. Shepherd and G. Wilson. Making chips that work. *New Scientist*, 1664:61–64, May 1989.
A general article containing information on the formal development of the T800 floating-point unit for the Transputer including the use of Z.

576. D. Sheppard. *An Introduction to Formal Specification with Z and VDM*. International Series in Software Engineering. McGraw Hill, 1995.

577. L. B. Sherrell and D. L. Carver. Z meets Haskell: A case study. In *COMPSAC '93: Proc. 17th Annual International Computer Software and Applications Conference*, pages 320–326. IEEE Computer Society Press, November 1993.

The paper traces the development of a simple system, the class manager's assistant, from an existing Z specification, through design in Z, to a Haskell implementation.

578. L. B. Sherrell and D. L. Carver. Experiences in translating Z designs to Haskell implementations. *Software—Practice and Experience*, 24(12):1159–1178, 1994.

579. L. B. Sherrell and D. L. Carver. FunZ: An intermediate specification language. *The Computer Journal*, 38(3):193–206, 1995.

580. T. K. Shih. A Z specification approach to multimedia modeling. *Computers and Artificial Intelligence*, 16(5):465–495, 1997.

581. T. K. Shih and F. Y. Lin. An operational semantics approach to disciplined exceptions in logic programming. *Computers and Artificial Intelligence*, 14(1):1–33, 1995.

582. T. K. Shih, C. C. Wang, and C. M. Chung. Using Z to specify object-oriented software complexity measures. *Information and Software Technology*, 39(8):515–529, 1997.

583. J. E. Sinclair and D. C. Ince. The use of Z in specifying securuty properties. In Habrias [303], pages 27–39.

584. R. O. Sinnott and K. J. Turner. Modeling ODP viewpoints. In H. Kilov, W. Harvey, and H. Mili, editors, *Proc. Workshop on Precise Behavioral Specifications in Object-Oriented Information Modeling, OOPSLA 1994*, pages 121–128, Portland, USA, 24 October 1994. OOPSLA.

585. R. O. Sinnott and K. J. Turner. Specifying multimedia binding objects in Z. In O. Spaniol, C. Linnhoff-Popien, and B. Meyer, editors, *Trends in Distributed Systems*, volume 1161 of *Lecture Notes in Computer Science*, pages 244–258. Springer-Verlag, 1996.

586. R. O. Sinnott and K. J. Turner. Specifying ODP computational objects in Z. In E. Najm and J.-B. Stefani, editors, *Proc. 1st IFIP International Workshop on Formal Methods for Open Object-based Distributed Systems*, pages 375–390. Chapman & Hall, March 1996.

587. R. O. Sinnott and K. J. Turner. Type checking in open distributed systems: A complete model and its Z specification. In J. Rolia, J. Slonim, and J. Botsford, editors, *Proc. IFIP/IEEE International Conference on Open Distributed Processing and Distributed Platforms (ICODP/ICDP)*, pages 85–96, Toronto, Canada, 26–30 May 1997. Chapman & Hall.

588. A. Smith. The Knuth-Bendix completion algorithm and its specification in Z. In Nicholls [502], pages 195–220.

589. A. Smith. On recursive free types in Z. In Nicholls [506], pages 3–39.

590. G. Smith. *An Object-Oriented Approach to Formal Specification*. PhD thesis, Department of Computer Science, University of Queensland, St. Lucia 4072, Australia, October 1992. A detailed description of a version of Object-Z similar to (but not identical to) that in [237]. The thesis also includes a formalization of temporal logic history invariants and a fully-abstract model of classes in Object-Z.

591. G. Smith. A object-oriented development framework for Z. In Bowen and Hall [91], pages 89–107.

592. G. Smith. Extending $\mathcal{W}$ for Object-Z. In Bowen and Hinchey [99], pages 276–295.

593. G. Smith. A fully abstract semantics of classes for Object-Z. *Formal Aspects of Computing*, 7(3):289–313, 1995.

594. G. Smith and R. Duke. Modelling a cache coherence protocol using Object-Z. In *Proc. 13th Australian Computer Science Conference (ACSC-13)*, pages 352–361, 1990.

595. P. Smith and R. Keighley. The formal development of a secure transaction mechanism. In Prehn and Toetenel [530], pages 457–476.

596. I. Sommerville. *Software Engineering*, chapter 9, pages 153–168. Addison-Wesley Publishing Company, 4th edition, 1992. A chapter entitled *Model-Based Specification* including examples using Z.

597. I. H. Sørensen. A specification language. In J. Staunstrup, editor, *Program Specification: Proceedings of a Workshop*, volume 134 of *Lecture Notes in Computer Science*, pages 381–401. Springer-Verlag, 1981.

598. I. H. Sørensen. Using B to specify, verify and design hardware circuits. In Bowen et al. [85], pages 60–65. Extended abstract.

599. J. M. Spivey. *Understanding Z: A Specification Language and its Formal Semantics*, volume 3 of *Cambridge Tracts in Theoretical Computer Science*. Cambridge University Press, January 1988.
Published version of 1985 DPhil thesis.

600. J. M. Spivey. An introduction to Z and formal specifications. *IEE/BCS Software Engineering Journal*, 4(1):40–50, January 1989.

601. J. M. Spivey. A guide to the zed style option. Oxford University Computing Laboratory, December 1990.
A description of the Z style option 'zed.sty' for use with the LaTeX document preparation system [408]. This early and influential style option is now largely superseded by fuzz.sty [603], oz.sty [398] and other style options.

602. J. M. Spivey. Specifying a real-time kernel. *IEEE Software*, 7(5):21–28, September 1990.
This case study of an embedded real-time kernel shows that mathematical techniques have an important role to play in documenting systems and avoiding design flaws.

603. J. M. Spivey. *The ƒUZZ Manual*. Computing Science Consultancy, 34 Westlands Grove, Stockton Lane, York YO3 0EF, UK, 2nd edition, July 1992.
The manual describes a Z type-checker and 'fuzz.sty' style option for LaTeX documents [408]. The package is compatible with the book, *The Z Notation: A Reference Manual* by the same author [604].

604. J. M. Spivey. *The Z Notation: A Reference Manual*. Prentice Hall International Series in Computer Science, 2nd edition, 1992.
This is a revised edition of the first widely available reference manual on Z originally published in 1989. The book provides a complete and definitive guide to the use of Z in specifying information systems, writing specifications and designing implementations. See also the draft Z standard [112].
Contents: Tutorial introduction; Background; The Z language; The mathematical tool-kit; Sequential systems; Syntax summary; Changes from the first edition; Glossary.

605. J. M. Spivey. The consistency theorem for free type definitions in Z. *Formal Aspects of Computing*, 8:369–375, 1996.

606. J. M. Spivey. Richer types for Z. *Formal Aspects of Computing*, 8:565–584, 1996.

607. J. M. Spivey and B. A. Sufrin. Type inference in Z. In Bjørner et al. [51], pages 426–438. Also published as [608].

608. J. M. Spivey and B. A. Sufrin. Type inference in Z. In Nicholls [502], pages 6–31.

609. P. Steggles and J. Hulance. Z tools survey. Imperial Software Technology Ltd. / Formal Systems (Europe) Ltd., June 1994.

610. S. Stepney. *High Integrity Compilation: A Case Study*. Prentice Hall, 1993.
Outlines a method for developing a high assurance compiler based on many concepts and notations, including denotational semantics, the Z specification language and the Prolog programming language based on a fully worked case study.

611. S. Stepney. Testing as abstraction. In Bowen and Hinchey [99], pages 137–151.

612. S. Stepney and R. Barden. Annotated Z bibliography. *Bulletin of the European Association of Theoretical Computer Science*, 50:280–313, June 1993.

613. S. Stepney, R. Barden, and D. Cooper, editors. *Object Orientation in Z*. Workshops in Computing. Springer-Verlag, 1992.
This is a collection of papers describing various OOZ approaches – Hall, ZERO, MooZ, Object-Z, OOZE, Schuman & Pitt, Z^{++}, ZEST and Fresco (an object-oriented VDM method) – in the main written by the methods' inventors, and all specifying the same two examples. The collection is a revised and expanded version of a ZIP report distributed at the 1991 Z User Meeting at York.

614. S. Stepney, R. Barden, and D. Cooper. A survey of object orientation in Z. *IEE/BCS Software Engineering Journal*, 7(2):150–160, March 1992.

615. S. Stepney, D. Cooper, and J. C. P. Woodcock. More powerful data refinement in Z. In Bowen et al. [85], pages 284–307.

616. S. Stepney and S. P. Lord. Formal specification of an access control system. *Software—Practice and Experience*, 17(9):575–593, September 1987.

617. P. Stocks. *Applying Formal Methods to Software Testing*. PhD thesis, Department of Computer Science, University of Queensland, St. Lucia 4072, Australia, 1993.

618. P. Stocks and D. Carrington. A framework for specification-based testing. *IEEE Transactions on Software Engineering*, 22(11):777–793, 1996.

619. P. Stocks and D. A. Carrington. Deriving software test cases from formal specifications. In *6th Australian Software Engineering Conference*, pages 327–340, July 1991.

620. P. Stocks and D. A. Carrington. Test template framework: A specification-based testing case study. In *Proc. International Symposium on Software Testing and Analysis (ISSTA'93)*, pages 11–18, June 1993.
     Also available in a longer form as Technical Report UQCS-255, Department of Computer Science, University of Queensland.

621. P. Stocks and D. A. Carrington. Test templates: A specification-based testing framework. In *Proc. 15th International Conference on Software Engineering*, pages 405–414, May 1993.
     Also available in a longer form as Technical Report UQCS-243, Department of Computer Science, University of Queensland.

622. P. Stocks, K. Raymond, D. Carrington, and A. Lister. Modelling open distributed systems in Z. *Computer Communications*, 15(2):103–113, March 1992.
     In a special issue on the practical use of FDTs (Formal Description Techniques) in communications and distributed systems, edited by Dr. Gordon S. Blair.

623. W. J. Stoddart. An introduction to the Event Calculus. In Bowen et al. [101], pages 10–34.

624. W. J. Stoddart. The specification and refinement of an environmental model. In Bowen et al. [85], pages 24–41.

625. W. J. Stoddart, C. Fencott, and S. Dunne. Modelling hybrid systems in Z. In Habrias [303], pages 11–25.

626. W. J. Stoddart and P. Knaggs. The Event Calculus (formal specification of real time systems by means of diagrams and Z schemas). In *Proc. 5th International Conference on Putting into Practice Methods and Tools for Information System Design*, Nantes, France, September 1992. University of Nantes, Institute Universitaire de Technologie.

627. A. C. Storey and H. P. Haughton. A strategy for the production of verifiable code using the B method. In Naftalin et al. [490], pages 346–365.

628. B. Strulo. How firing conditions help inheritance. In Bowen and Hinchey [99], pages 264–275.

629. B. A. Sufrin. Formal system specification: Notation and examples. In D. Neel, editor, *Tools and Notations for Program Construction*. Cambridge University Press, 1982.
     An example of a filing system specification, this was the first published use of the schema notation to put together states.

630. B. A. Sufrin. Towards formal specification of the ICL data dictionary. *ICL Technical Journal*, August 1984.

631. B. A. Sufrin. Formal methods and the design of effective user interfaces. In M. D. Harrison and A. F. Monk, editors, *People and Computers: Designing for Usability*. Cambridge University Press, 1986.

632. B. A. Sufrin. Formal specification of a display-oriented editor. In N. Gehani and A. D. McGettrick, editors, *Software Specification Techniques*, International Computer Science Series, pages 223–267. Addison-Wesley Publishing Company, 1986.
     Originally published in *Science of Computer Programming*, 1:157–202, 1982.

633. B. A. Sufrin. A formal framework for classifying interactive information systems. In *IEE Colloquium on Formal Methods and Human-Computer Interaction*, number 09 in IEE Digest, pages 4/1–14, London, UK, 1987. The Institution of Electrical Engineers.

634. B. A. Sufrin. Effective industrial application of formal methods. In G. X. Ritter, editor, *Information Processing 89: Proc. 11th IFIP Computer Congress*, pages 61–69. Elsevier Science Publishers (North-Holland), 1989.
    This paper presents a Z model of the Unix *make* utility.

635. B. A. Sufrin and He Jifeng. Specification, analysis and refinement of interactive processes. In M. D. Harrison and H. Thimbleby, editors, *Formal Methods in Human-Computer Interaction*, volume 2 of *Cambridge Series on Human-Computer Interaction*, chapter 6, pages 153–200. Cambridge University Press, 1990.
    A case study on using Z for process modelling.

636. B. A. Sufrin and J. C. P. Woodcock. Towards the formal specification of a simple programming support environment. *IEE/BCS Software Engineering Journal*, 2(4):86–94, July 1987.

637. P. A. Swatman. *Increasing Formality in the Specification of High-Quality Information Systems in a Commercial Context*. PhD thesis, Curtin University of Technology, School of Computing, Perth, Western Australia, July 1992.

638. P. A. Swatman. Using formal specification in the acquisition of information systems: Educating information systems professionals. In Bowen and Nicholls [102], pages 205–239.

639. P. A. Swatman, D. Fowler, and C. Y. M. Gan. Extending the useful application domain for formal methods. In Nicholls [506], pages 125–144.

640. P. A. Swatman and P. M. C. Swatman. Formal specification: An analytic tool for (management) information systems. *Journal of Information Systems*, 2(2):121–160, April 1992.

641. P. A. Swatman and P. M. C. Swatman. Is the information systems community wrong to ignore formal specification methods? In R. Clarke and J. Cameron, editors, *Managing Information Technology's Organisational Impact*. Elsevier Science Publishers (North-Holland), October 1992.

642. P. A. Swatman and P. M. C. Swatman. Managing the formal specification of information systems. In *Proc. International Conference on Organization and Information Systems*, September 1992.

643. P. A. Swatman, P. M. C. Swatman, and R. Duke. Electronic data interchange: A high-level formal specification in Object-Z. In *Proc. 6th Australian Software Engineering Conference (ASWEC'91)*, Sidney, Australia, July 1991.

644. K. Taguchi and K. Araki. The state-based CCS semantics for concurrent Z specification. In Hinchey and Liu [350], pages 283–292.

645. S. Thompson. Specification techniques [9004-0316]. *ACM Computing Reviews*, 31(4):213, April 1990.
    A review of *Formal methods applied to a floating-point number system* [35].

646. D. Till, editor. *6th Refinement Workshop*, Workshop in Computing. Springer-Verlag, 1994. The workshop was held at City University, London, UK, 5–7 January 1994. See [256, 411].

647. B. S. Todd. A model-based diagnostic program. *IEE/BCS Software Engineering Journal*, 2(3):54–63, May 1987.

648. B. S. Todd and W. L. Ledger. A computer-based flowcharting system for clinical protocols. *Medical Informatics*, 20(3):177–198, 1995.

649. R. Took. The presenter – a formal design for an autonomous display manager. In I. Sommerville, editor, *Software Engineering Environments*, pages 151–169. Peter Peregrinus, London, 1986.

650. I. Toyn. Formal reasoning in the Z notation using CADiZ. In *Proc. 2nd Workshop on User Interfaces to Theorem Provers, York*, July 1996.

651. I. Toyn. Innovations in standard Z notation. In Bowen et al. [85], pages 193–213.

652. I. Toyn and J. A. McDermid. CADiZ: An architecture for Z tools and its implementation. *Software—Practice and Experience*, 25(3):305–330, March 1995.

653. O. Traynor, P. Kearney, E. Kazmierczak, Li Wang, and E. Karlsen. Extending Z with modules. *Australian Computer Science Communications*, 17(1), 1995. Proc. ACSC'95.

654. S. Valentine. The programming language Z^{--}. *Information and Software Technology*, 37(5–6):293–301, May–June 1995.

655. S. H. Valentine. Z^{--}, an executable subset of Z. In Nicholls [506], pages 157–187.

656. S. H. Valentine. Putting numbers into the mathematical toolkit. In Bowen and Nicholls [102], pages 9–36.

657. S. H. Valentine. An algebraic introduction of real numbers into Z. In Habrias [303], pages 183–204.

658. S. H. Valentine. Equal rights for schemas in Z. In Bowen and Hinchey [99], pages 183–202.

659. S. H. Valentine. Inconsistency and undefinedness in Z – a practical guide. In Bowen et al. [85], pages 233–249.

660. M. J. van Diepen and K. M. van Hee. A formal semantics for Z and the link between Z and the relational algebra. In Bjørner et al. [51], pages 526–551.

661. K. M. van Hee, L. J. Somers, and M. Voorhoeve. Z and high level Petri nets. In Prehn and Toetenel [530], pages 204–219.

662. H. J. van Zuylen, editor. *The REDO Compendium: Reverse Engineering for Software Maintenance*. John Wiley & Sons, 1993.
An overview of the results of the ESPRIT REDO project, including the use of Z and Z^{++}. See in particular Chapter 16, also published in a longer form as [414].

663. M. Waldén and K. Sere. Refining action systems with B-tool. In Gaudel and Woodcock [280], pages 85–104.

664. M. Weber. Combining Statecharts and Z for the design of safety-critical control systems. In Gaudel and Woodcock [280], pages 307–326.

665. M. M. West. Types and sets in Gödel and Z. In Bowen and Hinchey [99], pages 389–407.

666. M. M. West and B. M. Eaglestone. Software development: Two approaches to animation of Z specifications using Prolog. *IEE/BCS Software Engineering Journal*, 7(4):264–276, July 1992.

667. C. D. Wezeman. Using Z for network modelling: An industrial experience report. *Computer Standards & Interfaces*, 17(5–6):631–638, September 1995.

668. C. D. Wezeman and A. Judge. Z for managed objects. In Bowen and Hall [91], pages 108–119.

669. R. W. Whitty. Structural metrics for Z specifications. In Nicholls [502], pages 186–191.

670. P. J. Whysall and J. A. McDermid. An approach to object-oriented specification using Z. In Nicholls [504], pages 193–215.

671. P. J. Whysall and J. A. McDermid. Object-oriented specification and refinement. In Morris and Shaw [487], pages 151–184.

672. J. M. Wing. A specifier's introduction to formal methods. *IEEE Computer*, 23(9):8–24, September 1990.

673. J. M. Wing. Hints for writing specifications. In Bowen and Hinchey [99], page 497.

674. J. M. Wing and A. M. Zaremski. Unintrusive ways to integrate formal specifications in practice. In Prehn and Toetenel [530], pages 545–570.

675. K. R. Wood. The elusive software refinery: a case study in program development. In Morris and Shaw [487], pages 281–325.

676. K. R. Wood. A practical approach to software engineering using Z and the refinement calculus. *ACM Software Engineering Notes*, 18(5):79–88, December 1993.

677. W. G. Wood. Application of formal methods to system and software specification. *ACM SIGSOFT Software Engineering Notes*, 15(4):144–146, September 1990.

678. J. C. P. Woodcock. Teaching how to use mathematics for large-scale software development. *Bulletin of BCS-FACS*, July 1988.

679. J. C. P. Woodcock. Calculating properties of Z specifications. *ACM SIGSOFT Software Engineering Notes*, 14(4):43–54, 1989.

680. J. C. P. Woodcock. Mathematics as a management tool: Proof rules for promotion. In *Proc. 6th Annual CSR Conference on Large Software Systems*, Bristol, UK, September 1989.

681. J. C. P. Woodcock. Structuring specifications in Z. *IEE/BCS Software Engineering Journal*, 4(1):51–66, January 1989.

682. J. C. P. Woodcock. Z. In D. Craigen and K. Summerskill, editors, *Formal Methods for Trustworthy Computer Systems (FM89)*, Workshops in Computing, pages 57–62. Springer-Verlag, 1990.

683. J. C. P. Woodcock. Implementing promoted operations in Z. In Morris and Shaw [487], pages 366–378.

684. J. C. P. Woodcock. A tutorial on the refinement calculus. In Prehn and Toetenel [531], pages 79–140.

685. J. C. P. Woodcock. The rudiments of algorithm design. *The Computer Journal*, 35(5):441–450, October 1992.

686. J. C. P. Woodcock and S. M. Brien. *W*: A logic for Z. In Nicholls [506], pages 77–96.

687. J. C. P. Woodcock and J. Davies. *Using Z: Specification, Proof and Refinement*. Prentice Hall International Series in Computer Science, 1996.
This book contains enough material for three complete courses of study. It provides an introduction to the world of logic, sets and relations. It explains the use of the Z notation in the specification of realistic systems. It shows how Z specifications may be refined to produce executable code; this is demonstrated in a selection of case studies.
The book strikes a balance between the formality of mathematics and the practical needs of industrial software development, following to the draft ISO standard for Z. It is based upon the experience of the authors in teaching Z to a wide variety of audiences. A set of exercises, solutions, and transparency masters is available on-line to complement the book.

688. J. C. P. Woodcock, P. H. B. Gardiner, and J. R. Hulance. The formal specification in Z of Defence Standard 00-56. In Bowen and Hall [91], pages 9–28.

689. J. C. P. Woodcock and P. G. Larsen, editors. *FME'93: Industrial-Strength Formal Methods*, volume 670 of *Lecture Notes in Computer Science*. Formal Methods Europe, Springer-Verlag, 1993.
The 1st FME Symposium was held at Odense, Denmark, 19–23 April 1993. Z-related papers include [103, 165, 254, 372, 447, 526].

690. J. C. P. Woodcock and P. G. Larsen. Guest editorial. *IEEE Transactions on Software Engineering*, 21(2):61–62, February 1995.
Best papers from the FME'93 Symposium [689]. See [49, 63, 168, 373].

691. J. C. P. Woodcock and M. Loomes. *Software Engineering Mathematics: Formal Methods Demystified*. Pitman, 1988.
Also published as: *Software Engineering Mathematics*, Addison-Wesley, 1989.

692. J. C. P. Woodcock and C. C. Morgan. Refinement of state-based concurrent systems. In Bjørner et al. [51], pages 340–351.
Work on combining Z and CSP.

693. I. M. Y. Woon and W. L. Loh. Formal derivation to object-oriented implementation of financial policies. *International Journal of Computer Applications in Technology*, 10(5–6):316–326, 1997.

694. R. Worden. Fermenting and distilling. In Bowen and Hall [91], pages 1–6.

695. J. B. Wordsworth. Teaching formal specification methods in an industrial environment. In *Proc. Software Engineering '86*, London, 1986. IEE/BCS, Peter Peregrinus.

696. J. B. Wordsworth. Specifying and refining programs with Z. In *Proc. 2nd IEE/BCS Conference on Software Engineering*, number 290 in Conference Publication, pages 8–16. IEE/BCS, July 1988.

697. J. B. Wordsworth. The CICS application programming interface definition. In Nicholls [504], pages 285–294.

698. J. B. Wordsworth. *Software Development with Z: A Practical Approach to Formal Methods in Software Engineering*. Addison-Wesley Publishing Company, 1993.
    This book provides a guide to developing software from specification to code, and is based in part on work done at IBM's UK Laboratory that won the UK Queen's Award for Technological Achievement in 1992.
    Contents: Introduction; A simple Z specification; Sets and predicates; Relations and functions; Schemas and specifications; Data design; Algorithm design; Specification of an oil terminal control system.

699. Xiaoping Jia. *ZTC: A Type Checker for Z – User's Guide*. Institute for Software Engineering, Department of Computer Science and Information Systems, DePaul University, Chicago, IL 60604, USA, 1994.
    ZTC is a type checker for the Z specification language. ZTC accepts two forms of input: LaTeX [408] with the oz.sty / zed.sty [398, 601] style options and ZSL, an ASCII version of Z. ZTC can also perform translations between the two input forms. This document is intended to serve as both a user's guide and a reference manual for ZTC.

700. W. D. Young. Comparing specifications paradigms: Gypsy and Z. In *Proc. 12th National Computer Security Conference*, Baltimore, Maryland, USA, 10–13 October 1989.

701. P. Zave and M. Jackson. Techniques for partial specification and specification of switching systems. In Prehn and Toetenel [530], pages 511–525.
    Also published as [702].

702. P. Zave and M. Jackson. Techniques for partial specification and specification of switching systems. In Nicholls [506], pages 205–219.

703. P. Zave and M. Jackson. Conjunction as composition. *ACM Transactions on Software Engineering and Methodology (TOSEM)*, 2(4):379–411, October 1993.
    Partial specifications written in many different specification languages can be composed if they are all given semantics in the same domain, or alternatively, all translated into a common style of predicate logic. A Z specification is used as an example.

704. P. Zave and M. Jackson. Where do operations come from? A multiparadigm technique. *IEEE Transactions on Software Engineering*, 22(7):508–528, July 1996.
    Z is supplemented, primarily with automata and grammars, to provide a rigorous and systematic mapping from input stimuli to convenient operations and arguments for the Z specification.

705. Y. Zhang and P. Hitchcock. EMS: Case study in methodology for designing knowledge-based systems and information systems. *Information and Software Technology*, 33(7):518–526, September 1991.

706. Z archive. URL: http://www.comlab.ox.ac.uk/archive/z.html, 1994 onwards.
    On-line information on the Z notation is available for use by anyone with World Wide Web (WWW) and anonymous FTP access. In particular, this Z bibliography [1] is available. The preferred method of access to the Z archive is under the 'URL' (Uniform Resource Locator) given above. Some of the archive (mainly older files) is accessible via anonymous FTP under the ftp://ftp.comlab.ox.ac.uk/pub/Zforum/ directory.

Comp.specification.z and Z FORUM
Frequently Asked Questions

Jonathan P. Bowen

The University of Reading, Department of Computer Science
Whiteknights, PO Box 225, Reading, Berks RG6 6AY, UK

Email: J.P.Bowen@reading.ac.uk
URL: http://www.cs.reading.ac.uk/people/jpb/

Abstract. This appendix provides some details on how to access information on Z, particularly electronically. It has been generated from a message that is updated and sent out monthly on the Internet. This information is issued each month on the comp.specification.z newsgroup and is available on-line on the following World Wide Web (WWW) hypertext page where it is split into convenient sections and updated each month:

http://www.cis.ohio-state.edu/hypertext/faq/usenet/z-faq/faq.html

1 What is it?

Z (pronounced "zed") is a formal specification notation based on set theory and first order predicate logic. It has been developed at the Programming Research Group at the Oxford University Computing Laboratory (OUCL) and elsewhere since the late 1970s. It is used by industry as part of the software (and hardware) development process in Europe, USA and elsewhere. Currently it is undergoing international ISO standardization.

The comp.specification.z electronic USENET newsgroup was established in June 1991 and is intended to handle messages concerned with Z. It has an estimated readership of tens of thousands of people worldwide. Comp.specification.z provides a convenient forum for messages concerned with recent developments and the use of Z. Pointers to and reviews of recent books and articles are particularly encouraged. These may be included in the Z bibliography (see below) if they appear in comp.specification.z. If you do not have direct news access, you can search for comp.specification.z articles on the World Wide Web using Deja News:

http://search.dejanews.com/dnquery.xp?QRY=comp.specification.z

2 What if I do not have access to USENET news?

There is an associated Z FORUM electronic mailing list that was initiated in January 1986 by Ruaridh Macdonald, RSRE, UK. Articles are automatically cross-posted between comp.specification.z and the mailing list for those whose do not have access to USENET news. This may apply especially to industrial Z users who are particularly encouraged to subscribe and post their experiences to the list. Please contact zforum-request@comlab.ox.ac.uk with your name, address and email address to join the mailing list (or if you change your email address or wish to be removed from the list). Readers are strongly urged to read the comp.specification.z newsgroup rather than the Z FORUM mailing list if possible. Messages for submission to the Z FORUM mailing list and the comp.specification.z newsgroup may be emailed to zforum@comlab.ox.ac.uk. This method of posting is particularly recommended for important messages like announcements of meetings since not all messages posted on comp.specification.z reach the OUCL.

A mailing list for the Z User Meeting educational issues session has been set by Neville Dean, Anglia Polytechnic University, UK. Anyone interested may join by emailing zugeis-request@comlab.ox.ac.uk with your contact details.

3   What if I do not have access to email?

If you wish to join the postal Z mailing list, please send your address to Amanda Kingscote, Praxis Critical Systems Ltd, 20 Manvers Street, Bath BA1 1PX, UK (tel +44-1225-466991, fax +44-1225-469006, email ark@praxis-cs.co.uk). This will ensure you receive details of Z meetings, etc., particularly for people without access to electronic mail.

4   How can I join in?

If you are currently using Z, you are welcome to introduce yourself to the newsgroup and Z FORUM list by describing your work with Z or raising any questions you might have about Z which are not answered here. You may also advertize publications concerning Z which you or your colleagues produce. These may then be added to the master Z bibliography maintained at the OUCL (see below).

5   Where are Z-related files archived?

On-line information relevant to the Z notation may be found as part of the World Wide Web (WWW) Virtual Library under the following URL:

http://www.comlab.ox.ac.uk/archive/z.html

This includes hyperlinks to many Z-related resources available on-line around the world. See also the following page on formal methods in general:

http://www.comlab.ox.ac.uk/archive/formal-methods.html

An older Z archive is also available via anonymous FTP under:

ftp://ftp.comlab.ox.ac.uk/pub/Zforum/

6 What tools are available?

Various tools for formatting, type-checking and aiding proofs in Z are available under:

> http://www.comlab.ox.ac.uk/archive/z.html#tools

This includes links to a number of LATEX style files which support the Z notation. Information on Object-Z LATEX macros ('oz.sty') may be found under:

> http://svrc.it.uq.edu.au/Object-Z/pages/latex.html

The FuZZ package, a syntax and type-checker with a LATEX style option and fonts, is available from the Spivey Partnership, 10 Warneford Road, Oxford OX4 1LU, UK. It is compatible with the 2nd edition of Spivey's Z Reference Manual. Access the following URL for brief information including ordering:

> http://www.comlab.ox.ac.uk/oucl/software/fuzz.html

Contact Mike Spivey (email Mike.Spivey@comlab.oxford.ac.uk) for further information.

CADiZ is a suite of integrated tools for preparing and type-checking Z specifications as professional quality typeset documents. The Z dialect it recognizes is evolving in line with the standard. The typesetting can be performed by either *troff* or LATEX for UNIX or Word for Windows. The mouse can be used to interact with a view of the typeset specification to inspect properties deduced by the type-checker, to see the expansion of schema calculus expressions, and to reason about conjectures such as proof obligations. The PC version is integrated with MS Word using OLE2, providing WYSIWYG editing of Z paragraphs directly in Word documents. (The *troff* and LATEX versions use ordinary text editors on ASCII mark-up.) Further development of the tools is ongoing. CADiZ is a BCS Award winning product available for Sun, SGI and PC machines from York Software Engineering Ltd, Glanford House, Bellwin Drive, Flixborough, Scunthorpe, North Lincolnshire, DN15 8SN, UK (email yse@cse-euro.demon.co.uk, tel +44-1724-862169, fax +44-1724-846256). URL:

> http://www.cse-euro.demon.co.uk/yse/products/cadiz/

ProofPower is a suite of tools supporting specification and proof in Higher Order Logic (HOL) and in Z. As an option, ProofPower also supports verification of SPARK-Ada programs against Z specifications using the Compliance Notation designed by DERA. Short courses on ProofPower-Z are available as demand arises. Information about Proof-Power can be obtained from the following location:

> http://www.trireme.demon.co.uk/

Please address enquiries to ProofPower-support@win.icl.co.uk or to Roger Jones, International Computers Ltd., Lovelace Road, Bracknell, RG12 8SN, UK (tel +44-1344-472000).

Zola is a commercial integrated support tool for Z on Sun workstations, for automated assistance at all stages of the specification construction, proving and maintenance process. It is intended for system developers and includes a WYSIWYG editor, typechecker and tactical theorem prover suitable for the creation and maintenance of large specifications. For further information, contact Chris Paine, Imperial Software Technology Ltd, Berkshire House, 252 Kings Road, Reading RG1 4HP, UK (tel +44-118-958-7055, fax +44-118-958-9005, email fms@ist.co.uk), or see:

```
http://www.ist.co.uk/products/zola.html
```

ZTC is a Z type-checker available free of charge for educational and non-profit uses. It is intended to be compliant with the 2nd edition of Spivey's Z Reference Manual. It accepts LATEX with 'zed' or 'oz' styles, and ZSL – an ASCII version of Z. ZANS is a Z animator. It is a research prototype that is still very crude. Both ZTC and ZANS run on Linux, SunOS, Solaris, HP-UX and DOS. They are available via FTP under:

```
ftp://ise.cs.depaul.edu/pub/ZTC/
```

```
ftp://ise.cs.depaul.edu/pub/ZANS/
```

Contact Xiaoping Jia `jia@cs.depaul.edu` for further information.

Formaliser is a syntax-directed WYSIWYG Z editor and interactive type checker, running under Microsoft Windows, available from Logica. Contact Susan Stepney, Logica UK Limited, Cambridge Division, Betjeman House, 104 Hills Road, Cambridge CB2 1LQ, UK (email `stepneys@logica.com`, tel +44-1223-366343, fax +44-1223-251001) or see on-line under:

```
http://public.logica.com/~formaliser/
```

The B-Toolkit is a set of integrated tools which fully supports the B-Method for formal software development and is available from B-Core (UK) Limited, Magdalen Centre, The Oxford Science Park, Oxford OX4 4GA, UK. For further details, contact Ib Sørensen (tel +44-1865-784520, fax +44-1865-784518, email `B@b-core.com`) or see on-line under:

```
http://www.b-core.com/
```

Nitpick is a freely available tool for fully automatically analyzing software specifications in (roughly) a subset of Z. See under:

```
http://www.cs.cmu.edu/~nitpick/
```

Z/EVES is an analysis tool for Z specifications, that can be used to check for syntax, type-correctness and 'domain errors' (are functions applied on their domain?), expand schemas, calculate preconditions and check for totality, and state and prove conjectures, with the aid of a heuristic theorem prover. It supports the 'zed'/'fuzz' style LATEX markup. and runs on SunOS, OS/2, Linux, Windows 3.1, Windows'95 and, with the appropriate compatibility package from Sun, Solaris. It is available electronically at no cost. Email eves@ora.on.ca or see:

```
http://www.ora.on.ca/distribution.html
```

Z fonts for MS Windows and Macintosh are available on-line. For hyperlinks to these and other Z tool resources see the WWW Z page:

```
http://www.comlab.ox.ac.uk/archive/z.html#tools
```

7   How can I learn about Z?

There are a number of courses on Z run by industry and academia. Oxford University offers industrial short courses in the use Z. As well as introductory courses, recent newly developed material includes advanced Z-based courses on proof and refinement, partly based around the B-Tool. Courses are held in Oxford, or elsewhere (e.g., on a company's premises) if there is enough demand. For further information, contact Jim Woodcock (email Jim.Woodcock@comlab.ox.ac.uk, tel +44-1865-283514, fax +44-1865-273839).

Logica offer a five day course on Z at company sites. Contact Susan Stepney (tel +44-1223-366343, fax +44-1223-322315, email stepneys@logica.com) at Logica UK Limited, Betjeman House, 104 Hills Road, Cambridge CB2 1LQ, UK, or see on-line under

http://public.logica.com/~formaliser/services/zcourse.htm

Praxis Critical Systems Ltd runs a range of Z (and other formal methods) courses. For details contact Anthony Hall on +44-1225-466991 or jah@praxis-cs.co.uk.

Formal Systems (Europe) Ltd run a range of Z, CSP and other formal methods courses, primarily in the US and with such lecturers as Jim Woodcock and Bill Roscoe (both lecturers at the OUCL). For dates and prices contact Kate Pearson (tel +44-1865-728460, fax +44-1865-201114) at Formal Systems (Europe) Limited, 3 Alfred Street, Oxford OX1 4EH, UK.

8   What has been published about Z?

A searchable on-line Z bibliography is available in BIBTeX format under:

http://www.comlab.ox.ac.uk/archive/z/bib.html

The following books largely concerning Z have been or are due to be published (in approximate chronological order):

• I. Hayes (ed.), Specification Case Studies, Prentice Hall International Series in Computer Science, 1987. (2nd ed., 1993)

• J. M. Spivey, Understanding Z: A specification language and its formal semantics, Cambridge University Press, 1988.

• D. Ince, An Introduction to Discrete Mathematics, Formal System Specification and Z, Oxford University Press, 1988. (2nd ed., 1993)

• J. C. P. Woodcock & M. Loomes, Software Engineering Mathematics: Formal Methods Demystified, Pitman, 1998. (Also Addison-Wesley, 1989)

• J. M. Spivey, The Z Notation: A reference manual, Prentice Hall International Series in Computer Science, 1989. (2nd ed., 1992) URL:

http://spivey.oriel.ox.ac.uk/~mike/zrm/

[Widely used as a de facto standard for Z. Often known as ZRM2.]

• A. Diller, Z: An introduction to formal methods, Wiley, 1990.

• J. E. Nicholls (ed.), Z user workshop, Oxford 1989, Springer-Verlag, Workshops in Computing, 1990.

• B. Potter, J. Sinclair & D. Till, An Introduction to Formal Specification and Z, Prentice Hall International Series in Computer Science, 1991. (2nd ed., 1996)

• D. Lightfoot, Formal Specification using Z, MacMillan, 1991.

• A. Norcliffe & G. Slater, Mathematics for Software Construction, Ellis Horwood, 1991.

• J. E. Nicholls (ed.), Z User Workshop, Oxford 1990, Springer-Verlag, Workshops in Computing, 1991.

- I. Craig, The Formal Specification of Advanced AI Architectures, Ellis Horwood, 1991.
- M. Imperato, An Introduction to Z, Chartwell-Bratt, 1991.
- J. B. Wordsworth, Software Development with Z, Addison-Wesley, 1992.
- S. Stepney, R. Barden & D. Cooper (eds.), Object Orientation in Z, Springer-Verlag, Workshops in Computing, August 1992. URL:

    http://public.logica.com/~stepneys/bib/ss/ooz/

- J. E. Nicholls (ed.), Z User Workshop, York 1991, Springer-Verlag, Workshops in Computing, 1992.
- D. Edmond, Information Modeling: Specification and implementation, Prentice Hall, 1992.
- J. P. Bowen & J. E. Nicholls (eds.), Z User Workshop, London 1992, Springer-Verlag, Workshops in Computing, 1993. URL:

    http://www.comlab.ox.ac.uk/archive/z/zum92.html

- S. Stepney, High Integrity Compilation: A case study, Prentice Hall, 1993. URL:

    http://public.logica.com/~stepneys/bib/ss/hic/

- M. McMorran & S. Powell, Z Guide for Beginners, Blackwell Scientific, 1993.
- K. C. Lano & H. Haughton (eds.), Object-oriented Specification Case Studies, Prentice Hall International Object-Oriented Series, 1993.
- B. Ratcliff, Introducing Specification using Z: A practical case study approach, Mc-Graw-Hill, 1994.
- A. Diller, Z: An introduction to formal methods, 2nd ed., Wiley, 1994.
- J. P. Bowen & J. A. Hall (eds.), Z User Workshop, Cambridge 1994, Springer-Verlag, Workshops in Computing, 1994. URL:

    http://www.comlab.ox.ac.uk/archive/z/zum94.html

- R. Barden, S. Stepney & D. Cooper, Z in Practice, Prentice Hall BCS Practitioner Series, 1994. URL:

    http://public.logica.com/~stepneys/bib/ss/zip/

- D. Rann, J. Turner & J. Whitworth, Z: A beginner's guide. Chapman & Hall, 1994.
- D. Heath, D. Allum & L. Dunckley, Introductory Logic and Formal Methods. A. Wall-er, Henley-on-Thames, 1994.
- L. Bottaci and J. Jones, Formal Specification using Z: A modelling approach. International Thomson Publishing, 1995.
- D. Sheppard, An Introduction to Formal Specification with Z and VDM. Mc-Graw Hill International Series in Software Engineering, 1995.
- J. P. Bowen & M. G. Hinchey (eds.), ZUM'95: The Z Formal Specification Notation, Springer-Verlag, Lecture Notes in Computer Science, volume 967, 1995. URL:

    http://www.comlab.ox.ac.uk/archive/z/zum95.html

- J. P. Bowen, Formal Specification and Documentation using Z: A Case Study Approach, International Thomson Compress Press, 1996. URL:

    http://www.comlab.ox.ac.uk/oucl/users/jonathan.bowen/zbook.html

- J. C. P. Woodcock & J. Davies, Using Z: Specification, proof and refinement, Prentice Hall International Series in Computer Science, 1996. URL:

```
http://www.comlab.ox.ac.uk/usingz.html
```

- A. Harry, Formal Methods Fact File: VDM and Z, Wiley, 1996.
- J. Jacky, The Way of Z: Practical Programming with Formal Methods, Cambridge University Press, 1997. URL:

```
http://www.radonc.washington.edu/prostaff/jon/z-book/
```

- J. P. Bowen, M. G. Hinchey & D. Till (eds.), ZUM'97: The Z Formal Specification Notation, Springer-Verlag, Lecture Notes in Computer Science, volume 1212, 1997. URL:

```
http://www.cs.reading.ac.uk/zum97/
```

- J. P. Bowen, A. Fett & M. G. Hinchey (eds.), ZUM'98: The Z Formal Specification Notation, Springer-Verlag, Lecture Notes in Computer Science, volume 1493, 1998. URL:

```
http://www.fmse.cs.reading.ac.uk/zum98/
```

See also an on-line list of Z books from Blackwells Bookshop under:
```
http://www.blackwell.co.uk/cgi-bin/bb_catsel?09_IBY
```

Formal Methods: A Survey by S. Austin & G. I. Parkin, March 1993 includes information on the use and teaching of Z in industry and academia. Contact DITC Office, Formal Methods Survey, National Laboratory, Teddington, Middlesex TW11 0LW, UK (tel +44-181-943-7002, fax +44-181-977-7091) for a copy.

OUCL Technical Monographs and Reports, including many on Z, is available from the librarian (email library@comlab.ox.ac.uk, tel +44-1865-273837, fax +44-1865-273839).

For information on formal methods publications in general, see:
```
http://www.comlab.ox.ac.uk/archive/formal-methods/pubs.html
```

9 What is object-oriented Z?

Several object-oriented extensions to or versions of Z have been proposed. The book *Object orientation in Z*, listed above, is a collection of papers describing various OOZ approaches – Hall, ZERO, MooZ, Object-Z, OOZE, Schuman&Pitt, Z^{++}, ZEST and Fresco (an OO VDM method) – in the main written by the methods' inventors, and all specifying the same two examples. A more recent book entitled *Object-oriented specification case studies* surveys the principal methods and languages for formal object-oriented specification, including Z-based approaches.

10 How can I run Z?

Z is a (non-executable in general) specification language, so there is no such thing as a Z compiler/linker/etc. as you would expect for a programming language. Some people have looked at animating subsets of Z for rapid prototyping purposes, using logic and functional programming for example, but this is not really the major point of Z, which is to increase human understandability of the specified system and allow the possibility of formal reasoning and development. However, Prolog seems to be the main favoured language for Z prototyping and some references may be found in the Z bibliography (see above).

11   Where can I meet other Z people?

The 11th International Conference of Z Users (ZUM'98) is being held in Berlin, Germany, 24–26 September 1998. A Call for Participation has been issued. For further information, please contact the Conference Chair: Mike Hinchey, Department of Computer Science, College of Information Science and Technology, University of Nebraska at Omaha, 6001 Dodge Street, Omaha, NE 68182–0500, USA (tel +1-402-554-4996, fax: +1-402-554-2975 email: michael.hinchey@ul.ie). See on-line information under:

http://www.fmse.cs.reading.ac.uk/zum98/

Information on Z User Meetings is issued on comp.specification.z and other related newsgroups, various specialist electronic mailing lists, and the Z postal mailing list. Previous proceedings for Z User Meetings have been published in the Springer-Verlag LNCS and Workshops in Computing series since the 4th meeting in 1989. For further on-line information on previous Z User Meetings, see the following URL:

http://www.comlab.ox.ac.uk/archive/z/zum.html

For a list of meetings with a formal methods content, see:

http://www.comlab.ox.ac.uk/archive/formal-methods/meetings.html

12   What is the Z User Group?

The Z User Group was set up in 1992 to oversee Z-related activities, and the Z User Meetings in particular. As a subscriber to either comp.specification.z, ZFORUM or the postal mailing list, you may consider yourself a member of the Z User Group. There are currently no charges for membership, although this is subject to review if necessary. Contact zforum-request@comlab.ox.ac.uk for further information. For on-line information, see the following URL:

http://www.comlab.ox.ac.uk/archive/z/zug.html

13   How can I obtain the draft Z standard?

The proposed Z standard under ISO/IEC JTC1/SC22 is available on-line. See under

http://www.comlab.ox.ac.uk/oucl/groups/zstandards/

for information and locations. An early version is also available in printed form from the OUCL librarian (email library@comlab.ox.ac.uk, tel +44-1865-273837, fax +44-1865-273839) by requesting Technical Monograph number PRG-107. For links to recent on-line information, see:

http://www.comlab.ox.ac.uk/archive/z.html#standards

14 Where else is Z discussed?

The BCS-FACS (British Computer Society Formal Aspects of Computer Science special interest group) and FME (Formal Methods Europe) are two organizations interested
in formal methods in general. Contact BCS FACS, Dept of Computer Studies, Loughborough University of Technology, Loughborough, Leicester LE11 3TU, UK (tel +44-
1509-222676, fax +44-1509-211586, email FACS@lut.ac.uk) for further information.

  A *FACS Europe* newsletter is issued to members of FACS and FME. Please send
suitable Z-related material to the Z column editor, David Till, Dept of Computer Science, City University, Northampton Square, London, EC1V 0HB, UK (tel +44-171-
477-8552, email till@cs.city.ac.uk) for possible publication. Material from articles appearing on the comp.specification.z newsgroup may be included if considered of sufficient interest (with permission from the originator if possible). It would
be helpful for posters of articles on comp.specification.z to indicate if they do not
want further distribution for any reason.

15 How does VDM compare with Z?

See I. J. Hayes, C. B. Jones & J. E. Nicholls, Understanding the differences between
VDM and Z, FACS Europe, series I, 1(1):7–30, Autumn 1993 available as an on-line
Technical Report from Manchester in compressed POSTSCRIPT format under:

  ftp://ftp.cs.man.ac.uk/pub/TR/UMCS-93-8-1.ps.Z

See also I. J. Hayes, VDM and Z: A comparative case study, Formal Aspects of Computing, 4(1):76–99, 1992. VDM is discussed on the (unmoderated) VDM FORUM mailing
list. Send a message containing the command 'join vdm-forum name' where name is
your real name to mailbase@mailbase.ac.uk. To contact the list administrator, email
John Fitzgerald on vdm-forum-request@mailbase.ac.uk.

16 How does the B-Method compare with Z?

B is a tool-based formal method for software development, conceived by the originator
of Z, Jean-Raymond Abrial, whereas Z is designed mainly for specification. See

  http://www.b-core.com/ZVdmB.html

for a comparison. See also

  http://www.comlab.ox.ac.uk/archive/formal-methods/b.html

for further information on B.

17 What if I have spotted a mistake or an omission?

Please send corrections or new relevant information about meetings, books, tools, etc.,
to J.P.Bowen@reading.ac.uk. New questions and model answers are also gratefully
received!

Author Index

Lecture Notes in Computer Science

For information about Vols. 1–1415

please contact your bookseller or Springer-Verlag

Vol. 1456: A. Drogoul, M. Tambe, T. Fukuda (Eds.), Collective Robotics. Proceedings, 1998. VII, 161 pages. 1998. (Subseries LNAI).

Vol. 1457: A. Ferreira, J. Rolim, H. Simon, S.-H. Teng (Eds.), Solving Irregularly Structured Problems in Prallel. Proceedings, 1998. X, 408 pages. 1998.

Vol. 1458: V.O. Mittal, H.A. Yanco, J. Aronis, R-. Simpson (Eds.), Assistive Technology in Artificial Intelligence. X, 273 pages. 1998. (Subseries LNAI).

Vol. 1459: D.G. Feitelson, L. Rudolph (Eds.), Job Scheduling Strategies for Parallel Processing. Proceedings, 1998. VII, 257 pages. 1998.

Vol. 1460: G. Quirchmayr, E. Schweighofer, T.J.M. Bench-Capon (Eds.), Database and Expert Systems Applications. Proceedings, 1998. XVI, 905 pages. 1998.

Vol. 1461: G. Bilardi, G.F. Italiano, A. Pietracaprina, G. Pucci (Eds.), Algorithms – ESA'98. Proceedings, 1998. XII, 516 pages. 1998.

Vol. 1462: H. Krawczyk (Ed.), Advances in Cryptology - CRYPTO '98. Proceedings, 1998. XII, 519 pages. 1998.

Vol. 1463: N.E. Fuchs (Ed.), Logic Program Synthesis and Transformation. Proceedings, 1997. X, 343 pages. 1998.

Vol. 1464: H.H.S. Ip, A.W.M. Smeulders (Eds.), Multimedia Information Analysis and Retrieval. Proceedings, 1998. VIII, 264 pages. 1998.

Vol. 1465: R. Hirschfeld (Ed.), Financial Cryptography. Proceedings, 1998. VIII, 311 pages. 1998.

Vol. 1466: D. Sangiorgi, R. de Simone (Eds.), CONCUR'98: Concurrency Theory. Proceedings, 1998. XI, 657 pages. 1998.

Vol. 1467: C. Clack, K. Hammond, T. Davie (Eds.), Implementation of Functional Languages. Proceedings, 1997. X, 375 pages. 1998.

Vol. 1468: P. Husbands, J.-A. Meyer (Eds.), Evolutionary Robotics. Proceedings, 1998. VIII, 247 pages. 1998.

Vol. 1469: R. Puigjaner, N.N. Savino, B. Serra (Eds.), Computer Performance Evaluation. Proceedings, 1998. XIII, 376 pages. 1998.

Vol. 1470: D. Pritchard, J. Reeve (Eds.), Euro-Par'98: Parallel Processing. Proceedings, 1998. XXII, 1157 pages. 1998.

Vol. 1471: J. Dix, L. Moniz Pereira, T.C. Przymusinski (Eds.), Logic Programming and Knowledge Representation. Proceedings, 1997. IX, 246 pages. 1998. (Subseries LNAI).

Vol. 1473: X. Leroy, A. Ohori (Eds.), Types in Compilation. Proceedings, 1998. VIII, 299 pages. 1998.

Vol. 1474: F. Mueller, A. Bestavros (Eds.), Languages, Compilers, and Tools for Embedded Systems. Proceedings, 1998. XIV, 261 pages. 1998.

Vol. 1475: W. Litwin, T. Morzy, G. Vossen (Eds.), Advances in Databases and Information Systems. Proceedings, 1998. XIV, 369 pages. 1998.

Vol. 1476: J. Calmet, J. Plaza (Eds.), Artificial Intelligence and Symbolic Computation. Proceedings, 1998. XI, 309 pages. 1998. (Subseries LNAI).

Vol. 1477: K. Rothermel, F. Hohl (Eds.), Mobile Agents. Proceedings, 1998. VIII, 285 pages. 1998.

Vol. 1478: M. Sipper, D. Mange, A. Pérez-Uribe (Eds.), Evolvable Systems: From Biology to Hardware. Proceedings, 1998. IX, 382 pages. 1998.

Vol. 1479: J. Grundy, M. Newey (Eds.), Theorem Proving in Higher Order Logics. Proceedings, 1998. VIII, 497 pages. 1998.

Vol. 1480: F. Giunchiglia (Ed.), Artificial Intelligence: Methodology, Systems, and Applications. Proceedings, 1998. IX, 502 pages. 1998. (Subseries LNAI).

Vol. 1481: E.V. Munson, C. Nicholas, D. Wood (Eds.), Principles of Digital Document Processing. Proceedings, 1998. VII, 152 pages. 1998.

Vol. 1482: R.W. Hartenstein, A. Keevallik (Eds.), Field-Programmable Logic and Applications. Proceedings, 1998. XI, 533 pages. 1998.

Vol. 1483: T. Plagemann, V. Goebel (Eds.), Interactive Distributed Multimedia Systems and Telecommunication Services. Proceedings, 1998. XV, 326 pages. 1998.

Vol. 1484: H. Coelho (Ed.), Progress in Artificial Intelligence – IBERAMIA 98. Proceedings, 1998. XIII, 421 pages. 1998. (Subseries LNAI).

Vol. 1485: J.-J. Quisquater, Y. Deswarte, C. Meadows, D. Gollmann (Eds.), Computer Security – ESORICS 98. Proceedings, 1998. X, 377 pages. 1998.

Vol. 1486: A.P. Ravn, H. Rischel (Eds.), Formal Techniques in Real-Time and Fault-Tolerant Systems. Proceedings, 1998. VIII, 339 pages. 1998.

Vol. 1487: V. Gruhn (Ed.), Software Process Technology. Proceedings, 1998. VIII, 157 pages. 1998.

Vol. 1488: B. Smyth, P. Cunningham (Eds.), Advances in Case-Based Reasoning. Proceedings, 1998. XI, 482 pages. 1998. (Subseries LNAI).

Vol. 1490: C. Palamidessi, H. Glaser, K. Meinke (Eds.), Principles of Declarative Programming. Proceedings, 1998. XI, 497 pages. 1998.

Vol. 1493: J.P. Bowen, A. Fett, M.G. Hinchey (Eds.), ZUM '98: The Z Formal Specification Notation. Proceedings, 1998. XV, 417 pages. 1998.

Vol. 1495: T. Andreasen, H. Christiansen, H.L. Larsen (Eds.), Flexible Query Answering Systems. IX, 393 pages. 1998. (Subseries LNAI).

Vol. 1497: V. Alexandrov, J. Dongarra (Eds.), Recent Advances in Parallel Virtual Machine and Message Passing Interface. Proceedings, 1998. XII, 412 pages. 1998.

Vol. 1498: A.E. Eiben, T. Bäck, M. Schoenauer, H.-P. Schwefel (Eds.), Parallel Problem Solving from Nature – PPSN V. Proceedings, 1998. XXIII, 1041 pages. 1998.

Vol. 1499: S. Kutten (Ed.), Distributed Computing. Proceedings, 1998. XII, 419 pages. 1998.

Vol. 1501: M.M. Richter, C.H. Smith, R. Wiehagen, T. Zeugmann (Eds.), Algorithmic Learning Theory. Proceedings, 1998. XI, 439 pages. 1998. (Subseries LNAI).

Vol. 1503: G. Levi (Ed.), Static Analysis. Proceedings, 1998. IX, 383 pages. 1998.

Vol. 1504: O. Herzog, A. Günter (Eds.), KI-98: Advances in Artificial Intelligence. Proceedings, 1998. XI, 355 pages. 1998. (Subseries LNAI).

Vol. 1510: J.M. Żytkow, M. Quafafou (Eds.), Principles of Data Mining and Knowledge Discovery. Proceedings, 1998. XI, 482 pages. 1998. (Subseries LNAI).